ROMANTIC DRAMA

A COMPARATIVE HISTORY OF LITERATURES
IN EUROPEAN LANGUAGES
SPONSORED BY THE
INTERNATIONAL COMPARATIVE LITERATURE ASSOCIATION

HISTOIRE COMPARÉE DES LITTÉRATURES
DE LANGUES EUROPÉENNES
SOUS LES AUSPICES DE
L'ASSOCIATION INTERNATIONAL DE LITTÉRATURE
COMPARÉE

ROMANTIC DRAMA

Edited by

GERALD GILLESPIE
Stanford University

JOHN BENJAMINS PUBLISHING COMPANY
AMSTERDAM/PHILADELPHIA

1994

TM infinity symbol

The paper used in this publication meets the minimum requirements of American National Standard for Information Sciences — Permanence of Paper for Printed Library Materials, ANSI Z39.48-1984.

Library of Congress Cataloging-in-Publication Data

Romantic drama / edited by Gerald Gillespie.
    p.   cm. -- (A Comparative history of literatures in European languages, ISSN 0238-0668 ; v. 9)
    Includes bibliographical references (p.) and index.
    1. European drama--19th century--History and criticism. 2. Romanticism--Europe. 3. Theater--Europe-
-History--19th century. I. Gillespie, Gerald Ernest Paul, 1933- . II. Series: Histoire comparée des littéra-
tures de langues européennes ; v. 9.
PN1851.R66   1993
809.2'9145--dc20
                                93-34838
ISBN 90 272 3441 8 (Eur.)/1-55619-600-8 (US) (Hb; alk. paper)   CIP

John Benjamins Publishing Co. · P.O. Box 75577 · 1070 AN Amsterdam · The Netherlands
John Benjamins North America · 821 Bethlehem Pike · Philadelphia, PA 19118 · USA

GENERAL PREFACE

This is one of a series of volumes in "Comparative History of Literatures in European Languages" (hereafter "Comparative Literary History") sponsored by the International Comparative Literature Association. The series is under the supervision of a coordinating editorial committee consisting of sixteen scholars from various countries. The committee appoints the directors of the particular research projects, issues general guidelines to them, monitors the genesis of the manuscript, and gives final approval before publication.

The "Comparative Literary History" series was launched by the International Comparative Literature Association in 1967. It is based on two fundamental premises: one, that the writing of literary history confined to specific nations, peoples, or languages must be complemented by the writing of literary history that coordinates related or comparable phenomena from an international point of view; two, that it is almost impossible for individual scholars to write such comprehensive histories and that we must now rely on structured teamwork drawing collaborators from different nations.

Within these principles and criteria, the scholars entrusted with each project are given the latitude needed to put together the best possible volume. Writing a comparative literary history by way of international teamwork is a revolutionary procedure in literary historiography. Few scholars can claim ability to cover the entire range of literature relevant to the phenomenon under study. Hence the need for partial syntheses, upon which more and more truly international syntheses will be built as our series progresses.

The "Comparative Literary History" series consists of volumes composed in either French or English. Most contributions will be originally written in these two languages, some will be translated into them from other languages. But we emphasize that the decision to write our volumes in English or French does not reflect a hierarchy of values. The literary specificities of every nation or cultural entity, large or small, acclaimed or neglected, will be valued. As a matter of fact, no discipline is as apt to do justice to the literatures of smaller diffusion as Comparative Literature.

The volumes in this series are collaborative projects of many scholars from different countries, cultures and procedures, but volume editors and the Coordinating Committee have worked to produce well defined historiographic systems of explanation that give literary scholarship a broader and more accurate assessment of the cultural past.

As the current President of the Coordinating Committee I have been entrusted with the responsibility of continuing and expanding the series of "Comparative Literary History" launched by Professor Jacques Voisine of the University of Paris III, and continued by Professor Henry Remak of Indiana University and brought up to its present level of achievement by Professor Jean Weisgerber of the Free University of Brussels.

Literary scholarship is indebted to the project directors for their scholarship, undaunted courage, patience and faith in the international community of scholars.

Mario J. Valdés
President, Coordinating Committee

CONTENTS

III. Affinity, Dissemination, Reception

IV. The Romantic Legacy

Gerald Gillespie

INTRODUCTION

I

Two centuries have not sufficed to exhaust the fascination. A good deal more than a bounteous critical literature attests to the lasting importance of Romanticism across virtually all the territories of the civilization named for better or worse after the goddess Europa; much of the literary art of the past two centuries reflects its reception and significance.

Part One of the present volume begins our consideration of Romantic drama by identifying large-scale changes observable in the later eighteenth century. These changes are analyzed as evidence of a deep paradigm shift spreading throughout all branches of literature that was accompanied by a revision of the canon and poetics of drama specifically. The chapters gathered under Part Two look at symptomatic subject-matters to which practicing Romantic playwrights turned, the structural means by which they expressed their view of the world, and their reshaping of dramatic genres. The chapters in Part Three then explore regional variations and peculiarities of the new drama. Part Four carries the history of its reception forward to connect at relevant points with literary phenomena in our own times. The Romantic experience of intertextuality and the dissolving of generic boundaries is one of the most important topics under Part Four.

Parts One and Four of the volume thus bracket a medley of distinct relationships examined under Parts Two and Three in a specific kind of comparative literary history – a history that is concerned with Romanticism as a movement of interactive currents within a larger polysystem, rather than as a limited period dominated by some construed singular master-ethos or dialectic. Although, in the editor's view, it would certainly be a legitimate exercise to divide specific decades into some supposed pattern of rising and falling Romanticism, such an operation involves a familiar kind of hermeneutic circularity. The use of such a paradigm would reflect and prolong the influence of Humanist, Enlightenment, and Romantic historiography as a cultural continuum that is self-reconfirming. That is, a preponderant emphasis on a developmental sequence of "periods" would contribute to the self-preservation of the historical vision *inherited* by the Romantics, but blunt our appreciation of certain seminal insights of Romanticism which tended, in the longer run, to challenge older "history" and suggest alternatives such as "myth."

Therefore, this volume admits the usefulness of tracing the energies and lasting appeal of certain elements of artistic practice and critical thought outside of the (locally variant) "normative" time bounds to which most national histories assign Romanticism. Our purpose includes paying some minimal attention to adaptations and transformations of primary structures and subject-matters of Romantic drama beyond the core decades from 1790 to 1830, even though yet newer cultural codings may meanwhile have determined (or altered) the sense and feel of things that in some earlier shaping were, on balance, "primarily" or "truly" Romantic. Of course, taking notice of recurrent or coopted Romantic phenomena may complicate the definition of other moments and movements in the nineteenth century – a very rich, polyphonic, and dynamic hundred years indeed. But our task here is only to acknowledge pertinent cases of persisting elements or their transference or reemergence, not to sort out the entire development and context of European literature over the course of the nineteenth century.

The paradoxical situation through which the collaborators of this volume had to find their way differs hardly at all from that described by Anna Balakian in the Introduction to *The Symbolist Movement in the Literature of European Languages* (1982). On one level, we were concerned with trends in dramatic literature that, as they grew more distinct, clearly acquired an international as well as multinational character. Yet, on another level, it was necessary to understand the ways that, now tepidly, now warmly, non-national impulses were absorbed into recipient cultures and naturalized. Such appropriations occurring on specific cultural soils were events that sometimes ushered in new national strains of poetic expression. At the same time, it was evident that certain giants (such as Goethe), who did not fit centrally within the Romantic forces, nonetheless had an enormous impact alongside more obvious categories of authors whom the label suited. Many major participants of the Romantic core or its periphery eluded any easy classification. Although we recognized we could not do any justice to more than a few of the larger figures, it seemed as wasteful to ignore the reality of their importance as to deny that creative bursts of Romantic experimentation appeared earlier in specific places, later in others. Our choice was not to flatten the heights, but to survey the historical landscape as a natural flow of energies.

This volume makes no pretense of inclusivity; it is not meant as an encyclopedia of Romantic dramatic literature nor is it a history of changes in the theater as an institution in European nations and the New World. Rather it attempts to highlight important strands of creativity in dramatic literature in which we can see the movement of Romantic ideas and their influence on poetic practice. It strives for a different order of comprehensiveness: for a supranational, crosscultural, and interlinguistic awareness of the creating and sharing of drama *as a literary art*. Instead of trying to convince readers of a neat thesis explaining all of Romantic drama or narrowing its varieties down to a single type, the volume faces the actual "messiness" of onflowing cultural life in Europe and in Europe's extensions overseas. (The latter territories, let us remember, were then two centuries closer to the foundational era of colonization, thus closer to their respective European mother countries.) Perhaps the most important critical choice by the editor has been to acknowledge that Romantic drama experienced particular fortunes in specific territories, and concomitantly to reject sweeping formalistic definitions that do not take the diachronic dimensions of these variant fortunes into account.

To bring out the authentic growth traits of branches within the larger cultural family of Europe and the New World, the volume offers not one but several essays examining the paradigm shifts in the generally recognized core decades from multiple perspectives – perspectives which, as the contributors show, were shaped by powerful forces associated with specific traditions. The objective of this collaboration is not to reach a collective, retrospective explanatory "theory" capturing Romanticism, but to suggest in outline the value of a polysystemic approach for assessing the effects of Romanticism on dramatic literature. There is a corollary to this proposition: The literary history of Romanticism includes, but is by no means limited to or by, those myriad, contemporaneous acts of

Romantic theorizing about literary processes already in action by the end of the eighteenth century. Our volume considers Romanticism as a series of events about which recipients in many related cultures – now we ourselves, two centururies later – have developed a *cumulative* appreciation. Therefore the concluding chapter, "The Past is Prologue," will review some of the relationships of the core Romantic decades, as established in the chapters, but will indicate later instances of their relevance as aspects of a Romantic heritage.

The special nature of this volume probing Romantic drama justifies brief mention of its history, a post-Romantic self-examination. The International Comparative Literature Association announced the grand design of a *Comparative History of Literatures in European Languages* in 1967. The series has been guided by an editorial board named the Coordinating Committee, newly elected every three years from the worldwide ranks of comparatists since its constitution under Jacques Voisine (University of Paris, Sorbonne) as its inaugural president. The second president of this supreme editorial council, Henry Remak (Indiana University, Bloomington), has chronicled the early evolution of its ambitious venture in a number of articles such as "A Literary History of Europe: Approaches and Problems," in the *Yearbook of Comparative and General Literature*, 17 (1968), 86-91, and "*A Comparative History of Literatures in European Languages*: Progress and Problems," in *Synthesis*, 3 (1976), 11-23. The idea of several volumes dedicated to Romanticism as an international phenomenon took root during the Remak years and began to reach fruition under the board's third president, Jean Weisgerber (Free University of Brussels).

Milan V. Dimić (University of Alberta-Edmonton) and Frederick Garber (State University of New York-Binghamton) suggested the ground-plan for a subseries in a report entitled "The Place of Romanticism within the *Comparative History of Literatures in European Languages*," published by *Neohelicon*, 3 (1975), 303-13. The nucleus of a Romanticism research group, hosted by Dimić, began meeting in Canada. The approach to Romanticism as a longer-term "movement" consisting of multiple currents gained clearer definition in these exchanges during the early 1980s. One of the binding points that emerged was the sense of differing with the concept of a Romanticism regarded first and foremost as a late climactic phase of an Enlightenment "period." This rival view was propounded by the shapers of the closely related ICLA project *Le Tournant du siècle des Lumières (1760-1820)*. Continuing friendly ties with the *Tournant* research group were established under Dimić's aegis.

Interest in collaborating on a volume dedicated to Romantic irony was sparked by a conference in April 1978 generously sponsored by the University of Alberta at Edmonton, with support by the Canada Council, ICLA, and other benefactors, and bringing together many European and North American consultants, as well as members of the future Romanticism editorial team. This First International Comparative Literature Symposium on Romanticism at Edmonton provided the model for the equally successful Second (1981) and Third (1984) Symposia on drama and poetry. Roger Bauer (University of Munich), director of the Theater volume in the *Tournant des Lumières* project, came the long distance to Western Canada to offer us a stimulating paper and collegial, sage commentary at the 1981 conference. The Drama Department of the University of Alberta sharpened our senses with its special production of Shelley's *The Cenci*, in Artaud's adaptation, directed by Brian Deedrick.

Following the Second Symposium, the Coordinating Committee asked me to coordinate all the Romanticism research efforts. I also took direct responsibility for planning a volume on *Romantic*

Drama. In practical terms, this double role has meant reporting regularly to the Coordinating Committee on all aspects of the preparation of our subseries. We hope this will eventually comprise *Romantic Irony, Romantic Drama, Romantic Poetry, and Romantic Prose* (narrative fiction, discursive writing, and other modes).

The Romanticism volumes have been enriched through dialogue with the editorial council of the *Comparative History* and with researchers in its other ongoing projects – not to speak of the helpful advice given by dozens upon dozens of colleagues around the world. It is infeasible to name more than a representative selection of persons who have assisted the project, but all who have encouraged our efforts are implicitly included in this expression of gratitude for their collegiality. The contributors to the drama volume typify the international mobility and openness of Comparative Literature. Many serve from time to time as guest professors or researchers in "foreign" nations. Many have migrated from an earlier homeland, in some cases to more than one new elective homeland. A few have changed their nationality or permanent residence while engaged in our project. Thus while a majority of the contributors to *Romantic Drama* currently work somewhere on the huge North American continent, by origin (or by way of an intermediary *Wahlheimat*) they "are" American, Argentinian, Austrian, Belgian, British, Bulgarian, Canadian, Czech, French, German, Hungarian, Israeli, Romanian, and Russian.

Our larger team's first commitment was to develop the already projected volume *Romantic Irony* under the editorial care of Frederick Garber. This collaboration was an important experiment, because instead of preparing a broad historical survey in terms of periodization or genre, we intended to illuminate the multitude of ways in which a Romantic literary principle informed a diverse range of artistic expression and in fact altered the very sense of genre. Our choice was not to proceed from a preconceived historical model of literary events and laws, but to pursue avenues marked by habits of mind and structural traits, while we remained engaged in a discovery process that had no prescribed terminal point. This approach seemed promising if it would allow collaborators on the volume *Romantic Irony* to follow the trace of key impulses beyond traditionally decreed time boundaries and to observe their absorption, transformation, and reinstantiation in later moments. Our hope was to write a more supple kind of literary history, skirting the pitfalls of any simplistic genetic or teleological thinking and following literary patterns and dynamics across linguistic and geocultural frontiers. The volume *Romantic Irony* made its appearance in 1988, published by Akadémiai Kiadó (Budapest). The value of discriminating family traits that appear in Romantic phenomena and phenomena of our own age as the Garber volume does has been independently corraborated in Ernst Behler's recent book, *Irony and the Discourse of Modernity* (Seattle: University of Washington Press, 1990).

The Garber project served a number of important functions. It went far in freeing literary history from a customary division into "national" blocks. It also revealed the usefulness – in fact, in the case of Romanticism, the urgent need – of essays that cut across older generic boundaries. The collaboration fostered the writing of several broader-gauged essays that explored narrative and drama as these were changing in Romanticism, and symptomatic analogies in music and the visual arts. I was assigned the task of writing two of these five cross-cultural "Syntheses" in the Garber volume. By virtue of the natural logic of Romantic innovation which it explored, my chapter on "Romantic Irony and the Grotesque" touched, among other things, on newer uses, forms, and ideas of drama (opera, puppet play, pageant, *commedia dell'arte*, the phantasmagoric, fantastic comedy, etc.). And my chapter on "Romantic Irony and Modern Anti-Theater" looked at "positive" and "negative" strains of a Romantic theater of the mind and of Romantic disillusionism that were to nourish lasting developments in the drama. I refer the reader to these two chapters in the Garber volume as a kind of preface anticipating my remarks here, as well as for commentary on the impact of Romantic irony and other pertinent topics. An example of relevant matters already broached in the Garber volume would be the structural and thematic use of theatricality in narrative fiction, notably the importance of theater as Romantic authors interpolated it in other modes as a central myth for treating modern consciousness and engaging questions of identity and fictionality ("Romantic Irony and Modern Anti-Theater," pp. 351-55).

The conceptual and cultural variety of the volume *Romantic Irony* was intended as a seedbed for future volumes that would be organized around broad generic notions (drama, poetry, narrative, etc.), tenacious cores that survived the Romantic experimentation with genre. It is no exaggeration to say that the Garber volume was the mother-project promising to bear many children. Once the irony project went to press, attention could be devoted to the drama project. It is my hope that the present volume on drama can play a similar part in its turn by suggesting ways to treat Romantic poetry and narrative.

Besides many fine articles published in recent years by contributors to *Romantic Drama* or the preceding Garber volume, several important books evidence the stimulus of participation in the ICLA Romanticism projects. These include Virgil Nemoianu's *The Taming of Romanticism: European Literature and the Age of Biedermeier* (1984), Lilian R. Furst's *Fictions of Romantic Irony* (1984), Jeffrey Cox's *In the Shadows of Romance: Romantic Tragic Drama in Germany, England, and France* (1987), and Frederick Burwick's *Illusion and the Drama: Critical Theory of the Enlightenment and Romantic Era* (1991).

II

The volumes of the *Comparative History* series are published in either French or English, the two principal working languages of the International Comparative Literature Association. Since the prospective readers of the volume *Romantic Drama* come from every continent, some clarification of the procedure in readying the chapters of such varied provenance for press will be helpful. In general, the attempt has been made to maintain continuity from the volume *Romantic Irony*; that is, punctuation, treatment of titles, footnoting, and bibliography have been adjusted to conform to a recognized American standard. But whenever a contributor has consistently employed British spelling (e.g., *favour, levelled, harmonise, centre, gaol*, as against *favor, leveled, harmonize, center, jail*), that original orthography has been preserved.

In certain cases, the spelling of a name or proper noun has been normalized to the form commonly used in English or in French. Sometimes names, titles, or other locutions have been transcribed into roman characters from another alphabet. (For example, in the case of Russian authors, the Anglicized form Fyodor Dostoevsky is more widespread than the transliteration Fëdor Dostoevskii; similarly, the German form Meyerhold is more current in English than the transliterated Russian spelling of the playwright's name as Meierkhol'd.) Several essays in this volume were written in another language and then translated into English. Whatever the initial habits of citation in any particular essay, the volume has been redacted for greater convenience; thus the titles of non-English works under discussion may be given either in their original form or in a form commonly used in English, as the context may allow. The contributors' choice of dating specific dramatic works according to the time of original writing, of first production, or of first publication has not been overridden.

Since the titles of works of dramatic literature and of eighteenth and nineteenth-century criticism are indexed according to their original form, the reader should not look for works in the Index under an English title unless they were originally published in English. In the Index, the names of cited authors are usually given in their original form, but some may appear in a common English form (e.g., Aeschylus). Authors who are known mainly by their pennames will be listed that way first in the Index, followed by their regular civil name (e.g., Voltaire: François-Marie Arouet). The system of citing the principal name in a shorter form by which an author is commonly known varies from language to language. In this volume, the standard English habit in the choice of the short form will prevail. But readers should be patient in looking up a fuller form. (For example, because of Luso-Brazilian naming customs, the actor João *Caetano dos Santos* would appear as Caetano, whereas the poet-playwright Domingos José *Gonçalves de Magalhães* would appear as Magalhães.)

In the text of the essays in this volume, upon first occurrence, titles and longer passages cited from works in languages other than English usually are translated; the English version may be immediately juxtaposed or appear in the annotations or in an appendix. Excepted are cognates, transparent or frequently borrowed terms, proper names, and non-English locutions whose semantic range is being directly analyzed in the essay in question.

As editor, I have taken into account the practical reality that, on the threshold of the twenty-first century, English is *de facto* the main medium of access for an extensive number of readers who have not yet acquired a mastery of other European languages, but would like to investigate European literature at large. For this reason, the general Bibliography appended to the volume offers a broader selection in English of works on special topics. These titles in English are complemented by choice works in other European languages, notably in French and German, for specialists in European literature. Readers are advised to consult the annotations and bibliographies of individual essays for further pertinent titles and for indications of the original sources used. The appended general Bibliography is not intended to be exhaustive by any means. It provides only a starting point for independent exploration into the comparative dimensions of Romantic drama. Although many excellent studies from earlier decades could be cited, the list has been restricted mainly to works published in more recent decades; of course, many of the newer titles cited furnish excellent bibliographic access to previous scholarship.

The appended Index Nominum is restricted principally to playwrights. Because of considerations of space, it will not carry the names of critics and scholars writing after the juncture of Symbolism and Modernism. Similarly, with rare exceptions, the Index Operum will not carry works of imaginative or critical literature that were published after the first few decades of the twentieth century.

III

Gloria Flaherty's chapter is reprinted by permission of *Theatre Research International*, where it appeared in a slightly shortened version; Harold Segel's chapter, by permission of *Theater Three*. Portions of Virgil Nemoianu's chapter are reprinted, by permission of the publishers, from *The Taming of Romanticism*, Harvard University Press, 1984.

I would like to salute here some of the persons whose help made the preparation of this volume less onerous. Among the many colleagues who took time out of busy schedules to advise on specific aspects of the volume were Claudio Guillén (Barcelona), René Wellek (Yale), Franco Meregalli (Venice), Karl Maurer (Bochum), Aleksander Flaker (Zagreb), Roger Bauer (Munich), Ernst Behler (University of Washington at Seattle), Elinor Shaffer (University of East Anglia), Milan V. Dimić (University of Alberta at Edmonton), Frederick Garber (State University of New York at Binghamton), Douwe Fokkema (Utrecht), and Virgil P. Nemoianu (Catholic University of America). Miroslav J. Hanak (East Texas State University) has kindly helped check the spellings of Slavic names and titles and made helpful comments about several essays. With his customary generosity, Albert Gérard (University of Liège) has suggested corrections and improvements throughout the volume.

The sympathy of Alexander Parker (Edinburgh University) was important during my preparatory experience of translating Ludwig Tieck's *Puss-in-Boots* (1974), as was subsequently the encouragement of Eric Bentley, Stanley Kaufmann, Martin Esslin, and Oscar Mandel as theater men. My English version of the play enjoyed its world première in April 1976 in a production mounted by Marvin Carlson at Cornell University; this was followed shortly in November 1976 by Charles Vicinus's production at Stony Brook; the West Coast première took place in January 1983 at the California Institute of Technology, under the direction of Alice Cronin-Golomb.

A word of thanks is due to the many staff members of Green Library and Information Resources at Stanford University for easing the burden of research. When my antique word processor burned out at a critical juncture in autumn 1991, my colleague Marsh McCall generously lent me his so that I could rescue large stranded pieces of the manuscript.

Thanks are likewise extended to Barbara H. Hyams and Carine Peelaers for help in assembling part of the Bibliography; to Simon Sreberny for translating the essay by Manfred Schmeling, and to Tracy Rich for translating the essay by Alexander Gershkovich; to Inez Drixelius, Kevin Langmuth, Barbara Gilbertson, and Karin I. Pagel for typing various parts of the volume manuscript; to Simon Sreberny, Karin I. Pagel, and Mark Lewis for proof-reading several essays, and to Mark Lewis also for assistance in preparing the indices.

Many contributors furnished their own English versions of non-English titles and citations. I have tacitly supplied these where lacking in other essays throughout the volume. I have also translated the essays by Carilla and Voisine-Jechova in their entirety and revised the translation of the essay by Schmeling.

Travel grants from the American Council of Learned Societies and the School of Humanities and Sciences of Stanford University enabled me to attend several of the valuable working meetings of the Coordinating Committee of the International Comparative Literature Association and the Division on Comparative Studies in Romanticism and the Nineteenth Century of the Modern Language Association of America.

I am grateful to Yola de Lusenet who has guided the production of the project at John Benjamins.

This volume of the Comparative History has been published on the recommendation of the International Council for Philosophy and Humanistic Studies (Conseil International pour Philosophie et les Sciences Humaines) of UNESCO.

Gerald Gillespie
Palo Alto, March 1992

I. RENEWAL AND INNOVATION

LILIAN R. FURST

SHAKESPEARE AND THE FORMATION OF ROMANTIC DRAMA IN GERMANY AND FRANCE

I

On the new curtain at the German National Theater in Hamburg in 1773 the figure of Shakespeare was prominently featured, seated at the foot of the goddess Truth on the uppermost steps leading into her temple, expectantly looking towards those about to approach her sanctum. Less than a year short of half a century later, in July 1822, a group of English actors presenting *Othello* in Paris were pelted with eggs, tomatoes, apples and oranges, and driven from the Théâtre Porte-Saint-Martin to an obscure, barn-like hall in the Rue Chantereine, where the performances were arranged on a private subscription basis. Though perhaps slight in themselves, these two incidents are in several important ways symptomatic of the response to Shakespeare in Germany and France.

They reveal first of all the temporal discrepancy between the two countries. Shakespeare attained the height of his influence in Germany in the twenty-five or so years following the publication of Gotthold Ephraim Lessing's (1729-81) *Briefe, die neueste Literatur betreffend* (Letters Regarding the Newest Writing, 1759). His presence is most strongly felt in the assertion of the Storm and Stress in the theater during the 1770s with the early plays of Johann Wolfgang Goethe (1749-1832) and Friedrich Schiller (1759-1805) and the dramas of Friedrich Maximilian Klinger (1752-1831), Jacob Michael Reinhold Lenz (1751-92), and Heinrich Wagner (1747-79). Theirs are the essential works in the thrust for a renewal of German drama. They mark simultaneously a break with the neoclassical practices imitated from French patterns, and an endeavor to rediscover an anterior native tradition. In this exploration of a less manicured and more robust theater Shakespeare was the commanding model. In France, on the other hand, it was not until the later 1820s and early 1830s that the impact of Shakespeare permeated the theater in a palpable fashion. The reasons for this delay[1] are as much political as literary: the upheavals of the French Revolution diverted immediate attention from aesthetic onto social questions, and when Napoleon became Emperor, he did his utmost to uphold the time-honored French heritage by personally supporting a revival of the neoclassical theater and vigorously blocking foreign importations. Yet despite this divergence in timing, Shakespeare aroused equally extreme passions in both countries; enthusiasm nothing short of bardolatry is offset by an animosity that could break out into active hostilities. The very fervor of the reactions to Shakespeare, positive or negative, is indicative of the momentum with which Shakespeare struck the Germans and the French alike. In the crystallization of a new dramatic ideal,

---

[1] For further discussion of the time-lag between Germany and France see Lilian R. Furst, *Counterparts: The Dynamics of Franco-German Literary Relationships 1770-1895* (London: Methuen; and Detroit: Wayne State Univ. Press, 1977), especially chapter 2, "The Emergence of the Romantic Movements" (pp. 7-46), and chapter 3, "The Storm and Stress and French Romanticism" (pp. 47-98).

Shakespeare was the primary activating catalyst, the "yeast"[2] which triggered the process of assessing and renewing dramatic theory and theatrical practice. Whether he was regarded as a savior or as an executioner depended on the viewpoint, the beliefs and the cherished traditions of the beholder. That he represented for all parties a serious challenge and a disturbing provocation is evident from the vehemence of the responses he elicited.

Because of the crucial position he occupies in the formation of Romantic drama, the reception of Shakespeare in both countries was one of the earliest topics of intensive research when the comparative study of literary history began to become established as an academic discipline. A fairly complete documentation is therefore available of the facts regarding Shakespeare's penetration into the German and French theater. It is not my purpose in this essay to rehearse what is already known from previous scholarship. My aim is rather to clarify an aspect of inner intellectual history. Since Shakespeare was the fulcrum of the visceral struggle underlying the emergence of Romantic drama in Europe, it is vital to understand the true nature of his impact. This can best be done by asking what was at stake for the combatants: what was the dominant image of Shakespeare? how was it formed? why did he evoke such violent feelings? what characteristics of Shakespeare's plays were selected for special praise or censure? what did Shakespeare signify to the Germans and the French? As a background and a basis for these central issues, a brief summary of his advent in each country will be helpful.

In Germany[3] "Saspar," as he was then called, appeared on the literary horizon in the early 1740s. Johann Jakob Bodmer (1698-1783), after singling him out for praise in his *Abhandlung über das Wunderbare in der Poesie* (Treatise on the Wondrous in Poetry, 1740), went on to translate a sample of *A Midsummer Night's Dream* in 1741. In the same year Caspar Wilhelm von Borck (1704-47) undertook a rendering of *Julius Caesar* which provoked the virulent opposition of the arch-conservative Johann Christoph Gottsched (1700-66) on account of its lack of a clear structural outline and, even worse, its interspersal of vulgar with edifying scenes. Johann Elias Schlegel (1718-49), in his *Vergleichung Shakespeares und Andreas Gryphs* (Comparison of Shakespeare and Andreas Gryphius, 1741), cautiously counters Gottsched's attack by conceding the English playwright's irregularities of construction, his tendency to bombast, and his mingling of the farcical with the sublime, while also expressing admiration for his capacity to draw characters and to portray emotion. The comparison with the highly idiosyncratic Baroque dramatist Gryphius (1616-64) gives Schlegel the occasion to point out Shakespeare's advantages. Even more significant in the long run is Schlegel's insistence on the affinity between Shakespeare and the German mentality which stemmed from his insight into the filiation between the German national heritage and Shakespearean drama. The natural rapport between Shakespeare and the German mentality is a central argument of Lessing's seventeenth *Literaturbrief*:

[2] Paul van Tieghem, *Le Préromantisme*, III: *La Découverte de Shakespeare sur le continent* (Paris: Sfelt, 1947), p. 179, "le levain."
[3] See Rudolf Genée, *Geschichte der Shakespeare'schen Dramen in Deutschland* (Leipzig: Engelmann, 1870); Marie Joachimi-Dege, *Deutsche Shakespeare-Probleme im 18.Jahrhundert und im Zeitalter der Romantik* (Leipzig: Haessel, 1907); Friedrich Gundolf, *Shakespeare und der deutsche Geist* (Berlin: Bondi, 1923); Roy Pascal, *Shakespeare in Germany 1740-1815* (Cambridge: Cambridge Univ. Press, 1937); Ernest Leopold Stahl, *Shakespeare und das deutsche Theater* (Stuttgart: Kohlhammer, 1947); van Tieghem, *Le Préromantisme*; Lawrence Marsden Price, *English Literature in Germany* (Berkeley: Univ. of California Press, 1953); H. Huesmann, *Shakespeare-Inszenierungen unter Goethe in Weimar* (Vienna: Böhlau, 1968); Wolfgang Stellmacher, ed., *Auseinandersetzungen mit Shakespeare* (Berlin: Akademie, 1976); Wolfgang Stellmacher, *Herders Shakespeare-Bild* (Berlin: Rütten & Loening, 1978); Julian Hilton, "Shakespeare: The Emancipator of German Drama 1750-1837," *Journal of European Ideas*, 2 (1981), 203-220.

daß wir mehr in den Geschmack der Engländer als der Franzosen einschlagen; daß wir in unsern Trauerspielen mehr sehen und denken wollen, als uns das furchtsame französische Trauerspiel zu sehen und zu denken giebt; daß das Große, das Schreckliche, das Melancholische, besser auf uns wirkt als das Artige, das Zärtliche, das Verliebte;[4]

(that we incline more to the taste of the English than of the French; that in our tragedies we want to see and ponder more than awesome French tragedy allows us to do; that the great, the terrible, the melancholy appeals to us more than the pretty, the dainty, the tender)

The critical breakthrough is accomplished as Lessing holds Shakespeare up as a model to be emulated in a bold proclamation of the reversal of hitherto accepted dramatic values, whereby the hegemony of French neoclassical conventions is condemned as baleful to the German theater.

From this turning-point onwards, Shakespeare's star was rapidly in the ascendant. Some two-thirds of his plays, twenty-two in all, were translated by Christoph Martin Wieland (1733-1813) in eight volumes between 1762 and 1766.[5] Notwithstanding its defects, Wieland's translation was the "agent for the passionate Shakespeare cult of the following years;"[6] or, as Gundolf puts it, though the translation was not "richtig" (correct), it was nonetheless "wirksam" (effective).[7] Even its shortcomings proved fruitful: under the impetus of his vexation at Wieland, Heinrich Wilhelm Gerstenberg (1737-1823) included a perspicacious review of Shakespeare in his *Briefe über Merkwürdigkeiten der Litteratur* (Letters on Peculiarities in Literature, 1766). With Lessing's mature and fuller discussion of Shakespeare in the *Hamburgische Dramaturgie* (Hamburg Dramaturgy, 1767) another important milestone was reached when the role of Shakespeare in Germany is defined in relation to the pressing problem of the establishment of a German national theater. Henceforth the fate of Shakespeare was closely identified with the future of German drama, of which he was regarded as the founding cornerstone. By the early 1770s the astute critical appreciation of the previous decade gave way to the fanatical adulation of Shakespeare characteristic of the young adherents of the Storm and Stress. The essay on Shakespeare by Johann Gottfried Herder (1744-1803) in *Von deutscher Art und Kunst* (On German Manner and Art, 1773) is the cardinal example of a subjective empathy with the idol so complete as to inhibit the method of historical criticism of which Herder was the first promulgator. The worship of Shakespeare led the *Stürmer und Dränger* to unabashed borrowings of motifs, such as the graveyard and the madness scenes from *Hamlet*, the balcony scene from *Romeo and Juliet*, or the witches' scene from *Macbeth*,[8] as well as of characters, notably the villain in the mode of Iago, Macbeth and Richard III, and also to extensive imitation of the richly imaged speech of passion. Shakespeare's naturalization into the canon of the German stage was confirmed by the performances in Berlin, in Hamburg, and in Vienna of *Hamlet, Othello, King Lear, Richard III*, and *Macbeth* under the brilliant direction of the actor-producer Friedrich Ludwig Schröder (1714-83) in the later 1770s.

---

[4] Gotthold Ephraim Lessing, *Sämtliche Schriften*, ed. K. Lachmann and F. Muncker (Stuttgart: Göschen, 1892), VIII, 43.

[5] This translation was completed by J.J. Eschenburg and published in twelve volumes under the title, *William Shakespeares Schauspiele. Neue Ausgabe* (William Shakespeare's Plays. A New Edition) in Zurich, 1775-77. Eschenburg's renderings, though scrupulously correct, were uninspired, and were superseded by the far superior version of seventeen plays in ten volumes produced under the leadership of August Wilhelm Schlegel and with the cooperation of Ludwig Tieck, Dorothea Tieck, and later Wolf von Baudissin.

[6] Pascal, p. 7.

[7] Gundolf, p. 186.

[8] See Edna Purdie, "Observations on some Eighteenth Century German Versions of the Witches' Scenes in *Macbeth*," in *Studies in German Literature of the Eighteenth Century* (London: The Athlone Press, 1965), pp. 47-61.

This total immersion in, and unqualified acceptance of Shakespeare in later eighteenth century Germany is of far-reaching importance for any consideration of his impact on the formation of German Romantic drama. Shakespeare was not in fact the immediate impetus for Romantic drama in Germany in the way that he was in France because the decisive and formative effect had come earlier. It is the dramatists of the Storm and Stress who are the primary heirs and exponents of Shakespeare in the German theater. The Romantics represent a second generation, already nurtured into an automatic endorsement of Shakespeare as an essential component of their national heritage. For this reason the German Romantics were in a position to explore other more subtle and sophisticated aspects of Shakespeare's artistry than their French counterparts. By the heyday of the Romantic movement in Germany, the strife and turbulence surrounding Shakespeare had died down; his greatness was no longer in dispute. It was for his profound knowledge of human nature and for the unsurpassed artistry of his technique that he was held in the highest esteem as one of the immortals of world literature. Ludwig Tieck (1773-1853), in his treatise *Shakespeares Behandlung des Wunderbaren* (Shakespeare's Treatment of the Wondrous, 1793), reveals his fascination with Shakespeare's handling of the marvelous; Friedrich Schlegel (1772-1829) considered him one of the masters of irony; and August Wilhelm Schlegel (1767-1845), in as series of essays beginning in 1796 and culminating in his *Vorlesungen über dramatische Kunst und Literatur* (Lectures on Dramatic Art and Literature, 1809), extolled him as the most consummately perfect dramatist of all time. Shakespeare was accorded a unique position, beyond contest and virtually beyond compare.

In France[9] the situation was quite different and far more complex. One of the main complicating factors was the involvement of French nationalistic patriotism in determining attitudes towards Shakespeare. As an Anglo-Saxon he had rapidly been adopted into a near native, family status in Germany.[10] But what endeared him to the Germans alienated the French. He was approached with the suspicion due to a representative of the inveterate foe, and with the outbreak of the Napoleonic wars this enmity was greatly intensified. Aggravating the rivalry was the French claim to supremacy in cultural matters; if competence in trade or government or even warfare might be conceded to the British, in questions of taste the French continued to arrogate the right to lay down the law as the final arbiters. So their national pride and their national honor seemed to the French to be threatened by the foreign invasion of the Parisian theater. A graphic report of this cultural chauvinism is given by Stendhal (Henri Beyle, 1783-1842) who cites the prevailing catcalls of the early 1820s: "*A bas Shakespeare! c'est un aide de camp du duc de Wellington!*" (*Down with Shakespeare! he is an aide-de-camp of the Duke of Wellington!*)[11] The private spheres of the library and the drawing room were thought less dangerous for the dissemination of subversive innovations than the public forum of the theater. The urge to defend the venerable institutions of French drama – established in the *grand* seventeenth century and sanctified since almost as articles of faith – against attack from overseas

---

[9] See J.-J. Jusserand, *Shakespeare en France sous l'ancien régime* (Paris: Colin, 1898); Fernand Baldensperger, "Esquisse d'une histoire de Shakespeare en France," in *Études d'histoire littéraire*, 2e série (Paris: Hachette, 1910), pp. 155-216; J.L. Borgerhoff, *Le Théâtre anglais à Paris sous la Restauration* (Paris: Hachette, 1913); C.M. Haines, *Shakespeare in France: Criticism Voltaire to Victor Hugo* (London: Shakespeare Association, 1925); *Shakespeare in France*, special issue *Yale French Studies*, 33 (1964); Monique Nemer, "Traduire Shakespeare," *Romanticisme*, 1-2 (1971), 94-101; Marion Monaco, *Shakespeare on the French Stage in the Eighteenth Century* (Paris: Didier, 1974).

[10] Jakob Michael Reinhold Lenz, in his *Anmerkungen übers Theater* (Notes on the Theater, 1774) speaks of Shakespeare as "unsers Landsmanns" (our compatriot) (*Gesammelte Schriften* [Munich and Leipzig, 1909], I, 92) while Goethe in his essay *Zum Schäkespears Tag* (On Shakespeare's Day, 1771) uses a decidedly German spelling.

[11] Stendhal, *Racine et Shakespeare* (Paris: Pauvert, 1965), p. 169. Italics are Stendhal's.

upstarts is a key element in the French stance towards Shakespeare. As Baudelaire (1821-67) pointed out in an essay of 1861 on Richard Wagner, in the reception accorded to "le vieux *Williams*" (old Williams) "la haine politique combinait son élément avec le patriotisme littéraire outragé" (political hate combined as an element with outraged literary patriotism).[12] This accounts for the often embittered, persistent, and apparently irrational opposition to him. He was cast as the uncouth barbarian come to destroy aristocratic decorum and rationality.

Yet, though clearly a barbarian in his infringement of all the proprieties, he was also recognized as a barbarian of genius. The early perplexity in France vis-à-vis this uncomfortable phenomenon is summarized in Voltaire's (1694-1778) verdict in his *Lettres philosophiques* (1734): "Shakespeare avait un génie plein de force et de fécondité, de naturel et de sublime, sans la moindre étincelle de bon goût, et sans la moindre connaissance des règles" (Shakespeare was a genius full of strength and fertility, of the natural and the sublime, without one slightest inkling of good taste, and without the least knowledge of rules).[13] The high esteem of *bon goût* (good taste), coupled with the distrust of *génie*, led to the grudging, rather disdainful and condescending posture generally maintained towards Shakespeare. Even the first complete translation into French (1776-82) by Le Tourneur (1737-88) made, ironically, fewer friends than enemies for Shakespeare among the French who were horrified, on closer acquaintance with the text, at such vulgarities as a reference to a handkerchief or to "a mouse stirring" in a tragedy. So long as he was to be judged by the yardstick of French neoclassical dramatic conventions, Shakespeare was bound to be deemed defective. Only after the aesthetic revaluations intrinsic to the Romantic revolution could Shakespeare attain any genuine acceptability among traditionally educated Frenchmen. His much readier acknowledgment as a popular melodramatist perversely fostered an image detrimental to his admission to loftier standing. Thus Rivarol (1753-1801) described Shakespeare in 1784 as "l'idole de sa nation et le scandale de notre littérature" (the idol of his nation and the scandal of our literature).[14] In an attempt to diminish that scandal, Jean-François Ducis (1773-1816), an actor with an ardent but wholly uncomprehending admiration for Shakespeare, did his utmost to remodel Shakespeare to French taste by squeezing his plays into the straitjacket of the three unities, and by replacing action with *récit* (narration) and *confidants* (confidents). It was in this emasculated format that *Hamlet* (1769), *Romeo and Juliet* (1772), *King Lear* (1783), *Macbeth* (1784), and *Othello* (1792) were first presented on the Parisian stage to a mixture of applause and derision.

By the turn of the century, therefore, when Shakespeare was securely enthroned in Germany, the struggle had hardly yet begun in France. Despite the perspicacity of such advocates as François-Thomas-Marie de Baculard d'Arnaud (1718-1805) and particularly Louis-Sébastien Mercier (1740-1814), whose two treatises, *Du théâtre ou nouvel essai sur l'art dramatique* (On the Theater, or New Essay on Dramatic Art, 1773) and *De la littérature et des littérateurs, suivi d'un nouvel examen de la tragédie française* (On Literature and Literators, Followed by a New Examination of French Tragedy, 1778) are pioneering pleas for the mingling of the comic and the tragic, the use of prose, and the expansion of the dramatic horizon, the entrenched French resistance to the alleged

---

[12] Charles Baudelaire, "Richard Wagner et Tannhäuser," in *L'Art romantique* (Paris: Garnier, 1962), p. 727.

[13] Voltaire, *Lettres philosophiques*, ed. Gustave Lanson (Paris: Cornély, 1909), II, 79.

[14] Antoine Rivaroli, known as Comte Rivarol, *De l'Universalité de la langue française, sujet proposé par l'Académie de Berlin en 1783, Oeuvres* (On the Universality of the French Language, Subject Proposed by the Berlin Academy in 1783. Works; Paris: Librairie des Bibliophiles, 1880), I, 34.

assassin of their cultural heritage remained unabated. The reactionary stronghold was reinforced by Napoleon's preference during his reign as Emperor for Corneille with his martial virtues. Out of political considerations even so enlightened a cosmopolitan as Benjamin Constant (1767-1830) had to practise caution as a matter of expediency. The *Étude sur Shakespeare* (Study on Shakespeare), which François Pierre Guillaume Guizot (1787-1874) prefaced to a new translation in 1821, marks an early effort at an understanding of Shakespeare within his cultural and historical context. But that barrage of eggs and tomatoes thrown at the English actors in 1822 was not an isolated occurrence. However, this incident did prompt the energetic counterattack initiated by Stendhal's *Racine et Shakespeare* (1823 and 1825). With the mustering of the *Cénacle* around Victor Hugo (1802-85) in 1827 and its consolidation of the Royalist and the Liberal avant-garde into a single powerblock, the climate began to change perceptibly. In Hugo's *Préface de "Cromwell"* (1827) Shakespeare is extolled as the very essence of drama with the same fervor and in much the same terms as among the *Stürmer und Dränger*. The second troupe of English actors who visited Paris in the winter 1827-28 received a more civil welcome, and were admitted to such prestigious theaters as the *Odéon* and the *Théâtre Italien*. But even after the noisy triumph of native Shakespearean drama with Hugo's *Hernani* in 1830, French qualms were by no means allayed. The third English company, which came to Paris in 1844-45, still shocked the French with their performances of *Othello, Macbeth*, and *Hamlet*. The strident tone and atmosphere of strife continued to surround Shakespeare in France throughout the Romantic period.

II

What then lies behind this checkered outer history? How well acquainted with Shakespeare were his admirers and detractors in France and Germany? Which were the aspects that attracted or repelled them? Above all, what did Shakespeare signify to them? At a remove of two centuries, such questions can best be answered through a scrutiny of the theoretical statements about Shakespeare for the evidence they contain of the extent and depth of the confrontation with his work as well as for the biases and emphases revealed in the rhetoric itself.

It is perhaps surprising, in view of the sound and the fury surrounding Shakespeare in Germany and France, to discover how scantily his works were actually known during the period of most intensive debate. By the later eighteenth and early nineteenth century, Elizabethan English was already sufficiently remote to present not inconsiderable obstacles to readers and even more so to audiences in the theater, particularly if they were not native speakers. Knowledge of English was more widely diffused in Germany than in France, partly because of the innate affinity between the Anglo-Saxon and German languages, and partly because German was still regarded as a semi-barbaric idiom. Germans were, therefore, under greater pressure to acquire facility in other tongues than were the French, whose language was the polite form of discourse throughout the European Continent and beyond. Lenz and Klinger, for example, though both of relatively modest social standing, knew English reasonably well. Moreover, since they lacked a distinctive literary heritage of their own at that time, the Germans were in the habit of seeking models and stimulus in other cultures. Gottsched had encouraged an orientation towards France. Lessing's championship of England and of Shakespeare involved a change of direction but not of mentality, such as would be required in

France, with its glorious dramatic patrimony, before Shakespeare's greatness could be acknowledged. Willingness to explore a foreign literature thus depends not only on linguistic competence; fundamental questions of attitude towards one's own culture play an important role in defining one's stance towards other cultures. The strong undertow of national pride and self-esteem in France, and, in contrast, the ambitious thrust for a new start in Germany are weighty factors in determining the degree of openness to Shakespeare.

However, willingness and indeed curiosity cannot take one very far without direct experience of the text. This is where the gravest obstacles reside to a genuine familiarity with Shakespeare in the late eighteenth and early nineteenth century. Given their linguistic limitations, most readers had perforce to have recourse to translations. That these became available quite early – 1762-66 in Germany, and 1776-82 in France – is an indication of the keen interest in Shakespeare. But both these translations fall so far short of the original as to give little idea of its poetic sublimity. Wieland, after rendering the first play he tackled, *A Midsummer Night's Dream*, into verse, gave up the effort and opted for prose. His versions were not only increasingly inaccurate and flaccid; they also made Shakespeare appear "formlos" (formless),[15] as Gundolf observed, thereby fostering the image of Shakespeare as a wild, turbulent genius. Le Tourneur's translation, too, was in prose except for the songs. In his anxiety to make Shakespeare palatable to his compatriots, Le Tourneur carried out more deliberate amendments than Wieland, cutting passages, embellishing phrases, stylizing the English into a closer approximation to French canons of good taste. As a result, the Shakespeare presented to the French had less crude realism, less comic verve, less primal energy than the Shakespeare offered to the Germans. Neither translation provided a satisfactory starting point for any deeper appreciation of Shakespeare's originality.

If the quality of Shakespeare's writing could hardly be evinced from the available renderings, his range and scope were not recognized either, certainly not in the initial stages of his advent into Germany and France. A small number of plays, at first almost exclusively tragedies, are the focus of interest and the bones of contention in both countries: *Hamlet, King Lear,* and *Othello* are by far the most commonly cited, followed by *Richard III, Romeo and Juliet, Macbeth,* and *The Tempest*. It is on this restricted repertoire that such leading exponents of Shakespeare as Lessing and Herder, Stendhal and Hugo draw. Virtually no heed is given to either the comedies or the chronicle plays, except for references to Falstaff, a character who patently caught the imagination. Guizot, in his *Étude sur Shakespeare* (1821) is voicing the general consensus of opinion when he maintains:

> On ne saurait douter qu'entre les pièces historiques et la tragédie proprement dite, le génie de Shakespeare ne se portât de préférence vers le dernier genre. Le jugement général et constant qui a placé *Romeo et Juliette, Hamlet* et le *Roi Lear, Macbet,* et *Othello* à la tête de ses ouvrages, suffirait pour le prouver. Parmi les drames nationaux, *Richard III* est le seul que l'opinion ait élevé au même rang; nouvelle preuve de mon assertion, car c'est aussi le seul ouvrage que Shakespeare ait pu conduire, à la manière de ses tragédies, par l'influence d'un caractère ou d'une idée unique.[16]

> (There can be no doubt that between historical plays and veritable tragedies, Shakespeare's genius tended by preference toward the latter. The general and constant judgment placing *Romeo and Juliet, Hamlet* and *King Lear, Macbeth,* and *Othello* at the head of his works, would suffice to prove this.

---

[15] Gundolf, p. 186.

[16] François Pierre Guillauem Guizot, *Oeuvres complètes de Shakespeare* (Complete Works of Shakespeare; Paris: Didier, 1860), I, 70.

Among his national dramas, *Richard III* is the only one that opinion has raised to the same level,
another proof of my assertion, for it is also the only work that Shakespeare was able to organize, like
his tragedies, around a single character or idea.)

Guizot was himself in fact a pioneer in his endeavors to expand the Shakespearean repertoire in
France by his analyses of such hitherto neglected plays as *Julius Caesar, The Merchant of Venice,
The Merry Wives of Windsor, King John, King Richard II, King Henry IV, King Henry V, King
Henry VI*, and *King Henry VIII*. This broadening of the Shakespearean spectrum came, however,
only relatively late in both countries. The more comprehensive coverage offered by Guizot in
France had been given in Germany by August Wilhelm Schlegel in the third book of his *Vorlesun-
gen über dramatische Kunst und Literatur* (1809), which is devoted almost in its entirety solely to
Shakespeare.

The evidence thus points to the inescapable conclusion that during the height of the controversy surrounding Shakespeare in Germany and France his works were not well known either by his
admirers or his detractors. A characteristic case is that of Lessing:

Lessing's attitude to Shakespeare is a perpetual mystery. He seems not to have known him well – in
the *Hamburgische Dramaturgie* he only refers to *Hamlet, Richard III, Romeo and Juliet*, and *Othello*.
But he refers to him always as a genius. And yet he never enters into a full discussion of Shakespeare,
and in his own theory of drama ignores him completely.[17]

This assessment is equally valid for Stendhal and Hugo, the foremost spokesmen of Shakespeare in
France. In *Racine et Shakespeare*, Stendhal mentions six Shakespearean plays: *Macbeth*, six times;
Othello, thrice; *Henry IV*, twice; and *Richard III, Coriolanus*, and *The Tempest*, once each. Yet he
has curiously little to say about his title figure, and his comments lack specificity: Shakespeare is a
genius who created masterpieces; he portrays the passions within the human heart; though he
violates conventions by his infringement of the three unities, he succeeds in conjuring up "courts
moments d'illusion parfaite" (brief moments of perfect illusion)[18] more often than Racine; in short,
he represents a model for Romantic tragedy to be studied, or imitated. Despite Shakespeare's prominent position in the title of Stendhal's treatise, he is no more than a shadowy silhouette looming on
the horizon; his function is that of a cudgel with which to beat new life into French tragedy. In
Hugo's *Préface de "Cromwell"* Shakespeare is assigned a similar role. Again, the standard plays are
cited: *Hamlet, Othello, King Lear, Richard III, Macbeth, Romeo and Juliet, The Tempest*, though
often in almost casual fashion, without any attempt at exegesis or interpretation. The apotheosis of
Shakespeare is even more grandiose than Stendhal's, and even more nebulous: "Shakespeare, c'est
le drame" (Shakespeare is drama);[19] "Shakespeare, ce dieu du théâtre" (Shakespeare, this god of the
theater, p. 81); "le pilier central" (the central pillar, p. 78) in the edifice of modern literature. The
procedure is identical to that of Stendhal, Lessing and Herder, and typical of the approach to
Shakespeare during this formative period: a narrow base of a few plays alluded to in indeterminate
terms constitutes the platform for quasi oracular pronouncements, as conspicuous for their general-
ity as for their magnitude. Shakespeare thus becomes not the object of analysis but the subject of a

---

[17] Pascal, p. 6.
[18] Stendhal, p. 42.
[19] Victor Hugo, *Préface de "Cromwell,"* ed. Annie Ubersfeld (Paris: Garnier-Flammarion, 1968), p. 75.

cult, enveloped in a mystique that serves in fact to elevate him above prosaic scrutiny. To a far greater extent than Goethe, Shakespeare was "un demi dieu honoré et deviné plutôt que bien connu" (a demi-god honored and intuited rather than well known).[20] This situations helps perhaps to account for the irrationality of many of the responses elicited by Shakespeare.

The paucity of concrete knowledge of Shakespeare was no deterrent to the spread of the debate about him in Germany and France. On the contrary, the absence of authentic information nurtured the growth of the Shakespeare myth. This found its precipitate in the conflicting images of Shakespeare which emerged in the course of the polemic.

The negative image is the less compelling, and for that reason it lost ground with the changing climate of opinion as the Romantic revolution gained in momentum. To the conservative adherents of neoclassicism in Germany and France alike Shakespeare was bound to appear as the arch-despoiler. The pattern of censure set by Gottsched in the early 1740s is repeated with little variation, and can be summarized in the single motif of his so-called "irregularity." He is said to be irregular in his disregard of the three unities, in his mingling of tragedy and comedy, in his shifts from verse to prose, in his juxtaposition of the lofty with the commonplace, in his barbaric offences to good taste. These criticisms are clearly predicated on the acceptance of a certain dramatic code. Within the context of that code, they are fully justified, and so they were inevitably reiterated as long as that code retained its authority. The defensiveness of its exponents tended naturally to increase in proportion to the threat they sensed to their own position. Only the most honest and forthright, such as Voltaire, had the courage to concede that Shakespeare, notwithstanding his irregularity, did possess genius. This was a dangerous compromise not only because it undermined the sacrosanct status of regularity as an ideal, but even more because it adumbrated the possibility of an alternative dramatic paradigm in which considerations other than regularity – such as genius – would be the paramount arbiters. This erosion from within weakened the pejorative image of Shakespeare, but what doomed it in the long run was its essentially negative thrust. As a reactionary, rearguard undertaking, it had no vital force or reinforcement to sustain it. Its primary impulse was to block, to impede, and to thwart. Its program came to appear as it indeed was: stale, vindictive, decrepit. Its energy spent, it atrophied into an occasional lone voice bent on an anachronistic mission to stem the rising tide.

The rising tide was that of Shakespeare's positive image. Curiously, and significantly, his supporters commended those very qualities to which his opponents objected. This clearly suggests that the controversy transcends the estimation of one particular dramatist, and embraces much larger and more fundamental questions regarding the dramatic ideal. The vocabulary of Shakespeare's partisans differs, of course, from that of his enemies. His advocates care nothing for regularity, rules, the unities, or even taste. Because they project an alternative code, they posit other standards of judgment. But despite the apparent divergence of concerns between the two camps and despite the distinctive idiom of each side, basically they are addressing the same issue. What separates them is not so much their preoccupations or their language as their underlying attitudes and beliefs. To put it bluntly, one man's irregularity is another man's genius. It is essential to realize that Shakespeare's friends do not in fact perceive him so very differently from his foes. The dividing line between them is not the actual perception, but the evaluation of that perception. The polemic about Shakespeare is

---

[20] Charles-Augustin Sainte-Beuve, "Lettre-Préface" to William Reymond, *Corneille, Shakespeare et Goethe* (Berlin: Luederitz, 1864), p. xi.

the manifestation of a profound revaluation of poetic values, specifically of the dramatic ideal. As such it is a direct and prominent expression of that total aesthetic re-orientation that is at the core of the Romantic revolution.

Irregularity was re-appraised into genius. Of all the many terms applied to Shakespeare by his admirers none occurs with as much frequency as "genius." In Germany, the association of Shakespeare and "Genie" was first made by Lessing in the seventeenth *Literaturbrief* in 1769. Thereafter, it was the pivotal concept of every single discussion without exception: Wieland, Gerstenberg, Herder, Lenz, and Goethe, writing in the years between 1759 and 1773, all capped their panegyric of Shakespeare with this magic and mysterious word. Introduced and quickly popularized together with Shakespeare, the notion of "genius" became in Germany the cornerstone of the new aesthetics. The Storm and Stress envisaged itself as the *Geniezeit* (Time of Genius) both on account of its apotheosis of the idea of genius and its nurturing of native geniuses. The fate of "genius" in Germany is a cogent illustration of the way in which the new terms and, above all, the new modes of thinking fostered by Shakespeare were instrumental in the shaping of the literary ideal. In France, too, "génie" is in intimate alliance with Shakespeare, but though it makes its debut in Mercier's *Du théâtre ou nouvel essai sur l'art dramatique* (1773), it does not swell into a resounding chorus, as in Germany, until the 1820s when it appears as a favorite prop of Guizot, Stendhal, Hugo, and Vigny.

The other dominant words in the Shakespearean constellation follow the same demographic pattern, invariably occurring fifty years later in France than in Germany. The vocabulary of approbation in the two countries testifies to a remarkable parallelism. The German *Natur* corresponds to the French *nature*, *Freiheit* (freedom) to *liberté*, *Leben* (life) to *vie*, *Wahrheit* (truth) to *vérité*, *Kraft* (strength) to *force* or *puissance*, *Leidenschaft* or *Gefühl* (passion or feeling) to *émotions*, *Schöpfer* (creator) to *créateur*, *Gott* (god) to *Dieu*, and *Volk* (people) to *peuple*. It is important to notice how many of these terms, like *Genie/génie* represent the laudatory equivalents (or opposites) to the disparaging "irregularity." "Nature," "freedom," "life," "strength," and "passion," used as vehicles of praise, denote an emancipation from the neoclassical yardsticks and a proclamation of a new aesthetic system ready to affirm turbulence as the price for renewed energy. This is common to Germany and France, and absolutely fundamental to the formation of Romantic drama. Again it becomes apparent how the revision of beliefs, polarized by the impact of Shakespeare, is the starting-point for the elaboration of an innovative dramatic ideal.

Although the vocabulary of assent is identical on the two banks of the Rhine, some differences of emphasis are discernible, apart from the recurrent time-lag. The Germans, more than the French, underscore Shakespeare's naturalness, passion and strength. These priorities are in close consonance with the creed of the Storm and Stress, which prized vigor, forcefulness and spontaneity. They also reveal how Shakespeare came to be interpreted at that time as the prototype of the "naive" poet, according to the categories enunciated by Schiller in his treatise *Über naive und sentimentalische Dichtung* (On Naive and Sentimental Poetry, 1795). This view of Shakespeare was considered a misreading by the German Romantics who departed from their predecessors in this respect, and who took pains to correct the earlier image of Shakespeare as a raw, instinctive creator by concentrating attention on the refinement of his artistry. The French, while paying due tribute to his *puissance* and his capacity to express emotion, set greater store than the Germans by Shakespeare's realism and his status as the people's poet. *Nature* signified to them less spontaneity than the ability to give a comprehensive picture of the world. Truth to life was a quality uppermost in the minds of many French adherents to Shakespeare. As in Germany, these preferences must be seen within the context of the indigenous scene. In a society where theater had become as aristocratic, exclusive, and stylized as it had in France, Shakespeare is invested as the incarnation of a broadly universal, realistic, and popular type of drama.

III

The debate about Shakespeare in Germany and France amounts to far more than a dispute about the merits or defects of a single playwright. It is the locus, and indeed the emblem, of the protracted and acrimonious clash between an old and a new dramatic ideal. That is the reason for the vehemence of the feelings aroused on both sides by this literary quarrel, and that also is the source of its importance for the formation of Romantic drama.

Once the conflict is envisaged in this broader context, it comes to matter little that few, if any, of the protagonists had a close acquaintance with Shakespeare's works. For the argument turned not on the historical persona William Shakespeare, author of tragedies, comedies, and historical chronicle plays. The actual Shakespeare was, so to speak, subsumed by a symbolical, quasi-mythical figure who could equally well be called Saspar, Schäkespear, or old Williams. In this situation, even the degree of genuine understanding of Shakespeare is almost beside the point. The crucial factor is not what Shakespeare really was, but what he meant and represented in the host countries – in other words, what was projected onto Shakespeare. In this final reckoning there is a fundamental congruence between Germany and France that transcends the multiple divergences between them in other respects. For if Shakespeare was the central bone of contention in both countries, it was because he formed the sounding board and the yardstick in the contest for control of the prevailing dramatic practice. Shakespeare became the cipher for the cultural revolution that was under way; his name itself was turned into an inspiring and provocative slogan in the fight for the liberation of the senses, the feelings and the imagination. As the prototype of independence Shakespeare was cast as the patron saint of the rebels against the status quo. The distorting simplification of such a perception is patently evident, as is its connection to the partiality (in both senses) in the appreciation of Shakespeare's works during the formative phase of Romantic drama. In fact, to quite a considerable extent Shakespeare's function in the crystallization of Romantic drama can be dissociated from the reality of his opus. It is as an almost abstract embodiment of a type of drama that Shakespeare has a decisive "programmatische Bedeutung" (programmatic significance).[21]

The attraction of that program lay in its evocation of a revolutionary dramatic vision. Liberty was to take precedence over rules, infinite vistas over finite neatness, a creative disorder over a stifling order. Two distinct principles of form and two contrary approaches to *imitatio* were arraigned in a battle that marks one of the major watersheds in the history of the European theater. Passions were so inflamed because the stakes were so high. What was at issue was nothing short of the switch from the traditional, Classical to a modern, nationalistic paradigm. A new poetics was being evolved that was to be of paramount importance far beyond the Romantic period. And its first and perhaps unsurpassable practical exponent was that mysterious genius called Shakespeare.

---

[21] Gundolf, p. 131.

It is in this way that Shakespeare was the liberating agent, the trigger of emancipation in both Germany and France. His plays implicitly challenged the need for rules, and at the same time offered powerful explicit exemplars of an alternative – and highly successful – dramaturgy. The electrifying impact of the encounter with Shakespeare is nowhere more poignantly described than in Goethe's essay of 1771, *Zum Schäkespears Tag*:

> Die erste Seite, die ich in ihm las, machte mich auf Zeitlebens ihm eigen, und wie ich mit dem ersten Stücke fertig war, stand ich wie ein Blindgeborner, dem eine Wunderhand das Gesicht in einem Augenblicke schenckt. Ich erkannte, ich fühlte aufs lebhafteste meine Existenz um eine Unendlichkeit erweitert; alles war mir neu, unbekannt, und das ungewohnte Licht machte mir Augenschmerzen. Nach und nach lernt' ich sehen, und, Dank sei meinem erkenntlichen Genius, ich fühlte noch immer lebhaft, was ich gewonnen habe.

> Ich zweifelte keinen Augenblick, dem regelmäßigen Theater zu entsagen. Es schien mir die Einheit des Orts so kerkermäßig ängstlich, die Einheiten der Handlung und der Zeit lästige Fesseln unsrer Einbildungskraft. Ich sprang in die freie Luft und fühlte erst, daß ich Hände und Füße hatte.[22]

> (The first page of his that I read turned me into a lifelong devotee, and when I had finished the first play, I stood like a person born blind to whom a wondrous hand has suddenly given sight. I recognized, I felt my existence most vividly expanded by an infinite measure; everything was new and unknown to me, and the unaccustomed light troubled my eyes. Gradually I learned to see, and thanks to my recognizing genius, I still felt vividly how much I had gained.

> I did not hesitate for a second to renounce regular theater. The unity of place seemed to me as frighteningly restricted as a prison, the unities of action and time as bothersome shackles to our imagination. I sprang into the free air, and felt only then that I had hands and feet.)

The imagery of this passage invokes not only the release from a state of imprisonment ("kerkermäßig ängstlich" [as frightening as a prison], "Fesseln" [shackles], "freie Luft" [fresh air]) but also the experience of a sudden astonishing revelation ("wie ein Blindgeborner, dem eine Wunderhand das Gesicht in einem Augenblicke schenckt" [like a person born blind to whom a wondrous hand has suddenly given sight]). This was indeed not the least important aspect of Shakespeare's magic touch: that he struck with the force of a religious epiphany. His admirers were like converts, spreading their newly discovered gospel and seeking further proselytes with an ardent devotion. That their conversion stemmed from an intuitive recognition rather than from cognitive knowledge in no way diminished its impelling effect.

The advent of Shakespeare in Germany and France was, therefore, the occasion when the power struggle between the old and the new dramatic ideals erupted into an open conflict. Shakespeare was the primary instrument in precipitating this clash because his plays were the models that threw all the neoclassical assumptions into question. So he became the rallying-point for the opposition to what seemed stale and worn, and the flag under which the apostles of renewal and innovation mounted their campaign. What is more, Shakespeare's status as the bearer of a cultural revolution was subtly reinforced by the political implications particularly of his historical chronicles, in which he overtly examines the nature of government and the distribution of responsibilities within the state. Thus Shakespeare became the touchstone of the deep aesthetic and moral transformations

---

[22] Pascal, pp. 98-99.

that were at the core of the Romantic movement. As a model, as a stimulus for liberation, and as a kind of projection screen for the incoming ideals, Shakespeare was the vital spark for the formation of Romantic drama. The debate about Shakespeare was in fact the forum for the discussion of the shape of the drama of the future.

Douglas Hilt

THE RECEPTION OF THE SPANISH THEATRE IN EUROPEAN ROMANTICISM

Writers, alas, may but rarely determine the environment in which they pen their works. This was certainly true of Spain in the first third of the nineteenth century. For reasons beyond their control – Napoleon's invasion leading to a protracted war, the subsequent suppression and censorship of Ferdinand VII's despotic reign – conditions were hardly propitious for Spanish authors to create original works. The Spanish Romantic movement, in effect, dates from about 1830, the famous year of the tumultuous first performance of Victor Hugo's *Hernani*.

But, one might object, was not French Romanticism itself of late flowering if – especially in the theatre – its high point is considered to coincide roughly with the reign of the bourgeois Louis Philippe (1830-48)? Yet some fundamental differences north and south of the Pyrenees immediately spring to mind. Beyond a doubt Spanish Romanticists were greatly indebted to their northern neighbor; Larra, brought up in France, spoke French before Spanish, while Espronceda manned the Paris barricades during the 1830 revolution. For his part Zorrilla was familiar with many of the habitués of the literary salons. Generally speaking, as with Rivas and Martínez de la Rosa, their writings came too late to have any marked influence in France. The truth is that Spanish Romantic dramatists provided the source material for more Verdi operas – Rivas's *Don Alvaro o La fuerza del sino* (Don Alvaro, or The Power of Fate, 1835), García Gutiérrez's *El trovador* (The Troubadour, 1836) and *Simón Bocanegra* (1843) are the most obvious – than for any French plays of the period. In fact, the vast majority of French littérateurs were unacquainted with Spanish Romanticism. Far more important, what later was to pass for such were actually the theatre and romances of the seventeenth-century *siglo de oro* (Golden Age), introduced to northern Europe through German and Swiss intermediaries. A cheerful ignorance about literature in Spain, often resulting in hopeless confusion as to dates and even authorship, let alone any first-hand knowledge of the country or its language, did not prevent the Iberian nation from becoming the reputed Romantic land par excellence.

Often those writers who waxed most enthusiastically about Spain, for example the Schlegel brothers, August Wilhelm and Friedrich, never set foot in the country, and those who did went there merely to confirm their preconceptions. Spain was viewed as a vast colorful stage replete with guitar-strumming gypsies, audacious brigands and bullfighters, the inspiration of Goya's canvasses, an exotic land caressed by the zephyrs of Africa from whence had come the noble Moors. Returning French soldiers regaled their listeners with accounts of passionate women and fanatical priests; that the Inquisition was only finally suppressed in 1835 merely lent further credence to the *leyenda negra* (Black Legend) and tales of cruelty and barbarism. Even the excesses of Ferdinand VII were seen in their grotesque forms to be Romantic. The country soon "served as the archtype for all places foreign or medieval [...]. Spain came to embody the irrational violent forces that haunted

Hugo [...]. It is as if Spain had become a kind of home of the willful and sinister unconscious."[1]

Writers who did cross the Pyrenees had a definite notion as to what Spain should be. Fact and fiction thereupon became hopelessly entwined. Alexandre Dumas *père* went determined to ferret out a notorious bandit, and felt somehow cheated not to have confronted him at pistol point. "Ohé! Les voleurs de Castro de Río, où sont-ils?" (Ole! The robbers of Castro de Río, where are they?) he shouted in best Romantic fashion.[2] At least Dumas had seen the country, however superficially. The young Alfred de Musset, in his *Contes d'Espagne et d'Italie* (Stories of Spain and Italy) was able to describe Madrid in glowing terms without ever having viewed the city:

> Madrid, quand tes taureaux bondissent,
> Bien des mains blanches applaudissent,
> Bien des écharpes sont en jeux:
> Par tes belles nuits étoilées,
> Bien des señoras long-voilées
> Descendent tes escaliers bleus![3]

(Madrid, when your bulls rear up, many a white hand applauds and many a scarf is waved. In your beautiful starry nights many long-veiled señoras descend your blue steps.)

Small wonder, then, that Spain soon became known as "La péninsule de la passion." Here, perhaps, a brief digression is in order. Has not Spain been regarded as a land of exotic contrasts from the time of Corneille to the present day? Are not Hemingway's Spanish novels an extension of an over-romanticized vision of a country that existed mainly in his – and others' – imagination? The French Romanticists were merely following in a long tradition of uncritical clichés and preestablished "facts." As the critic Sainte-Beuve observed of his contemporaries, "Même lorsqu'on imitait, il y avait une certaine ignorance première, une demi-science qui prêtait à l'imagination et lui laissait sa latitude" (Even when they imitated there was a certain initial lack of knowledge, a semi-science which fed the imagination and gave it some scope).[4] As to the "certaine ignorance première," how many people today can name any Spanish figure of either the eighteenth or nineteenth century, with the exception perhaps of Francisco Goya? How many have ever heard of Galdós, the Spanish Balzac or Dickens? It is as if Spain's sole historical purpose were to provide a dazzling backdrop, an anonymous chorus, full of passionate sound and fury, but strangely incapable of providing any individual of note in any endeavor. In the first half of the nineteenth century ignorance of facts was to prove no barrier; on the contrary, all writers and tourists from northern climes felt secure in their knowledge of Spain.

French dramatists had always borrowed heavily from their Hispanic neighbor. Thus, *Le Menteur* (The Liar) is greatly indebted to Alarcón's *La verdad sospechosa* (Suspect Truth), but committing the type of mistake to be repeated through the centuries, Corneille believed the play to be the work of Lope de Vega. *Le Cid* is a considerable improvement over Guillén de Castro's episodic *Mocedades del Cid* (The Cid's Youthful Adventures), but the theme of honor and epic grandeur without question reflects its Spanish heritage. Claude Abraham notes:

---

[1] John Porter Houston, *Victor Hugo* (New York: Twayne, 1974), p. 14.

[2] Alfred de Musset, *Contes d'Espagne et d'Italie* (London: Athlone Press, 1973), p. 12 of Introduction by Margret Rees.

[3] Musset, p. 103.

[4] Paul Hazard, *Le Romantisme et les lettres* (Paris: Montaigne, 1929), p. 96.

The true genius of Corneille is made manifest in every aspect of the adaptation from the Spanish model which is a long, rambling dramatic poem in which the tragic rubs elbows with the comic, the trivial with the epic, and the tasteless with the sublime.[5]

Yet it was precisely these defects which later would be hailed as the very essence of Spanish "Romanticism."

As was later to occur with Hugo's *Hernani*, the first performance of *Le Cid* caused a furor, followed by the famous *querelle*. Scudéry in his *Observations sur le Cid* objected to the play on the following grounds:

> Qu'il choque les principales règles du poème dramatique;
> Qu'il manque de jugement en sa conduite;
> Qu'il a beaucoup de méchants vers;
> Que presque tout ce qu'il a de beautés sont dérobées.

(It conflicts with the basic rules of dramatic poetry; it lacks judgement in its behavior; it contains many bad lines; nearly all it has of beauty has been stolen.)

Scudéry's points are debatable. Less so are the decidedly emotional exchanges between Rodrigue and Chimène, as in Act III, Scene iv, that foreshadow future Romantic intensity and freer dramatic technique:

CHIMÈNE	Hélas!
RODRIGUE	Écoute-moi.
CHIMÈNE	Je me meurs.
RODRIGUE	Un moment.
CHIMÈNE	Va, laisse-moi mourir.
RODRIGUE	Quatre mots seulement: Après ne me réponds qu'avecque cette épée.

(CHIMÈNE	Alas!
RODRIGUE	Listen to me.
CHIMÈNE	I'm dying.
RODRIGUE	Just one moment.
CHIMÈNE	Go, let me die.
RODRIGUE	A few words only. Then only answer me with this sword.)

For his part, that liberated spirit, Molière, owed as much to Italian adaptations and other sources for his *Dom Juan* as he did to Tirso de Molina. Even so, already in the French classical age, the Spanish "romantic" theatre was having a noticeable influence.

During the eighteenth century Spain was temporarily forgotten. Le Sage was an exception; generally the Enlightenment regarded Spain as decadent and fanatical, even under French Bourbon rule. Calderón, if known at all, was dismissed as narrowly Catholic and provincial in an age that strove to broaden horizons. The paucity of original theatrical material on the Madrid stage (the *refundiciones*

---

[5] Claude Abraham, *Pierre Corneille* (New York: Twayne, 1972), p. 98.

were labored reworkings of Golden age plays to conform with imposed classical taste) merely confirmed French opinion that little was to be gained from a study of Spanish drama. The new theatre of Moratín *hijo* (the younger) was largely ignored; Beaumarchais's *Le Barbier de Séville* and *Le Mariage de Figaro* were political in intent, and the purpose of the supposed Spanish background was as much to placate the censor as anything else.

By contrast, in both countries, often played on stages with no great pretensions, a more popular fare, in the form of *comédies larmoyantes* (tearful comedies) and outright melodrama oblivious to any set of rules, was being performed before a delighted public. Totally unconcerned with observing the hallowed three unities, these modest plays were precursors of future more ambitious Romantic offerings:

> Intrigues ténébreuses et compliquées, coups de théâtre, style emphatique, favorable à la déclamation vibrante, rien n'y manque en effet. C'est un mélange de tragédie, de comédie larmoyante, de drame bourgeois, de pantomime, de musique même et de danse. Par son pathétique facile, par sa prose triviale ou solennelle, par ses libertés, par le spectacle, par l'exploitation des romans en vogue et du répertoire étranger, il paraît souvent un romantisme de la veille.[6]

> (Dark and complex plots, theatrical effects, bombastic style, inclined toward emotive declamation – indeed, nothing was missing. It is a mixture of tragedy, tearjerker, of bourgeois drama, pantomime, even some music and dance thrown in. Through its cheap pathos, its prose at times trivial and solemn, liberties taken, through the use of spectacle, using novels in fashion and also taken from foreign lists, it often appeared to be the harbinger of Romanticism.)

The melodrama was to continue unabated into the new century. Guilbert de Pixérécourt wrote over one hundred such popular plays from 1798 to 1834; one entitled *Le Pèlerin blanc* (The White Pilgrim), a veritable "succès de larmes," ran for several months. In 1827, a scant three years before the epochal presentation of *Hernani*, the celebrated actors Fréderick Lemaître and Marie Duval scored a notable success in *Trente ans dans la vie d'un joueur* (Thirty Years in the Life of an Actor) before an enthused public. The themes for these potboilers were drawn from any source available, including similar works produced in Spain.

Such performances notwithstanding, some momentous event was needed to renew the historical ties between the two countries. This was inadvertently provided by Napoleon's invasion of the Peninsula in 1808. On a more literary level, the involvement of a major author was required to focus public attention. That figure was Chateaubriand:

> Spain, always known to the French, made a strong re-entry into French literature with Chateaubriand, who needed its sumptuous settings for his melancholy. With the vogue of the troubadour, the romanticists as a whole came face to face with a country overflowing with lore, heroic and still medieval. The colorful legends of violent passions led them to add to the misconceptions of Spanish life which the nation had inherited from the past.[7]

In *Les Aventures du dernier des Abencérages* (The Adventures of the Last of the Abencerrajes) Chateaubriand presented a vision of the idealized Moor, fighting for liberty, ancient rights, and the soil of his ancestors. This evocation of bygone chivalry, not published until 1826, was already com-

---

[6] Jean Giraud, *L'École romantique française* (Paris: Colin, 1947), p. 100.
[7] Albert Joseph George, *The Development of French Romanticism* (Syracuse: Syracuse Univ., Press, 1955), p. 32.

posed in 1810 and known among a select group. Though not a play, the ringing images and stirring deeds depicted by the leading writer of the age were not lost on later aspiring dramatists. If Chateaubriand set the mood, it was left to others from Germany and Switzerland to provide securer underpinnings – at least outwardly – for a more embracing image of a Romantic Spain.

As in France, most German writers lacked firsthand acquaintance with the Spanish theatre of the eighteenth century. Having to all intents and purposes but recently created a literature of their own, the passionate debate that was to be waged elsewhere over the relative merits of Classicism and Romanticism seemed largely irrelevant. Both Goethe and Schiller, who in their youthful outpourings had precipitated the *Sturm und Drang* (Storm and Stress), a shrill forerunner of Romanticism, with rousing plays including *Götz von Berlichingen* and *Die Räuber* (The Bandits), in later years professed to be above the fray. German critics such as Bouterwek and the Schlegel brothers found themselves in an especially favorable position:

> La littérature allemande venait seulement de découvrir l'antiquité, elle n'a pas donc à lutter contre le classicisme antique, elle l'absorbe au contraire, et nous voyons quelques-uns des théoriciens du romantisme allemand passionément admirateurs de l'antiquité. Du reste, au lieu de se séparer de la littérature classique de l'âge précédent, le romantisme allemand cherche aussi à l'absorber; au lieu de contredire le XVIIIe siècle, il le suit.[8]

> (German literature had only just discovered antiquity, and therefore felt no need to struggle against ancient Classicism. On the contrary, it absorbs the latter, and we see some of the theorists of German Romanticism become passionate admirers of the ancients. Moreover, instead of distancing itself from the classical literature of the previous age, German Romanticism endeavors to absorb it; rather than contradicting the eighteenth century, it follows in its wake.)

In the case of Germany with its fledgling literature such a perspective afforded a distinct advantage. This simply was not possible in France; even in the most romantic of Hugo's plays, the classical element was never totally absent.

German enthusiasm for the Spanish *siglo de oro* entered with the new century. Tieck's monumental translation of the *Quixote* between 1799-1801 had first opened German eyes to the hitherto unsuspected depth and extent of Spanish seventeenth-century literature. Soon the attention of German critics turned to the works of the leading playwrights, notably Calderón. One day in 1802, Goethe, in his capacity as Director of the Weimar court theatre, read the manuscript of August Wilhelm Schlegel's translation of Calderón's *La devoción de la cruz* (Devotion to the Cross) under its new title *Andacht zum Kreuze*. Goethe's extravagant response was to declare the play superior to any of Shakespeare's;[9] in truth, the English dramatist's decisive influence among writers on the Continent was never in doubt. Yet for the first time the Spanish stage was embraced as a parallel source of inspiration.

In sheer exuberance over the Spanish drama, no German writer surpassed August Wilhelm Schlegel. His praise of Calderón in particular was ecstatic and for a time verged on the idolatrous:

> Calderón [...] ein Dichter, wenn je einer den Namen verdient hat. In weit höherem Grade erneuerte sich das Wunder der Natur, der enthusiastische Beifall und die Beherrschung der Bühne [...] in ihm

---

[8] Joseph Aynard, "Comment définir le romantisme," *Revue de la littérature comparée* (1925), p. 649.

[9] Werner Brüggemann, *Spanisches Theatre und deutsche Romantik* (Münster: Aschendorffsche Verlagsbuchhandlung, 1964), I, 190.

hat das romantische Schauspiel der Spanier den Gipfel der Vollendung erreicht.[10]

(Calderón [...] a poet, if ever one deserved the name. The miracle of Nature was renewed to a far higher degree, as well as enthusiastic applause and the mastery of the stage [...] in him the Romantic Spanish theatre has reached the peak of perfection.)

In a letter addressed to Goethe, Schlegel proudly declared himself the "erste Missionar Calderóns in Deutschland."[11]

Already in 1798 and again in 1801 Wilhelm von Humboldt had visited Spain, and on his return wrote to Goethe that the country had the appearance of Europe in the sixteenth century, having retained its customs and true identity.[12] Soon visitors from England and France were perceiving similar Romantic features in the Peninsula. Schlegel never journeyed to Spain, but for years it was to remain the land of his ideals. To him Spain was the nation that had freed itself from the Muslim invader, thus saving Christianity (an ambivalent attitude toward the Moors was no impediment among the Romantics). During this stirring period the individual nature and heroism of the people had found its true expression in the *romance* and later in the national poetic drama of Lope de Vega and Calderón. This "brennende Nationalität" (burning national character) is the essence of Schlegel's concept of the Romantic theatre, the vital expression of a people's inner self, neither limited by epoch nor geography. These ideal conditions had been found in Spain during the *siglo de oro*, for Schlegel the Romantic period nonpareil:

Hier war alles günstig gewesen. Religion und Mythos, Geschichte und Legende, ritterliche Tapferkeit und edle Liebe zu den Frauen, echt romantische Motive, waren lebendig und mitwirkend bei der Geburt der Nationalpoesie. Und das spanische Theatre, von Ursprung an modern und romantisch, hat alle diese Elemente in sich. So ist Calderón (und mit ihm die anderen spanischen Dramatiker) neben Shakespeare und Dante einer der Väter der modernen Poesie, speziell der modernen Dramatik.[13]

(Here everything was favorable. Religion and myth, history and legend, chivalrous bravery and noble love toward ladies, true Romantic motifs, all were alive and helping at the birth of national poetry. And the Spanish theatre, modern and Romantic right from the beginning, contains all these elements in itself. Thus Calderón [and with him the other Spanish playwrights] together with Shakespeare and Dante is one of the fathers of modern poetry, especially of modern drama.)

In more practical terms Schlegel's younger brother Friedrich led the way in 1802 with his dramatic poem *Conde Alarcos* (Count Alarcos), based on the well-known Spanish ballad. August Wilhelm followed in 1803 with the first volume of the *Spanisches Theater* containing his translations of several Calderón plays which eventually were to include *La devoción de la cruz* (Devotion of the Cross), *El mayor encanto amor* (Love Is the Greatest Enchantment), *La banda y la flor* (The Sash and the Flower), *El príncipe constante* (The Steadfast Prince), and *La puente de Mantible* (The Bridge of Mantible). Schlegel attempted to reproduce the original verse forms with meticulous accuracy. This required the introduction into German literature of the *romance* (with assonance), the *redondilla*, the *quintilla*, and the *décima* (in the five plays selected by Schlegel there were no *liras*

---

[10] August Wilhelm Schlegel, *Vorlesungen über dramatische Kunst und Literatur* (Bonn and Leipzig: Schroeder, 1923), pp. 272, 275.
[11] Gerhart Hoffmeister, *Spanien und Deutschland* (Berlin: Schmidt, 1976), p. 128.
[12] Brüggemann, p. 206.
[13] Schlegel, p. 42.

or *endechas*). Generally speaking, assonance in German is less effective than in Spanish. It is not recognized immediately, and after the initial enthusiasm for Calderón had run its course, assonance failed to establish itself to any large degree in the German theatre. Significantly, the "new" Spanish verse forms had little effect in France; the majority of the Romantic dramas composed in verse continued to use the classical alexandrine, albeit in a more liberated form.

However, it was not Schlegel but Tieck, the translator of the *Cid*, who was the first to announce the new "évangile calderónien." Already the *Aufzug der Romanze* (The Pageantry of the Romance, the Prologue to Tieck's mystery play *Kaiser Oktavian*) written in 1804 is a faithful copy – at least in spirit – of a Calderonian *auto sacramental*. The influence of Calderón even extends to the incorporation of characteristically Spanish motifs and the use of a great variety of rhythms found in the Golden Age drama. Probably the Prologue to *Kaiser Oktavian* represents the apogee of Calderón's direct influence on Germany, even though other writers, notably Grillparzer and Eichendorff, were to fall under his spell for considerable periods.

Soon the Calderón cult had passed from theoretical treatises and translations to actual performances. *La vida es sueño* (Life Is a Dream) had been performed in Königsberg as early as 1809, and in the translation of Einsiedel and Riemer it was produced in Weimar in 1811. The German and Austrian stage during this period presents a bewildering array of translations, adaptations, and imitations of original Spanish plays. Schlegel's translation of *El príncipe constante* enabled the play to be successfully performed first in Weimar in 1814 and later in Berlin in 1816, on both occasions under Goethe's direction. During the period 1816-34 *La vida es sueño* was given an impressive 269 performances in Germany and Austria;[14] small wonder that the young Grillparzer was so familiar with Calderón's masterpiece. Only in later years were Tieck and Grillparzer to become disenchanted with the "Spanish Shakespeare" and lift Lope de Vega from the near total obscurity into which he had fallen as a result of the one-sided praise heaped upon Calderón.

The Napoleonic invasion of Germany, the patriotic fervor and nationalism stirred up by the adherents of Fichte, the resultant awakening sense of reality – all of these factors contributed to the later lessening of interest in Calderón.[15] The *Junges Deutschland* (Young Germany) movement had little affection for the Spanish "poet-priest," and parodies began to appear, including doggerel and satire by Heine. In later years the Schlegels turned their enthusiasm elsewhere and barely bothered to defend their Spanish exemplar. Yet ironically, just as the inevitable reaction to the Spanish "romantic" theatre gathered strength in Germany, the writings of the Schlegels and other critics were to have their profoundest influence in France.

Within the space of three years the French reading public was to be introduced to fresh influences from abroad, this despite the ill-concealed hostility of Napoleon's censorship. Already in 1811 Madame de Staël (A.W. Schlegel's patroness) had prepared the way with *De l'Allemagne* (On Germany) for an acceptance of Romantic views. The following year saw the translation of Bouterwek's *Geschichte der schönen Literatur in Spanien* (History of Belles Lettres in Spain, originally published in 1804) as the *Histoire de la littérature espagnole*. For the first time the Spanish stage was depicted in its medley of *graciosos* (fools, clowns), saints, devils, and allegorical figures, all

---

[14] J.J. Bertrand, *L. Tieck et le théâtre espagnol* (Paris: Rieder, 1914), p. 133.

[15] Ernst Behler, "Calderón and the German Romantics," in *Studies in Romanticism*, Vol. 20, No. 4 (Winter 1981), p. 441, is of the opinion that "This political motivation [underlying the German romantic devotion to Calderón] [...] is clearly directed against the military despotism of Napoleon," and therefore increased, rather than lessened interest in the Spanish dramatist.

freely expressing themselves in the most extravagant language, ranging from elaborate metaphor to popular speech. Though Sismondi's *De la littérature du Midi de l'Europe* (On the Literature of Southern Europe, 1813) was more classical in its restraint (only the third volume out of four dealt with Spain), he too finally championed the *comedia* against all artificial rules. Sismondi, a Swiss Calvinist, hardly knew any Spanish, but relied for his sources on Bouterwek and Schlegel.

By far the most effective influence was the translation by Madame Necker de Saussure of A.W. Schlegel's 1808 Vienna lectures which appeared in 1814 as *Cours de littérature dramatique*. Schlegel was a dedicated scholar with a sound grasp of the Spanish language and an effective style, and soon his views regarding the *siglo de oro* as the true spirit of Romanticism found wide acceptance. Never mind that Schlegel was francophobe in outlook and that his comprehension of Spanish culture was largely secondhand; in Restoration France, as Van Tieghem has pointed out, "la connaissance de la littérature étrangère, soit directement, soit, le plus souvent, à travers des traductions, invitait, sinon à l'imiter, du moins à faire aussi bien" (an acquaintance with foreign literature, either direct or, as was more often the case, through translations, was an invitation if not exactly to imitate then at least to do just as well).[16] Foreign literature beyond the confines of the classics was now all the rage; few questioned the authenticity of Scott's novels, the historical veracity of Schiller's plays, or the background of the Spanish "Romantic" theatre.

Presently French writers were making their own contributions. In 1814, taking advantage of Napoleon's fall, Creuzé de Lesser published a collection of verse entitled *Le Cid, romances espagnoles, imitées en romances françaises*, with further editions in 1823 and 1836. Insofar as possible he retained the passion and vigor of the original Spanish epic poems, so dramatic in their late medieval form. These and other *romances* had also been the source material for many of the plays of the Golden Age:

> De l'épopée surtout: car ces admirables romances offrent l'exemple d'une création spontanée. Retourner à la poésie populaire: tout est là; oublier la poésie savante, toujours artificielle, toujours fausse, pour recueillir sur les lèvres du peuple le cri de la nature, voilà le plus nécessaire effort. Admirable rencontre! Cette épopée primitive, jaillie du sol, l'Espagne la possède, il suffit de l'écouter. Et les Français de s'appliquer à faire goûter à leurs compatriotes cette poésie populaire, qui est, comme l'on sait, un des mythes du romantisme.[17]

> (Above all, the epic: for these admirable ballads provide the example of spontaneous creation. We need to return to the poetry of the people: everything is there; forget erudite poetry which is always artificial and false, go and gather the cry of Nature from the lips of the people, that's where we have to bestir ourselves. Happy encounter! This primitive epic, sprung from the soil, Spain has it, just listen to it. And the French have to apply themselves to let their compatriots taste this poetry of the people which is, as we know, one of the myths of Romanticism.)

In 1822 Abel Hugo published his *Romances historiques traduites de l'espagnol* which introduced his countrymen, among them his famous brother, to Spanish historical figures such as Bernardo del Carpio, Fernán González, Alvaro de Luna, and Rodrigo, the last of the Goths. Abel Hugo sincerely believed that these Christian exploits recalled the Bible, even so far as the metre of the poetry. When Abel Hugo compiled his *Histoire de la campagne d'Espagne en 1823* earlier

[16] Philippe Van Tieghem, *Le Romantisme français* (Paris: Presses Universitaires de France, 1968), p. 27.
[17] Hazard, p. 88.

memories of atrocities and torture had ceded to a Chateaubriand vision of Spain as a bulwark of Christianity, aided by the "cien mil hijos de San Luis" (The Hundred Thousand Sons of Saint Luis). In 1827 Esménard and La Beaumelle translated the *Chefs-d'oeuvre des théâtres étrangers* (Masterpieces of Foreign Theatres), marked more by patient accuracy than any Romantic spirit, but which at least made several Spanish plays accessible to a wider public. Furthermore, La Beaumelle's *Vie de Lope de Vega* helped right the imbalance which had stood so long in favor of Calderón.

By now Spanish studies were all the rage. In 1828, Émile Deschamps, a close friend of Victor Hugo, published his *Études françaises et étrangères* (French and Foreign Studies), of which the central part consisted of the *Romances sur Rodrigue, dernier roi des Goths, imitées de l'espagnol* (Ballads, Imitated from the Spanish, on Rodrigo, Last King of the Goths). Deschamps carefully described how new blood might be added to the impoverished old traditions:

> Ce poème est tiré de ces admirables romances espagnoles, qu'on a si bien nommées une Iliade sans Homère. J'en ai traduit quelques-unes, j'en ai inventé quelques autres, en m'inspirant de toutes les chroniques du temps, et en me servant surtout de l'excellent travail de M. Abel Hugo sur la poésie espagnole. J'ai conservé la forme lyrique des romances, en ayant soin de varier continuellement les rythmes comme les tons; et j'ai tâché de coordonner tous ces matériaux de manière à présenter un intérêt suivi, une espèce d'action dramatique ayant son exposition, son noeud et sa catastrophe.[18]

> (This poem is taken from one of these admirable Spanish ballads which have so rightly been dubbed "An Illiad without Homer." I have translated a few of them, a few others I have invented, drawing inspiration from all the chronicles of the period, and above all by availing myself of the excellent work of Mr. Abel Hugo in Spanish poetry. I have retained the lyric form of the ballads, taking care always to vary the rhythms as well as the sounds; and I have tried to coordinate all this material in such a way so as to present a constant flow, a sort of dramatic action with its exposition, its complication, and its unraveling.)

In other words, the Spanish *romance* and theatre were virtually interchangeable, both being charged with lyricism and powerful dramatic effects.

It was but a short step from translations to original plays. In 1825 Pierre Lebrun's *Cid d'Andalousie* was staged, written in verse, though disregarding the unity of place. The drama was largely an adaptation of Lope's *Estrella de Sevilla* (Star of Seville), but without the part of the *gracioso* and imbued with a large measure of sentimentality. In his preface Lebrun stated quite candidly that Lope "peut nous aider à fonder en France un théâtre comme le sien, national" (can help us to found a theatre in France like his own, that is to say, national).[19] Lebrun's play immediately ran into difficulties. The censor took objection to a scene in which the young King of Spain, surprised on a nocturnal romantic foray, received several sword blows on his back from an outraged brother. Worse still, the actors fell to quarreling among themselves, and a segment of the public objected to the style of versification and other liberties, including the unadorned use of the plebeian word "chambre." On March 7, 1825 the critic of *Le Globe* took Lebrun to task:

> À en croire le grand nombre de nos journalistes, rien de plus commun, de plus lâche, de plus prosaïque que la diction du *Cid d'Andalousie* [...]. Les vers de comédie abondent dans son ouvrage; il aime appeler les choses par leur nom [...]. Plus les sentiments sont élevés, plus ils se produisent avec

---

[18] Émile Deschamps, *La Préface des Études françaises et étrangères* (Paris: Presses Françaises, 1923), p. 67.
[19] Hazard, p. 88.

simplicité et franchise. Voilà ce qui a été chez lui le principal objet du blâme.[20]

(To believe the large number of us journalists there is nothing more common or more despicable, nothing more prosaic than the diction of *The Cid of Andalucia* [...]. Comic verse permeates his work; he likes to call a spade a spade [...]. The more elevated the sentiments, the more they are expressed with simplicity and openness. That is where the main fault lies.)

Whatever the play's shortcomings, real or supposed, it was nevertheless a direct precursor to *Hernani*.

Later that same year appeared a bizarre pot-pourri of short plays entitled *Théâtre de Clara Gazul, comédienne espagnole*, allegedly translated from the original Spanish. In fact the young perpetrator of the hoax was Prosper Mérimée, later renowned as the author of *Carmen*. Mérimée was not a dramatist by nature, his sketches being designed more for the salon than the stage. Though only twenty-three years old, he had visited Spain in 1823 and had acquired a substantial knowledge of the language, enabling him to lampoon the traditional *comedia*. If the biting satire on the Inquisition and the priests' love affairs reflect the author's Voltairean attitudes, at least he made sound use of his Spanish sources. One critic noted that "[il] unissait parfois à la liberté shakespearienne la fantaisie de Calderón, pastichant curieusement le vieux drame d'outre-Pyrénées" (sometimes he would combine Shakespearean freedom with Calderonian imagination, creating a curious pastiche of the traditional drama beyond the Pyrenees).[21]

The playlets, half serious, half ironical, owe as much to Byron and Molière as to anything perceptibly Spanish. In a brief introduction by a certain Joseph L'Estrange (Mérimée in the thinnest of disguises) Clara's origin is explained: "Je suis née sous un oranger sur le bord d'un chemin, non loin de Motril, dans le royaume de Granade" (I was born under an orange tree by the side of the road, not far from Motril, in the kingdom of Granada).[22] Her "Moorish" background is merely a pretense for Mérimée to deliver some anticlerical thrusts; Clara flees the convent to which she has been assigned, and after many adventures finally becomes an actress performing in Moratín's *La Mojigata* (The Prude). The opening lines of the Prologue in *Clara Gazul* set the mood for much that follows:

LE GRAND	– Enfin vous êtes habillée!
LE POÈTE	– Et toujours jolie comme une ange.
LE CAPITAINE	– Et quoi! sans basquina et sans mantilla?
CLARA	– C'est que je n'ai pas à jouer un rôle espagnol.[23]

(THE GRANDEE	– At last you're dressed!
THE POET	– And still pretty as an angel.
THE CAPTAIN	– What! No skirt and no mantilla?
CLARA	– It's just that I don't have to play a Spanish role.)

Clearly the self-mocking tone of such scenes, written in prose, is far removed from the spirit of the *comedia*. One of the collection, *Les Espagnols au Danemark* (The Spaniards in Denmark), is even

---

[20] Pierre Martino, *L'Époque romantique en France*, 1815-1830 (Paris: Hatier, 1944), p. 128.
[21] Giraud, p. 102.
[22] Prosper Mérimée, *Le Théâtre de Clara Gazul* (Paris: Larousse, 1949), p. 12.
[23] Mérimée, p. 21.

divided into "journées" in imitation of the original "jornadas," but in all of the eight short plays the distance from the Spanish seventeenth century is immense. Only later in his *Lettres d'Espagne* and above all in *Carmen* did the mature Mérimée give true expression to the passionate warmth he felt for the wild beauty of Spain, so different from what he considered to be the dull existence of his native country. Yet how much he owed to the *romance* or to the drama of the *siglo de oro*, let alone to dreamy German theorists, is open to question; in *Colomba* and other tales the exotic background is as much the result of artistic imagination as of conscious research.

The same observations apply even more to Théophile Gautier. An *artiste manqué*, in his *Voyage en Espagne* in 1843 (as well as in the 43 poems collected under the title *España* in 1845) he evoked the sensuous appeal of the country, down to the very color of the food. Originally entitled *Tra los montes* (Beyond the Mountains), an indication of the author's rudimentary Spanish, much of the travelogue was shamelessly invented. Whatever the fanciful quality of the whole enterprise, the sweep of the canvas is memorable, as in the following description of a performance of *Hernani* which Gautier, a participant in the original *bataille*, witnessed in Valladolid:

> Le lendemain, on jouait *Hernani* ou *l'Honneur castillan*, de Victor Hugo, traduit par don Eugenio de Ochoa; nous n'eûmes garde de manquer pareille fête. La pièce est rendue, vers pour vers, avec une exactitude scrupuleuse, à l'exception de quelques passages et de quelques scènes que l'on a dû retrancher pour satisfaire aux exigences du public. La scène des portraits est réduite à rien, parce que les Espagnols la considèrent comme injurieuse pour eux, et s'y trouvent indirectement tournés en ridicule. Il y a beaucoup de suppressions dans le cinquième acte. En général, les Espagnols se fâchent lorsqu'on parle d'eux d'une manière poétique; ils se prétendent calomniés par Hugo, par Mérimée et par tous ceux en général qui ont écrit sur l'Espagne: oui... calomniés, mais en beau. Ils renient de toutes leurs forces l'Espagne du Romancero et des Orientales, et une de leurs principales prétentions, c'est de n'être ni poétiques ni pittoresques, prétentions, hélas! trop bien justifiées.[24]

> (The next day, *Hernani* or *Castillian Honor* by Victor Hugo was being performed in the translation of Eugenio de Ochoa. We made sure we did not miss such an occasion. The play was rendered, line by line, with scrupulous accuracy, with the exception of a few passages and a scene or two which they had to omit to oblige local demands. The scene with the portraits is reduced to nothing as the Spaniards consider it insulting, finding themselves obliquely made to look ridiculous. There are quite a few cuts in the fifth act. In general the Spaniards get annoyed when one talks about them in a poetic way; they claim that they have been slandered by Hugo, by Mérimée and by all those who in general have written about Spain: yes... slandered, indeed. They repudiate with all their energy that Spain of the *Romancero* and the *Orientales*, one of their main claims being that they are neither poetic nor picturesque, claims, I fear, only too well justified.)

On his return to Paris, Gautier produced a vaudeville sketch entitled *Un voyage en Espagne*, a lighthearted self-parody full of amorous intrigue, which had a run of thirty-four performances.

If Gautier at least had visited Spain to fire his poetic muse, no such consideration bothered the young Alfred de Musset. Not yet twenty, the precocious poet in 1830 swelled the rising Romantic tide with his *Contes d'Espagne et d'Italie*. Often the Italian settings are interchangeable with the Spanish; only a gondola is needed to indicate Venice, while the rustle of a mantilla serves to place the poem south of the Pyrenees. Yet the audacity of his verse, the *enjambement* from one stanza to the next, and other dramatic effects were all calculated to shock the literary public on the eve of

---

[24] Théophile Gautier, *Voyage en Espagne* (Paris: Charpentier, 1894), p. 64.

Hernani. Nor was that all. The fiery passions of duped lovers bent on exacting a terrible revenge, and similar overwrought scenes set against an exotic canvas – all led to Musset being declared an authority on Spain, in turn inspiring credulous visitors to seek the exact location of each poem. The influence of Byron is writ large on every page; one can only sympathize with the long-suffering Spaniard who plaintively asked a tourist, "Quand donc sera terminé cet éternel portrait de l'Espagne stéréotypé par nos voisins?" (When will this eternal portrait of stereotyped Spain painted by our neighbors ever come to an end?)[25]

No French writer devoted more time and enthusiasm to Spain than did Victor Hugo. As an impressionable child of eight he had spent a year at the Collège des Nobles in Madrid, the city where his father was a general in Napoleon's army of occupation. Together with his brother Abel, the young Victor had witnessed a nation rise in defense of its liberties, a spontaneous *levée en masse* of primeval force. The rebellion, chaotic and futile at times, desperate, often without hope, men women, and children against the ordered ranks of the French – here on a vast stage was adumbrated the Romantic revolt against imposed authority. Already in 1818 the young Victor Hugo had dashed off a three-act melodrama entitled *Inez de Castro*; his last play, *Torquemada*, written in 1869 but never performed during his lifetime, reverted to a cherished Spanish theme set in the period of Fernando and Isabel. Many of the longer novels, for example, *Notre Dame de Paris* with its gypsy Esmeralda, again reveal a Spanish interest.

In *Les Orientales* the spirit of Spain pervades the whole, whatever the supposed location of each individual poem. One critic has aptly noted that "the orientalism of Hugo is, in fact, his imaginative description of the Spain that he had visited during his youth [...]. The mosques, gardens, and steps that he describes are conveyed in such picturesque language that we are ready to ignore their essentially Spanish flavor."[26] Though the majority of poems are set in Greece and Turkey (only *Romance mauresque, Grenade, Les Bleuets* [Cornflowers], and *Fantômes* are specifically located in Spain), in the Preface Hugo evokes sensuous images of "ces belles vieilles villes d'Espagne, par exemple, où vous trouvez tout [...] car l'Espagne c'est encore l'Orient; l'Espagne est à demi asiatique" (these beautiful old Spanish towns, for example, where you can find everything [...] for Spain is still the Orient; Spain remains half Asian).[27] One can easily quibble at the anachronisms and misconceptions that crept in; Hugo, as a result of his brother Abel's translation, thought that the original of the *Romance mauresque* was truly written by a Moorish poet, and likewise misunderstood the legend of the Seven Sons of Lara. The great Spanish critic Menéndez y Pelayo was generally not impressed; Hugo's readers, on the other hand, were enthralled by the daring evocation of sultry passions and memories of a storied past.

The famous *Préface* to *Cromwell*, the clarion call of French Romanticism, needs no reiteration here. The ideas contained in the declaration were already common currency, and in a capital habituated to melodramatic offerings were less of a shock than has been commonly supposed. Hugo's indebtedness to the Spanish Golden Age drama is moot. He specifically quoted from Lope's *Arte nuovo de hazer Comedias en este tiempo* (A New Way of Writing Plays Today) with enthusiasm:

[25] Musset, p. 12 of Introduction.

[26] Robert T. Denommé, *Nineteenth-Century French Romantic Poets* (Carbondale: Southern Illinois Univ. Press, 1969), p. 94.

[27] Victor Hugo, *Les Orientales* (Paris: Garnier-Flammarion, 1968), Préface, pp. 320, 322.

> Cuando he de escribir una comedia
> Encierro los preceptos con seis llaves[28]

(When I have to write a play I lock up the rules with six keys.)

But the extent to which Hugo followed Lope's precept is debatable. Hugo gave dry Classicism a sound drubbing, but without delivering a mortal blow. In both *Hernani* and *Ruy Blas* there is no innovative use of the varied Spanish verse forms, nor is there any Shakespearean admixture of prose and verse. In both plays the hallowed alexandrine (contemptuously dismissed by Stendhal as a "cache-sottises" [hiding place for follies]) is retained, even though in the *Préface* Hugo had specifically pleaded for a greater freedom of verse. True enough, the alexandrine was bestowed a free caesura; and enjambement, hitherto the exception, now became commonplace. Yet when all is said and done, is not *Hernani* ultimately more indebted to Corneille than to either Shakespeare or the Spaniards?

The first vociferous performance of *Hernani*, with Hugo's supporters dressed *à l'espagnole* and Théophile Gautier, flamboyantly bedecked in his *gilet rouge*, well to the fore, has passed into literary history. Gautier later boasted that "pour notre génération *Hernani* a été ce qui fut *Le Cid* pour les contemporains de Corneille" (for our generation *Hernani* represented what *Le Cid* had been for the contemporaries of Corneille).[29] The tickets for admission consisted of slips of red paper with the word "hierro" superimposed, inspired by "hierro, ¡despiértate!" (sword, awaken!), the war cry of the medieval Spanish *almogávares*. Certainly Hugo succeeded in recreating onstage the atmosphere of Spain in 1519, even though the factual history of *Hernani* (the name of a small town near San Sebastian where the young Victor had stayed one night with his mother in 1811) was on insecure foundations. Hugo himself felt unease on this score, and took pains to quote an excerpt from an obscure Spanish chronicler to justify his unconventional characterization of the youthful Charles V in the play.

Hernani assuredly *looks* Spanish; all the external trappings are there in profusion. The play is typically *capa y espada* (cloak and dagger), and the audience is frequently reminded that the setting and emotions are authentically Spanish. Yet Hernani's suicide to uphold *pundonor* (point of honor) is unconvincing; the Calderonian social value system is not for export. As a noted critic observes, "Talk of honor makes it 'Spanish,' of course, a Spain with no particularly characteristic diction, nothing but a show of place names to individualize it for purposes of the play. The manners come from the Gothic novel, not from Hugo's reading of Spanish writers of the seventeenth century."[30] Similarly, despite Hugo's protestations to the contrary, *Ruy Blas* not only is inaccurate historically but is also a pastiche drawn from many sources, some entirely non-Spanish, such as Bulwer-Lytton's *The Lady of Lyons*. Hugo, of course saw it otherwise: "Entre *Hernani* et *Ruy Blas*," he wrote on November 25, 1838, "deux siècles de l'Espagne sont encadrés. Dans *Hernani* le soleil de la maison d'Autriche lève; dans *Ruy Blas* il se couche" (Between *Hernani* and *Ruy Blas* two centuries of Spain are contained. In *Hernani* the sun rises on the house of Austria; it sets over *Ruy Blas*).[31]

The idea of a valet disguising himself as a gentleman does indeed occur in dramas of Calderón and Rojas, but Hugo could well have drawn on the recent example of Manuel Godoy, the guards-

---

[28] Victor Hugo, *La Préface de Cromwell* (Paris: Société Française d'Imprimerie et de Librairie, n.d.), p. 253.
[29] Martino, p. 134.
[30] Houston, p. 55.
[31] Ernest Martinenche, *L'Espagne et le romantisme français* (Paris: Hachette, 1922), p. 134.

man from the provinces, who became the Queen's lover and royal confidant. Undeniably Hugo's "Spanish" plays are written with panache, the versification is magnificent, many of the scenes are memorable tours de force. But to rely solely on Castillian honor does not make either play truly authentic (nor for that matter are his other plays convincingly English or Italian). Yet all shortcomings to the contrary, the Romantic theatre had won the day, as the *Mercure du XIXe siècle* readily conceded:

> Là, rien de convenu, rien de travaillé, rien qui sente le métier [...]. Chacun parle le langage qui lui convient, la passion se révèle, comme dans la nature, par des mots vifs et spontanés et non par de froides analyses de sentiments; tout s'enchaîne, tout marche vers un même but [...]. C'est ainsi que l'art dramatique pourra se régénérer en France, et que la querelle des classiques et des romantiques se terminera.[32]

> (There, nothing is conventional, nothing studied, nothing that smells of technique [...]. Everyone speaks the language best suited to him, passion, as in nature, is revealed through lively and spontaneous words, and not through the cold analysis of emotions; everything is linked together and strides toward the same goal [...]. This is the way dramatic art could revive in France, and how the squabble between the Classicists and the Romantics will come to an end.)

Martínez de la Rosa, then living in Parisian exile, was not surprised at the outcome. His *Abén Humeya ou la Révolte des Maures sous Philippe II* (Aben Humeya, or The Moorish Revolt in the Reign of Philip II) was performed before an enthusiastic audience at the Porte Saint-Martin later in 1830, and the following year on his return to Spain he carried the completed manuscript of *La conjuración de Venecia* (The Venitian Conspiracy) in his luggage.[33]

The wild success of *Hernani* produced a spate of imitations that sought to mine the Spanish lode. On November 5, 1831, *La Reine d'Espagne* (The Queen of Spain) by Henri de Latouche was performed at the Comédie Française. This violent and crude drama, bordering on the farcical, was rightly whistled off the stage. A better effort was that of Casimir Delavigne whose *Don Juan d'Autriche* (Don Juan of Austria) had some real dramatic merit. On December 15, 1839, he tried again with *La Fille du Cid* (The Cid's Daughter), written in three acts, but retaining the alexandrine. Both plays fell wide of the mark despite Delavigne's good intentions. Far more grotesque – but not in the Romantic sense envisioned by Hugo – was an absurd play by Mallefille entitled *Les Infans de Lara* (The Infantes of Lara), in which the *romancero* was outrageously distorted in order to provide cheap melodramatic effects. Characters were invented, relationships changed, and the pious intentions stated in the Preface were simply not observed. By the time Alexandre Dumas penned *Don Juan de Manara* with its false evocation of Spain, it is all but impossible to discern any relationship with the Golden Age; rather a *pot-pourri* of Shakespeare, Byron, *Faust*, and Schiller, fueled by the author's powerful imagination, was predominant.

How much influence did the drama of the Golden Age, metamorphosed into Romanticism by Schlegel and his coterie, have on the French theatre? Spanish models replete with freedom of expression and exotic settings permeated the atmosphere, yet as to any real discernible influence, the answer is – not very much. The telling voices came from the north, Shakespeare foremost, but also

---

[32] Jules Marsan, *La Bataille romantique* (Paris: Hachette, 1912), p. 137.
[33] Maryse Bertrand de Muñoz, "*Hernani* de Victor Hugo et le théâtre romantique espagnol," *Mosaic: A Journal for the Comparative Study of Literature and Ideas*, 10 (1976), 92.

those with something new to say: Scott, Byron, the young Goethe, and Schiller. Paul Hazard concludes: "Ainsi l'Italie et l'Espagne ne pourraient prétendre qu'à des revendications modestes, et devraient se contenter d'un rôle effacé" (Thus Italy and Spain could only make modest claims, and would have to remain content with a secondary role).[34] Whatever their interest in Spain, the majority of French dramatists sought their inspiration elsewhere; thus the young Musset, in a letter to his friend Paul Foucher (Hugo's brother-in-law) declared: "Je ne voudrais pas écrire, ou je voudrais être Shakespeare ou Schiller" (Either I don't want to be a writer, or else be Shakespeare or Schiller).[35]

The legacy of the Spanish stage in France is one of overall spirit, rather than any specific contribution or lasting effect. Hazard, somewhat in conflict with his view cited above, perceives a certain indebtedness:

> Nous avons longtemps crié: liberté; mais nous manquions de modèles dégagés et admirables, capables de nous donner l'exemple d'une création vraiment indépendante, capables de s'opposer au prestige des chefs-d'oeuvre anciens et de le balancer: Dante, Lope de Vega, Calderón, et les autres, nous ont fourni ces exemples indispensables, nous ont appris qu'il existait un art qui n'avait rien de commun avec les règles du pseudo-classicisme, une poésie qui était autre chose que le calcul arithmétique des syllabes, une dramaturgie qui était autre chose que le jeu des trois unités; ils ont aidé les novateurs à combattre nos préjugés, à briser nos chaînes: ils sont l'origine de notre délivrance.[36]

> (For a long time we have shouted "liberty!"; but we lacked unfettered and admirable models capable of providing us the example of a creative work truly independent, models capable of resisting the prestige of the classical masterpieces and of offering a counterweight. Dante, Lope de Vega, Calderón, and the others have provided us with these indispensable models and have taught us that an art existed that had nothing in common with the rules of pseudo-Classicism. This was a poetry different from the mathematical counting of syllables, a dramatic art something other than the game of the three unities. They have helped the innovators to fight our prejudices and to break our chains; they are the source of our liberation.)

Perhaps. But is a theatre of passion and literary freedom, however exotic and intense, sufficient in itself to lay the groundwork for a new drama in an alien culture? A more accurate assessment may be that of Van Tieghem:

> L'âme de la littérature espagnole, dans ses aspects les plus essentiels, dans sa nature la plus profonde, a-t-elle inspiré nos romanciers et nos poètes? Bien peu, en somme. Autant la couleur locale espagnole a coulé à flots de 1825 à 1850, autant l'âme secrète de l'Espagne a peu inspiré nos écrivains.[37]

> (Did the soul of Spanish literature in its most basic aspects, its deepest nature, really inspire our novelists and poets? Very little, on the whole. As much as local Spanish color flowed in torrents between 1825 and 1850, just as little did the secret soul of Spain inspire our writers.)

If the Spanish theatre had failed to impress the French, what then were the chances in England, the traditional enemy, the instigator of the *leyenda negra*? Surprisingly, the theatrical heritage of the two countries shared much in common. In both England and Spain popular taste predominated in

---

[34] Hazard, p. 69.
[35] Musset, p. 147.
[36] Hazard, p. 97.
[37] Philippe Van Tieghem, *Les Influences étrangères sur la littérature française* (Paris: Presses Universitaire de France, 1961), pp. 212-13.

the theatre from an early date, to the general exclusion of the scholars who naturally looked to the ancients for their models. The corollary was that the English stage, already liberated through Shakespeare and his successors, had no need for Spanish examples to free it from the rigors of classical unities and was indeed the inspiration for the rest of Europe. Ironically, the English theatre at the beginning of the nineteenth century was itself in dire need of renewal, the victim of capricious censorship and of gross commercial considerations. The local wags gibed that there was more rewarding drama offered in parliament than at either Covent Garden or Drury Lane, and who was there to gainsay them?

Other factors predominated in 1822 when the *comédiens anglais* crossed the Channel to perform in Paris. Stendhal, among others, left a graphic account of the disaster that befell the English company at the Porte Saint-Martin theatre. If nothing else, the rowdy Paris audiences followed in the tradition of the groundlings who vociferously greeted the efforts of Shakespeare, Lope, and Calderón. But five years later in 1827 Charles Kemble and his company were accorded an enthusiastic reception. Kemble swept all before him as Hamlet, Othello, and Romeo, while Macready as Macbeth, and Kean in the role of Shylock enjoyed similar acclaim. The impressionable Berlioz fell head over heels in love with Harriet Smithson, the leading actress, and Dumas hastened to pen his epochal *Henri III* while still affected with emotion. Significantly, Émile Deschamps, the earlier defender of the Spanish theatre, now rendered *Romeo and Juliet* and *Macbeth* into improved French versions.

If the English theatre was in no need to be liberated from classical shackles, that by no means precluded a widespread interest in the Spanish drama. Both Lord Holland and the diplomat Hookham Frere had firsthand experience of the Peninsula and the Spanish language, as did the poet Southey. A scant three years after Trafalgar, following Napoleon's invasion of the Peninsula, Spain had become England's ally rather than the hereditary enemy. But even before this reversal of traditional roles there had been a reawakening of interest in Lope de Vega, Calderón, and the *romance*. As early as 1803 Southey had translated and abridged a number of medieval legends beginning with *Amadis of Gaul*, followed by *Palmerin of England* (1807) and *The Chronicle of the Cid* (1808). Six years later appeared his own version of *Roderick, the Last of the Goths*, a "tragic poem" that extended over one hundred pages. Southey was an industrious scholar rather than an inspired poet, but his two visits to Spain did enable him to assemble an extensive library of original works. Hookham Frere translated parts of the *Cid*, while Southey's friend, the colorful exile Blanco White published the periodical *El Español* for his compatriots in England. As early as 1809 an anonymous writer expressed the hope that Spanish literature would soon obtain "as many readers and admirers [...] as French and German."[38]

Following the failure of the liberal revolt in Spain in 1823 more émigrés found their way to England. The next year Lockhart's *Spanish Ballads* were published, and a few years later Washington Irving's *Conquest of Granada* and *The Alhambra*. In England the great Romantic generation virtually ended with the death of Scott in 1832, just as the movement began to flourish in Spain. Thus Coleridge, Scott, and Keats among others had no opportunity to become acquainted with the poetry and plays of Rivas, Espronceda, Martínez de la Rosa, and Zorilla; in any case, most of them found sufficient inspiration in the medieval ballads of their own country and Scotland without having to draw on foreign sources.

---

[38] Ian Jack, *English Literature, 1815-1832* (Oxford: Clarendon Press, 1963), p. 397.

But what of the Spanish drama? In 1846 the literary critic George Henry Lewes could look back and observe: "The richness of the Spanish Drama is proverbial; yet it has occupied the attention of students and critics less than the drama of almost any other nation."[39] Indisputably the English theatre during the first three decades of the new century was far more blessed with outstanding actors than with gifted playwrights. Yet most of the writers of the period, whether poets, diarists, or novelists, were keenly aware of what the Spanish stage had to offer. Unfortunately, their interests and peculiar talents did not enable them to derive any real benefit from that exposure.

Already in the summer of 1809 Byron, then a sentient young man of twenty-one, traveled through southern Spain during his first Mediterranean odyssey. The first two cantos of *Childe Harold's Pilgrimage* are a fantasized chronicle of that early journey, yet the reader searches in vain for any lasting impression left by the country; as with most of his generation, Byron was far more enthralled by Italy. True enough, he did translate a moving Spanish ballad, *Woe is me Alhama*, but then who of the English Romantics did not essay his hand at dabbling in foreign languages? Again, as did most of his poetic friends, Byron had aspirations to become a successful dramatist, but not even his friendship with John Hookham Frere could awaken a real interest in the Spanish drama. Thus *Manfred* owes more to *Faust*, while *Beppo*, like most of his work, is clever satire rather than effective theatre. Even *Don Juan*, despite its Spanish origins, soon finds more congenial settings elsewhere. Only in Canto the First, while evoking the memory of Don Juan's mother, is there any mention of the Spanish theatre:

> Her memory was a mine: she knew by heart
> All Calderón and greater part of Lope,
> So, that if any actor missed his part,
> She could have served him for the prompter's copy.[40]

Clever, to be sure, but hardly an in-depth familiarity with either playwright! Byron, the master of audacious rhymes and verse forms, certainly had little to learn from the Spaniards as to literary freedom. Moreover, his unconventional lifestyle and scandalous conduct assured him a diligent following throughout Europe; the English lord, far from requiring foreign models, was himself the embodiment of Romantic freedom.

So, to a lesser extent, was Shelley. Like Byron, he also secretly longed to be a recognized dramatist. If *Prometheus Unbound* was well-nigh unperformable, Shelley held high hopes for the success of *The Cenci*. Not only did he translate scenes from *Faust*, but also rendered three scenes from Calderón's *El mágico prodigioso* (The Wonderworking Magician) into passable verse, some twenty pages in all.[41] The result is more a literary exercise than an original work, and of marginal significance in the totality of his output.

Clearly, conditions in England were unpropitious for any meaningful cult of Lope or Calderón to establish itself. The Spanish theatre was recognized as a fertile source of incident and intrigue, as it always had been from the time of the Elizabethan dramatists, but ultimately it was found wanting in character and penetrating psychology. Lewes summed it up best of all:

---

[39] George Henry Lewes, *The Spanish Drama, Lope de Vega and Calderón* (London: Knight, 1846), p. 5.

[40] Sir Leslie Stephen, ed., *The Complete Poetical Works of Lord Byron* (New York: Macmillan, 1927), p. 969.

[41] Roger Ingpen and Walter Peek, eds., *The Complete Works of Percy Bysshe Shelley* (New York: Gordian Press, 1965), IV, 299-320.

Considering the immense influence exercised over the European stage by the Spanish dramatists, it is a matter of some surprise that no selection and translation of *chefs-d'oeuvre*, no accurate and satisfactory account of these dramatists exists in our language. The German critics have eulogized them with fervour; the French have been scarcely less ardent; many English writers have exhibited a satisfactory knowledge, and great admiration; and yet the Spanish drama remains a mystery to all not acquainted with its language.[42]

Enthusiasm everywhere; and yet little of permanent impact. Perhaps the Spanish theatre was too exotic a flower to survive beyond its own borders, perhaps it could not acclimatize itself to more austere northerly environments. Whatever the cause, it had its day in the sun and bloomed in all its splendor, only to fade, then wither away.

[42] Lewes, p. 10.

MANFRED SCHMELING

"THEATER IN THE THEATER" AND "WORLD THEATER": PLAY THEMATICS AND THE BREAKTHROUGH OF ROMANTIC DRAMA

1. Poetological Presuppositions of the Romantic Concept of "Play"

The severe critical judgment that August Wilhelm Schlegel rendered of the German theater in the year 1808 in his *Lectures on Dramatic Art and Literature* now strikes us as having been hasty, one-sided and polemical: Schiller's *Die Räuber* (The Bandits) is deemed to be a "failed imitation of Shakespeare"; some plays of Goethe, antiquarian "imitation"; and *Faust I*, the work of an author who "has infinite dramatic, but not quite as much theatrical talent." Most devastating is the verdict on German comedy:[1]

> Auf hundert Komödienzetteln wird der Name romantisch an rohe und verfehlte Ereignisse verschwendet und entweiht; es sei uns erlaubt, ihn durch Kritik und Geschichte wieder zu seiner wahren Bedeutung zu adeln.

> (In a hundred play-bills the name Romantic is wasted and desecrated on rough and misconceived happenings; permit us to ennoble it again to its true meaning through critical analysis and historical fact.)

It is clear that, on the one hand, Schlegel was rooted in the Romantic movement and that, on the other, he encountered a *Lebenswelt* marked by absolutism in a Germany still far from the closed condition of a nation-state. Once we reconsider his critique in this intellectual and political context we must evaluate his statement as addressing a problem of national identity rather than as an expression of genuine cultural concern. The idea governing the last of Schlegel's *Lectures* is the aim of winning over the heterogeneous productive powers in drama on behalf of the ideal of a "National Poetry" that will embody the Romantic aesthetic. To be sure, this focus on what is "national" is not free of ambivalence. The paradigms which Schlegel invokes – in particular Aristophanes, Shakespeare, and Calderón – speak for themselves: "What a field for a poet, who like Shakespeare would know how to grasp the poetic side of great world-events."[2]

Such laments are typical for what could be called the paradox of Romanticism in regard to the theater. The truly "Romantic" play is above all merely a "phantom," a construct played out not on

---

[1] August Wilhelm Schlegel, *Vorlesungen über dramatische Kunst und Literatur*, ed. Edgar Lohner (Stuttgart: Kohlhammer, 1967), II, 281, 279, and 290. The first three citations in this paragraph read in the original: "verfehlte Nachahmung Shakespeares"; "Nachgesang"; "[eines Autors, der] zwar unendlich viel dramatisches, aber nicht ebenso viel theatralisches Talent besitzt."

[2] A.W. Schlegel, p. 291: "Welch ein Feld für einen Dichter, der wie Shakespeare die poetische Seite großer Weltbegebenheiten zu fassen wüßte."

the stage (except in the form of Shakespeare productions) but in criticism and in aesthetics.[3] At the beginning of the Romantic period it is not contemporary theater practice, but rather literary history and aesthetics, the nostalgic admiration of old masters, and – at least implicitly – the provisions of a Romantic poetology anchored in the philosophy of Fichte and Schelling et al., that engender something like the "prototype" of this genre.[4] Romantic theater practice is at best only an approximation to the animating concepts of Romantic poetics: the "ludic impulse," "phantasy," the "universal," the "union of opposites," the "absolute I," and much more.

Critics now generally agree that a Romantic poetology could scarcely have developed as it did without the corresponding headstart[5] – Schlegel counted Fichte's *Wissenschaftslehre* (Science of Knowledge, 1794-98), along with Goethe's novel *Wilhelm Meister*, and the French Revolution, among the "greatest tendencies of the age."[6] Fichte's central category of the "Absolute I" is taken up, criticized, modified again and again by the Romantics: "As the absolute, the I is the basis of all knowledge and of every being [...]. The consciousness of the split between object and subject is the starting point, while the resolution of this split is the goal of Romantic striving."[7] What keeps this I permanently in motion is the yearning for identity with the "Universe," with the "Infinite" – and for Romanticism that means: with the "Divine." This I should, as it were, participate actively in divine Creation, a Creation that never attains completion, but is enacted anew again and again in human cognition, in progressive self-consciousness.[8]

It is no coincidence that this idea of a human co-responsibility for Creation emerges in connection with the idea that the world is a theater, or, as in Schelling's *System of Transcendental Idealism*, that "history [is a] play."[9] This old topos nicely suited both the tendency of Romanticism to aestheticize Creation and its complementary belief in the absoluteness, the universality of art.[10] Just as World History represents, as it were, an act of "joint production" between God and man, so does the relationship between the divine poet of the Drama of Humanity and the human performers thereof rest on the principle of universal analogy: man is the "co-author of the whole":[11]

Ist er nicht, unabhängig von uns, sondern offenbart, und enthüllt er sich nicht sukzessiv durch das Spiel unserer Freiheit selbst, so daß ohne diese Freiheit auch er selbst nicht *wäre*, so sind wir Mitdichter des Ganzen, und Selbsterfinder der besonderen Rolle, die wir spielen.

(If he *does* not exist independently of us, but reveals and discloses himself successively through the very play of our own freedom, so that without this freedom even he himself *would not be*, then we are co-authors of the whole and have ourselves invented the particular roles we play.)

---

[3] Characteristic in this regard is Friedrich Schlegel's view that "Calderón [...] is to be seen as the last Romantic," in his *Geschichte der europäischen Literatur*, in *Wissenschaft der europäischen Literatur*, vol. XI of *Kritische Friedrich-Schlegel-Ausgabe*, ed. Ernst Behler (Munich: Schöningh, 1958), p. 166. This edition will be referred to henceforth as *KFSA*.

[4] F. Schlegel, *KFSA*, XI, 166. On Shakespeare as 'Romantic' see pp. 172ff and 339f, note 439.

[5] A basic statement of this issue is to be found in Armand Nivelle's *Frühromantische Dichtungstheorie* (Berlin: de Gruyter, 1970).

[6] Friedrich Schlegel, *Athenäum-Fragmente*, in *Charakteristiken und Kritiken I (1796-1801)*, vol. II of *KFSA* (Munich: Shöningh, 1967), Fragment 216 (1798), p. 198: "größten Tendenzen des Zeitalters." English edition: Friedrich Schlegel, *Dialogue on Poetry and Literary Aphorisms*, trans. and ed. Ernst Behler and Roman Struc (University Park/London: Pennsylvania State Univ. Press, 1968), p. 143.

[7] Nivelle, p. 30

[8] See the corresponding texts cited in Nivelle, pp. 35ff.

[9] F.W.J. Schelling, *System des transzendentalen Idealismus* (Hamburg: Meiner, 1957), p. 271: "Wenn wir uns die Geschichte als ein Schauspiel denken [...]" (Stuttgart edition, III, 602). English edition: *System of Transcendental Idealism*, trans. Peter Heath, ed. Michael Vater (Charlottesville: Univ. Press of Virginia, 1978), p. 210

[10] Nivelle, p. 184. Nivelle is referring to Novalis.

[11] Schelling, *System*, German ed., p. 271; English ed., p. 210, translation slightly emended.

Here already is an indication of the direction in which at least some Romantics propose to reinterpret the idea of the *theatrum mundi* inherited from the Baroque. Above all the assumption, anchored in Christian dogma, of the limitedness of the human role is discarded. One can better understand from this perspective Schelling's admiration for Shakespeare as a dramatist who was able to represent the "totality," "universality," the "entire infinity of art and nature."[12] Thus the heart of the Romantic idea of the world theater – which we shall discuss more explicitly in a moment – is not the concept of "role" and "play" as such, but rather the characterization of this play as universal and as even "mythological" in that it harmonizes all natural oppositions. Hence the Romantic enthusiasm for an art which, for all "diversity" and "mixing of contraries," can mirror the "one world," whose "absolute formlessness" nonetheless signifies "highest, absolute form."[13]

In his commentary on Aristophanes' "pure comedy" Friedrich Schlegel, in almost literal agreement with Schelling, also uses the concept of "formlessness" positively: "The formlessness is only apparent, the non-form itself is here the highest art and represents the true essence of the genre."[14] In his *Discourse on Mythology* he calls for a poetic reappropriation of the "original chaos of human nature."[15] The demand raised in these and other statements on the art of Romantic poetry must necessarily lead to a sundering of theory and practice. The vague connections that Friedrich Schlegel made between the comedies of Aristophanes and Tieck's *Zerbino* (1798) with respect to the ludistic component – the "purposelessness" of the play, the "wit" and the "phantasy" – could scarcely disguise the fact that drama around 1800 was only very inadequately able to comply with such idealist(ic) demands.

This is not a specifically German problem. In the *Préface* (1827) to his play *Cromwell* Victor Hugo bemoans at length that his epoch lacks a Dante or a Shakespeare, "that god of the theater," that is, lacks poets with the power to lend form to the *scenae vitae*, the universal, the conflicting elements of being, the sublime and the grotesque, terror and comedy, body and soul, lived life, as a *single* unity, without imposing the classicist Unities. Though he remains a little more distanced from irrationalism than do the German Romantics, Hugo comes in the *Préface* to an entirely comparable concept of "reality":[16]

> le réel résulte de la combinaison toute naturelle de deux types, le sublime et le grotesque, qui se croisent dans le drame, comme ils se croisent dans la vie et dans la création. Car la poésie vraie, la poésie complète, est dans l'harmonie des contraires.
>
> (the real results from the quite natural combination of two types, the sublime and the grotesque, which intersect in the drama as they intersect in life and in creation. For true poetry, complete poetry, is in the harmony of contraries.)

Not only does this elemental connection between "the sublime" and "the grotesque" result, for Hugo, in a mixing of the dramatic genres (tragedy and comedy) within the modern genus "drama,"

---

[12] F.W.J. Schelling, *Philosophie der Kunst,* reprint of edition of 1859 (Darmstadt: Wissenschaftliche Buchgesellschaft, 1980), pp. 367 and 369 (Stuttgart ed. (1859), V, 723 and 725).

[13] Schelling, *Philosophie der Kunst*, pp. 90, 109, 362ff. (Stuttgart ed., V, 446, 465, 718ff.).

[14] Friedrich Schlegel, "Charakteristik der griechischen Komödie," in *Wissenschaft der europäischen Literatur*, vol. XI of *KFSA*, p. 89: "Die Formlosigkeit ist nur scheinbar, die Unform selbst ist hier die höchste Kunst und bezeichnet das echte Wesen der Gattung."

[15] F. Schlegel, *KFSA*, II, 311ff.: "[...] des ursprünglichen Chaos der menschlichen Natur." English edition: "Talk on Poetry," in *Dialogue on Poetry*, p. 86.

[16] Victor Hugo, "Préface de Cromwell", in *Théâtre complet* (Paris: Gallimard, 1963), I, 425.

but dramatic form itself is also, as it were, impressed onto the universe as outer and inner form of existence ("the drama of life and the drama of consciousness"), as the form in which history and action manifest themselves. To be sure: one must see this as a dialectical process, that means, see it, at the same time, also the other way round. Because the world offers us a play in which we humans are participants – "All Cromwell is at stake in this comedy which is played out between him and England"[17] – the drama within a drama almost seems to be the "natural" form of theater. In accordance with the Romantic striving for autonomy of the self, man can thus transcend his determination as a passive player in a divine plan of salvation (a role which already in the Baroque – in Gracián, for example – carries the negative implication of the "nugatory" play) and can assume his co-responsibility in the spectacle of History.[18] This modified conception of history and its transfer to theater via metaphors from drama and puppetry find expression also in Hugo's thesis that art intervenes to some extent as a *corrective*, bringing order to the course of events: "art [...] re-establishes the play of the strings of providence among the human marionettes."[19] He was certainly not the first to hold this view; it recalls Schelling's dictum of 1800 – not long after the French Revolution – that we humans are the "co-authors of the totality." This new consciousness of the I, however, manifests itself no longer exclusively on the heights of transcendental philosophy or pure aesthetics but is also increasingly mediated by a moral and socio-political understanding of the nature of man as actor. That Romanticism formulated no decisive answer to the question whether man as *homo ludens* is an autonomous agent or is plagued by destiny seems typical of an epoch which is shaped by intellectual and political upheavals, but in which forces of innovation – including those in the drama – assert themselves only quite gradually.

2. Theater within the Theater: From Purposeless Play to Dramatized Critique

As heterogeneous as the group of dramatists active between 1770 and 1840 may seem – one thinks of Sheridan, Goethe, Tieck, Eichendorff, Kleist, Büchner, Shelley, Bulwer-Lytton, Musset, Hugo, an many more –, the trend toward "metatheater," that is, toward a doubling of the dramatic situation, surely counts as one of the essential structural and substantive features permitting an approach toward the ideal of a specifically "Romantic" theater. It is no coincidence that precisely those poets count as Romantic paragons whose program embraced aspects of playfulness and metadrama, namely Aristophanes, Shakespeare, and Calderón. In this context we must distinguish two typical functions of dramatized self-consciousness of play, which may but need not coalesce: satire or critique of the theater on the one hand, and symbolic referentiality on the other. The latter concerns the antithesis of being and appearance, and its appropriate rhetorical form is metaphor (life as a stage, dream, or masquerade; man as marionette). The former has to do with the antithesis of tradition and innovation and formulates their conflict in aesthetic categories (by thematizing, for example, dramatic genres, illusion, certain historically derived poetological categories such as

---

[17] Hugo, p. 446: "Tout Cromwell est en jeu dans cette comédie qui se joue entre l'Angleterre et lui."

[18] Rainer Hess presents the intellectual-historical development of the motif in his "Wandel der Schauspiel-metaphorik," in *Studia Iberia: Festschrift für H. Flasche*, ed. K.-H. Körner and K. Rühl (Bern-Munich: Francke, 1953), pp. 247-66.

[19] Hugo, p. 437: "l'art [...] rétablit le jeu des fils de la providence sous les marionnettes humaines." Compare Hess, p. 254.

"reason," "feeling," etc.). Of course such self-thematization of the play within the play is not specific to Romanticism; it is in fact a possibility at all times. Such instances as these come readily to
mind: the play-within-the-play tradition in the Elizabethan theater, the whole English "rehearsal"
tradition, the theater taking stock of itself in French Classicism (Molière's *L'Impromptu de Versailles*, 1663), in Italian Rationalism (Goldoni's *Il teatro comico*, 1753), or on the German stage of
the eighteenth century. Despite the general historical availability of this artistic device, we must
acknowledge that the self-interrogation of the theater in terms of the two functions named above
enjoyed a new flowering in Romanticism, and we must seek out the aesthetic, ideological, historico-
political or psycho-social factors responsible for it.

The scope of our paradigmatic investigations is as wide as the polyvalence of the thematics of
play. Thus it is evident, for example, that a play like Sheridan's *The Critic* (1779), based on the burlesque "rehearsal" tradition, in stressing the artistic or artful component, the artifice, of the play, has
quite different intentions from those of Musset's *Lorenzaccio* (1834), which presents the world
theater as a human masquerade and political game of intrigue. Other works, however, such as
Tieck's *Die verkehrte Welt* (The Land of Upsidedown, 1798), can scarcely be limited to any single
function. In them burlesque, satire, Romantic play of wit, and the presentation of a world-view all
interact. Toward the end of the eighteenth century several plays, such as *The Critic*, attacked certain
tendencies of theatrical art, which, whether traditional or recent, had congealed into a style without
content. These plays bear witness that auto-thematizing drama functions both as satire about the
theater and, in the best cases, also as genuine criticism. The developments in France, England and
Germany run parallel here. Stage rehearsal and thematization of the dramatic situation were not just
a favored medium of direct, *explicit* confrontation with theater culture. Because of their anti-illusionist implications they showed up above all in *mixed forms* such as burlesque, parody, farce,
comic opera, etc., and thereby they rendered an *implicit, structural* contribution to the liberalization
of the stage in the post-Classical period. The Romantic sense of a new beginning and Romantic
ideals of freedom were significantly bound up with practices of aesthetic subversion: the grotesque
was juxtaposed to the sublime, buffoonery to Classicist pathos. There had of course been such
"manifestations of a breaking-up" before – for example, in Lesage's parody of Racine's *Les
Souhaits* (Wishes, 1723), in George Villiers's *The Rehearsal* (1671) or in Fielding's *Pasquin*
(1736). As of the end of the eighteenth century such forms were all the more appreciated – especially by Friedrich Schlegel and Ludwig Tieck – for their correspondences to the Romantic conception
of art. "Arbitrary" play, anti-illusionism, the ironising of fiction, contraventions of the Unities, the
mixing of serious and comic, etc., could not have a better channel for uninhibited development than
a theatrical art in which the play was problematized and performed consciously as play.

Such reflexive art was based on thoroughly *critical* intentions. In Sheridan's *The Critic, or a
Tragedy Rehearsed* no aspect of the theater is left untouched. In the first act foolish authors fight
about whose work is better, accuse each other of plagiarism, and bribe the critics. In the second and
third act the poet rehearses his tragedy *The Spanish Armada*, a play within the play, which functions
simply as grotesque anti-theater. Here the author Puff rehearses the death scene several times (a
play within the play, ironising fiction), and the speaker of the prologue is instructed in the use of the
kerchief (allusion to the "sentimental comedy"). The lack of originality, the schematic division of
tragedy into main- and sub-plot, the exaggerated motivation, the unthinkable "aside," and allegorical magic of the conventional stage (the Thames and its two "banks" appear) are all produced and

made ridiculous through parodistic exaggeration. In this play within the play the destructive aspect clearly predominates. Only rarely do new impulses really emerge from this kind of theatrical self-reflexion.

This is also true for a further group of works that stand in the same metadramatic tradition and constitute to some extent an alternative program to the lyric dramaturgy of the self of a Byron or a Shelley. The latter was of more immediate appeal to the British and European reading public interested in Romantic ideas. The apodictic judgment of Allardyce Nicoll on the English dramatists of this epoch is not altogether unjustified: "not one produced a dramatic masterpiece which can be looked upon as the starting point for further art development."[20] The following exemplify the burlesque play within the play: David Garrick's *A Peep Behind The Curtain; or, The New Rehearsal* (1767), Frederick Reynold's *The Dramatist* (1789), Thomas Dibdin's *Melodram Mad! or, A Hit If You Like It* (1825). Not infrequently such "rehearsals" have a theater-political significance. Some plays of Planché, for example, put on stage the confrontation of "legitimate" and "illegitimate" drama and thus call in question the artistic monopoly of the classical genres – the "legitimate" and financially subsidized genres. We know such experiments from French theater (to some extent in the tradition of Martial): titles such as *La Querelle des théâtres* (Lesage and Lafont, 1718) or *L'Opéra-Comique assiégé* (Lesage, 1730) speak for themselves.[21] We also know the German attacks in the form of a play within a play on the "Gottschedians," who wanted to ban Harlequin and thus the burlesque popular tradition from the German stage.[22]

A dramatic form that had conquered the European stages from France and had found particular resonance in contemporary society played an important role in this tradition of dramatized critique: the *melodrama*. It had become securely anchored in entertainment-culture, as had the no less popular parodies, harlequinades, comic operas, etc. The passions, absolutized as "monsters," stand opposed to the virtues of the "honnête homme." This extreme constellation also appealed to the *historical* thinking of Romanticism, and that is not one of the least reasons why it engenders sufficient emotion to guarantee the success of melodramatic art: "The Classical will to sobriety, to litotes, had been succeeded by the emphasis on and search for the pathetic, whether the pathos of horror or the pathos of the sentiments."[23]

Michel de Cubière's *La Manie des drames sombres* (1777) is an exemplary dramatization of the discontent with melodrama. Indirectly the commitment to criticize taste also reflects a critical consciousness of ideology: alongside the forms of dramatic expression of the genre, the "melodramatic social order"[24] of the early Romantic epoch is also put on the stage. The critique finds expression through the parodistic recreation of a degenerate art form in which the serious concerns of the bourgeois drama (for example, of Diderot) had been reduced to sensational "faits divers," to effects of horror and Brigand-Romanticism, to whimpering gestures – melodramatic strategies in no way inferior to those of the "Dallas" and "Denver" soap-operas of our own TV-age. The corres-

---

[20] Allardyce Nicoll, *A History of English Drama, 1660-1900* (Cambridge: Cambridge Univ. Press, 1960), IV, 63.

[21] See on this Manfred Schmeling, *Das Spiel im Spiel* (Rheinfelden: Schauble, 1977), pp. 78ff.

[22] Schmeling, *Das Spiel im Spiel*, pp. 111ff.

[23] Jacques Truchet, *Théâtre au XVIIIᵉ siècle* (Paris: Gallimard, 1972), p. xxvii: "A la volonté classique de sobriété, à la litote, avaient succédé l'emphase et la recherche du pathétique, qu'il s'agît du pathétique de l'horreur ou du pathétique des sentiments."

[24] On the development of melodrama and the socio-political background see Winfried Wehle, "Französisches Populardrama zur Zeit des Empire und der Restauration," in *Europäische Romantik II*, ed. K. Heitman, vol. 15 of *Neues Handbuch der Literaturwissenschaft* (Wiesbaden: Akademische Verlags-Gesellschaft Athenaion, 1982), pp. 153-170.

pondingly negative mediating role in *La Manie des drames sombres* is played by a certain Prousas (alias Sébastien Mercier); he is the dramaturge of *Le Brigand vertueux*. One can already discern the polemic intent in the title of this play within the play. The motif of the "noble brigand" recalls the conflict, typical of the time, between the bourgeois sense of virtue and the 'autonomous' principle of evil – a conflict that fascinated the German Storm and Stress (Schiller) as much as later French Romanticism (Musset, Hugo). But it is precisely here that the tendency toward the clichéd is unmasked: the black and white strategies are but the automatic course of a game in which the triumph of the moral-social order is guaranteed from the start.

Comparable dramatic procedures are also evident in both early and high German Romanticism: the play within the play is developed into a critical-satirical discourse *about* theater, into a medium of *intertextual* confrontation. Here too the theater tradition is brought, in a burlesque way, to trial, as are the "Philistines" – their trial is a specifically German contribution. In these works the favorites of the eighteenth- and early nineteenth-century public are pulled to pieces and the public itself is deprecated, whether for its inability to comprehend "illusionist" stage practices (as in Tieck's *Der gestiefelte Kater* [Puss-in-Boots, 1797]) or for its petit-bourgeois striving, its assiduous pursuit of cultivation (as in Eichendorff's *Krieg den Philistern* [War on the Philistines, 1823]). The absurd, the irrational, and play "for the sake of play" are affirmed in opposition to the approved canon of contemporary rationalist taste. What Mercier, La Harpe, and Pixérécourt were for the French, Kotzebue and Iffland were for the Germans. Because these propagators of established morality, of the patriarchal system, of the ethical and respectable in family and society, were immovably established and solidified into a cultural institution, they almost necessarily became an object of parody, of satirical belittlement. To be sure, there is in this nothing radically new. In as much as self-thematizing Romantic theater makes transparent certain constituents of dominant theater practice in a burlesque manner (the banning of Harlequin mentioned above was also a central point for criticism here), it takes up corresponding models from the past.

Such "subversive practices" based on the involution and exponentiation[25] of dramatic forms always emerge at times in which the contents and forms of expression of drama have historically outlived themselves, have ended up a canon of boredom, with corresponding social implications. Metadramatic reflexion thus provides its own "artistic" contribution to literary historiography. In the ironically distanced intercourse of the theater with itself historical transformation becomes materially tangible. Tieck's "comedies" have been characterized not unjustly as *literary* satires: they live to a considerable extent, though not exclusively, on *cultural reminiscence*; they need the tradition in

---

[25] In the original: "auf der Basis von potenzierten Spielformen." *die Potenz* [Lat. *potentia*, It. *potenza*, Fr. *puissance, potence*]: potency, capacity, generative power; [plural] social or political powers; [in mathematics] exponent, power to which a base number is to be raised; whence the verb *potenzieren*: exponentiate, raise to a higher power, involute, potentialize, intensify. This favorite terminology from early German Romanticism has entered the modern German critical language. As John Neubauer has shown in *Symbolismus und symbolische Logik: Die Idee der ars combinatoria in der Entwicklung der modernen Dichtung* (Munich: Fink, 1978), Novalis and Friedrich Schlegel adapted *Potenz/potenzieren* from Leibnizian thought about potentiality to express their own concept of the heightening brought about by poetic reflection. Novalis defines the "Romanticizing of the world" as "nothing but a qualitative exponentiation (*Potenzierung*)." "The lower self becomes identified with a better self in this operation. Just as we are ourselves such a qualitative exponential series (*Potenzreihe*)" (*Schriften*, ed. Paul Kluckhohn and Richard Samuel, 2nd ed. (Stuttgart: Kohlhammer, 1960), II, 545). In his influential *Athenäum* fragment 116, Schlegel relates exponentiation to his key concept of progressive universality: "Romantic poetry is a progressive universal poetry. [...] free from all real and ideal interest, it can also float on the wings of poetic reflection midway between the represented and the representer. It can even exponentiate this reflection (*diese Reflexion* [...] *potenzieren*) and multiply it over and over again as in an infinite series of mirrors" (*KFSA*, II, 182f; compare English edition: p. 140f.). [G.G.]

order to be able to distance themselves from it. Both artistically and historically, as is evident already from their recurrent treatment of the problem of revolution, they belong to a literature of transition. What is distinctive is that these transitions, rich in conflicts, are not simply "performed," but are rather expressly brought to consciousness, brought into the limelight through the play with the play. On the one side stand the Enlightenment bourgeoisie, rooted in rationalist thinking, and its utilitarian and moralizing art establishment. On the other is a Romantic urge toward the unbounded, with its clearly irrational(ist) aspects. The narcissistic reflexive structure of theatrical play must be counted among the primary cultural forms of Romantic expression, and so also must the conflict between practical life and the striving of art toward autonomy. This may sound very abbreviated and formulaic, but it does completely correspond to the dialectical model underlying most of the plays discussed here.

Already in Tieck's little dramatic effort *Ein Prolog* (1797) one encounters such newer structures. This play rejects the usual practice of rationalistic theater in that the "prologue," performed before a lowered curtain by several figures, becomes an "absolute" overture: nothing follows, the play itself does not take place. This is a thoroughly Romantic idea, which we shall explain further in connection with the often encountered phenomenon of the fragmentary or *negated* play. In addition, contradictory expectations and interests are explicitly enacted. The conformists look forward to illusionistic theater of the old school, to a "family play," in which life is shown as "in a mirror" and one perceives "nothing theatrical" – requirements which are certainly already carried *ad absurdum* through the *hic et nunc* of the "prologue." A less rationalistically cast figure, called, jokingly, Bounder (*Rüpel*), takes the side of Fichte and the philosophy of the absolute I; he considers his I to be a singular, ideal reality, of which other people are but emanations. Finally there is also Scapin, who advocates "poetry," and the sceptic Melantus and the pessimist Anthenor, who meditate on their wretched situation as role-players "in the theater" and on the "future purposes" of their existence, as well as Hanswurst, who would like to link all opposing tendencies "into one whole." In Tieck's *Prolog* essential features of the dramatic concept of his fairy-tale plays are already prefigured. This shows that the metadramatic play cannot be reduced to its satirical-critical function. All too often the reflexive gesture shifts from the concrete historical theater world to poetic, jocose examination of the play "in itself." The particular authentic contribution of the Romantics to the tradition of the theater within the theater lies above all in this last trend. Both the Romantic dividedness of self and the attempt to overcome this state are reflected in the dramatic self-consciousness of role-playing. What appears in the real world as the utopian element in Romantic thinking, that grasping for the infinite and the absolute, the attempted fusion of immanence and transcendence, all this is, as it were, simulated on the stage in the form of a play constituted of self-transcending moments.

No doubt this observation also fuels further critical probing. For if I am correct, this kind of play would live only from its own dynamic, would be interested in nothing but itself, remote from the lived practice of life. Friedrich Schlegel invokes repeatedly the "purposelessness" of the play, for example, in the discussion of Aristophanes in his *Vorlesungen*. If Schlegel ranks Tieck's *Zerbino* on a par with the comedies of Aristophanes (whose political meaning he clearly underestimates),[26] he does so above all because he believes Tieck to have fulfilled the necessary requirements of such drama of "wit, gags and playfulness," "without any purposes or intention," "com-

---

[26] F. Schlegel, *KFSA*, XI, 94.

pletely nonsensical, silly and clownish."[27] Schlegel obviously does not appreciate here the ambiguity in Tieck's concept of play. This resides in the contradiction between, on the one hand, a reflexive art that conceives its object – the naive-rationalist audience – as a cultural reality and illumines it critically and satirically, and, on the other, a type of art that, as play with play, as potentiated illusion, has itself as goal and is thus "pure" poetry. Apart from the fact that Tieck's comedies predate the relevant poetological considerations of Schlegel, it is also their cultural political engagement, which compromises their purposelessness as play, and renders problematic the claim that Tieck's dramas are, so to speak, "applied Romantic irony."

All the same, structural parallels cannot be overlooked. Schlegel writes in the *Athenäum-Fragmente*:

> [die Romantische Poesie kann] am meisten zwischen dem Dargestellten und dem Darstellenden, frei von allem realen und idealen Interesse auf den Flügeln der poetischen Reflexion in der Mitte schweben, diese Reflexion immer wieder potenzieren und wie in einer endlosen Reihe von Spiegeln vervielfachen.
>
> (Romantic poetry [...] can soar, free from all real and ideal interests, on the wings of poetic reflection, midway between the work and the artist. It can even exponentiate this reflection and multiply it as in an endless series of mirrors.)

It aims to "portray itself with each of its portrayals; everywhere and at the same time, it should be poetry and the poetry of poetry."[28] Schlegel claims that such art is "critical" in this transcendental sense of an endless mirroring of itself – which unquestionably means something quite different from the satirical critique of empirical states of affairs, as Tieck offers it in *Der gestiefelte Kater* (1797). The latter's figures, conscious of art in a destructive way, abstracted to their poetological function, battle very concretely for a play adequate to the theater. In the process, the play within the play, *Der gestiefelte Kater*, demonstrates the *casus belli*. The ironising of fiction played out between the frame and the interpolated performance, the falling-out-of-role, the incessant oscillation between discourse within the theater and discourse *about* the theater, the interruptions, convolutions, breaks of illusion, artful protean transformations (superimposition of roles), the thematizing of the machinery of theater, etc. – all this subserves the satirical polemic against the real contemporary theater world and the intellectual, moral, and social values of the eighteenth century. Tieck knew the theater world very well – in Hamburg, Berlin, and Dresden. He knew Kotzebue and Iffland just as well as Shakespeare, Calderón, or Gozzi. They are all presented in *Der gestiefelte Kater*, the former in a negative light, the latter in a positive light.

There exists also an immediate connection between the concept of theater presented theoretically in Tieck's critical writings and the metadramatic reflexions within his fairy-tale plays. In addition there is the general enthusiasm of the period for the theater, boosted by the "discovery" of Shakespeare. This enthusiasm was translated in art not only into dramatic works but also into novels, such as *Wilhelm Meister, Anton Reiser*, and *William Lovell*. While a tendency to artistic self-reflexion is manifested also in novels, it does not rest on the same structural presuppositions as those of a typology of genres; the involvement of the novel with the theater has no consequences. It

---

[27] F. Schlegel, *KFSA*, XI, 89: "Witz, Scherz und Spiel," "ohne allen Zweck und alle Absicht," "durchaus unsinnig, närrisch und possenhaft."

[28] F. Schlegel, *KFSA*, II, 182 and 204; Fragments 116 and 238.

is a quite different matter in drama, where such references to the dramatic situation can be a vehicle for *epic* features, as for example in Tieck's *Zerbino*.[29]

In a lengthy commentary on the state of contemporary theater Tieck writes of *Der gestiefelte Kater*:[30]

> Alle meine Erinnerungen, was ich zu verschiedenen Zeiten im Parterre, in den Logen oder den Salons gehört hatte, erwachten wieder, und so entstand und ward in einigen heiteren Stunden dieser Kater ausgeführt [...], was mir als das Alberne und Abgeschmackte erschien, wurde als solches mit allen seinen Widersprüchen und lächerlichen Anmaßungen hingestellt, und an einem eben so albernen, aber lustigen Kindermärchen deutlich gemacht.
>
> (All my memories of what I had heard in the stalls, the boxes, the lounges reawakened, and so this tomcat was born and worked out during several cheerful hours [...], what seemed to me ludicrous, dull and tasteless was presented as such, with all its contradictions and ridiculous pretensions, and made visible by means of an equally ludicrous but entertaining fairy-tale.)

What Tieck judged to be "dull and tasteless" is concretized in the protestations of the audience of *Der gestiefelte Kater*. Their demands for a supposedly apodictic "reasonable illusion," a "proper play," which must not be a "revolutionary play," etc., reflect the value system of rationalism. Appropriateness and good taste – these are not merely aesthetic problems for the age of Kotzebue and Iffland, as the following short dialogue indicates.

A member of the audience, Schlosser, utters the crucial slogan – "a tasteful piece!":[31]

DICHTHER:	Von welcher Sorte? Von welcher Farbe?
MÜLLER:	Familiengeschichten.
LEUTNER:	Lebensrettungen.
FISCHER:	Sittlichkeit und deutsche Gesinnung.
SCHLOSSER:	Religiös erhebende, wohltuende geheime Gesellschaften!
WIESENER:	Huissiten und Kinder!
NACHBAR:	Recht so, und Kirschen dazu, und Viertelsmeister!

(THE AUTHOR:	Of what kind? Of what complexion?
MÜLLER:	Family stories.
LEUTNER:	Rescues.
FISCHER:	Morality and German sentiments.
SCHLOSSER:	Religious upliftingfly beneficent secret societies!
WIESENER:	Huissites and children!
NEIGHBOUR:	That's right, and cherries too, and quartermasters!)

---

[29] In his detailed review of my book *Das Spiel im Spiel* Gerald Gillespie has drawn attention to the ideological connection between the problematic of the theater in the novel and the play within the play on the stage. See *Komparatistik in Österreich*, Jahressonderband of *Sprachkunst*, 10 (1979), pp. 241-48.

[30] Quoted from *Ludwig Tieck*, ed. Uwe Schweikert, vol. 9, part 1 of *Dichter über ihre Dichtungen* (Munich: Heimeran, 1971), pp. 142-43.

[31] Ludwig Tieck, *Der gestiefelte Kater*, in *Die Märchen aus dem Phantasus. Märchen*, vol. II of *Werke in vier Bänden*, ed. Marianne Thalmann, 2nd ed. (Munich: Winkler, 1978), p. 210. Bilingual German-English edition: Tieck, *Der gestiefelte Kater. Puss-in-Boots*, ed. and trans. Gerald Gillespie (Edinburgh: Edinburgh Univ. Press, 1974), cf. pp. 40f. The published translation differs textually in this passage.

The funny drifting away from the topic here turns into an alibi. The whole joke aims to render innocuous the real historical connections, as do also the ubiquitous phantastic-fabulous events and the comical ironising of fictionality. The author is a cover for the real critic, the playful arbitrariness (itself, of course, a rationally contrived "arbitrariness") hides the potential of cultural and social criticism. Typical of such retraction is Tieck's commentary of 1851 on the role of the foolish king (in the theater within the theater): "Some eccentric royalists expressed the opinion that through this simple joke one wanted to denigrate royalty. I claim that the power of the king is the most natural, well-grounded and beneficent of all political institutions."[32] This reminds one of Goethe who later distanced himself from the revolutionary tone of his *Prometheus* and characterized it as "youthful sin." The fact is however that Tieck, by using the device of the play within a play – behind the pretext of it all being, so to speak, only theater and only lighthearted – rehearses, if not rebellion, then at least as change of governance: for the king functions as fool. The gift of a rabbit provides the sovereign with "material for our world history,"[33] the burned roast becomes a political issue, the king raves (in the form of quotations from Schiller), the public is outraged, the Pacifier has to calm both king and audience. The monarchy as a theme for humour is almost a commonplace in dramatic literature before and after the French Revolution. F.M. Klinger already makes use of the harlequin in his *Prinz Seidenwurm der Reformator oder die Kronkompetenten* (1780) in order to "rehearse" by means of a theater within the theater various forms of government. The fool as the *deus movator* of the theatrical play and of the political intrigue certainly does not, with his revolutionary ideas, contribute to an authentic political solution. At the end of this "moral drama," performed for the "education of the nations," all characters rule together, including the fool.

In Tieck, allusions to the Revolution abound – from *Der gestiefelte Kater* through *Die verkehrte Welt* to *Zerbino*. Yet Tieck's position is as hard to determine as Klinger's; the political message is dispersed in the back and forth of play and non-play, fiction and reality, jest and seriousness. Hinze the cat can oblige with slogans and events out of the immediate historical reality ("Freedom and Equality! – The law has been eaten up! Now indeed will the third estate, Gottlieb, assume the government"), but *within* the play the wheel of history can still be rolled back (Schlosser: "Stop! A revolutionary play! [...] It should be performed from the beginning! Stop this unholy racket!").[34] The real problems of the time are treated as problems of art, abandoned to the dictates of taste and the narrow-mindedness of the playgoing public. The tumult in the theater becomes formal, explainable as the reaction of the audience to the preposterousness of the play within the play. Also typical of such doubling of points of reference is the role of the Pacifier whom the perplexed author summons after the disaster of the play within the play for "just a little mediating criticism."[35] A final conciliatory spectacle with music from *The Magic Flute* and a mythological tableau restores order.

The satirist is of course permitted such aesthetic skirmishes and playful lack of commitment, above all when the target of attack is in the cultural sphere. But there is something more. That is the Romantic tendency to judge the world altogether according to aesthetic criteria, to "poeticize" it. To

---

[32] Schweikert, ed., p. 147: "Einige exzentrische Royalisten sprachen die Meinung aus, man habe durch diesen einfachen Scherz das Königtum erniedrigen wollen. Ich behaupte, daß die Macht des Königs die natürlichste, begründetste und wohltätigste von allen politischen Einrichtungen ist."

[33] Tieck, *Kater*, p. 234: "Materie für unsere Weltgeschichte." Bilingual ed., pp. 82f.

[34] Tieck, *Kater*, p. 262: "Freiheit und Gleichheit! – Das Gesetz ist aufgefressen! Nun wird ja wohl der Tiers état Gottlieb zur Regierung kommen." "Halt! Ein Revolutionsstück! [...] Es sollte lieber von vorn gespielt werden! Nur nicht weltlich getrommelt!" Compare bilingual ed., pp. 122f.

[35] Tieck, *Kater*, p. 264: "ein weniges vermittelnde Kritik." Omitted from bilingual ed., pp. 124f.

that extent Tieck's *Die verkehrte Welt* is more thoroughgoing than *Der gestiefelte Kater*. The words
of "Adagio" at the beginning of the second act of *Die verkehrte Welt* express what becomes evident
– in theme, structure and atmosphere – as the basically poetic vision of the play: "Oh, you weak,
fragile mortal! I always want to think of you as a work of art [...]."[36] This play also proceeds dialectically, indeed in the spirit of Martial. Scaramuz, one of the many "commedia dell'arte" figures that
Tieck inserts in the reflexive plot strands of the play, has driven the poet-god Apollo, the king of
poetry, off Parnassus. In his empire "Reason," "Morality," and "Prose" rule: "Now however, the
Age of Enlightenment has caught on, and I'm in charge."[37] At the end, after a grotesque decisive
battle, Apollo is restored to his former estate, but some members of the audience still have not
grasped the message of this theater on the stage. This all belongs just as much to Tieck's satirical
attacks on bourgeois art appreciation as do the provoking endless mirrorings of the theater, in which
the naive audience loses its bearings:[38]

> SCÄVOLA: Es ist gar zu toll. Seht, Leute, wir sitzen hier als Zuschauer und sehn ein Stück; in jenem
> Stück sitzen wieder Zuschauer und sehn ein Stück, und in jenem dritten Stück wird jenen dritten
> Akteurs wieder ein Stück vorgespielt.
>
> (LOPSIDE: This is too crazy. Look – here we sit watching a show; in this show more people sit watch-
> ing another show, and in this third show, the third actors are watching still another show!)

In Tieck's *Prinz Zerbino; oder, Die Reise nach dem guten Geschmack* (Prince Zerbino, or the
Journey to Good Taste, 1798) the infinite structures of the play within the play (whose phases
recapitulate the journey itself) also lead into the irrational and phantastic. The journey of the prince
seems to confound through irony the rationalist or utilitarian clichés of the *Bildungsroman*. Poetry
and play stand in opposition to a life led in accordance with rules of reason – a "boring" life, which
makes Zerbino plaintive and melancholy. However there is no therapeutic or compensatory outcome at all in this play, it mounts rather toward aesthetic suicide and teeters on the brink of the
void. This is a characteristic result of the contradictions inherent in the Romantic concept of the
play. This tendency to self-negation can be considered the dramaturgic complement to Romantic
world weariness (*Weltschmerz*).[39] It is manifested in the role of Zerbino:[40]

> Durchdringen will ich durch alle Szenen dieses Stücks, sie sollen brechen und zerreißen, so daß ich
> entweder in diesem gegenwärtigen Schauspiele den guten Geschmack antreffe oder wenigstens mich
> und das ganze Schauspiel so vernichte, daß auch nicht eine Szene übrigbleibt.
>
> (I want to penetrate all the scenes of this play, they should break and tear so that I either meet good
> Taste in this present play or at least annihilate myself and the whole play so that not a single scene
> remains.)

---

[36] Ludwig Tieck, *Die verkehrte Welt*, in *Die Märchen aus dem Phantasus. Märchen*, vol. II of *Werke in vier Bänden*,
p. 287: "Ach du schwaches, zerbrechliches Menschenleben! Ich will dich immer als ein Kunstwerk betrachten [...]." This
passage is omitted from the English edition: *The Land of Upside Down*, trans. Oscar Mandel and Maria Kelsen Feder
(Rutherford, New Jersey: Fairleigh Dickinson Univ. Press, 1978).

[37] Tieck, *Die verkehrte Welt*, p. 285: "Jetzt aber hat die Aufklärung um sich gegriffen, und ich regiere." English ed.,
p. 48.

[38] Tieck, *Die verkehrte Welt*, pp. 323f. English ed., p. 87.

[39] See on this Dieter Arendt, *Der "poetische Nihilismus" in der Romantik*, 2 vols. (Tübingen: Niemeyer, 1972).

[40] Ludwig Tieck, *Prinz Zerbino; oder, Die Reise nach dem guten Geschmack*, in vol. 10. of *Ludwig Tieck's Schriften*
(Berlin: Reimer, 1828), Act VI, p. 329.

Such statements provide important material for a Romantic poetology – a poetology composed in part of mutually contradictory and in part of complementary constituents. Epic and dramatic structures, satire and purposelessness, the rational and the irrational, potentiated play and Romantic irony are assembled here into a type of cultural production that, with its inner and outer plurality, could only exist in an atmosphere of intellectual and socio-political upheaval. Discontent with traditional culture then seems to be only one aspect of the confrontation with an altogether, and therefore also politically, "topsy-turvy" world. The attempt to master it requires the help of irony and satire, such means as potentiated illusion, masks and marionettes, the figure of the fool.

Also after the turn of the century one finds sufficient examples of the double strategy, identified here, of comedy as jocose play with the play and also as play with reality. Although the elements pioneered in Tieck subsequently enjoy a variable degree of importance, a continuous tradition can nonetheless be discerned. It is exemplified by Brentano's *Gustav Wasa* (1800), Grabbe's *Scherz, Satire, Ironie und tiefere Bedeutung* (Jest, Satire, Irony, and Deeper Significance, 1822), Eichendorff's *Krieg den Philistern* (1823), *Die Freier* (The Wooers, 1833), *Das Incognito* (c. 1840), and Büchner's *Leonce und Lena* (1836). These plays, like those of Tieck, also embody the idea of the world as stage, mask, etc., a motif not only deployed comically, but certainly also often reflecting the tragicomic world view of the authors. Here the world theater idea comes to be the vehicle for approaching a more serious underlying philosophy, a more pessimistic view of society and history. Primarily the concept of play of Büchner, but also that of Musset, Shelley, and Bulwer-Lytton, will be investigated here in this connection.[41]

Eichendorff's *Krieg den Philistern* comes closest to the *satirical* implications of Tieckian theater; it is a piece in which the play within the play asserts itself once again as an "art of war." The conflict results, as the title indicates, from the opposition between philistinism and the Romantic view of art and the world, a theme that preoccupied the Romantics – Clemens Brentano and E.T.A. Hoffmann, for example.[42] In Eichendorff's satire, the allegory of the storming of the philistine city by "the poetic party" reduces the play within the play more or less to a mere vehicle. Self-consciousness of play and falling-out-of-the-role are here, among other things, a modus operandi for satirical overturning of the philistine role: "the whole piece comes to a standstill," because some of the characters denounce their own "prosaic principle" and prefer to give themselves up to poetic pleasures. Once tasted, this nectar "suddenly turned their innards quite inside out, and once the little bit of understanding is drowned, there's nothing left of such a philistine."[43] The critique of philistinism has as its object not only the prosaic, reasonable discourse of the Enlightenment, but also everything, whether in literature or in society, that recalls the uncritical, conventionalized, and clichéd self-satisfaction of bourgeois existence: in literature, for example, nostalgic "Teutonising," the "sense of virtue," "the touching" and "tragic effect," "learnedness" and "humanism," and much

---

[41] Goethe's *Faust* also belongs in the history of the world theater motif, though it can only in a limited sense be considered "Romantic theater." For practical and substantial reasons we have foregone a discussion of Goethe's concept of world theater. Gerhard Hoffmeister offers an informative discussion of its influence, which complements this essay, in "Goethe's *Faust* and the *theatrum mundi* – Tradition in European Romanticism," *Journal of European Studies,* 13, No. 40/50 (1983), 45-55.

[42] See Clemens Brentano, "Philister-Rede," a talk he held in the Jena circle of Caroline Schlegel-Schelling, and "Der Philister vor, in und nach der Geschichte," in vol. III of *Brentanos Werke,* ed. Max Preitz (Leipzig-Vienna: Meyers Klassiker-Ausgaben, 1914). On Hoffmann see K.L. Schneider, "Kunstlerliebe und Philistertum im Werk E.T.A. Hoffmanns," in *Die deutsche Romantik,* ed. Hans Steffen (Göttingen: Vandenhoeck & Ruprecht, 1967), pp. 200-18.

[43] Joseph Freiherr von Eichendorff, *Krieg den Philistern,* in vol. I of *Neue Gesamtausgabe der Werke und Schriften* (Stuttgart: Cotta, 1957), p. 572: "[...] das ganze Stück gerät ins Stocken." "[Der Nektar] hat ihnen auf einmal recht das Inwendige herausgekehrt, und ist das bißchen Verstand ersoffen, so ist an so einem Philister gar nichts mehr dran."

more; in society and politics, every form of conformity and amenability, according to the motto: "There is nothing like a well-fed state, that stands steady on its feet. The *Zeitgeist* can storm it as it will, it won't stir or budge." [44]

It would be an exaggeration to characterize Eichendorff's satire as a "sharp-sighted critique of his time focussed on the fundamentals."[45] It is not precise enough for that. Apart from the fact that the grotesque play within the play can be used for certain noncommittal explorations and paradoxes, the concept "philistine," which "as biblical name for the enemies of Israel already denoted the opponents of a chosen group,"[46] remains in Romanticism a truly vague and all too pat paraphrase for the disagreeable spirit of the age. To be sure, it fits the Romantic view of history in that the life of the philistine, a life whose characteristics are the night-shirt, the night-cap, and the pipe of tobacco, embodies the negative side of historical processes. It means, therefore, more than the mere continuance of a convention when Eichendorff presents on stage the "drama of the philistine" as a play within the play. The "doubled" theatrical event becomes here the artistically reduced image of the world play. It is not by chance that the fool has the last word in this play, for he is the actual *deus movator* and in this function also the symbol of the desperateness and meaninglessness of the age, understood in a quite unmetaphysical way. In the final analysis, he has only held up to the audience the distorting mirror of these roles that they themselves play on the stage of their bourgeois lives:[47]

> Es war ein Spiel nur, und die hier Gestorbenen stehn alle wieder auf ganz unverdorben und treiben's nun zu Hause ruhig weiter, in anderen Kleidern nur und etwas breiter. Ihr seid so gut wohl, tut dasselb' zu Haus, so spielet fort das Stück und spielt nie aus.

> (It was only a play, and those who died here will all get up again quite unharmed and will now carry on at home as usual, only in other clothes and a little looser. Be so good, do the same yourself at home, so the play will continue and never be played out.)

3. Romantic World Theater: From Aesthetic Idealism to Historical Nihilism

In sociology and social psychology metaphors of the play and the simile of the theater serve to elucidate the status of people as players of social roles: "There must be something in the constitution of society itself that always elicits this comparison."[48] Sociology was certainly not the first to define human interaction as social role-behavior. The metaphor of life as play and as role is almost as old as literature; it would be superfluous to list the sources – in Plato, Seneca, Paul's Epistles to the Corinthians, in mediaeval plays (as evident in the stage-construction), in baroque literature, etc.[49]

---

[44] Eichendorff, *Krieg den Philistern*, p. 532: "Es geht doch nichts über einen wohlgenährten Staat, der so recht breit auf den Beinen steht. Den mag der Zeitgeist anrennen, wie er will, das rührt und rückt nicht."

[45] Jürgen Brumack correctly describes Brentano's "Philister-Rede" in this way in his "Komödie und Satire der Romantik," in *Europäische Romantik I*, ed. K.K. Mandelkow, vol. 14 of *Neues Handbuch der Literaturwissenschaft* (Wiesbaden: Akademische Verlags-Gesellschaft Athenaion, 1982), p. 285.

[46] Brumack, p. 285.

[47] Eichendorff, *Krieg den Philistern*, p. 606.

[48] Uri Rapp,*Handeln und Zuschauen* (Darmstadt: Luchterhand, 1973), p. 29.

[49] See the following works for the numerous sources: E.R. Curtius, *Europäische Literatur und lateinisches Mittelalter*, (Bern: Francke, 1948); English edition: *European Literature and the Latin Middle Ages* (New York: Pantheon, 1953); H.O. Burger, "Dasein heißt eine Rolle spielen," in *Studien zur deutschen Literaturgeschichte* (Munich: Hanser, 1963), pp. 75-93; Rainer Hess, "Wandel der Schauspielmetaphorik" (cited in note 18); Manfred Karnick, *Rollenspiel und Welttheater* (Munich: Fink, 1980); Franz Link, "Götter, Gott und Spielleiter," in *Theatrum Mundi*. Sonderband of *Literaturwissenschaftliches Jahrbuch*, ed. Frank Link and Günter Niggl (Berlin: Duncker & Humblot, 1981), pp. 1-47.

The history of the changing meanings of this motif is so complex that we have to refrain from discussing it here. I shall just say that the decisive turning point comes in the eighteenth century, with the broadening intellectual reception of Copernican discoveries. The idea that man is no longer the center of divine Creation led not only to a new self-consciousness but also to a feeling of being lost in the cosmos. One must keep the latter point in mind even if one can agree with Hans Blumenberg that modern dialectical consciousness was an enduring source for the self-emancipation of the subject.[50] The negative side effects of the Copernican turn find expression in the changing metaphors of man's position in the world: for example, in spatial metaphors – in particular, the world as "labyrinth" – or in theatrical metaphors – life as a stage, mask, puppet-play, etc. Such images are used in modernity not only with emancipatory intent; they also have a dimension of "horror vacui," scarcely found in epochs with a "closed world view," when man could "relate the goodness and wisdom of God the Creator, the meaning of the world to himself."[51]

Already in the eighteenth century, and particularly in the postrevolutionary period, the consciousness of role and play denotes an at least problematic, if not explicitly negative, individual or social experience – one speaks of the division between subject and object, of a crisis of identity and alienation. This crisis finds its adequate artistic form in the doubling of the stage, or, more precisely, in the "conflict" between the various levels of theater. It is a crisis that has since been further radicalized, as one can see from the metadramas of Jean Genet, Peter Weiss, and Tom Stoppard.[52]

According to the theocentric baroque conception of the *theatrum mundi*, exemplified by Calderón's strictly, hierarchically constructed *El gran teatro del mundo* (c. 1635), human role-playing was an expression of the vanity of earthly existence, but as such it had a meaning and a sense in the divine plan of salvation. The moralists – La Bruyère, for example – considered the play of life to be a rationally conducted social game determined tactically and with worldly wisdom. Their expositions are indeed also concerned to unmask the illusoriness of life – however, with the difference that their premise is not a transcendental but an earth-bound and social conception of being. Only since Rousseau explicitly denounced the masquerade of existence in *Émile, ou: De l'éducation* (1762) as human self-alienation, has consciousness of the problem entailed real existential compulsions, leading to the modern doubt about the meaning of life altogether.[53]

Such negative implications certainly also arise among the Romantics. In the idealist contemplations of the early German Romantics, however, one finds at first a completely "positive" concept of play. Their new problematic explains this: theological, moral and paedagogic viewpoints make way for *poetic* reflexion, for the aestheticization of the world by the contemplative I. When Friedrich Schlegel in his *Gespräch über die Poesie* (Conversation on Poetry, 1800) indicated the direction in which Romantic art was to develop, he was certainly not thinking of any negative states of being that might result from the involvement of man in a reality for which the element of play is consti-

---

[50] Hans Blumenberg, "Der kopernikanische Umsturz und die Weltstellung des Menschen," *Studium Generale*, 8 (1955), pp. 637-48. Blumenberg claims that the new knowledge "had rather a triumphal and elevating significance" (p. 641). To refuse disconnected outcastness (*Geworfenheit*) to "drive away crudescent existential anxiety, became the deepest impulse of a new epoch." This view has to be relativized at least with regard to the feeling of emptiness and meaninglessness thematized by means of the analogy of world and stage in the Romantic theater (e.g., in Büchner).

[51] Blumenberg, p. 641.

[52] On the modern see Manfred Schmeling, *Métathéâtre et intertexte* (Paris: Minard, 1982), in particular the chapter "Le Théâtre dans le théâtre sous le signe de l'avant-garde," pp. 47ff.

[53] J.-J. Rousseau, *Émile, ou: De l'éducation* (Paris: Garnier, 1964), p. 271: "L'homme du monde est tout entier dans son masque [...]. N'étant presque jamais en lui-même, il y est toujours étranger."

tutive. "We demand that events, men, in short, the play of life, be taken as play and represented as such."[54] To present the play *as play* means two things here: first, the reflexive gesture, the ironic playing with the play, the "transcendental buffoonery" (and to that extent one can talk of a dialectically operative "negativity" of play); second, it means that the poet participates artistically in Creation, that he take himself back once again, as it were, into the "original chaos," and that he has the world play come into existence anew in the play world. Although Schlegel's ideal of "life as play" is formed more by poetic than by theatrical elements (it is not by chance that he uses the concept "dramatic *poetry*"), his views do also characterize the Romantic concept of world theater.[55] Indeed it is in the context of theater-historical reflections – on Aristophanes, Shakespeare and Tieck – that the components of this concept of play emerge in Schlegel's texts: "arbitrariness," "plurality," "phantasy," etc. "World theater" has here of course quite another meaning than in the Baroque. Romantic participation in the world play signifies fulfillment, a heightening of the I. While the baroque *theatrum mundi* "uncovers the nullity of the world behind its theatrical glitter, here the nullity of everyday life cloaks itself in image, in a liberating intensification."[56]

These poetic components of the world theater are also to be found in Wackenroder's *Fragment aus einem Briefe Joseph Berglingers* (posthumous, 1799), where it is written that "the teeming world all around me seemed to me like a drama which I myself had created [...]."[57] But this already indicates a shift of emphasis. The mood of the observer in Wackenroder's text is ambiguous: a certain melancholy is mixed into the divine feeling of being author of the cosmic drama. Doubt as to the meaning of it all is hinted at: "the entire, hitherto so lively natural scene was dissolved into a gentle fever of melancholic sadness," the play of life comes to an end, only "to break out again tomorrow anew: – and thus, on and on, into the most distant mists of the ages, where we can see no end."[58] This position has been called "pessimistic reflectiveness."[59] The concept is not totally unproblematic to the extent that, ultimately, it levels the essential paradox of potentiation and annihilation, of intensification and destruction, mirth and listlessness. This paradox, recalling the mannerist principle of "concordia discors," concerns both the formal means (play vs. non-play, role vs. negation of role) and also the content, the historical-ideological message of the "tragical humorist,"

---

[54] Friedrich Schlegel, "Gespräch über die Poesie," in vol. II of *KFSA*, p. 323: "Wir fordern, daß die Begebenheiten, kurz das ganze Spiel des Lebens wirklich auch als Spiel genommen und dargestellt sey." English edition: *Dialogue on Poetry*, p. 89.

[55] One must of course see this mood of poetic upheaval in historical context. The world is also presented in Romantic transfiguration in the *Rede über die Mythologie* (1800). The aestheticization of the idea of revolution is typical. Schlegel speaks of the "great process of general rejuvenation," the "principles of eternal revolution" etc. Twenty years later, after the counterrevolution, he uses quite a different language and criticizes "the revolutionary unrest," "whose false birth pangs are not able to bring forth anything enduring, but lead only to moral death and to the chaotic dissolution of all that existed earlier and all that exists no longer alive." (In *Die Signatur des Zeitalters*, in vol. VII of *KFSA*, p. 537.) This corresponds rather to the pessimistic idea of history of the later Romantics, especially of Büchner with his woe-begone world theater conception.

[56] Arendt, I, 85.

[57] Wilhelm Heinrich Wackenroder, "Fragment aus einem Briefe Joseph Berglingers," in vol. I of his *Werke und Briefe*, ed. Friedrich von der Leyen (Jena; Diederichs, 1910), pp. 178ff.: "[...] und die wimmelnde Welt um mich her kam mir wie ein Schauspiel vor, das ich selbst gemacht [...]." English edition: "Fragment of a Letter by Joseph Berglinger," in *Confessions and Fantasies*, trans. and ed. Mary Hurst Schubert (University Park-London: Pennsylvania State Univ. Press, 1971), p. 187.

[58] Wackenroder, p. 179: "[...] die zuvor so lebendige Natur war in ein leises Fieber melancholischer Wehmut aufgelöst [...]." "[Das Spiel des Lebens geht zuende,] um morgen von neuem wieder loszubrechen: – und so immer fort, bis in die fernsten Nebel der Zeiten, wo wir kein Ende absehen –."

[59] Arendt, I, 91.

for whom "history is at the same time tragedy and comedy."[60]

Textual evidence for this is already to be found in the by no means "pure" comedies of Tieck. In *Zerbino*, for example, Helikanus exclaims, "I've had enough of this disgusting empty play." Tieck's comment on the dramatic situation (in which the play on the stage of life is reduced to the play within the play) is made in terms of boredom and melancholy.[61] We encounter such thematizations of existential emptiness throughout the Romantic epoch, from Schiller's *Die Räuber* (1781), in which Karl Moor gives voice to his "disgust" with "this age of scribblers," in numerous theatrical metaphors ("stage lightning, not flame enough to light a pipe of tobacco"),[62] up to Büchner's *Leonce und Lena* (1836) and Musset's *Fantasio* (1833-34). Only the specific context can elucidate the exact meaning of this set of images in each work. For if the play of life is such that it causes us a hangover, then a Karl Moor draws different conclusions from that fact than do Tieck's artificial figures, always acting on the field of theatrical satire, or the tragicomic heroes of the later Romantics. But the theme of melancholy asserts itself increasingly as a negative connotation of the idea of play. The problematic of world *theater* and of world *weariness* (*Weltschmerz*) arise out of one and the same feeling about life. Of course it remains possible to have comedy – like "resolutions" – in Eichendorff's *Die Freier* (1833), for example. In this comedy all the characters appear as actors: Count Leonard because his "residence is too boring" and he wants to captivate Countess Adele; the countess, because she wants to unmask his play-acting through a counterplay/ploy; the chamberlain (*Hofrat*), because he wants to observe the whole show, etc. In this comedy, reason can once again triumph over the play-impulse, "the world's common drive," and everything gets assembled into a tidy proper ending – a marriage.

Using a similar scheme of intrigue Brentano's comedy *Ponce de Leon* had already called into question life as a masquerade. Here too the play becomes a trajectory of flight, a measure taken against paralyzing boredom, the sickness for which the aristocracy in the postrevolutionary period seemed to be predestined. Tieck's Prince Zerbino also suffers from it, as, of course, does Büchner's Leonce; they all look for what they are seeking in the illusory world of the play. When Ponce gets his Valeria after endless complications that disturb the "plans" of the intriguer Sarmiento, it is less the accomplishment of the puppeteer's art and of masquerade, cunning and theater, than an expression of genuine feelings. The world of feelings enters into competition with the play world, though of course the aesthetic and existential fronts are not clearly staked out. Here too the principle of mixing the comic and the serious reigns, and in the process the play's melancholic in-between notes actually cross over to buffoonery, even to "madness."[63]

In Tieck, especially in *Der gestiefelte Kater*, the fool is in some respects still the spontaneous figure from the *commedia dell'arte*, but also one who mischievously mediates between sense and nonsense, a fool on whom the Enlightenment had left its mark despite its animosity toward him. One seeks in vain such a comical and critical mediating figure in the later comedies of Roman-

---

[60] K.J. Obenauer, *Die Problematik des ästhetischen Menschen in der deutschen Literatur* (Munich: Beck, 1933). See the chapter "Die Welt als Bühne," pp. 53ff. Obenauer documents his thesis with numerous passages on the *theatrum mundi* in the works of Jean Paul (p. 62, note 2).

[61] Tieck, *Prinz Zerbino*, Act II, p. 72.

[62] Friedrich Schiller, *Die Räuber* (Stuttgart: Reclam, n.d), I.ii, p. 15: "Ekel"; "[dem] tintenklecksenden Sekulum"; "Theaterfeuer, das keine Pfeife anzündet." In English: *The Robbers*, in *The Robbers. Wallenstein*, trans. F.J. Lamport (Harmondsworth: Penguin, 1979), p. 35.

[63] See Brentano, *Ponce de Leon*, in vol. IV of *Brentanos Werke*, p. 6.

ticism. There it is not the individual fool but an absolutized folly, for which not even traditional religious beliefs are taboo, that convulses the world.

Although Büchner's *Leonce und Lena* evokes hilarity through brilliant verbal wit and intertextual play (the model was Brentano's *Ponce de Leon*), the theater of the fool appears here rather in a tragic light, as expression of destroyed hopes and fractured illusions. Sinking into the world of endless mirrorings, Leonce risks that everything will disintegrate "into pieces" and that there will be "nothing but the bald bare wall around me."[64] Typical Romantic motifs and structures – the mirror in the mirror, the doubling of the theater, the motif of boxes one inside another ("and in the smallest there's nothing at all"[65]) – are de-idealized; they have become ciphers for the world as existential abyss. They recall early Romantic reflexive art only in structure. The nihilist set of images can be expanded indefinitely: the empty ballroom, masks, helpless automata, etc. They are all tainted with the deathly aura of the effigy, of the merely illusory, of evil. Although there is also talk of God, it is of a God who lets the world turn into a pub and who plays cards with the devil out of pure boredom: "you're the king," says Valerio to his prince, "and I'm the knave, all we need is a queen [...]."[66] This gloomy constellation, which has been correctly interpreted as the "mythical *Abbreviatura*," as the "cosmic dimension" of boredom, also dominates the microcosm of the marriage comedy.[67] The protagonists do not conceive themselves as subjects, but rather as objects of the play. Multiplying itself again and again, the play congeals into a grotesque automatism, in which even Valerio, the stage-manager, only leads the life of an automaton, a life become independent of his will – for "they're only *making* me talk and it's nothing more than cogs and airpipes that are saying all this."[68] The world of love, which for Brentano had still seemed to be an authentic counterweight, is now derived from a negative myth of Creation: it is merely a product of the bored god. There remains only the "mechanism of love."[69] Marriage is rehearsed again and again, and the whole procedure seems all the more fated as it is associated with hanging, a well-known occurrence on the contemporary political stage, that was thematized in *Dantons Tod* (Danton's Death) as "just a playing" of history.[70] Upon the dissolution of the masquerade there follows a new one: "for tomorrow the fun will begin all over again, though at your leisure and convenience."[71]

We can only hint at the complex links between the thematics of play and world view. I have tried to show with a few exemplary texts that Büchner no longer stands firmly within Romanticism to the extent that he radically turns away from the idealist concept of play. To be sure the aesthetic view of the world is not abandoned as such, but a deeply pessimistic turn has reshaped it. Para-

---

[64] Georg Büchner, *Leonce und Lena*, in *Dichtungen und Übersetzungen*, vol. I of *Sämtliche Werke*, ed. Werner R. Lehmann, 2nd. ed. (Munich: Hanser, 1979), II.i, p. 118: "in Scherben"; "[daß] ich vor der kahlen, nackten Wand stünde." English edition: in *Leonce and Lena. Lenz. Woyzeck*, trans. Michael Hamburger (Chicago-London: Univ. of Chicago Press, 1972), p. 17.

[65] Büchner, *Leonce und Lena*, II.l, p. 119: "in der kleinsten ist gar nichts." English ed., p. 18.

[66] Büchner, *Leonce und Lena*, II.ll, p. 122: "Ihr seid der Kartenkönig und ich bin ein Kartenbube, es fehlt nur noch eine Dame [...]." English ed., p. 20.

[67] Karl S. Guthke, *Die Mythologie der entgötterten Welt*, (Göttingen: Vandenhoeck & Rupecht, 1971), p. 171.

[68] Büchner, *Leonce und Lena*, III.lll, p. 131: "[weil] man mich nur so reden läßt, und es eigentlich nichts als Walzen und Windschläuche sind, die das Alles sagen." England ed., p. 30.

[69] Büchner, *Leonce und Lena*, III.lll, p. 131: "der Mechanismus der Liebe." English ed., p. 30.

[70] Georg Büchner, *Dantons Tod*, in *Dichtungen und Übersetzungen*, vol. I of *Sämtliche Werke*, I.ii, p. 15: "Nur ein Spielen." Compare English edition: *Danton's Death* in *The Plays of Georg Büchner*, trans. Victor Price (London: Oxford Univ. Press, 1971), p. 11.

[71] Büchner, *Leonce und Lena*, III.lll, p. 133: "denn morgen fangen wir in aller Ruhe und Gemütlichkeit den Spaß noch einmal von vorn an." English ed., p. 32.

doxical as it may sound, Büchner's stage of life is structurally closer to the baroque *theatrum mundi* than to the world play as conceived by Schlegel or Tieck. In seventeenth-century allegory, sublunary life, with its contradictions and natural array of roles, was planned out in the ready made and imperturbable scenario of a transcendental power; Büchner simultaneously takes over and perverts this model in proclaiming melancholy as universal principle and in projecting the meaninglessness inherent in life back onto an equally empty god. The intellectual and political-social preconditions for asserting the autonomy of the subject, man's participation in the divine role, and his creative collaboration in the world drama, were particularly lacking in the endphase of Romantic parodic comedy.

A similarly radical commentary on the symptoms of contemporary dissolution is only to be found in the anonymously published *Die Nachtwachen des Bonaventura* (The Night Watches of Bonaventura, 1804):[72]

Der Totenkopf fehlt nie hinter der liebäugelnden Larve, und das Leben ist nur das Schellenkleid, das das Nichts umgehängt hat, um damit zu klingeln und es zuletzt grimmig zu zerreißen und von sich zu schleudern.

(The death's head is never missing behind the ogling mask and life is only the cap and bells which the Nothing has draped around to tinkle with and finally to tear up fiercely and hurl from itself.)

In the fullness of its arsenal of motifs – world theater, mask, melancholy, madness, king and fool, god and devil, etc. – the *Nachtwachen* anticipates much of what is to be found thirty years later in Büchner or in French Romantic drama – for example, in Musset's *Fantasio* (1833-34) and Hugo's *Le Roi s'amuse* (1837). The spirit of absolute contradiction of the *Nachtwachen* does not even spare its own discourse. It is an anarchic discourse that both has command of the laws of Romantic poetry and conceives itself as a critique of Romanticism; in the same breath it proclaims and negates its ideological message – an apologia for nothingness (the fool says, "If one were ready to take the like consideration seriously [...]"[73]); it judges the world according to aesthetic and metaphysical criteria and yet comprehends the sufferings of the actors on the stage of the world in an historical and directly political way. The politicization of the image of the puppet in the *Nachtwachen* makes one doubt the originality of Büchner's *Danton*. The marionettes rattle in their box "as if they were producing a French Revolution for amusement."[74]

In conclusion, I shall address this political aspect. The regularity with which the motif of revolution appears precisely in plays that have the structure of a play within a play is remarkable – consider Klinger's *Prinz Seidenwurm* (Prince Silkworm), written before the French Revolution. Revolution and play, world history and world theater run their course according to the same mechanisms. Of course these mechanisms are evaluated in a variety of ways. Tieck had already called his *Verkehrte Welt* an "historical drama" and had alluded intermittently to revolution, thus giving a certain historical resonance to the stage revolt rehearsed in the play (as play within the play). It would

---

[72] *Nachtwachen von Bonaventura*, ed. Wolfgang Paulsen (Stuttgart: Reclam, 1964; with new introd., 1977), 8. Nachtwache. Bilingual German-English edition: *Die Nachtwachen des Bonaventura. The Night Watches of Bonaventura*, ed. and trans. Gerald Gillepsie (Edinburgh: Edinburgh Univ. Press, 1972), Eighth Night Watch, pp. 140f.

[73] *Nachtwachen*, 8. Nachtwache: "Wollte man dergleichen ernsthaft nehmen [...]." Bilingual ed., Eighth Night Watch, pp. 140f.

[74] *Nachtwachen*, 15. Nachtwache: "wie wenn sie eine französische Revolution zum Zeitvertreibe aufführte." Bilingual ed., Fifteenth Night Watch, pp. 222f.

however be a mistake to want to see in this mix of poetry, mythology, and satire on philistinism an allegory on the political conditions after 1789. Tieck's conception of world theater is rather a reflection of early Romantic positions, exemplified by Friedrich Schlegel's *Fragments* and *Talk on Mythology*. Appreciation of the political processes that had been triggered by the events of 1789 came slowly; only somewhat later could *real* historical revolutionary conditions be represented (the same Schlegel pictures them in 1822 from a reactionary standpoint in his *Signatur des Zeitalters*).

Play as history and history as play: virtually all Romantic dramatizations of the stage of life are organized around this dialectical principle. Nonetheless it makes a difference, whether contradictory sequences of events are taken to be manifestations of an, as it were, "natural" chaos and as poetic-mythological artifice – as in Tieck's *Verkehrte Welt* and in his comedy of fate, *Fortunat* (1815) – or whether the poet addresses political reality directly in his understanding of history. Büchner asserts the latter position in a letter to his family about his play *Dantons Tod* (1835), claiming that he "had to remain true to history and present the men of the revolution as they were, bloody, dissolute, forceful, and cynical."[75]

Dantons Tod, giving even higher profile to the tragic aspect of the stage of life than *Leonce und Lena*, thematizes a conflict of the postrevolutionary period also considered crucial by historians: the confrontation between Robespierre and Danton. At issue was the political direction of the revolutionary movement but also – and Büchner stresses this – personal power, "private hatred and private passions."[76] If Robespierre counts today as "the symbol of loyalty to principles and revolutionary radicalism," then Danton counts as "the moderate," who was "ready to trade the queen for recognition of the revolution throughout Europe."[77] The fact that Danton falls victim to an intrigue and is guillotined in 1794 belongs as much to the paradoxes of that period as does, later, the coronation of Napoleon, who had himself proclaimed emperor in order to secure the achievements of the Revolution. Büchner does not take up the historical material of the Robespierre-Danton conflict in order to prepare a history lesson, but rather because the material is of an exemplary character with respect to the question whether the ends of social revolt sanctify any – even the bloodiest – means used ("virtue has to reign by terror"[78]) and also because it provides occasion for philosophical and psychological discussion of the contradictions of human existence in general. Büchner pursues in his own way beyond what Enlightenment skepticism articulated, for example, in Rousseau's complaint about life as masquerade and alienation. The crisis of the subject arises from the feeling of being the plaything of a divine non-comedy: "We are puppets, our strings pulled by unknown forces; nothing, we ourselves are nothing!"[79] It can no longer be compensated for aesthetically, that is, through a Romantic withdrawal to ludistic or ironic positions. The play can no longer heal itself. Play and death are now synonyms for the metaphysical forsakenness of humanity addressed by Danton in one of the most famous lines of world literature: "The world is chaos. Nothingness is the world-god

[75] Georg Büchner, "An die Familie," 5 May 1835, in *Vermischte Schriften und Briefe*, vol. II of *Sämtliche Werke*, ed. Werner R. Lehmann, 2nd. ed. (Munich: Hanser, 1980), p. 438: "[daß er] der Geschichte treu bleiben und die Männer der Revolution geben mußte, wie sie waren, blutig, liederlich, energisch und zynisch."

[76] Büchner, *Dantons Tod*, II.vii, p. 43: "Privathaß und Privatleidenschaften." Compare English ed., p. 39

[77] Louis Bergeron, François Furet et al., eds., *Das Zeitalter der europäischen Revolution 1780-1848*, vol. 26 of *Fischer Weltgeschichte* (Frankfurt: Fischer, 1969), p. 67.

[78] Büchner, *Dantons Tod*, I.vi, p. 26: "die Tugend muß durch den Schrecken herrschen." Compare English ed., p. 22.

[79] Büchner, *Dantons Tod*, II.v, p. 41: "Puppen sind wir von unbekannten Gewalten am Draht gezogen; nichts, nichts wir selbst!" Compare English ed., p. 37.

yet to be born."[80] If, as we have indicated, discussion of role-playing and world theater often depended on a mythification of the relationship of man and world, then this de-rationalization of the play becomes in Büchner a sort of anti-myth. It takes place within the context of a radically negative mythology of Creation that subordinates historical and political processses to the laws of cosmic "ennui," to the idea of the purposelessness and nullity of all being – including God.

It is not surprising that one finds parallel views in Alfred de Musset's *Lorenzaccio* (1834). Not only because this French author had himself experienced the consequences of the Revolution, including the Paris July revolution of 1830, but also because the myth of evil was flourishing in the literature of the epoch – in de Sade and Stendhal, in Byron and Shelley. Musset's drama was prompted by George Sand's *Une Conspiration en 1537*, a play about the republican conspiracy against Alessandro de Medici described by Benedetto Varchi (1503-65) in his *Storia Fiorentina* (1721). The way in which Musset's Lorenzo is characterized as a "revolutionary" and in which his failure is psychologically evaluated shows that this play goes beyond the Romantic demand for an "historical drama" that realistically conveys "the grotesque and the sublime" (Hugo) and that it concerns itself with actual contemporary problems. The *tactical masquerade* and the *consciousness of dividedness* that together determine the development of Lorenzo reflect the disillusionment following the revolutionary turmoil, the reactionary tendencies of 1830 that supersede Napoleonic messianism, and in general the entire political and social life revealed and masked in evil. At first Lorenzo serves the republican cause of Strozzi out of pure idealism, but, as confidant of the despotic Alexandre de Médicis, he takes an increasing pleasure in his role as "modern Brutus," to the point that the mask becomes nature and he seeks to put an end to this "hideous comedy" by murdering Alexandre. Of course, the right moment has passed: a new tyrant arises, the hero is felled by a myrmidon's death-blow, and the people's cry of "Vive Médicis!" sets its seal symbolically on the senselessness of the revolutionary deed.[81]

In Musset's play world, as in Büchner, political resignation and a somber view of history fuse with an idea of evil as an autonomous principle – and therefore as mythical. It would however be risky to reduce what here stands out as the *satanic principle on the stage of life* to an anthropological schema.[82] The hermeneutic potential of a dramaturgy conceived as world theater and masquerade existence, and of its *modus operandi*, the play within the play, can only be appreciated with respect to its particular intellectual and socio-political contexts. To be sure, this dramaturgy amounts to rewriting a topos. However, in contrast to the Baroque and in contrast also to Rousseau who conceives the human masquerade as a *cultural* malady, this malady is here rendered absolute. With certain qualifications this is already true of Schiller's *Die Verschwörung des Fiesko zu Genua* (Fiesco's Conspiracy in Genoa, 1783), that "republican *Trauerspiel*," to which the tragedy *Lorenzaccio* is deeply indebted, and the hero of which unites in himself the dialectic of "Spielen und Gespieltwerden" (playing and being played), freedom and tyranny – a conflict that thoroughly corre-

---

[80] Büchner, *Dantons Tod*, IV.v, p. 72: "Die Welt ist das Chaos. Das Nichts ist der zu gebarende Weltgott." English ed., p. 67.

[81] Alfred de Musset, *Lorenzaccio*, in *Oeuvres complètes*, ed. Philippe van Tieghem (Paris: Seuil, 1963), pp. 316-60. The exclamation is in V.vii, on p. 358.

[82] See Bernard Masson, *Musset et son double* (Paris: Minard, 1978). Masson anthropologizes evil and clearly underestimates the topical historical meaning of *Lorenzaccio*. In the chapter "Le monde est un spectacle" (pp. 135ff) he asserts that Lorenzo's self-reproaches "put in question less a society that surrenders itself to servitude or a political regime that favors this than the world of men in general delivered up by nature to omnipotent evil" (p. 138).

sponds to the political and psychological circumstances of a (still) absolutist age.[83] This is true above all of English Romanticism: Percy Bysshe Shelley's horror tragedy *The Cenci* (1819) is exemplary. It is a reworking of Renaissance material crammed with atrocious deeds. The pride of the devil – the tyrannical Count Francesco Cenci, who rapes his daughter Beatrice, is triumphant at the death of his sons, and himself falls victim to a conspiracy – manifests itself here also in the context of a world of absolute appearance. In the "Preface" it is said of Beatrice, "The crimes and miseries in which she was an actor and a sufferer are as the mask and the mantle in which circumstances clothed her for her impersonation on the scene of the world."[84] When Shelley makes "circumstances" responsible for the roles and sufferings, he is not invoking some abstract concept of destiny common at all times and cherished especially in Romanticism, but rather the same environment of revolution in which Büchner's and Musset's concepts of world theater too are grounded. The fact that the diabolic play of masking and unmasking occurs also in comic versions is certainly not the least indication of the hermeneutic breadth of this motif. Exemplary is Edward Bulwer-Lytton's comedy *Money* (1840), in which the "great comedy of life" is transposed to the bourgeois life of Victorian society, and the power of evil prevails, not in the political intriguer or the tyrant, but in the form of a new money-aristocracy.

Thus the play within the play and the world theater have developed internationally into extremely complex models of dramatic form and of theatrical modes of being. Even though reflexive theater has always been historically present, precisely because of its exemplariness, there can be no doubt that it reached its highpoint both quantitatively and qualitatively in Romanticism – an epoch that had to a great degree freed itself from poetological and ideological dogma. Indeed reflexive theater contributed decisively to the formation of a specifically Romantic form of drama. An interesting question – that we cannot pursue but have discussed elsewhere – is, to what extent twentieth-century metaliterature, the virtually irrepressible trend to reflexivity in art and to the so-called "mise en abyme," is indebted to this Romantic tradition.[85]

Let us once more highlight the two functions of metadramatic expression in the epoch under discussion: the critical and the symbolic. In the critical function the contradictions – and more rarely the innovations – of a development immanent in culture are proclaimed. That means, the content of the autothematic plays is precisely the theater, literature, art, culture in general. This involves an explicit form of intertextuality. Of course, it does not preclude a secondary process by which social structures and ideological oppositions are conveyed. A typical example of this is the confrontation of the Romantics with the philistinism surviving from the age of utilitarianism into the nineteenth century. The playing with dramatic illusion, with reason, and with "good taste" staged as reactions by the public, virtually constitutes a satirical chapter in reception-history: it unmasks bourgeois habits of thought and life through the dramatization of horizons of expectation. In the symbolic function, the events played out within art refer paradigmatically to no less playlike events outside art, to the historical or existential factors of human acting and suffering. The issue is the relationship between the self and the world, the specific circumstances that, according to the Romantic point of

---

[83] Friedrich Schiller, *Die Verschwörung des Fiesko zu Genua*, in vol. II of *Sämtliche Werke in zehn Bänden. Berliner Ausgabe*, ed. H.-G. Thalheim et al. (Berlin: Aufbau, 1981). See on *Die Verschwörung* Karnick (cited in note 49), p. 49.

[84] Percy Bysshey Shelley, "Preface," *The Cenci*, in *Shelley's Poetry and Prose*, ed. Donald H. Reiman and Sharon B. Powers (New York: Norton, 1977), p. 242.

[85] See Manfred Schmeling, "Autothematische Dichtung als Konfrontation: Zur Systematik literarischer Selbstdarstellung," *Zeitschrift für Literaturwissenschaft und Linguistik (LiLi)*, 8 (1978), 77-97, and the monograph *Métathéâtre et intertexte* cited above.

view, determine the fate of man as *homo ludens* on the world stage. To the extent that this view is still idealist, as it is among the early Romantics (because the world play turns out for the author to be "nature's work of art"), this relationship of self and world is represented only in terms of an aesthetic controversy.[86] Although they always also cultivate the aesthetic side of theatricality and of life as masquerade (prefiguring the artist-as-dandy of the second half of the century), the later Romantics do stress more strongly real historical, existential, or psychological connections. The actor's consciousness of play now stands, however, clearly in the service of a fundamentally new, and from a Christian perspective negative, experience of being. It is not by chance that among its philosophical descendants are counted Kierkegaard and Nietzsche.

(Translated from the German by *Simon Sreberny*, with *Gerald Gillespie*.)

---

[86] F. Schlegel, "Rede über die Mythologie," in *KFSA*, II: "Kunstwerk der Natur." Compare the English ed.: "Talk on Mythology," in his *Dialogue on Poetry*, p. 86.

FREDERICK BURWICK

ILLUSION AND ROMANTIC DRAMA

Like many of their eighteenth-century predecessors, the Romantics stressed illusion as one of the principal attributes of the drama. At odds with such statements during the Enlightenment period, however, the new generation of critics endeavored to redeem illusion from that irrationality of emotional excess in which the feelings were said to overwhelm the understanding. A.W. Schlegel, Coleridge, and Hugo set forth criteria for the drama which emphasize the simultaneity of intellectual scrutiny and imaginative participation. Illusion in Romantic theory of the drama is consciously and deliberately conjured by the imagination (it was in accord with such principles that Coleridge defined "poetic faith" as "a willing suspension of disbelief for the moment"). If the drama of the Romantic period rests upon a new set of presumptions about illusion, the question naturally follows whether the theoretical concern with illusion had relevant consequences in shaping the drama during the period. In spite of the persistent objection that dramatic illusion is merely an indulgence of subjectivism and escapism, the Romantic model of dual perception was in fact utilized to claim a grander province for the individual consciousness. While drama has always revealed tensions between individual experience and the hegemonic order, the mediation of illusion in the plays of Kleist, Byron, Shelley, and Hugo involves an experimentation with representation which does not passively surrender to that hegemony.

Illusion, as conceived by eighteenth-century critics, required that the spectator should perceive the artistic representation as reality. To create illusion, the playwright must adhere as closely as possible to "real" conditions. Fantasies and masques, whatever value they might otherwise have for pageantry, spectacle, and celebration, were considered extraneous, perhaps even disruptive. Attention was directed, instead, to verisimilitude. Although generally conceded to be impossible to attain, "perfect illusion" was nevertheless a goal toward which dramatic production might strive. Marian Hobson, in her excellent account of artistic illusion in eighteenth-century criticism, describes the prevailing theories as either bipolar or bimodal: "'Illusion' will either cover the whole experience, the two parts being complementary and the mind oscillating between them (bimodal); or illusion will be applied to only one pole of the experience, which will never be contaminated by an awareness that art is art (bipolar)."[1]

Because bimodality assumes an alternation or oscillation between the awareness of art and the indulgence in its illusion, the experience must be engaged voluntarily. Thus Marmontel argued that the spectator must be able to shift attention between two different perspectives, one fully aware of the artifices of acting and staging, the other engaged in the representation. Because the experience is

[1] Marian Hobson, *The Object of Art. The Theory of Illusion in Eighteenth-Century France* (Cambridge: Cambridge Univ. Press, 1982), p. 43. See also: Otto Haßelbeck, *Illusion und Fiktion* (Munich: Fink, 1979); Frederick Burwick, *Illusion and the Drama. Critical Theory of the Enlightenment and Romantic Era* (College Park, PA: Penn State Univ. Press, 1991).

voluntary, Marmontel explains, illusion should neither be "perfect" nor long sustained. The spectator should be at liberty to reflect upon the effects.[2] Diderot, in contrast to Marmontel, advocates such intensity and spontaneity of feeling that the reason temporarily succumbs. In order to seduce the spectator's involuntary submission to illusion, art must make itself invisible and imitate even the minute details of reality. Although Diderot himself plays games with the conventions of representation in his *Entretiens sur "Le Fils naturel,"* he nevertheless argues that drama should eliminate all elements which might distract from the illusion.[3]

In Romantic theories of the drama there is a concerted effort to banish the arguments of involuntary illusion and to elaborate the case for conscious and creative control of the aesthetic experience. The old psychological opposition of reason vs. emotion no longer defines the contrasting modes or poles of aesthetic experience. Both reason and emotion are mediated through the imagination. Nor is illusion still deemed dependent on the mimetic representation of external nature. Among Tieck's early studies in the drama was his essay on Shakespeare's use of the marvelous. As we have already noted, eighteenth-century critics dismissed fantastic spectacles as disruptive of dramatic illusion. Tieck was among the first to address the conditions of non-mimetic illusion.[4] This dimension in Romantic criticism, as Thomas McFarland has described it, turns from the *mimetic* to the *meontic*: "the imitation is not of what is there, but of what is not there."[5]

What, then, should the spectator expect to behold when the curtain rises? How does one dramatize what is not there? The *meontic* problem has always been relevant to dramatic representation. Indeed, Aristotle himself implicated it in the very process of *mimesis*. When he called for the imitation of human action, his emphasis was not simply on action as *praxis*, but rather on the invisible conditions which lead up to that visibly demonstrable moment. In the workings of human action, after all, *proairesis* precedes *praxis*, and the playwright is called upon to imitate these subjective pre-conditions of action in a character's responding, deliberating, and choosing.[6] The representation

---

[2] Jean-François Marmontel, "Illusion," in *Encyclopédie, ou Dictionnaire raisonné des sciences, des arts et des métiers*, 3rd. ed., 36 vols. (Geneva: Pellet, 1777-99), XVIII, 353-57. "C'est ainsi qu'au spectacle deux pensées sont présentes à l'âme. L'une est que vous êtes venu voir représenter une fable, que le lieu réel de l'action est une salle de spectacle, que tous ceux qui vous environnent viennent s'amuser comme vous, que les personnages que vous voyez sont des comédiens, que les colonnes du palais qu'on vous représente sont des coulisses peintes, que ces scènes touchantes ou terribles que vous applaudissez sont un poëme composé à plaisir; tout cela est la vérité. L'autre pensée est l'*illusion*; savoir, que ce palais est celui de Mérope, que la femme que vous voyez affligée est Mérope elle-même, que les paroles que vous entendez sont l'expression de sa douleur. Or, de ces deux pensées, il faut que la dernière soit la dominante; et par conséquent le soin commun du poëte, de l'acteur, du décorateur doit être de fortifier l'impression des vraisemblances et d'affaiblir celle des réalités."

[3] Denis Diderot, *Entretiens sur "Le Fils naturel"* (1757) and *Discours sur la poésie dramatique* (1758), in *Oeuvres complètes*, ed. J. Assézat and M. Tourneaux, 20 vols. (Paris: Garnier, 1875-77), VII, 85-168, 299-394. VII, 330: "L'illusion n'est pas volontaire. Celui qui dirait: Je veux me faire illusion, ressemblerait à celui qui dirait: J'ai une expérience des choses de la vie, à laquelle je ne ferai aucune attention." VII, 328: "C'est lui [le poète] qui crée, qui tire du néant; avec cette différence, que nous n'entrevoyons dans la nature qu'un enchaînement d'effets dont les causes nous sont inconnues; au lieu que la marche du drame n'est jamais obscure; et que, si le poëte nous cache assez de ses ressorts pour nous piquer, il nous en laisse toujours apercevoir assez pour nous satisfaire." VII, 345: "Et l'acteur, que deviendra-t-il, si vous vous êtes occupé du spectateur? Croyez-vous qu'il ne sentira pas que ce que vous avez placé dans cet endroit et dans celui-ci n'a pas été imaginé pour lui? Vous avez pensé au spectateur, il s'y adressera. Vous avez voulu qu'on vous applaudît, il voudra qu'on l'applaudisse; et je ne sais plus ce que l'illusion deviendra."

[4] Ludwig Tieck, "Shakespeare's Behandlung des Wunderbaren" (1793), in *Kritische Schriften*, 4 vols. (Leipzig: Brockhaus, 1848-52; rpt. Berlin: de Gruyter, 1974), I, 37-74. In contrast to Tieck's endorsement of a creative fecundity liberated under the subjective guidance of an inherent, self-consistent dream-logic, Johann Jacob Bodmer insisted upon external constraints and criteria; see: Bodmer, *Critische Abhandlung von dem Wunderbaren in der Poesie* (Zurich: Orel, 1740; rpt. Stuttgart: Metzler, 1966), pp. 14-18, 150, 166-67.

[5] Thomas McFarland, *Romanticism and the Forms of Ruin* (Princeton: Princeton Univ. Press, 1981), p. 384.

[6] Aristotle, *Poetics,* chs. vi, xv; in *The Basic Works of Aristotle*, ed. Richard McKeon (New York: Random House, 1941), pp. 1462, 1469.

of what is visibly demonstrable must somehow reveal as well what is invisibly operative. Amidst the turmoil of that revolutionary period which was the significant watershed between Enlightenment and Romanticism, what factors were invisibly operative?

On the stage, no less than in the streets, in court or council, the individual began to assert himself more vigorously against the controlling order of state authority. And governing authority, at least in some dramatic fictions, began to recognize the urgency and power of the individual mind. The turn to the *meontic* mode was a part of that effort to lay claim to the larger province of subjectivity. It was not enough simply to detail those struggles of *proairesis* bound to a *praxis* sanctioned or constrained by the hegemony of ruling authority or "destiny." The integrity of consciousness and all the human capacities to doubt, to dream, to speculate, or to aspire, should have their just place in dramatic representation. That integrity, to be sure, had previously managed to express itself in the arts. In the Romantic period it acquired unprecedented primacy.

When Schlegel, in his *Lectures on Dramatic Art and Literature* (1809-11), boldly championed Shakespeare as literary model of the modern age, he built his case for the freedom of English drama at the expense of the rigidity of French neoclassicism.[7] As Jonathan Bate has reminded us, Schlegel's lectures are imbued with the fervor of patriotic resistance to French domination. Following the defeat of the Austrian army at Ulm in 1805, there was no adequate military force to counter Napoleonic hegemony in continental Europe. With the political power of the Hapsburgs effectively checked under the terms of the Treaty of Pressburg, Napoleon soon extended his control throughout the German states. The Prussian army was defeated at Jena in October 1806, and the Peace at Tilsit, in July 1807, left Prussia open to the French. The attempt of the Austrians to rally against Napoleon was crushed at Wagram in July 1809. It was in this context that Schlegel forwarded his distinction, soon to be repeated by Coleridge, between the "mechanic" and the "organic." It is a distinction, Bate observes, fraught with ideological tensions.[8]

Schlegel's theory of the drama builds upon a set of basic premises: drama is poetic dialogue; as poetry, it develops through the imagination, not through the reason. The theater grows out of cultural traditions and national values; therefore, each country must encourage its own playwrights rather than relying on foreign models. From these same premises, Schlegel derived his most often cited distinctions: the classic and the romantic, the plastic and the picturesque, the organic and the mechanic. Classical art, as it emerged in ancient Greece, values the ideal, the simple, the finite; romantic art, as evident in Christian Europe, prefers the mystical, the complex, the infinite. The forms of classical art are plastic: the artist approaches his material as the sculptor his marble. In the plays of Aeschylus, Sophocles, Euripides, dramatic character is shaped with the same exterior constraint as we witness in Attic sculpture. Romantic art, however, is picturesque, attending more to content than to form.[9] Both the classic and the romantic are organic, for they grow naturally out of

---

[7] August Wilhelm Schlegel, *Vorlesungen über drmatische Kunst und Litteratur*, 2 vols. in 3 (Heidelberg: Mohr & Zimmer, 1809-11). For the German text I cite: *Kritische Schriften und Briefe*, ed. Edgar Lohner, 7 vols. (Stuttgart: Kohlhammer, 1965-74), V and VI. Edgar Lohner bases his text of Schlegel's *Vorlesungen* on the posthumous 3rd edition in *Sämtliche Werke*, ed. Eduard Böcking, 12 vols. (Leipzig: Weidmann, 1846-47), rpt. 16 vols. (Hildesheim: Olms, 1971-72).

[8] Jonathan Bate, "The Politics of Romantic Shakespearean Criticism: Germany, England, France," *European Romantic Review*, 1, No. 1 (July 1990), pp. 1-25. See also: Bate, *Shakespearean Constitutions. Politics, Theatre, Criticism 1730-1830* (Oxford: Clarendon Press, 1989).

[9] Schlegel, *Kritische Schriften und Briefe*, repeats the comparison of classical poetry to sculpture and modern poetry to painting: II, 86, 101, 104-108; V, 45, 69-71, 73, 79, 99, 209-10; VI, 28, 112-13. The comparison derives from Lessing's *Über das Laokoon* and was appropriated by Jean Paul in his *Vorschule der Ästhetik* as well as by both August Wilhelm and Friedrich Schlegel; Paul Kluckhohn, *Das Ideengut der deutschen Romantik* (Tübingen: Niemeyer, 1953), pp. 163-68.

the cultures in which they are engendered. That art is mechanical which appropriates the forms of another culture, defines them according to rational principles, advocates imitation and opposes imaginative play. The French pretensions to the classic, then, are mechanic rather than organic.

Worse than the merely aesthetic error of relying on foreign models, however, is the French presumption in attempting to legislate their mechanical rules and forms throughout Europe and to deny other cultures their freedom of organic expression. When Schlegel turns to Shakespeare, he recapitulates these distinctions between the organic and mechanic, classic and romantic, plastic and picturesque (II, 109-12). Shakespeare is not merely a great English playwright, he provides a model of the organic process in art which may inspire German artists, Schlegel hopes, to break from neoclassical tyranny and develop their own "native species" of drama (II, 114, 251). Under the mechanical precepts of French neoclassicism, illusion required an imitation of reality which could only be secured by strict adherence to the "three unities." Illusion, Schlegel counters, does not deceive the spectator with counterfeit images of reality, rather it is engendered through the involvement of the imagination.

Der Begriff der Täuschung hat in der Kunsttheorie große Irrungen angerichtet. Man hat oft darunter den unwillkürlich gewordenen Irrtum, als ob das Dargestellte wirklich sei, verstanden. Dann würde sie bei den Schrecknissen des Trauerspiels eine wahre Plage sein, ein Alpdrücken der Phantasie. Nein, die theatralische Täuschung, wie jede poetische, ist eine wache Träumerei, der man sich freiwillig hingibt. Um sie hervorzubringen, müssen Dichter und Schauspieler die Gemüter lebhaft hinreißen; die berechneten Wahrscheinlichkeiten helfen nicht im mindesten dazu. Jene Forderung der buchstäblichen Täuschung, aufs Äußerste getrieben, würde alle poetische Form unmöglich machen.[10]

(This idea of illusion has occasioned great errors in the theory of art. By this term there has often been understood the unwittingly erroneous belief that the represented action is reality. In that case the terrors of Tragedy would be a true torture to us, a nightmare oppressing the fancy. No, the theatrical as well as every other poetical illusion, is a waking dream, to which we voluntarily surrender ourselves. To produce it, the poet and actors must powerfully agitate the mind, and the probabilities of calculation do not in the least contribute towards it. This demand of literal deception, pushed to the extreme, would make all poetic form impossible.)

How illusion is engendered and propagated is crucial to Schlegel's account of dramatic art as organic process. Shakespeare, he argues, overcomes the barriers between representation and reality by insisting on the reality of representation. The play-within-a-play is only one such device for exploiting the reality of role-playing. His characters put on disguises and feign other parts. By thematizing illusion, Shakespeare secures the audience participation in the illusion-making process.

In contesting the presumption of the French critics, Schlegel denies that the probability provided by the "three unities" is necessary. Illusion, he argues, is neither involuntary misapprehension, nor a confusion of the represented with the real. If either were the case, then the scenes of horror in tragedy would work as a nightmare upon the fantasy. Instead, like all poetic illusion, theatrical illusion is a waking dream which we engage voluntarily. Coleridge, too, counters the French

---

[10] Schlegel, *Kritische Schriften*, VI, 22-23. The English quotation is from: *Lectures on Dramatic Art and Literature*, trans. John Black (London: Balwin, Cradock & Joy, 1815); rev. A.J.W. Morrison (London: Bell, 1889). Because Black mistranslated "ein Alpdrücken der Phantasie" as "an Alpine load on the fantasy," I have amended the phrase to "a nightmare oppressing the fancy."

critics, distinguishes illusion from delusion, stresses the voluntary over the involuntary, and compares the experience to a waking dream.

The parallels are striking. Nevertheless, Coleridge formulated this position while preparing his notes on Shakespeare for his first lecture series (15 January to 8 June 1808) – before Schlegel delivered his lectures in Vienna (31 March to 10 May 1808). When Coleridge did subsequently borrow from the *Vorlesungen*,[11] he left virtually untouched the account of illusion. Schlegel's emphasis on audience participation through thematization of illusion had little in common with his own attention to the imagination and the controlling will in engendering and modulating illusion. While Bate is certainly right in asserting that Coleridge kept the political implications intact when he imported Schlegel's distinction between the "mechanic" and "organic,"[12] Coleridge forwards a very different account of illusion – one that is far more conscientiously "organic" than Schlegel's. However effectively it might be propagated through Shakespeare's themes of role-playing, illusion is always subservient to the will of the spectator and must be understood in terms of the mental processes through which it is cultivated. Coleridge thus turns to Schlegel's demonstration of Shakespeare's "excellent judgment" and his arguments about the playwright's "intentionality" and "purpose" to augment his case for the constitutive nature of the imagination.

In his preparatory notes for the 1808 lectures, Coleridge discussed a "temporary Faith which we encourage by our own Will" and a "suspension of the Act of Comparison" which brought the spectator into a "negative Belief."

> Stage Presentations are to produce a sort of temporary Half-Faith, which the Spectator encourages in himself & supports by a voluntary contribution on his own part, because he knows that it is at all times in his power to see the thing as it really is. [...]
> The Subject of Stage-Illusion is so important, and so many practical Errors & false criticisms may arise, and indeed have arisen, either from reasoning on it as actual Delusion – (the strange notion, on which the French Critics built up their Theory, and the French Poets justify the construction of their Tragedies) – or from denying it altogether, (which seems the butt of Dʳ Johnson's reasoning and which, as Extremes meet, would lead to the very same Consequences by excluding whatever would not be judged probable by us in [our] coolest state of feeling with all our faculties in even balance) that a short digression will, I hope, be pardoned, if it should serve either to explain or illustrate the point.[13]

The distinction between illusion and delusion, already proposed by Kant,[14] disencumbers critical theory of the notion that with the excitation of the senses and passions, reason may be subdued and the spectator convinced of the reality of the events on stage. Such an involuntary, irrational response is delusion, not illusion. If art is mistaken for reality, the experience might well rest upon ardent

---

[11] Anna Augusta Helmholtz-Phelan, *The Indebtedness of Samuel Taylor Coleridge to August Wilhelm Schlegel* (Madison: Univ. of Wisconsin Press, 1907; rpt. New York: Haskell House, 1971). As evidence of plagiarism, George Henry Lewes printed four parallel examples from Coleridge's *Literary Remains* and Black's translation in his review of the French edition of Schlegel's *Essais littéraires et historiques* for the *Foreign Quarterly Review*, 32 (1843), 87-99. Sara Coleridge, in her edition of Coleridge's *Lectures upon Shakespeare and other Dramatists* (London: Pickering, 1849; New York: Harper, 1854), pp. 457-488, attempted to document all similarities to Schlegel.

[12] Bate, "The Politics of Romantic Shakespearean Criticism," p. 11.

[13] *Lectures 1808-1819: On Literature*, ed. Reginald A. Foakes, 2 vols., in *The Collected Works of Samuel Taylor Coleridge*, 5 (Princeton: Bollingen, 1987), 129-136; from British Museum, Add Ms 34225 f56.

[14] Immanuel Kant, *Anthropologie in pragmatischer Hinsicht* (1798), *Werke*, ed. Wilhelm Weischedel, 6 vols. (Darmstadt: Wissenschaftliche Buchgesellschaft, 1975), VI, 412-58, and 526-29. See esp. §11, "Von dem künstlichen Spiel mit dem Sinnenschein" (VI, 440ff).

conviction but it can have no aesthetic significance. Delusion is a false belief and remains blind, whether for a moment or for the duration of the performance, to the play as a work of art. As his reference to Dr. Johnson makes clear,[15] Coleridge seeks to extricate the concept of illusion from skeptical disbelief as well as from false belief. To escape the constraints of both "belief" and "disbelief," Coleridge proposes "a sort of temporary Half-Faith, which the Spectator encourages in himself & supports by a voluntary contribution on his own part."

What is entailed, here, is a mental shift from judgment to speculation, from determining validity to conjecturing possibilities. With this shift, the meontic becomes not merely coequivalent with the mimetic, it vastly extends the horizons of artistic representation. Kendall Walton missed the point when he proposed that illusion depends on "pretending belief" rather than "suspending disbelief."[16] As Thomas McFarland has argued, "that willing suspension of disbelief for the moment, which constitutes poetic faith" cannot be accurately paraphrased as "that temporary belief, which constitutes poetic faith." As Coleridge himself makes explicit, "Images and Thoughts possess a power in and of themselves, independent of that Judgment or Understanding by which we affirm or deny the existence of reality correspondent to them." As in a dream, "we neither believe it or disbelieve it." In dreams, however, not just "the comparing power" but also the will is inoperative. Poetic faith, like the dream, involves suspending acts of affirmation or denial, but, unlike the dream, the will remains active and determines the very decision whether the judgment should be exercised.[17] The crucial term in Coleridge's account of illusion is *faith*: the "Half-Faith" of the definition in 1808, the "poetic faith" in the more famous formulation of 1817. This faith – speculative, conditional, intuitive – shares the same philosophical ground, as McFarland demonstrates, which Coleridge affirmed against Hume's notorious indictment of miracles.[18] Illusion is no abrogation of reason but, rather, a calling forth of the "as if" ("als ob") mode of intuitive reason in place of the verificational mode of the discursive understanding.

In surveying the history of Spanish theater, Schlegel noted the emergence of formative conventions identical to those which shaped the drama in England, specifically in the handling of scene changes. When the stage was left empty for a moment and another set of characters appeared through another entrance, the audience was prepared to imagine a complete change in time or place. Before stage design was introduced and elaborated, spectators were accustomed to rely on their own imagination in order to fill in a lapse of time or to provide a different setting. The act of aesthetic complementation (or, as Schlegel calls it, "die ergänzende Phantasie") underlies all the pleasures of participation in illusion. In aesthetic complementation, the spectator is called upon to join the playwright as a fellow poet in co-authoring the dramatic effects. Thus the response cannot be passive; it must be active and conscious. It must also be concentrated and focussed:

---

[15] Samuel Johnson, "Preface to Shakespeare," *The Works of Samuel Johnson*, 16 vols. (Cambridge, Mass.: Harvard Coöperative Society, 1912), XII, 9: "The truth is, that the spectators are always in their senses, and know, from first act to last, that the stage is only a stage, and that the players are only players."

[16] Kendall Walton, "Appreciating Fiction: Suspending Disbelief or Pretending Belief?" *Dispositio*, V, No. 13-14 (1980), 1-18; see also: Walton, *Mimesis as Make-Believe* (Cambridge, Mass.: Harvard Univ. Press, 1990).

[17] To Daniel Stuart (13 May 1816), *Letters of Samuel Taylor Coleridge*, ed. Earl Leslie Griggs, 6 vols. (Oxford: Clarendon Press, 1956-71), IV, 641; cf. *Biographia Literaria*, ed. James Engell and Walter Jackson Bate, 2 vols., in *The Collected Works of Samuel Taylor Coleridge*, VII (Princeton: Bollingen, 1983), II, 6, 134.

[18] McFarland, "The Willing Suspension of Disbelief," in *Shapes of Culture* (Iowa City: Univ. of Iowa Press, 1987), pp. 114-145; Burwick, "Coleridge and De Quincey on Miracles," *Christianity and Literature*, 40, No. 1 (Autumn 1990), pp. 7-33.

Die wahre Täuschung besteht eben darin, wenn man durch die Eindrücke der Dicht- und Schauspielkunst so hingerissen wird, daß man die Nebensachen übersieht und die ganze übrige Gegenwart ver-
gißt.[19]

(That is the true illusion, when the spectators are so completely carried away by the impressions of the
poetry and the acting, that they overlook the secondary matters, and forget the whole of the remaining
objects around them.)

Schlegel notes that these priorities are often turned about: the misdirected fascination with costumes
and settings results in treating the primary concerns – good plays and good players – as if they were
secondary. He goes on to lament the plight of the spectator who suffers from an impotent imagination, who sees only the holes in the fabric of illusion. Lacking the power of aesthetic complementation, he learns to take a perverse pleasure as an unbelieving skeptic at the shrine of the imagination.
He preys upon the imperfections and inadequacies of the performance, not realizing that the sublime
effects of the drama can never be fully represented on the stage. An impotency of the imagination
thus results in an inability to engage illusion ("die Unfähigkeit getäuscht zu werden"). A vocal
skeptic does not simply deprive himself of pleasure, he may well disenchant others as well. Just as
illusion is enriched through the mutual contagion among the spectators, so too a prosaic disbelief
("prosaische Unglaube") can undermine the conditions favorable to dramatic effects (VI, 216-17).

Although Schlegel takes no steps to elaborate an intuitive ground, his objection to the destructive effects of a "prosaische Unglaube" nevertheless has a bearing on Coleridge's insistence upon "a
willing suspension of disbelief" and a "poetic faith" in illusion. Indeed, this was the very passage
from which Coleridge quoted in his second lecture at Bristol (2 November 1813). *Macbeth* was
Coleridge's subject, and his notes acknowledge his intention to use Schlegel in his conclusion. He
repeats some of Schlegel's commentary on the hallucinations of the guilty mind. Schlegel, again
discussing the thematization of illusion, addresses the problems in staging the "ghost" scenes. Coleridge is concerned, instead, with the psychology of illusion vs. delusion, and that meontic mode
which makes it possible to dramatize delirium.[20]

Since Schlegel and Coleridge both propose their defintions of illusion in opposition to French
criticism, it may seem surprising that Romantic theory in France should adopt the same strategy. Of
course, it had to await the passing of the Napoleonic era, and even then the political tensions were
extreme. The circumstances which provoked Stendhal to pen his pamphlet, *Racine et Shakespeare*
(1823), were much the same as those which, four years later, prompted Hugo to write his polemical
"Preface" to *Cromwell* (1827). Although Hugo's "Preface" to *Cromwell* became the important
manifesto of Romanticism in France, Stendhal's dialogue between the Academician and the Romantic had already set forth the major issues. To be sure, Schlegel and Coleridge had already proposed
Shakespeare as the model for Romantic drama. In France, however, the reception of Shakespeare
was a difficult matter. In 1822, when a company of English actors in Paris attempted to perform
Othello, they were hooted by a hostile audience.[21] An English Shakespeare on the French stage too

---

[19] Schlegel, *Kritische Schriften*, VI, 217.

[20] Coleridge, *Biographia Literaria*, II, 6; *Shakespeare Criticism*, ed. T.M. Raysor, 2 vols. (London: Constable, 1930;
2nd ed. London: Dent, 1960), I, 70-71; *Lectures 1808-1819: On Literature*, ed. R. Foakes, I, 528. The unidentified quotation,
"Das spottische auflauern ob nicht ein umstand der wirklichkeit widerspricht," is from Schlegel, *Kritische Schriften*, VI, 217:
"Das spöttische Auflauern hingegen, ob nicht irgendein Umstand der scheinbaren Wirklichkeit widerspricht."

[21] Roger Fayolle, "Criticism and Theory," in *The French Romantics*, ed. D.G. Charlton, 2 vols. (Cambridge: Cambridge Univ. Press, 1984), II, 260. Cf. the start of Furst's essay in this volume.

blatantly represented the intrusion of political and aesthetic values at odds with tradition. France, after Wellington's defeat of Napoleon and the restoration under Louis XVIII, was chary of intrusions on tradition.

Stendhal addresses the conflict of Romantic and Classic as essentially ideological, an opposition between the values of the Modern Age and the Ancien Régime:

> Le *romantisme*. L'art de présenter aux peuples les oeuvres littéraires qui, dans l'état actuel de leurs habitudes et de leurs croyances, sont susceptibles de leur donner le plus plaisir possible.
> Le *classicisme*, au contraire, leur présente la littérature qui donnait le plus grand plaisir possible à leurs arrière-grands-pères.[22]

> (*Romanticism* is the art of presenting nations with the literary works which, in the present state of their customs and their beliefs, are capable of giving them the greatest possible pleasure.
> *Classicism*, on the contrary, offers them the literature which gave the greatest possible pleasure to their great-grandfathers).

He then proceeds to examine the divergence in aesthetic views which derive from basic ideological differences. The debate over the respective merits of Racine and Shakespeare concerns the power of the drama to conjure a "perfect illusion." The Academician assumes that he can win his case for Racine simply on the grounds of an adherence to the three unities. An audience in England or Germany, he declares, cannot really imagine that whole months pass while they are in the theater watching *Macbeth*. Nor could a French audience, replies the Romantic, believe that twenty-four hours pass during a performance of *Iphigénie en Aulide*.[23] Clearly, illusion requires something more than merely constraining lapses in time or shifts in place. What, the Academician and the Romantic must ask, constitutes illusion? Does the word mean the same to each of them?

The first point to be established is whether we are capable of analyzing how our senses react to the events on stage. The Romantic attempts to placate the Academician who insists that he experiences perfect illusion in beholding the plays of Racine.[24] The Academician is surprised that the Romantic insists that theatrical illusion experienced in *Macbeth* is the same as in *Iphigénie en Aulide*. To establish a common ground for interpreting the drama, the Romantic offers an academic definition of illusion, quoting from François Guizot, leader of the *doctrinaires*. "Illusion refers then to the action of a person who believes the thing that is not, as in dreams for example."[25] Stendhal thus far endorses much the same argument that Marmontel had forwarded a half-century earlier. The dream-like state of illusion is experienced only for brief moments. It is a deception, but the alternating awareness of reality prevents the spectator from being utterly duped.

---

[22] Stendhal (= Henri Beyle), *Racine et Shakespeare* (1823), in *Oeuvres complètes*, 79 vols. (Paris: Le Divan, 1927-37), XIII, 64.

[23] Stendhal, XIII, 12-14.

[24] Stendhal, XIII, 14: "Ne nous fâchons pas, et daignez observer avec attention ce qui se passe dans votre tête. Essayez d'écarter pour un moment le voile jeté par l'habitude sur des actions qui ont lieu si vite, que vous en avez presque perdu le pouvoir de les suivre de l'oeil et de les voir *se passer*. Entendons-nous sur ce mot *illusion*. Quand on dit que l'imagination du spectateur se figure qu'il se passe le temps nécessaire pour les événements que l'on représente sur la scène, on n'entend pas que l'illusion du spectateur aille au point de croire tout ce temps réellement écoulé."

[25] Stendhal, XIII, 15: "Avoir des illusions, être dans l'*illusion*, signifie se tromper, à ce que dit le dictionnaire de l'Académie. Une *illusion*, dit M. Guizot, est l'effet d'une chose ou d'une idée qui nous déçoit par une apparence trompeuse. Illusion signifie donc l'action d'un homme qui croit la chose qui n'est pas, comme dans les rêves, par exemple. L'illusion théâtrale, ce sera l'action d'un homme qui croit véritablement existantes les choses qui se passent sure la scène."

The Romantic tells the story of an American soldier on sentry duty at a Baltimore theater during a performance of *Othello*. Upon beholding the black man about to murder the white woman, the outraged soldier fired a gun shot which shattered the actor's arm. This, declares the Romantic, is the consequence of perfect illusion. Most spectators manage to extricate themselves from the depths of the spell.

> Il est impossible que vous ne conveniez pas que l'illusion que l'on va chercher au théâtre n'est pas une illusion parfaite. L'illusion *parfaite* était celle du soldat en faction au théâtre de Baltimore. Il est impossible que vous ne conveniez pas que les spectateurs savent bien qu'ils sont au théâtre, et qu'ils assistent à la représentation d'un ouvrage de l'art, et non pas à un fait vrai.[26]

> (It is impossible for you not to admit that the illusion which one goes looking for in the theater is not a perfect illusion. The *perfect* illusion is that one of the soldier on guard at the theater in Baltimore. It is impossible for you not to admit that the spectators know well that they are in the theater and that they witness the representation of a work of art and not a true fact.)

Since a perfect illusion, if sustained, would reduce the spectator to the same sort of madness that gripped the Baltimore soldier, then the desired effect in the drama must be either scattered moments of perfect illusion or an imperfect illusion, in which our response to the drama is less intense and immediate. The Academician is led to admit that Racine's use of rhetorical declamations frequently disrupt the experience of illusion. Admiration for the acting or the poetic language cannot co-exist with perfect illusion, nor can the awareness of our own emotional response to the dramatic experience. Amidst the longer duration of imperfect illusion, a play may successfully solicit brief moments of perfect illusion. These moments of perfect illusion, argues the Romantic, are less frequent in Racine than in Shakespeare. Racine emphasizes the formal attributes of time, place, and action, but his lengthy speeches interrupt rather than enhance illusion. Shakespeare, however, gathers emotional force and, in spite of his want of regular form, the moments of perfect illusion occur with greater frequency.

Hugo's "Preface" to *Cromwell* develops a more complex distinction. The tensions are not merely the classic vs. the romantic. At stake is the fundamental conflict between soul and body. Art does not presume to duplicate nature. Through a rapport with nature, it strives to represent ideal as well as material life. It represents essences by bringing together the opposing tendencies of nature. Like Schlegel, Coleridge, and Stendhal, he saw in Shakespeare the model for Romantic drama: "Shakespeare is drama; and the drama, which is based on the grotesque and the sublime in the same breath, tragedy and comedy, such drama is the appropriate form for the third period of poetry, the literature of the present."[27] The grotesque and the sublime, the real and the ideal, the natural and the imaginative all contribute to the dramatic illusion. Through the tension of opposites, the spectator recognizes the real. Drama, then, may hold up a mirror to nature, but it is a concentrating mirror which focuses and intensifies the light of its images. The stage is an optical point. Our perception of reality tends to be scattered and diffused, whereas our perception of the drama is concentrated. This paradoxical combination of the poetical and the natural is what engenders dramatic illusion: "it

---

[26] Stendhal, XIII, 15-16.

[27] Victor Hugo, *Préface de Cromwell*, in *Oeuvres dramatiques et critiques complètes*, ed. Francis Bouvet (Paris: Pauvert, 1963), pp. 139-53; p. 144: "Shakespeare, c'est le Drame; et le drame, qui fond sous un même souffle le grotesque et le sublime, la tragédie et la comédie, le drame est le caractère propre de la troisième époque de poésie, de la littérature actuelle."

imparts to it that vitality of truth and brilliancy which gives birth to illusion, that prestige of reality which fascinates the spectator."[28]

Imaginary scenes, imbued with the same "couleur" as the actual historical events, actually sharpen rather than blur the historical verisimilitude. This is because the combination of the natural and the poetic reveals the body as well as the soul. The focus is so sharply defined that we see the inner workings as well as the outer actions.[29] Whereas perception in the real world is baffled by surfaces, perception in the theater penetrates to the very core, revealing both the deeds and the motives. This does not mean that the mimetic is less important that the meontic; for Hugo, both modes are caught up in the eternal conflict between physical and spiritual being. In terms of staging, the physical setting is not merely a back-drop; the characters in his play interact with the "props." He advocates detailed attention to local color. The spectator will notice the difference in atmosphere when the curtain rises, but his perception will be so thoroughly entranced by historical fidelity to time and place that, upon accepting its conventions, he will not be distracted by the difference again until he leaves the theater, when he will find it necessary to re-adjust to "la couleur locale" in his own world outside the theater. Local color is sustained by "une ardente inspiration" and the illusion can only be disrupted by a lapse into the commonplace.

As may be surmised from Hugo's attention to local color, he is much more concerned with stage design than either Schlegel or Coleridge. They chose to praise the bare stage of the Globe Theatre as enforcing a reliance on dramatic illusion rather than on the gimmickry of stage illusion. For Hugo, the illusion conjured through the imagination and the illusion wrought through the actor's physical engagement with the setting were the soul and body of the drama. His formula for Romantic drama required the dual awareness of mind and matter. While the theories of Schlegel, Coleridge, and Hugo by no means exhaust the manifold deliberations on illusion during the period, they are broadly representative of the principal issues. All three oppose the doctrine of illusion as delusion, mistaking art for reality. Schlegel stresses the thematization of illusion, Coleridge explores illusion as imaginative process, Hugo defines illusion as the interaction of man's grotesque and sublime nature. All three, and we may add Stendhal as well, drew their examples from Shakespeare as model for the modern drama. If these critical theories had any influence at all in the contemporary theater, one might reasonably expect Shakespearean resonances. Too, one might anticipate self-reflexive themes about creating illusion, meontic explorations of the mind's imaginings, contests between real and ideal, flesh and spirit. Such expectations are not misplaced, for these are in fact the stuff of Romantic drama.

The problematic relation of illusion and reality, for example, directs the action in Kleist's *Amphitryon* (1807).[30] To seduce Alcmene, Jupiter must disguise himself as her husband Amphitryon. For Plautus this had provided appropriate matter for sexual ribaldry and comedy of errors. For Molière the seduction plot served as a humorous apology for the monarch's presumption of nuptial rights. But for Kleist the problem is truly one of perception and illusion. Alcmene sees in her "transformed" husband only the idealization she has always perceived. Jupiter cannot seduce her in

---

[28] Hugo, p. 148: "lui donne cette vie de vérité et de saillie qui enfante l'illusion, ce prestige de réalité qui passionne le spectateur."

[29] Hugo, p. 149; "l'extérieur, par leurs discours et leurs actions; l'intérieur, par les *a parte* et les monologues; de croiser, en un mot, dans le même tableau, le drame de la vie et le drame de la conscience."

[30] Heinrich von Kleist, *Werke*, ed. Erich Schmidt, with Georg Minde-Pouet and Reinhold Steig, 5 vols. (Leipzig and Vienna: Bibliographisches Institut, 1904-5); English quotations are from: *Heinrich von Kleist: Five Plays*, trans. Martin Greenberg (New Haven: Yale Univ. Press, 1988).

his own person, for she is absolutely devoted to Amphitryon. The dramatic conflict, then, does not arise from the adulterous intrigue. Alcmene is aware of no adultery, denies it even when confronted with the presence of two Amphitryons. The conflict is, rather, the internal one of Alcmene's discovery of the physical intensity of her passion for the husband she has envisioned only as an ideal.

The play, however, is not for this reason any the less a play about loyalty and fidelity. Loyalty and fidelity are basic Kleistian themes, informing such works as *Die Hermannsschlacht* (1808), say, or *Prinz Friedrich von Homburg* (1811). Indeed, in both of these plays, allegiances are challenged sexually as well as politically. It may well be a mistake, therefore, to grant that Molière's play provides an ideological critique in satirizing Louis XIV's most recent sexual affair, and then go on to insist that Kleist's play avoids ideological implication and focuses, instead, on the purely subjective dilemma of love and desire. Some critics, to be sure, have observed in the play autobiographical shadows of his broken engagement to Wilhelmine von Zenge and her subsequent marriage to Wilhelm Traugott Krug.[31] Or of his rivalry with Goethe.[32] But it is equally relevant to consider the work in the context of the French invasion.

After the French vanquished the Prussian army, Kleist became a staunch defender of the nationalist cause. His earlier political position, vis-à-vis Napoleonic France, was a fickle matter. He was a boy of fourteen when he entered military service in 1792. His regiment was on the Rhine at the time of the Siege of Mainz, 1793. Relatively peaceful years between Prussia and France followed upon the Treaty at Basel, March, 1795. Kleist advanced to Second Lieutenant in 1797, but during the following year difficulties with his commanding officer, General Rüchel, prompted his request for discharge, granted in April, 1799. His attempt at university study lasted three semesters. He began preparations for civil service, but soon grew disaffected with the routine. He spent five months in Paris in 1801. His engagement to Wilhelmina von Zenge, a curious relationship even if we read *cum grano salis* the account she wrote for the benefit of her future husband, ended in May, 1802.[33] After several months of sickness, Kleist returned to several of the literary works he had begun earlier in the year.

In April, 1803, he met Johann David Falk, who had drafted an adaptation of the Amphitryon comedy.[34] According to the account of Ernst von Pfuel, Kleist began his version at this time, and it was apparently among his papers when the two travelled to Paris that October. In Paris, Pfuel reports, Kleist was mentally distraught and quarrelsome. Kleist burned his manuscript of *Robert Guiskard*, then left for the north coast of France to join the French army stationed in St. Omer and Boulogne. Because he was travelling without a pass, he was sent back to Potsdam.[35] The years

---

[31] Hanna Hellmann, "Kleists Amphitryon," *Euphorion*, 25 (1924), 241-51. If Kleist intended to identify himself as Jupiter and Krug as Amphitryon, as Hellmann argues, he was an egotistical rogue. Possibly, he identified with Amphitryon and shared the male fear of failing to satisfy female sexual desire; for speculations on Kleist's "Masturbation and Anxiety," see Sander Gilman's account of Kleist's reaction to masturbatory insanity during his visit to the Julius-Hospital in Würzburg in 1800: "Kleist and the Iconography of Onanism," *Diseases and Representation: Images of Illness from Madness to AIDS* (Ithaca: Cornell Univ. Press, 1988), pp. 67-73.

[32] Katharina Mommsen, *Kleists Kampf mit Goethe* (Heidelberg: Stiehm, 1974), p. 18.

[33] *Heinrich von Kleists Lebensspuren. Dokumente und Berichte der Zeitgenossen*, ed. Helmut Sembdner (Munich: dtv, 1969), pp. 48-53. Hans Joachim Kreutzer, *Die dichterische Entwicklung Heinrichs von Kleist: Untersuchungen zu seinen Briefen und zu Chronologie und Aufbau seiner Werke*, Philologische Studien und Quellen, 41 (Berlin: Schmidt, 1968).

[34] Helmut Sembdner, *Johann David Falks Bearbeitung des Amphitryon-Stoffes. Ein Beitrag zur Kleistforschung* (Berlin: Schmidt, 1971), pp. 16-17.

[35] *Heinrich von Kleists Lebensspuren*, pp. 90-96; Hilda M. Brown, "Kleist in Paris 1804," *Seminar: A Journal of Germanic Studies*, 13 (1977), 88-98; Hermann F. Weiss, *Funde und Studien zu Heinrich von Kleist* (Tübingen: Niemeyer, 1984), pp. 68-93.

immediately following his discharge from military service are obviously marked with false starts and misdirections. His gesture toward enlisting in the French army was an act of desperation, not of political enthusiasm. Napoleon had become Consul for Life in 1802, and assumed the imperial title in 1804. It was not until 1805 that Napoleon increased his military action in Germany. Kleist may have been ready to join the French army in 1803, but in January 1807 he was arrested by the French in Berlin and held prisoner until June at Fort de Joux and Châlons-sur-Marne.[36] From prison a final draft of *Amphitryon* was sent to his friends in Dresden. Just a month after his step-sister, Ulrike, negotiated his release, the play was published.

Kleist asserts his political opposition to the French in his very decision to rewrite Molière for a German audience. Molière had already been accused as a playwright who pandered to the corrupt morality of Paris. That charge could not be made more vigorously or more devastatingly than Rousseau had made it in his reply to D'Alembert.[37] Molière may have gently mocked his monarch, but he remained very much an apologist for the prevailing rule. His play may satirize, but it wittily sanctions rather than denounces the abuse of power. By insisting on the complete identity of the two Amphitryons, Kleist exonerates his Alcmene of adultery. More importantly, and this is the purpose of the dialogue between the divine and the mortal Amphitryon in the final scene, Kleist elevates his Jupiter above any taint of guilt. His play is not about the abuse of power, but about its proper exercise.

While there is more than just a hint of Mary, Joseph, and the Immaculate conception in Kleist's play,[38] Kleist keeps the seduction in the material world. As part of his insistence on the physical rather than the spiritual, he has provided a sub-plot with the two Sosias (Amphitryon's servant and Mercury as Jupiter-Amphitryon's servant) in which Sosia's wife Charis expresses her sexual frustrations in terms, albeit more blatantly bawdy, clearly echoing the high eroticism of Alcmene's desire. Further, he has made Alcmene, far more than any of his literary predecessors, a woman of intense passion. Filled with love and longing for her husband, who has been absent five months (only a few days in Molière's play), Alcmene has nurtured visions of an idealized Amphitryon. Jupiter, as god become flesh, perfectly realizes those visions. He is no impostor, no counterfeit, but precisely the incarnate fulfillment of her imaginings. If Schlegel is right in arguing that audience participation in illusion is secured through the thematization of illusion, Kleist's play is well designed to seduce the spectator's participation in the illusions of Alcmene. Although Goethe may have been right in claiming that Kleist's play, in contrast to Molière's, aimed at a "confusion of the feelings," the illusions of identity involve no less crucial confusions of perception and intellect.[39] Kleist's play demands a confrontation with illusion on moral, social, and political levels no less than on the emotional level.

As Hesiod told the tale, Jupiter, wishing to sire a Theban hero, had chosen Alcmene precisely because she was incorruptible. She is to give birth to Hercules, who will be a champion against all

---

[36] *Heinrich von Kleists Lebensspuren,* pp. 113-12; Weiss, pp. 103-22.

[37] Jean-Jacques Rousseau, *Lettre à d'Alembert sur les spectacles,* in *Oeuvres,* 18 vols. (Paris: Deterville, 1817), VIII, 50-66.

[38] Henri Plard, "'Gottes Ehebruch'?: Sur l'arrière-plan réligieux de l'*Amphitryon* de Kleist," *Etudes Germaniques,* 16 (1961), 335-74.

[39] Johann Wolfgang Goethe, *Tagebücher,* in *Gesamtausgabe,* ed. Peter Boerner, 45 vols. (Munich: dtv, 1963), XLIII, 232: (13 July 1807) "Der antike Sinn in Behandlung des Amphitryon ging auf Verwirrung der Sinne, auf den Zwiespalt der Sinne mit der Überzeugung. [...] Molière läßt den Unterschied zwischen Gemahl und Liebhaber vortreten, also eigentlich nur ein Gegenstand des Geistes, des Witzes und zarter Weltbemerkung. [...] Der gegenwärtige, Kleist, geht bei den Hauptpersonen auf die Verwirrung des Gefühls hinaus."

foes of Thebes. Jupiter's mission is to preserve Thebes from foreign conquest. He comes not to corrupt Alcmene and cuckold Amphitryon, but to help them wreak vengeance on the Taphians and Teleboans who had killed Alcmene's brothers.[40] The proud nationalism of Hesiod's tale is not suppressed in Kleist's play, but its overt expression is delayed until the concluding scene.[41] There are other problems to be dealt with first, and these are problems complicated by the illusions of popular perception. Not everyone in Kleist's audience would applaud a Jupiter come to preserve Prussia against France. It was by no means clear, even after the defeat of the Prussian army at Jena, that Napoleon's intervention should not be welcomed as a liberation from the old order.[42] In testing the problems of loyalty and fidelity, Kleist keeps Jupiter's true identity as much a secret from his audience as he does from Alcmene. Jupiter declares his motives only at the end.

As the play opens, Sosia arrives in Pharissa to inform Alcmene of Amphitryon's victory and to announce his return. The circumstances, past, present, and future, are revealed in this first scene as Sosia rehearses an imaginary dialogue with Alcmene. In the second scene he encounters – Sosia. Mercury, as Sosia's double, challenges his identity, his right to claim that the wife and house of Sosia, or even the name of Sosia, are his.

> MERKUR   Du sprachst, du hättest dich Sosias sonst genannt?
> SOSIAS   Wahr ist's, daß ich bis diesen Augenblick gewähnt,
>   Die Sache hätte ihre Richtigkeit.
>   Doch das Gewicht hat deiner Gründe mich
>   Belehrt: ich sehe jetzt, daß ich mich irrte.
> MERKUR   Ich bin's, der sich Sosias nennt.
> SOSIAS   Sosias – ?
>   Du – ?
> MERKUR   Ja, Sosias. Und wer Glossen macht,
>   Hat sich vor diesem Stock in acht zu nehmen. (I.ii)[43]

> (MERCURY   You said your name
>   was Sosia once?
> SOSIA   It is true that till today
>   I had supposed that there were some grounds for thinking
>   so. But now the force of your close
>   reasoning has quite persuaded me –
>   I see I erred.
> MERCURY   *I* am the one whose name
>   is Sosia.

---

[40] Hesiod, *De scuti Herculis*, ed. F. Stegemann (1904), 1-65; cited in *The Oxford Classical Dictionary*, ed. N.G.L. Hammond and H.H. Scullard, 2nd ed. (Oxford: Clarendon Press, 1970), pp. 39, 55, 511.

[41] Several contemporary reviews observe that, whereas Molière had treated the Greek myth frivolously, Kleist not only preserves but metaphysically resolves the mythic sense of divine immanence. See especially: August Klingemann, *Zeitung für die elegante Welt* (Leipzig, 19 June 1807); Karl Friedrich von Jariges, *Allgemeine Literaturzeitung* (Jena, 24 July 1807); in *Heinrich von Kleists Lebensspuren*, pp. 127-31.

[42] Max Braubach, "Entstehung und Ausbreitung der nationalen Bewegung," *Von der Französischen Revolution bis zum Wiener Kongress*, in *Gebhardt. Handbuch der deutschen Geschichte*, ed. Herbert Grundmann, 7th ed., 22 vols. (Munich: dtv, 1985), XIV, 96-104; 96: "Es hat im ersten Jahrzehnt des 19.Jh. nicht wenige Deutsche gegeben, die in der Herrschaft Napoleons keine Schmach für ihr Vaterland sahen, die ihr vielmehr zustimmten als der Verwirklichung einer dem alten Reich überlegenen Ordnung und der Anbahnung einer europäischen Gemeinschaft."

[43] Kleist, I, 214.

SOSIA   Sosia – you?
MERCURY   Yes, me. And any
    one who thinks it calls for comment on his part
    had better watch his step – and this stick here.)

As Kleist plays out his several variations on the confusions of identity, the opposition of doubles is resolved. The two become one. But the opening scene effectively sets up the anticipations of antagonism: one not only becomes two, false and true, but the disguised role threatens to usurp the true identity. Because Mercury-Sosia drives off the actual Sosia, it may be anticipated that Amphitryon will suffer the same fate. But in the central scenes, Alcmene, in spite of Jupiter's goading and Amphitryon's dumfounded response to her account of their grand night of love making, steadfastly denies any difference between the two Amphitryons. When Jupiter, as Amphitryon, asks her to distinguish between husband and lover, she responds that only her sacred bonds with her husband enable her to embrace him as her lover. She grants no possibility of a false Amphitryon. In the final scene, however, she is confronted by what she has all along denied – two Amphitryons.

    This is a scene of encounter, of revelation, and of decisions. It is a time to question and sort out loyalties. Amphitryon stands before the palace among his officers, soldiers, and the people; Jupiter-Amphitryon steps forth with Alcmene at his side. Sosia is convinced that Amphitryon is to be disamphitryonated just as he, Sosia, has been dissosiated ("Und kurz ich bin entsosiatisiert,/ Wie man Euch entamphitryonisiert.") But Jupiter's purpose is just the opposite. He comes not to divide but to unite.

JUPITER   Die ganze Welt, Geliebte, muß erfahren,
    Daß niemand deiner Seele nahte,
    Als nur dein Gatte, als Amphitryon. (III.xi)[44]

(JUPITER [to Alcmene]   Your husband, Lord Amphitryon,
    and *no one else* has ever been allowed
    within the precincts of your soul –
    and I wish the world to know it.)

Amphitryon himself commands the people to destroy the impostor, but they are baffled. When Alcmene is called upon by the officers to distinguish the true from the false, she concludes that only the Amphitryon whom she has embraced can be her husband. The Amphitryon who stands among the people must be the deceiver. When Amphitryon is called upon by Jupiter-Amphitryon to declare his identity, the situation is more charged. His own troops are divided now in factions. If he denies that the Amphitryon before him is the true Amphitryon, he is charging his own people with treason, accusing his own wife of adultery, and compromising even his own identity. Amphitryon begins to comprehend the dilemma. After first denying that the divine Amphitryon is Amphitryon, he must concede that to Alcmene he is indeed Amphitryon. When he calls upon his double to reveal his identity, the answer seems only to echo his own confusion:

AMPHITRYON   Jetzt einen Eid selbst auf den Altar schwör' ich,
    ...   .
    Daß er Amphitryon ihr ist.

---

[44] Kleist, I, 302.

JUPITER   Wohlan! Du bist Amphitryon.
AMPHITRYON   Ich bin's! –
    Und wer bist du, furchtbarer Geist?
JUPITER   Amphitryon. Ich glaubte, daß du's wüßtest.
AMPHITRYON   Amphitryon! Das faßt kein Sterblicher.
    Sei uns verständlich. (III.xi)[45]

(AMPHITRYON   Even upon the altar I now swear
    [...] to her he is Amphitryon.
JUPITER   Just so! And you're Amphitryon.
AMPHITRYON   I am – Then, awful spirit, who are you?
JUPITER   Amphitryon. I thought you understood.
AMPHITRYON   Amphitryon! But that's too much for mortal wits.
    Do make more sense.)

What Amphitryon has not understood is that his true identity is now fully realized in Jupiter-Amphitryon. To make more sense, Jupiter in a blast of thunder and lightning reveals his divine presence. The paradox of Amphitryon as divine transformation is resolved only in Amphitryon's own fulfillment of the divine triumph:

JUPITER   [...] öffne dem Triumph dein Herz.
    Was du, in mir, dir selbst getan, wird dir
    Bei mir, dem, was ich ewig bin, nicht schaden. (III.xi)[46]

(JUPITER   welcome with
    an open heart the triumph which is yours.
    The injury that you, in me, inflicted
    on yourself, no injury is, in my
    eternal Allness.)

Rather than capitulate to a trespassing monarch, Amphitryon acquires new power and a larger identity. Jupiter's true identity, after all, is that he has indeed become one with Amphitryon. The implication is clear: the German people, too, must assert their national identity. Thebes is united, its boundaries secure, and, with the promise of a strong leader as Amphitryon's heir, future years will bring continuing prosperity to the country.

Byron's *Sardanapalus* (1821) has a similar multistability. It, too, is a play entangled in illusion that seems to invite an autobiographical as well as a political reading. In 1820, the Prince Regent brought his estranged queen back from the continent to put her on trial for adultery. Since "the Prince of Pleasure" had not been leading a life of celibacy at Brighton, there was considerable public outrage at his making a public scandal of the Queen's behavior. With the death of the old, insane king, the Prince Regent was crowned George IV in 1821. The characters in Byron's play – Sardanapalus, Queen Zarina, and Myrrha, the king's concubine – provide an obvious parallel to King George, Queen Caroline, and Lady Conyngham (of whom, incidentally, it was said that she held her sway as the King's favorite by making it clear that "in her conviction he was a compound

---

[45] Kleist, I, 308-9.
[46] Kleist, I, 310.

of Sardanapalus and Louis XIV").[47] But the play also echoes Byron's own domestic turmoil of 1816, when he left England amidst the scandal of divorce and whispered charges of incest with his half-sister Augusta Leigh. In Italy the Countess Teresa Guiccioli had become his intimate companion. Sardanapalus, Queen Zarina, and Myrrha not noly figure forth the public and political affairs of England, but also expose Byron's private reflections on his relationship with Lady Byron and Countess Guiccioli.

The tragedy of the effete king, as it had been developed in Marlowe's *Edward II* and Shakespeare's *Richard II*, clearly informs Byron's characterization of Sardanapalus. Paradoxically, however, Byron's Sardanapalus draws his heroic strength from his feminine, not to say effeminate, sensibility.[48] He rationalizes his voluptuary existence as a rejection of the masculine brutality of his warrior ancestress, Semiramis. Byron builds, of course, on the popular reception of *Sémiramis*, Voltaire's powerful dramatization of the bloody queen and her incestuous passion for her son.[49] It is her image that terrifies him in the dream-scene which provides the dramatic turn at the beginning of Act IV. The dream forces him out of his hedonistic self-indulgence into heroic action. His naive belief in goodness and pervading peace is destroyed.[50] He must confront the grim truth of greed and war. Byron negates the concept of the dream as soul-assuaging solace and affirms the dream as truth. What the conscious mind typically ignores or represses in waking experience, breaks through in dreams to torment the dreamer – not with delusions, but with discomforting truths. The dream is not an escape but a confrontation.

The escapist notion is proffered conditionally by Myrrha, who watches over the slumbering Sardanapalus. Sleep, she soliloquizes, is a balm and bliss. Perhaps the pleasant dreams of sleep foreshadow the eternal dream of death. Just as in this life "we are happiest" in sleep, so we shall be "happiest of all" in death, sleep's "unawakening twin." Sardanapalus, however, is not in happy sleep; he is in the throes of a tormenting nightmare. He tosses upon his couch and his features grimace in pain. Still Myrrha hesitates to rouse him for fear that the pain of waking will prove more insufferable than the pain of sleep. When Sardanapalus suddenly awakens, he continues to speak to the phantoms of his dream. "The hunter and the crone," Nimrod and Semiramis, do not vanish from his vision as raises himself upon his couch. He struggles to exorcise their meontic persistence:

SARDANAPALUS [awakening]   Not so –
                 although ye multiplied the stars

[47] J.B. Priestley, *The Prince of Pleasure and his Regency 1811-20* (New York: Herper & Row, 1969), p. 280.

[48] Julie Carlson, "Impositions of Form: Romantic Antitheatricalism and the Case Against Particular Women," Byron and the Drama of Romanticism, Yale University, New Haven, 30 March 1990. With reference to *Sardanapalus*, as well as to a number of other Romantic works, Carlson observes a gender transfer in character description (feminine men, masculine women). Henry Fuseli, who was inclined to worry about such matters, expressed his concern with the phenomenon in Aphorism §226: "In an age of luxury women have taste, decide and dictate; for in an age of luxury woman aspires to the functions of man, and man slides into the offices of women. The epoch of eunuchs was ever the epoch of viragos." *The Mind of Henry Fuseli*, ed. Eudo Mason (London: Routledge & Kegan Paul, 1951), p. 145; originally published in *Aphorisms* (1788-18), *Life and Writings of Henry Fuseli*, ed. John Knowles, 3 vols. (London: Colburn & Bentley, 1831).

[49] Voltaire's *Sémiramis*, as translated by George Edward Ayscough, first played in England at Drury Lane (13 December 1776). Charles-Simon Catel's opera, *Sémiramis* (libretto by Disriaux after Voltaire) was performed in Paris (3 May 1802), but it was Rossini's *Semiramide* that won international acclaim (it opened in Venice, 3 February 1823, and first played in London at the Haymarket Theatre, 15 July 1824).

[50] In the production of *Sardanapalus*, directed by Murray Biggs at Yale University (29 and 31 March, 1 April 1990), Brian Price gave an excellent performance in the lead role, making the character readily accessible to a modern audience by playing the sybaritic king much in the manner of a "flower-child" of the sixties. The implicit "make love not war" credo seemed aptly suited to the character of Sardanapalus. Cameron Meyer, as Myrrha, gave her role an Ionic constraint that effectively contrasted with the lascivious effusions of Sardanapalus in company with his other concubines.

> And gave them to me as a realm to share
> From you and with you! I would not so purchase
> The empire of eternity. Hence – Hence –
> Old hunter of the earliest brutes! and ye,
> Who hunted fellow-creatures as if brutes!
> Once bloody mortals – and now bloodier idols,
> If your priests lie not! An thou, ghastly beldame!
> Dripping with dusky gore, and trampling on
> The carcasses of Inde – away! away!
> Where am I? Where the spectres? (IV.i.24-34)[51]

The nightmare images fade, and he discovers Myrrha at his side. He explains the terror that has overwhelmed him. "I dream'd myself here – here – even where we are," he tells her, and he describes grasping hands with the fearsome hunter, only to have the spectre vanish like "the memory of some hero." He describes, too, the bloody Semiramis, "sneering with the passion/ Of vengeance, leering too with that of lust." Although he shrinks from her embrace, her "noisome kisses" burn upon his lips, "as if,/ In lieu of her remote descendent, I/ Had been the son who slew her for her incest!" In this dream, he must confront the past which haunts the present, "here – even where we are."

The dream exposes the evil legacy which, as Sardanapalus knows, haunts his kingship. He has inherited a bloody throne. In classical drama, dreams are used as symbolic or prophetic revelations. In the meontic mode of Romantic drama, the images of dreams become active and animating forces. In Kleist's *Kätchen von Heilbronn* (1808), Kätchen's actions are motivated by her dream under the elder bush. Friedrich's dream of glory in the opening somnambulist episode sets in motion that chain of cause-and-effect which brings him blindfolded before the firing squad, so he thinks, in the penultimate scene of *Prinz Friedrich von Homburg* (1811). Sardanapalus, too, acts upon his dream. The fears which he has denied in his life of sensual abandon have escaped from the darkness of his repressed subconscious and have stalked him back into his waking world. His life has been escapism. The dream reveals the idle delusion of his waking hours: "Myself a host that deem'd himself but a guest,/ Willing to equal all in social freedom" (IV.i.80-81). That fond hope of freedom is dashed by the ghastly figures of lust and greed that threaten, not his mind, but his kingdom. Social freedom cannot flourish, as he has fatuously presumed, unnourished and unattended. The hunter and the crone continue to spread their poison among the people.

The terror of the dream stirs the king to action. He is aroused too late. Rebellion is at his gates, and corruption has infiltrated his palace. Although his heroic action cannot turn back the siege, his efforts are not futile. Macbeth, who is certainly as much persecuted by horrible dreams as any tragic hero, may cower in his private agonies, but he will not accept the name "coward" from Macduff. He cannot redeem his crimes, but he can reassert his self-respect as a soldier. The death of Sardanapalus is far more complex, nor does the parallel to *Edward II* or *Richard II* persist after the pivotal opening scene of Act IV. Byron devotes the 173 lines of that scene to the exposition of the dream that then takes hold of Sardanapalus and directs his action through the final acts. While Byron had adapted from Shakespeare and Marlowe his representation of the effete king, there is a crucial dif-

---

[51] George Gordon, Lord Byron, *Poetical Works* (London: Oxford Univ. Press, 1945; rpt. 1967), pp. 453-92; at the time of writing, I could not make use of the new edition of the text in *The Complete Poetical Works of Lord Byron*, vol. 6, ed. Jerome McGann and Barry Waller (London: Oxford Univ. Press, 1990).

ference: Edward had his Gaveston, Richard his Bolingbroke. Sardanapalus is foiled neither by corruptor nor by rival. Arbaces and Beleses plot against him, but they are less manipulators than opportunists.

Sardanapalus is his own enemy. He himself, in his neglect of duty, is responsible for the civil unrest that explodes into rebellion. He is surrounded by faithful friends, each of whom might have some right to be an enemy, who tell him what his own benumbed conscience has failed to tell him. Myrrha his slave, Zarina his estranged wife, Salemines her brother, all remain loyal, all seek to rouse him to action. Instead, like George IV in his retreat to Brighton, Sardanapalus prefers to lounge with his concubines in a flowery pavilion. Salemines warns him: "I would have recall'd thee from thy dream;/ Better by me awaken'd than rebellion" (I.ii.200-1). Salemines cannot shake Sardanapalus from the idle dream of his waking hours. It takes the dream rising up from his own repressed conscience to shatter his fond delusions that he can rule with "songs, and lutes, and feasts, and concubines."

Once roused by that dream of the awful curse of Nimrod and Semiramis, Sardanapalus has but one course of action. In Act IV, he saves his wife and children from the looming insurrection. In Act V, he battles against the rebel army that storms his castle. Like Macbeth, he is valiant even though he knows death is inescapable. But Sardanapalus does not die in battle. He holds off the invasion only to cover the escape of his retinue. He then prepares his throne as a grand funeral pyre. Myrrha, who has refused to leave him, ascends the pyre with him. Resignation? Defeat? Suicide? Sardanapalus gives his action a very different rationale:

> the light of this
> Most royal of funereal pyres shall be
> Not a mere pillar form'd of cloud and flame,
> A beacon in the horizon for a day,
> And then a mount of ashes, but a light
> To lesson ages, rebel nations, and
> Voluptuous princes. Time shall quench full many
> A people's records, and a hero's acts;
> Sweep empire after empire, like this first
> Of empires, into nothing; but even then
> Shall spare this deed of mine, and hold it up
> A problem few dare imitate, and none
> Despise – but, it may be, avoid the life
> Which led to such a consummation. (V.i.436-49)

It is with this sense of a moral lesson to posterity that Sardanapalus welcomes the flames. It is a lesson to "Voluptuous princes" as well as to "rebel nations." He cannot dispel the curse of Nineveh's murderous progenitors, but his martyrdom will echo through history as the moral counterpart and corrective to their record of cruelty and slaughter.

Conflicting sources of illusion also provide thematic and dramatic motifs in Byron's *Manfred* (1817), where his "vigil" of self becomes a mandate for all other characters whom he directs to "Look upon me," "Watch me, or watch me in my watchings." While the meontic illusionism may be enhanced by the supernatural encounters with Spirits (I.i), or the visit to the Hall of Arimanes (II.iv), it is the "continuance of enduring thought," announced in the opening lines, that enables

Manfred to assert his ground in the subsequent scenes. The encounters with the Chamois Hunter, the Witch of the Alps, the Abbot of St. Maurice are, after all, a series of debates in which Manfred must pit his convictions against opposing philosophies. The very "vigil" that is darkened by his self-recriminations provides the ground of his self-assertion, even in meeting the demons at his death. The subjective truth becomes the only enduring truth. Precisely because it seems to repeat his own guilty dream, Ulric, in Byron's *Werner* (1822), is aghast at Ida's dream of Strahlenheim's murder (IV.i.192-202). He may claim, "All dreams are false," but he fears their awful truth will reveal his crime. Kleist, like Byron, dramatizes the subjective, the intuitive, the introspective.[52] Penthesilea's dream that she has failed to fulfill the law of the Amazons may be "sweet" when defined in accord with its own subjective conditions (xiv.1556-62), but she cannot make the dream accord with her waking world. She sees in the waking world what she has been taught to see; in the dream she sheds the delusions of her waking experience and beholds the truth of her own desires.

Shelley conceived his *Charles the First* (1821) as an elaborate metadramatic effort to turn dramatic illusion into a critique of those subjective illusions by which the mind constructs reality. Stuart Curran describes the incomplete play as Shelley's attempt "to present a drama that looked continually into itself as into a mirror even as it represented itself to readers or auditors as a spectacle to contemplate and through which to comtemplate themselves." Shelley adapted the self-reflexive techniques of Calderón to dramatize the psychological dilemma of illusion, "the sense that everywhere you look in the world you are victimized by your own illusions as well as the illusions of others."[53] Shelley's opening scene clearly endorses and exploits the Romantic premise that illusion, as opposed to delusion, is deliberately and consciously engaged. Illusion acquires its leverage by working against certain counter-forces: illusion as opposed to delusion, illusionism, anti-illusion, as well as to "reality."

Shelley's play opens upon a group of spectators who watch two spectacles: first a theatrical masque, then a royal procession. His characters, as in the fable of the blind men and the elephant, each perceive a different aspect of the scenes before them. The First Citizen, while not a Royalist, upholds the *status quo* with optimistic hopes for better times. The Second Citizen condemns the corruption of the Court and the Popish inclinations of the Monarch. The Third Citizen, a Puritan Dissenter, quotes from the Book of Revelations in prophesying the wrath about to fall upon the "papists, atheists, tyrants, and apostates." A Youth, the son of the Second Citizen, beholds the proceedings with a sense of wonder and awe. A Law Student also speaks, more as passive observer than as critic of the events. Throughout the dialogue, as an intrusive refrain, are heard the commands of the Pursuivant and the Marshalsman to "Give place, give place!"[54]

The setting is one of bustle and jostle, as the people, sharply divided into opposing factions, try to maintain their own places even as they are being pushed aside to make room for the royal pageantry. The contrasts and tensions, significantly enough, derive not from the differences between the two spectacles – the masque and the royal procession – but from the political vantages of the various spectators. The straggling "troop of cripples, beggars, and lean outcasts," who follow after

---

[52] See: Friedrich Koch, *Heirich von Kleist: Bewußtsein und Wirklichkeit* (Stuttgart: Metzler, 1958); Elmar Hoffmeister, *Täuschung und Wirklichkeit bei Heinrich von Kleist* (Bonn: Bouvier, 1968); Hermann Reske, *Traum und Wirklichkeit bei in der Welt Heinrich von Kleists* (Stuttgart: Metzler, 1969).

[53] Stuart Curran, "Shelleyan Drama," in *The Romantic Theatre*, ed. Richard Allen Cave (Gerrards Cross: Smythe, 1986), pp. 68-71.

[54] Percy Bysshe Shelley, *Poetical Works*, ed. Thomas Hutchinson, rev. G.M. Matthews (London: Oxford Univ. Press, 1970), pp. 488-507.

the royal procession are called the anti-masque by the Youth, who wishes to give some artistic sanction to the pitiful sight. In part, the opening scene declares that the display of royalty is no less illusionary and theatrical than the masque being performed at the Inns of Court. But the illusionism is even more encompassing, for the spectators themselves, as the Second Citizen reminds the awestruck Youth, are also actors in the drama being played in British politics. The Youth is warned to be wary of "that stage-scene" taking place even at the moment. Clearly, Shelley intends the admonition to apply to his contemporary audience as well.

The second scene, set in Whitehall where the King and Queen meet with their followers to discuss problems of state, continues the self-reflexivity established in the opening scene. Archy, the court fool, provides the ironic leverage of the aloof spectator. He readily confesses that, because he is a fool, he is an unreliable witness. But he sees well enough to observe how the king's perception is being distorted by those around him. In response to the Queen's haughty comments on the "quaint pageant" and her recollection of the superior theater of Paris, St. John tells her that "the love of Englishmen can make/ The lightest favour of their lawful kind outweigh a despot's. – We humbly take our leaves,/ Enriched by smiles which France can never buy" (ii.29-32). He not only rejects her pretensions of French superiority, he even suggests that the French monarch is a despot. When he departs, the king remarks worriedly that Archbishop Laud should "Mark what spirit sits in St. John's eyes." This is Archy's cue for a discourse on the problems of perception and illusion;

> Yes, pray your Grace look: for, like an unsophisticated [eye] sees everything upside down, you who are wise will discern the shadow of an idiot in lawn sleeves and a rochet setting springes to catch woodcocks in haymaking time. Poor Archy, whose owl-eyes are tempered to the error of his age, and because he is a fool, and by special ordinance of God forbidden ever to see himself as he is, sees now in that deep eye a blindfold devil sitting on the ball, and weighing words out between king and subjects. One scale is full of promises, and the other full of protestations: and then another devil creeps behind the first out of the dark windings [of a] pregnant lawyer's brain, and takes the bandage from the other's eyes, and throws a sword into the left-hand scale, for all the world like my Lord Essex's there. (ii.36-47)

The Fool apparently sees a good deal more than the King sees. He sees that blindfold Justice is being perverted, and that "devils" have come between the King and his subjects. The King can neither see nor act for himself. He has become a blind puppet who merely acts a role and recites the lines that are given him by his counsellors. The villains of this historical tragedy are Archbishop Laud and Queen Henrietta. Shelley has taken his history largely from Hume, but he has drawn widely from other sources, including the collection of Charles I's treaties distributed in *Eikon Basilike*.[55] Subsequent scenes record the cruel "justice" administered by the Star Chamber (scene iii), Hampden's departure from England (scene iv), and Archy's farewell, banished from Court by Laud (scene v). Shelley apparently intended to focus the dramatic action on Laud's fanatic zeal, the struggles of the "Long Parliament," and Strafford's execution in 1641. In some accounts, it had been suggested that the King deliberately betrayed Strafford. Shelley seeks to show, rather, a King manipulated by the Archbishop and the Queen, and unable to keep his promise to protect his friend.

When Hugo takes up the problem of representation in the concluding section of the *Préface*, he once more addresses the evocation of illusion. He refuses to separate scene and situation. Setting

---

[55] R.B. Woodings, "Shelley's Sources for *Charles the First*," *Modern Language Review*, 69 (1969), 267-75; Woodings, "'A Devil of a Nut to Crack': Shelley's *Charles the First*," *Studia Neophilologica*, 11 (1968), 216-37.

participates in dramatic action. Thus he speaks of the "séduction qu'exerçait sur l'imagination de l'auteur cette vaste scène de l'histoire" – and he adds, "De cette scène il a fait ce drame." Plot and staging, no less than character, enable the drama to represent the subtle oppositions of the sublime and the grotesque in the political struggle for worldly power between the rival religious factions. The grotesque is abundantly manifested throughout the play, most notably in the antics of Cromwell's quartet of jesters, the bungling of his son Richard, the prophecies of the necromancer Manesse, and the religious fanaticism of Carr.

As immediately becomes clear in the play, Hugo's sense of historical fidelity clearly has more to do with "la couleur locale" than with fidelity to fact, for *Cromwell* (1827) opens with a radical twist of history: the Cavaliers and the Roundheads are gathered together in a tavern conspiring to assassinate the Lord Protector. Cromwell, it is feared, aspires to have himself crowned king – a situation which might fit Napoleon more nearly than Cromwell.[56] The dialogue involves a delightful display of stylistic virtuosity. Hugo has the Cavaliers speak like the court poets of Louis XIV, while his Puritans quote the Bible like Huguenots and reason about Divine Will like eighteenth-century Deists or Mechanists. In Act III the jesters sing demonic songs, and Lord Rochester (the Rochester of Dryden's day, not of Milton's) engages in a debate with Milton on the nature of poetry. The play also involves a complicated game of disguises. Rochester, the most zealous of the Cavaliers, pretends to be a devout Puritan come to serve Cromwell as personal chaplain. Learning of the plan to drug and kidnap him, Cromwell plays along with his "chaplain," drugs his would-be drugger, and re-disguises him as Cromwell. Cromwell then puts on the uniform of sentinel guarding his own gate and watches as the conspirators carry off the wrong victim.[57] The final grotesquery of Act IV is Rochester's confusion upon awakening: he thinks he has died and gone to Hell. The active use of stage setting, a factor to become more prominent in Hugo's dramaturgy,[58] is effectively used in Act V. Carpenters are on stage building a platform, a platform to be used for a coronation – and an execution. The platform serves throughout Act V as a major symbol for the rise and fall of rulers. The carpenters' macabre reflections are followed, first, by the Roundheads' threat to behead their leader should he go through with the coronation and, then, by Cromwell's trance-like reverie on royal power. He seems ready to mount the platform, but them comes to his senses and restores political order.

Confessing that his play is lengthy and crowded, Hugo nevertheless maintains that the history plays of Shakespeare have been his model. Just as one would not want to watch a Shakespearean play abridged to a two-hour comic opera or farce, a French audience might take a lesson from the English and Germans and learn to devote a whole evening in the theater to a single play. What if it should take six hours to perform his *Cromwell*! It would not be six hours of tedium or monotony. His very formula of opposition and contrast would prevent that. His Cromwell is not merely "warrior and statesman," he is also "the theologian, the pedant, the bad poet, the visionary, the buffoon, the father, the husband, the human Proteus, in a word, the two-fold Oliver Cromwell, *homo et vir*."[59] Hugo not only dramatizes the many masks of body and soul, he makes his dramatic illusion interact

[56] Maurice Descotes, *L'Obsession de Napoléon dans le Cromwell de Victor Hugo* (Paris: Lettres modernes, 1967).
[57] On Hugo's use of masks, disguises, and stage charlatanry: Jean-Bertrand Barrère, *La Fantaisie de Victor Hugo*. 3 vols. (Paris: Corti, 1949-60).
[58] Burwick, "Stage Illusion and the Stage Designs of Goethe and Hugo," *Word and Image*, 4, No. 3-4 (July-December 1988), 692-718.
[59] Hugo, pp. 151-52, 149.

with stage illusion. Political and theatrical illusions are exposed in a peculiarly self-reflexive way when Hugo has his carpenters construct the multiple-function "props" on the stage.

While Hugo took the circumstances of the Cromwellian Interregnum as setting for his critique of Napoleon's aspirations to Empire, Shelley used the events just prior to the rise of Cromwell to comment on the political recoil that followed Napoleon's fall. In Archy's anachronistic reference (ii.360-62) to Coleridge's one-time scheme to found a Pantisocracy and to Gonzalo's vision of an ideal colony in *The Tempest* (II.i.147-56), Shelley reminds his contemporaries of those who have abandoned their Jacobin enthusiasm and have succumbed to the manipulations of Anti-Jacobin authority. There is an immediately relevant message about the nature of political illusions in Shelley's dramatization of the inability of Charles I to resist the French pretensions of his Queen and the zealous machinations of his Archbishop.

Private illusions, no less than public illusions, emerge and even dominate the stage in Romantic drama. The introspections and invisible fantasies of Sardanapalus, or of Manfred, assert the meontic impulse as determinate constituents of the action. Kleist, too, transforms the invisible world of personal fantasy into a seemingly palpable presence on the stage. The myth of Theban nationalism redefines and gives moral purpose to what had been mere "libertine" excesses in Molière's comedy. Resonances of Shakespeare's *Measure for Measure* inform the structure of *Prinz Friedrich*.[60] Like Claudio, Friedrich falls prey to a cowardly fear of death; and like Isabella, Natalie visits him in prison and subsequently pleas that his life be spared. Like Shakespeare's "Duke of dark corners," the Elector manipulates the course of action. As mortal counterpart to the genius of Friedrich's dream, the Elector literally reaches into that dream in the opening scene, and in the finale he reconstructs it and provides its happy consummation.

Illusion in Romantic drama, as recommended by the Romantic critics, exploits self-reflexive themes about creating illusion. Not "reality" but the human mind becomes the object of dramatic representation, and the shift to the meontic mode is manifest in the new dramatic explorations of the mind's imaginings. Just as Schlegel, Coleridge, and Hugo had prescribed, the playwrights of the age allowed their plots to reveal, rather than conceal, their efforts at illusion-making. In the plays of Kleist, Byron, Shelley, and Hugo the conjurings of subjective illusions vie with, and often displace, the illusions of the objective world.

---

[60] Hellmann, "Kleists *Prinz von Homburg* und Shakespeares *Maß für Maß*," *Germanisch-Romanische Monatsschrift*, O.S. 11 (1923), 288-96.

W.D. HOWARTH

ASSIMILATION AND ADAPTATION OF EXISTING FORMS IN DRAMA OF THE ROMANTIC PERIOD

I

For a variety of reasons, the French contribution to the history of Romanticism in the European theatre was the most striking at the time, and remains the most significant to us today. Not only were certain events – the "battle" of *Hernani* and other confrontations between Old and New – highly sensational, but the theatre attracted virtually all the major imaginative writers of the day; particularly in the case of Victor Hugo, the plays themselves were supported by a challenging body of theoretical writing, and the *Préface de Cromwell* still counts as one of the most important aesthetic manifestos of the nineteenth century; the number of French dramatic works of the period which continue to attract a major interest, on the stage and in the study, is more considerable than is the case with any other corpus of drama texts from the same period; and the lasting influence of Romantic modes of feeling and expression in the theatre derives almost exclusively from the French example. It is altogether too easy, therefore, to overlook the fact that what we are dealing with here is a European phenomenon; that the same sort of development that was taking place in France can also be illustrated from the literary and theatrical history of England, Germany and Italy; and that the gradual throwing-off, throughout Europe, of the narrow and exclusive neoclassical aesthetic which was one of the signs of French eighteenth-century cultural hegemony anticipates the much slower process in France itself of catching up with more liberal and eclectic aesthetic attitudes that had already gained acceptance elsewhere. For most of the eighteenth century the French had been allowed to sustain the role of cultural arbiters of Europe, exporting the derivative formulas that pro-duced verse tragedies like Addison's *Cato* or Johnson's *Irene*, Gottsched's *Der sterbende Cato* (The Death of Cato) or the plays of Maffei and Alfieri, and maintaining the patronising disdain for the freer aesthetic of Elizabethan or Golden Age drama that can be seen in Voltaire's writings over half a century or so. Any progress towards the cultural relativism of which Madame de Staël was to show herself capable in *De la Littérature* (1800) and *De l'Allemagne* (1810) was slow indeed in France.

In the meantime, Voltaire's own tragedies, and those of his contemporaries and successors, continued to abide slavishly by the unities of time, place and action – and, even more fatal to the creative imagination, the fourth, unwritten, unity of *tone*. The most crippling of all conventions was that of *le style noble*: a highly selective idiom full of abstraction, from which all concrete, technical or everyday terms were banned. Voltaire's rendering of Hamlet's "To be or not to be [...]" into alexandrines in 1734 is a good illustration of this; even more indicative is his scornful rejection in 1776 of the homely "Not a mouse stirring" from the opening of the same play as totally unworthy to bear comparison with Racine's 'noble' evocation of a still night: "Mais tout dort, et l'armée, et les vents, et Neptune" (But everything is asleep: the army, the winds, and Neptune himself).[1] Voltaire's positive achievement was to pioneer a change in the subject-matter of tragedy. The kind of subject from national history that seems perfectly natural in the English – or Scottish – context of Hume's *Douglas* (1756) was a notable breakthrough in plays like Voltaire's *Tancrède* (1760) or De Belloy's *Le Siège de Calais* (1764); while the use of the dramatic form to express the humanitarian ideals of the Enlightenment, that one can take for granted in Johnson's *Irene* (1749), Lessing's *Nathan der Weise* (1779) or Goethe's *Iphigenie auf Tauris* (1787), represents a much more daring innovation in Voltaire's *Mahomet* (1742) and even in M.-J. Chénier's *Charles IX* (1789). However, genuine local and historical colour was impossible, as was the forceful expression of topical ideas, as long as the neoclassical attitude to *language* prevailed; and at a time when English and German poets were free to use the full range of contemporary vocabulary, their French counterparts had perforce to have recourse to the most outlandish of circumlocutions in order to express even quite ordinary concepts. As late as 1823 Stendhal was to complain that the word *pistolet* "ne peut absolument pas entrer dans un vers tragique" (is quite unacceptable in tragic verse); and he quotes the dilemma of the poet Legouvé, who in his tragedy dealing with Henri IV (1806) had been unable to render the monarch's celebrated wish, that all his subjects might be able to enjoy "la poule au pot le dimanche" (a fowl to roast on a Sunday), otherwise than by this laboured periphrasis:

> Je veux enfin qu'au jour marqué pour le repos
> L'hôte laborieux des modestes hameaux
> Sur sa table moins humble ait, par ma bienfaisance,
> Quelques-uns de ces mets réservés à l'aisance.[2]

(My wish is that on the day set aside for rest, the hardworking denizen of the humblest hamlet should enjoy by my charity, at a less frugal meal, some of the dishes normally reserved for my wealthier subjects.)

In Britain, the Shakespearean masterpieces, certain plays of Marlowe and other contemporaries, and later products of dramatists who did not subscribe to the neoclassical formula such as Rowe's *Jane Shore* (1714), remained part of the literary and theatrical heritage throughout the eighteenth century, even if David Garrick's Shakespearean productions showed a cavalier disregard for the text that would not have been tolerated in a later age. On the Continent, however, where the neoclassical aesthetic had a much firmer hold, there was a correspondingly greater sense of polemic and confrontation in the challenge presented by the champions of irregular drama.

In France, there were of course honourable exceptions to the narrow-minded, patronising attitude to Shakespeare represented by Voltaire. As early as 1747 Hénault, in the Preface to his *François II*, writes a discerning appreciation of the Shakespearean history-play; Mercier's historical dramas, set in the period of the Wars of Religion, are inspired by Shakespeare's dramatised account of the Wars of the Roses; and Ducis who, composing the only theatrically viable versions of Shakespeare's own plays in French before the end of the eighteenth century, however imperfect his renderings into the prevailing neoclassical idiom inevitably remained, nevertheless provided the texts by which Talma was to effect the first impact of Shakespeare on the Parisian stage. The conscientious prose translations of Letourneur (1776-83) not only provided an essential service for

---

[1] *Lettres philosophiques*, Letter 18; *Lettre à l'Académie française*.
[2] *Racine et Shakespeare*, ed. H. Martineau (Paris: Divan, 1928), p. 47.

Ducis (who knew no English), but remained the only version of Shakespeare accessible to the French until improved on by the scholarly Guizot in the 1820s. Similarly in Italy, although there were minor dramatists towards the end of the century who assimilated the influence of Shakespearean tragedy in a creative manner, it was not until Manzoni's *Conte di Carmagnola* (1820) and *Adelchi* (1822), accompanied by his *Lettre à M. Chauvet sur l'unité de temps et de lieu dans la tragédie*, that the Italian public was presented by a major writer with a reasoned alternative to the neoclassical formula, based on the Shakespearean model.

However, it was in Germany that the influence of Shakespeare made the earliest real impact, and produced the most substantial results. Here, Wieland's translations (1762-66), coupled with Herder's critical essay in the influential *Von deutscher Art und Kunst* (On German Style and Art, 1773), met with a much more fruitful response from the young *Stürmer und Dränger* than Letourneur's translation was able to do in France; while Lessing, complementing the work of his contemporaries in the *Literaturbriefe* (1759-65) and the *Hamburgische Dramaturgie* (1767-68), drew on both the Shakespearean example and that of Spanish Golden Age drama as support for his campaign against the French neoclassical theatre and its prolonged and excessive influence in Germany.

If the term "preromantic" has any critical validity, it would seem proper to use it to denote that period of fifty years or so during which, under the influence of Rousseau's anarchic individualism, the various struggles throughout Europe for political freedom and social justice, and new forms of sentiment propagated by Young and others, what might be called the Romantic sensibility already existed, although writers – particularly dramatists, and particularly in France – lacked the proper medium for its expression. However, once we look at the situation in Germany during the same period, we can see straightaway that there were fewer inhibitions; and that the greater liberty of the theatres (one of the cultural advantages of the fragmentation of Germany, whatever its political drawbacks), the growing resistance to French domination in the arts, and especially the characteristic difference between the two languages and the lack of that hierarchical attitude to literary style that was so crippling to originality and spontaneity in French, combined to offer the aspiring young dramatist a far freer choice of dramatic style and linguistic idiom than his counterpart in France enjoyed. As a result, *Sturm und Drang* drama possesses a vigour not to be found elsewhere in the European theatre at the time, and a formal variety to match. Above all, the German example shows a refreshingly eclectic attitude towards tone, as the essential determinant of genre. Whereas French theory and practice still maintained a rigorous opposition between tragedy and comedy (for *drame bourgeois*, despite Diderot's pleas for a "genre intermédiaire," was in effect little more than "comédie sérieuse"), and between "literary" and "popular" in the theatre, the *Sturm und Drang* playwrights were free to mix contrasting moods and styles as they wished: at least partly in conscious imitation of those features in Shakespeare's drama which even his most favourable interpreters in France tended to omit as repugnant to national taste. Lenz, in his *Anmerkungen über das Theater* (Remarks on the Theatre, 1774), goes further than Lessing in rejecting the separation of comedy and tragedy; but Benjamin Constant, translator of *Wallenstein* into French and sympathetic spokesman for the German theatre generally, has this revealing comment to make in 1809:

> Les auteurs allemands peuvent employer, pour le développement des caractères, une quantité de circonstances accessoires qu'il serait impossible de mettre sur notre théâtre sans déroger à la dignité requise: et cependant ces petites circonstances répandent dans le tableau présenté de la sorte beaucoup de vie et de vérité. Dans le *Goetz de Berlichingen* de Goethe, ce guerrier, assiégé dans son château par

une armée impériale, donne à ses soldats un dernier repas pour les encourager. Vers la fin de ce repas, il demande du vin à sa femme, qui suivant les usages de ce temps, est à la fois la dame et la ménagère du château. Elle lui répond à demi-voix qu'il n'en reste plus qu'une seule cruche qu'elle a réservée pour lui. Aucune tournure poétique ne permettrait de transporter ce détail sur notre théâtre: l'emphase des paroles ne ferait que gâter le naturel de la situation, et ce qui est touchant en allemand ne serait en français que ridicule.[3]

(German authors are able, in developing character, to use a host of accessory traits that we could not show on our stage without impairing the essential dignity [of tragedy]; nevertheless, such traits help to give the dramatic portrait more life and truth. In Goethe's *Goetz von Berlichingen* that warrior, besieged in his castle by the Emperor's army, offers his soldiers a last meal to encourage them. Towards the end of the meal he asks his wife, who according to the practice of the time is both chatelaine and housekeeper, for more wine. She replies in a whisper that there is only one pitcher left, which she has been reserving for his own use. No poetic turn of phrase could possibly convey this detail on the French stage: the grandiloquence of the expression would destroy the naturalness of the situation, and what we find touching in the German would be ridiculous in French.)

It was not only a question of literary tone, of course: the *dramatic* idiom of *Götz von Berlichingen* (1773) is thoroughly imbued with the liberating influence of Shakespeare; and Goethe's play, with its battle-scenes, its kaleidoscopic picture of an age, and the characterisation of the hero as a forceful figure whose portrait is intimately related to that of the age in which he lived, is the most distinguished of the eighteenth-century historical dramas written according to the Shakespearean formula.

In France, by the time of the Revolution, which accelerated the breakdown of the neoclassical system by undermining the status of the Théâtre Français as a monopoly theatre, the "middle" genre of *drame bourgeois* had an established place in the theatrical repertory. However, its potential as an expression of the ideology of the Enlightenment was slow to be exploited, and the watchfulness of the censor prevented this from ever being fully realised; so that the moral platitudes of *Le Philosophe sans le savoir* (The Unwitting Philosopher) or *La Brouette du vinaigrier* (The Vinegar-seller's Wheelbarrow) remain all too typical of the middle-class challenge to the élitist prestige of tragedy. "Bürgerliche Tragödie," on the other hand, fulfilled a much more provocative role as a means of challenging the prejudices of birth and breeding. While Lessing's *Miss Sara Sampson* retains the domestic atmosphere of Richardson's novels, and fails to escape the melodramatic clichés of Lillo's *London Merchant*, his *Emilia Galotti* already prefigures Schiller's *Kabale und Liebe* in the way in which private misfortunes are related to matters of public concern: the closed world of *Clarissa Harlowe* is replaced by a wider arena, in which a ruler's morality is held up to scathingly critical scrutiny. The idiom of eighteenth-century domestic drama made an undoubted contribution to the achievements of *Sturm und Drang*: it helped Schiller to develop the maturity and subtlety of character analysis that are to be seen in his later plays, themselves among the most distinguished products of that classical interlude between the subversive turbulence of Sturm und Drang in a wholly German context and Romanticism as a more complex, and truly European, phenomenon some fifty years on. There was no such development in the French theatre. There, far from enriching the traditional literary forms by an input of new ideas or feelings, the result of the challenge from *drame bourgeois* was to reinforce the contrast between élitist and popular forms of drama, by providing the latter with a foundation on which the *mélodrame* of Pixérécourt and others was to build at the turn of the century.

---

[3] *Wallstein*, ed. J.-R. Derré (Paris: Les Belles Lettres, 1965), pp. 52-53.

For one thing seems to be certain in the long-standing critical debate about the origins of this popular genre: that whatever other elements it may have assimilated, it reproduces in a simplified form, and for an uncultured audience – "j'écris pour ceux qui ne savent pas lire" (I write for those who are unable to read), wrote Pixérécourt – features of literary style, tendencies in characterisation and above all the moralistic impulse, with which more literate playgoers in France had been familiar for thirty years or more. The polarisation of characters into black and white; plot seen as a mani-chaean struggle between the forces of light and darkness; the pervading sententiousness of the dia-logue:[4] all of these can be found in abundance in the dramas of Mercier and his contemporaries, and carry over into much Romantic drama of the 1830s – a continuity proclaimed by Nodier in his edi-tion of Pixérécourt,[5] and more recently recognised by Peter Brooks, who goes so far as to identify the "melodramatic mode" as the hallmark of all Romantic literature.[6] A similar tendency can be de-tected, it is true, in some of the German forerunners of Romantic drama: not only in the case of *Miss Sara Sampson*, but also in Schiller's *Die Räuber*; but the simplification is seldom as crude as in the French melodrama: since the latter play focuses, not on the melodramatic villain Franz Moor, but on the more complex and morally ambivalent figure of Karl, it satisfies Hegel's prescription for the dialectical basis of tragedy, and the criterion which, according to Albert Camus, serves to distin-guish tragedy from melodrama:

> Les forces qui s'affrontent dans la tragédie sont également légitimes, également armées en raison. Dans le mélodrame ou le drame, au contraire, l'une seulement est légitime. Autrement dit, la tragédie est ambiguë, le drame simpliste. Dans la première, chaque force est en même temps bonne et mau-vaise. Dans le second, l'une est le bien, l'autre le mal (et c'est pourquoi de nos jours le théâtre de pro-pagande n'est rien d'autre que la résurrection du mélodrame). Antigone a raison, mais Créon n'a pas tort [...]. La formule du mélodrame serait en somme: "Un seul est juste et justifiable" et la formule tra-gique par excellence: "Tous sont justifiables, personne n'est juste."[7]

> (The two forces confronting each other in tragedy are equally legitimate, they appeal equally to our reason. In melodrama (or in *drame bourgeois*), on the other hand, one only is legitimate. In other words, tragedy is ambiguous, while melodrama is simplistic. In the former, each force is at once good and bad. In the latter, one stands for good, the other for evil – and that is why today's propaganda drama is merely melodrama in a new guise. Antigone has right on her side, but Creon is not wrong [...]. The characteristic formula of melodrama would be: "One only is right, and can be shown to be right"; while that for tragedy is "All can be shown to be right, none *is* right.")

II

The period between the French Revolution and 1830 was marked in Germany by the achievements of that "high classicism" which successfully blended the French neoclassical influence with that of

---

[4] See my articles: "The Playwright as Preacher: Didacticism and Melodrama in the Theatre of the Enlightenment," *Forum for Modern Language Studies*, 14, (1978), 98-115; and "Word and Image in Pixérécourt's Melodramas: The Drama-turgy of the Strip-cartoon," in *Performance and Politics in Popular Drama*, ed. D.J. Bradby et al. (Cambridge: Cambridge Univ. Press, 1980), pp. 17-32.
[5] Pixérécourt, *Théâtre choisi*, ed. C. Nodier (Nancy: The Author, 1841-43). See the quotation on page 40 below.
[6] See *The Melodramatic Imagination: Balzac, Henry James, Melodrama and the Mode of Excess* (Yale: Yale Univ. Press, 1976).
[7] *Théâtre, récits, nouvelles*, (Paris: Gallimard, 1962), p. 1703.

Shakespeare, and by the beginnings of the vogue for a "fate tragedy" which paid homage to the Greek example, but in a distinctly melodramatic manner. In England, it was marked on the one hand by the importation of popular melodrama from the Continent, and on the other by the self-conscious efforts of poets to create a new form of literary drama, absorbing contemporary European influences as well as looking back to Elizabethan and Jacobean models. In France, the continued polarisation of contrasting literary and popular forms gave little hint of the cultural revolution that was to come.

The name of Schiller is cited by Hans Eichner as an illustration of the inherent difficulty of reaching an agreed definition of "Romantic" and "Romanticism." "French historians of German literature," he says, "call Schiller a romantic with the same air of inevitability with which German historians refuse to consider him under that heading."[8] The reason is surely that this playwright is a prime example of the eclecticism that characterises the achievements of German drama from the *Sturm und Drang* years through to the 1830s. It is indeed impossible to label his theatre simply and unequivocally in terms of the acceptance or rejection of eighteenth-century neoclassical influences, or of those of Shakespeare and other dramatists outside that tradition. His own influence on the next generation of playwrights is equally difficult to assess. What Walter Pater sees in Goethe may apply in general terms to Schiller as well:

> A union of the Romantic spirit, in its adventure, its variety, its profound subjectivity of soul, with Hel-
> lenism, in its transparency, its rationality, its desire for beauty – that marriage of Faust and Helena, of
> which the art of the nineteenth century is the child.

Nevertheless it would be wrong in Schiller's case to speak, as Pater does in Goethe's, of "the predominance in this marriage of the Hellenic element."[9] In Schiller's theatre, the union is more nearly one between equal partners; and although the individual plays may reflect classical restraint and pre-Romantic desire for freedom in differing degrees, nowhere does Schiller achieve the austere concentration, reminiscent of Greek tragedy, that had inspired Goethe in his *Iphigenie auf Tauris*. However, he seems unwilling to adopt the complete licence of the Shakespearean model, as is abundantly clear from his adaptation of *Macbeth* for the Weimar stage, in which Shakespeare's witches are much modified and the porter eliminated. The Shakespearean inspiration is strongest, perhaps, in the *Wallenstein* trilogy (1800). The broad historical sweep of the whole subject, which could never even have been contemplated by a contemporary French dramatist; the homely realism of *Wallensteins Lager* (Wallenstein's Camp); and the complexity of the central character: all these features reflect, not a slavish imitation, but the liberating influence of Shakespeare's historical dramas – especially when compared with *Don Carlos* (1787) and *Maria Stuart* (1800) whose tighter construction, and more conventional pattern of personal relationships, remain nearer to the formulas of Voltaire's tragedy. *Die Jungfrau von Orleans* (The Maid of Orleans, 1801) is subtitled "eine romantische Tragödie": a challenging label at this early date, when Schlegel's critical use of the term, in the sense of "poetic," "imaginative" (and with a polemical connotation of "anti-classical," "anti-French"), was only just beginning to gain general currency. Seen in the light of Schlegel's definition – "das [...] was uns einen sentimentalen Stoff in einer fantastischen Form darstellt" (whatever presents us with sentimental subject-matter in a fanciful form) – *Die Jungfrau von Orleans* is "roman-

---

[8] *"Romantic" and its Cognates: The European History of a Word*, ed. H. Eichner (Manchester: Manchester Univ. Press, 1972), p. 15.

[9] Quoted in L. Magnus, *A History of European Literature* (London: Nicholson & Watson, 1935), p. 272.

tic" both in the fanciful, or imaginative, treatment of a historical subject (visions, miracles, the apparition of the Black Knight, the liberty taken with well-known historical fact concerning Joan's death) and in the "poetic" form adopted by the playwright: episodic in structure, the play is full of contrasts of style and tone. A modern critic writes of the "fairy-tale stylisation" that characterises it;[10] and altogether, *Die Jungfrau von Orleans* shows Schiller at his most independent, equally free from the influences of neoclassical and Shakespearean models. The genre-label for *Wilhelm Tell* (1804) – "Schauspiel" (spectacle, play) – likewise serves to indicate the play's uniqueness by contrast with the rest of Schiller's *oeuvre*; however, *Die Braut von Messina* (The Bride of Messina), in 1803, despite its links with later fate-tragedies of a wholly Romantic character, is a "Trauerspiel mit Chören" (tragedy with choruses), and Schiller's introductory essay proclaims his intention to create a modern equivalent of the way in which tragic fate works in a play like Sophocles' *Oedipus*, where the characters' every move is frustrated by a hostile supernatural force. Like *Oedipus*, the whole play is strongly marked by tragic irony; but it is the general opinion of modern readers that *Die Braut von Messina* does not live up to the author's aspirations. Schiller's aim was a play in which "das Interesse nicht sowohl in den handelnden Personen als in der Handlung liegt, so wie im *Oedipus* des Sophocles" (the interest lies not so much in the protagonists as in the dramatic action, as in Sophocles' *Oedipus*) – but chance, rather than a properly tragic fate, seems to control the action, and the play is melodrama rather than tragedy. *Wilhelm Tell* is very different, in both form and inspiration. It has the form of a chronicle-play: not a play without a hero, but one in which the hero's assertion of moral liberty is related to the struggle of a whole people for political independence. Structurally, *Wilhelm Tell* lacks that classical concentration on a moral dilemma that had marked *Don Carlos*, for instance: it is recorded that the dramatist was influenced by a performance of Shakespeare's *Julius Caesar* at Weimar when he was beginning to compose his play, and it is not difficult to see something like the English playwright's manner in the treatment of a body of diffuse historical material. But as well as looking back to the Shakespearean chronicle-play, *Wilhelm Tell* also looks forward, and embodies in theme and spirit the nationalist aspirations that we associate with the Romantic generations that were to come.

Classical and Romantic characteristics – or at any rate, characteristics that would be termed "classical" and "Romantic" in the wider context of European cultural history – are similarly mixed in varying proportions in the plays of Kleist. Subjects taken from classical mythology (*Amphitryon*, *Penthesilea*) are treated in an intensely personal manner; imitation of Shakespeare is combined (in *Die Familie Schroffenstein*) with the extravagance of the late eighteenth-century gothic; *Das Käthchen von Heilbronn* anticipates much later Romantic writing, in the novel and for the theatre, with its romanesque, idealising treatment of the Middle Ages; while *Die Hermannsschlacht* (Hermann's Battle) and, to some extent, *Prinz Friedrich von Homburg* are inspired by that nationalist feeling which, at the time of Napoleon's domination of Europe, was one of the features of European Romanticism. Since our brief requires us to pay particular attention to the Romantic playwrights' attitudes to the forms and fashions inherited from their predecessors, two plays of Kleist's seem to call for closer examination. In *Die Familie Schroffenstein* (1803) it is *Romeo and Juliet* that provides the theme, and the substructure of plot; but this is so overlaid by contrived incident, by parallels and symmetries involving members of the two warring branches of the Schroffenstein family, that the freshness and spontaneity of Shakespeare's masterpiece are replaced by an excessively

---

[10] L. Löb, *From Lessing to Hauptmann: Studies in German Drama* (London: University Tutorial Press, 1974), p. 118.

mechanical demonstration of the operation of chance, aided by human capacity for misunderstanding; and the plot of Kleist's play almost suggests a parody of the gothic novel. *Amphitryon* (1807) takes up the Romantic theme of deceptive appearances, and of human fallibility in interpreting the evidence of the senses; in this play too, theme, plot and dramatic form are closely based on a particular model, and Kleist's "Lustspiel nach Molière" (Comedy after Molière) illustrates the real continuity of subject-matter going back, via Rotrou, to Plautus. However, the interpretation is wholly original, with a greater emphasis on Alkmene's position than in previous versions, and a new poignancy is given to the theme of misunderstanding. Since the senses no longer provide a reliable basis for rational judgement, the stability of the classical universe is shaken, and both Alkmene and Amphitryon are victims of a more capricious order of things created by the pessimistic imagination of the Romantic dramatist. None of Kleist's plays reflects the feverish and tormented individualism of his novelle *Michael Kohlhaas*; but in *Prinz Friedrich von Homburg* (1811) the dramatisation of a subject from history provides a framework not only for anti-Napoleonic propaganda, but also for the highly personal treatment of a theme appealing to the sensibility of the age: the conflict of a complex individual's nature with the demands of law and authority, representing the real world in which he must live. Perhaps more Romantic in tone than any other of Kleist's plays, *Prinz Friedrich* does not depend to anything like the same extent on borrowings of plot or style, and this poetic expression of contemporary sensibility in the context of a patriotic historical drama avoids the extravagant *Sturm und Drang* inspiration of *Die Familie Schroffenstein* as well as the idealised presentation of history shown in the "Ritterschauspiel" (chevalric drama), *Das Käthchen von Heilbronn*.

A similar pattern is to be seen in Grillparzer's theatre, in spite of the difference in characteristic tonality between the works written by the two dramatists. Like Kleist in *Schroffenstein*, Grillparzer paid homage to the gothic tradition in *Die Ahnfrau* (The Ancestress, 1817), normally seen as responsible for consolidating the vogue for fate tragedy that had been inaugurated in 1810 by Werner's *Der vierundzwanzigste Februar* (The 24th of February). J.G. Robertson sees in *Die Ahnfrau* "the real poetry of terror,"[11] while the dramatist himself insists in his Preface that it was not his purpose to lend support to a "neues System des Fatalismus." However, in spite of the role of the ghostly ancestress in linking the sensational events, we are more likely to think in terms of chance than of genuine predestination. The gothic cult of horror is not one of the profounder aspects of literary Romanticism, and as is the case with *The Monk* or *Frankenstein*, modern readers find it difficult to treat these originals with much more reverence than their cinematic progeny. Grillparzer's major historical drama, *König Ottokars Glück und Ende* (King Ottokar's Fortunes and Finish, 1825), is strongly marked by the influence of Shakespeare: the Shakespeare of *Richard III*, in which a vivid picture of a complex historical scene serves as framework to the analytical study of the downfall of a central character, destroyed by his own ambition. The theme of overreaching ambition was a topical one, and Grillparzer himself indicates the link with Napoleon's career; but his is also a positive celebration of the triumph of the forces of right ("Wir stehen am Eingang einer neuen Zeit" [We stand at the threshold of a new era), and an expression of Austrian nationalism very much in the spirit of the Romantic age. A different sort of reaction to the dramatic traditions of the past is to be seen in *Das Goldene Vlies* (The Golden Fleece, 1820). The plot, and the formal shape, of earlier versions (largely taken over by Corneille from Euripides) are more or less preserved in *Medea*, the third play of Grillparzer's trilogy, but the decision to go back to the beginnings of the legend and to

---

[11] *A History of German Literature* (Edinburgh: Blackwood, 1933), p. 523.

dramatise the capture of the fleece, the courtship of Jason and Medea and the flight from Colchis in the first two plays, *Der Gastfreund* and *Die Argonauten*, indicates not only the dramatist's desire to portray on stage the build-up of fate and tragic guilt symbolised in the fleece, but also his readiness to experiment with dramatic form. In the event, this was only partially successful: the first two plays contain much that is epic and narrative in character rather than properly dramatic, and Grillparzer's own later criticism of the trilogy form is confirmed by customary practice in the modern theatre, which is to limit performance to the third play of the three.

Neither Kleist nor Grillparzer can be unreservedly identified with the Romantic movement in Germany, whose favourite media were in any case the more subjective and reflective genres of lyric poetry, the novel and the short story, better able than drama to handle the fantasy and the metaphysical dimension that characterised main-line German Romanticism. On the other hand, the wider perspective of Romanticism considered as a European phenomenon must inevitably give a relatively greater importance to chronological criteria, and place less emphasis on the distinctive features that the movement may have taken on in a national context; and in any survey of European drama of the Romantic period, both Kleist and Grillparzer must stand beside Schiller as representing the most distinguished contributions by German playwrights.

Drama was similarly not central to the activities of the English Romantics – or at any rate to their achievements, viewed from a historical perspective; and although Coleridge and Southey, Wordsworth, Shelley, Byron, and Keats all showed a keen interest in the theatre, in no case was this a major part of the poet's creative output. Coleridge's translation of *Wallenstein* antedated that of Benjamin Constant by several years – it was in fact published in 1800, within months of the original – yet as Lilian Furst shows in "Two Versions of Schiller's *Wallenstein*," it made no impact in England, where Schiller's play, whose excessive licence Constant would be obliged to modify for French taste, "simply lacked the interest of novelty."[12] In other words, the English poets' experiments with historical drama should be seen against the background of a familiarity with the Shakespearean example that was non-existent in France, and insofar as it did exist in Germany, was so recent as to possess a lively polemical character. On the other hand, the English Romantics' obsession with the Shakespearean and Jacobean theatre was one of the principal factors responsible for their failure as dramatists. More clearly in England than elsewhere, Romanticism aspired to rival past glories in the theatre by the close imitation of those very glories – with the result that, as George Steiner writes, "from Coleridge to Tennyson, nearly all English poetic dramas are feeble variations on Shakespearean themes."[13] The imitation of Shakespeare's manner makes of Wordsworth's *The Borderers* (1795) an obscure succession of turgid tirades, and Keats's *Otho the Great* (1819) is a poor pastiche of Shakespeare, both in its structure and in its diction. By the general consent of scholars, only Shelley in *The Cenci* (1819) and Byron in *Marino Faliero, Sardanapalus,* and *The Two Foscari* (all 1821) manage to come to terms adequately with techniques and conventions, and to distance themselves sufficiently from the Shakespearean models, to be able to express Romantic themes in an acceptably independent and individual manner.

Shelley had little experience of the theatre as a playgoer – none at all, we are told, of the recent and contemporary repertory. *The Cenci* was conceived as closet drama; its Webster-like subject-matter, and Shelley's familiarity with Shakespeare and his contemporaries, have commonly led to

---

[12] *The Contours of European Romanticism* (London: Macmillan, 1979), p. 107.
[13] *The Death of Tragedy* (London: Faber, 1961), p. 145.

the view that this was an exercise in the Jacobean manner. Swinburne wrote in 1869 that *The Cenci* was "the one great play written in the manner of Shakespeare's men that our literature has seen since the time of these."[14] The unities of time and place are rejected, though relatively discreetly; the structure has none of the tight logic of neoclassical dramaturgy, though it is certainly not as episodic as many representative examples of Shakespearean practice. However, it is surely reminiscences of theme and characterisation that have been responsible for the traditional view that Shelley was reviving the dramatic style of two hundred years earlier: the conception of consummate evil in the character of Count Cenci inevitably reminds the reader of the heroine's brothers in *The Duchess of Malfi* – indeed, the imaginative horror of Shelley's creation far surpasses Webster – and there are borrowings from *Macbeth* both in the banquet scene and in the manner of Cenci's murder. On the other hand, *The Cenci* could be said to portray Jacobean evil through a gothic filter: at any rate the influence (of gothic novels, if not the gothic drama, suggests B. Evans[15]) is everywhere apparent; though Shelley's horror is no superficial seeking after effects, and his "gothic" affinities are with the metaphysical evil of Maturin, and with the perversions chronicled by Sade.[16] Moreover, the more closely one examines the dramatic means by which Cenci's character is presented, the more clearly it will be seen that these are the means of the neoclassical dramatist. Bagehot, writing in 1856, says that one difficulty for the English reader is that of accepting "the existence of beings, all of whose actions are unmodified consequences of a single principle,"[17] and this same fundamental point – the playwright's *a priori* conception of his characters – is made by Stuart Curran, who suggests that comparison with Shakespearean practice reveals "two vastly different approaches to the writing of tragedy," since Shelley "enlarges the moral considerations sequentially, not simultaneously [...] Shelley's approach is more Greek than Elizabethan."[18] The predominant impression made on a reader of *The Cenci* is of a manichaean universe in which good is powerless against the overwhelming presence of evil, portrayed with a singleness of purpose that sets Shelley apart from his Romantic contemporaries, and with a poetic intensity that redeems what might otherwise be no more than melodrama.

In Byron's case, his independence of Shakespearean models was no doubt largely due to his awareness of the dangers inherent in too slavish an imitation. This was expressed in the most provocative fashion when he declared Shakespeare to be "the worst of models, though the most extraordinary of writers"; and in a letter of 1821 he offered this formula for the revival of English tragedy:

> [...] writing naturally and *regularly,* and producing *regular* tragedies, like the Greeks; but not in *imitation* – merely the outline of their conduct, adapted to our own times and circumstances, and of course *no* chorus.[19]

Although it has been convincingly analysed as "the high romantic expression, in dramatic form, of

---

[14] Quoted by S. Curran, *Shelley's "Cenci": Scorpions Ringed with Fire* (Princeton: Princeton Univ. Press, 1970), p. 23.

[15] B. Evans, *Gothic Drama from Walpole to Shelley* (Berkeley and Los Angeles: Univ. of California Press, 1947), p. 230.

[16] Mario Praz, *The Romantic Agony* (1933; rpt. London: Collins, 1960), pp. 132-34.

[17] Quoted in Curran, p. 22.

[18] Curran, p. 48.

[19] Quoted by Steiner, *The Death of Tragedy*, pp. 202, 203.

the Gothic spirit,"[20] *Manfred* is at best a "dramatic poem," of similar inspiration to Part II of Goethe's *Faust*. It did in fact reach the stage after the poet's death, but its fame as the most celebrated expression of a typically Romantic theme rests on the appeal made to a generation of impressionable readers by the cryptic portrait of the sombre hero, victim of an unexplained destiny. *Sardanapalus* and the last group of Byron's "sacred dramas" were also conceived of by the poet as examples of a "mental theatre"; so that the fact that the former offers in its construction a perfect illustration of the regular play is perhaps less important than the quality of its dramatic verse: in *Sardanapalus*, says Steiner, Byron "comes near to writing the only dramatic blank verse in the English language from which the presence of Shakespeare has been entirely exorcised."[21] No dead pastiche, this closet drama combines classical dramaturgy with Romantic feeling, for the death of the seemingly effeminate Assyrian king, who finds his true identity in a courageous suicide with his devoted mistress Myrrha, possesses the same power to move us as the denouement of *Hernani* or the finale of *Aida*: the fulfilment of the lovers' death-wish, at the same time as it marks their defeat by a hostile world, preserves their love in an ideal form, free from the corruption of reality. The two Venetian plays similarly present what Steiner calls a "conjunction of classic craftsmanship with the romantic temper."[22] *The Two Foscari* was staged only posthumously, and *Marino Faliero* was a failure when performed in 1821; but they are less idiosyncratic in style than the later plays, and their historical subject-matter gives them common ground with other European dramas of the period.

It is particularly interesting to compare Byron's *Marino Faliero* with the play on the same subject by Casimir Delavigne, performed in 1829. By 1829, we are on the very threshold of the Romantic "revolution" in French drama. The visit of the English actors to Paris had already revealed Shakespeare to a highly appreciative public, and Dumas's *Henri III et sa cour* and Vigny's *More de Venise* both also date from 1829. The time was ripe for a frontal attack on the Théâtre Français by means of an original verse drama in the new idiom defined by Hugo in the *Préface de Cromwell* (1827) – but it must have been clear that Delavigne was not the man to lead such an attack, and in the Preface to *Marino Faliero* he adopts a neutral position:

> Deux systèmes partagent la littérature. Dans lequel des deux cet ouvrage a-t-il été composé? C'est ce que je ne déciderai pas, et ce qui d'ailleurs me paraît être de peu d'importance [...].
>
> (Our literature is divided by two schools of thought. Which of them has presided over the composition of this work? I shall not decide: moreover, the question seems to me to be relatively unimportant.)

This is no 'oeuvre de combat,' then; but an attempt by an intelligent and skilful dramatist to carry modification of the existing system as far as possible without disrupting that system. The most original feature is perhaps the diffusion of dramatic focus: we are no longer asked to concentrate exclusively on the dilemma of a single tragic hero, but to sympathise with the fortunes of a group of characters, none of whom is the *a priori* stereotype of neoclassical dramaturgy. Delavigne goes as far as the staging conventions of the time will allow (there is a change of scene before each act) towards showing the city of Venice, with its various castes and factions, as making a vital contribution to both the action and the atmosphere of the play; and the playwright's handling of the alexandrine, if

---

[20] Evans, p. 232.
[21] Steiner, pp. 206-7.
[22] Steiner, p. 208.

less boldly innovative than Hugo's was to be, exploits its possibilities with a pleasing flexibility. A contemporary reviewer wrote:

> Le talent d'écrivain que M. Delavigne a montré dans cette pièce suffirait pour faire regarder *Marino Faliero* comme le plus grand événement de l'histoire de l'art dramatique en France depuis Voltaire.[23]
>
> (The literary talent shown by M. Delavigne in this play would be enough to establish *Marino Faliero* as the most important event in the history of dramatic art in France since Voltaire.)

And P.J. Yarrow, in an interesting article, has suggested that what this play of 1829 lacked, in order to satisfy "all, or very nearly all, the requirements of the innovators,"was the stage-management and sense of publicity that Hugo was to bring to the "bataille d'*Hernani*" in the following year.[24] By the side of Delavigne's play, Byron's has a somewhat reactionary appearance. In spite of the fact that Byron exploits the greater freedom of the English staging conventions, changing scene not only between the acts but also within each act, his play concentrates more than Delavigne's on the individual catastrophe of a central figure. Byron's Faliero gives a greater impression of *a priori* characterisation: while he remains the hero of a neoclassical tragedy, Delavigne's counterpart is the dramatic focus of a play approximating more nearly to the new conception of historical drama; he assumes the paradoxical character of a rebel Doge gradually as the play progresses, whereas Byron's hero represents that paradox from the beginning. In any case, while both of these distinguished works were composed by dramatists consciously aiming at a judicious amalgamation of tradition and innovation, nevertheless in the context of English Romanticism Byron's *Marino Faliero* (together with *Sardanapalus* and *The Two Foscari*) marks the limit of such experiments in poetic drama, whereas Delavigne's moderate reformism was soon to be overtaken by the more revolutionary programme, and the highly organised campaign, of Hugo and his colleagues.

III

At the time of the "bataille d'*Hernani*," the Romantic breakthrough was felt on all sides to be imminent: indeed, the general expectation of a confrontation between partisans of the rival schools must have been an essential factor in helping to produce the challenge that did occur in February 1830. Of the three outstanding plays of 1829, *Henri III et sa cour*, although produced at the Théâtre Français, was a historical melodrama in prose, and as such, offered no direct competition to neoclassical tragedy; *Le More de Venise* was a translation, not an original work; and as we have seen, *Marino Faliero* was a prudent compromise, performed in any case at the Porte-Saint-Martin. Hugo's own *Marion de Lorme* had been accepted at the Théâtre Français, but was banned by the censor on political grounds; and it is arguable that a production of this play, of somewhat soberer inspiration than *Hernani*, in 1829 would have paved the way for a readier acceptance of the plays to come.[25] *Marion de Lorme* is less deliberately provocative: the verse is less flamboyant, the central figure of Marion, though conceived in the light of the same antithetical formula, presents a less arti-

---

[23] Quoted in R. Bray, *Chronologie du romantisme (1804-1830)* (Paris: Bovin, 1932), p. 214.
[24] "Three Plays of 1829, or Doubts about 1830," *Symposium*, 23 (1969), 373-83.
[25] See my article "Victor Hugo and the 'Failure' of French Romantic Drama," *L'Esprit Créateur*, 16 (1976), 247-56.

ficial synthesis of sublime and grotesque than does that of Hernani, and the play is altogether nearer to the coherent dramatic structure of Voltairian historical tragedy than to the operatic impressionism of *Hernani* or *Le Roi s'amuse*. At its best, in *Marion de Lorme*, Hugo's characterisation, while it can be seen as a variant on neoclassical tragedy's *a priori* approach to character, does achieve a sympathetic balance between innocence and guilt, free will and determinism: this is not the black-and-white characterisation of melodrama. In *Le Roi s'amuse*, however, the amalgam of sublime and grotesque in Triboulet is particularly unsubtle; and in the three prose plays of the mid-1830s Hugo lapses into the vigorous crudity we associate with melodrama. The opposition between innocence and guilt is now no longer internal to the character, but manifests itself in conflict between characters: Lucrèce Borgia and Gennaro, Marie Tudor and Jane, Angelo and his long-suffering Duchess. *Lucrèce Borgia* (1833), for all its melodramatic clichés and the gothic inspiration of certain scenes, was in many ways the most successful of all Hugo's plays, and perhaps Gautier's comment helps to account for this:

> Si la pièce alla aux nues, c'est peut-être justement qu'elle plaisait aux romantiques par sa couleur et aux classiques par la construction régulière qu'ils y trouvaient.[26]

> (The reason for this play's extraordinary success is perhaps that it appealed to the Romantics by its colour, and to the Classics by the regularity of its construction.)

The same is no doubt true of *Ruy Blas* (1833), by far the most successful of Hugo's verse plays. The eponymous hero, a Romantic character in the style of Hernani, is placed between the unashamedly melodramatic pair of the Queen, a typically passive heroine, and Don Salluste, as black a "traître" as the "boulevard du crime" could ever have mustered; but quite apart from the quality of the verse (*Ruy Blas* is an excellent illustration of Nodier's claim in 1841: "La tragédie et le drame de la nouvelle école ne sont guère autre chose que des mélodrames relevés de la pompe artificielle du lyrisme" [The tragedy and the *drame* of the new school are little more than melodramas embellished by the artificial pomp of lyric poetry]),[27] contemporary spectators must also have appreciated the traditional structure of a historical drama which made hardly any greater demands on the conservative taste of the theatre-going public than those of Delavigne or Soumet.

Despite the importance of Hugo's assault on the Théâtre Français with *Hernani*, this play was far less iconoclastic than *Cromwell*, that blueprint for a panoramic – one might almost say cinematic – presentation of a historical subject. There were certain deliberate provocations in *Hernani* – the King hiding in a cupboard, the scene in Charlemagne's tomb – but the construction of the play was on the whole traditional, and the revolution it brought about was essentially a linguistic one. There is little difference between the basic dramatic structure of *Hernani* (and Hugo's other verse plays) and that of *Marino Faliero*; there is all the difference in the world, however, between Hugo's alexandrine and the way in which this verse-form had been handled by every French dramatist who had preceded him. Here at last was a play written by a poet, not a versifier; "le style noble" was swept away, and replaced by the linguistic medium defined in the *Préface de Cromwell*:

> [...] un vers libre, franc, loyal, osant tout dire sans pruderie, tout exprimer sans recherche; passant d'une naturelle allure de la comédie à la tragédie, du sublime au grotesque; tour à tour positif et

---

[26] Quoted by P. Berret, *Victor Hugo* (Paris: Garnier, n.d.), p. 311.
[27] Pixérécourt, *Théâtre choisi*, in Nodier, ed., I, vii.

poétique, tout ensemble artiste et inspiré, profond et soudain, large et vrai [...].

(a verse-form that shall be free and uninhibited, daring to say everything without prudishness, and to express everything without affectation; slipping easily and naturally from comedy to tragedy, from the sublime to the grotesque; by turns factual and poetic, at once decorative and inspired, profound and spontaneous, far-reaching and true to life.)

It is Hugo the poet who masks the occasional infelicities and ineptitudes of structure and characterisation of Hugo the dramatist, and who gives his verse plays the emotional appeal of all great Romantic art; and this only makes the more remarkable his descent to the bathos of melodrama in the plays he chose to write in prose.

However, even if "Romantic drama" in a French context suggests to most of us in the first place the idealising poetic historical genre illustrated by *Hernani* or *Ruy Blas*, the Romantic ideology of the 1830s was given more direct – and possibly more effective – expression by dramatists who preferred to write in prose, and who adopted the medium of bourgeois drama as a vehicle for the topical message they wanted to bring home to their audience.

The name of Diderot, those of Lillo and Lessing, appear nowhere in the *Préface de Cromwell*. Hugo envisaged Romantic drama as drawing on the past, not mirroring the present, and he regarded history much as Voltaire or M.-J. Chénier, Lemercier or Delavigne, had done: that is, as a repertory of episodes and events to be treated not in the manner of a factual chronicle but in such a way, through the exercise of the poet's imagination, as to move, uplift, or persuade the reader or spectator. To Vigny, the results of such an attitude showed it to be irresponsible: in his own historical drama, *La Maréchale d'Ancre* (1831), he substituted a historian's erudition for the imagination of a poet, with the aim of extracting a valid philosophical lesson from the events of the regency of Marie de Médicis, soberly recorded; and in the prefatory letter to *Chatterton* he takes pains to dissociate himself from Hugo's manner:

Maintenant que l'amusement des yeux par des surprises enfantines fait sourire tout le monde au milieu même de ses grandes aventures, c'est, ce me semble, le temps du DRAME DE LA PENSÉE.

(Now that spectacular entertainment by means of childish surprises makes us all smile even in the midst of our more important preoccupations, the time seems to me to be ripe for a drama of ideas.)

Chatterton, played in 1835, and Dumas's *Antony* of 1831 are very different in textual flavour as well as in spirit; yet between them they exemplify a more successful exploitation of the formula of *drame bourgeois* than anything produced by Diderot and his fellow-dramatists before the Revolution – or indeed by their immediate successors. Since the turn of the century, the domestic idiom of *drame bourgeois* had been annexed by *le mélodrame*; and there is nothing in the native French theatre in the early nineteenth century to compare with Kotzebue's *Menschenhass und Reue* (Misanthropy and Remorse, 1789) as an example of domestic drama with more elevated literary pretensions (insofar as Kotzebue himself was played, and imitated, in France, he belongs firmly to that line of descent which, by-passing the "grands romantiques," links Pixérécourt with Scribe). Vigny's purpose in *Chatterton*, he tells us, was to portray "l'homme spiritualiste étouffé par une société matérialiste" (the spiritual faculties of man stifled by the materialism of society); but of these two elements it is the latter which, perhaps inevitably, receives the more convincing dramatic treatment. The objective portrait of John Bell, the successful businessman "rouge de visage, gonflé d'ale, de porter et de roastbeef, étalant dans sa démarche l'aplomb de sa richesse" (red-faced, swollen with ale, porter and roast beef, his manner advertising the self-assurance of the wealthy man), is wholly in the eighteenth-century *drame* tradition: an example of Diderot's "conditions" if there ever was one; and generally speaking, the other characters surrounding Chatterton also carry conviction (even if the aged Quaker, "vieillard de quatre-vingts ans," is something of a cliché from contemporary melodrama). But one problem inherent in the portrayal of artistic or literary genius on the stage is that it has to be taken on trust: it is virtually impossible to show it in action. Chatterton himself is too much of a symbolic abstraction – "Le poète était tout pour moi; Chatterton n'était qu'un nom d'homme" (the poet was all-important to me: Chatteron was merely an individual's name), Vigny wrote – and although he must presumably have struck a chord in the ardent young spectators of 1835 which remains silent in the reader of today, this character derives from the subjective imagination of the playwright rather than from his objective observation of the world around him.

Antony is the one play in which Dumas rose above the purely mechanical appeal to quick and easy box-office success, and finding a theme which expressed to perfection the dynamic, anti-social aspect of Romantic individualism, he was inspired to write a masterpiece. Like *Chatterton, Hernani, Ruy Blas*, and like so many other major works of Romantic art, *Antony* takes as its premise the incompatibility of a shared, idealised love with the demands of a hostile society, and our sympathies are engaged not just with Adèle as victim, but with the ill-starred couple of Adèle and Antony. In spite of certain outdated expressions of the contemporary sensibility, it is still possible today to be carried away by the lovers' exaltation, as well as to appreciate the skill with which Dumas, operating within the tradition of serious domestic drama, has portrayed the superficial respectability of the society against whose code Adèle offends. As a serious attempt at *drame bourgeois*, as a play of ideas (a much more eloquent plea on behalf of the illegitimate than either Diderot's *Fils naturel* or Dumas *fils*'s play of the same name) and as a vehicle for the lyrical expression of passionate feeling, *Antony* must count among the small handful of truly successful Romantic dramas in France.

At the same time as the poetic myth of a shared love, crushed by a hostile society and finding its true consummation in death, was to inspire Hugo, Vigny, and Dumas to create the sort of Romantic tragedy whose analogue in Shakespearean terms would no doubt be *Romeo and Juliet*, a remarkably gifted young German dramatist chose to portray the hopeless struggle of a solitary individual with the world he lives in, and produced a tragedy whose intensity of feeling and suffering has earned it a comparison with *King Lear*. Since *Woyzeck* was left in an incomplete state on Büchner's death in 1837 at the age of 23, with no indication as to the overall shape of the projected work, it is difficult to discuss in a meaningful way the play's formal qualities. Suffice it to say that Büchner took the existing genre of "bürgerliche Tragödie" – domestic drama in a prose idiom – and went far beyond the examples of Diderot, Lessing, Mercier, and Kotzebue in presenting as his hero a simple, inarticulate representative of the common people – "a proletarian outcast," as M.B. Benn calls him.[28] He succeeded in the *gageure* of turning a squalid episode from the low life of his day

---

[28] M.B. Benn, *The Drama of Revolt: A Critical Study of Georg Büchner* (Cambridge: Cambridge Univ. Press, 1976), p. 217. Cf. H. Lindenberger's comment on Hebbel's *Maria Magdalene*: "As a 'bourgeois tragedy' it is actually a late example of a German form which, deriving from Lillo and Diderot, includes such distinguished examples as Lessing's *Emilia Galotti*, the early Schiller's *Kabale und Liebe* and, to name a work which easily towers above its predecessors, Büchner's *Woyzeck*" (*Historical Drama: The Relation of Literature and Reality* (Chicago: Chicago Univ. Press, 1975), p. 126).

into a moving, and poetic, portrayal of human suffering; and it is the texture of his play, with its simple speech-rhythms, its interpolated fragments of song, and its complete lack of conventional rhetoric, that has led Brecht and others to see in *Woyzeck* the beginnings of truly modern theatre. It is no doubt true that according to traditional classification Büchner is, as Benn insists, "not a Romantic";[29] but in the context of Romantic drama on a European scale it seems proper to recognise *Woyzeck* as a work that could have been produced only by a playwright of Büchner's generation, imbued with the historical pessimism and the metaphysical despair that were common to some, at any rate, of the thinkers of his age, and to see this essential link between the bourgeois drama of the Enlightenment and the Naturalism and Expressionism of the late nineteenth century as a peculiar contribution of the Romantic *Zeitgeist*.

The affiliation of Büchner's *Dantons Tod* with "main-line" Romantic drama is clearer still. Büchner knew his Shakespeare; and although he translated *Lucrèce Borgia* and *Marie Tudor*, the model for his own historical drama was Shakespearean rather than Hugolian. There is the same sequence of short episodic scenes; the central character is not presented in terms of an *a priori* dilemma to which all else is subordinated, but is built up piecemeal as the play proceeds, as we see him in his various relationships with Julie, Camille, Hérault, and Marion, and in his determined opposition to the policies of Robespierre and Saint-Just; and Büchner's historical narrative has something of the diffuse perspective of Shakespeare's histories, rather than the concentrated focus imposed on the hero of a neoclassical tragedy. To use the image applied by Kenneth Tynan to Brecht's historical drama, Büchner "uses the wrong end of the telescope as well."[30] In addition to being a convincing representation of the historical figure, Büchner's Danton is also a tragic hero in the contemporary mould: fatally cursed by *ennui*, the "mal du siècle" which forms the opposite pole in Romantic sensibility to the dynamism of a Manfred or an Antony, he rouses himself from his initial passivity too late to counter Robespierre's challenge, and it has been said that Danton's tragedy is the tragedy of his own death-wish.[31]

Published in 1835, *Dantons Tod* was not performed until 1902. *Lorenzaccio*, the other great historical drama of the 1830s which reflects a playwright's sympathetic understanding of the Shakespearean manner, was to have a similar fate: although it was published in 1834, it had to wait until well into this century for a production that did full justice to Musset's treatment of the subject. However, since *Lorenzaccio* was conceived as an example of "armchair drama," Musset was able to write with complete freedom from the constraints of contemporary stage practice. As a result, the five acts of his play contain thirty-seven changes of scene, and this Shakespearean structure is absolutely essential to his purpose of building up by juxtaposition and contrast a colourful picture of Renaissance Florence with its corrupt court, its patrician families, and the various factions among the republican opposition. Sarah Bernhardt's production in 1896, which rearranged Musset's material on the model of Hugo's plays, with a single setting for each act, produced a travesty of the original, and it was not until Gérard Philipe's production at Avignon in 1952 that Musset's intentions were fully respected. The shifts of focus in the first two acts are of course essential to the playwright's purpose: to create a Lorenzo who is as much of an enigma to the spectator as he is to the courtiers and conspirators whose conflicting reactions we see; indeed, it is not until the central

[29] Benn, p. 255.
[30] *The Observer*, 17 July 1960.
[31] Benn, p. 120.

scene of the middle act that Lorenzo emerges unambiguously as the principal focus of our interest, as he begins to give a coherent account of his motivation. There is surely no better example in any dramatic literature of that cumulative approach to characterisation that Shakespeare bequeathed to the more understanding among his followers; for after bringing Lorenzo to the fore in the long confessional scene with Philippe Strozzi, Musset then, through a series of masterly soliloquies by Lorenzo, converts us from uncomprehending hostility to complete indentification with a character conscious of having reached an extreme limit of human experience. Like Büchner, Musset integrates the individual tragedy of the Romantic hero (or anti-hero, for more clearly than Hugo's characters, Büchner's Danton and Musset's Lorenzo call into question heroic attitudes that had been taken for granted for centuries) with the convincing portrayal of period and place, which become far more than "background" and play a vital role in their own right. If what we mean by historical drama is that kind of dramatic writing which persuades us of the specific nature of the historical event, as the product of unique process of cause and effect, then we can say that the two masterpieces of the genre in the Romantic period were created by playwrights who, inspired by the Shakespearean example, finally succeeded in rejecting neoclassical attitudes to plot and character. Both *Dantons Tod* and *Lorenzaccio* were generations ahead of the taste of their time, but critical opinion in our day has at last given them the recognition they deserve.[32]

[32] For a more detailed analysis of *Lorenzaccio*, see my *Sublime and Grotesque: A Study of French Romantic Drama* (London: Harrap, 1975), pp. 294-307.

II. THEMES, STYLES, STRUCTURES

ANDRÉ LEFEVERE

SHAKESPEARE REFRACTED: WRITER, AUDIENCE, AND REWRITER IN FRENCH AND GERMAN ROMANTIC TRANSLATIONS

Conventional wisdom runs roughly as follows: Shakespeare was introduced to the French by Voltaire, who was dissatisfied with some of the more soporific aspects of neoclassical drama, and wanted to rejuvenate the French "tragédie" by transplanting some of Shakespeare's vigor to the French stage, while filtering out his "barbarousness." Shakespeare was introduced to the Germans by Lessing, who needed a foreign model to counterbalance Gottsched's prescription of neoclassicism for the German stage. In both cases Shakespeare triumphed, after some initial opposition in Germany, after stronger and longer-lived opposition in France.

The persistence of that conventional wisdom is rather amazing, especially if we pause to reflect that what Hansjürgen Blinn says about the study of the reception of Shakespeare in Germany also largely holds true for the reception of Shakespeare in France:

> [es] fehlt eine neuere wissenschaftliche Untersuchung die – die bisherigen Forschungsergebnisse zusammenfassend – eine gründliche und tiefgehende Analyse der literaturkritischen Diskussion um Shakespeare von den Anfängen seiner Wirkung in Deutschland im 18. Jahrhundert bis in die Gegenwart hinein [...] in Angriff nimmt. (Blinn I, 9)[1]

> (a newer scientific analysis is lacking, which would summarize the results of research to date and attempt a fundamental and thorough-going analysis of the critical discussion on Shakespeare from the beginning of his impact on Germany in the eighteenth century until the present.)

Blinn goes on to say that "die bisherigen Arbeiten von unterschiedlichen methodischen Ansätzen ausgehend sind z.T. überholt, z.T. ihrem Unfang nach unbefriedigend" (the works we have now, which take their bearings from different methodological perspectives, are in part obsolete, in part unsatisfactory in size) (Blinn I, 9). Yet some of the older attempts at painting the total picture are the works we have to rely on for the "facts" in the "case" of Shakespeare in France and Germany. More recent "detailed" studies tend to be so detailed that they contribute little that is new. The fact that some of the older works may appear "dated" by now does not invalidate the factual information they provide.

As was to be expected, the true story of Shakespeare in France and Germany is much more complicated and also much more fascinating, if only because the audiences supposed to have been influenced by Shakespeare never really got to see and hear Shakespeare himself. Neither did the writers who prescribed him for the masses. They read him, in the best case, and not a few among

---

[1] References to Hansjürgen Blinn, ed., *Shakespearerezeption*, 2 vols. (Berlin: Schmidt, 1982, 1988), will be indicated in the text by the abbreviation Blinn with volume and page number within parentheses. My translations will follow within parentheses after the original.

them, such as Goethe, were or became convinced that it was simply impossible to act out his plays on the stage itself.

In both France and Germany, the celebrated "struggle for Shakespeare" was not really "for" or "against" Shakespeare at all. Rather, "Shakespeare" became shorthand for the emerging new drama, which was to be accepted or resisted. It would be inaccurate to say that Shakespeare, or "Shakespeare," brought this new drama into being. The real "father" of the new drama was Diderot. Both in France and Germany "Shakespeare" was wielded as a weapon against neoclassical theater. In Germany there were two or three competing "Shakespeares" for a while, Lessing's "Shakespeare" to be put to judicious use in the creation of a German "bourgeois drama" à la Diderot, the "Shakespeare" of the *Sturm und Drang* designed to go beyond this, and Schröder's "Shakespeare," the one who actually got staged and was much closer to Lessing than to the *Sturm und Drang*. France also had three "Shakespeares," though not exactly the same ones. There was Voltaire's "Shakespeare," designed to rejuvenate the flagging "tragédie," Le Tourneur's "Shakespeare" moving into the direction of Diderot, and the "Shakespeare" invoked as the model for Victor Hugo's history-based plays that finally exploded the neoclassical rules on the French stage – much as the *Sturm und Drang* "Shakespeare" had been the model for Goethe's history-based play *Goetz von Berlichingen.*

Shakespeare himself and his works took second place, more so in France, which never had a relatively early "philological" translation of his entire works, of the kind provided by Eschenburg to the Germans. Before pointing an accusing finger at Shakespeare's translators and adaptors in both France and Germany though, we would do well to remember what kind of Shakespeare these rewriters themselves found in England. The Shakespeare they could go see was the one adapted by Garrick, not the one published by Theobald and other early commentators. In Chateaubriand's words: "En théorie, admirateurs sans réserve de Shakespeare, leur zèle en pratique est beaucoup plus circonspect: pourquoi ne jouent-ils pas tout entier l'oeuvre du dieu? Par quelle audace ont ils réservé, rogné, altéré, transposé des scènes?" (They admire Shakespeare unreservedly in theory, but their zeal is much more circumspect in practice: why do they not stage the work of their god in its entirety? How dare they tighten it, gnaw at it, change it, transpose scenes in it?) (*Oeuvres complètes* XI, 580 – this and all subsequent translations mine).[2] Ironically, the Shakespeare French travelers brought back from England (and the Shakespeare who migrated through France to Germany) was a Shakespeare already adapted to their own French neoclassical "goût," or at least to a somewhat anglicized version of it.

It should also be pointed out, in no uncertain theoretical terms, that the "wagging" of "accusing fingers" is utterly pointless in any process of attempted historical reconstruction. Of course everybody who touched Shakespeare in England, France, and Germany in the eighteenth and early nineteenth centuries got it "wrong." But that is not the point. The real question to be answered is: what influence did these "wrong" interpretations of Shakespeare exert. In literature as in politics "right" does not change history.

This anglicized version of "goût" led to the production of such neoclassical plays as Otway's *Venice Preserved*, and Young's *The Revenge* – which may be said to be based loosely on *Othello* – on the English stage. These plays came close to Voltaire's objective: they contained enough Shakespearian elements to keep the audience interested – with action taking precedence over "messenger's

---

[2] References by volume and page number in parentheses are drawn from the edition François René de Chateaubriand, *Oeuvres complètes*, 12 vols. (Paris: Garnier Frères, n.d.).

speeches" wherever possible – without proving offensive to the "goût" itself. This controlled change from one poetics to another was what Voltaire ideally hoped to achieve with "Shakespeare." His opponents, on the other hand, wanted to use "Shakespeare" as a counter-model to the "tragédie." Voltaire's *Zaïre* was an attempt to show what a French neoclassical Othello could be like, just as his *La Mort de César* was to be a neoclassical, "correct" rewriting of Shakespeare's *Julius Caesar* – a text rewritten according to the rules.

The "struggle for Shakespeare" is, on one level, a struggle over the rules. The first and most obvious set of rules is that of the rules of neoclassical drama, the well-known unities of time, place, and action, which the "romantic" dramatists reduce to one rule only, and one they have no quarrel with: "l'unité d'action ou d'ensemble, la seule vraie et fondée, était depuis longtemps hors de cause" (the unity of action or of the whole, the only real and well-founded one, has not been subject of discussion for a long time) (Hugo II, 34).[3] In both France and Germany the second, or political, set of rules supported the first, though much less strongly in Germany, and in different ways. Moreover, in Germany political support for the "rules" never really stifled any attempts to go beyond them, although some attempts at censorship were made. Goethe raises the question of the relationship between the rules of poetics and those of politics in his *Gespräche mit Eckermann* (1826): "Hätte aber Shakespeare für den Hof zu Madrid oder für das Theater Ludwigs des Vierzehnten geschrieben, er hätte sich auch wahrscheinlich einer strengern Theaterform gefügt" (If Shakespeare had written for the court in Madrid or for the theater of Louis XIV, he would probably have submitted to a stricter form of theater) (in Pascal 122).[4] In other words: if institutional circumstances had been different, Shakespeare would have written a different kind of theater. This implies that the first set of rules, the unities, is not universally valid, as Wieland had already hinted in his *Theorie und Geschichte der Red-Kunst und Dicht-Kunst* as far back as 1757: "Es ist vielleicht noch nicht so ausgemacht, ob die Einheit der Zeit und des Orts unverletzliche Regeln eines dramatischen Stücks sind" (Maybe it is not an established fact, whether the unities of time and place are rules of a dramatic piece beyond all attack) (in Blinn I, 69). What was a cautious remark in Wieland would become the main strategy for vindicating Shakespeare among the writers associated with the *Sturm und Drang* movement.

The Germans were prepared to admit the relativity of the unities rather early on – even though Frederick II, King of Prussia, and therefore guardian of the political rules, wrote sternly about Shakespeare: "Ich beurtheile diese Stücke so hart, weil sie wider alle Regeln des Schauspiels sündigen. Diese Regeln sind nicht willkürlich" (I judge these plays so harshly, because they sin against all rules of the theater. These rules are not arbitrary) (in Blinn I, 151-52). Arbitrariness in the theater, one may be tempted to infer, might lead to arbitrariness in the world of politics as well. Like all other German princes, Frederick II was not exactly taken with the latter concept. As it turned out, he did not have to worry overmuch, since the German theaters became attached to princely residences after it had become clear that the emerging bourgeoisie was unwilling or unable to support them. A theater that had turned "zur Institution des aufgeklärten Absolutismus" (into an institution of enlightened absolutism) (Meyer 210) could even afford to stage less "regular" plays once in a

---

[3] References by volume and page number in parentheses from Victor Hugo, *Oeuvres complètes*, 48 vols. (Paris: Hetzet-Quantin, n.d.).
[4] References by page number in parentheses from Roy Pascal, *Shakespeare in Germany* (Cambridge: Cambridge Univ. Press, 1937).

while.[5]

For a long time the French were definitely not prepared to follow the German example. As late as 1801 Chateaubriand maintains in one of his *Mélanges littéraires*:

> Il faut donc se persuader d'abord qu'écrire est un art; que cet art a nécessairement des règles, et que chaque genre a des règles. Et qu'on ne dise pas que ces règles et les genres sont arbitraires: ils sont nés de la nature même. (*Oeuvres complètes* VI, 389)

> (We must therefore convince ourselves first that writing is an art and that this art, of necessity, has rules, just as each genre has its rules. And nobody should tell us that the rules and the genres are arbitrary: they are born from nature itself.)

It is understandable that a king would rise to the defense of rules, since rules are in the final analysis what helps keep him on his throne. It is less understandable that a French critic of noted intellectual ability would stoop to defend the unities twelve years after the Revolution. Except if we identify what Chateaubriand calls "nature" with what the French used to call "goût" both before and after the Revolution. In his preface to *Zaïre* (1732) Voltaire had already called the French

> le peuple le plus sociable et le plus poli de la terre; et cette politesse n'est point une chose arbitraire, comme ce qu'on appelle civilité; c'est une loi de la nature qu'ils ont heureusement cultivée plus que les autres peuples. (*Oeuvres complètes* II, 553)[6]

> (the most sociable and polite people on earth; and this politeness is not an arbitrary matter, not like what is called "civility"; it is a law of nature they have happily cultivated to a greater extent than other people.)

Almost a hundred years later, in *Racine et Shakespeare* (1824) Stendhal still calls the unities of time and place: "une habitude française, *habitude profondément enracinée,* habitude dont nous nous déferons difficilement, parce que Paris est le salon de l'Europe et lui donne le ton" (a French habit, and a *habit deeply entrenched*, a habit we will not easily rid ourselves of, because Paris is the salon of Europe and sets the tone) (*Oeuvres complètes* X, 9).[7]

The "goût," then, appears to be perilously close to the central core of what the French consider their own sense of self; hence the ferocious resistance against any attempt to tamper with any aspect of it, the more so since France, having cultivated the "goût," felt obliged to be "Europe's salon," to defend it against all the rest of Europe, not least the British. Yet the French attitude toward the British was also ambiguous. The British might be blessed with less "goût," but they were also blessed with a form of government in which the bourgeoisie had more real rights and real power than in France – or Germany, for that matter. The problem for the French writers and intellectuals was then to move closer to the British politically, while safeguarding more of the "goût" than the British had been willing to take over from France.

Chateaubriand could therefore point out in all seriousness: "le penchant pour Shakespeare est bien plus dangereux en France qu'en Angleterre. Chez les Anglois il n'y a qu'ignorance; chez nous

---

[5] References by page number from Reinhart Meyer, "Von der Wanderbühne zum Hof- und Nationaltheater," in vol. III of *Hansers Sozialgeschichte der deutschen Literatur*, ed. Rolf Grimmiger, 4 vols. (Munich, Vienna: Hanser, 1980).

[6] References by volume and page number from the edition, Voltaire, *Oeuvres complètes*, 52 vols. (Paris: Garnier Frères, 1881).

[7] References by volume and page number from the edition Henry Beyle Stendhal, *Oeuvres complètes*, 27 vols. (Paris: Champion, 1925).

il y a dépravation" (the penchant for Shakespeare is much more dangerous in France than in England. The British are simply ignorant; we are subject to depravity) (*Oeuvres complètes* VI, 373). Barbarians cannot help being barbarians; the guardians of civilization itself should know better.

Since the German sense of self was not nearly so outspoken in the eighteenth century, resistance against tampering with the unities was much less violent. In fact, whereas France clearly saw itself as the central culture in Europe, a culture unquestioningly supported by both the declining aristocracy and the rising bourgeoisie, the German bourgeoisie looked increasingly to England, thereby exchanging one possible model for another, but with little loss of its own self-esteem. Germany – or one should really say – "some German men of letters" began to use "Shakespeare" to undermine the neoclassical "rules" propagated in Germany by Gottsched, who wanted to create a German theater on the French neoclassical model. But there were really two "Shakespeares" in Germany, in chronological succession. The older "Shakespeare," was pressed into service by Lessing, as noted above. Lessing attacks Gottsched on the unities and the necessity for the tragedy to put only noble characters on the stage, but he "festigt auch die neuen Positionen Gottscheds: vor allem das Postulat der Wahrscheinlichkeit, Natürlichkeit und Notwendigkeit" (also strengthens Gottsched's new positions, especially the postulate of verisimilitude, naturalness, and necessity) (Meyer 206). As noted above the "younger Shakespeare" was used a good two decades later by the *Sturm und Drang* writers. Since the "rules" were much less bound up with the German image of what their culture should become than with the French image of what their culture was, "Shakespeare" was able to win over Germany much sooner than France. Yet in both countries "Shakespeare's" victory contributed little or nothing to a better knowledge and understanding of the real Shakespeare.

In both France and Germany, though, a third "Shakespeare" appeared, whose impact on the audience at large was much greater than that of the writers, critics, and intellectuals. Or one could look at the phenomenon from the opposite angle and state, not untruthfully, in my opinion, that in both cases the audience not only largely ignored the "learned" arguments of those who tended to write voluminous books on tragedy, "während das theaterpraktisch viel wichtigere Lustspiel und Drama (Schauspiel) theoretisch weitgehend unbetrachtet bleibt" (while the comedy and the drama [or 'play in which things happened'], much more important in terms of practical performance in the theater, remained largely unnoticed in theoretical writings) (Meyer 206), but also greatly limited the options of the translators/rewriters of Shakespeare by indicating, in no uncertain terms, which deviations from the established "goût" it was willing to tolerate, and which deviations it was determined to reject. That audience had its translators and producers rewrite Shakespeare into the "Shakespeare" described by Ludwig Tieck in the following terms: "wie man sich einen Dichter dachte, der das menschliche Herz kannte, wie man immer von ihm gerühmt hat, übrigens sich in den Schranken einer billigen Prosa hielt" (the way one could imagine a poet who knew the human heart, a feature for which he had always been praised, but kept well within the boundaries of cheap prose) (in Blinn II, 123). Because, one might add, "cheap prose" was what the bourgeoisie was familiar with, and liked. Especially the newly educated women of the rising bourgeoisie "dürfen [...] sich hauptsächlich mit Belletristik [...] versorgt haben" (must have provided themselves mainly with belles-lettres) (Martino/Stützel-Prüsener 53).[8] The "struggle" for or against Shakespeare was there-

---

[8] References by page number from Alberto Martino and Marlies Stützel Püsener, "Publikumsschichten, literarische und Lesegesellschaften, Leihbibliotheken," in vol. IV of *Deutsche Literatur: Eine Sozialgeschichte*, ed. Ralph-Rainer Wutenow, 4 vols. (Reinbek bei Hamburg: Rowohlt, 1980).

fore not decided by "the most advanced of the critics (who) reserved for their privacy the English originals," but rather by the authors of the "adaptations, bowdlerizations (that) were produced for the public" (Pascal 1). The present essay attempts to highlight the role rewriters played in this and, by extension, in any transplantation of a writer into a different literature and a different culture.

The process of transplantation usually unfolds as follows: a need is felt in the potential receiving literatures, mainly because the dominant literary discourse (the "tragédie" in France and its Gottschedian avatar in Germany) is found to be lacking in some quality or qualities. Once the dominant literary discourse is indeed perceived as lacking, it can no longer be considered absolute, which means that it can be tampered with, on condition that is not so ideologically marked that political power would intervene to stifle any discussion or "tampering." If this is not the case, those who "tamper" are even allowed to proceed with a relative impunity which contributes to the creation of a climate of receptiveness for the foreign, especially that part of a foreign literary discourse that seems to possess what the native literary discourse has been perceived as lacking. This climate of receptiveness is more easily created when the foreign culture as a whole is perceived as also possessing non-literary elements the native culture is perceived as lacking. The actual transplantation of the foreign element (a writer, a genre or, in the case under discussion, both) is then perceived to be the work of one influential literary figure (Voltaire in France, Lessing in Germany), who is usually given all the credit in literary histories. The (political) powers that circumscribe the literary discourse, as they circumscribe all others, may promote or prevent a smooth transplantation. The German princes, for instance, recuperated Shakespeare, while Napoleon tried to keep him off the French stage and the Restoration allowed his plays to be performed again.

In France "the most minute details as yet printed in French are given (seventeen years before Voltaire's "Letters") on the English drama, and especially on Shakespeare," (Jusserand 183) in an anonymous article published in the *Journal Littéraire* in 1717. Shortly afterwards Prévost spoke of Shakespeare "with a freedom and audacity much greater than Voltaire's, but which attracted much less attention" (Jusserand 216). But Prévost did not have anything like the status enjoyed by Voltaire, nor did he work in the canonized orbit of tragedy. His translations of Richardson, for instance, passed into French literature without arousing any controversy whatsoever, and contributed greatly to the cult of sensibility canonically associated with Rousseau. The resistance to "Shakespeare" is mainly the resistance to any change in the "tragédie." If his proponents had been content with carving out a niche for Shakespeare in the opera, where works for the stage not neoclassical in nature had migrated, they would have encountered significantly less resistance. For this very reason, some of those experimenting with new forms of work for the stage tried to avoid confrontation by calling their works "drames" in spite of Cubières and Desfontaines who proposed to name them "*romanédies*" (Jusserand 318-19),[9] hoping no doubt to profit from some of the freedom awarded the "*roman*."

Voltaire perpetuated his own myth. In his *Appel à toutes les nations de l'Europe*, in which he asks the nations to sit in judgment over Corneille and Shakespeare, he speaks of himself in the third person, saying that M. de Voltaire "nous apprit, il y a environ trente ans, les noms de Milton et de Shakespeare" (taught us the names of Milton and Shakespeare some thirty years ago) (*Oeuvres complètes* XXIV, 201). And so he did, in his *Lettres Philosophiques* of 1734, which rode the crest

---

[9] References by page number from J.J. Jusserand, *Shakespeare in France* (New York, London: Putnam & Unwin, 1899).

of the *anglomanie*, or fascination with England, then washing over France. But it is in the preface to his *Brutus* that Voltaire lists his reasons for introducing "Shakespeare" to the French. The first reason goes beyond poetics: "à rendre à ma langue cette force et cette énergie qu'inspire la noble liberté de penser" (to give to my language that power and that energy inspired by the noble freedom of thought) (*Oeuvres complètes* II, 311). The second reason is perhaps the most weighty one in terms of poetics itself: "la sévérité de notre poésie, et l'esclavage de la rime" (the strictness of our poetry, and the bondage of rhyme) (*Oeuvres complètes* II, 312). Later, in the *Appel*, Voltaire expands on this even more: the problem raised by the alexandrine is compounded by a style of acting dominated by "declamation," which "mettait encore un obstacle à ces emportements de la nature qui se peignent par un mot, par une attitude" (put another obstacle in the way of those transports of nature painted by a word, an attitude) (*Oeuvres complètes* XXIV, 219). The third deals with the lack of action in the French "tragédie." Whereas "les pièces les plus irrégulières" (the most irregular plays) produced in England "ont un grand mérite: c'est celui de l'action" (have one great merit: that of action), the French "délicatesse excessive nous force quelquefois à mettre en récit ce que nous voudrions exposer aux yeux" (excessive delicacy sometimes forces us to put into a story what we would have liked to expose to the eyes) (*Oeuvres complètes* II, 315).

Voltaire wanted to administer a sensible dose of "Shakespeare" to remedy those ills of the "tragédie," but he could not control what he had set free or, in Chateaubriand's words: "Il vit qu'en relevant les beautés des barbares, il avoit séduit des hommes qui, comme lui, ne sauraient pas séparer l'alliage de l'or. Il voulut revenir sur ses pas: il attaque l'idole qu'il avait incensée; mais il était déjà trop tard" (He realized that in pointing out the beautiful features of the barbarians he had seduced people who, like him, were unable to separate the gold from the alloy. He retraced his steps: he attacked the idol he had burnt incense for; but too late) (*Oeuvres complètes* VI, 385). In more prosaic terms, what really happened was that Voltaire had lost his monopoly on Shakespeare to La Place, who published the first French "translations" subsequent to Voltaire's own translation of *Julius Caesar*. We should note that La Place's "translations" were in reality a series of synopses of various plays, supplemented by actual translations of key scenes.

To limit the damage, Voltaire gave his wholehearted approval to the Shakespeare adaptations of Ducis, which turned Shakespeare into the "Shakespeare" described by Tieck and insisted on by "une nation accoutumée à tourner en ridicule tout ce qui n'est pas d'usage." (a nation used to ridicule whatever is not customary) (Voltaire, *Oeuvres complètes* II, 315). A few years later Le Tourneur published his own Shakespeare translations, cunningly using a combination of translation and "criticism" to launch an attack on neoclassicism itself. The translations are accompanied by sections of "criticism" purportedly written by English critics, but most likely ghost-written by Le Tourneur himself, who enlisted both "Shakespeare" and his "critics" in the same cause. In doing so, however, Le Tourneur went too far for Voltaire, who turned against him, vehemently, in his *Lettre à l'Académie Française*. Le Tourneur's translation was not reissued until 1821.

The almost incredible stubbornness with which the French literary establishment clung to the sacrosanct "tragédie" is also illustrated by the vicissitudes of Schiller's *Wallenstein* in Benjamin Constant's translation. That translation, called *Wallstein*, was given a public reading in 1808. The play was not well received and therefore never produced on the stage. Yet when Constant managed to get the play published in 1810 the first edition sold out very quickly, less on account of the play itself, than of the preface. The actual translation of the play reflects Constant's "determination to squeeze the vast German historical drama into the bounds of the regular French Neoclassical form" (Furst 77).[10] Schiller's *Wallenstein* consists of two plays and a half. Constant's *Wallstein* consists of five acts. Moreover, the action, which takes years in Schiller, is compressed into one day by Constant. The German dialogue, which did not sound too unnatural to the German ear at the time, is translated into a French heavily tributary to neoclassical vocabulary, and much of the action is not shown on the stage, but told by "messengers" in the time-hallowed form of the "récit," or tale of what has happened off-stage.

In the preface, on the other hand, Constant pointed out in unmistakable terms the extent to which French dramatists of his time were still captives of a neoclassical poetics that had been left behind in both England and Germany. Accordingly, the importance of the 1810 *Wallstein* edition "lies in the very contradiction between the timidity of Constant's practices and his extraordinarily perspicacious insight into the dilemma facing French dramatists" (Furst 77). Constant's success rested on his assuming a Moses-like pose: showing French dramatists some kind of "Promised Land," but not entering it himself.

In some ways, Voltaire tried to use "Shakespeare" to bridge the gap between "highbrow" and "lowbrow" audiences, or to widen the appeal of the "tragédie," much as "ein Haufen ästhetischer Individuen" (a crowd of aesthetic individuals) (Christian Dietrich Grabbe, *Ueber die Shakespearo-Manie*, cited in Blinn II, 210) tried to do in Germany. Yet both the French and the German audiences went against the "aesthetic individuals," which is Grabbe's shorthand for the writers, critics, and intellectuals referred to above, who wrote about and discussed the Shakespeare they read, but whose plays were never performed in their entirety, with the result that the "aesthetic individuals" ultimately began to prefer Shakespeare adaptations that made "Shakespeare's" plays "zu wahren Familienstücken aus der Diderot-lessingischen Schule" (into real family plays from the Diderot-lessing school) (Grabbe in Blinn II, 210).

Voltaire, who did try to introduce some new elements in the "tragédie," resented the reaction to his and all other similar attempts aptly described by Mme de Staël in *De l'Allemagne*, perhaps partly under the influence of the fate that had befallen Constant's *Wallstein*, for we must keep in mind that Constant was her lover for a number of years: "Si l'on vouloit risquer en France, dans une tragédie, une innovation quelconque, aussitôt on s'écrieroit que c'est un mélodrame" (if anyone tried to hazard any kind of innovation in a tragedy in France, the audience would immediately shout that it was a melodrama). Voltaire even went farther than most of his colleagues and did try "de savoir pourquoi les mélodrames font plaisir à tant de gens" (to find out why so many people like melodramas) (de Staël II, 256).[11] But he was not prepared to abandon the "tragédie," or rather, the "goût," in order to rejuvenate the "tragédie," even though he was prepared to make concessions that went a fair way towards "Shakespeare":

> Toutes ces lois, de ne point ensanglanter la scène, de ne point faire parler plus de trois interlocuteurs, etc., sont des lois qui, il me semble, pourraient avoir quelques exceptions parmi nous, comme elles en ont eu chez les Grecs. Il n'en est pas des règles de la bienséance, toujours quelque peu arbitraires, comme des règles fondamentales du théâtre, qui sont les trois unités. (*Oeuvres complètes* II, 319)

---

[10] References by page number from Lilian R. Furst, *The Contours of European Romanticism* (Lincoln: Univ. of Nebraska Press, 1979).

[11] References by volume and page number from the edition Germaine de Staël, *De l'Allemagne*, 4 vols. (Paris: Hachette, 1958).

(All those laws: not to spill blood on the stage, not to have more than three characters speak at the same time, are laws which, I think, could brook some exceptions among us, as they could among the Greeks. The rules of civility, which are always somewhat arbitrary in nature, should not be treated with the same reverence as the fundamental rules of the theater, the three unities.)

In the end the battle for the romantic drama was won in France when its final bastion fell. It was a bastion built into the "tragédie" from its very inception, beyond unities and characters: "La pompe des alexandrins est un plus grand obstacle encore que la routine du bon goût, à tout changement dans la forme et le fond des tragédies françaises" (The pomp of the alexandrines is an even bigger obstacle than the routine of good taste to any kind of change in the form and substance of French tragedies) (de Staël II, 248). Victor Hugo's description of the new medium in his preface to *Cromwell* has nothing in common any more with the "sévérité de notre poésie, et l'esclavage de la rime" (the strictness of our poetry and the bondage of rhyme) mentioned by Voltaire (*Oeuvres complètes* II, 312). Hugo writes "un vers libre, franc, loyal, osant tout dire sans prudence, tout exprimer sans recherche; passant d'une naturelle allure de la comédie à la tragédie, du sublime au grotesque" (free verse, frank, loyal, daring to say everything without prudishness, without artifice; moving naturally from comedy to tragedy, from the sublime to the grotesque) (*Oeuvres complètes* XXIV, 54).

Once the battle for the romantic theater was won, "Shakespeare," or rather, his work, lost its potential value as a weapon. The work no longer needed to be translated, or rewritten in such a way that it could be made to serve the objectives of one faction or another. In other words, "Shakespeare" could become Shakespeare again. In 1829, five years after Stendhal's *Racine et Shakespeare*, which advised young playwrights to follow in Shakespeare's footsteps, rather than in Racine's, Alfred de Vigny published one of the first complete French translations of a Shakespeare play: *Othello*, without prefacing his translation – as Voltaire had done for his own translation of *Julius Caesar* – with an elaborate apology or riddling it with footnotes pointing out the "uncouth" nature of the original. Shakespeare was no longer a model to be accepted or rejected. Rather, Vigny published his translation, "non comme un modèle pour notre temps, mais comme la représentation d'un monument étranger, élevé autrefois par la main la plus puissante qui ait jamais créé pour la scène, et selon le système que je crois convenable à notre époque" (not as a model for our time, but as the representation of a foreign model, erected long ago by the most powerful hand that ever created for the stage, and according to a system I think fitting for our era) (*Oeuvres complètes* I, 265).[12] Later on in the preface, Vigny expresses the hope that the French will soon be able to read Shakespeare in a translation similar to that produced by Schlegel and Tieck in Germany. It is significant to note, in this respect, that August Wilhelm Schlegel translated thirteen Shakespeare plays between 1797 and 1801, and then one more in 1810, after which he refused to translate any more plays. The translation was completed by Tieck or, more accurately by his daughter Dorothea and Count Baudissin, from 1825 onwards, after the battle for the romantic theater had been won. Schlegel's translations may well have been inspired by the *Sturm und Drang* "Shakespeare," and he may equally well have lost his enthusiasm for the whole endeavor after the waning of the *Sturm und Drang* and with the growing realization that his translations would not be staged any time soon. In any case, it is totally

---

[12] References by volume and page number from the edition Alfred de Vigny, *Oeuvres complètes*, 3 vols. (Paris: Calmann-Lévy, 1897).

incorrect to state – as do many (comparative) histories of literature that the Schlegel-Tieck transla-tion struck the final blow for Shakespeare in Germany. Rather, the complete translation appeared when there were no more blows to be struck.

This is hardly surprising, since the basic story of Shakespeare's fortunes is rather similar in Germany. A well-known critic, Lessing, was perceived as Shakespeare's champion; he could fall back on a fashion of German "anglomania," just as Voltaire could ride the crest of French "anglo-mania." In Germany, Blinn notes, "wurden die englischen 'Moralischen Wochenschriften' ver-schlungen, Richardsons Romane als 'Offenbarungen' gefeiert, das bürgerliche Trauerspiel berief sich vorwiegend auf englische Vorbilder, englische Philosophen und Literaturkritiker wurden über-setzt" (the English 'Moral Journals' were devoured, Richardson's novels acclaimed as 'revelations,' the bourgeois drama appealed to English models, English philosophers and literary critics were translated) (I, 20). Yet, just like Voltaire, Lessing is not interested in Shakespeare, but in "Shakes-peare": "Mit seiner Konzeption stand er ganz in der didaktischen, ein neues Humanitätsideal anstre-benden Tradition der Aufklärung" (his concept located him squarely in the didactic tradition of the Enlightenment, which aspired to a new image of man) (Blinn I, 21). Since not too many plays of Shakespeare actually exhibit the humanitarian ideal of the Enlightenment, Lessing himself does not translate Shakespeare; he translates the more acceptable Diderot instead.

Wieland did translate Shakespeare, but as "Shakespeare": the notes he adds to his translations could just as easily have come from Voltaire's – they show the same condescension towards the original. Wieland writes about a passage in *Midsummer Night's Dream*, for instance: "Ich habe mich genötigt gesehen, einige ekelhafte Ausdrücke aus diesem Gemälde in Ostadens Geschmack wegzulassen" (I saw myself forced to omit a few revolting expressions from this painting executed to suit Ostade's taste) (V, 731).[13] Writers like Gerstenberg, Herder, the young Goethe, and Lenz, on the other hand, created another "Shakespeare" for themselves, one who would take them beyond the "bourgeois drama" advocated by Lessing and his followers. In his *Anmerkungen übers Theater* (Ob-servations on the Theater), Lenz states that Shakespeare has perfected the kind of play that finds its own "unity" time and again, in different ways, all of them far beyond any of the rules of the neo-classical theater, which lose all their relevance precisely because Shakespeare's plays have been written. Rather than listening to critics, "Der Dichter und das Publikum müssen die eine Einheit fühlen aber nicht klassifizieren" (Poet and audience have to feel this one unity without classifying it) (21).[14]

To create their own "Shakespeare," the writers of the German *Sturm und Drang* did in the sixties and seventies of the eighteenth century what Hugo did in France in the twenties of the nine-teenth century. They took the neoclassical rules out of timelessness and reinserted them into history. Gerstenberg does so primarily to apologize for Shakespeare's perceived "Unregelmässigkeiten" (ir-regularities). When the imaginary addressee of his *Briefe über die Merkwürdigkeiten der Literatur* (Letters on the Remarkable Features of Literature) laments: "Schade, dass ein so vollkommenes Genie (Shakespeare) einen so fehlerhaften Geschmack haben musste!" (pity that such a perfect genius had to have such faulty taste), Gerstenberg is quick to answer: "Und dreimal schade, setze

[13] References by volume and page number from the edition Christoph Martin Wieland, *Werke*, ed. Fritz Martini and Hans Werner Seiffert, 5 vols. (Munich: Hanser, 1968).
[14] References by page number from Jakob Michael Reinhold Lenz, "Anmerkungen übers Theater," in *Anmerkungen übers Theater: Shakespeare-Arbeiten und Shakespeare-Übersetzungen*, ed. Hans-Günther Schwarz (Stuttgart: Reclam, 1976).

ich hinzu, dass es nicht anders sein konnte wenn wir ihn beständig nur auf unser Jahrhundert beziehen" (a threefold pity, I must add, that it could not be otherwise if we keep discussing him only in terms of our century) (97).[15] Lenz, on the other hand, eschews all apologies and mounts a frontal attack on Aristotle, the perceived source of the unities himself, by coolly declaring: "Aristoteles konnte nicht anders lehren, nach den Mustern, die er vor sich hatte" (Aristotle could not teach in any different way because of the models he had before him) (17).

It should of course be noted in this respect that the writers of the *Sturm und Drang* did not have a "Comédie Française" to contend with, wielding the invincible alexandrine and supported by the full weight first of the king, and later of the emperor. On the contrary, the writers of the *Sturm und Drang* were writing at a time when the German bourgeoisie was still convinced it could, and eventually would, subsidize and cultivate its own "Nationaltheater."

Yet in the end neither Lessing's "Shakespeare" nor the "Shakespeare" of the *Sturm und Drang* really prevailed on the German stage. They were both superseded by a third "Shakespeare," introduced to Germany by Friedrich Ludwig Schröder, who based his Shakespeare adaptations for the stage on the more plodding and pedantic Eschenburg translations, not on the more literary translations made by Wieland. Schröder was to the German "Shakespeare" what Garrick was to his English homonym. He probably had to be, since even his watered-down versions of the original, the "abgemildert inszenierten Shakespeare-Aufführungen der siebziger Jahre" (adapted Shakespeare productions of the seventies) led to "Ohnmachtsanfällen, Frühgeburten, u. ä." (fainting spells, premature births, etc.) (Blinn I, 22) in the audience composed mainly of the rising and newly educated middle class which expected to see men and women fighting their passions, though not necessarily to the extent they do in Shakespeare's plays. Some of Shakespeare's protagonists and their actions could not be considered "human" by a bourgeoisie that could cultivate in the theater – and there only – its illusion of fundamental human values that "transcended" the sociological line separating it from the nobility. "Im Theater illusionär der gesellschaftlichen Wirklichkeit enthoben, entkleiden die Bürger auch die Figuren auf der Bühne ihres sozialen Standes – de facto machen sie sie damit zu Bürgern, die mehr oder weniger zufällig Könige sind; im bürgerlichen Selbstverständnis bedeutet dies: zu 'Menschen'" (in the theater the bourgeoisie is transported out of social reality in an illusionary manner; the bourgeois therefore also divests the characters on the stage of their social status – turning them de facto into bourgeois who happen to be kings more or less by chance; in the bourgeoisie's understanding of itself that means turning them into "human beings") (Meyer 211).

The "Shakespeare" actually performed in the German theaters was more often than not Schröder's "Shakespeare," quite openly designed to appeal to the taste of the bourgeoisie, and subjected to radical transformation to do so, to the point where it remained customary to "die Dramenausgänge ins Postive zu wenden" (change the endings of the plays in a positive sense) (Blinn I, 36). Hamlet marries Ophelia, Cordelia is reunited with Lear and Lear reascends his throne. No wonder Grabbe's "aesthetic individuals" felt betrayed by the "taste-lag" that separated them from the majority of the audience in the theaters, whose limited comprehension of Shakespeare tended to drive Goethe, for instance, to despair.

Since the German middle class would not accept the "real" Shakespeare, Goethe felt it necessary to "läugnen [...] und zwar zu seinen Ehren, dass die Bühne ein würdiger Raum für sein Genie

---

[15] References by page number from Heinrich Wilhelm von Gerstenberg, "Aus dem Versuch über Shakespeare's Werke und Genie (14.-18. Brief)," in Gerstenberg, *Ugolino*, ed. Christoph Siegrist (Stuttgart: Reclam, 1977).

gewesen" (deny, and to his honor, that the stage has been a worthy space for his genius) (in Blinn II, 190). Goethe's "Shakespeare" (and the "Shakespeare" of many intellectuals disappointed in the middle class) became a supreme poet, whose misfortune it was to have been forced to write for the theater in a barbaric age, and who could therefore not be adequately staged any longer.

It is interesting to note how the "historicism" of the older Goethe represents quite a step backward when compared to that of Lenz, and probably also the Goethe who was, for a while, a *Sturm und Drang* writer himself. That Goethe had used the *Sturm und Drang*'s image of "Shakespeare" to justify and defend the writing of his own *Goetz von Berlichingen*. The older Goethe complains that Elizabethan staging has "keine Spur von der Natürlichkeitsforderung, in die wir nach und nach durch Verbesserung der Maschinerie und der perspectivischen Kunst und der Garderobe hineingewachsen sind" (not a trace of the demand for naturalness we have gradually grown into because of improvements of a technical nature combined with improvements in the art of perspective and of costuming) (in Blinn II, 190). It would be unthinkable even for Shakespeare to lead the German theater of Goethe's time back "in die Kindheit der Anfänge" (to the childhood of beginnings) (in Blinn II, 190). It will be remembered that the *Sturm und Drang* Shakespeare was precisely supposed to be the beginning of a new theater in Germany.

Since the middle class did not like Shakespeare (compare the French middle class's preference for "mélodrame" over "tragédie"), they had to be satisfied with the "Shakespeare" they got. Goethe praised Schröder because he "hielt sich allein ans Wirksame, alles andere warf er weg, ja sogar manches Nothwendige, wenn es ihm die Wirkung auf seine Nation, auf seine Zeit zu stören schien" (just stuck to what worked, throwing away all the rest, even much that was necessary, when it seemed to distract from Shakespeare's effect on his nation and his time) (in Blinn II, 191). And since Schröder seemed to work, there was no need for Schlegel or Tieck: all attempts to stage Shakespeare word for word, "durch eine vortreffliche genaue Übersetzung veranlasst, wollten nirgends gelingen" (occasioned by an excellently faithful translation, never did succeed anywhere) (in Blinn II, 191).

Still the Germans had an accurate translation much earlier than the French did: not Schlegel-Tieck, at first, but Eschenburg. Those who were not satisfied with "Shakespeare" could read Shakespeare first in his translation, later in Schlegel's and Tieck's. Hence probably Goethe's somewhat resigned statement, "Durch's lebendige Wort wirkt Shakespeare, und dies lässt sich beim Vorlesen am besten überliefern" (Shakespeare works through the living word, and that is best transmitted through recitation) (in Blinn II, 184), echoed by Mme de Staël's "il vaut mieux lire ses pièces que les voir" (his plays are better read than seen) (*De l'Allemagne* II, 251).

In Germany, as in France, therefore, Shakespeare can be said to have remained the purview of critics, whereas the bourgeoisie went to see "Shakespeare," Schröder's or Ducis's. Shakespeare's undeniable influence on the transition from neoclassical to romantic drama in both France and Germany was exerted to a far greater extent through rewriters like Schröder and Ducis than through great "aesthetic individuals," like Goethe and Voltaire. In the final analysis, it would seem, the audience controlled the pace of the change taking place on the stage, not by submitting to the demands of genius, but by calling forth adaptors, rewriters who were able to slowly guide the audience to Shakespeare, via "Shakespeare".

The audience did this because it was most interested in a form of drama that would try "den Bürger über sich selbst und seine soziale Situation aufzuklären, ihn moralisch zu bessern und ihm

Handlungsanweisungen anzubieten" (inform the bourgeois about himself and his social situation, improve him on the moral level, and offer him instructions on behavior) (Meyer 201). There was really little need for Shakespeare in this respect, except that plays produced according to this model tended to be rather dull, and that allowances had to be made for both "Vergnügen" (enjoyment) and "Lust an der Neuigkeit" (desire for new things) (Meyer 205). This is where Shakespeare was brought in, not primarily for his own sake, but to liven up both the emerging bourgeois drama and the languishing "tragédie." In Germany Schröder's "Shakespeare" managed to do exactly what was expected of him; in France the "tragédie" complicated matters, mainly because the self-image of the bourgeoisie was different in literary matters in France and Germany.

The German bourgeoisie was much more open-minded, since it had just begun to look on itself as "gebildet," or educated, and since Germany had no literary and cultural tradition that could rival France's in any way. The German bourgeoisie was therefore quite prepared to take in the Diderot-Lessing type of bourgeois drama, with Shakespearian icing and all. In France, on the other hand, acceptance of the bourgeois drama was thwarted by the enormous cultural prestige of the "tragédie," which had become the transparent discourse of the theater to such an extent that it could live on long after it had lost its actual power-base in society. Since attacks on the transparent discourse of any facet of a society raise questions about the nature of other aspects, the resistance to "Shakespeare" was much fiercer in France than in Germany, also because the French were well aware of their dominant position in European culture. Once the bourgeoisie had been given a "Shakespeare" it could live with, the road was open for Grabbe's "aesthetic individuals" to further discover and propagate the "real" Shakespeare, as printed and finally staged in his entirety, whose integration into French and German literature lagged significantly behind that of his "bourgeois" avatars.

In a type of literary studies dominated by reverence for either the "aesthetic" or the "great writer," or both, the rewriter's input is nearly always overlooked. Ducis's translation can still be found in libraries, whereas it is alsmost impossible to find Schröder's adaptations. In contrast, special editions exist of all Voltaire ever said about Shakespeare. In what precedes I have tried to redress this injustice somewhat.

MIROSLAV J. HANAK AND NADEŽDA ANDREEVA-POPOVA

FOLKLORE AND ROMANTIC DRAMA

The Romantic interest in folklore represents a stage in a continuous cultural-historical development. When Europeans passed beyond the boundaries of their own continent and discovered new lands – when the Crusaders entered the Near East and the great seafarers of the Renaissance found the New World and reached the Far East – a process was initiated in which the reappraisal of European civilization became connected with the study and interpretation of folklore. This process reached a major peak in nineteenth-century Romantic literature, both through the intensive collecting and publishing of folklore materials and through the creation of folkloric studies. The very core of Romantic thought and aesthetics became positively oriented to the primitive folk art of the past and sought there inspiration, models, and confirmation of its own ideals. The attraction to folklore has its parallels in Romantic fascination for the "night side" of the psyche and such cultural practices as shamanism. Artistic predilection for the immediacy of folk expression after the mid-eighteenth century exhibits a gradual return of prerational values and a partial reversal of centuries of privileging the Platonic-Aristotelian direction of European metaphysics. This essay proposes to explore this central Romantic interest in, and sense of kinship with, folklore as a widespread European phenomenon, with special attention to the Slavic nations.

The success of literary scholarship in defining the concept of Romanticism is still in question. Nonetheless, it is helpful to consider several important attempts to characterize the ideological "center" of the movement and to reduce the variety of its traits to a generalizing formula. It seems it was easier to do this in the past, i.e., in the late eighteenth century, throughout the nineteenth, and in the first half of the twentieth century. Traditional historiography usually defined Romanticism as the antipode of Enlightenment, that is, either as a reaction to it, or as a flight from reality and from society. This reaction or flight was often thought to express the mood of the European intelligentsia after its disappointment with the results of the French Revolution. Both definitions depend on the thesis that reason and feeling are opposed. The first definition emphasizes the rhythmic alternation of the predominance of these forces in literature, while the second focuses on the degree of commitment to the life of society. However, the formula "Romanticism against Enlightenment" often implies a closed circle, an endless oscillation, which cannot explain the complex literary-historical processes. However, the imputation of a flight from reality cannot easily be reconciled with such important traits of Romantic literature in certain countries as patriotism, national consciousness, a new sense of history, and liberal political views.

This polarization between Enlightenment and Romanticism is not useful for analyzing the relationship between the Romantic interest in folklore and the formation of national literatures. It also fails to account for the ties between the Romantic movement and the Enlightenment on the one hand and nineteenth-century Realism on the other. These ties were especially strong and significant in the literatures of the countries of Central, East, and Southeast Europe, which were then fighting for social and political emancipation.[1]

Recent research has demonstrated the extent and the uniformity of the spirit of Romantic literature within much wider territorial and temporal boundaries than those traditionally accepted. It has illuminated the close relationship between certain trends in the Enlightenment and in Romanticism, and between the latter and Realism, a relationship that is manifested in the works not only of certain Late, but also in most Early Romantics, who are usually considered the most alien both to the Enlightenment and to Realism.

It has become clear that it is hard to speak of a flight from reality where the efforts of most writers were, in fact, directed toward the attainment of a deeper knowledge of reality and toward its improvement, both spiritual and material. It is now also clear that the subtlety and sensitivity of the Romantics do not exclude but rather imply a heightened intellectual activity; that, in the main, their flights of imagination begin with *Selbstanschauung* (self-contemplation) and end in a philosophical contemplation of the world, especially of the darkly intuited, undefinable, but existentially necessary World Ground. The Romantics did not simply reject culture or oppose "Geist"/"Spirit" and structuring consciousness, but were instead thoughtful artists who believed in the power of the Spirit, and also longed for the return to Nature, the latter being their first and foremost goal. The Romantics were, in the words of Oskar Walzel, *überbewußt* (meta-conscious).[2] This would imply transcending reality, without remaining – unlike the Baroque ego – in the beyond, nor a flight from reality due to its coldness to enthusiasm and intuition. Walzel saw Romantic synthetic mediation, encapsuled in the triad *naturhafte Unbewußtheit – Bewußtheit als Ergebnis der Kultur – bewußte Wiedererlangung naturhafter Haltung* (unconsciousness attuned to nature – consciousness resulting from acculturation – conscious recovery of a nature-attuned attitude) as the attempt to achieve this ultimate synthesis. With the weapons of culture the Romantics fought against the harm its inevitable rationalist alienation from nature had done. Their highly organized consciousness strove to penetrate the sphere of the unconscious, to awaken Nature, and to create according to her rationally "incognizable" laws. Definitions of Romanticism as, for example "Urgegensatz der Aufklärung" (radical opposite to the Enlightenment),[3] the denial of reality, anti-Classicism, or anti-Rationalism, have proved to be not merely insufficient, but also, to a certain extent, untrue. In the best case they show what the Romantic movement was not – but not what it was.

Today there are at our disposal comprehensive characterizations of Lovejoy[4] and of Wellek,[5]

---

[1] Struggles for political independence, national identity and the recovery of a once glorious past appeared all over *Southern* Europe, viz. the explosion of the "new" Romantic theater in Spain after the death of Fernando VII in 1833, the Italian *risorgimento* and Mazzini's Giovane Italia (after 1831), the Serbian uprising against the Turks in 1804 and Stefanović Karadžić's edition of folk songs (1814-36), and the Greek War of Independence 1821-29 and the Ionian School (Kalvos, Solomos) of "freedom poetry" after 1821.

[2] Oskar Walzel, "Wesensfragen deutscher Romantik," rpt. in *Begriffsbestimmung der Romantik*, ed. Helmut Prang (Darmstadt: Wissenschaftliche Buchgesellschaft, 1972), p. 186.

[3] Hermann August Korff, "Das Wesen der Romantik," in Prang, ed., p. 197.

[4] Arthur O. Lovejoy, "On the Discrimination of Romanticism," rpt. in *Essays in the History of Ideas* (Baltimore: Johns Hopkins, 1948). Lovejoy points out three kinds of Romanticism: a naturalistic Romanticism (primitivism and simplicity), p. 252; a transcendental (self-transcedence, diversity and complexity), p. 244; and an ethical (the ideal of Christianity and of endless progress), pp. 248-49.

[5] René Wellek, "The concept of Romanticism in Literary History: The Unity of European Romanticism," rpt. in *Concepts of Criticism*, ed. and with an Introduction by Stephen G. Nichols, Jr. (New Haven and London: Yale Univ. Press, 1962). Wellek selected three groups of ideas: the theories of imagination of the Romantic poets, pp. 178-82; the Romantic conception of nature, pp. 182-88; and the poetic practice ("all the great romantic poets are [...] symbolists"), pp. 188-92.

the formulations of Peckham[6] and of Remak,[7] the observations of Neupokoyeva on the interaction between Romanticism and Classicism, and between Romanticism and Realism,[8] the periodization of the Romantic movement by Sőtér and his account of its relationship to *Sturm und Drang* and of its development in Central and Southeast Europe.[9] Taken together, they delineate the Romantic movement in three ways – as an attunement to Spirit, i.e., to the *Zeit- und Volksgeist* (spirit of the age and ethnic folk spirit), as a literary phenomenon, and as a trend in aesthetics; they outline its ideological core[10] and extend its domain to the whole of Europe – and beyond – and to the entire century from 1780 to 1880. These achievements make our conception of Romanticism considerably more meaningful. Upon them, though without any pretense to completeness, a general characterization of the Romantic creator can be established – one which often involves the interest in folklore. These are then the most important concerns of Romanticism, aside from the above-mentioned goal of *awakening Nature*: a *longing for the unfamiliar* and a *desire to be free of the bonds of empirical reality*; a *desire to approach truth, absolute beauty, and harmony*, in order to find there *the fullest realization of unique human individuality*.

Before it was embraced by Romanticism as one of its chief points of departure, the concept of folklore had undergone a long development, whose principal stages, according to Giuseppe Cocchiara,[11] can be seen in the appearance of the myth of the "virtuous savage" in the Renaissance, and in the opposition of Nature to civilization in the Enlightenment, the fascination for "natural man," "the natural state," and "natural religion," and the idealization of "primitive" peoples. During the eighteenth and well into the nineteenth century, we see the search for "Nature" embodied in the fascination with the American Indian, with the mysterious "veiled" East, Hebrew thought and religion (the Bible), ancient Hellas (Homer), and finally, in Europe proper, with Old German poetry. The new organicist vision of history entails the rejection of Classicism as alien and untrue, and the discovery of national ethnicity as the root of cultural development. A return to the beginnings does not mean imitation of Classical models, but appreciation of the origins of one's own history, the childhood of one's people, as a source of spontaneous artistic creativity.

Consequently vision can now turn inward, from the foreign to what is one's own, and poetic energy no longer imitates but creates authentically. As the eighteenth century ended, Europeans east and south of France were discovering on home grounds beauty, purity, and power that seemed

---

[6] Morse Peckham, "Beitrag zu einer Theorie der Romantik," in Prang, ed., pp. 362-76: "dynamischer Organizismus," "positive" and "negative" Romanticism.

[7] Henry H.H. Remak, "Ein Schlüssel zur westeuropäischen Romantik," in Prang, ed. For Remak the most characteristic features of Romanticism are Primitivism and Introversion; he formulates his concept of Romanticism as "[...] Versuch, den Bruch im Universum zu heilen [...] die schmerzliche Erkenntnis des Dualismus verbunden mit dem Drang nach Lösung in einem organischen Monismus [...]," pp. 436, 438. ([...] An attempt to heal the breach in the universe [... and] the painful realization of dualism linked to the drive to solution in an organic monism [...].)

[8] Irina Neupokoyeva, "General Features of European Romanticism and the Originality of Its National Paths," rpt. in *European Romanticism*, ed. I. Sőtér and I. Neupokoyeva (Budapest: Académiai Kiadó, 1977), p. 27: "Some General Typological Problems of European Romanticism."

[9] I. Sőtér, "Romanticism: Pre-History and Periodization," rpt. in *European Romanticism.*

[10] Ideology in the socio-political sense would be hardly thinkable as a core of Romantic consciousness. Yet Dmitrij Čiževskij speaks of "specific ideological fundamentals of the Romantic Weltanschauung and of the adoption of the new [i.e., Romantic] ideology." *Comparative History of Slavic Literatures*, trans. R.N. Porter and M.P. Rice, ed. S.A. Zenkovsky (Nashville: Vanderbilt Univ. Press, 1971), p. 120. Ideology is a necessary condition for the rebirth of national-cultural collective consciousness of peoples in Central, Southern, and Eastern Europe struggling for self-determination.

[11] Giuseppe Cocchiara, *Storia del folklore in Europa*, 2nd ed. (Turin: Einaudi, 1954), or in the English version, *The History of Folklore in Europe* (Philadelphia: Institute for the Study of Human Issues, 1981).

lacking in the art of Classicism, formed after foreign models, i.e., French *classicisme*. The attitude to classical antiquity also changed: Hellas was no longer the strict lawgiver but represented rather the ideal of unviolated harmony. The folklore of other peoples was taken to exemplify the same ideal. Nationalistic thinking should teach the European nations, according to Madame de Staël, to "use one another as guides," rather than "to deprive one another of the lights they could loan one another [...]. It would be to the advantage of every country to absorb foreign thoughts."[12]

The Romantics neither discovered the corpus of folklore nor founded folklore. They were, however, the first to systematize the collecting, study, and interpretation of the wealth of folklore of their own and of other peoples. The diverse trends of Romantic aesthetics were reflected and refracted in their love of folklore. Poets and critics frequently looked to folklore for proof and illustration of their principles, in the variegated array of Romantic literary theory.[13]

The interest of Romantic writers in folk poetry and folk stories remained constant, overarching the particularity of individual nations. It was not restricted to the English Lake Poets and Sir Walter Scott, nor to the Heidelberg circle – Arnim, Brentano, Görres, and the Grimm Brothers. The writings of the Jena circle, those of Tieck and Novalis above all, found inspiration in medieval tales and legends that lead to a sophisticated *Nachdichtung* (artistic re-creation) of the untutored spontaneity of the creative *Volksgeist*, the matrix of ethnic self-consciousness. The common interest in folklore was one of the most important features of the aesthetic and metaphysical kinship between the earlier *Sturm und Drang* and Romanticism. Herder and his followers buttressed their philosophy of history through extensive research in folklore. They defined poetry as the voice of nature and the *Volk* (Nation) as the expression of a particular national spirit. The Romantics accepted Herder's philosophy of history and extended it on their own path to a "high-literature" re-creation of the originally unconscious spontaneous outpouring of Nature-attuned emotions. They saw embodied in folklore an ideal model of composition that suited their own aesthetic creed, which, once consciously identified, strove for the reawakening of primitive folk creativity.

The Romantic longing for the unknown led to a new knowledge of the world, including that of the psyche. The words of Coleridge in *Biographia Literaria* are a Romantic confession, not an assertion of Enlightenment Rationalism:

> For facts are valuable to a wise man, chiefly as they lead to the discovery of the indwelling law, which is the true being of things, the sole solution of their modes of existence, and in the knowledge of which consists our dignity and our power.[14]

For the Romantics it is poetry, that is, the creative principle, that leads to knowledge, rather than science, which they understood as dry ratiocination. For Coleridge, "Poetry is not the proper anti-

---

[12] Mme. de Staël, *De l'Allemagne*, ed. la Comtesse Jean de Pange (Paris: Hachette, 1959), III, 352-53.

[13] Henry H.H. Remak, "West-European Romanticism: Definition and Scope," in *Comparative Literature: Method and Perspective*, ed. Horst Frenz and Newton P. Stallknecht (Carbondale, Illinois: Southern Illinois Univ. Press, 1961), as quoted by Lilian R. Furst, "Further Discriminations of Romanticism," *Neohelicon*, 3, Nos. 3-4 (1975), p. 18, lists the characteristics of Romanticism thus: "imaginativeness, cult of strong emotions, restlessness and boundlessness, individualism, subjectivism, introversion, cult of originality, interest in nature, greater emphasis on religion, mysticism, *Weltschmerz*, liberalism, cosmopolitanism, nationalism, interest in folklore and primitivism, medievalism, anti-neoclassicism, interest in Nordic mythology, supremacy of lyrical moods and forms, historical drama and novel, reawakening of national epic, greater flexibility of form, irony, 'vagueness,' symbolism, rhetoric, exoticism and realism in local color."

[14] Samuel Taylor Coleridge, *Biographia Literaria; or Biographical Sketches of My Literary Life and Opinions* (London: Bell, 1884), p. 169.

thesis to prose, but to science."[15] For Shelley, poetry "is at once the centre and circumference of knowledge; it is that which comprehends all science, and that to which all science must be referred. [...] It makes us the inhabitants of a world to which the familiar world is a chaos."[16] Most of the Romantics found in folklore a model for such poetry.

The four often cited principal ideological-aesthetic aspects of Romanticism – its anti-Rationalism, primitivism, its invocation of the national spirit, and a markedly metaphorical style – do make comprehensible the Romantic turn to folklore; as such they deserve closer attention.

Although anti-Rationalism has usually been interpreted as opposition to the Enlightenment, the numerous ties of Romanticism to the preceding epoch show that it did not oppose or reject the "spirit" of the Enlightenment but, realizing the limitations of "rational" knowledge, sought to pursue the Enlightenment's quest with new means. The Romantics did not reject logical thought, but looked for ways to approach truth, which were both more powerful than the senses and more penetrating than reason. Thus they discovered imagination and its boundless possibilities, the secrets of the unconscious, and the free play and untapped power of intuition. Out of this matrix emerged also their "cult of feeling," of the strong and original personality, and their unceasing interest in all regions of metalogical experience – religion, instinct, and faith in the beyond.

Primitivism was a nucleus of ideas that determined the Romantic *Weltbild* (world view). It implied an interest in nature, in the sources of life, in childhood, folk art, the creative act, the past (Hellas, the Orient, the New World, the Middle Ages, Christianity – specifically Roman Catholicism), and in the recovery of ethnic origins, "originality," that moment in which the essences of being were most purely and fully revealed. In Romantic ideology, ethnicity was not a political category, but the name of that which is primordially true of a people, and which directs its fate – even when unrecognized. The "nation" was an expression of nature and often clashed, therefore, with civilization, with its institutions, ethics, and art. Alienation from the national spirit was, for the Romantics, equivalent to being torn from one's roots, to the desiccation of life, to barrenness, and spiritual doom. For Herder and the *Sturm und Drang*, and for most of the Romantics as well, Nature was the divine principle revealed in and through creation. Therefore to turn away from one's ethnic background was to forfeit not only the sources of all knowledge, but also the spiritual principle of all existence – that is, the God behind or in Nature. Hegel's Absolute Spirit/Knowledge is a Romantic echo of Spinoza's "baroque" pantheism of *Deus sive natura*. Folk poetry is one of the purest and truest voices of Nature. It is the spontaneous expression of man's need to reveal his soul; through it a people gives form to its national identity. Herder's triad *Volk* – Nature – God was developed in many directions in Romantic thought. It was the basis of Romantic love of "the peoples" and the echo of their "voices," and the admiration for the "national genius." When the historical development of a people and the social and political situation in their country created the necessary conditions – in periods of struggle for national liberation, for example – these beliefs gave impetus to a lofty concept of patriotism and didactic historical drama, to a passion for collecting, popularizing, and interpreting folklore.

The Romantics discerned precedents in folklore for certain means of expression characteristic of Romantic style – e.g., symbol and myth. Folk legends, historical sagas, ballads, and tales pro-

---

[15] Samuel Taylor Coleridge, "Definition of Poetry," in *Lectures and Notes on Shakespeare and Other English Poets* (London: Bell, 1884), p. 183.
[16] Percy Bysshe Shelley, "A Defense of Poetry," in *Shelley's Poetry and Prose*, ed. Donald H. Reiman and Sharon B. Powers (New York: Norton, 1977), pp. 503 and 505.

vided much material for the building of Romantic literary works. Romantic authors transformed the wealth of stories and images in the historical, heroic, and religious myths of folklore into metaphors, which addressed the task of conveying the sense of their own – non-folkloric, Romantic – world view. By the same token, folk poetry became for many of the Romantics the prototype of F. Schlegel's *Poesie der Poesie* (the Poetry of Poetry)[17] which they themselves desired to create, and which aimed to set itself apart from literature bearing the names of the traditional poetic genres and, above all, from *das Gedicht* (the Poem) of the preceding epochs of Classicism and Enlightenment. "Wenn man manche Gedichte in Musik setzt, warum setzt man sie nicht in Poesie?" (If many a poem is set to music, why are poems not set to poetry?) asks Novalis in *Fragment 1252*, opposing the *Gedichte* of his contemporaries to *Poesie*, which was alien to them. The essence of the poetical in the newer sense of *Poesie* is its "fabulous" quality. Civilized peoples had long ago lost the childlike state,[18] that "unknown land of wonders yet undiscovered." Folklore, however, had been created in the childhood of mankind, it was *die Natur selbst* (Nature herself).[19] It was also naive, in Schiller's sense, that is, inwardly united and still unacquainted with tragic separation and loss of harmony.[20] For these reasons folklore was able to give the Romantics the model, the ideal, of the tale.

Folklore also gave the Romantics a mode of poetry apparently "without rules," for it knew nothing of the strict, normative regulation of Classical art. It was close to Shelley's above-mentioned ideal of poetry "to which the familiar world is a chaos." The antithesis to Shelley's chaos, what he considers harmony, is of another order than the considered measures of literature created in accordance with preestablished rules. The examples of folklore encouraged the Romantics to create supposedly by submitting themselves to no laws but Nature's. They construed these laws to be also those of the soul, unintelligible to reason, laws which allowed the creation of works independent of logical coherence and sometimes fragmentary and senseless, like dream visions. "Nichts ist mehr gegen den Geist des Märchens als ein moralisches Fatum, ein gesetzlicher Zusammenhang" (Nothing opposes the spirit of the fairy tale more than moral fate, a connection according to a law), wrote Novalis in *Fragment 1260*. "Im Märchen ist echte Naturanarchie: abstrakte Welt, Traumwelt, Folgerungen von der Abstraktion u.s.w. auf den Zustand nach dem Tode." (In the fairy tale rules genuine anarchy: an abstract world, a dream world, conclusions drawn from abstraction etc. as to the state after death.) The tendency of many Romantics to overlook the actual rules of folk art can be attributed to their position as heirs of Classical poetics; they were extending Classical dicta through their eagerness to accept that any work which did not correspond to Classical rules was free of rules altogether.[21]

Since this essay focuses mainly on the mutual cross-pollination of the Romantic spirit and folklore resulting in a Romantic drama in Central, Eastern, and Southeastern Europe, it necessarily must address first of all the other genres that were more directly impacted by this symbiosis. Dramatic

[17] Friedrich Schlegel, *Literary Notebooks, 1797-1801*, ed. Hans Eichner (London: Athlone Press, 1957), no. 579.

[18] "Die Kinder sind Antiken. Nicht alle Kinder aber sind Kinder." (Children are works of classical art. Not all children are, however, children.) Novalis, *Fragment* 740.

[19] "Kinder sind noch terrae incognitae." (Children are still *terrae incognitae*.) Novalis, *Fragment* 741.

[20] On the basis of Schiller's conception of the naive and the sentimental Novalis wrote (*Fragment* 1300): "Das Naive ist nicht polarisch. Das Sentimentale ist es." (The naive is not polarized. The sentimental is.)

[21] "Ein Märchen ist wie ein Traumbild, ohne Zusammenhang. Ein Ensemble wunderbarer Dinge und Begebenheiten, z.B. eine musikalische Phantasie, die harmonischen Sorgen einer Aeolsharfe, die Natur selbst" (*Fragment* 1259). (A fairy tale is like a dream vision, without cohesiveness. An ensemble of wondrous things and occurrences, as, for instance, a musical fantasy, the harmonic cares of an aeolian harp, Nature herself.)

literature and dramaturgy were not among the fortes of the Romantic creative process in the regions of Europe addressed here.[22] Not unlike earlier in Scotland, England, and Germany, it was the genres of lyric, epic, and lyrico-epic poetry (Robert Burns, Walter Scott, Macpherson's *Ossian*, Shelley, Coleridge, young Goethe, Schiller, Brentano, Arnim, Tieck, Heine) with the folk ballad as core of inspiration and re-creative imitation that allowed the poetic genius of Romanticism to shine the brightest. In England and Germany, the Romantic drama came into its own, respectively, thanks to the genius of Shelley and the Classicist, oft Romantically tinged, endeavors of Goethe and Schiller. Only Goethe's *Faust* and Schiller's *Freiheitsdramen* (dramas of freedom) proved stageworthy in the long run. The rest of Romantic dramaturgy remained in the category of *Lesedramen*, dramatic *literature*, often fascinating (Tieck) and quite enjoyable, but too avant-garde for the tolerance of the theatrical audience of their age, nor resistant to the test of time.[23]

Because of their preeminent importance during this era, lyric and epic poetry, and a combination of the two *qua* Romantic ballad, must be addressed first in the so-called major Slavic literatures, i.e., literary works in Russia and Poland. A sketch, however brief, of non-Slavic poetic efforts (e.g., in Hungarian, Rumanian, Greek, and Albanian letters) is beyond the scope of this essay.

Aleksandr S. Pushkin's (1799-1837) quickly maturing talent produced lyrical gems representing a perfect blend of high literature and folk inspiration ("Zimniy večer," Winter Evening, 1825; "Zimnaya doroga," Winter Road, 1826; "Běsy," The Fiends, 1830). These last three are perfect examples of folklorically inspired high poetry which becomes "nationalized," i.e., adopted by the enthusiastic admirers as a new addition to Russia's folk patrimony. Yet Pushkin could also write straight imitations of folk poetry, ballad-like epic cameos ("Pěsň o věščem Olegye," The Lay of Oleg the Sagacious, 1822), and penned a series of brief "Sketches of Folk Songs" (1824) dedicated to Stenka Razin, the seventeenth-century Cossack rebel-hero.

Nostalgia and a macabre *horror mortis* are the hallmarks of the other briefly flashing star in the constellation of Russian poetic geniuses, Mikhail Y. Lermontov (1814-41). Both Pushkin and Lermontov fed their Muse on the primitive, exotic, and majestic beauties of the Caucasus and its peoples, the genuine *nobles sauvages* hailed by their Romantic sensibility. Lermontov was also receptive to the allurements of Hebrew lore, and produced faithful stylistic and metric imitations of Ossianic and Old-Russian bardic rhapsodies ("Ataman," 1831). The culminating work in this sub-genre is the long epic poem *Pěsnya pro carya Ivana Vasilyeviča, molodogo opričnika i udalogo kuptsa Kalašnikova* (A Song about Czar Ivan Vasilyevich, His Young Retainer, and the Valiant Merchant Kalashnikov, 1837).

"Ballada" (Ballad, 1831) evokes the misery suffered by Russian peasantry in Tartar raids; another *ballada* of 1832 is an impressionist vignette of men off to war taking leave from their girl-

---

[22] Notable exceptions to this are Pushkin's *Boris Godunov* and the dramas of Mickiewicz, Słowacki, and Krasiński in Poland. More on this later in the text.

[23] The major difference between Romantic dramaturgy in Western Europe and in the regions here investigated comes to the fore in the stageworthiness of the West-European drama for which there is no equivalent in the East and the Southeast of Europe. France, Spain, and Germany (*the* center of Europe, excepting the bilingual – i.e., Czech and German culture of Bohemia) had a long tradition of theater sophistication and grandeur in both dramatic creativity and audience receptiveness. In Spain, the giants of the *siglo de oro* (Golden Age: Lope, Tirso, Calderón) were easily awakened from their century-long sleep by the Duque de Rivas (*Don Alvaro*, 1835), García Gutiérrez (*El trovador*, 1836), Hartzenbusch (*Los amantes de Teruel*, The Lovers of Teruel, 1836), and, of course, by the master of explosive stage theatricality, Zorrilla (*Don Juan Tenorio*, 1844). Victor Hugo's unstageable *Cromwell* (1827) gave French Romantics an aesthetic canon in its famous "Preface"; *Hernani* (1830), a rallying call; *Ruy Blas* (1838) survives to this day on the stage, as does Musset's genteel-decadent *On ne badine pas avec l'amour* (Don't Trifle with Love, 1834).

friends; yet another ballad of the same year deals with the tragedy of an interracial affair between a Jewish girl and her Russian lover. This last ballad is more a *costumbrista* piece (a term used by Hispanists for realist sketches of typical public and private behavior among certain social and ethnic groups), than what is traditionally conceived as Romanticism's echo of folk traditions.

In his *Comparative History of Slavic Literatures*, Dmitrij Čiževskij shows a connection between interest in folklore and in what are the mythical, rather than documented origins of the Slavs:

> The Slavic romantics' pursuit of folklore grew out of the interest in prehistory and its residue in superstition and in the "prejudices" that were especially hated by the Enlightenment. The first good collections of fairy tales, songs, [and] proverbs [...] belong to the achievements of Slavic Romantic scholarship.[24]

Čiževskij mentions the fairy-tale collector A. Afanasev's efforts "to reconstruct Slavic mythology on the foundation of folklore."[25]

As for the popularity enjoyed universally by the ballad in the Romantic repertory, Čiževskij states:

> The ballad appeared as a new genre, the value of which was seen in the possibility of manufacturing national and popular materials. The mostly short, lyrical poem was widely spread.[26]

What Čiževskij apparently means by "manufacturing" is coopting folklore to "high literature," rather than "fabricating"; as will be shown presently, the latter "possibility" was certainly exploited to the fullest by the authors of the apocryphal MSS of Czech prehistory Hanka-Linda-Svoboda.

The Romantic penchant for the *Nachtseite* (night aspect) of the soul, for the unconscious[27] – including the instinctual and splenetic life weariness – found its fondest expression in the elegy, but also in the romance. The latter is a tale in verse set in the Middle Ages elaborating legendary, gallant, or miraculous themes in the language of Courtly Love, but usually avoiding the ballad's bent for the macabre and demonic annihilation of the good and innocent. A specific example of cross-pollination between West and East is Nikolai Michailovič Karamzin's (1766-1826) loose translation of a Spanish *romance*[28] entitled "El almirante Guarinos." Karamzin's Russian "Graf Guarinos" (Count Guarinos, 1789) was sung, according to a footnote by Agustín Durán, editor of the *Romancero general*, by Russian *muzhiks* in Siberia.[29] Both Pushkin and Lermontov wrote romances (the best known among Pushkin's is the one dedicated to the "rytsar bedniy," the ascetic knight-votary of the Marian cult, 1830); Lermontov's "Romans" of 1832 is a personal complaint about slanderous tongues that had brought about a separation with a lady friend.

---

[24] Čiževskij, p. 128.

[25] Čiževskij refers to the important nineteenth-century expert A. Afanasev, *Poetic Views of the Slavs on Nature* (1865ff.).

[26] Čiževskij, p. 129.

[27] Čiževskij points out that the Romantics' exploration of the unconscious does not necessarily mean the "subconscious" of modern psychology but rather sinister forces of nature in which the individual shares and "which can break into the normal psychic life from below and even from above [...]" (p. 124). Čiževskij cites V.F. Odoevskij's *Russian Nights* (1844) as explorations of the sinister and uncanny in which the borderline between sanity and insanity tends to disappear (pp. 123ff.).

[28] The Spanish romance is an anonymous octosyllabic lyrico-epic composition of some length, in which the even verses are assonated; Karamzin's Russian version ignores the assonance.

[29] *Romancero general. Colección de romances castellanos anteriores al siglo XVIII*, Biblioteca de autores españoles, ed. Agustín Durán, vol. X (Madrid: La Real Academia Española, 1945), pp. 265-67.

Another species of the ballad subgenre is the bridegroom-revenant, or specter-bridegroom which draws on the universally applauded and imitated *Lenore* (1773) by Gottfried August Bürger (1747-94). In Russia, Pushkin's "Ženikh" (Bridegroom, 1825) is subtitled "Prostonarodnaya skazka" (A Simple-Folks Tale); it is cast in dialogue form. "Utoplennik" (The Drowned Man, 1828) bears the same subtitle. Vasiliy Andreyevich Zhukovsky (1783-1852), a neoclassicist precursor of Romanticism and translator of Thomas Gray's *Elegy Written in a Country Churchyard* (1750-51) which appeared in 1802 under the title *Selskoye Kladbišče* (A Country Churchyard), produced an autochthonous version of the specter bridegroom in *Svyetlana* (1808, pb. 1812). In the similar vein of the *Schauerballade* (ballad of horror), he composed *Lyudmila* (1808), a reflection of folk belief, still widely accepted in Zhukovsky's time, in the direct intervention of the usually demonically-oriented beyond.[30]

A convert to Romanticism, Pavel Alexandrovič Katenin (1792-1853), in spite of his aesthetically ultra-conservative views and attacks on the linguistic innovations of Karamzin's and Zhukovsky's *Schauerballaden*, did nevertheless cultivate the ballad mode, albeit in a soberly-realist style worthy of this last defender of Russian neoclassicism. His ballad "Olga" (1816) was an unfeigned condemnation of the mystical raptures and daydreams à la Zhukovsky. Other ballads (*Nataša*, 1814, pb. 1832; *Ubiytsa*, The Murderer, 1815, pb. 1832) show a definite leaning toward realism. Anton Antonovič Delvig (1798-1831), Pushkin's classmate and another member of the circle gathering about the latter, cultivated, in addition to high-literature genres (the sonnet, ode, elegy, idyll, Anacreontic lyrics) also the creative imitation of Russian folksongs such as "Solovyey" (The Nightingale), "Nye osienniy mielkiy doždičok" (Not the Fine Drizzle of the Fall), edited by A.F. Smirdin in 1852. Brilliant poems like "Dvye doli" (Two Destinies), "Istina" (Truth), "Vodopad" (Waterfall), all dating from 1824, are typical of the early work of Evgeniy Abramovič Baratynsky (1800-44). The tale in verse *Cyganka* (Gypsy Girl), originally titled *Naložnitsa* (Concubine, 1831) deals with the Romantic commonplace of Gypsy free-spiritedness. Gradually, the poet's Muse succumbed to pessimism and, eventually, benightedness.

In this sketchy review of Russian lyric and epic poetry of the Romantic era in terms of its interdependence with folklore it is proper to adduce Čiževskij's insights concerning the Romantics' predilection for euphony, a principal device of folk poetry for the evocation of moods and atmosphere. Although "euphony did *not always* let itself be united with precision and clarity of expression,"[31] it certainly heightened the force of the intuitive faculty as a tool of cognition in defiance of Classicist reason and logic. Čiževskij finds close links between euphony and "the extensive use of the *epitheta ornantia*, the decorative epithets of folk literature" by the Romantics. He speaks of

> a gradual infiltration of folkloristic elements into the language and style of the literary works [...] not only in song and fairy tale, but in works of other genres as well.[32]

---

[30] Zhukovsky was a prolific translator of Byron, W. Scott, Southey as well as of Schiller's ballads and of poems by Goethe, Uhland, Rückert, and Bürger; he also brought to the Russian reader *The Odyssey*, and selections from Persian and Indian literature. He tried, not always successfully, to exercise a tempering influence on Pushkin's restless genius. Belinsky claimed that Zhukovsky introduced "the spirit of Medieval Romanticism into Russian literature." Cf. *Bolšaya Sovyetskaya Enciklopedia*, ed. B.A. Vyedenskiy, 2nd ed. (Moskva: Kniga, 1953), XVI, 226.

[31] Čiževskij, p. 142.

[32] Čiževskij, p. 141.

The preceding outline of the development of non-dramatic Romantic genres in Russian literature will permit the treatment of the same phenomena in the rest of the Slavic literatures in a more summary form.

Polish letters of the Romantic era contributed to world literature a poetic genius comparable in his originality, scope, and sweep to Pushkin: Adam Mickiewicz (1798-1855). His first fruits, *Ballady i Romanse* (Ballads and Romances, 1822-23), though undistinguished compared to his mature poetry, excelled, according to Manfred Kridl, "any Ballads [sic] written in Poland before [him]."[33] One of them, "Pan Twardowski," is a variant on the Faust saga. The ode-like *Romantyczność* (Romanticism, 1822) is more than a "programmatic poem."[34] According to Krzyzanowski, since "analogous" to Bürger's *Lenore*,[35] it is a variant of the "specter-bridegroom" ballad. "Mad" from the viewpoint of the "enlightened scholar,"[36] a girl speaks with her dead lover in the presence of a crowd of country folk who join her in tearful prayer, for they too sense the spectral presence. Kridl maintains that the Byronic epic *Konrad Wallenrod* (1828) which deals with an eventual military and moral victory of the Lithuanian hero over the Teutonic Order is "unprecedented [...] in language and style in Polish poetry."

Mickiewicz's younger contemporary Julyusz Słowacki (1809-49) was a man of letters pure and simple. His fame springs from his being the creator of modern Polish drama; however, Byronic tales in verse, published in 1832, two years after his self-exile to France, bear also the clear imprint of Mickiewicz. The turbulent history of clashes between Cossacks and Turks, rather than folklore per se, inspired one tale entitled *Zmija* (The Viper).

Zygmunt Krasiński (1812-59) and Cyprjan Norwid (1821-83) were virtuosos of form and daring, innovators, rather than artful adapters of folkloric naiveté.

Taras Hryhorovič Ševčenko (1814-61) was the father of modern Ukrainian literature as well as the embodiment of the century-old rage of his race directed against both Poland and Russia. Gifted painter and poet, his artistic inspiration fed upon the violent ups and downs of the Ukranian past.

Few men of letters in the Slav world identified as closely as Ševčenko with the plight of the poor country folk, their customs, and the cruel hopelessness of their servitude. The tale in verse *Kateryna* (Catherine, 1838) elaborates a rather commonplace tragedy of a seduced and abandoned serf girl, but the beauty of the verse and unfeigned compassion make it a poetic jewel. "Perebendia" (1838-40) is the first avatar of the Ukrainian *kobzar*, the bandura (lute-playing) folk bard who appears as "wretched and blind," whom "no one in the world welcomes [...]. Like the sun, he is alone among men."[37] Yet he is the most important link to the Ukrainian folk past and the chief mainstay of Ukrainian ethnic consciousness. As a folk institution, he is immortalized in the eponymous *Kobzar* (1840). This folk tale in verse saw three subsequent reworked and expanded versions. C.A. Manning calls it the poet's heart pouring out "the sufferings of his people and of their past."[38] Pavlo Fylypovič contrasts Ševčenko's unabashedly Romantic ballads ("Prychynna," The Bewitched

[33] Manfred Kridl, ed., *An Anthology of Polish Literature* (New York: Columbia Univ. Press, 1957), p. 161.
[34] Čiževskij, p. 122. Here Čiževskij also refers to this poem as a "glorification of madness" which became a sought-after feature of the Romantics' predilection for the psyche's *Nachtseite*.
[35] Julian Krzyzanowski, *Polish Romantic Literature* (Freeport, NY: Books for Libraries Press, 1968), p. 46.
[36] Čiževskij, p. 122.
[37] Ivan Franko, "Foreword to Shevchenko's *Perebendia*," in George S.N. Luckyj, ed., *Shevchenko and the Critics 1861-1980*, trans. by Dolly Ferguson and Sophia Yurkevich (Toronto: Toronto Univ. Press, 1980), p. 102.
[38] Clarence A. Manning, *Ukrainian Literature: Studies of the Leading Authors* (Freeport, NY: Books for Libraries Press, 1944), p. 47.

Woman, 1841; "Topolia," The Poplars, 1839; "Lileia," Lily, 1846) with other nations' ballads popular in Ševčenko's time:

> In form, they are simpler than [...] Bürger's "Lenore," Zhukovsky's "Svetlana," Mickiewicz's "Ucieczka" or "Lilia." They lack the characteristic ballad structure – the reliance on repetition [...] the fantastic elements are not overdrawn and are far removed from mysticism.[39]

The tale in verse *Haidamaki* (The Haidamaks, 1841), indisputably the greatest epic work of Ukrainian literature, deals sympathetically with the 1768 peasant uprising against the Polish aristocratic serfholders.

Panteleimon Kulish (1819-97) showed early interest in Ukrainian peasant folklore, especially in songs and tales. The collection *Kievlyanin* (1840) reflects the interest of a collector, rather than that of a poetic re-creator of Ukrainian peasant lore; a cycle of poems *Ukraina* (1843) expands the efforts of a collector to include his own poetry. He gravitated toward a gradually more conservative bourgeois nationalism which made him see the warlike Cossack past in a less positive light than Ševčenko's passionate idealization. *Čorna rada* (The Black Council, 1857) is a historical novel dealing with the turbulent months that followed Bogdan Chmielnicki's[40] demise during which Poland and Russia took advantage of the power struggle between the Cossack colonels and divided the Ukraine between the right (Polish) and left (Russian) banks of the Dnieper. Kulish's *Zapiski o iužnoi Rusi* (Notes on the South Rus, 1856-57) are dedicated to the role of the *kobzar* as preserver of Ukrainian folk traditions. The *kobzar*'s "poetic and philosophic frame of mind" is a constant reminder "of God and good deeds."[41] The work is an encompassing repository of Ukrainian oral traditions.

The reawakening of national consciousness, strong enthusiasm for ethnological activities, the search for a glorified past that did not shy from plagiarism on a truly epic scale, as well as the impact of the cult of Romantic sensibility from the West all combined in the genesis of a new, robust, though usually less frenetic literature in the territories of the traditional crown lands of Bohemia and Moravia.

The Slovak pastor Jan Kollár (1793-1852) produced in Czech[42] the first Panslavic epos *Slávy dcera* (The Daughter of Sláva, 1824). In the mystic-majestic world of a past idealized by enthusiasm rather than backed by objective fact, Kollár's resonant sonnets evoke "Slavdom's history [...] monumentalized along Herderian lines." In Arne Novák's words,

> the military and cultural exploits of the Slavs, projected back, fantastically, to the very threshold of the Middle Ages, invoke Slavic pride, but the fate of the persecuted and decimated Slavs on the Elbe and on the Baltic cries for revenge [...] the whole is organized [... as] a sentimental journey through various Slavic lands [... on the plan] reminiscent of *Childe Harold*, and later supplemented by a Slavic *Inferno* and *Paradiso* à la Dante.[43]

[39] Pavlo Fylypovych, "Shevchenko and Romanticism," in Luckyj, ed., pp. 173-74.
[40] Bohdan Chmielnicki (1595?-1657) was a Cossack colonel who first served loyally the Polish Crown, though he tried to support Ukrainian and Cossack interests. Eventually he seems to have been forced by the Poles into open rebellion. Even though he was usually victorious on the battlefield, dissension and unruliness of the Cossack hosts made him seek Moscow's aid. By recognizing the Czar's sovereignty, he guaranteed the loss of Ukrainian independence.
[41] Franko, in Luckyj, ed., p. 107.
[42] Finding himself early in the minority, Kollár considered Czech the proper writtten language of Slovakia.
[43] Arne Novák, *Czech Literature*, trans. Peter Kussi, ed. William E. Harkins (Ann Arbor: Michigan Slavic Publications, 1976), p. 132.

Kollár's idealization of the past and call for a more hopeful future stirred little controversy compared to the "discovery" of the *Rukopis královédvorský* (The Královédvorský MS), allegedly found in 1817, and the *Rukopis zelenohorský* (The MS of Zelená Hora) which emerged a year later. The authenticity of the two MSS (the first dating back supposedly to the ninth, the second, to the fourteenth century) sparked a controversy that was to stretch out through most of the nineteenth century, resulting in divisive acrimony along political and ideological lines drawn by the patriotic fervor and blindness of practically every faction at work in Bohemia's public life. Today the MSS are universally viewed as Ossianesque forgeries, produced *con amore* by the Slavist and poet of questionable talent Václav Hanka (1791-1861), the classical philologist V.A. Svoboda (1791-1849), and the able journalist and author of historical novels Josef Linda (1789-1834).[44] According to A. Měšťan, both texts "have considerable esthetic value and represent important documents of Czech pre-romantic fiction." It is now generally believed that the main author had to be Linda the novelist, the only one of the trio capable of producing poetic texts of such high quality.[45]

Full-fledged Romantic enthusiasts for Czech and Slav folklore were František Ladislav Čelakovský (1799-1852) and Karel Jaromír Erben (1811-70). The first produced what Měšťan calls *Widerhall-Lyrik*, or "echo-lyricism," owing to the fact that this "grandson of Goethe" gathered Czech folksongs in the same fashion that Kollár did their Slovak equivalents.[46] Eventually, Čelakovský published in three volumes *Slovanské národní písně* (Slavic Folk Songs, 1822-27). Aside from selectively editing his materials, he added "his own poems, written in the spirit of authentic folk songs." Hence the title of his next cycle reads *Ohlas písní ruských* (Echoes of Russian Songs, 1833) which imitated the Russian *byliny*, Old Russian sagas, equivalent to the heroic epic in the West. *Ohlas písní českých* (Echoes of Czech Songs, 1839) followed.

> A major portion of the *Czech Songs* are ballads and in comparison with the *Echoes of Russian Songs*, the poet recast the Czech folk materials in a rather free [i.e., personally creative] fashion [...]. The term "echo" is, consequently, warranted only to a small degree – what we have here is to a great extent high-literary *Kunstlyrik* [a highly personalized and premeditated lyrical expression].[47]

Růže stolistá (Centifoliate Rose, 1840) "took as point of departure the philosophy of nature of German Romanticism," meaning primarily Herder and Schelling. In this "Čelakovský determined in a decisive way the development of Czech Slavistics." This process was further intensified by the *Mudrosloví národu slovanského v příslovích* (The Wisdom of the Slavic People in Proverbs, 1852).

> For the period of thirty years he has collected 15,000 proverbs in circulation among Slavic nations, using a comparative approach involving proverbs of other European nations.[48]

Karel Jaromír Erben, archivist of the City of Prague, spent his life researching and collecting every facet of Czech folklore: songs, fairy tales, customs, and, especially, ballads. An expert in paleography, he was an exacting researcher. Novák points out that

---

[44] For the latest status of the now acknowledged forgery, see Mojmír Otruba "Rukopisy královédvorský a zelenohorský. Dnesní stav poznání," *Sborník Národního muzea v Praze* 100-13/14 (Prague: n.p., 1969), and Miroslav Ivanov, *Záhada rukopisu královédvorokého* (Prague: n.p., 1970).
[45] Antonín Měšťan, *Geschichte der tschechischen Literatur im 19. und 20. Jahrhundert* (Köln: Böhlau Verlag, 1984), p. 63. This and the following quotations from Měšťan are my translations.
[46] Měšťan, p. 75.
[47] Měšťan, p. 76.
[48] Měšťan, pp. 76-77.

the ethnographer in Erben showed the poet how to combine various versions of folk material and how to select [... the best]. It inspired him to supplement Czech materials with poetry taken from the common Slavic treasury; it convinced him that behind the richness of imagination there was something deeper and more significant, perhaps remnants of an old mythology, or the ethical wisdom of Christianity.[49]

Písně národní v Čechách (Folk Songs in Bohemia, 1842-45) attempted successfully to capture the "soul of the nation." Měšťan draws the difference between the gathering efforts of Čelakovský and those of Erben: the latter "is concerned exclusively with collecting genuine folk songs"; the result is an ethnographically accurate record, "while [the poet's own creations], the echoes, are no longer included in the collection."[50]

Erben the poet left us only one slim book of his own folk-inspired poetry. *Kytice* (The Bouquet, 1853) contains only twelve ballads, but they assured their author a lasting place in the Romantic Pantheon. "Svatební košile" (Wedding Gowns) is one of the best variants on the "specter bridegroom" theme of *Lenore*. It comes close to outdoing the paradigm of the gruesome irruption of demonic forces into the simple, pious life of an innocent bride-never-to-be. Novák comments on the *Bouquet*:

Destructive passions and mysterious guilts drive human fate into the embrace of [...] dark forces, so that man finds himself at the very edge of tragedy.

The influence of Bürger, Herder, and Goethe is obvious. However, "Erben the moralist and humanist"

found optimistic solutions, allowing the world of darkness and passion to be conquered by a clear moral Christian order.

Vying with the labors of the Brothers Grimm, Erben published *České pohádky* (Czech Fairy Tales, 1863-65), again a faithful *Nacherzählung*, "tale-retelling, in the spirit of the nation from which they had been born."[51]

The only master poet to emulate Erben's brilliant but scant contribution was the quintessential Romantic and *beau ténébreux*, Harel Hynek Mácha (1810-35). His *Máj* (May, 1836) "a lyrico-epic poem with balladic interludes," according to Měšťan, may have

scandalized contemporaries [... but] it is today generally regarded as the starting point of a totally new development in Czech poetry.

It is also the first work of modern Czech letters which, with the exception, perhaps, of Erben's *Bouquet*, found a deserved place among masterpieces of world literature. As to its classification, it belongs to the category of *Burg-und-Schauerromantik* (castle-and-horror Romanticism); aside from personally-inspired lyricism it is a product of a glorified knightly past only slightly molded by folk-

---

[49] Novák, pp. 151-52.
[50] Měšťan, p. 81.
[51] Novák, p. 152.

loric materials. Although Mácha's early inspiration can be traced to Czech folksongs, the predominant strain that guides his Muse is the dilemma between

> the loveliness and indifference of Nature [which he experienced] just as passionately as the bondage of his enslaved nation, powerless in the face of a glorious, elegiac past.[52]

Perhaps nowhere else did the marriage of folklore, truly heroic history, the rise of Romantic enthusiasm, and ethnic renascence produce a more intensive creative surge than in the cultural sphere of the former Yugoslavia. Vuk Stefanović Karadžić (1787-1864), founder of the modern Serbo-Croatian literary language, published in Vienna *Mala prostonarodna Slaveno-serbska pesnarica* (Little Slaveno-Serbian Songbook for the Common Folk, 1814). The self-styled "Illyrians,"[53] a group of enthusiasts for their hard-tried Slavonian, Croatian, and Dalmatian past, launched a manifesto in Zagreb entitled *Danicza Horvatzka, Slavonzka y Dalmatinzka* (The Croatian, Slavonian, and Dalmatian Day-Star, 1835). It set off a vogue of collecting folkloric materials among all Southern Slav ethnic groups. The first slim volume was followed by a second in 1815, until, in Albert B. Lord's words, "a classical collection began to appear in 1823."[54] Petar II Petrović Njegoš (1813-51), Prince Bishop and spiritual as well as secular leader of Montenegro, collected his region's epic songs. Lord summarizes the collecting efforts aimed at reviving the ethnic consciousness through folkloric materials in Croatia. Somewhat later (in 1850),

> *Bosanski Prijatelj* (The Bosnian Friend), under the editorship of I.F. Jukić Banjalučanin, published a number of folk epics [...]. In 1879, the Matica Dalmatinska Society published a *Narodna pjesmarica* (Popular Songbook) [...]. The popular poetry, especially the Vuk [Karadžić] collection, had an important impact on Croatian, Serbian, and Montenegrin literature. It was widely imitated, and its form was influential in shaping the style of literary poetry, both narrative and lyric, throughout the century and even later. Some of its subjects – Kosovo, Marko Kraljevic, the *hayduk* (lore),[55] [... were] used by the Illyrian Petar Preradović (1818-72).[56]

France Prešeren (1800-49), the national poet of Slovenia, went for the plot of his epic *Krst pri Savici* (Baptism – actually Conversion – at the Savica [River], 1836) back to ancient Slovene his-

---

[52] Novák, p. 159. Actually measured by the norm of the recently terminated Communist-imposed bondage that has lasted forty-one years, the demeaning second-rate citizen status that the Czechs faced under the Austro-Hungarian empire could be hardly called enslavement. The term of a three-century long nightmare that bores one to a slow death might be in order as definition of the Czech nation's lot under the inept Habsburg rule.

[53] Illyria was an ancient region in Southeastern Europe encompassing Slavonia (North-Western Yugoslavia), Western Croatia, and Dalmatia, a 350-mile long coastal strip on the eastern shore of the Adriatic Sea.

[54] Lord obviously utilizes the term classical not in the sense of a literary movement such as *Klassik-classicisme*, or one denoting works of Graeco-Roman antiquity, but rather in what regards first-rate historical significance and exemplarity. Albert B. Lord, "The Nineteenth-century Revival of National Literatures: Karadžić, Njegoš, Radičević, the Illyrians and Prešeren," in *The Multinational Literature of Yugoslavia*, ed. Albert B. Lord, *Review of National Literatures*, V, no. 1, (Spring 1974), pp. 101-11.

[55] Kosovo Polye, the plain of Kosovo, located in today's Autonomous Province of Kosovo-Metohija, is a 50 mile long plain, where in 1389 Murad I's Turkish host defeated the Serbs, Albanians, and Bosnians under Lazar I, Czar of Serbia. The defeat put an end to the Serbian state and brought the nation under Turkish suzerainty. Marko Kraljević (Prince Marko) was a semi-legendary hero of Serbian and Bulgarian epic lays. The oldest record in which appears Marko's name are the writings of the sixteenth-century chronicler P. Hektorović of Dubrovnik. Marko was supposedly a son of King Vukašin (1356-71), the next-to-last ruler of independent Serbia. Right after the disaster at Kosovo, some half a dozen epic folk songs sprang up, sung by the wandering *guslars* (bards). This "Kosovo cycle" complements the Marko Kraljević cycle. Hayduks were outlaw patriots that carried on guerilla warfare in the centuries-long resistance of Balkan Christians against the Turkish occupants.

[56] Lord, in Lord, ed., pp. 105-6.

tory: the Christians conquer a heathen fortress and obtain the enemy chieftain's voluntary conversion to Christianity.

The Serbian poet Branko Radičević (1824-53) published his first lyrical poems in 1847. A passionate revolutionary in the turbulent years of 1848-49, he also seconded the linguistic reform efforts of Vuk Karadžić. Although influenced by Byron, Heine, and the neoclassicist Serbian lyric poetry of the eighteenth century, his optimistic, simple and spontaneous lyrical vein paralleled linguistically and stylistically folk poetry. He alternated explicit love lyrics with Romantic epics such as *Hajdukov grob* (The Hayduk's Grave), a defiant last stand of a *hayduk* and his girlfriend, who choose suicide over surrender to the Turks. Petar Preradović (1818-72) was a Croatian in Austrian military service and author of fervent patriotic lyrics such as *Pyervyye pesni* (First Songs, 1847) and *Novye Pesni* (New Songs, 1851). Lord describes Preradović's "Djed i unuk" (Grandfather and Grandson) as a poem breathing with

> romantic spirit of times when men saw the folk epic and the one-string *gusle* as symbols of the heroic and the heritage of the past.[57]

His lyrical works *Prvenci* (The First Ones, 1846) and *Nove pjesme* (New Songs, 1851) round out the Romantic flowering of poetry as reverberation of a powerful and lasting folksong patrimony among the South Slavs.

Romanticism was late in coming to Bulgaria. Its inception is closely tied to the struggle for independence from the Turkish yoke and the stabilization of Bulgarian as a literary language. All these efforts and concerns were embodied in the person of the Macedonian-born Petko Račov Slaveikov (1827-95),[58] who gained fame as publicist, rouser of Bulgarian ethnic consciousness, and moving force in the genesis of modern national literature. After the liberation of Bulgaria from Turkish rule (1878), he became head of the Liberal Party. He published his first book of poetry in 1850.

His *Smesena Kitka* (Mixed Bouquet) of fervent patriotic lyrics, couched in the style of folk song and ballad, came out in 1852. Another significant figure in the struggle for independence, Georgi Stoikov Rakovski (1818-67), revolutionary publicist, organizer of partisan warfare against the Turks, historiographer, ethnographer, archeologist, political agitator, author of fantastic works *tour à tour*, produced one work of lasting significance titled *Gorski Putnik* (The Forest Traveler, 1855-58), which summarized its author's principal activity, that of a revolutionary writer and activist, who patterned his life and work after the time-honored proud and uncompromising way of the *hayduk*, the Balkan answer to Robin Hood.

From the above review of Slavic literatures emerges a basic question whether the correspondences between folklore and characteristic traits of Romanticism express genuine affinity, or an attraction born of deeper mutual differences. Although literary historiography more frequently emphasizes the affinities than the differences, the literature of Romanticism obviously is not identical with folklore, even when it successfully imitates it, and folklore does not become Romantic literature just because the latter moment in the development of literature bears the mark of earlier times. Although the restoration of forgotten values was part of the Romantic program for modern civilization, not one of the Romantics thought that he could by himself become a folk-singer or folk-storyteller – with the exception, perhaps, of the Ukrainian Ševčenko.

---

[57] Lord, in Lord, ed., pp. 110-11.
[58] Čiževskij (p. 151) classifies Slaveikov as a realist, "with tendencies toward modernism."

The differences between Romantic high literature and folklore stand out more clearly if a work of Romantic literature is compared to a literature still connected with folklore. In countries of Southeast Europe the process of disengaging literature from its ecclesiastical, scholarly, and folkloric foundation culminated in the second half of the eighteenth and the early nineteenth century. Thus the new artistic production of the transition period had a *Volkscharakter* (national character), but it also had many of the features of the early Enlightenment – notably a cruder realism and a moralizing tendency. Because it still exhibited folkloric elements, this literature has sometimes been erroneously considered Romantic, whereas in fact Romanticism proper only appeared in these countries when literature completely broke away from folklore. Once the connection to folklore ceased to exist, some new link had to be consciously forged out of the perceived need of reclaiming the essence of something valuable that had been lost. In the actual cultural development in the European East, Romanticism was not the heir but the rediscoverer of folklore. It reshaped folklore elements aesthetically into literature. Romanticism represented the third stage of a triadic movement toward synthesis: folklore – literature – literature and folklore.

The Romantic interest in folklore examined here found specific expression in drama. Although Romanticism did not create a great theater like the Renaissance, Classicism, and the Baroque, it nonetheless dominated the European stage for a considerable time. Its achievements were greatest in intellectual comedy, historical plays, and especially in drama of myth and legend.

As a source for drama, myth was, of course, not a new discovery. The playwrights of Antiquity, the Middle Ages, and Classicism made extensive use of Graeco-Roman myth and Biblical legend. The Romantics differed, however, from all of the preceding dramatic elaborations of myths both in their choice and in their interpretation of mythological material. They chose primarily myths that had become familiar through their own national traditions, and used Hellenic and other ancient mythical motifs mainly in order to exhibit their own philosophical ideas.

Drama with a mythic-legendary foundation was largely the creation of early German Romanticism.[59] Although its immediate effect on European Romantic literature was small, its longer-range influence on Symbolism and twentieth-century Modernism was significant. In the West, the most characteristic dramatizations of myth are the *Romantische Dichtungen* (Romantic Fiction, 1799-1800) of Ludwig Tieck, among which the tragedy *Leben und Tod der heiligen Genoveva* (Life and Death of St. Genoveva, 1800) deserves special attention. It has, with good reason, been considered the highpoint of Tieck's early period and has enjoyed unusual popularity.[60] The kinship of early Romanticism and *Sturm und Drang* is reflected in the work's origin, while in its reception outside Germany we observe the transformation of this example of folkloristic writing into an instrument of national consciousness and liberation. It is known that Tieck became acquainted with the story of Genoveva from the manuscript of *Golo und Genoveva*, a play by the *Sturm und Drang* writer Friedrich Müller (1749-1825), known as Maler Müller.[61] What is less well-known is that Tieck's play

[59] Introduction by Jakob Minor, to Ludwig Tieck, *Werke*, I, ed. J. Minor, in *Deutsche National-Literatur, Historischkritische Ausgabe*, ed. Joseph Kürschner, series 1, vol. 144 (Stuttgart: n.p., n.a.; facsimile rpt., Tokyo: Sansyusya, 1974).

[60] See Nadežda Andreeva, "Mnogostradalna Genoveva – ot srednovekovnata legenda do balgarskata vasroždenska szena" (Long-suffering Genevieve – From the Medieval Legend to the Bulgarian Renascence Stage), *Yearbook of the Advanced Institute for Theatrical Art* (Sofia), 5 (1961). Actually, according to Mme. de Staël, Schiller and A.W. Schlegel were familiar with Tieck's *Genoveva* version as early as 1801, although Tieck's drama was not published until 1811 (*De L'Allemagne* II, 225). In fact Mme. de Staël wrote her own drama on the subject, titled *Geneviève de Brabant* in 1808 (*Oeuvres complètes* XVI).

[61] *Golo und Genoveva*, in *Maler Müllers Werke* (Heidelberg: Mohr & Zimmer, 1811).

was disseminated in translation and adaptation in Southeast Europe, where it played a considerable role in stimulating the development of theater in the period of National Revival. It is remarkable that this one folkloric legend received many and very different dramatic interpretations – the impact of which varied greatly from nation to nation – throughout Europe during the eighteenth and nineteenth century. Among them are the *Volksschauspiele* (Popular Plays) and puppet plays, school plays in Latin, melodramas, operas, and operettas.[62]

Based on a *Volksbuch* about Countess Genevieve of the Rhine Palatinate, Tieck's version dramatizes a popular legend, the historical authenticity of which cannot be fully established. The folk-

---

[62] Genoveva of Brabant was one of the most famous figures of popular German literature. A daughter of the Duke of Brabant, she was married to the Count Palatine Siegfried. Accused falsely of adultery, she spent six years as a hermit with her infant son in a forest cave, until her husband, by then convinced of her innocence, found her while hunting and reinstated her. The Jesuit René de Cérisier, chaplain of Louis XIV, wrote a novel entitled *L'Innocence reconue* (Innocence Recognized) which elaborated the Genoveva legend (*L'Innocence reconue*, Paris: Bibliothèque Bleue, 1638). The following is an incomplete list of editions, re-editions and recastings of the Genoveva legend.

German editions:
> Christoph von Schmid, *Genovefa* (Augsburg: Veith, 1825).
> Christoph von Schmid, *Genoveva* (Leipzig: Anton, n.d.).
> Friedrich Hebbel, *Genoveva*, Tragödie, 1843.
> Robert Schumann, *Genoveva*, Oper in vier Akten nach Tieck und Friedrich Hebbel (Leipzig: Peters, 1880).
> *Genoveva*, nach Christoph von Schmid (Hillsboro, Kansas: Fast, 1898-1904).
> Hanna Rademacher, *Golo und Genovefa*, Drama in drei Aufzügen (Leipzig: Wolf, 1914).
> *Genoveva, nach Christoph Schmid und Ludwig Tieck* (Gordonville, PA: Gordonville Print, 1969).

Spanish editions:
> H.C. Granch, *Genoveva de Brabante por el canónigo Schmid* (n.p.: Maucci/Spain, n.d.).
> Christoph von Schmid, *Genoveva de Brabante* (México D.F.: Medina, n.d.).
> Alfonso de Lamartine, *Genoveva* (Madrid: Ramos, 1900, 1990).
> Cristóbal Schmid, *Genoveva de Bratante* (San Antonio, TX: Librería de Quiroga, 1920, 1929).
> Cristóbal Schmid, *Genoveva de Brabante* (San Antonio, TX: Lozano, 1924).
> Christoph von Schmid, *Genoveva* (México, D.F.: Hermano, 1944).
> Christoph von Schmid, *Genoveva de Brabante* (Santiago de Chile: Zig-zag, 1950).
> Christoph von Schmid, *Genoveva de Brabante* (México, D.F.: El Libro Español, 1960).
> Christoph von Schmid, *Genoveva* (México, D.F.: Cuauhtemoc, 1960, 1968).
> Christoph von Schmid, *Genoveva de Brabante* (Barcelona: Mateu, 1965).
> Christoph von Schmid, *Genoveva de Brabante* (Barcelona: Bruguera, 1956, 1970, 1956, 1972).
> Christoph von Schmid, *Genoveva de Brabante* (México, D.F.: Latino-Americana, 1973, 1981).
> Christoph von Schmid, *Genoveva de Brabante* (Buenos Aires: Difusión, 1977).
> Christopher Schmid, *Genoveva de Brabante* (Barcelona: Editors, S.A.).
> Christopher Schmid, *Genoveva de Brabante* (Barcelona: Ediciones Toray, 1981).

Swedish:
> Christoph von Schmid, *Genovefa* (Chicago: Holmberg, 1888).
> *Genoveva* (Stockholm: Askerberg, 1910).

Croatian:
> Christoph von Schmid, *Genoveva* (Zagreb: n.p., n.d.).

Polish:
> *Genowefa*: powiastka moralna z dawnych czas. (n.pl., n.p., 1910).

Slovene:
> Christoph von Schmid, *Genovefa*; povest iz starih časov: (Ljubljana: Blaznik, 1890).

Ukrainian:
> *Genovefa* (Winnipeg, Manitoba: Ruskoi Knygarni, 1919).
> *Genovefa* (Kyiv: Ukrainska nakladnia, 1917/1977).

Lithuanian:
> Christoph von Schmid, *Genovaite* (Kaunas: Sviesos, 1937).

Sorbian:
> Christoph von Schmid, *Genovefa* (Bautzen/Germany: Znak, 1861).

lore material is treated freely and in an original way, despite the evident influence of Shakespeare, Goethe, and Müller. The play manifests familiar elements of Romanticism: a return to the past (in this case, the Middle Ages); an interest in history (the campaigns of Charles Martel against the Islamic world); a cult of feeling; a mystic faith in providence (Golo); a quest for the unusual and exceptional that transcends the boundaries of human capacities (Golo, Genoveva); and a childlike experience of religion. Moreover, the dramatic form also typifies Romantic aesthetics: the abandonment of Classical poetic rules; the dissolution of the boundaries between drama, lyric, and epic; the union of poetry with music and painting; and the device of a play within the play.

The folk legend, with its formal uncommittedness, proved to be a most favorable material for the construction of a Romantic drama, although Tieck's experimental effort struck the general public of the nineteenth century as hard to stage and hard to read.

A brief yet systematic catalog is in order of Romantically inspired dramas which were an integral part of the effort to revive a past more grand than the political, social, and cultural hardly satisfactory *status quo* of the Slav countries in the age of the unfolding Romantic spirit.

Discussion of the Russian and Polish drama (as was the case with the lyric and epic folklorizing poetry) should initiate the analysis of the function of the theater among Slavs for two reasons. These literatures evidence most clearly the debt to Western thought and the impact of high literature on public opinion.

Pushkin's *Boris Godunov* (1831), a powerful drama of the haunted usurper of the Russian throne, outshone not only the poet's own dramatic efforts like *Kamyennyy Gost* (The Stone Guest, 1825; 1830), a brief, four-scene version of the Don Juan legend,[63] and *Rusalka* (The Water Nymph, 1832) which draws on Slav folklore, but became an archetype of Romantic drama elsewhere in Central and Eastern Europe. His *Cygany* (The Gypsies, 1827) is a dramatized tale in verse; attuned to the Romantic yen for vagabond existence, direct action, and scorn for logically explicable motivation, it would hardly qualify as a playable drama. Lermontov's juvenilia – *Ispancy* (The Spaniards), the German-titled *Menschen und Leidenschaften* (Men and Passions), and *Strannyy čelověk* (A Strange Man), written between 1830-36 – combine, according to Guy Daniels,

> passionate "social protest" with dramatization of that metaphysical revolt which [...] is at bottom the subject of all [of Lermontov's] works.[64]

The characters are unidimensional and all "black and white"; needless to say, Lermontov's teenage drama made precious little *bruit* in the theatrical world anywhere. Far from drawing for inspiration on folklore, his *Maskarad* (Masked Ball, 1842) belongs to the subgenre of gambler-dramas[65] à la Pushkin's tale *The Queen of Spades* (1833).

Polish drama of the Romantic period reflects a bent for a collective-hero-martyr concept of that nation's past. Parts II and IV of Mickiewicz's *Dziady* (Forefathers' Eve), both published in 1823, are characterized by Manfred Kridl as a typical product of the inspiration provided by

---

[63] Pushkin followed Da Ponte's operatic libretto more closely, rather than Tirso de Molina's version of 1616.
[64] Guy Daniels, ed., *A Lermontov Reader* (New York: Macmillan, 1965), p. 25.
[65] M.J. Lermontov, *Sobraniye sochinyeniy*, vol. III, Dramy (Moskva: Khudozhestvennaya Lityeratura, 1965), p. 548.

the realm of folk beliefs [... Part II features] three dramatized ballads [that offer a] kind of operatic spectacle.[66]

Though obviously not stageworthy in their basically balladic form, the high quality of language, verse, and inspiration, unusual even for a poet of Mickiewicz's caliber, qualifies them as a model of dramatic achievement, inspired by a folklorically rich past.

The princes of the bona-fide stage drama in Romantic Poland are indisputably Słowacki and Krasiński. The first is the father of modern Polish drama. *Kordian* (1834) is an anti-heroic tableau of the Polish generation of Słowacki's contemporaries. *Balladyna* (1834, pb. 1839) evokes Poland's prehistory. A dramatic legend, its tenor owes more to Shakespeare than to Polish folklore. Other plays like *Horsztyński* and *Złota czazka* (The Golden Skull), both dating from 1840, are classified by Kridl as "romantic realism."[67] *Mazepa* (1840) harks back to the power play between the Cossack *hetman* Mazepa, Peter the Great, and the political ambitions of Sweden's Charles XII.[68] *Ojciec Marek* (Father Mark, 1843) dramatizes the spiritual triumph of the Polish Confederation over the Russians achieved with supernatural help.[69] Krasiński's *Nieboska komedia* (The Undivine Comedy, 1833, pb. 1835) is, according to Kridl,

[a] mixture of the natural and supernatural worlds [where figure] symbolic and fantastic characters [mixed with] lyrical elements [...] The Romantic accessories disappear almost completely [...]. Presented here is a truly prophetic vision of the social class struggle, of the conflict [without compromise ... between] the remnants of the moribund aristocracy [... and] the masses of the disinherited, exploited and suffering [...].[70]

Like *Irydion* (1836), an embodiment of Hellenism attempting to crush Rome, Krasiński's *Undivine Comedy* reached beyond the Romantic mode and folk inspiration.

What has been said about Norwid's innovative experiments in language and poetic approach in his non-dramatic works applies likewise to his dramas. Plays like *Kleopatra* (in *Chimera*, 1829) and *Tyrtej* (Tyrtaeus, 1865)[71] present not so much great personalities as the power of tradition, beliefs, and sociopolitical conditions.[72] Norwid's efforts drew widely on world history and axial ages of cultural flowering, rather than on moments of concretized popular tradition.

Ševčenko's predecessor in the shaping of modern Ukrainian literature was Ivan Kotlyarevsky (1769-1838) who wrote a Ukrainian spoof on Vergil's *Aeneid* (*Eneida*, 1798) that became an instant success. He produced, in 1819 in his own theater at Poltava, his *Natalka Poltavka*, "an opera in two acts," which is, actually, a sort of operetta. Manning indicates it "contains many elements [...] typi-

---

[66] Kridl, p. 161. The ex-post-facto reestablished part I of *Dziady*, couched in narrative form, explains the title of all four parts as derived from "an ancient folk ceremony indigenous to [... Novogrodek, a little town in Lithuania] where the poet was born, held in honor of the memory of dead ancestors." (p. 166.)

[67] Kridl, p. 210.

[68] Ivan Stepanovič Mazepa (1644?-1709) was a Polish-educated scion of a Ukrainian noble family who rose to *hetman* (military commander and political leader) of Cossack Ukraine. At first Peter the Great's ally against the Turks and Swedes, Mazepa threw in with Charles XII of Sweden, hoping to stave off Russia's expansionist policy. Defeated together with the Swedes at Poltava in 1709, he assured what he was trying to prevent: the permanent crushing of Ukrainian autonomy.

[69] Like the drama *Horsztyński* (1840) and the dramatic fragment *Beniowski* (1841) the Polish Bar-Confederation at the time of the First Partition of Poland by Prussia, Austria, and Russia in 1772 attracted Słowacki's dramatic Muse.

[70] Kridl, p. 278.

[71] Tyrtaeus was a seventh-century Greek elegiac poet, commander-in-chief of the Spartans in the Second Messenian war, and author of popular marches.

[72] Kridl, p. 248.

cal of the Franco-Italian plays of the period," as well as stock characters that go back to classical antiquity; nevertheless, in a non-heroic way, Kotlyarovsky "boldly emphasized various qualities of the Ukrainian temper."[73] *Moskal Charivnik* (The Muscovite Wizzard) was produced in the same year as *Natalka*. It exercises indirect literary criticism (the Moskals-Muscovites do not know how to depict the Ukrainian character and manners) and ridicules Russified Ukrainians. Hryhorii Kvitka-Osnovianenko (1778-1843) wrote dramas for the Kharkov stage. His *Šelmenko denščik* (Shelmenko the Orderly, 1831) is a sort of bilingual comedy, in which the hero consistently speaks Russian, while the orderly Šelmenko usually speaks Ukrainian. The villain, a corrupt village clerk, who has maneuvered the hero into military service, typifies the Ukrainian upstarts who shy from nothing to escape their Ukrainian-peasant background. The comedy *Priyesči iz stolicy* (The Man Who Came from the Regional Capital, 1827, pb. 1840) may have inspired Gogol's *Inspector General*. Ševčenko himself tried his hand at drama. Zaitsev notes that by 1842, Ševčenko

> tried to translate into Ukrainian *Danilo Reva* or *Nazar Stodolia*, a play he had written in Russian [... in order to stage it] by Easter of 1843. [...] It is doubtful whether *Nazar Stodolia* had actually been performed.[74]

As evident from the above examples, Romantic drama in the Ukraine did not expand beyond the field of comedy.

The Czech drama of the Romantic era did not actually grow out of the country's rich folkloric substratum per se. As in Spain after the end of the *década ominosa* (the "Ominous Decade" of political and cultural reaction) which ended with the death of Fernando VII in 1833, it drew on a glorified mythical and medieval past. Unfortunately, the Czech lands could not fall back on the rich and deeply rooted dramatic tradition of a *Siglo de oro*, which made the renascence of the Spanish national theater a matter of legitimate national pride. Czech theater of the early eighteen hundreds, the period of national reawakening and cultural renascence, did not produce a world-class grand tragedy, nor, for that matter, a comedy that would bear periodic restaging. For plots the authors of national "historic" plays had recourse to Bohemia's Romanticized prehistory and, predominantly, to the Middle Ages. The comic-didactic genre showed realist traits from the start: the Czech no-nonsense approach to just about everything under the sun showed sobriety tinged with hope in a brighter future especially in drama, while the lyrico-epic genres developed more closely along the lines of the *Burg-und-Nachtromantik* (Castle-and-Night Romanticism) that flourished in the rest of Europe, both East and West. Biedermeier aesthetics and an encouraging *costumbrismo*, rather than the comedy of manners,[75] would best describe the chief traits and thrust of Czech Romantic theater.

Václav Kliment Klicpera (1792-1859), professor at a Prague Academic Gymnasium (the equivalent of the French *Lycée*-prep-school) had nurtured a number of future poets of Bohemia, many of whom, like Jan Neruda (1834-91), were destined, by inclination and their age, to embrace the tenets of literary realism. Měšťan lists among Klicpera's contributions

---

[73] Manning, p. 31. The play came back to be staged off and on for the next hundred years.

[74] Pavlo Zaitsev, *Taras Shevchenko: A Life*, ed. and trans. by George S.N. Luckyj (Toronto: Univ. of Toronto Press, 1988), pp. 109-10.

[75] While *costumbrismo*, as indicated in the text, represents, usually in a flattering manner, the way certain ethnic groups of a nation, certain classes, and professions behave, including some quaint, innocuous aberrations, it usually lacks the barbs with which the comedy of manners bristles, unless, of course, such *costumbrismo* loses its predominant, descriptive objectivity, giving way to a prescriptive, vituperative attack on specific vices.

historical narratives in W. Scott's spirit; yet of the highest merit are his numerous plays which were staged starting in 1818. The pre-Romantic bent of his dramas and topics from Czech mythology and history assured him the same great popularity, as did his comedies laced with satire and farces [lashing out at] his age. A few of his plays are performed to this day.[76]

His historical tragedy *Blaník*[77] (1813, premiered 1816) would not bear a stage production in the twentieth century. Arne Novák calls the plays representing four decades of Klicpera's "theatrical adaptation" of Czech "historical events and legends" crude, due to their lack of "compositional unity and psychological depths."[78] However, the farces *Divotvorný klobouk* (The Wonderworking Hat, 1817), *Rohovín Čtverrohý* (a proper name that is an untranslatable alliterative calembour, something in the order of "Corniform Foursquare," 1812), *Hadrián z Římsů* (another calembour, roughly, Hadrian Fitzcornice, 1821), and *Komedie na mostě* (The Comedy on the Bridge, 1826) have, according to Novák, "vitality in spite of a patina of quaintness more than a century old."[79]

Josef Kajetán Tyl (1808-56) was undoubtedly the most gifted among the Romantic playwrights of Bohemia. This pupil of Klicpera's was "a proper representative of sentimental Romanticism" and the closest to a folk-inspired artist. Unlucky as a state official,

journalist, director of the State Theater [in Prague], actor and head of a traveling theatrical company, he was destroyed by the very segment of society he chose to depict [i.e., the petty bourgeoisie].[80]

This selfless, passionate idealist in the service of Czech national reawakening was repeatedly attacked, often savagely, by his fellow-patriots. His populist *Fidlovačka* (May Fest or Spring Festival, 1834) not only gave Bohemia, and, eventually, Czechoslovakia, its anthem "Kde domov můj?" (Where is My Homeland?); it was a farcical representation of lower- and middle-class *costumbrismo*, rather than a mirror of folk ways.[81] The topics of his historical dramas tapped the turbulent fifteenth century's religious and social upheavals filled with conflicts between the Utraquist Hussite countryside and the predominantly Catholic burghers.[82] These dramas focused on the plights of the miners of Kutná Hora, on the martyrdom of Jan Hus and the Lord's Hussite mace Jan Žižka. Tyl addressed the late-medieval generation gap in *Měšťané a studenti* (Burghers and Students, 1850). Another dramatic subgenre that Tyl brought to near perfection was the dramatic fable, a well-balanced mix of realist detail and the irruption of the magical. The ambience of *Strakonický dudák* (The Bagpiper of Strakonice, 1846) belongs to this twilight sphere.[83] With it, Tyl succeeded in tapping the deep founts of Czech folklore. Novák claims affinity for Tyl's synthesis of "dream, illusion and life" with the Viennese popular theater of Ferdinand Raimund (1790-1836). These plays might be

---

[76] *Měšťan*, p. 90 n.

[77] Like Mount Kyffhäuser (Thuringia) in German lore, which houses the sleeping Emperor Friedrich Barbarossa and his knights, who will rise when Germany's need will be most pressing, Mount Blaník is the shelter of King Venceslas and his knights, who will ride again in Bohemia's hour of direst distress.

[78] Novák, p. 154.

[79] Novák, p. 154.

[80] Novák, p. 154.

[81] Bourgeois life and crises are the topic of *Paličova dcera* (The Incendiary's Daughter, 1846) and *Pražský flamendr* (The Prague Carouser, 1846).

[82] The Utraquists or Calixstenes insisted on communion in both species (of bread *and* wine) and basically demanded reforms in the 1420s that were to be introduced by Vatican II.

[83] *Jiříkovo videní* (Georgie's Vision, 1846) belongs to the same semi-spectral realm.

the final outcropping of the Baroque drama in Bohemia, a drama not of the Shakespearean but Calderonian type otherwise so rare in [... the Bohemian] land. [Yet ...] not even [these] dramatic fables left a
permanent imprint upon Czech theatrical tradition.[84]

Tyl's bourgeois background provided no firsthand experience with the world of the aristocracy. His
drama *Poslední Čech* (The Last Czech, 1844) failed because of "schematization and barren stereo-
typing" in its characterization of the *beau monde*. The "patriotic clichés"[85] of the play brought down
on Tyl the wrath of the younger, more Realist-oriented generation.

Karel Hynek Mácha's lyrico-epic genius was not given enough time to mature into the epic
sweep and psychological depth needed for great drama. He planned historical dramas on the grand
scale of a Shakespeare and Schiller, representing the tragic fate of key figures of Czech history.
Měšťan indicates that the extant fragments show an extremely loose handling of historical fact.

One cannot deny this aficionado of the theater and amateur actor the feel for the dramatic. [He knew
full well] that he would have by far outdone all that had been so far achieved in Czech dramatic production [...] Yet he never finished a single one of his dramatic projects.[86]

With Mácha's death perished all chances for the Czech Romantic drama to reach the level of world
literature.

The most significant playwright among the Southern Slavs during the Romantic age was without doubt the Prince-Bishop Njegoš of Montenegro. His chef d'oeuvre *Gorski Vijenac* (The Mountain Wreath, 1847) is, in Lord's words,

solidly based on the folk epic, which he himself had collected and imitated. [... It] is his most arresting
work, a poetic drama written around a historic event of the latter part of the eighteenth century, the
killing of the Moslemized Montenegrins by their Christian brothers under Prince-Bishop Danilo.

Lažni car Sćepan Mali (The False Czar Stephen the Little, 1851) is Njegoš's last drama, depicting
the arrival in Montenegro of "an impostor pretending to be the fugitive Russian Czar Peter III."
Though tighter knit than the *Wreath*, and equally powerful in the evocation of "the Montengrin
heroic milieu [...], it does not reach the heights of [the earlier drama]."[87]

Two more dramas of the period worth mentioning are both by the Croatian Petar Preradović
(1818-72). Like Njegoš's plays, they are poetic dramas dealing with the glorious if bloody and sad
past of the Southern Slavs. *Marko Kraljević* (Prince Marko, 1851) is cast in the role of a militant
secular Messiah, coming to save his oppressed people. *Vladimir i Kosara* (Vladimir and Kosara)
dramatizes a tale

told in the *Ljetopis Popa dukljanina* collection of the twelfth century, a story of love and intrigue and
tragic betrayal and vengeance.[88]

The verve, sweep, and powerful language of these dramas certainly warrant a place for them in
world literature in spite of their relative inaccessibility due to the language barrier.

---

[84] Novák, pp. 155-56.
[85] Novák, p. 156.
[86] Měšťan, p. 88.
[87] Lord, in Lord, ed., pp. 108-9.
[88] Lord, in Lord, ed., p. 111.

In Bulgaria *Mnogostradalna Genoveva* (Long-suffering Genevieve), a dramatization of the novella *Genovefa* by Christoph von Schmid (1768-1854),[89] enjoyed continuous success over several decades ever since the première of its Bulgarian adaptation in 1875. This Bulgarian version, the first public staging of any play in Bulgaria under Turkish rule, at first attracted attention by its sentimental moralizing content; later – for a very short period – it came to epitomize the dream of political liberation by being interpreted as a naive revolutionary allegory.[90] One reason for the spread of this drama and its lasting presence on the stage was without doubt the folkloric character of its subject, for although the legend refers to foreign events, it contained many elements familiar in European folklore in general, e.g., the motif of the slandered wife, of persecuted and triumphant innocence, frequently encountered in Southern Slavic folk poetry, a basic age-old dramatic conflict recognizable to Bulgarian audiences. However, the Bulgarian struggle for national liberation urged an interpretation of the subject matter very different from that of Tieck and Early German Romanticism. This new attitude, though not alien to Romanticism, pushed the Romantic concept of national spirit more emphatically in a political direction, allowing the articulation of the emerging self-consciousness of oppressed peoples in patriotic Romantic literature.[91]

The Bulgarian drama of the National Revival period is a good example of the social *engagement* of the Romantics and their sense for history. The process of awakening a national consciousness and the struggles for political liberation were guiding forces of the cultural development in the early period of approaching independence. They determined the specific character of Bulgarian literary Romanticism and its attitude to folklore and history. Hence links with foreign literatures were a necessary condition for Bulgarian literature becoming integrated into the general European literary process. However, artistic phenomena developed largely in an independent fashion and showed kinship of a typological rather than a genetic variety with parallel phenomena in other European countries. It is interesting to note that the historical dramas by Drumiev and Voinikov,[92] whose

---

[89] Christoph von Schmid, *Leben und sonderbare Schicksale der frommen Gräfin Genovefa die heilige genannt* (Solbrug: n.p., 1806).

[90] Dobri Vičev's essay "Methodologische Fragen der Rezeption der deutschen Literatur in Bulgarien bis 1878. Christoph von Schmid und die bulgarische Wiedergeburt," *Bulgaronemecki literaturni i kulturni vzaimootnošenia pres XVIII i XIX vek* (Sofia: Izdatelstvo na Bulgarskata Akademia na naukite, 1985), p. 152, n. 14, indicates that

> claims (like N. Andreeva's study of 1960), concerning the staging of *Genoveva* in the age of the Bulgarian Rebirth, that the play [...] stimulated revolutionary feelings in the Bulgarian audience (due to the content, absent from the text itself, but which the audience read into the play), may have relevance in this particular case, but may not be regarded as a rule and thus be generalized [...]. Likewise no one would have tried in 1875 [i.e., three years before Bulgaria's gaining independence from Turkey] to present a play instigating to rebellion, such as Voinikov's *Voivoda Stojan*, and disguised under the title *The Much-Suffering Genoveva*, in order to deceive Turkish authorities. (Translation by M.J.H.).

Vičev does not mention the name or names of the translator or adaptor of Schmid's play, but supplies us at least with the date of its première. Vičev stresses Schmid's popularity in Bulgaria, which equalled that of the German *Volksbücher* (chapbooks) and had "a relatively strong impact on public opinion":

> a dramatized version of Schmid's sentimental-Romantic tale *Genoveva* [enjoyed extreme popularity] and this not entirely due to the fact that it was the very first theatrical presentation in Bulgaria [... for] it allowed the Bulgarian audience to identify with the lot of the hard-tried countess, offering hope for [eventually] seeing right and justice done. (p. 152, n. 14).

[91] Byron notes that he had himself heard the tale of the *Giaour* from a native story-teller: "[...] I heard it by accident recited by one of the coffeehouse story-tellers who abound in the Levant, and sing or recite their narratives." *The Poetical Works of Lord Byron* (London: Warner, New York: Scribner, Welford, and Armstrong, n.d.), p. 187.

[92] Drumiev was a direct participant in Bulgaria's national liberation movement. Politically he was a Russophile militating for closer ties between Bulgaria and Russia; the world view and style of his dramas was, however, realist. Voinikov, aside from being a playwright and dramatic producer was, generally speaking, an enlightener of the Bulgarian people. In spite of their artistic mediocrity, his plays served as a beacon in Bulgaria's liberation movement.

education and varied cultural associations made them susceptible chiefly to the influence of French literature, stood nevertheless closer to Scott and Shakespeare, than to Hugo and Corneille. It is true that the national-patriotic element was a dominant factor, but, at the same time, the dramas of these Bulgarian patriots breathe with the spirit of history, the same as the novels of Walter Scott, something that is absent in the historical drama of French *classicisme* and Romanticism. Bulgarian dramas of the Romantic period evolved under the influence of folkloric creativity and imagination, drawing on historical legends and songs about *yunaks* (heroes), *hayduks*, and *tsars* of the past in the same manner that Scott's fiction was enriched by his appreciation of the Scottish folk ballad. Quite often the historical tale displaces historical truth, but even then the plot is fed by the heroic and the historical, rather than by the mythical *vis epica*. Much later, after Bulgaria's liberation (1878), there emerges a drama informed by a national mythology and folklore. And yet, the Romantic spirit is absent; in its stead, general trends in modern aesthetics assert themselves, characteristic of the whole of European literature at the turn of the nineteenth and twentieth centuries.

Perhaps the most interesting part of Romantic dramaturgy is the so-called "Theater of the Mind." Its preferred genre was comedy, and its principal medium Romantic irony. Here, too, folklore could offer advantages to Romantic authors whose aesthetic code insisted on creative freedom. Tieck was among those who grasped the new generic logic of breaking all the rules of rationalist drama and asserting the primacy of the imagination. By creating a theatrical game, apparently subject only to the alogical rules of children's games and stories, and by indulging in the lost pleasures and satisfactions of childhood, the poet unabashedly reveals the nature of dramatic illusion and explores our inner, uncensored relation to art. The theater plays with itself, with reality, and with the spectators, swinging them between the poles of knowledge and ignorance. Romantic drama often realizes the denial of all canons of traditional aesthetics and the unmasking of all illusion founded on reason – including theatrical illusion – by means of the "play within the play." The rather demanding theater of the mind (demanding because of its avant-garde nature) had no impact on the Slavic world in the Romantic era, with the brilliant exception of Krasiński's *The Undivine Comedy*, the chief inspiration for which was Goethe's *Faust*.

The tracing and identification of a variety of connections between the Romantic drama and folklore, and the different ways in which they manifested themselves, contribute not only to the elucidation of the relationship Romanticism-folklore; they also serve to make more precise the periodization of Romanticism as a literary movement and the assessment of its connections with the preceding and the following literary periods, as well as its propagation over the entire European continent.

MARVIN CARLSON

NATIONALISM AND THE ROMANTIC DRAMA IN EUROPE

The roots of modern nationalism and Romanticism are closely intertwined. The Romantic dramatist found in national history, legend, and myth a fertile source of subject matter and in the struggles for national freedom and identification important sources of dramatic power, while the emerging nationalist consciousness found in the Romantic drama a highly useful means for encouraging national enthusiasm, pride, and solidarity. The mainstream of Enlightenment thought ran counter to the separatist spirit of nationalism, viewing a primary identification with a specific people as an out-moded idea, to be replaced by the concept of the citizen of the world, who, as Goethe suggested, placed humanity above all nations. Nevertheless even writers within this mainstream, such as Lessing, contributed significantly to the erosion of the international neoclassic style and thus helped prepare the way for the diverse national expressions of Romantic drama. This was not of course their intention; they attacked the neoclassic style because they felt it was not in fact international enough – it imposed an artificial national taste, the French, on art, which should recognize no such limitations.

The later eighteenth century, however, also saw the rise of a much more radical view, which also attacked French neoclassic hegemony, but precisely in order to allow other specific cultural groups their own possibility of expression. Central to the formulation of this position, as to so much of the counter-tradition that developed into Romanticism, were the theories of Jean-Jacques Rousseau, whose vision of the nation as a confederation of free individuals led him to place a major new moral emphasis on love of the fatherland and on virtue inspired by the commonweal. From Rousseau also came the concept, shared by Montesquieu and developed in French dramatic theory as early as Saint-Evremond, that climate, environment, and historical circumstances created significant differences among the nations. Man is everywhere so modified by religion, government, laws, and customs, Rousseau observed in the *Lettre à M. D'Alembert*, that one can suggest only what sort of theatre "is good in such and such a time or in such and such a country."[1] For Geneva he advocated open-air festivals, gymnastics, and other such innocent celebrations as a reinforcement of communal spirit, but he made quite different recommendations for national festivals in his *Considérations sur le Gouvernment de Pologne*, reflecting the very different circumstances of that nation. Here was a vast country with a rich historical heritage, but surrounded by hostile neighbors and with no natural barriers to their aggression. Rousseau felt that in such circumstances political independence could never be certain and that the Poles should study the means for surviving as a nation even when under the domination of others. "You may not be able to prevent them from swallowing you up, but at least make it impossible for them to digest you." In this 1777 essay he deplored the eighteenth-

[1] Jean-Jacques Rousseau, *Oeuvres*, 25 vols. (Paris: Dupont, 1823-26), II, 21.

century cosmopolitanism that he felt was removing the distinctive features of the French, Germans, Spanish, even the English, and making them all Europeans with "the same tastes, the same passions, the same mores, since none have received a national form through a particular institution."[2] He urged the Poles to set a counter-example, maintaining their national identity, even if conquered, by honoring symbols of their past and Polish historical heroes and by celebrating distinctly Polish national festivals.

In France and in England during the eighteenth century there was a close correspondence between a moderately homogeneous linguistic and cultural group and existing state boundaries. This of course was not at all true of Germany, where ties of language and cultural traditions cut across a complex web of principalities, duchies, and republics, ranging in size from large states to individual cities. Here the ideas of Rousseau took on a coloring quite different from their interpretation in France or England, and emphasis shifted from a distinction between early "natural" confederations and corrupt modern international urban society to one between the "natural nation" – an eternal, organic, almost sacred entity to which people belonged by birth – and the artificial and arbitrary "state," the product of historical accident, dynastic wars and marriages, and political intrigue.

The influence of Rousseau in Germany after the middle of the eighteenth century was immense, and the pre-Romantic *Sturm und Drang* authors drew heavily upon him. His observations on national literature reinforced a growing interest in specifically German poetry, most strikingly represented in the early patriotic odes of Friedrich Gottlieb Klopstock. As early as 1745 Klopstock delivered an address deploring the lethargy of the German people in poetic endeavors and calling for national poetry.[3] The appearance of the Ossian poems in German translation in the early 1760s provided Klopstock and many in his generation with a powerful new stimulus for such activity, and Klopstock's historical drama *Hermanns Schlacht* (Hermann's Battle, 1769) was characterized by its author himself as "bardic." In 1784 and 1787 he added two further plays to complete a trilogy on Hermann, the subject of earlier literary treatments but here presented for the first time as a mythic national hero in drama, protecting the rights and liberties of his people and leading them to victory against the decadent Romans.

In the final number of the *Hamburgische Dramaturgie* (Hamburg Dramaturgy, 1768) Lessing complained of the futility of attempting "to create a national theatre, when we Germans are not yet a nation."[4] Klopstock's *Hermanns Schlacht*, created the following year, was conceived as a means of using theatre itself to aid in the development of this nation. For Klopstock this involved not simply establishing a German national consciousness, but of setting that national consciousness in direct competition with those of rival nations. His reading of Rousseau encouraged Klopstock to see Germany as arising from a people of primeval strength and uncompromised nature, as exemplified by Hermann, while other Romanized states represented the effects of decadent civilization. The emerging German nation he saw as already engaged in "a heated and extended struggle" for supremacy in the intellectual and cultural world against France and England, a struggle that Germany, closer to nature, would inevitably win.[5]

---

[2] Rousseau, V, 257-60.
[3] Friedrich Gottlieb Klopstock, *Sämmtliche sprachwissenschaftliche und ästhetische Schriften*, 6 vols. (Leipzig: Back & Spindler, 1876), IV, 31-35.
[4] Gotthold Lessing, *Gesammelte Werke*, 2 vols. (Munich: Hanser, 1959), II, 759.
[5] Klopstock, *Sämmtliche Werke*, 10 vols. (Leipzig: Göschen, 1854), X, 442.

This concept of the potential superiority of Germanic culture could also be found in the critical writings of Johann Herder, who hailed Klopstock as an original genius equal to Shakespeare and Ossian. In fact, Herder was concerned with the importance of national cultural expression for all peoples, hence his wide-spread importance in subsequent generations to oppressed language groups – the Czechs and Letts, the Serbs and Finns – seeking a cultural identity. "Every nation has its individuality of character and spirit, as of land [...] No man, no country, no people, no history of a people, no state is like any other," he wrote in his *Journal meiner Reise im Jahre 1769* (Journal of My Travels in the Year 1769), devoting several pages to the inevitable differences in the drama of Italy, France, Germany and Russia, reflective of the organic development of each culture.[6]

The young Goethe's interest in the sixteenth-century German figures Götz von Berlichingen and Faust grew directly from his exposure to Herder in 1770 and 1771. Götz, like Hermann, is a free spirit, struggling in vain against an encroaching and inferior new order, who dies betrayed but with the word "Freedom" on his lips. The year 1771 saw, besides Goethe's play, the publication of Herder's collection of essays *Von deutscher Art und Kunst* (Concerning German Style and Art), generally regarded as the manifesto of the *Sturm und Drang*. Its importance in arousing national and patriotic consciousness was at least as important as its solidification of certain literary and artistic trends. Among the essays were one on German architecture by Goethe, one on German folk songs by Herder, and one on German history by Julius Möser, who surpassed Klopstock in arousing the interest of the Germans in their historical heritage.

The German historical dramas of the late eighteenth century however tended to emphasize artistic liberty, in their form, and political liberty, in their depiction of heroic martyrs, rather than the development of a distinctly German consciousness. Schiller speaks in his essay *Die Schaubühne als eine moralische Anstalt betrachtet* (The Stage as a Moral Institution, 1784) of the "enormous influence" of a permanent theatre on the "national spirit of a people,"[7] but even in such apparently patriotic works as *Die Jungfrau von Orleans* (The Maid of Orleans) and *Wilhelm Tell* he was clearly more concerned with the struggle of a Rousseauesque hero against an established despotism than with the possible function of these stories as national or cultural myth. The philosopher and poet, he wrote in 1795, belong "to no people and to no time," but are the "contemporaries of all times."[8]

Goethe, looking back on Klopstock's *Hermann* dramas and his own *Götz* in *Dichtung und Wahrheit* (Truth and Poetry, 1811-12) admitted the potential of such plays to "awaken self-consciousness in a nation," but he considered that the "martial feelings of defiance" they stimulated were dangerous in times of peace, since they encouraged a spirit of rebellion against all authority, legitimate or not.[9]

The obvious conservative bias of this observation does not rob it of a certain validity. In the 1770s and 1780s the German states lacked both a sense of common concern and a common enemy that might have encouraged such a sense. As a result, the spirit of revolt in the *Sturm und Drang* dramas tended to be individualistic, even whimsical. In the early years of the next century, however, the crushing defeats inflicted upon the German states by Napoleonic armies served as a powerful

---

[6] Johann Herder, *Sämtliche Werke*, 33 vols. (Hildesheim: Olms, 1967), IV, 478. In the original: "Jede Nation ihre Reichthümer und Eigenheiten des Geistes, des Characters, wie des Landes hat [...] Kein Mensch, kein Volk, keine Geschichte des Volkes, kein Staat ist dem andern gleich."

[7] Friedrich Schiller, *Werke*, 38 vols. (Weimar: Bohlaus, 1943-75), XX, 99.

[8] Schiller, *Briefe*, 7 vols. (Stuttgart: Deutsche Verlags-Anstalt, n.d.), IV, 111.

[9] J.W. von Goethe, *Aus meinem Leben*, 2 vols. (Berlin: Akademie-Verlag, 1970), I, 442-43.

catalyst for the creation of a German national consciousness. On this question the first generation of Romantics, gathered around the Schlegel brothers at Jena in the years just before the Napoleonic wars, continued to take essentially eighteenth-century positions. Often their thought continued initiatives that were not beholden mainly to French rationalism, but were associated rather with the British and German interest in authentic non-classical attributes of native peoples and in an organic view of cultural evolution. Friedrich Schlegel wrote in his *Jugendschriften* (Youthful Writings, 1797) that the drama should be completely free from national bonds, quite in the spirit of eighteenth-century cosmopolitanism,[10] while his brother August Wilhelm in the *Vorlesungen über die schöne Literatur und Kunst* (Lectures on Literature and Art, 1801-3) echoed Klopstock in idealizing the early Germans and stressing their distinction from the Latin peoples.

After the Jena group dissolved, the center of Romantic activity moved to Heidelberg, where the dominant figures of Clemens Brentano and Achim von Arnim took up with enthusiasm the cause of German culture in their *Des Knaben Wunderhorn* anthology (The Boy's Magic Horn, 1805-8), collecting folk songs and *Märchen* and looking to national myths and legends for poetic inspiration. In his letters to Brentano, Arnim spoke of such material as a means of national education of the German people and of promoting the German language and culture, if necessary even at the expense of rival cultures.[11] Even so, the short-lived Romantic era in Heidelberg was far less oriented toward patriotism than was its successor in Berlin, where both Brentano and Arnim located in 1809. Here the Napoleonic victories over Prussia created a strong community of authors and theorists who firmly rejected the frequently favorable view of the French Revolution held by the early Romantics. Instead they approvingly quoted the condemnations of Edmund Burke and sought to counter the Napoleonic threat with a stimulation of militarism and national pride in the Prussian state.

Schleiermacher, who delivered a series of patriotic sermons in Halle before appearing in Berlin in 1807, and Fichte, who presented here his famous *Reden an die Deutsche Nation* (Address to the German Nation) in 1807 and 1808, were the leaders in this orientation, but most of the literary world in Berlin shared their views. August Schlegel wrote in March of 1806 to Friedrich de la Motte-Fouqué, soon to join the Berlin circle, that "for poetry to have a living function, it must always bear a direct relationship to its historical situation," and that for contemporary Germany this meant the creation of an "alert, direct, energetic, and above all patriotic poetry."[12]

The young Danish poet Adam Oehlenschläger arrived in Germany in 1805, attaching himself first to Schleiermacher in Halle, then to Fichte in Berlin. Under this stimulation he created his Scandinavian tragedy *Hakon Jarl* in 1807 and noted in the preface published with it that every nation "ought to have its own peculiarly national dramas. The peculiarly national is the finest flower of poetry."[13] In his *Selbstbiographie* (Autobiography, 1838) Oehlenschläger claimed as his particular interest as a dramatist the heroic stories of "my own fatherland, that had not yet been individually represented in poetry."[14] His acquaintance with August Schlegel and Mme de Staël, with whom he sojourned in 1809, clearly reinforced this dedication, and on his return to Denmark Oehlenschläger served as the major model there for subsequent nationalist and Romantic drama. Mme de Staël

---

[10] Friedrich Schlegel, *Werke*, 10 vols. (Vienna: Mayer, 1822-25), I, 176.

[11] Reinhold Steig, *Achim von Arnim und Clemens Brentano* (Stuttgart: Cotta, 1894), pp. 37-39.

[12] Friedrich de la Motte-Fouqué, *Briefe* (Berlin: Adolf, 1848), p. 357.

[13] Quoted in P.M. Mitchell, *A History of Danish Literature* (New York: American-Scandinavian Foundation, 1958), p. 112.

[14] Adam Oehlenschläger, *Werke*, 21 vols. (Berlin: Mar, 1839), II, 72.

observed in *De l'Allemagne* that he had "created a completely new career, by taking as the subject of his plays the heroic traditions of his fatherland," and that if others were to follow his example "Nordic literature could someday become as celebrated as that of Germany."[15]

August Schlegel's famous *Vorlesungen über dramatische Kunst und Literatur* (Lectures on Dramatic Art and Literature), delivered in 1809 in Vienna, sounded the same challenges as his letter to La Motte-Fouqué. The true potential of Romantic drama will not be realized in Germany until it becomes deeply national and historical, depicting "what the Germans of olden times were and what they should become again." He views the sweep of German history from the Roman wars to the establishment of the Empire, the houses of Hohenstaufen and Hapsburg, as rich in material for a German Shakespeare who could through the dramatization of this history aid his countrymen "to feel their indestructible unity as Germans."[16]

Joseph von Hormayr, in his periodical *Archiv* (founded in 1810), called for a "turning of art toward patriotic concerns."[17] and himself provided a rich mine of such material for subsequent dramatists in his *Österreichischer Plutarch* (Austrian Plutarch, 1807-14). An 1811 article by Matthäus von Collin in *Archiv* entitled *Über die nationale Wesenheit der Kunst* (Concerning the National Essence of Art) similarly urged subjects drawn from German history, and Collin in fact embarked on an ambitious project to depict the history of thirteenth century Austria in a cycle of twelve plays. Unfortunately Collin's dramatic skill did not match his historical enthusiasm, and these works remained unproduced, but other contributions to the new patriotic/historical drama fared much better. The dramaturg of the Vienna court theatre, Theodor Körner, enjoyed a major success with his *Zriny* (1812), the popular novelist Caroline Pichler produced several such dramas, led by *Rudolf von Habsburg* (1814), and Kotzebue, ever responsive to the latest fashions in drama, offered *Rudolf von Habsburg und König Ottokar von Böhmen* (1815).

In Berlin, Schlegel's observations reinforced the patriotic exhortations of Fichte and Schleiermacher, and La Motte-Fouqué, following Schlegel's suggestion, immersed himself in German and Scandinavian legends to create the first modern treatment of the Niebelungen story, *Sigurd der Schlangentöter* (Sigurd the Dragon Slayer, 1808) as well as *Sigurds Rache* (Sigurd's Revenge) and *Aslauga*, published together with a dedication to Fichte in 1810. A far more significant dramatist, Kleist, was inspired by the political events of 1808 to write the most chauvinistic of his plays, *Die Hermannsschlacht* (Hermann's Battle), and on 20 April, 1809, a month after Austria declared war on France, he wrote to a potential producer of his play in Vienna urging immediate production there of the drama "that was calculated solely and alone for this moment." To speed up the process he waived all negotiations about his own repayment, donating the production "to the German people."[18]

In Prague in 1809 Kleist developed plans for a new journal, *Germania*, that according to the opening sentence of the proposed *Einleitung* (Preface) was to be "the first breath drawn by German freedom."[19] The defeat of Austria at Wagram dashed hopes for this project, but the following year in Berlin Kleist found a more sympathetic hearing. The return of the King and Queen late in 1809

---

[15] Germaine de Staël, *Oeuvres complètes*, 3 vols. (Geneva: Slatkine, 1967), II, 136.

[16] August W. Schlegel, *Kritische Schriften und Briefe*, 7 vols. (Stuttgart: Kohnhammer, 1967), VI, 289-90.

[17] Kurt Adel, ed., *Joseph Freiherr von Hormayr und die vaterländische Romantik in Österreich* (Vienna: Bergland, 1969), p. 36.

[18] Heinrich von Kleist, *Sämtliche Werke und Briefe*, 5 vols. (Munich: Hanser, 1952), II, 860.

[19] Kleist, V, 39.

stimulated a wave of Prussian patriotism and a dream in the minds of many that Prussia might serve as the nucleus of a new German nation. In the enthusiasm of this period Kleist created his most famous play, *Der Prinz von Homburg*, planning for the work to be presented in the national theatre and published with a dedication to the Queen. Yet despite the play's championship of Brandenburg, the Prince's fear in the face of death displeased the authorities and the play was in fact neither printed nor performed during Kleist's lifetime.

By way of consolation, Kleist did manage to fulfill in Berlin his hitherto frustrated dream of founding a journal to promote nationalist spirit. This was the *Abendblätter* (Evening News), edited by Kleist and Adam Müller, which first appeared in 1810. The following year writers and the main supporters of the new journal founded a society, the Christlich Deutsche Tischgesellschaft, that counted among its members Kleist, Müller, Arnim, Brentano, and Fichte. Out of this group, and from other literary colleagues sympathetic to their aims, came many Romantic historical dramas during the next few years. La Motte-Fouqué undertook a history cycle, the first two dramas of which appeared in 1811 under the title *Vaterländische Schauspiele* (National Plays). Arnim published his *Schaubühne* (Stage) in 1813, the centerpiece of which was *Die Vertreibung der Spanier aus Wesel im Jahre 1629* (The Expulsion of the Spanish from Wesel in the Year 1629), in which the emancipation of Wesel stood as an obvious allegory for the emancipation of modern Germany. It closed with the exhortation: "God has broken the chains laid on free Wesel by the Spanish, and you were the hammer of God. Men, help yourselves, and God will help you!"

At this same time Brentano, who had been much impressed by the city of Prague on visits there in 1810 and 1812, began his major drama *Die Gründung Prags* (The Founding of Prague) as the first part of a projected trilogy on the early history of Bohemia. Although Brentano's work was written in German, it coincided with the beginnings of a modern national consciousness in Bohemia and helped to make the legend of Libussa central to this consciousness. The next decade saw a flowering of patriotic and historical work in the Prague theatres, led by Conradin Kreutzer's popular opera *Libussa* (1823).[20] Smetana's later (1881) opera on the same subject, the opening work of the National Theatre, has become a central expression of Czech consciousness. Such expressions as Libussa's final prophesy, "My beloved Czech nation will not perish; gloriously she will vanquish the terrors of Hell," led to the suppression of the work under Nazi occupation. The commemorative revival of the opera in 1975, marking the thirtieth anniversay of the end of that occupation, was a deeply moving experience even for the non-Czechs (among them the present author) in the audience, and the performance of *Libussa* was naturally a central event in the exultant celebrations of a newly freed Czechoslovakia in 1989.

The immediate post-Napoleonic period in Hungary also saw a new generation of authors attempting to establish a national consciousness by promoting Hungarian instead of German as their cultural and political language and by turning for literary inspiration to the events of Magyar history. The first great Hungarian drama, József Katona's *Bánk Bán* (Governor Bánk, 1814), portrayed a thirteenth-century rebellion of Hungarian nobles and populace against German oppressors, a subject that not surprisingly offended Austrian censors to such an extent that the play was not produced during its author's lifetime. Charles Kisfaludy, however, managed to present a variety of episodes from Magyar history, beginning with *A Tatárok Magyaroszágon* (A Tartar in Hungary, 1819)

---

[20] Matthias Murko, *Deutsche Einflüsse auf die Anfänge der Slavischen Romantik*, 2 vols. (Graz: Styria, 1897), I, 99.

which, with less obvious contemporary and political overtones, were tolerated by the censors and enjoyed great popularity.

The struggles in Bohemia and Hungary during the early years of the nineteenth century to establish a national literary expression drawn from the language and the historical experience of the people paralleled contemporary movements in many parts of Europe, but most notably in Spain, Italy, and Russia, where the dominant alien literary language and tradition to be overcome was French rather than German. The full impact of Romanticism did not reach Spain until 1833, when the emigrants exiled during the absolutist reign of Ferdinand VII returned, bringing with them recent French inspiration, but certain elements of the movement appeared in the previous genera-tion, tied here as elsewhere to a rising spirit of liberalism and patriotism. Napoleon's annexation of Spain in 1808 set off a war for independence that lasted until the restoration of the monarchy in 1814 and inspired a host of historical dramas, having little to commend them but patriotic enthu-siasm, from *La gloriosa defensa de Gerona por el valor catalán* (The Glorious Defense of Gerona by Catalan Valor, 1808) to *La gran batalla de Arapiles* (The Great Battle of Arapiles, 1813). Unhappily the restoration here as elsewhere brought with it severe censorship of the theatre, but the ideas of German Romantics, and particularly those of August Schlegel, began to be championed in Spain by a German merchant in residence at Cádiz, Böhl von Faber. Schlegel's advocacy of national drama in general, and his admiration for Calderón in particular, were repeated by Böhl in various patriotic journals in Cádiz between 1810 and 1820, particularly in the *Diario Mercantil*. These observations aroused protest from champions of the eighteenth-century tradition, led by José de Mora, resulting in Spain's first taste of the Classic-Romantic debate. Interestingly, Mora also argued from patriotic motives, calling Romanticism an attempt to impose alien German ideas on Spain, whose "natural" literature was developing in a neoclassic direction.

Mora followed Voltaire in viewing the Renaissance Spanish authors, like Shakespeare, as dan-gerous models, Calderón being "like all, without rules, and worse yet, a defect embraced by all the ancient writers, to have little moral sense."[21] Böhl was not particularly successful in opening Spanish literature to full Romantic experimentation, but his campaign for the re-establishment of the Golden Age writers fared much better, and his election to the royal Academia Española in 1820 was essentially a recognition of this. The same year he published a collection of his articles under the title *Vindicaciones de Calderón y del teatro antiguo español contra los afrancesados en literatura* (Vindication of Calderón and the Classic Spanish Theater against the Literary Francophiles), the preface to which observed that "There is no true patriotism without a love for national literature."[22]

Romanticism as such did not appear in Russia until about 1820, but as in Spain, certain elements of the Classic-Romantic debate were anticipated in the early nineteenth-century version of a controversy dating back to the time of Peter the Great between those who wished to open Russian culture to the West and those who wished to retain its traditional Slavic character. As the century began, the Western orientation was championed by authors like Karamzin, who looked for inspira-tion to French Classicism and beyond it to classic Greece and Rome, while authors like Chichkov and Lomonosov sought sources in native Russian religious and popular observances. Both parties, as in Spain, were strongly affected by the nationalist spirit aroused by the Napoleonic wars, and

---

[21] *Diario Mercantil de Cádiz*, 7 January, 1818, cited in E.A. Peers, *Historia del Movimiento Romántico Español*, 2 vols. (Madrid: Gredos, 1954), I, 198. In the original: "como todos sin reglas, y lo que es peor y defecto que a todos los anti-guos comprende, de no muy buena moral."
[22] Quoted in Peers, I, 200.

Karamzin, appointed imperial historiographer in 1803, worked until his death in 1826 on the twelve volume *Istoriya gosudarstva rossiyskago* (History of the Russian State). This, like Naruszewicz's *Historya narodu polskiego* (History of the Polish Nation) and Hormayr's *Österreichischer Plutarch*, served as a central work in the definition of a national consciousness and as a rich source for Romantic ballads, novels, and dramas.

Alexander I at first warmly approved these patriotic expressions, but after 1818, as the government grew more repressive, and as many of the young patriotic writers of the period became associated with emerging resistance organizations, the liberal inclination of much of the new literature increasingly disturbed the authorities. Pushkin, the major literary figure of the new generation, avoided direct contact with any of the revolutionary groups, but his sympathies with both patriotic and liberal concerns were clear. He shared with many of his contemporaries a fascination with the concept of *narodnost* which Prince Vyzvemsky introduced in an essay of 1819 as a literary ideal combining the French concepts of *nationale* and *populaire*.[23] Pushkin's critical notes from this period observe that *narodnost* does not necessarily require the use of subject matter from national history, but in fact he drew heavily upon Karamzin's history for his own dramatic work. In 1818 he noted enthusiastically in his diary that "Karamzin discovered ancient Russia as Columbus did America,"[24] and from Karamzin came the subject of his first attempt at tragedy, *Vadim*, which reflected contemporary political concerns in a depiction of a ninth-century national-republican revolt against a foreign oppressor.

Late in 1824 Pushkin read the tenth and eleventh volumes of Karamzin's work while seeking fresh inspiration for national literature. "We still have no literature, no books," he wrote this same year. "We have from our childhood derived all our knowledge, all our notes from foreign books; we have accustomed ourselves to think in a foreign language."[25] The following year Pushkin completed the first great tragedy of Russian literature, *Boris Godunov*. Though less openly political than the unfinished *Vadim*, it was far too liberal for the imperial censor. It was not published until 1830, and then in highly altered form, and not staged (even with expurgation) until 1870. Nevertheless during Pushkin's own lifetime his drama, like many other Romantic dramas preaching messages unacceptable to the ruling powers, achieved considerable renown through private, and essentially illegal, readings.

The defeat of Napoleon meant for northern Italy essentially the replacement of one foreign occupying power, France, by another, Austria, but this shift nevertheless brought with it a distinct increase in patriotic feeling. German influence in early nineteenth century Italy played a highly ambiguous role, since the same forces that brought political oppression also introduced to this area current German Romantic thought, the patriotic and nationalistic elements of which proved particularly stimulating here. The political unification of the Italian people was an ancient dream, dating back to Dante, Petrarch, and Machiavelli, but two events in the eighteenth century brought new life to this vision. First was the creation of the essentially independent Kingdom of the Two Sicilies in southern Italy and then the Napoleonic invasions and French occupation at the end of the century.

---

[23] Günther Wytrzens, *Pjotr Andreevic Vhazenskij* (Vienna: Verlag Notring der Wissenschaftlichen Verbände Österreichs, 1961), p. 101.

[24] *Iz autobiografischeskikh zaposik*, IV, 377, quoted in E.J. Simmons, *Pushkin* (Cambridge, MA: Harvard Univ. Press, 1937), p. 86.

[25] Quoted in Ivan Luppoi, *Pushkin* (Moscow: U.S.S.R. Society for Cultural Relations with Foreign Countries, 1939), p. 15.

Napoleon shrewdly cast himself in the role of liberator of Italy from its patchwork order of petty states suffering under the conflicting claims of Austria and Spain. His introduction of a uniform legal system, his building of new roads, and his suppression of customs barriers all contributed significantly to creating a new sense of unity in the peninsula. For the Italian patriots who had welcomed the French as liberators, however, these positive benefits were quite outweighed by the fact that politically the French proved as oppressive as the powers they replaced. The leading poet and dramatist of this generation, Alfieri, greeted the French Revolution with celebrative odes, but in his final years wrote bitterly anti-French works denouncing their betrayal of republican ideals. The presentation of his own tragedies in praise of liberty, *Virginia* and *Bruto Primo*, in the occupied cities of Italy caused Alfieri particular anguish, but the French who felt these dramas could be used to stimulate anti-Austrian feelings in Italy were ultimately as mistaken as the Austrians, who in their turn replaced the French army of occupation and attempted to enlist Alfieri's work for their own cause. As the pressure for Italian freedom and unification grew, Alfieri was increasingly regarded as the first great modern spokesman for the emerging Italian nation-state, opposed equally to the political interests of all other European national powers.

The Austrian occupiers who replaced the French also followed the French lead in attempting to solidify their political dominance by cultural indoctrination. Translations of German writers were encouraged and new journals, like the *Biblioteca Italiana* in Milan, were established to focus upon Germanic letters and culture. Romanticism being at this moment the leading literary movement in Germany, its doctrines inevitably were a central part of this importation, and since a significant element in German Romanticism was a revolt against the cultural dominance of France, the Austrian authorities in Italy at first looked favorably upon this development.

Their enthusiasm soon waned. Italian patriots eagerly embraced the political elements of Romantic thought, translating the German rebellion against French hegemony into their own needs for an Italian consciousness opposed to both French and German. The article by Mme de Staël, *Sulla maniera e l'utilità delle traduzioni* (On the Manner and Usefulness of Translations), generally credited with launching the Italian Romantic movement, affirmed that Italian authors must seek to discover and express the vital spirit unique to their own nation, an idea reinforced in the drama by the plea for a national theatre that closed Schlegel's *Vorlesungen*, translated into Italian in 1817.

After its experience with Mme de Staël, the *Biblioteca Italiana* viewed Romanticism much more warily and the Italian Romantics gathered around a new Milanese journal, *Il Conciliatore*, founded in 1818. Its editor, Silvio Pellico, achieved great success with his Alfierian tragedy *Francesca da Rimini* (1815), a success due in no small part to the drama's openly nationalistic appeal. Not only was the plot drawn from Dante (specifically quoted in places), but stirring patriotic passages punctuated the work, such as Paolo's famous

> Per te, per te, che cittadini hai prodi
> Italia mia, combatterò, se oltraggio
> Ti moverà la invidia. E il più gentile
> Terren non sei di quanti scalda il sole? ?
> D'ogni bell'arte non sei madre, o Italia?
> Poive d'eroi non è poive tua?"

> (For you, for you, my Italy, who has heroes
> As citizens, I will fight

When outrages move you to anger.
Are not the noblest lands those so warmed by the sun?
Are you not mother of all the fine arts, O Italy?
Is not your dust the dust of heroes?)

This nationalist spirit, reinforced by such authors as de Staël and Schlegel, permeated the pages of *Il Conciliatore*. "What are the heroic actions most important for Italy to celebrate?" asked Pellico rhetorically in one of the first issues. "Native or foreign? Historical or mythological? The most ancient or the least removed from our own century?"[26]

The answer was obvious, as Pellico demonstrated in a subsequent issue, calling historical tragedy "the most instructive, the most effective, the most philosophic type of tragedy," which took as its concerns "our forefathers and our national glory."[27] "Why pretend that we are Greeks or Romans rather than Italians," asked Giuseppe Pecchio in a typical passage comparing modern Italy's relation to its classics to that of the American colonies to Great Britain, "sons, indeed, but youths at their time of independence, ready to pursue new interests."[28] Such references to independence, patiotism, and nationalism, which appeared constantly in the *Conciliatore* pages, naturally aroused the antagonism of the Austrian officials, and the journal, after thirteen months of steadily increasing censorship, was at last forced to cease publication.

Still its spirit remained strong in Milan, both artistically and politically. Manzoni's *Il Conte de Carmagnola*, published just three months after the final issue of the journal, dealt with an historical subject precisely of the sort that Pellico and others urged, and although it was not allowed public performance in Milan, it was widely read and quoted, especially the patriotic chorus ending the second act:

D'una terra son tutti: un linguaggio
Parlan tutti – fratelli li dice
Lo straniero: il comune lignaggio
A ognun d'essai dal volto traspar.
Questa terra fu a tutti nudrice,
Questa terra di sangue ora intrisa,
Che natura dall'altre ha divisa,
E ricinta con l'alpe e col mar.[29]

(All are of one land, all speak
A common language – foreigners call
them brothers: a common lineage
Is revealed in the features of each.
This land nursed them all
This land now united by blood,
This land that nature has set off from the rest
And enclosed by the Alps and the sea.)

---

[26] *Il Conciliatore: Foglio Scientifico-Letterario*, ed. Vittore Branca, 3 vols. (Florence: Monnier, 1965), I, 135. In the original: "Quali sono le azioni eroiche che più importa all'Italia di celebrare? Le patrie o le straniere? Le mitologiche o le storiche? Le antichissime o le meno remote dal nostro secolo?"

[27] *Conciliatore*, II, 507.

[28] *Conciliatore*, II, 286.

[29] Alessandro Manzoni, *Opere* (Bologna: Zanichelli, 1967), p. 792.

The spirit expressed here and in the pages of the suppressed *Conciliatore* erputed into an uprising in Milan in 1821, but it was ruthlessly crushed. The leaders of the young Romantic movement were arrested or dispersed, Pellico spending the next decade as a political prisoner in the notorious Spielberg castle.

The rising spirit of liberalism and patriotism in Italy that led to the uprisings of 1821 had a powerful effect on two young non-Italian leaders of Romanticism now in residence in Italy, Byron and Stendhal. Stendhal, much disheartened by the events in Milan in 1821, returned to Paris, taking with him, as we shall presently observe, many of the ideals of Milanese Romanticism. Byron remained in Italy, closely watched by the authorities as a known radical with republican sympathies. It was in his life and writings that English Romanticism touched most closely on the wide-spread European sentiments of liberal and republican concern, although as early as 1809 Wordsworth had advanced in his treatise *The Convention of Cintra* a powerful plea for nationalism, patriotism, and political freedom.

Though the focus of this essay was the recent attempt by Spanish revolutionaries to throw off French domination, Wordsworth extended his concern to other stifled nationalities in Europe, calling for the unification and political independence of both Germany and Italy. For Byron this ideal became an inspiration for practical activity as well as poetic expression. He joined the underground Carbonari movement in Italy, supplying them with arms and encouragement, and when the uprisings of 1821 were put down, continued his support of other nationalist movements in Spain and in Greece. In 1823 he went to Greece to sacrifice his fortune, his energy, and a year later his life in the cause of Greek independence. Henceforth for many Europeans Byron provided the central example of the link between Romanticism, nationalism, and political liberty.

Among Byron's first acquaintances in Italy were Silvio Pellico and the Milan circle of Romantics, and although Byron as a dramatist shared the general indifference of the English Romantics to the continental battle over the unities and dramatic rules, he was totally in harmony with Pellico on the matter of political freedom. In 1819 when the Milan Romantics were being closely monitored by the police, Byron, in Romagna, was organizing cells of the Milanese Società Romantica, ostensibly a literary society but in fact, as the authorities well knew, a subversive political organization as well.[30] At this same time Byron created his *Marino Faliero*, based on the 1355 revolt of a Venetian Doge against the entrenched power of the ruling aristocracy. To his conservative publisher Murray, Byron wrote that despite appearance *Marino Faliero* was not a political drama, but at the same time he confessed to his liberal friend Kinnaird that the drama was "full of republicanism."[31] Two other political/historical dramas rapidly followed, *Sardanapalus* and *The Two Foscari*, both published in 1821. In the latter Byron returned to Venetian history for another confrontation between a liberal spirit and an unyielding and uncaring aristocracy. Dramaturgically these works, with their determined neoclassic orientation and insistence on the unities, had little to offer the Italian Romantics, but politically their liberal republican message was precisely in tune with Romantic thought. On these grounds Byron, like Alfieri, was accepted and even adulated by the Italian Romantic authors. Rossini's opera, *Mahomet the Second*, a failure in Naples in 1820, was revived in 1826 with a new Byronic title, *Le Siège de Corinth* (The Siege of Corinth), and with many Byronic references. The choruses of the besieged Corinthians, ready to sacrifice their lives resisting their oppressors, became

---

[30] See *Byron, Letters and Journals*, ed. R.E. Prothero, 6 vols. (London: Murray, 1898-1900), IV, 454-64.
[31] *Lord Byron's Correspondance*, ed. John Murray, 2 vols. (London: Murray, 1922), II, 156.

the most popular passages in a now highly successful work. The two greatest operatic composers of the next generation turned to Byron's political dramas for inspiration, Donizetti for *Marino Faliero* (1834) and Verdi for *I due Foscari* (The Two Foscari, 1844).

In the decade after the supression of liberal ideas in Milan, from 1821 to 1831, many authors with Romantic sympathies, such as Manzoni, found Florence, whose Duke Leopold II was at least somewhat more tolerant than the rulers of neighboring states, a place of refuge, and her Romantic nationalism continued to develop, though with distinctly more subdued expression. The leading dramatist of this Florentine phase of Romanticism was Giovan Battista Niccolini, professor of history and mythology at the Accademia di Belle Arte. Niccolini began his dramatic career with a series of neoclassic tragedies on Greek themes, but after 1815 he began to follow with interest the new Romantic trends, turning to historical and national subjects.

The first fruit of this new orientation was *Giovanni da Procida*, written about 1817, which used the historical background of the Sicilian Vespers for a main action involving the unwittingly incestuous love of a brother and sister. In 1823 Niccolini wrote to a friend that "Mythological plots have become anti-poetical for our era."[32] This echo of *Conciliatore* thought is supported by his *Antonio Foscarini*, written about this same time with another Italian historical setting, the Venetian Republic of 1450, and a plot devoting attention both to thwarted love and to political repression. *Antonio Foscarini* and *Giovanni da Procida* were both performed in Florence, the first in 1827 and the second in 1830, with great success. The outspoken championship of liberty in *Antonio Foscarini* caused it to be forbidden public presentation in Milan, Venice, and elsewhere, however. *Giovanni da Procida* was permitted for a time in Milan, probably because its ostensible subject was French oppression, but the Austrian authorities soon recognized that the tumultuous applause that greeted lines urging the French to return to their own soil applied equally well to themselves. After the triumphant first performance in Milan, the French ambassador is said to have complained about the play to an Austrian colleague, only to receive the reply: "Don't be upset. The envelope is addressed to you, but the contents are for me."[33]

A new series of popular uprisings in Italy in 1831 and 1832 brought new Austrian troops in to restore order, and although Tuscany was not directly affected, the turbulence in neighboring states ended the relative literary freedom enjoyed here during the previous decade. Liberal journals were suppressed, censorship strengthened, and although Niccolini was able, after great difficulty, to get his *Ludovico Sforza* published in 1834, performance was out of the question. He turned during the rest of this decade to subjects with no clear political overtones, but in his final plays, *Filippo Strozzi* and *Arnaldo da Brescia*, produced his strongest political/dramatic statements, knowing that such works could not possibly be openly circulated or performed in the Italy of his own day. *Arnaldo da Brescia* was printed in Marseilles in 1843, read in secret throughout Italy, and its fiercely patriotic passages memorized by the men of the *Risorgimento*. "If I have not written a great tragedy," observed its author, "I believe I have performed a courageous act."[34]

Among the concerns of the Milan Romantics that the young Stendhal brought back with him to Paris in the early 1820s was an interest in national history as a major source for Romantic tragedy. In *Racine et Shakespeare II* (1825) he defines this new genre as a "prose tragedy that lasts several

[32] Guido Mazzoni, *L'Ottocento*, 2 vols. (Milan: Vallardi, 1934), I, 831.
[33] Arthur James Whyte, *The Evolution of Modern Italy* (Oxford: Blackwell, 1944), pp. 42-43.
[34] Mazzoni, I, 935.

months and takes place in various settings," and suggests that many of the great events of French history would lend themselves to such treatment.[35] France, having long since achieved the political cohesiveness and national independence still lacking in Italy, had little interest in such drama as a stimulation for national spirit; but many French Romantics, headed by Victor Hugo, nevertheless were able to make common cause with the Italian Romantics on the grounds of political liberalism, and it was with this orientation that the French Romantic historical drama developed. The preface to *Hernani* called Romanticism "liberalism in literature" and accused the "Classicists and monarchists" of working together to stifle revolutionary changes "of all types, social and literary."[36] When Hugo's *Marion de Lorme*, previously censored, was freed for presentation by the revolution of 1830, Hugo saw this as confirmation of his theory, and in a new preface to the work, written in 1831, claimed that 1830 would eventually be recognized as "a literary date no less than a political date." After the events of 1830, poetry was free to work for a more humane order and the dramatist to attempt "the creation of a theatre vast yet simple, one and varied, national in its historical interest, popular in its truth, human, natural, and universal in its passion."[37] His subsequent works, from *Le Roi s'amuse* (The King Amuses Himself, 1831) to *Ruy Blas* (1838) may be seen as contributions to this sort of national drama.

During the 1830s this concept of drama as a weapon for liberal thought as well as for national consciousness spread out from Paris through much of Europe, appearing perhaps most clearly in the writings of *Das junge Deutschland* (Young Germany), a new generation of German authors whose name was taken from the dedication of Ludolf Wienbarg's book *Ästhetische Feldzüge* (Aesthetic Campaigns, 1834), which became a central manifesto of this movement. Throughout Wienbarg's book the word "national" appears, but he carefully distinguishes this new nationalist literature from that of the earlier German Romantics. Drama must arise, like all the noblest poetry "directly from the people, from the national spirit, from national customs."[38] For Wienbarg however this did not mean a return to the mystic nationalism of the early nineteenth-century Germans, but to a modern, liberal, politically engaged nationalism as represented by such figures as Hugo and Byron.

This program was followed as faithfully as the times would allow by such dramatists as Karl Gutzkow and Heinrich Laube, who used historical subjects less to promote national pride, as dramatists of the Napoleonic era had done, than to explore contemporary political concerns, especially those involving repression and censorship. Both Laube's *Die Karlsschüler* (The Karl School Students, 1846), dealing with Schiller, and Gutzkow's *Das Urbild des Tartuffe* (The First Version of Tartuffe, 1845), dealing with Molière, were essentially pleas for artistic freedom. Such dramas, however, had to speak cautiously to pass the still powerful censor, and it is clear that historical subjects were sometimes employed, as in Laube's *Mondaleschi* (1841), set at the court of Christian of Sweden, to remove their subjects from too immediate an identification with current politics. Robert Prutz, whose *Moritz von Sachsen* was banned in Berlin in 1844, accompanied the published version of the play with an essay, *Über das deutsche Theater* (Concerning the German Theater), which suggested that significant historical drama was not possible in contemporary Germany and that dramatists must see themselves not as the epigones of Goethe and Schiller, but as the "progones" of

---

[35] Henri Beyle (Stendhal), *Oeuvres*, 35 vols. (Paris: Divan, 1927-47), XIII, 89.
[36] Victor Hugo, *Oeuvres*, 18 vols. (Paris: Club français du livre, 1967-70), III, 922.
[37] Hugo, IV, 456-66.
[38] Ludolf Wienbarg, *Ästhetische Feldzüge* (Berlin: Aufbau-Verlag, 1964), p. 157. In the original: "aus dem Schoß des Volks, des nationellen Geistes, der nationellen Sitte."

the great historical dramas of the future, which would be able to present "complete historical existence in the clear light of freedom."[39]

As the nineteenth century progressed, the concerns of historical drama became increasingly varied and complex. Strictly nationalist subjects sometimes gave way, as in the dramas of Byron, to historical dramas carrying a message of freedom from oppression to all audiences, whatever their nationality. Eugène Scribe popularized historical drama as a form of escapist intrigue comedy. Ferdinand Lassalle attempted, with advice from Marx and Engels, to create historical drama demonstrating the dynamics of the historical process itself, of which nationalism was only one aspect.[40] The historical drama with a specific nationalist focus was, however, a particular concern of the Romantic period when the modern concept of the nation-state was developing. How far this approach is removed from the eighteenth century idea of the generalizability of human actions or from specific historical events used to illuminate more general questions or processes is clearly illustrated by Coleridge's observation: "In order that a drama may be perfectly historical, it is necessary that it should be the history of the people to whom it is addressed."[41]

By the middle of the nineteenth century this relationship between Romantic idealism, political liberalism, and an emerging national consciousness had begun to bear fruit not only in the creation of national plays but in the founding of national theatres with a national repertoire. We see this manifested, for example, in the organization in 1849 of a National Theatre at Bergen, Norway, where the young Henrik Ibsen for the next six years devoted his developing dramatic skills to treating the materials of Norwegian legend and history, and fifty years later in the organization and repertoire of the Abbey Theatre in Dublin. Indeed few of the emerging national/cultural groups of the post-Romantic period neglected to utilize the drama as a powerful tool for awakening a people to a common heritage and, not infrequently, encouraging them through an awareness of this heritage to seek both national identity and national liberty in opposition to the demands of dominant and external political and cultural influences. For good or ill, the Romantic drama thus contributed in no small measure to the shaping and development of modern nationalism.

[39] Robert Prutz, *Dramatische Werke*, 4 vols. (Leipzig: Weber, 1847-62), IV, 5.
[40] For an extended study of various attitudes of dramatists, readers, and audience to the dramatic use of historical material, see Herbert Lindenberger, *Historical Drama: The Relation of Literature and Reality* (Chicago: Univ. of Chicago Press, 1975).
[41] *Coleridge's Shakespearean Criticism*, ed. T.M. Raysor, 2 vols. (Cambridge, MA: Harvard Univ. Press, 1930), I, 138.

JEFFREY N. COX

ROMANTIC REDEFINITIONS OF THE TRAGIC

Tragedy seems to demand a closed world, a world from which the hero cannot (or will not) escape, a world that has narrowed to the point where choice and fate name two facets of the same act. The unities of place, time, and action, often defended on the grounds of verisimilitude, work less to make the tragic world believable, than to shield it from the possibilities that might lead away from tragedy. Even when the unities are violated, we usually experience a movement into an enclosed world. Othello leaves Venice behind to travel to Cyprus, but in doing so he journeys from a courtly, Christian society that has witnessed his marriage to a primitive claustrophobic land that provides the backdrop for murder and suicide. Hamlet, who escapes briefly from the hothouse of the Danish court to wander in the romance world of pirates, returns to the confines of Elsinore and so to certain death. Sophocles' Oedipus perhaps best reveals the tragic hero's fated affinity for a closed world. Because he seeks to avoid tragedy by fleeing his assumed parents and becoming a wanderer, he ironically returns to Thebes, the tragic place from which he cannot escape. The variations may be as many as the ways of genius, but tragedy always returns to a closed world at its climactic moments.

Many have argued that the Romantic age must therefore be anti-tragic; for it seems to demand an open world.[1] Following the simultaneously liberating and destructive work of the Enlightenment, Romanticism's vision was forged during what R.R. Palmer has called "the age of the democratic revolution," between 1760 and 1800;[2] it was further tempered by the tumultuous years of the early nineteenth century, marked by the Napoleonic Wars, Restoration and repression, and further revolution. This vision was shaped in particular in the fires of the French Revolution, perceived as enacting the previous century's attacks upon the hierarchies, immutable laws, and mythic repetitions that had defined both traditional society and the literary forms like tragedy it had supported. Born in this era, Romanticism celebrates the liberated individual. It embraces new lands, remote times, and strange experiences. It delights in new and open literary forms that seek to reflect a world of endless possibilities; one thinks of the unending travels of Byron's Don Juan, of the kaleidoscope of modes and moods in Schlegel's *Lucinde*, or of the encyclopaedic reach of Goethe's *Faust* and Hugo's *La Légende des siècles*.

Romanticism brought, after all, the rebirth of romance and thus of the quest that breaks out of the enclosed world of tragedy. This opposition between tragedy and romance had appeared as early

---

[1] See, for example, R.B. Sewall, *The Vision of Tragedy* (New Haven: Yale Univ. Press, 1959), p. 84; George Steiner, *The Death of Tragedy* (London: Faber & Faber, 1961), *passim*; and Geoffrey Brereton, *Principles of Tragedy* (Miami: Univ. of Miami Press, 1968), pp. 183-88. The present essay is based extensively upon chapter one of Jeffrey N. Cox, *In the Shadows of Romance: Romantic Tragic Drama in Germany, England, and France* (Athens, OH: Ohio Univ. Press, 1987).

[2] R.R. Palmer, *The Age of the Democratic Revolution: A Political History of Europe and America 1760-1800*, 2 vols. (Princeton: Princeton Univ. Press, 1959 & 1964).

as the Homeric epics: the Greek and Trojan heroes can only seek a tragic death while their armies are locked in combat between the city and the sea, but Homer's great anti-tragic figure, Odysseus, can leave behind the confines of the tragic world to make his life into a romance as a wanderer always moving on to new adventures, always able to avoid the identification with a single act or place that leads to tragedy. In adopting the romance, Romanticism explores a potentially anti-tragic theme, that of personal change and development. From the growth of the poet's soul in Words-worth's poetry to the evolution of Satan in Hugo's *Fin de Satan* (Satan's End), the Romantics seek paths for the individual to follow out of or around limits. Such poems defeat tragic closure in pursuit of imaginative romance.

But what if this quest fails? While Romanticism seeks a world made new by the imagination, it begins with an awareness of what was lost in the collapse of a prior order – whether it be the loss of the innocent state of nature imagined by Rousseau and Schiller, of the perfection of morals and art that Shelley found in ancient Greece, or of the hierarchical and organic "age of faith" admired by Novalis and Carlyle. The Romantics may have celebrated the independent individual, but they were only too aware that his new freedom brought with it the isolation and alienation of intense self-consciousness. Romanticism inherited the Enlightenment's struggle to free man from religious, political and ideological oppression, but the Romantics also knew that this struggle had resulted in the Revolution and its literal and violent destruction of the traditional way of life ruled by Monarch and Priest. What happens when man finds that he has destroyed the closed world of the traditional order, but that he is unable to break through to the open world of the Romantic imagination? Is there not, in this moment between the fall of the enclosed but meaningful order of the past and the creation of a new Romantic order, occasion for a peculiarly modern tragedy? Is there not a tragic drama lurking in the shadows of imaginative romance?

Certainly critics like George Steiner do not believe so. Steiner contends that tragedy became impossible after rationalism and secular metaphysics undermined the traditional world view of providential and hierarchical order. For Steiner, tragedy must reveal a divine realm. The plot must follow a providential script, whether that of the Greek oracles or that of the Christian God. A hierarchical social order defines the hero, for it establishes as heroic those who occupy the summit of the order, it reveals the significance of their fall from such a height, and it insures that this fall will have a public significance. Steiner argues that Romantic drama lacks a sense of the divine, that it orders its plots only by drawing upon the moralistic melodrama, and that it sought tragedy not in the fall of great personages but in the private troubles of inward-turned individuals.[3]

There is much truth in Steiner's description of what was lost in the movement from traditional culture to that of the modern, Romantic age. However, his normative definition of tragedy prevents him from seeing that the Romantics transformed the tragic by grounding it in the very fact of that loss. Like most students of tragedy, he establishes a set of criteria and rejects as non-tragic any work that does not meet it. If an author – Romantic or otherwise – offers an innovative tragedy, he more likely than not will be seen as a contributor to the "death" of the form. There are, of course, other critics who completely reject such restrictive definitions, arguing that each new play that calls itself tragic must alter our idea of tragedy. Morris Weitz, for example, in his *Hamlet and the Philosophy of Literary Criticism*, concludes that, "The concept of tragedy, thus, is perennially debatable."[4] We

---

[3] Steiner, pp. 193-98.
[4] Morris Weitz, *Hamlet and The Philosophy of Literary Criticism* (Chicago: Univ. of Chicago Press, 1964), p. 307.

need to steer a middle course between the prescriptions of Steiner and the relativism of Weitz. The desire to write tragedy is present in every period of our literature; many artists have felt they were writing tragedies even if we do not agree that they succeeded. Each age has had to confront the issues central to tragedy, issues like the idea of the hero, the relationship between man and whatever lies beyond him, and the fact of man's mortality. Each age faces these issues anew and tries a different way of making real the dream of a tragic art. Rather than criticizing the Romantics for failing to be Sophocles or Shakespeare, we should instead appreciate the bold spirit with which they offered their redefinitions of tragedy.

The simplest approach to the Romantic effort in tragedy is to see it as a rejection of the rules set down by neoclassical theorists – primarily the unities, but also the strictures of decorum on style and subject matter and the insistence on "moral" tragedy embodied in the doctrine of "poetic justice." However, we miss the heart of the Romantic revision of the tragic if we focus too narrowly upon formal issues. The Romantics were not merely opposing a particular set of rules. They were protesting against the idea that formal features define a genre. The Romantic attack on the rules was not so much a debate on formal features as an attempt to replace a definition of the form of tragedy with a definition of the tragic vision. This movement from form to vision is revealed not only in demands for the end of generic distinctions – as in Gerstenberg's call, "Weg mit der Classification des Drama" (Away with the classification of the drama) – but also in attempts, like that of J.S. Mill, to define genres in relation to the central emotion they each express, or, as in the case of A.W. Schlegel, to discuss comedy and tragedy in relation to the "tone of mind" that lies behind them.[5] As the comments on tragedy by writers like Hegel, Schopenhauer, Shelley, and Hugo suggest, the Romantics also sought to replace the moral emphasis of the doctrine of poetic justice with what Raymond Williams, in discussing Hegel's theory, has called "a metaphysic of tragedy."[6] For the Romantics, the tragic was no longer identified with a particular aesthetic form, but rather with a vision or philosophy of life.

This divorce of vision from form in part explains the stylistic experimentation of Romantic drama, an experimentation that led writers to attempt virtually every possible dramatic style, from Greek tragedy (e.g., Goethe's *Iphigenie auf Tauris* or Shelley's *Hellas*) to Shakespearean historical drama (e.g., Schiller's *Wallenstein* or Musset's *Lorenzaccio*), from the medieval mystery play (e.g.,

---

[5] Heinrich Wilhelm Gerstenberg's comment is from his *Briefe über Merkwürdigkeiten der Litteratur* (1766), and is quoted in René Wellek, *A History of Modern Criticism: 1750-1950* (New Haven: Yale Univ. Press, 1955), I, 177. Mill's genre theory, set forth in his essays "What is Poetry?" and "The Two Kinds of Poetry" (1833), is discussed by M.H. Abrams, in *The Mirror and the Lamp* (New York: Norton, 1958), esp. pp. 23-24, 148. Mill's ideas owed much to Wordsworth's prefaces to *Lyrical Ballads* and to the 1815 edition of his poetry; on Wordsworth, see Abrams, "Wordsworth and Coleridge on Diction and Figures," *English Institute Essays: 1952* (New York: Columbia Univ. Press, 1954), pp. 171-201. A.W. Schlegel's discussion of tragedy and comedy as "tones" of mind is found in his *Vorlesungen über dramatische Kunst und Literatur*, vol. V of *Kritische Schriften und Briefe*, ed. Edgar Lohner (Stuttgart: Kohlhammer, 1966), pp. 41-43; *Course of Lectures on Dramatic Art and Literature*, trans. John Black (London: Bohn, 1846), pp. 45-46.

[6] Raymond Williams, *Modern Tragedy* (Stanford: Stanford Univ. Press, 1966), p. 32. Hegel argued against the "false notion of guilt or innocence" in tragedy; Hegel, *Vorlesungen über die Ästhetik*, in *Werke* (Frankfurt: Suhrkamp, 1970), XV, 545-46; *Hegel on Tragedy*, ed. Anne and Henry Paolucci (New York: Harper & Row, 1975), pp. 70-71. Schopenhauer attacked the notion of poetic justice and found the "true sense of tragedy" in man's atonement for "the crime of existence itself"; *Die Welt als Wille und Vorstellung*, in *Sämtliche Werke* (Munich: Piper, 1924), I, 299-300; *The World as Will and Idea*, trans., R.B. Haldane and J. Kemp (New York: Doubleday, 1961), p. 265. Hugo's account of modern drama as a merger between the sublime and the grotesque renders it morally as well as aesthetically mixed; and Shelley in the preface to *The Cenci* (1819) contended that tragedy had to eschew "what is vulgarly termed a moral purpose"; in *Poetical Works*, ed. Thomas Hutchinson, rev. G.M. Matthews (Oxford: Oxford Univ. Press, 1970), p. 276. All references to Shelley's plays are from this edition; act, scene, and line number will be given in the text.

Byron's *Cain*) to the Spanish miracle play (e.g., Tieck's *Leben und Tod der heiligen Genoveva* [Life and Death of Saint Genoveva]). We also find Romantic writers drawing upon contemporary theatrical forms, with *Manfred* owing a great deal to the gothic drama and *Hernani* having ties to the melodramas of Pixérécourt. Even neoclassical tragedy could become an influence in Goethe's *Die natürliche Tochter* (The Natural Daughter) or Byron's *Marino Faliero*. These works could not, of course, revive earlier forms, though we might note Beddoes's immersion in Jacobean drama and Hölderlin's attempts to recapture the spirit of Greek tragedy in the various versions of *Der Tod des Empedokles* (The Death of Empedocles) and *Empedokles auf dem Ätna* (Empedocles upon Aetna). However, the Romantics emulated traditional models only to revise them, thus demonstrating the distance between the traditional tragic vision and that of the Romantic dramatist. It is clearly not the form of the various plays written by the Romanticists that makes them Romantic. What they share is a revisionary turn against the past that seeks a new tragic vision.

This pursuit of a tragic vision needs to be placed in relation to the project of Romanticism as a whole, which – in the words of Robert Langbaum – "starts with the acknowledgement that the past of official tradition is dead. But it seeks beneath the ruins of official tradition an enduring truth, inherent in the nature of life itself, which can be embodied in a new tradition, a new Mythus."[7] The Romantic dramatist also searches through the "ruins" of past tragic forms for the true tragic vision. However, he does not discover the new Mythus of a visionary or imaginative order. This Mythus is the creation of the central works of Romanticism, but Romantic tragic drama arises in the moment between the loss of traditional culture and the creation of a Romantic one. We can perhaps see more clearly this relationship between Romantic tragic drama and the key visionary works of Romanticism, if we glance at two quite different plays by Shelley. His *Prometheus Unbound* is one of the essential testaments to the Romantic Mythus. After completing the third act of his great visionary drama, Shelley turned to write *The Cenci*; and in the dedication to that play, he pointed to the distance between his celebrations of the imagination – his "dreams of what ought to be or may be" – and his tragic drama: "The drama which I now present to you is a sad reality."[8] Romantic tragic drama reveals the nightmares that haunt the imagination's dreams of what ought to be. It suggests that the quest for a new Mythus might fail, that man might have to live in the ruins of the old world without being able to construct a new order for life. Romantic tragic drama presents Romanticism's investigation of the failure of its own central literary mode – the visionary quest romance. In their poetry, the Romantics imagined man and his world remade. In their dramas, they portrayed men and women caught in the dangerous lures of the self and the violence of revolutionary history.

While Nietzsche did not preach the death of God until late in the nineteenth century, theistic tragedy was already moribund when the Romantics first began to write at the close of the eighteenth century. In traditional tragedy, the gods rule the world. Like Aeschylus' Prometheus or Marlowe's Faustus, the hero acts in violation of a divine order and perhaps, like Oedipus, finally becomes reconciled to it. His heroic struggle is defined by the tensions between the human and the divine, and the tragic shape of his life is determined by their resolution. The Romantic protagonist, however, does not face a divine order but the chaos that follows its collapse. The God invoked by Shelley's Count Cenci, the cosmological order sought by Schiller's Wallenstein, and the vague sense of fate

---

[7] Robert Langbaum, *The Poetry of Experience* (1957; rpt. New York: Norton, 1971), p. 12.
[8] Shelley, "Dedication" to *The Cenci*, in *Poetical Works*, pp. 274-75.

embraced by Hugo's Hernani are all revealed as being at best weak echoes of an earlier theistic vision and at worst emblems of an oppressive world, Blakean Nobodaddies.

This point is perhaps made most emphatically in those Romantic plays like Byron's *Cain* that still ostensibly engage a theistic world view and thus seem to contradict our sense that the Romantics could no longer dramatize the gods or God. However, Byron's heterodox play focuses not upon the divine, but upon Cain's sense of loss in being kept from Paradise and thus direct contact with God. Cain desperately wants to discover a divine plan for life, but Jehovah's rule appears to him as oppression, not order. He longs for the divine presence, but like Goethe's Faust meets only a demonic messenger. As the play reaches its climax – with Cain's sacrifice over-turned by the wind – we are presented with a moment that the pious Abel sees as an instance of divine revelation but which Cain knows to be open to multiple interpretations: the scattering of the sacrificed fruits upon the ground can appear as both a sign of divine displeasure and as an appropriate return of the fruits to their source in the soil. An argument ensues and the murder of Abel. The clarity of divine revelation is replaced by the uncertainty of man's quest for meaning through interpretation.

This shift receives a more positive treatment in another play where the gods still seem present, Goethe's *Iphigenie auf Tauris* (Iphigenia at Tauris). In Goethe's play, the characters at first follow Apollo's oracle which apparently demands the return of his divine sister's statue, a demand that would lead to bloodshed between the Greek Orestes and the Tauridians who have sheltered his sister Iphigenia as Diana's priestess. However, Iphigenia and Orestes offer a new interpretation of the god's words that replaces the goddess Diana with the woman Iphigenia, thus moving the characters from violence to the creation of a new human community. Like *Cain*, then, the play charts a shift from a world defined by the will of the gods to one in which man must discover his own way through human vision and interpretation.

With the loss of a providential plan that is chronicled in such plays, society's hierarchical organization ceases to provide a meaningful structure for human life. While the traditional character was a hero who lived in a world that supported his heroism by granting him fame and a lofty place in society, the Romantic character must struggle to create himself as a hero in opposition to an unheroic world. Many Romantic plays explore explicitly the contrast between a traditional, heroic society and the modern, unheroic age.

As Hegel notes, Goethe and Schiller were especially concerned with dramatizing the transition between these two periods. In *Götz von Berlichingen*, Goethe portrays the moment when the feudal society of heroes gave way to the modern bourgeois world lacking a heroic sense of life. As a representative of the knightly class and its *Faustrecht*, Götz yearns for the traditional social system in which he had obligations only to his people and his Emperor. Now, he finds that a new social order made up of princes, churchmen, and lawyers constrains his proud spirit, enclosing his field of action within the fences of the law. Finally, destroyed by a world in which he no longer belongs, Götz foresees a future of pettiness and betrayal, a future without heroes: "Es kommen die Zeiten des Betrugs, es ist ihm Freiheit gegeben. Die Nichtswürdigen werden regieren mit List, und der Edle wird in ihre Netze fallen" (V.xiv, "Gärtchen am Turn") (The times of humbug are coming, and to it licence is given. The base will rule by craftiness, and the noble man will fall into their nets).[9]

---

[9] All quotations from Goethe's works are taken from *Goethes Werke*, Hamburger Ausgabe in 14 vols. (Hamburg: Wegner, 1948ff.). *Götz* and *Egmont* are found in vol. IV, *Faust* in vol. III. Act, scene (and, where appropriate) line numbers will be given in the text. Hegel's comments on Goethe's and Schiller's treatment of historical themes is found in *Werke*, XIII, 255-57; *On Tragedy*, pp. 110-12.

Egmont undergoes a similar dislocation of his identity as his society changes. A hero in the past when battling against his homeland's enemies, he believes in a political order in which he owes allegiance to his King and Emperor, but where his own privileges are assured by his status as a Knight of the Golden Fleece. The world around him, however, is changing, and his heroic self-conception, grounded in the old social reality, is undermined; his fall is catalogued in the play's crowd scenes which first reveal the people proclaiming Egmont as their heroic protector (I.i, "Armbrust-schiessen") only to later show them finally afraid to even whisper the name they once raised in joyous toasts (V.i, "Strasse. Dämmerung").

Schiller's *Die Räuber* (The Bandits) stages the contrast between a heroic past and a debased present even more bluntly. Schiller has Karl Moor revolt against his "puny age" for it lacks the heroic grandeur he finds in reading Plutarch. While Moor's difficulties may originate within the private sphere (his misunderstandings with his father, his struggle with his brother), he attempts to resolve them by adopting the public role of a heroic liberator; he comes to understand the gap between his revolt and the stand of the traditional hero, however, when he discovers that in pursuing his heroic dream he must become a robber – not society's defender but its potential destroyer. We find a similar concern for a lost heroic past elsewhere. We hear Moor's call for Plutarchan heroics echoed by Musset's Lorenzaccio as he seeks to cast off the debasing role he has had to play and thus to reveal himself as a hero, a new Brutus. Like Goethe's Götz, Byron's Marino Faliero finds himself at a pivotal moment in his society's history when the structures that have supported his heroic self-image as Doge begin to collapse and he is forced to a join a rebellion against the society he nominally rules. The Romantic protagonist does not find himself as a hero within society, but – like Hugo's Hernani – as an outcast in revolt.

The world of Romantic tragic drama, then, is defined by the lack of both the social order that supported the traditional hero and the providential order that shaped the tragic plot. Still, in an important sense, the Romantic protagonist wants to live in the heroic, tragic world of traditional drama; for then he would be a hero and human existence would again possess the rich, mysterious order found in providential tragedy. He finds himself, however, to be a titan in a bourgeois society and a questor after meaning in the midst of chaos. His heroism can only be a struggle to become heroic. The order of his world must be one he creates. The tragedy of Romantic man arises in the gap that separates him from the fully meaningful world of gods and heroes, a gap he has often helped to create. Romantic man's heroic project is to forge an equivalent meaning for his own life and for his world. He is in the situation of Faust: "Du hast sie zerstört/ Die schöne Welt/ [...] Mächtiger/ Der Erdensöhne,/ Prächtiger/ Baue sie wieder,/ In deinem Busen baue sie auf!" (I.1608-9, 1617-21) (You have destroyed the beautiful world [...] Mighty son of earth, more brilliant build it again, in your heart build it again). This project involves him in an inward turn to discover a new vision of life within the self and an outward turn to alter the world through revolt; both of these turns pose dangers that can bring tragic destruction down upon him.

Isolated in a world without meaningful order, the Romantic protagonist first seeks within his own selfhood a vision to project upon his world. Vigny's Chatterton wrapped in his silence, the Faust-like Manfred alone in his study, and Hölderlin's Empedokles moving ever further up Mount Aetna are all images of the mind seeking within for some idea of order; as Manfred puts it, "in my heart/ There is a vigil, and these eyes but close/ To look within" (I.i.5-7).[10] However, when the

[10] Byron, *Poetical Works*, ed. Frederick Page, rev. John Jump (Oxford: Oxford Univ. Press, 1970); additional references to Byron's plays will be to this edition; act, scene, and line numbers will be given in the text.

Romantic protagonist turns inward, he discovers a chaos of passion and thought, spiritual longings and physical appetites. Neither providence nor society provides him with the means to structure the complexities of the self. He has no map to chart out the regions of the intellect, the will and the appetites, nor a role to shape his personality. Musset's Lorenzo, for example, can discover no fixed identity for himself. He has haunting memories of an innocent past of learning and pastoral pleasures. He has dreams of a heroic future as a Brutus liberating his country. But in the present he has only a mask, that of Lorenzaccio, the debauched companion of a vice-ridden ruler. His public persona does not reveal his inner identity; there is no connection between his past, present, and future identities.

Hoping to conquer the inner Babel that threatens Lorenzo, the Romantic protagonist seeks in the form of his own selfhood a model of order for his world. As Hegel says of these characters, "Hier vor allem muß daher wenigstens die formelle Größe des Charakters und Macht der Subjektivität gefordert werden, alles Negative auszuhalten" (What we require therefore above all in such cases is at least the formal greatness of character and power of the personal life which is able to ride out everything that negates it); they want to be "freie[...] Künstler[...] ihrer selbst" (free artists of themselves), creating from the chaos of the self an artful identity that is fully human and that has the imaginative power to envision a new world.[11] Whether he is Byron's Manfred struggling to be true to his divided nature as "half dust, half deity," or Kleist's Homburg pursuing an ideal in his wish-fulfilling dreams, or Hugo's Hernani claiming to mold the tumultuous passions within him into "une force qui va" (a force that goes), the Romantic protagonist strains to mold his selfhood into a power capable of remaking the world in its own image.

As Schiller's Moor and Musset's Lorenzaccio in their desire to be like Plutarch's heroes suggest, this drive to create an integrated and forceful identity is defined as an attempt to become a hero. But this attempt to emulate past heroes merely emphasizes the distance that lies between them and the Romantic protagonist. While we talk of figures like Musset's Lorenzo, Schiller's Wallenstein, and Byron's Manfred as modern Hamlets, Macbeths, and Fausts, Romantic playwrights in fact evoke heroic archetypes in order to measure the gap that opens between the traditional hero and the Romantic would-be hero. The very freedom that enables the Romantic protagonist to be an "artist" of his own identity also prevents him from acquiring the firm character of the traditional hero. The Romantic protagonist must define himself and this self-definition can never command the recognition nor possess the authority awarded to the traditional character whose heroism arises within an objective order. Hugo's Cromwell exemplifies this plight. He is portrayed as a self-made man who has defined himself in opposition to the order that had structured English society in the past. Yet Cromwell is obsessed by one desire: to become king. An absolute ruler in fact, he wants to be granted the hierarchical and even providential role that marked the great man in the past. However, as a Romantic rebel, he will never attain the heroic status offered within the traditional order that he, ironically, helped to destroy. The play ends with Cromwell, triumphant over his enemies, but still musing, "Quand donc serai-je roi?" (V.xiv) (When then will I be king?).[12]

The Romantic protagonist cannot win his way back to the world of the past. But neither can he win his way through to a future made new by the visionary imagination. Romantic poetry typically

---

[11] Hegel, *Werke*, XV, 537, 562; *On Tragedy*, pp. 61, 86. The comment on characters as "free artists of themselves" comes in reference to Shakespeare who was for Hegel and other writers of the period a Romantic playwright.

[12] Hugo, *Théâtre complet*, ed. J.-J. Thierry and Josette Mélèze (Paris: Gallimard, 1963), vol. I.

moves through self-consciousness and alienation to an imaginative reunion with a renovated world. The protagonist of Romantic drama, however, finds himself trapped within the present, left to shoulder the burdens of the self. He has not vision, but his own selfhood; and in finding his ideal within the heroic identity he creates for himself, he must betray the central Romantic quest for a truly visionary identity. In the very act of creating himself as a hero in the present, he tragically closes himself off to the visionary future.

Beddoes's Isbrand in *Death's Jest-Book* confronts just this tragic impasse. He has sought to create himself as a heroic superman: "It was ever/ My study to find out a way to godhead":

> And on reflection soon I found that first
> I was but half created; that a power
> Was wanting in my soul to be its soul,
> And this was mine to make. (V.i.47-50) [13]

Needing to remake himself, he also hopes to transform his society in his own image, "To chisel an old heap of stony laws,/ The abandoned sepulchre of a dead dukedom,/ Into the form my spirit loved and longed for" (V.i.14-16). However, he is unable to free himself from his own selfhood with its past habits and present crimes; he cannot break through to the future because he is wrapped up in "that poisonous reptile,/ My past self," as another character terms it (IV.iii.15-16). He has not renovated himself or his world, but merely usurped the Duke's role for which he has neither the power nor the authority. Like Cromwell, he has destroyed the order of the past but has no stable new order within which to define himself. He has sought to transform life, but has in fact betrayed himself to the world of death that for Beddoes lies waiting within the selfhood of every man.

While he may not break through into a visionary future, the Romantic protagonist who forges a heroic identity for himself does escape some of the more debilitating modes of consciousness and subjectivity. Seeking to control his inner life, Romantic man may become lost in gazing inward. Endlessly fixated upon the self, torn between this thought and that desire, he may become a Romantic Hamlet, incapable of action and – in Goethe's words – "ohne die sinnliche Stärke, die den Helden macht" (without the strength of nerve which forms a hero).[14] We find many such figures from Schiller's Wallenstein forever postponing decision to Büchner's Danton awaiting Robespierre's attack. Again, Romantic man's struggle to know the self may lead him to betray his full humanity and to accept a reductive sense of himself. Schiller puts on stage a series of men and women who, in order to control the self, identify themselves with only a portion of their full human potential: the brothers in *Die Braut von Messina* (The Bride of Messina) suggest the dangers of unrestrained passion; the Marquis of Posa is a portrait of the enthusiastic reformer as fanatic; and Fiesco is a role-player who becomes lost within his role.[15]

As Schiller's Franz Moor suggests, the isolated and alienated intellect poses a special danger; for Romantic man – as exemplified by Wordsworth's Oswald in *The Borderers* or Coleridge's Ordonio in *Remorse* – is tempted to adopt a destructive mode of analytic consciousness that defines it-

---

[13] Beddoes, *Plays and Poems*, ed. H.W. Donner (Cambridge, MA: Harvard Univ. Press, 1950); additional references will be cited by act, scene, and line number in the text.

[14] Goethe, *Wilhelm Meisters Lehrjahre*, in *Werke*, VII, 246; *Wilhelm Meister's Apprenticeship*, trans. Thomas Carlyle, vol. 23 of *The Works of Thomas Carlyle in Thirty Volumes*, Centenary Edition (1899; rpt. New York: AMS, 1969), p. 282.

[15] On this point, see Ilse Graham's *Schiller: A Master of the Tragic Form* (Pittsburgh: Duquesne Univ. Press, 1974) and *Schiller's Drama: Talent and Integrity* (New York: Barnes & Noble, 1974).

self by severing all the ties that link the individual to others. He may then become an intellectual nay-sayer, a demonic spirit of negativity like Goethe's Mephisto or Byron's Lucifer in *Cain*; Lucifer embraces self-involved isolation as the goal of such figures: "Think and endure, – and form an inner world/ In your own bosom – where the outward fails/ So shall you nearer be the spiritual/ Nature, and war triumphant with your own" (II.ii.463-66). Romantic man may further discover that a dependence upon the analytic intellect leaves the individual unprepared to defend himself against his baser desires. Seeking to submit his self and his world to an intellectual idea, he may find himself in fact under the sway of an unconscious will. Kleist's Prince Friedrich – who is so wrapped up in the self and its dreams that he can no longer tell reality from fantasy – and Musset's Lorenzaccio – who comes to believe that "je corromprais ma mère, si mon cerveau le prenait à tâche" (IV.v) (I would corrupt my mother, if the idea came into my head)[16] – embody key instances of the Romantic tragedy of selfhood in which the protagonist struggles, in the absence of imaginative redemption, to overcome the lures and deceptions that lie within the self.

Shelley's *The Cenci* investigates all of these dangers of what he calls "self-anatomy":

> [...] 'tis a trick of this same family
> To analyse their own and other minds.
> Such self-anatomy shall teach the will
> Dangerous secrets: for it tempts our powers,
> Knowing what must be thought, and may be done,
> Into the depth of darkest purposes. (II.ii.108-13)

Self-anatomy marks all of Shelley's central characters. Its key exponent is the evil Count Cenci who pursues every desire he can uncover within himself:

> All men delight in sensual luxury,
> All men enjoy revenge; and must exult
> Over the tortures they can never feel –
> Flattering their secret peace with other's pain.
> But I delight in nothing else. I love
> The sight of agony, and the sense of joy,
> When this shall be another's and that mine. (I.i.77-83)

The very rhythm of his speech follows Cenci's mind as it divides the world between the joys of the self and the pain it inflicts on others. Fully in the grip of the family "trick," he finds he must act upon "any design my captious fancy makes" (I.i.99). Cenci has thus "progressed" beyond the delights of lust, he tells us; for he has found in torturing another and in finally destroying him the means of proving his self's power. Cenci can ensure himself through the pain of others that he lives fully and contentedly, thus proving his "secret peace with other's pain." His most recent desire, his final attempt to impose the self upon the other, is to rape his daughter, Beatrice.

Cenci unleashes the self's energies when he turns within, but his son Giacomo is paralyzed by self-anatomy. He loses the ability to act when he looks within to discover his desire to kill his oppressive father; he is even afraid to give voice to his hidden wishes:

---

[16] The text of *Lorenzaccio* used is found in *La Genèse de Lorenzaccio*, ed. Paul Dimoff, rev. ed. (Paris: Didier, 1964); act and scene numbers will given in the text.

> I am as one lost in a midnight wood,
> Who dares not ask some harmless passenger
> The path across the wilderness, lest he,
> As my thoughts are, should be – a murderer. (II.ii.94-97)

Again, the priest Orsino, who plots to marry Beatrice, finds that self-scrutiny has "made me shrink from what I cannot shun,/ Show a poor figure to my own esteem,/ To which I grow half reconciled" (II.ii.116-18). Having fallen half in love with the vicious desires he finds within, he betrays his love for Beatrice, adopting a reductive vision of himself as a clever schemer, a pygmy Cenci.

Only Beatrice herself can confront the self without falling prey to its dangerous lures. Orsino tells us of her command of self-examination, but he makes it clear that she attempts to bend the will away from the self's desires:

> Yet I fear
> Her subtle mind, her awe-inspiring gaze
> Whose beams *anatomize* me nerve by nerve
> And lay me bare and *make me blush to see*
> *My hidden thoughts.* (I.ii.83-87; my emphasis)

Beatrice's much disputed innocence lies not in virtuous action – she does after all plot her father's murder – but in her struggle against the dangers of self-analysis. While she shares with her family the turn to the self, she remains heroic in her attempt to master the inner world.

Even if the Romantic protagonist creates a heroic mode of self-consciousness, it is only his first step. For once he has completed his journey into the interior of the self, he must then turn outward to discover a mode of action through which to body forth his heroic self-consciousness and to remake his unheroic world. Given the nature of his world, this outward turn must take the form of revolt. As in his struggle with the self, this confrontation with the world can be defined in relation to an ideal Romantic pattern. The Romantic poet turns out from the self in the hopes of transforming his world through the visionary imagination and love. *Prometheus Unbound* successfully completes this encounter when the world is made new through the imagination as Prometheus and Asia come together in love; Jupiter overthrown – and with him social, personal, and mental oppression – man finds that "human love" "makes all it gazes on Paradise" (IV.127-28) and that language, the voice of the imagination, has become "a perpetual Orphic song,/ Which rules with Daedal harmony a throng/ Of thoughts and forms, which else senseless and shapeless were" (IV.415-17).

The protagonist of Romantic tragic drama, however, does not find such a harmonious resolution to his movement into the world. Even Hölderlin's Empedokles, whose status as poet-prophet should make him another Prometheus, finds that the balance between man and the world that he has in part disrupted can only be regained through his sacrificial death. Most Romantic protagonists, lacking the imaginative powers of Prometheus and Empedokles, find their sacrifices less availing. The typical Romantic protagonist brings not Orphic vision but his heroic self-definition, and he faces a world that sees him as a dangerous outcast not a victorious liberator. He finds that he must struggle to remake his world through revolt not imagination and that his relationship with others is defined by violence rather than love.

From the rebellion of Schiller's Robber to that of the bandit Hernani, from the metaphysical plaint of Byron's Cain to the social protest of Dumas's Antony, from the conspiracy of Schiller's

Fiesco to the revolution planned in Musset's *Lorenzaccio*, revolt dominates the action of Romantic tragic drama. While the difficulties of subjectivity lie at the heart of Romantic drama's characterization, revolt shapes its plot. Clearly, Romantic drama could no longer draw its plots from myth. Instead Romantic man must plot his own life. He does not live in a mythic world where the fates chart his rise and fall. Rather, he lives in historical time, where the future seems uncharted, ready to be shaped by the human will. Confronting a world from which the gods have departed, the Romantic protagonist participates in a revolt that thrusts him into history with the hope he can plot its course towards an ideal human future.

However, if the future seems open to a heroic ideal, it is in the unheroic present that the protagonist must act. He is tragically caught in the structure of historical time. A rebel within his own society, he would be a hero only in the ideal world he would create in the future through revolt. Seeking to transform the world, he still must adopt the violent means of his present sad reality and thus betray the ideal for which he fights. Schiller's Wallenstein, for example, hopes to create a peaceful and unified Germany, but to do so he must revolt against his Emperor and violate his oath of loyalty. Knowing his path into the future is uncertain, Wallenstein watches the stars anxiously, waiting for a heavenly signal, the kind of revelation that came to heroes in the past. Living in a post-providential age, he searches in vain. At the very moment when he believes he has finally found the conjunction of the stars that will enable him to act, he discovers that the action of other men – of the Emperor and his tool, Octavio, of the impetuous rebels Illo and Terzy – have already produced a situation in which his actions are constrained, in which he must act upon his dreams even though he knows action will now bring defeat. In seeking providential assurances, he has allowed history to move past him. As Hugo says of his Cromwell, the commitment to realizing one's dream in the present is "le moment où sa chimère lui échappe, où le présent lui tue l'avenir" (the moment when his chimera escapes him, when the present kills the future for him).[17]

Other figures find that their attempt to stage a revolt involves them in self-falsification, a destruction of some essential part of their identity. Byron's Marino Faliero turns against the government of Venice when he realizes that his position as Doge is merely ceremonial and that he does not even possess the power to avenge personal wrongs committed against him by the aristocrats who truly rule. His sense of himself as a great warrior and strong leader threatened, he joins a plebeian rebellion. However, the identity he fights to protect is bound up with the very nobles he must kill. He is, after all, an aristocrat himself; he comes to realize that destroying his noble enemies will entail the destruction of a part of himself: "Each stab to them will seem my suicide" (III.ii.402).

The Romantic tragedy of revolt is perhaps clearest in Musset's *Lorenzaccio*. Lorenzo dreams of being a Brutus and of killing one of the tyrants who oppress his city. He thus plots to kill Alexandre de Medicis, hoping that such an assassination will lead to an ideal Florence:

> Je vais tuer Alexandre; une fois mon coup fait, si les républicains se comportent comme ils le doivent, il leur sera facile d'établir une république, la plus belle qui ait jamais fleuri sur la terre. (III.iii)

> (I am going to kill Alexandre; once my strike is made, if the republicans act as they should, it will be easy for them to establish a republic, the most beautiful one that has ever flourished on earth.)

---

[17] Hugo, "Preface" to *Cromwell*, in *Théâtre Complet*, I, 446.

However, Lorenzo does not live in that ideal republic but in the decadent Florence of Alexandre. To accomplish his purpose, he must thus don the disguise of Lorenzaccio. To his dismay, he finds he can no longer distinguish between his role and his true self: "Le vice a été pour moi un vêtement, maintenant il est collé à ma peau" (III.iii) (Vice used to be a cloak for me; now it has become glued to my skin). In seeking the means to change his world within the present confines of society, he betrays the ideal self that could only be forged in the fires of revolt.

Lorenzo does kill the Duke, but no revolution follows; and he finds himself in exile, without purpose, without a sense of who he is. His friend Philippe had dreamed of Lorenzo killing Alexandre, giving up his disguise, and revealing himself to be "d'un métal aussi pur que les statues de bronze d'Harmodius et d'Aristogiton" (III.iii) (of a metal as pure as that in the bronze statues of Harmodius and Aristogiton), heroic enemies of tyranny. But Lorenzo finds himself instead to be a "statue de fer-blanc" (V.vi) (a tin statue), emptied of his heroic dreams. If Lorenzo convinces us that he possesses his own brand of heroism, it is because he finally escapes any reductive sense of self. He leaves his identity open to the future, a future in which he had hoped to define himself but towards which he can only gesture through the violence that finally engulfs him along with his enemy.

The double task of the Romantic protagonist, then, offers him opportunities to create himself as a hero but also occasions for tragic failure. He wants to discover for himself a heroic identity; but when he turns inward to order the chaos of his self, he cuts himself off from a visionary solution to the problems of consciousness. He also seeks to remake his world in accordance with an ideal vision within which he is heroic and his world humanely significant; but when he revolts against the turmoil and oppression that surround him, he finds that he has isolated himself in violence, trapping himself in the present in his very attempt to create the future. It is an interesting fact about the criticism of Romantic tragic drama that the introspection of its protagonists is seen as a weak imitation of Hamlet; that the historical emphasis of these plays has struck many as a feeble attempt to pit Shakespearean historical drama against neoclassical tragedy; and that the violence of these plays has appeared as mere gothic theatricality. It should be clear, however, that subjectivity and the violence of historical revolt were problems central to Romanticism as a whole. In confronting them, Romantic playwrights did not merely borrow bits and pieces of the dramatic tradition; rather they sought to discover the potential tragedy within the modern, Romantic world. They discovered the Romantic tragedy that is the counterpart of visionary romance.

Romantic tragic drama lies between traditional tragedy and twentieth-century tragicomedy. Traditional, providential tragedy had always affirmed both man's greatness and an ultimate order that transcends man. Tragicomedy, modern man's equivalent to the great form of the past, finds man's greatness an illusion in a world that lacks order. The Romantic dramatists struggled to affirm man's heroic stature and to discover an order for their world, but they already confronted the problems that have produced tragicomedy. The Romantics realized that they no longer had heroes supported by a hierarchical world order, or plots derived from divine myth, or a vision of providential order; but they sought to find a hero in the man who seeks his full humanity, a modern equivalent to myth in the processes of revolutionary history, and a replacement for providential order in a vision of a humanized world. Soon, however, this vision of Romantic tragic drama would begin to waver in the face of the three great reductions of modern culture: the reduction of the self to its lower drives, of history to socio-economic forces beyond man's control, and of man's imaginative ideals to the rhetoric of language games. We may continue to insist that the Romantic attempt to define tragedy was a mistake, that they should have been the writers of forward-looking tragicomedies not backward-looking tragedies. But if Romanticism's redefinitions of the tragic represent a mistake and perhaps even a failure, they were also a glorious gamble risked in the hopes of creating a vision of man and his world that would preserve the nobility and richness of life at the very moment when the providential guarantees of such qualities were collapsing.

GERHART HOFFMEISTER

THE ROMANTIC TRAGEDY OF FATE

The easiest approach to this complex topic would doubtless be to declare at the outset: the Romantic tragedy of fate does not exist – thus sweeping it off the table, along with some disputed Romantic movements of a national brand, such as the Spanish, Italian, or Russian variety. But these plays are, as von Platen sarcastically put it, "zum Entsetzen meisterhaft. Zum Fressen schön" (masterful in a ghastly way. So beautiful they're good enough to eat).[1] The fact is that, between 1809 and 1817, *Schicksalstragödien* were quite fashionable in the German-speaking lands.[2] Scholars have differed in their evaluation of this literature. Some have recognized in these plays, next to Romantic irony, one of the essential forms of literary production and reception of the period;[3] others have regarded them as a uniquely German contribution to European drama;[4] while still others have played down their literary significance.[5] Whether *Schicksalstragödien* have a distinctive character, whether they go beyond a mere German manifestation or, on closer inspection, take on European dimensions, and whether some common generic features can be established – these are the problems that I shall try to answer.

Without going into the intricate history of the philosphical concept of fate among the various schools of thinking in ancient Greece,[6] Latin *fatum* (for which the Greeks used four different terms: *ananke, heimarmene, moira* and *tyche*) conveys the sense that human will is not in control but is determined by impersonal and supernatural powers. Fate is characterized by blind necessity and inevitable force; it is omnipotent, inflexible, and amoral; it is the prime cause of fated events, determining their succession or sequence and their outcome ("doom" or "lot" apportioned to an individual). In Greek mythology fate is sometimes conceived as *Moira*, the personal goddess of destiny (Hesiod), who even controls the Olympian gods (see Goethe's poem "Prometheus"). As to Greek tragedy, Euripides and Aeschylus stress the omnipotence of merciless *ananke*; to attempt to escape one's lot is to be guilty of pride or *hybris* and to call down the *nemesis* of the offended powers.

Sophocles' *Oidipos Tyrannos* has been regarded as exemplary of Greek fate tragedy but it has received varying interpretations. I believe Oedipus falls victim to fate through a combination of his

---

[1] *Der romantische Oedipus* (1829), Act V, l. 1285.

[2] Actually some literary historians have gone to the extreme of viewing *Schicksalstragödie* as synonymous with German Romantic drama in general; see, e.g., Robert F. Arnold, ed., *Das deutsche Drama*, (Munich: Beck, 1925; rpt. Hildesheim and New York: Olms 1972), p. 543.

[3] See Herbert Kraft, *Das Schicksalsdrama: Interpretation und Kritik einer literarischen Reihe* (Tübingen: Niemeyer 1974), p. 45.

[4] For example, Jakob Minor, "Zur Geschichte der deutschen Schicksalstragödie und zu Grillparzers *Ahnfrau*," *Jahrbuch der Grillparzer-Gesellschaft*, 9 (1899), 1-85.

[5] See Paul Hankamer, "Schicksalstragödie," *Reallexikon der deutschen Literaturgeschichte*, 2nd ed. (Berlin: de Gruyter, (1955f.), p. 628.

[6] For details see Johannes Hoffmeister, ed., *Wörterbuch der philosophischen Begriffe*, 2nd ed. (Hamburg: Meiner, 1955), "Schicksal".

ignorance of the true situation and his own strength and courage, believing that he can outwit the decree of the gods, making sure that it will not come true. To some extent, Oedipus brings about the catastrophe because initially he (like his parents) tries to escape destiny by proving the decree wrong. Destiny here, however, is not only the mark of an innocent criminal who kills his father and commits incest with his mother, but also the mark of an outstanding hero. As Hegel remarks "der alte Räthsellöser zwingt das Wissen über sein eigenes Schicksal heraus" (the inveterate solver of puzzles forces the knowledge about his own fate to come out);[7] by unflinchingly seeking the truth about his past at whatever personal cost, Oedipus loses his happiness and power, but gains knowledge about himself and his gods. In this sense he regains control over his fate or at least he becomes equal to it: he unmasks and sentences himself, being criminal, prosecutor, and judge at the same time, a noble man and worthy counterpart of the gods. Blinding himself obviously restores him to the divine level of blind Tiresias. This opens the door to the restoration of his former human dignity and his eventual salvation by the gods in *Oedipus at Colonus*. (His reconciliation with the gods does not yet amount to the transfiguration of the soul brought about by providence, but remains on the level of ethics.) Oedipus falls victim to fate and saves himself subsequently, thus illustrating Heraclitus' sentence: man's *ethos* (character) is his *daimon* (personal fate).

At least two major interpretations of Oedipus seem possible to me: on the one hand, he appears as the fated victim of Apollo's hatred (cf. line 515, Tiresias speaking: "you and your fate belong to Apollo"), according to which all actions except his self-willed blinding and exile come from outside powers; on the other hand, Oedipus can be viewed as not waiting for his fate to overcome him, but challenging the gods, believing that he is master of his own life, in control of his fate, a free agent of his actions (on stage) for which he accepts full responsibility (cf. line 1414: "this horror is mine and none but I is strong enough to bear it"). In this light, Oedipus could be regarded as the first *homme fatal*, since he is "cursed by his own curses" (line 1669), "destroyer and destroyed, the man whose life is hell for others and for himself" (line 1748f.).

It is obvious that *Oedipus* aroused the interest of West European playwrights who were raised on the axiom of the paradigmatic value of the ancients in a classicist tradition. Yet their reception of Sophocles and Greek tragedy in general experienced many changes from the Middle Ages to Romanticism. First, the perception of ancient tragedy shifted considerably because Christian theology substituted divine providence for pagan fate, replacing destiny by the doctrine of predestination, which affirms the sovereignty of the divine will without eliminating the need of the human will to choose between Good and Evil. According to God's providence, everything works together to fulfill the plan of salvation. In this light a Christian tragedy of fate would be a contradiction in terms. Both fate and authentically classical "Greek" tragedy were generally inconceivable to poets from the Middle Ages to the Age of Goethe. Thereafter, however, loss in faith resulted in a return to the widespread conviction in the inevitability of fate. This belief is based on a materialistic conception of the universe, in which everything happens according to the laws of nature. Although this idea is already found in the Stoic philosophy, it was revived at the dawn of modern science.[8] An important question is whether the determinism of modern science caused the tragedy of fate to flourish around 1800, or whether additional or other motives were at work.

---

[7] Hegel, *Sämtliche Werke*, ed. Glockner (Stuttgart: Fromanns, 1928), XIV, 558.

[8] See Roger Bauer on the shifting perception of tragedy and fate since Aristotle in "'Das gemißhandelte Schicksal': Zur Theorie des Tragischen im deutschen Idealismus," *Euphorion*, 58 (1964), 243-59. See also Roger Bauer, ed., *Inevitabilis Vis Fatorum: Der Triumph des Schicksalsdramas auf der europäischen Bühne um 1800* (Bern: Lang, 1990).

Second, any purist approach that tries to explain the revival of fate tragedy by linking it directly to *Oedipus* as the major model, is doomed to failure. To be sure, as Gerald Gillespie and Martin Mueller[9] have aptly demonstrated, one road on which a direct knowledge of Oedipus arrived in Germany from the 1750s onward "was bordered by translations and editions" by well-known writers such as Bodmer and Gessner (both in 1761), Stolberg (1787), and Solger (1808). Hölderlin's translation (and treatise on) *Ödipus der Tyrann* (1804) is only one example of widespread interest in Sophocles. Schiller and Kleist, too, went straight to the source when they decided to rival the Greek playwright in *Der zerbrochene Krug* (The Broken Jug) and *Die Braut von Messina* (The Bride of Messina).[10] "The other road, however, on which perhaps Oedipus sped his approach even more swiftly was by way of France. For, through translations, despite Lessing's anti-Gallic thrusts, the enormous vogue in Germany around 1750 of Racine, of Corneille (to a lesser extent), and then of the great contemporary Voltaire, lent sufficient impetus to carry Oedipus into the nineteenth century."[11] As an example such as Goethe's *Iphigenie* shows, "the tyranny of Greece over Germany" (E.M. Butler, 1935) in the later eighteenth century rivalled that of France earlier in respect to the prior modelling of German plays on Racine and Corneille. The preceding French vogue strengthened in turn the pervasive indirect influence from Sophocles (Corneille, *Oedipe*, 1659; Voltaire, *Oedipe*, 1718, German translation 1748).[12]

With the shift from the French drama to Shakespeare promoted by Lessing, the English treatment of the Oedipus myth opened a third road to German perception, not at all negligible in comparison to the French impact, since *Hamlet* and *Macbeth*, both unthinkable without *Oedipus* (e.g., incest-motif, father-son-conflict, oracles), generated much enthusiasm for Shakespeare in the Storm and Stress period and in the Romantic movement.[13] Actually, a Hamlet-version had been performed by the English Comedians in Germany since 1626.[14] Shakespeare's play was translated by Eschenburg in 1762, by Wieland in 1775, enacted by F.L. Schröder in 1776, discussed in Book V of *Wilhelm Meisters Lehrjahre* (Wilhelm Meister's Apprenticeship), and, in a curious conflation of Sophoclean and Shakespearian motifs, adapted to prose narratives by writers such as Novalis, Brentano, Hölderlin, and Bonaventura.[15]

A fourth road, frequently overlooked, although of tremendous importance for German Romantic playwrights, was the reception of Calderón's philosophical and religious *comedias*, which gained momentum with A.W. Schlegel's translations in *Spanisches Theater*, 1803f.[16] Calderón's *La vida es sueño* (Life is a Dream) evidences strong links to the Oedipus myth as does *La devoción de la cruz* (Devotion to the Cross), as we see in primary shared motifs: father-son conflict, the "dark birth" and

---

[9] Mueller, *Children of Oedipus and Other Essays on the Imitation of Greek Tragedy 1550-1800* (Toronto: Univ. of Toronto Press, 1980).

[10] In England, Lillo who inaugurated the European fashion of fate tragedies with his *Fatal Curiosity* (1735) apparently read a Sophocles translation, and several generations earlier, Dryden and Nathaniel Lee collaborated on a dramatic version of the story by inserting literal translations from Sophocles (in 1679).

[11] Gerald Gillespie, "Romantic Oedipus," *Goethezeit: Festschrift Stuart Atkins*, ed. G. Hoffmeister (Bern: Francke, 1981), p. 331.

[12] Mueller, pp. 109f., 131f.

[13] See Friedrich Gundolf, *Shakespeare und der deutsche Geist*, 9th ed. (Bad Godesberg: Küpper, 1947).

[14] Date according to W. Creizenach, ed., *Die Schauspiele der englischen Komödianten*, DNL 23 (Berlin and Stuttgart: Spermann, 1888; rpt. Darmstadt: Wissenschaftliche Buchgesellschaft, 1967), p. 129.

[15] On this Oedipus-Hamlet connection, see Gillespie, in Hoffmeister, ed., pp. 333-45.

[16] On *Calderonismus*, see G. Hoffmeister, *Spanien und Deutschland: Geschichte und Dokumentation der literarischen Beziehungen*, Grundlagen der Romanistik, 9 (Berlin: Schmidt, 1976), pp. 128-34; Spanish transl. *España y Alemania*, Estudios y Ensayos, 302 (Madrid: Gredos, 1980), pp. 178-88.

incest-motif, fatal encounters and properties, the analytical form, as well as the major theme of free will versus predestination. In Calderón's plays Walter Benjamin discovered the rule of an "astral or magic fate" present in both a Sophoclean and Catholic tradition, a juxtaposition perhaps inspired by Schelling's interpretation of Eusebio (*La devoción de la cruz*) as a Christian Oedipus.[17]

Following any one of the above mentioned routes which Oedipus took to reach Germany entails a considerable shift in the concept of fate. While for Sophocles fate remains a religious power beyond human control and therefore severely restricting personal responsibility, Corneille under Neo-Stoic influence presents the will as ultimately triumphant over fateful circumstances (*Oedipe* II.v), while Racine under Jansenist influence shows it as feeble and vacillating. According to the prevailing Romantic view, whereas Shakespeare's Hamlet represents a reluctant instrument of vengeance torn between father and mother, between thinking and acting, Calderón overcomes the fatal mechanism of accidents and crimes by stressing divine destiny (providence), which intervenes at the last moment if the protagonist is ready for God's grace. His Christian fate tragedy is based on the sequence of sin (original sin) and expiation.[18]

The literary evidence shows it was not the determinism of modern science that caused the fate genre to flourish, but (at least in Germany) a conscious effort on the part of writers to produce plays in the spirit of the Greek masters. This was especially true of the Oedipus myth, certainly a difficult undertaking, since Oedipus had traveled so many different roads which, by the time of European Romanticism, had led to a conflation of French Classical nuances, of Shakespearian motifs, and of Sophocles translated.[19] The admixture of ingredients fluctuated. Lessing for instance thought Shakespeare and Lillo closer to the ancients than the French were. Attempting to transplant the Greek fate tragedy to Germany in theory (*Hamburgische Dramaturgie*, Nos. 74ff.), Lessing developed his concept of the sentimental middle-class tragedy out of his admiration for Lillo's *Fatal Curiosity*. His dramatic fragment *Das Horoskop* shows his failure to put his misconceived idea of a "Greek" fate tragedy into practice, using devices such as murder of relatives, and the chain of events determined by mantic oracles, curses, and horoscopes, in order to arouse terror and pity.[20]

A similar discrepancy between intention and execution occurs in Schiller's *Die Braut von Messina*, a play closely modelled on *Oedipus* as far as parallels in the unravelling of the plot,[21] the revival of the chorus, and the rule of fate are concerned. Although this tragedy is celebrated as a re-creation of Greek tragedy, Schiller did *not* establish fate as an omnipotent, transcendent power beyond human control in it. On closer examination fate appears throughout "as the consequence of morally culpable actions,"[22] i.e., the characters' jealousy and secrecy. By conceiving fate as character, Schiller was able, toward the end of the play, to introduce his concept of individual freedom, responsibility, and will. Despite frequent references in the play about the rule of fate,[23] it is finally

---

[17] See Ernst Behler, "The Reception of Calderón among the German Romantics," *Studies in Romanticism*, 20 (1981), 437-60, especially p. 456f.

[18] See Swana L. Hardy, *Goethe, Calderón und die romantische Theorie des Dramas* (Heidelberg: Winter, 1965), p. 62f.

[19] Cf. Gillespie, in Hoffmeister, ed., p. 332.

[20] See Paul Hankamer, p. 628.

[21] See "Erläuterungen" in Schiller, *Werke*, National-Ausgabe, ed. J. Petersen et. al. (Weimar: Böhlaus Nachfolger, 1943ff.), vol. X (1980), pp. 341-54.

[22] Mueller, p. 137.

[23] For instance, I, 1: "Aus unbekannt verhängnisvollem Samen"; II, 5: "Ist's Wahl, wenn des Gestirnes Macht den Menschen Ereilt in der verhängnisvollen Stunde?"; IV, 5: "wie die Seher verkündet, so ist es gekommen, Denn noch niemand entfloh dem verhängnisvollen Geschick."

reduced to individual guilt (see last line), which can be overcome or defeated by a courageous act of cathartic self-sacrifice. Schiller's characters determine their own fate negatively through their petty actions, from the chain of which only Caesar is able to break away.[24] For artistic purposes, Schiller employed the notion of "fate" as a metaphor for past guilt haunting a family in the present. His approach was meant to be analytical (see his letter to Goethe, Oct. 2, 1797), yet it is not past horrors that are discovered by a process of inquiry, but "rather, past events, having remained latent, realize their full destructive potential as they interact with present circumstances to bring about the cata-strophe."[25]

"Fate," manifesting itself as a generational curse in this case, a curse inherited by two rival-brothers with an inclination to rash violence, was a theme which had gained literary currency among the dramatists and novelists of the Gothic persuasion. Characteristic of their works, which flourished in the last quarter of the eighteenth century, is their setting in medieval castles inhabited predominantly by villainous tyrants who abuse their paternal authority by oppressing noble heroes and innocent heroines. To achieve the highest degree of gloom and terror, these victims are struck down at the very instant when the mystery is about to be revealed. "None of this is in *Oedipus Rex*, but all of it can be found in *Die Braut von Messina*."[26] Schiller's plot appears to be a variation on Walpole's *The Mysterious Mother*, the first Gothic tragedy (1758), in that Adelize, like Beatrice, grows up in a convent, until her mother reveals the family secret and she meets her relatives there for the first time.[27] An ancestral curse sets the mechanism of fateful events in motion in *Die Braut von Messina* (I.viii). Thus, although Schiller's intention was ostensibly Sophoclean in origin, al-though the vacillating and feeble will of his protagonists reminds one of Racine's characters, fate as a "Gothic monstrosity"[28] seems to have gained the upper hand in his play. Certainly the recognition of this monstrosity lies at the root of Bonaventura's travesty of *Die Braut von Messina* in *Die Nachtwachen* (The Night Watchers, chapters 4 and 5).[29]

It is not our intention to dwell further on the genesis of the German *Schicksalstragödie* nor to discuss insignificant plays at any length, but rather to look at paradigmatic plays which show the conflation of various strains in the onrolling reception of fate tragedy. While Schiller seemed to pre-pare the way for a more lyrical drama by introducing a chorus, it was Friedrich Schlegel who tried to fuse ancient fate and Calderonian providence in his *Alarcos*. But Schlegel, too, failed to support his weak plot, relying finally on Gothic elements: the murder of a wife who, upon her deathbed, inflicts on her rival a curse which is fulfilled within three days. Her rival dies of grief, as a white ghost in female shape appears at her deathbed, whereupon Alarcos, tormented by the furies, com-mits suicide. Until the very end, he shirks all responsibility for his deed, but then the ghost steps in as a *deus ex machina* to take revenge.

Inspired by Shakespeare's *Romeo and Juliet*, Kleist wrote his *Die Familie Schroffenstein* (1803), a tragedy of fate[30] which reduces all deadly misunderstandings to the banality of a cut-off

---

[24] According to Walter Benjamin, *Urpsrung des deutschen Trauerspiels* (Berlin: Rowohlt, 1928), "Kern des Schicks-alsgedankens [ist] die Überzeugung, daß Schuld [=original sin, not a moral guilt] [...] Kausalität als Instrument der unaufhalt-sam sich entrollenden Fatalitäten auslöst," p. 124.

[25] Mueller, p. 140.

[26] Mueller, p. 146.

[27] Schiller, in Petersen et. al., eds, X, 348.

[28] Mueller, p. 146.

[29] See Gillespie, in Hoffmeister, ed., p. 338.

[30] According to Gerhard Fricke, *Gefühl und Schicksal bei Heinrich von Kleist* (Berlin: Juncker u. Dünnhaupt, 1929; rpt. Darmstadt: Wissenschaftliche Buchgesellschaft, 1963), p. 55; Georg Lukács, "Die Tragödie Heinrich von Kleists," *Deutsche Realisten des 19. Jahrhunderts* (Bern: Francke, 1951), pp. 19-48.

child's finger. "If you kill each other, it is by mistake," thus concludes the play. In this case, fate actually consists in a meaningless, confusing chain of deceptive accidents, which reduce the protagonists to blind puppets and the tragedy to a farce. The ultimate source of this farcical tragedy in which the clearsighted lovers fall victim to the superstitions, distrust, and prejudices of their parents is not an external mysterious power but rests with the inability of the individual to see through words and misleading evidence. Kleist's characters are caught up in their own shortcomings and gain true knowledge only through the experience of death.[31]

Zacharias Werner's play *Der vierundzwanzigste Februar* (The Twenty-Fourth of February), inaugurated in 1809 a fashion of about twenty-five German dramas of this type. Goethe as well as Werner were well aware of the ancient model when discussing this play. The theme of the curse is reinforced by the terrifying atmosphere and such props of fate as the recurrent fated date, the scythe, the birthmark, and the knife. But in spite of the fatalistic features of his work, Werner was not interested in presenting fatalism as a way of life. As he states in his prologue:

> So schafft das Schicksal weder Lust noch Leiden
> Den Weisen, die, mag Hölle blinken, blitzen,
> In treuer Brust des Glaubens Schild besitzen.
>
> (Thus fate provides neither pleasure nor pain
> To the wise who, though hell glower and glare,
> Rely on their shield of faith for protection.)

He was, however, concerned with the idea of transforming the curse into Christian grace through atonement and forgiveness. Fate was for him an artistic device, not a power beyond the protagonists, but within the reach of their responsibility. The curse can only become reality, because man, fallen from grace and submitting to superstitions, fulfills it himself. Fate is the deed of man. No wonder then that some scholars prefer to speak about the "so-called" *Schicksalstragödie*.[32] Of course, there are external similarities between Werner's play and *Oedipus*: a curse plaguing a family for generations, the analytical structure, etc., but fate as decreed by the gods has been replaced by a sequence of fateful events and recurrent devices which do not result in an overall transcendental world view, but in a chain of unfortunate coincidences linked for the purpose of bringing about retribution. The accidental element in *Oedipus* (the criminal aspects) has become the center of attention in Werner's play. But both protagonists are deemed responsible for their doom and subsequent redemption, Oedipus facing his destiny squarely and thus regaining control over it, Kunz succumbing to it by falling ever deeper into a state of sin from which only Christian grace can save him, and this grace is invoked by his dying son, who is the instrument of providence.

Thus, Werner's play is, at least in intention, linked to *Oedipus* as well as to Calderón (trochaic verse, transfiguration). It would have been possible for the protagonists to save themselves if they had only believed in God's guidance; in effect, however, Werner's play leaves the impression of a dark, claustrophobic world ruled by "a Gothic monstrosity of fate." For Werner's epigones, Müllner

---

[31] See Walter Müller-Seidel, *Versehen und Erkennen: Eine Studie über Heinrich von Kleist* (Köln: Böhlau, 1967), p. 218.
[32] For example, Friedrich Sengle, "Die Braut von Messina," *Arbeiten zur deutschen Literatur 1750-1850* (Stuttgart: Metzler, 1965), pp. 94-117; Zdenko Skreb, "Die deutsche sogenannte Schicksalstragödie," *Grillparzer-Gesellschaft*, 9 (1972), 193-237.

and Houwald, it was an easy matter to turn his devices into even more effective means for writing fashionable "fate tragedies." In Müllner's *Der neunundzwanzigste Februar* (The Twenty-Ninth of February, 1815), for instance, Schiller's *Die Braut von Messina* and Werner's play seem to fuse, because he blends Gothic influences[33] with Calderonian mysticism, verse technique, and professed belief in divine justice (Preface).

The German fashion reached a climax with Grillparzer's first play, *Die Ahnfrau* (The Ancestress, 1817), an intriguing mix of the Oedipus myth (parricide, incest, tragic analysis), as it had been passed on through German and Spanish intermediaries, and the Gothic tradition as represented by M.G. Lewis's *Ambrosio or the Monk* (1796). For example, the curtain rises upon a terrifying night scene with a rusty dagger on the wall of a Gothic hall. The ghost of the adulterous ancestress clad in a white veil appears, to signify the doom of her family which she can foresee but not prevent. A generational curse seems to engulf the protagonists who appear to be completely at its mercy. Jaromir dies in despair.[34] Yet essentially, fate reveals itself to the reader or spectator not as an objective demonic power but as a poetic image for an inescapable mixture of guilt, coincidence, and expiation, or, as the Preface says, a "Verkettung von Schuld und unglücklichen Ereignissen" (chain of guilt and unlucky coincidences) which turns "fate" into a somewhat subjective "instrument of imminent justice." Fate has been replaced by moral and hereditary justifications and thereby loses its overpowering function.[35] In effect, such a fate leaves enough room for personal responsibility, free will, and the belief in divine justice.[36]

Apart from Kleist's comedy *Der zerbrochene Krug*, a brilliant "parody of Oedipus' enquiry,"[37] the so called German *Schicksalstragödie* from Schiller to Grillparzer did not generally fulfill the intentions of their authors to regenerate Greek fate tragedy or at least to blend ancient fate with Christian providence successfully. Almost all the artistic devices of *Oedipus* were employed, either by going directly to the source or translation (e.g., Schiller) or by conflating influences of the "Children of Oedipus" (e.g., the French classicists Corneille, Racine), Calderón, Shakespeare, and the Gothic tradition. The best example for the fusion of different sources is the already mentioned *Die Ahnfrau*.[38] Again we find an analytic structure, a dramatic process which leads from blindness to final realization, a constant invocation of fate which is used as an artistic device to promote the coherence and the mysterious effect of the plot.

But in spite of the Romantics' preoccupation with the dark and irrational aspects of existence, the so-called *Nachtseiten* (night side), their fate, without the foundation of a corresponding world view, degenerates into a sequence of accidental events and intrigues, a mechanical correlation between an injustice, a curse, and revenge or retribution that is nothing more than a semblance of Greek *tyche*. In effect, Romantic protagonists, although apparently acting of their own free will, fall victim to their own false assumptions, which they alone are to be blamed for. In contrast to Oedipus, they turn out to be rather irresponsible criminals (e.g., the anti-heroic figures in plays by Kleist, Schlegel, Grillparzer). Oedipus has decayed into a poetic alibi.

---

[33] See, for instance, the fatality of dates in Walpole's play of 1768.

[34] See the count's speech, Act IV, lines 2382f.: "Willst Du mit den Kinderhänden/ In des Schicksals Speichen greifen?"

[35] About these justifications see Roger Bauer, "*Die Ahnfrau* et la querelle de la Tragédie Fataliste," *Études Germaniques*, 27 (1972), 174f.

[36] See *Die Ahnfrau*, V, lines 3300f.: "Durch der Schlüsse Schauernacht/ Sei gepriesen ew'ge Macht!"

[37] Mueller, p. 118.

[38] Calderonian trochaic verse, providence, conflict of essence and appearance, lines 400f.; Jaromir as Hamlet, lines 2776f.

Is the so-called *Schicksalstragödie* a uniquely German or a European phenomenon with specific generic features? The Gothic influences on plays from Schiller to Grillparzer suggest to us that
there must exist a closer relationship between the British and German tragedies of the period. However, hardly anything is known about Gothic plays as compared with Gothic novels. Gothic plays
were first developed in "pre-Romantic" classicist times, usually by the adaptation of novels. Walpole published *The Castle of Otranto* in 1764 and then dramatized its key motifs in *The Mysterious
Mother* in 1768. Interesting in this context is "Monk" Lewis's *The Castle Spectre* (1797) which had
begun as a Gothic novel and "took final shape as a Gothic play, inspired respectively by Walpole,
Mrs. Radcliffe and the horrors supped in Germany," as B. Evans states in his book on *Gothic
Drama from Walpole to Shelley*.[39] As late as 1829, this play was turned into a prose romance by
Sarah Wilkinson – demonstrating that occasionally the reverse adaptation process could take place.

At first glance, these plays, with their emphasis on supernatural elements in medieval setting,
may appear to be different from the *Schicksalstragödie*, but both types provide protagonists who set
in motion, or fall victim to, a mechanism of cause and effect, of sin and retribution, sometimes a
generational curse. Both kinds furnish studies of evil, and stress an atmosphere of horror, gloom,
and mystery. Not surprisingly the spectators of the British plays adopted the epithet "German"
instead of Gothic to indicate the apparent source of this type of horrific tragedy. But Coleridge protested strongly against this misnomer: "The so-called *German* drama [...] is *English* in its *origin*,
English in its materials, and *English* by re-adoption,"[40] meaning that the Gothic play had already
fully developed its own national brand of horrors from 1768 on before some German "improvements" (Coleridge) did reach England in the 1790s.[41] As Evans explains: "Given a common
impulse, each country developed its own horrors in its own way," the German Gothic branch combining elements of the robber-drama of the Storm-and-Stress period with the "novel of terror"
inspired by Walpole.[42] "Up to 1798 the stream of influence flowed from England to Germany,"[43]
afterwards the flow reversed itself and brought with it a rush of dramatic adaptations, translations,
and borrowings of a specifically German (i.e., more magic and mysterious) character based on blue
flames, ghosts, beloved ladies as skeletons, all of which are responsible for the misnomer "German"
drama. Oedipus' fate as "an expression of the way things are" faded into the background of these
playwrights' consciousness and was replaced by fate as a metaphor of time, "the oppressive power
that the past is seen as holding over present and future" through a generational curse, "a *sine qua
non* of Gothic fate."[44] Only indirectly, watered down to dramatic devices of suspense, is Oedipus
still present in studies of evil which for inspiration turned to the "children of Oedipus" of the Elizabethan and Jacobean tragedy, above all Shakespeare (Hamlet, Macbeth, Othello), whose German
fortunes are well-known.

Disregarding the pre-Romantic, still mostly neoclassical Gothic plays of trivial character, I
want to compare briefly three literary manifestations of the Gothic tradition in English Romanticism. Starting with Wordsworth's *The Borderers* (Ms. 1795, published 1842), it is extremely
interesting to see that Oswald represents an Iago-like satanic seducer who makes his own laws. He

---

[39] B. Evans, *Gothic Drama from Walpole to Shelley* (Berkeley: Univ. of California Press, 1947), p. 132.
[40] *Biographia Literaria*, ed. by John Calvin Metcalf (New York: MacMillan, 1926), p. 360.
[41] Evans pinpoints first noticeable German influences in Lewis's play (1797), p. 124.
[42] Evans, p. 119.
[43] Evans, p. 124.
[44] Mueller, p. 145.

is not only the instrument for the unravelling of the plot, but also an *homme fatal* for others and himself. Man is his own fate: Oswald tries to prove it and fails unrepenting. While in *The Borderers* "the villain tries to destroy the hero's remorse, and fails; in Coleridge's play *Remorse*, the hero tries to arouse the villain's remorse and succeeds."[45] It is a Gothic tragedy of revenge with an admixture of fate, set in the period of Moorish border wars. Ordonio, "proud and gloomy" (I.i), acts as the fatal agent before the consequences of his deeds catch up with him. He actually appears as a "self-created God" (III.i).

And finally there is Shelley's *The Cenci* (1819). Here Beatrice's father becomes her fate. By the third act she realizes that she, an innocent victim of incest, has been trapped by circumstances beyond her control and feels called upon to avenge her lot as an "angel of wrath," an agent of divine justice taking the law into her own hands. The victim turned rebel dispenses with human justice and in her *hybris* sets herself up as an avenging demi-god, a step which brings her very close to her tyrannical father. She has become personally responsible, but her spiritual status is fraught with ambivalence. And in this sense fate constitutes itself as a combination of circumstance (i.e., criminal father, corrupt pope, Orsino, etc.) and character, which determines how she, her father's daughter, reacts to a desperate situation. Shelley fused the trivial motifs from the so-called German Gothic tradition with Shakespeare's *Macbeth* in order to achieve his own poetic and political ends.[46]

In sum, the English and German fate tragedies have the following features in common:

1. They employ similar devices in order to bring about an effect of Gothic mystery and horror: dreams, curses (not in Wordsworth), fated props, the suspense between disguise and revelation, revenge and murder by a close relative.

2. Fate is man-made, consisting of a combination of character and circumstances, which makes man responsible for his deeds. While the protagonist metes out death on account of greed, lost love, or some kind of revenge, thus acting as an *agent fatal*, his victim, who is usually passive, upholds the voice of providence (Werner, Wordsworth, Coleridge), surmounting senseless fate, or reinforces it by ending in complete despair (Kleist, Shelley).

A distinction lies in the greater reliance of the British authors on Gothic elements along with the Iago-type villain from the Elizabethan revenge tragedy, who has no counterpart in German Romanticism, unless we include the pre-Romantic *Sturm und Drang*. The German *Schicksalstragödie* portrays its protagonists as driven by curses, superstitions, and prejudices, yet ultimately responsible for whatever happens; whereas the English heroes take control of their fellow-men's affairs, usually avenging an earlier injustice, despite a misconception about their own role.

There is also a French variety. According to Evans, English "Gothic materials went to Germany and returned to overwhelm their own sources under German; just so, they went to France and returned to bury them under melodrama," or rather, Gothic melodrama.[47] Examples are "Monk" Lewis and Holcroft, who drew on British Gothic plays, German robber-tales, and French *mélodrame*. The best-known French author of popular and sensational *mélodrames*, Pixérécourt, adapted plays from English Gothic novels, e.g., *Les Mystères d'Udolphe* (1798) from Mrs. Radcliffe, there-

[45] Evans, p. 220.
[46] On Shelley's play, see for example: Joseph W. Donohue, "Shelley's Beatrice and the Romantic Concept of Tragic Character," *Keats-Shelley Journal*, 17 (1968), 53-73; Melvin R. Watson, "Shelley and Tragedy: The Case of Beatrice Cenci," *Keats-Shelley Journal*, 7-8 (1958-59), 13-22; Robert F. Whitman, "Beatrice's Pernicious Mistake in *The Cenci*," *PMLA*, 74 (1959), 249-53.
[47] Evans, p. 164.

by introducing foreign Gothic settings to the French stage. In these dramas he blended the direct enactment of murder and violence, tragic and comic styles, the depiction of vice (villainy) and virtue (persecuted innocence) in black and white, the suspended secret identity, the conflict of passion and honor, and the final victory of the latter.[48] Artistic devices such as the violent incident and exaggerated sentiment which are the hallmark of this second-class theater, had considerable impact on such French dramatic writers of the Romantic period as Victor Hugo and Dumas père in the 1830s. Their plays frequently center around the motif of mistaken identity with incest as a possible added motif (*Lucrèce Borgia* by Hugo, 1833; Marguerite in Dumas père, *La Tour de Nesle* [The Tower of Nesle, 1832]) and murder by a close relative as a prominent feature (Otbert in Hugo's *Les Burgraves*, 1843; his Lucrèce; Dumas's Marguerite). Basically, an aura of fated events arises from the very beginning; a victim of circumstances, such as education, milieu, or prejudice, rebels and decides to take fate into her own hands. I say her, since it is usually the heroine who seeks revenge on somebody responsible for her fall from grace and reputation (besides Lucrèce, see the fallen angel of *Marion Delorme* by Hugo, 1831, and his Guanhumara in *Les Burgraves*). Vengeance catches up with the perpetrator, but the fatal agent, too, is punished by an ironical fate (Lucrèce; and Buridan in *La Tour de Nesle*; Guanhumara).

Since these plays consist of intrigue and counter-intrigue, agent and victim, the concept of fate seems to have two aspects. For the agent, fate is identical with his desire and force of revenge. It is the *homme fatal* in whose web the victim is caught. This fate is the result of a mixture of milieu, character, and opportunity (chance). The plot progresses according to cause and effect laid out like an algebraic equation. But even for the most intelligent protagonist some blind spots (*até*) exist which will bring him down. On the other hand there is the victim, usually a man in love (Otbert, Didier, Gennaro, Walter) who accepts his fate passively, even allies himself with it by becoming an instrument of revenge for someone else. He sees fate as an external force imposed on him and beyond his control, a set of circumstances actually brought about by the *homme fatal*.[49]

Obviously elements of Gothic *mélodrame*, i.e., a curious fusion of the British tradition of horror and the French type of sensational drama, have survived in these plays. But these elements do not determine the character of the whole subgenre; for instance, in France a shift takes place from the concern with social order and justice in the *mélodrame* to a psychological interest in a complex hero who combines the forces of vice and virtue in his psyche. Also, distant echoes of the ancient tragedy of fate, which have trickled down through Corneille, Racine, and Voltaire (e.g., suspense between curse, prophecy, and fulfillment; search for identity), are present, although Hugo and Dumas père may not have been particularly conscious of them as such. But they were enthusiastic admirers of Schiller's virtuous heroines, of his art of building dramatic suspense, and of his presentation of national history,[50] so that we can establish their links to German Classical plays, as well as to the lesser German contributions to the international baggage of Gothic writers of *mélodrame*.

Spanish contributions also merit consideration. Some of the leading Romantic plays of Spain were written under the impact of French literature.

---

[48] See Winfield Wehle, "Französisches Populardrama zur Zeit des Empire und der Restauration," in *Europäische Romantik II, Neues Handbuch der Literaturwissenschaft*, 15, ed. Klaus Heitmann (Wiesbaden: Athenaion, 1982), pp. 153-70.
[49] See Samia Chahine, *La Dramaturgie de Victor Hugo* (Paris: Nizet, 1971), pp. 162f.
[50] About Schiller's impact on French romanticism see G. Hoffmeister, *Deutsche und europäische Romantic* (Stuttgart: Metzler, 1978), p. 65f.; or 2nd ed. (1990), p. 75f.

One of the best-known protagonists is the title figure in Duque de Rivas's *Don Alvaro o la Fuerza del Sino* (Don Alvaro or the Force of Fate, Ms. 1832). That he is responsible for the slaughter of an entire family has been the view of numerous critics who nonetheless consider Don Alvaro's persecution by a merciless Greek fate to be the work of a blind and chaotic force.[51] There are also those who interpret him as a Christian Oedipus in the Spanish Catholic tradition.[52] It seems to me, however, that Rivas shows Don Alvaro's fate as determined much rather by the social conditions and prejudices that prevailed among the Spanish upper class, which did not permit upstarts in their circle and therefore compel Don Alvaro to hide his mestizo descent until the very end. Don Alvaro appears as an *homme fatal*, a dark catalyst who brings about the destruction of a family and himself. But this happens in reaction to social conventions he is faced with; just as convention motivates the long search by Leonora's brothers for him, a quest of revenge, in each case based on a conscious decision to kill for honor's sake. Rivas's play is in the Spanish tradition, but there are also strong echoes of other Europeans, above all the French and English (Byron, Shelley) Romantics. Alvaro differs radically from the Oedipus type in that he knows everything about his own background, yet his enemies do not.

Also in García Guitiérrez's *El trovador* (The Troubadour, 1836) and Hartzenbusch's *Los amantes de Teruel* (The Lovers of Teruel, 1836) fate can only be perceived as the lot apportioned to a hero because of a disastrous combination of character and insurmountable circumstances. In *El trovador*, man is his own fate, Luna finds out in the end, after having executed his brother Manrique, whom he has mistaken for a gypsy's son. Diego too, in *Los amantes de Teruel*, deems himself responsible for his lost opportunity.

Conclusions:

Does the "Romantic tragedy of fate" exist on some discernible cross-cultural footing in Western Europe? With certain qualifications, I believe, it is justifiable to establish a subgenre called tragedy of fate, very different from the Greek conception and exhibiting national variations in accord with strong indigenous literary traditions and tastes. Thus we encounter the Gothic conventions alongside the Elizabethan tradition of the revenge play in England; in France, a clear emphasis on the historical drama with Gothic melodramatic effects; in Spain, the deeply entrenched themes of honor and revenge. But in spite of the above differences, the following similarities are striking:

1. *The motif:* Most of the plays surveyed here have drawn at least some of their inspiration from the Oedipus myth, although direct links to Sophocles are extremely rare (e.g., Schiller). In most cases where there is such a link, the authors' intention of recreating the Greek fate tragedy falls short of our expectations (e.g., even Schiller, Kleist, Werner). Such direct attempts at imitation were adulterated by the strong assertion of later indigenous, i.e., Gothic, or other current foreign fashions, such as the literary influences established by Calderón or Shakespeare (e.g., in the case of Grillparzer). Distant echoes of Oedipus sometimes are a mere ingredient of a long tradition of writing plays of terror and pity.

---

[51] Juan Alborg, *Historia de la literatura española*, (Madrid: Gredos 1980), IV, 488f., quotes Pastor Diaz.
[52] Alborg refers to Pacheco and Menéndez Pelayo, p. 489.

As a result of this conflation, the Romantic tragedy of fate extols a protagonist who frequently becomes the instrument (voluntarily or not) of erasing a family, as Don Alvaro does, or a parent who kills his offspring (in plays by Werner, Kleist, Grillparzer, Hugo, Dumas père). In a reversal of roles, the children rebel against their parents (*The Cenci, Les Burgraves*), or a brother against his brother (*Die Braut von Messina, Remorse, El trovador*). If it is not a close relative, then at least it is a lover who commits a murder – sometimes unwittingly, e.g., under the delusion of a mistaken identity (*El trovador*).

2. *The protagonists* either fall into the category of passive pawns in the hands of a superior force (French lovers, English and Spanish heroines), who are often used as tools of someone else's revenge (French) and as victims of a strange curse (German). Or they belong to the class of the Romantic superman or -woman, adamant personages, who, victimized early in their lives, have turned into fallen angels of satanic revenge, meting out doom and destruction to their supposed enemies, but by a twist of fate also to themselves. Above all, the English heroes (cf. also Don Alvaro) and the French heroines turn into superagents of death or *hommes/femmes fatales*, characteristics which are all but unknown to the German Romantic tradition of playwrighting.

3. *The mood* of mystery, gloom, and terror is prominent in these dramas, but especially in those plays which have that Gothic frame of reference (English, French, German). Sometimes an element of time racing toward the catastrophe contributes to the atmosphere of suspense and terror (Werner, Shelley, Dumas, Hartzenbusch). The technique of suspense between error and revelation is employed almost without fail to increase the mood of mystery. Mantic devices such as curses and prophecies abound, as well as the motif of incest (Schiller, Grillparzer, Shelley, French plays).

4. *The concept of fate* is a complex one. But nowhere (except perhaps in the messianic Polish play *Lilla Weneda* by Słowacki, 1840) does it manifest itself as a religious power in the Greek sense. In spite of frequent invocations of fate or destiny, it has by and large degenerated into a secularized force, either into the "Gothic monstrosity" of a generational curse, sometimes heriditary in nature, which haunts the children of a criminal until his or her guilt is expiated (German plays). Or "fate" amounts to the mechanism of an intrigue instigated by a fatal agent who, as a rule, seems to be determined by his character (i.e., a frustrated passion turns into revenge) and by the effects produced on him by time, milieu, and chance. Social conventions and blindness about one's own role, prejudices, etc., are often the ultimate causes of an intricate plot of death and destruction (French and English examples). Fate has become the deed of man. Whether he submits to it passively (German) or whether he directs it, he becomes responsible and often the object of ensuing guilt and remorse. Once set in motion, this man-made fate is controlled by the principle of cause and effect, decision and execution, or frustration of purpose. What sometimes looks to the victim like an external force beyond his control is frequently nothing but a misconception of his role in society (mainly in plays other than German).

Does fate ever appear as a christianized version of providence? Under the impact of Calderonism German playwrights from Schlegel to Grillparzer tried, at least according to their best intentions, to fuse ancient fate and Christian providence, but generally failed to express adequately the victory of divine justice over the dark forces and to change the catastrophic outcome.[53] Alarcos as

---

[53] See Schreyvogel's "Vorbericht" to the orginal edition of Grillparzer's *Die Ahnfrau*: "Die Sophisterei der Leidenschaften, welche der Verfasser seinen tragischen Personen in den Mund legt, ist nicht sein Glaubensbekenntnis."

well as Jaromir die in despair, Werner's protagonist in *Der 24. Februar* becomes an instrument of providence too late, providence is completely negated in Kleist's *Die Familie Schroffenstein* as it is in Shelley's *The Cenci*, and in the French and Spanish examples. Only Hugo's Barbarossa (*Les Burgraves*) and Coleridge's Alvaro become successful and convincing instruments of divine justice, thereby thwarting their opposing fatal agents.

5. *The condition of the world*: We can speculate that the idea of a generational curse did lend itself well to express the anxieties of the Revolutionary period which was troubled by the question of "the oppression of youth by age," "paternal authority," and the past wielding undue power over the present and future.[54] Certainly, too, since the *Sturm und Drang*, the loss of religious faith has grown inversely with the gain in scientific determinism and the belief of the individual in his own "demonic" or intellectual powers (e.g., the literary figures Werther, Prometheus, Faust). Tieck's William Lovell (in the novel by that name of 1795-96) speaks for many when he asserts that he does not know what rules the world, yet he feels that he is in the center of strange coincidences without knowing what to do with them.[55] Therefore he takes his "fate" into his own hands. Quite often murder and suicide are to be read as acts of protest against the apparent senselessness of life without any guiding providence.[56] While pessimism gains the upper hand among many playwrights and prompts them to turn their protagonists into helpless victims or fatal agents of dark powers incomprehensible to them, others see a ray of hope in a rededication of Christianity. Only Schiller, the idealist, shows how the chain of guilt and punishment can be broken by a courageous act of self-sacrifice.

[54] Mueller, p. 145f.

[55] Hankamer, p. 630-31.

[56] Having demonstrated the complexity of this Romantic subgenre, it would be inadmissable to reduce it, for instance, to Mesonero Romanos's parody which divides plays of this type into the following six acts: "Un crimen, El veneno, Ya es tarde, El panteón, 'Ella' and 'El'" (in "El Romanticismo y los románticos," *Escenas matritenses*, in *Obras*, ed. C.S. Serrano [Madrid: Atlas, 1967], II, pp. 65f.); nor to Platen's "stich zu, stich zu!" and the concomitant reply: "Ich getraue mich nicht, stich selber zu, hier hast du die Gabel" (in *Die verhängnisvolle Gabel*, 1826, Act V, ll. 1238-39).

GLORIA FLAHERTY

EMPATHY AND DISTANCE:
GERMAN ROMANTIC THEORIES OF ACTING RECONSIDERED*

Works dealing with the actor proliferated during the early decades of German Romanticism. Actors had come to be viewed as role models whose very costumes, hairstyles, and mannerisms often influenced prevailing fashions or, at least, gave them specific labels from particular plays.[1] Popular interest in everything having to do with people of the theater was seconded by contemporary poets, playwrights, painters, philosophers, professors, and physicians. While some of their writings concentrated on historical and philosophical concerns, others investigated anthropological and psychiatric as well as medical ones. And contemporary actors themselves contributed publications about the ways, means and consequences of playing roles in public.

Such writings raised questions about the essence of theater that had been asked intermittently since remotest antiquity. One such question was whether professional acting dealt in lies or in truths. Another was whether it was a form of art or only a craft. Another pondered the transitoriness of performance. Yet another had to do with the degree of illusion and the kind of aesthetic reality created by theatrical performers. Of all the questions raised, those dealing with the actor's relationship to his role, both on-stage and off-stage, seemed to be most significant for the Romantics. In short, should the actor empathize to such a degree that his own personality would be overcome by the role, or, should he distance himself emotionally so as to enliven the role? Would the paradox of acting that Denis Diderot identified ever be resolved? Could Heinrich von Kleist's bear and god somehow live together? Or, was there no artistically possible way of fusing the unconscious spontaneity of emotional identification with the conscious discipline of intellectual study? Would what was to be called method acting remain eternally separated from what Bertolt Brecht was to term *Verfremdung* (alienation)?

Although the answers to these questions were in some instances the same offered by the ancients and their Renaissance commentators, the Romantics applied them in different contexts, thereby giving them new and far-reaching implications. The topos of *theatrum mundi*, for example, remained in full popular consciousness, but with broader meaning. No longer was the actor just a metaphor for the human being. The actor was made synonymous with the highest of human potentialities, the genius. He was a poet-performer like Plato's rhapsodist Ion, who transferred

* My thanks go to the Ford Foundation and Bryn Mawr College from making this research possible.
[1] Edward P. Harris, "From Outcast to Ideal: The Image of the Actress in Eighteenth-Century Germany," *German Quarterly*, 56 (March 1981), 177-87, and, "Mirrors of Change: The Actor in Eighteenth-Century Germany," *The Stage in the Eighteenth Century*, ed. J.D. Browning, Publications of the McMaster University Association for 18th-Century Studies, no. 9 (New York and London: Garland, 1981), pp. 54-69. See also, Hans Knoll, *Theorie der Schauspielkunst: Darstellung und Entwicklung ihres Gedankens in Deutschland von Lessing zu Goethe* (Greifswald: Able, 1916); Hans Oberländer, *Die geistige Entwicklung der deutschen Schauspielkunst im 18. Jahrhundert*, Theatergeschichtliche Forschungen, no. 15 (Hamburg and Leipzig: Voss, 1898).

inspiration from the divine to the audience through a series of magnetic rings. Much of the glory of his performance resulted from the creative furor or divine frenzy that possessed him and sometimes happened to take him to the brink of madness.[2] Drug abuse, alcoholism, and suicide were quite prevalent among Romantic actors, the best known cases being Ludwig Devrient (1784-1832) and Edmund Kean (1787-1833). On the other hand, many admirers of ancient comedy, especially those of Aristophanes, maintained that irony reduced such risks and prevented being carried away by the role. Their point of view contributed to the development of the concept of "Romantic irony."[3] Others aspects of aesthetic speculation, critical theory, and applied criticism were similarly affected by such questions and answers, as was the very production of literary works, not only dramas, but also novels and other forms of fiction.

My objectives are threefold. First, I should like to illuminate the decisive shift in theoretical preference from empathy to distance in acting, or, to what was considered a safe, yet artistic combination of the two. Second, I should like to redirect attention to performance as a significant constituent in the history of aesthetics. Neglecting it has produced many unfortunate misconceptions. One is that divine frenzy was something that descended on the creative genius while alone in his study during the middle of the night rather than when he was enjoying some kind of communal or tribal unity with his fellows. Another is that only the audience was to experience catharsis. My third objective in this chapter is to show how the basic stuff of literary productivity, namely that which excites and drives the poet's imagination to create, did indeed develop out of theoretical debates, just as Friedrich Schlegel predicted in the 116th fragment of the *Athenaeum*. My procedure will be to start with those writers espousing empathy in acting and move to those who advised distance. While providing that sampling, I shall as of necessity include discussion of some works of Romantic literature that have to do with the theatrical milieu.

Many factors contributed to the development of Romantic acting theories. Among the most important was the increasing knowledge about human behavior and cultures that came from the firsthand experiences of explorers and travelers. Carl Ludwig Fernow (1763-1808), a devoted student of things Italian and an expatriate in Rome before being called back to Weimar, supported Plato's concept of the performing artist. In "Über die Begeisterung des Künstlers" (On Enthusiasm in the Artist), he maintained that all artists, whether performers, poets, or painters, were "Söhne des Apollo, heilige Seher der Zukunft, Männer Gottes" (sons of Apollo, sacred seers of the future, men of God).[4] He compared their creative process to the explorers' descriptions of initiatory rites in the New World. Using the kind of imagery that eventually found its way into the paintings of George Catlin (1796-1872) and Karl Bodmer (1809-93), Fernow wrote that genuine artists felt as strung-out and incapable of painless, free movement as the adolescent American Indians undergoing their initiation into tribal mysteries:

Er ist der Zustand der Weihe; der Moment der geistigen Zeugung. In ihm werden ewige Wahrheiten entdekt, erhabene Thaten beschlossen, unsterbliche Kunstwerke empfangen.[5]

---

[2] Gloria Flaherty, "The Dangers of the New Sensibilities in Eighteenth Century German Acting," *Theater Research International*, 8 (1983), 95-100.
[3] Ingrid Strohschneider-Kohrs, *Die romantische Ironie in Theorie und Gestaltung*, 2nd rev. and enl. ed. (Tübingen: Niemeyer, 1977), p. 131. Actors rarely come up.
[4] Carl Ludwig Fernow, *Römische Studien*, 3 parts (Zurich: Gessner, 1806-8), I, 304.
[5] Fernow, I, 263.

(His is the state of initiation, the moment of spiritual generation. In him eternal truths are discovered, sublime deeds determined, immortal artworks conceived.)

The effects of such transport out of and beyond the self fascinated Fernow so much that he took up the issue in other works. In the one about the *commedia dell'arte*, "Über die Improvisatoren" (On Improvisors), he explained that the performer was able to transmit his enthusiasm to the spectators and infuse them with it:

Ja es scheint, daß die Dichtkunst wirklich ihre Gewalt auf das Gemüth nicht mächtiger erweisen könne, als in Dichtungen dieser Art, wo der Dichter, im Augenblicke der schaffenden Begeisterung, seinen Gesang unmittelbar in die Sele [sic] des von ihr ergriffenen Hörers hinüberströmt.[6]

(Indeed it seems that the poetic work really cannot evidence its power over the heart and mind more powerfully than in poems of this kind, when the poet, in the moment of creative inspiration, lets his song stream over directly into the soul of the listener likewise gripped.)

Although Italy was his subject, Fernow acknowledged that such dramatic urges were basic to all cultures the world over at certain stages of social development.

The practice of relating the archaic rites of extant pagan societies to Greek mythology had begun with the reports of the very earliest explorers.[7] It increased proportionately as the explorations spread out to include not only the New World and the South Seas but also Africa and Siberia. The fields of comparative mythology, linguistics, ethnograpphy, and anthropology profited greatly. And, so did aesthetics. The main reason was that the German Romantics had no alternative but to come to terms with the grand surge of exciting new information right at the moment of its arrival. That so many of them spent some time or had very close contacts in Göttingen, Jena, and Berlin, cities at the forefront of the rapidly emerging social sciences, seems to be more than mere coincidence.

Johann Gottfried Herder (1744-1803) was one of the first to apply to the arts the prodigious number of ideas he had assimilated from the constantly increasing new information. For him, the actor was a shaman, that is, a poet, singer, prophet, seer, healer. He cited numerous illustrations from different cultures in several epochs, but he repeatedly came back to the original singer, Orpheus, as the epitome. In "Von Ähnlichkeit der mittlern englischen und deutschen Dichtkunst" (On the Similarity of Middle English and German Poetry) which concentrated on minstrels, troubadours, skalds, and bards, he mentioned that the Greeks had also been savages before their civilization blossomed, and that even after it did, they remained more closely attuned to nature than contemporary European intellectuals would allow. And the Greek poets, he maintained, were never completely separated from nature. He continued, writing, "wenn *Arion, Orpheus, Amphion* lebten, so waren sie edle griechische Schamanen" (if Arion, Orpheus, Amphion lived, then they were noble Greek schamans).[8]

The shaman's ability not only to reach the imagination of his fellow tribesmen but to gain complete sway over it interested Herder more than the various means employed to induce the frenzy or the trance. Unlike so many others who reviewed this archaic phenomenon in the eighteenth century,

---

[6] Fernow, II, 304.
[7] Frank E. Manuel, *The Eighteenth Century Confronts the Gods* (Cambridge, Mass.: Harvard Univ. Press, 1959), pp. 15-16.
[8] Johann Gottfried Herder, *Sämtliche Werke*, ed. Bernhard Suphan (Berlin: Weidmann, 1880), IX, 522-34.

Herder did not find the chanting and dancing to the tambourine, the ventriloquism, legerdemain, and other artful tricks contemptible. His discussion of Bileam in "Vom Geist der ebräischen Poesie" (On the Spirit of Hebrew Poetry) stressed the importance of emotional receptivity or psychic rapport:

> Auch in diesem Ereigniß sehe ich nichts, was nicht der Seele eines Schamanen ähnlich wäre. Man lese Reisebeschreibungen aller Länder, wo es noch dergleichen giebt: mit Erstaunen sieht man welcher gewaltsamen Zustände der Einbildung sie fähig sind. Ihre Seele wandert aus dem Körper, der leblos daliegt, bringt Nachrichten, was sie an dem, an jenem Ort, wo sie jetzt gewesen, gesehen habe? Das sind sodenn ihre Weissagungen, die das Volk verehrt, und bei denen oft die klügsten Reisenden staunten. Alle nehmlich bewunderten die Anstrengung dieser Menschen, einen gewaltsamen Zustand, gegen den diese Vision Bileams ein Kinderspiel ist.[9]

> (Also in this instance I see nothing that would not be similar to the soul of a shaman. One should read travel accounts about all the countries, where there still are shamans; with astonishment one learns what powerful states of imagination they are capable of. Their soul wanders out of their body, which lies lifeless, brings news about what they saw at this and that place where they were. Those are then their prophecies, which the people revere, and at which often the smartest, most rational travellers are amazed. All namely admire the exertion of these people to induce such a state, against which this vision of Bileam is child's play.)

Herder was not alone in viewing the actor as the shaman of higher civilization. The inundation of reports that the phenomenon still existed in many regions in various stages, ranging from archaic purity to civilized decline, saw to it that the idea caught on mightily in the last quarter of the eighteenth century. Many intellectuals, as a result, began looking closer to home. Some, like Christian Sigismund Grüner (1758-1808), who wrote "Über die Wahl des Schauspielerstandes" (About the Choice of the Acting Station, 1788), thought each nation had a moral obligation to revive the pristine dignity of the shaman's position since drama had, after all, evolved out of religious mysteries and had had good intentions from the very beginning.[10] Relating shamanism specifically to the Judeo-Christian tradition was not something that the anonymous reviewer of *Von der Schauspielkunst* (On the Art of Acting, 1780) exactly approved of doing. Therefore he queried:

> Hat die Schauspielkunst nicht den Zauberstab jener Hexe in der Hand, die Helden aus ihren Gräbern rufte und stehts nicht in ihrer Gewalt die Zuseher durch ihre Schwarzkünstlerey so zu erschüttern, daß sie wie Saul in Ohnmacht fallen?[11]

> (Has not the art of acting in its hand the magic wand of that witch who called forth the heroes from their graves, and does it not stand in her power so to shake the viewers through her necromancy that like Saul they fall unconscious?)

Even the arch-conservative August Wilhelm Iffland (1759-1814) did not choose to sidestep the issue. He confronted it head-on by writing that some people were simply imbued with ultra-sensitive faculties of perception and communication. Usually they were not the hyper-cultured, urban types. Again and again the tracking instincts of those who lived in the wild were cited. The Ameri-

---

[9] Herder, XII, 159.
[10] In *Neue Litteratur und Völkerkunde*, 2, no. 10 (1788), 367.
[11] In *Baierische Bayträge* (October 1780), pp. 1210-11.

can Indian was repeatedly used as an example. Such people knew how to find, according to Iffland, "oft ohne Worte die deutlichste Sprache der Seele zu der Seele" (often without words the most coherent language of soul to soul).[12] In regard to professional acting, Iffland was appalled, as he wrote in the "Briefe über Schauspielkunst" (Letters on Acting, 1781), that so many Europeans demeaned the phenomenon by brushing it aside as mere "Taschenspielergeheimnis" (tricks of side-show magicians).[13] Johann Jakob Engel (1741-1802) held those same views, and, as might be expected of a solid, but less than brilliant mind, he did not take them any further. He simply included them in *Ideen zu einer Mimik* (Ideas on Imitation, 1785-86), the textbook that was to influence several generations of aspiring young German actors. Engel's own reading of the explorers' reports focussed on matters to be learned from the war dances and other pantomimic reenactments of the American Indians.[14]

Ludwig Tieck (1773-1853), who shared his older colleagues' concerns about improving the quality of theater in the German lands, was profoundly influenced by the on-going intellectual debate about what had already come to be labeled as shamanism. He, unlike Engel, did take what he learned further. As early as his student days in Göttingen, the leading anthropological center, Tieck was already incorporating many of the terms and ideas from that shamanistic debate into his own critical writings. His essay, "Shakespeare's Behandlung des Wunderbaren" (Shakespeare's Treatment of the Wondrous, 1793), singled out the self-induced trance and its transmission to audiences that were even skeptical or unwilling. It explained,

> daß der Dichter nicht unsere Gutmüthigkeit in Anspruch nimmt, sondern die Phantasie, selbst wider unsern Willen, so spannt, daß wir die Regeln der Aesthetik, mit allen Begriffen unsers aufgeklärten Jahrhunderts vergessen, und uns ganz dem schönen Wahnsinn des Dichters überlassen; daß sich die Seele, nach dem Rausch willig der Bezauberung von neuem hingibt und die spielende Phantasie durch keine plötzliche und widrige Überraschung aus ihren Träumen geweckt wird.[15]

> (that the poet does not stake a claim on our goodnaturedness, but, even against our will, so harnesses the fancy that we forget all the rules of aesthetics with all the concepts of our enlightened century and give ourselves over entirely to the poet's beautiful madness; such that the soul, after intoxication, willingly surrenders to the enchantment anew and playing fancy is not wakened from her dreams by any sudden or untoward surprise.)

Shakespeare always succeeded where others failed because, Tieck argued, he knew how to enoble and elevate "den gemeinen Aberglauben zu den schönsten poetischen Fictionen" (common superstitions into the most beautiful poetic fictions).[16] Shakespeare reached his spectators because he sensed their needs and satisfied them. In other words, he invited them to join him and to play along with him: "er weiht in diesen Stücken den Zuschauer in seine Zauberwelt ein und läßt ihn mit hundert magischen Gestalten in eine vertrauliche Bekanntschaft treten" (in these pieces he initiates the spectator into an enchanted world and has him enter into an intimate acquaintance with a hundred magi-

---

[12] August Wilhelm Iffland, comment cited in *Die Protokolle des Mannheimer Nationaltheaters unter Dalberg aus den Jahren 1781 bis 1789*, ed. Max Martersteig (Mannheim: Bensheimer, 1890), p. 94.

[13] Iffland, "Briefe über Schauspielkunst," *Rheinische Beiträge zur Gelehrsamkeit*, no. 10 (1780), p. 367.

[14] Johan Jakob Engel, *Ideen zu einer Mimik*, 2 vols. (Berlin: n.p., 1786) II, 19 and 25.

[15] Ludwig Tieck, *Kritische Schriften*, 4 vols. (Leipzig: Brockhaus, 1848-52), I, 37-38.

[16] Tieck, *Kritische Schriften*, I, 39.

cal figures).[17]

Tieck tried to do the same to do the same in *Ein Prolog* (1796). This hilariously funny dramatic piece pokes good-natured fun at just about everything involved with going to the theater. And most of the issues – as anyone who has ever had a subscription anywhere will attest – are timeless. First, there is the self-conscious way the average burgher and his wife, both dressed to the hilt, enter the empty auditorium, find their places, take their seats, gain confidence, greet the people who have the same series, and then, lastly, make the acquaintance of new people. As latecomers climb over those already seated, questions arise about the kind of play to be performed.

The ubiquitous refreshment vendors, a standard feature in most eighteenth-century continental theaters – often depicted by painters as juggling oranges – are summoned by a number of spectators who become increasingly vociferous because they have to wait their turn. As more and more of the burghers question whether or not there will be any kind of performance at all, the similarities to the prologue of Kalidasa's *Sakuntala* and the "Vorspiel" to Goethe's *Faust* come to the reader's mind.[18] While the commotion among the spectators intensifies, the orchestra begins tuning instruments, and the lamplighters arrive to carry out their duties. The actor then emerges as the person to sum up the entire situation and put it into perspective:

> Wenn ich das Ganze überlege,
> So können wir Nachbarn allewege
> Hier gar nicht im Theater sein,
> Es ist nur Lug und Trug und Schein.[19]

> (When I think about the whole thing,
> Then, neighbors, we can't in any way
> At all be in the theater here;
> It's just lie, trick, and illusion.)

The actor continues, insisting that he is the only one who really does exist:

> Ich bin der einz'ge hier, der existirt,
> Und sich die andern nur imaginirt
> Dann steht es billig kaum zu begreifen,
> Wie ich so kann Erfindung auf Erfindung häufen,
> Und daß ich hier so eingepresset sitze,
> Und das Gedränge macht, daß ich schwitze,
> Und doch kann ich's verfluchte Imaginiren
> Nicht lassen, ich muß dies alles produciren.[20]

---

[17] Tieck, *Kritische Schriften*, I, 41. See also Tieck's letter to Karl Wilhelm Ferdinand Solger of October 16, 1814, *Nachgelassenen Schriften und Briefwechsel*, eds. L. Tieck and Friedrich von Raumer, 2 vols. (Leipzig: Brockhaus, 1826), I, 322-23.

[18] Tieck, *Schriften*, 28 vols. (Berlin: Reimer, 1828-54), XIII, 245-47. In the Preface to *Schriften*, I, Tieck mentions that in France, where spectators traditionally sat on the stage, there were plays in which they were allowed to participate. Theodore Gish demonstrates Tieck's early dramatic strategies convincingly in *Vorspiele auf dem Theater*: Dramatic and Theatrical Elements in Ludwig Tieck's *Straussfedern*," *Theatrum Mundi: Essays on German Drama and German Literature*, Houston German Studies, no. 2 (Munich: Fink, 1980), pp. 52 and 58.

[19] Tieck, *Schriften*, XIII, p. 261.

[20] Tieck, *Schriften*, XIII, p. 262.

(I'm the only one here who exists
And is just imagining the others;
But you'll grant it's hard to grasp
How I can pile invention on invention,
And that I sit here so tightly squeezed
And the crowd makes me sweat.
And yet I can't leave off this accursed
Imagining; I have to produce all this.)

Although the curtain never rises in this wonderful spoof, Tieck did manage to demonstrate his deep concern about the essence of theatrical reality.

Such concern comes up again and again in *Phantasus* (1812-16), the collection of works, some written much earlier, that he brought together within a framework resembling that of Boccaccio's *Decamerone*. It is especially evident in the introductory dialogue that Tieck wrote in 1811. One speaker admits concern about maintaining sobriety after having drunk "aus dieser Quelle des heiligen Wahnsinns" (from this source of holy madness), an expression that is like a refrain in late eighteenth-century writings about acting.[21] Then, he confesses, he succumbed to the wantonness of the emotionally stimulating orgy and wished to do nothing except show reverence for the seer or shaman. Before concluding with an attempt to explain what ecstasy is, another speaker claims, "Erregt ein wahrer Schauspieler diesen Zustand in uns, so ist er uns ein hoch verehrtes Wesen" (If a true actor excites this state in us, he is to us a highly honored being). Such an accomplishment, he quickly adds, had been "ein Theil der Zauberkraft Homers und der Nibelungen Helden" (part of the magical power of Homer and the Nibelungen heroes).[22] In the last pages of Tieck's introduction, Lothar, who has a bad case of theater mania, articulates an uncanny understanding of the whole configuration of ideas. He says,

daß die geistigste und witzigste Entwickelung unserer Kräfte und unsers Individuums diejenige sei, uns selbst ganz in ein anderes Wesen hinein verloren zu geben, indem wir es mit aller Anstrengung unsrer geistigen Stimmung darzustellen suchen.[23]

(that the most spirited and witty development of our energies and individuality is that of letting ourselves get quite lost in another being, in seeking to present it with every effort of intellectual attunement.)

Whenever Tieck himself performed or gave dramatic readings, he apparently did just that. Reports were that he was no longer himself. In one there is the description that,

die Täuschung wurde zur Wahrheit, er wandelte sich in den fremden Charakter um. Er glaubte die Person zu sein, welche er darstellte, und war es auch nach dem Eindrucke zu schließen, welchen er auf seine Freunde, auf die Zuschauer machte.[24]

(the deception turned into truth, he transformed himself into the foreign character. He believed to be the person whom he represented, and was such, too, judging by the impression which he made on his friends and the audience.)

---

[21] Tieck, *Schriften*, IV, 32.
[22] Tieck, *Schriften*, IV, 98.
[23] Tieck, *Schriften*, IV, 100.
[24] Rudolf Köpke, *Ludwig Tieck, Erinnerungen*, 2 vols. (Leipzig: Brockhaus, 1855), I, 86.

Another maintained that he once got

> eine innere Wut, ein solches Außersichsein im eigentlichen Sinne des Worts, daß Wackenroder, der den Kaiser spielte, und seine Umgebung sich scheu vor ihm zurückgezogen, weil sie im Ernst fürchteten, er könne ein Unheil anrichten.[25]

> (into an inner fury, such a state of being beside himself in the true sense of the expression, that Wackenroder, who was playing the emperor, and his entourage drew back from him timidly because they feared in earnest that he could do some mischief.)

Included in the second part of *Phantasus* was a play originally written in 1798 to examine the comic rather than the tragic possibilities of being carried away by a role. *Die verkehrte Welt: Ein Historisches Schauspiel in fünf Aufzügen* (The Land of Upside Down: A Historical Drama in Five Acts) was designed to be a living, three-dimensional compendium of theatrical history. Tieck took great delight in toying with diverse kinds of theatrical works and their particular levels of aesthetic reality. Among them are the pastoral, heroic tragedy, bourgeois tragedy, opera, melodrama, monodrama, *Bardiet* (bardic lay), comedy, farce, slapstick revue, and *commedia dell'arte*, the last being the most prominent. Tieck also experimented with different styles and demonstrated every possible kind of scene in the contemporary repertory, including the love scene, the mad scene, the battle scene, and the suicide scene. Spectators take the role of performers and vice versa. All the possible walls separating illusion from reality either do not exist or are ignored or are destroyed.

The action of *Die verkehrte Welt* begins amidst great confusion because here once again the play is not ready. Nor are the players, most of whom embody one or another aspect of current acting theories. Skaramuz, refusing to remain type-casted as a comic actor, demands the role of Apollo. An actor, he insists, does not have to be in real life what he only pretends to be on-stage and the other way around. Pierrot wants to test that idea by making the great leap across the footlights into the parterre, "um zu sehen, ob ich entweder sterbe, oder von einem Narren zu einem Zuschauer kurirt werde" (to see whether either I die or I am cured of being a fool by becoming a spectator).[26] After his successful leap, Pierrot becomes the actors' exponent among the spectators. He also gives away their secrets; the most important one is that they have already agreed on a happy end so that no one really has to die. On the other hand, Grünhelm, a spectator who has long hankered to display his histrionic talents in public, climbs onto the stage to assume the role of the comic figure.

The second act develops such ideas about acting still further by taking up the relationship of the actor to his audience. While Grünhelm complains how strenuous it is to be funny, Skaramuz remodels Apollo's realm, and the spectators demand still greater scenic effects. After the thunder and lightning of the machinist's storm, the scene shifts to an inn, which delights the innkeeper who has been bemoaning the new theatrical tastes that demand private homes or prisons as locales. In the following scene on Mount Parnassus, total disorder erupts. The baker, at one point a peaceful spectator, tells Skaramuz the reason: "Der Brauer ist ganz unschuldig, aber in der poetischen Begeisterung suchten die Gäste Händel" (The brewer is quite blameless, but in poetic enthusiasm the guests picked a quarrel).[27] Acknowledging the transparency of that reason, Skaramuz warns the brewer not

---

[25] Köpke, I, 86.
[26] Tieck, *Schriften*, V, 294. Raymond Immerwahr, *The Esthetic Intent of Tieck's Fantastic Comedy* (St. Louis: Washington Univ. Press, 1953), pp. 67, 80, and 116, compares Tieck to Aristophanes, whose plays still are stageworthy.
[27] Tieck, *Schriften*, V, 329.

to make his beer so strong, "sonst gerathen mir meine Unterthanen doch noch auf die Dithyrambe" (otherwise my subjects will stumble into dithyrambics on me yet).[28] As the curtain falls, the word-music describes the effect of the performance on the audience:

> In welcher Trunkenheit jauchzt unser Geist, wenn es ihm einst vergönnt ist, tausend wechselnde, bunte, schwebende, tanzende Gestalten zu erblicken, die stets erneut und verjüngt in ihm aufsteigen.[29]
>
> (In what drunkenness our spirit exults once it is granted the glimpse of a thousand shifting, gay, hovering, dancing shapes which rise up in it continually renewed and rejuvenated.)

Empathy, however, must be balanced by distance: "Ja, könnten wir in dieser Fülle nur immer schwelgen, müßten wir nicht auch im Wahnsinn nüchtern und mäßig sein" (Yes, could we but ever revel in this plenitude, we would not have to be sober and moderate even in madness).[30]

The poet's lament begins the third act. The folk with its mundane, provincial, tasteless demands has destroyed the genuine adoration of Apollo:

> Nichts darf ich mehr im kühnen Schwunge schreiben
> Und wenn der holde Wahnsinn mich bethört
> Wenn durch die Adern sich Dein Feuer gießt,
> Und hoher Klang von meiner Lippe tönt....[31]
>
> (Nothing more may I write in bold verve
> Albeit gracious madness befool me,
> Thy fire pour through my veins,
> And lofty tone sound from my lips....)

This act comprises so many plays within plays that everybody, including the reader, becomes pleasantly confused, if not in doubt about his own sanity or sobriety. In addition to the sketch of a wandering troupe, there is an illumination, a masquerade, and various scenarios requiring improvisation. When one of the spectators in the play exclaims, "Leute, bedenkt einmal wie wunderbar! Wir sind hier die Zuschauer, und dorten sitzen die Leute nun auch als Zuschauer" (People, just think how marvelous! We are the spectators here, and there the people are sitting, too, as spectators), Pierrot responds with "Es steckt immer so ein Stück im andern" (There is always some play stuck inside another play).[32]

One of the more revealing pieces is the pastoral staged by two lovers in order to extract permission to marry from the girl's reluctant father. Modeled on the eighteenth-century psychiatric view of theater as a therapeutic measure, it portrays their actual situation so intensely and convincingly that the father mistakes illusion for reality and happily acquiesces. The act concludes as one of the confused spectators wishes he had become an actor: "aber um nur zur Ruhe zu kommen, hätt' ich mich gern aus meinem jetzigen Zuschauerstande in die letzte versificirte Komödie als Akteur hineingeflüchtet. Je weiter ab vom Zuschauer, je besser" (but just to gain peace, I would gladly have left my

---

[28] Tieck, *Schriften*, V, 329.
[29] Tieck, *Schriften*, V, 336.
[30] Tieck, *Schriften*, V, 337.
[31] Tieck, *Schriften*, V, 338.
[32] Tieck, *Schriften*, V, 356. Compare also, p. 372.

present station as spectator and taken refuge in the last versified comedy as an actor. The further from spectator, the better).[33]

The fourth act presents the effects of Skaramuz's reign as Apollo. Everything – law and order, marriage and the family, education and religion, taste and style – has become topsy-turvy. The dramatic highlight of this act is a sea battle fought by Pantalon against Harlekin and refereed by Skaramuz, who has become so smitten with his role as Apollo that he no longer recognizes any of his old colleagues. The director cannot reawaken him to the reality of the world, fails in his attempt to fire him, and, furthermore, worries that he is so far gone as to have fixed on the idea, "das Stück gar nicht zu beendigen, damit er nur immer an der Regierung bleiben [kann]" (not to end the play at all so that he can go on ruling forever).[34]

The overthrow of Skaramuz is the subject of the fifth and last act. As the Muses sing a *Bardiet*, Apollo and his co-conspirators claim victory. The audience, however, unite with Skaramuz, insisting that the battle be done over again so that they can fight by his side. At that point, Apollo loses all patience and tells them that they are all totally confused because they got carried away by the performance and forgot themselves: "Sie vergessen in Ihrem Enthusiasmus, daß wir alle nur Schauspieler sind, und daß das Ganze nichts als ein Spiel ist. Und damit wäre denn das Stück völlig zu Ende" (They forget in their enthusiasm that we are all merely players and that the whole business is nothing but a play. And thereupon the play would then be fully at its end).[35] The curtain descends to an empty auditorium, for the spectators have rallied to Skaramuz's defense and – like modern groupies or fans – have hastened backstage to join him.

A lengthy discussion of *Die verkehrte Welt* and the numerous issues it raised followed so as to place the play within the framework of *Phantasus*. Lothar, the young man who is so stage-struck, considers small bands of wandering players fascinating because they perform works "die längst verschollen sind, uralte Traditionen, von denen man oft nicht begreift, woher sie sie haben können" (which are sunk into oblivion, age-old traditions of which one often does not comprehend whence they could have them).[36] He firmly believes that they and all other actors must empathize, must have the exact same feeling as the character they are to portray. He himself claims to have had experiences as an actor whereby "meine Entzückungen nicht selten in eine Art von Wahnsinn ausarteten" (my raptures not infrequently degenerated into a kind of insanity).[37]

Lothar's preference for empathy is most apparent in his analysis of Johann Friedrich Fleck (1757-1801). Unsuited for cerebral roles by virtue of his "produzierende Phantasie," Fleck not only excelled, but also achieved superhuman greatness in depicting characters with whom he felt attuned. As Lothar explains to the others:

> In jenen Schauspielen, die Flecks Sinne zusagten, floss ihm der ganze Strom der hellsten und edelsten Poesie entgegen, umfing und trug ihn in das Land der Wunder, als Vision trat alles auf ihn zu, und diese Poesie und Begeisterung schufen, ihn tief bewegend, durch ihn so große und erhabene Dinge, wie wir schwerlich je wieder sehen werden.[38]

---

[33] Tieck, *Schriften*, V, 372. Ernst Nef, "Das Aus-der-Rolle-Fallen als Mittel der Illusionszerstörung bei Tieck und Brecht," *Zeitschrift für deutsche Philologie*, 83 (1964), pp. 214-15, thinks the differences are greater than the similarities.

[34] Tieck, *Schriften*, V, 408.

[35] Tieck, *Schriften*, V, 431.

[36] Tieck, *Schriften*, V, 437.

[37] Tieck, *Schriften*, V, 448.

[38] Tieck, *Schriften*, V, 466.

(In those plays agreeable to Fleck's mind, the whole stream of the most lucid and noble poetry flowed his way, embraced him and bore him into the land of wonders; everything encountered him as vision, and moving him deeply, this poetry and inspiration created such grand and sublime things through him as we shall scarcely ever again see.)

It was as though a higher genius spoke through him. Since that genius seemed to be so fickle, Fleck's performances were understandably of very uneven quality. After questioning the dangers of empathy, the friends who are assembled, more or less agree that the very worst thing that could happen would be for the Germans to accept the opposite extreme, the distance of the French declamatory style.

Tieck, who was enormously knowledgable about world theater, continued to ponder the disadvantages as well as the advantages of losing selfhood while on-stage. In "Die geschichtliche Entwicklung der neueren Bühne und Friedrich Ludwig Schröder" (The Historical Development of the Recent Stage and Friedrich Ludwig Schröder, 1831), he admitted the possibility of madness or some other mental health problem as a result. As a matter of fact, he jocularly called the question about levels of madness an ancient one: "Daß die Menschen zur Freude sagen: 'du bist toll!' ist schon eine alte Krankheit" (That persons say for joy, 'You're crazy!' is a very old sickness).[39] He believed genuine theater, much like the games children play, always had controls, set forms, or regulations so that no one individual got out of hand without having the entire group or team notice and take action.

As far as theater during the Middle Ages was concerned, "jener erhabene Wahnsinn, jene geregelte Trunkenheit der begeisterten alten Welt konnte sich auch nicht einmal in der Erinnerung, in diesen Hütten der Bürger und Bauern melden" (that sublime madness, that orderly drunkenness of the inspired ancient world could hardly put in an appearance even as recollection in today's burgher and peasant cottages).[40] What the descendants of the Roman mimes perpetrated in order to gain a livelihood beclouded, in Tieck's estimation, the quasi-religious mission of the shaman-actors. The result was that all those who performed and did tricks in public began to meld in the consciousness of the citizenry as an undesirable element. In Tieck's own words,

Wie alt in Europa jene herumziehenden Banden der Komödianten waren, die von den eben bezeichneten Spielern ganz unterschieden sind, wissen wir nicht mit Genauigkeit anzugeben, da sie zu allen Zeiten mit Bänkelsängern, Taschenspielern, Jongleurs, Grimassenschneidern, ja selbst mit Dieben und Vagabunden aller Art zusammenfallen und eins werden.[41]

(How old those strolling troupes of comedians in Europe were who are quite distinct from the just designated players, we are unable to indicate with exactness, since in every era they coincide and become one with saltimbanques, carnival tricksters, jugglers, mimes and cutups, indeed even with thieves and vagabonds of every sort.)

The healthy, socially productive period of German theater, according to Tieck, began as Goethe came into his own. It was then that Schröder, who happened to be a juggler, an acrobat, and a

---

[39] Tieck, *Kritische Schriften*, II, 320. William J. Lillyman, *Reality's Dark Dream: The Narrative Fiction of Ludwig Tieck* (Berlin and New York: de Gruyter, 1979), p. 32, explains Tieck's ideas on consciousness by comparing life to a painting that is constantly to be examined but not so that one is totally absorbed.
[40] Tieck, *Kritische Schriften*, II, 318.
[41] Tieck, *Kritische Schriften*, II, 319.

dancer as well as an actor, made his best contributions as "der Erklärer der Natur" (nature's explicator).[42] Tieck concluded his article with unreserved praise for Alexander Pius Wolff (1782-1828) and his wife, both of whom Goethe trained in Weimar to keep their distance.

Wilhelm von Humboldt (1767-1835) admired the Wolffs (who moved on to Berlin) and heartily approved of the stylized acting that Goethe was assiduously advocating. Nevertheless, like his brother Alexander von Humboldt (1769-1859) and other Göttingen classmates, he was enamored of the inspired, enthusiastic style. In scrutinizing ideas about empathy and divine madness among actors, Wilhelm produced a number of sonnets. While not one qualifies as great literature, each and every one is valuable because of the theoretical stance it reveals. There is, for example, "Die Schauspielerin" (The Actress), which underscores the emotional transference and confusion of many eighteenth-century actresses:

> Der Bühne Bretter sind mein wahres Leben,
>   das eigentliche hab' ich aufgegeben,
>   und den Geliebten nur ans Herz ich drücke,
>   den mir der Tag zuführt in jedem Stücke.
> Doch dies der nackten Wirklichkeit Entheben
>   ist nur ein reiner ahndend Wahrheitsstreben.[43]

> (The stage's boards are my true life;
> real life I have given up
> and I only press to my heart the beloved
> whom the day brings me in each play.
> Yet this exemption from naked reality
> is but a purer premonitious striving for truth.)

Putting a stop to that kind of extended reverie or intoxication by introducing emotional distance is the theme of "Der Schauspieler":

> Wenn ich in manchen Stücken Rollen spiele,
>   wo ich ausdrücken soll, was selbst ich fühle,
>   wenn ich im Leben bin mir überlassen,
>   so kann ichs schwer in reine Kunstform fassen.
> Viel leichter steigert man zu Dichtungsstile,
>   was magisch schon nie vor im Leben fiele,
>   als daß Natur und Kunst zusammen passen
>   in dem, was wirklich lieben wir und hassen.
> Man kann auf Stunden wohl, was einem eigen,
>   ablegen und sich wahr in Fremden zeigen;
>   allein sein eigen Wesen so zu heben,
> daß es im reinen Äther scheint zu schweben,
>   da es auf Erden sonst prosaisch schleichet,
>   das selten Studium und Talent erreichet.[44]

---

[42] Tieck, *Kritische Schriften*, II, 374.

[43] Wilhelm von Humboldt, *Gesammelte Schriften*, 17 vols. (Berlin: Behr, 1903-36), *Werke*, ed. Albert Leitzmann, XII (1912), p. 192, no. 141, lines 1-6.

[44] Humboldt, p. 205, no. 184.

(When I am playing roles in some plays
where I am supposed to express what I myself feel,
if I am left to my own devices in life,
then I can hardly put it into a pure art form.
One raises to poetic style far more easily
what magically never before occurred in life,
while nature and art rarely join
in what we really love and hate.
One can probably put aside one's own self
for hours and show oneself truly in strangers;
only, to lift one's own being
so that it seems to tremble in the pure ether,
when otherwise it crawls prosaically on earth,
study and talent seldom attain that.)

Humboldt's experiences in Paris, where he frequented the theater, led to the essay that Goethe published in the *Propyläen* (1800), "Über die gegenwärtige französische tragische Bühne" (On the Contemporary French Tragic Stage). The acting of the internationally acclaimed François Joseph Talma (1763-1826) served as the focal point. In explaining what the actor is and does, Humboldt supported an idea that was very popular at the time. He maintained that during performance the actor was both the artist and the work of art. The demands of being simultaneously producer and product were enormous. The actor not only had the strain of summoning up emotions, but he then also had to keep control over those emotions so as to channel them for aesthetic purposes:

Es ist in der That eine ungeheure Aufgabe, alle Gefühle der Menschheit zu erregen, die tiefsten und mächtigsten Kräfte der Natur zu beschwören, und sie doch nur als Kunst wirken zu lassen und ästhetisch zu beherrschen.[45]

(It is in fact a colossal task to excite all the feelings of humanity, to conjure the deepest and mightiest forces of nature, and yet to have them work only as art and control them aesthetically.)

Humboldt distinguished the French style of acting from the German according to the way that aesthetic effect was produced. The French, he wrote, stressed artistry, therefore performing in a painterly, reflective, emotionally distant manner. They were like dancers going through a carefully choreographed routine. The Germans, on the other hand, stressed nature, which meant performances with expressive gestures, heartfelt sentiments, and emotional appeal. Humboldt wrote that the French actor, "zeigt und malt den ganzen Zustand der Seele, die Empfindung, die Leidenschaft, den Entschluß, aber nicht das von Empfindungen zerrissne, von Leidenschaften bestürmte, zu kühnen und raschen Entschlüssen gestählte Herz selbst" (shows and paints the soul's whole condition, sentiment, passion, decision, but not the heart itself torn by feelings, stormed by passions, steeled for bold and rash decisions).[46] This controlled French style could lead to boredom or affectation that was neither nature nor the ideal, but it could never lead to confusion with everyday reality: "An eine eigentliche Verschmelzung des Menschen mit dem Künstler im Schauspieler ist in Frankreich nicht zu denken" (A true fusion of human being with artist in the person of the actor cannot be considered

---

[45] Humboldt, II (1904), 394-95.
[46] Humboldt, II, 394.

in France).[47] Humboldt, like Goethe and an increasing number of their contemporaries, feared that the fusion of role and personality was becoming dangerously commonplace in German theater.

August Wilhelm Schlegel (1767-1845) acknowledged the danger inherent in such fusion. He was a scholar and a critic rather than a medical professional, so, instead of worrying about the emotional health of the actors and their audiences, he expended his efforts to stem what he considered the runaway tide of naturalism on the German stage. His emphasis was on the kind of sophisticated artistry that forced audiences into a make-believe world where they partook of the creative process. The very vocabulary he used, as we see, for example, from his various poems to or about actresses, was what had become standard. In "An die Rhapsodin" (To the Female Rhapsodist), there was not only the effortless breathing of life into a work, but also the magic, the ecstasy, the illusion, and the intoxication.[48] The poems to Friederike Unzelmann (ca. 1760-1815) mentioned the transitoriness of the performing arts as well as the magical transference of the dream-like effect to the audience. In one poem, he spoke of her as though she were a latter-day female version of Plato's *Ion*:

> Die Bühne Kunst glänzt vor der Mitwelt Augen,
> Die Zauber einer fremden Welt umstrahlen
> Den Augenblick des Jubels, der Entzückung,
> Und tausend hingeriss'ne Herzen glüh'n.[49]

> (Stage art is splendid in Midgarth's eyes,
> The enchantments of a strange world wrap in rays
> The moment of jubilation and delight,
> And a thousand beating hearts glow.)

The one other actress who ranked as high in his estimation was Anne Louise Germaine Necker, Baroness de Staël-Holstein (1766-1817). And at that, she was only a dilettante, as he admitted in his essay, "Über einige tragische Rollen von Frau v. Staël dargestellt" (About Several Tragic Roles Portrayed by Mme de Staël, 1806). Her achievements were, in his opinion, manifold, for she knew how to organize and train a supporting cast as well as make a fabulous appearance, enunciate a faultless French, and perform the given role with absolute conviction. He described her actual performance as completely governed by empathy:

> Frau von Staël gehört nicht zu den besonnenen Schauspielern, welche das, was sie einmal als das Richtige oder Vortheilhafteste berechnet haben, immer auf gleiche Weise ausführen. Nachdem sie ihre Rolle sorgfältig durchdacht und geübt, überläßt sie sich bei der Aufführung ganz den Eingebungen des Augenblicks. Sie verliert sich in die vorgestellte Person, ringt mit streitenden Gefühlen, leidet, verzagt, entsetzt sich, sinkt in Ermattung, faßt neuen Muth oder wird zum letzten Entschluß der Verzweiflung hingetrieben; kurz alles, wodurch die tragische Poesie die Gemüther bewegt und erschüttert, fühlt sie bis zur Täuschung, als gienge es mit ihr selbst vor.[50]

> (Madame de Staël does not belong among those circumspect actors who always execute in the same manner what once they have calculated to be correct or most advantageous. After she has carefully thought through and practiced her role, during performance she abandons herself entirely to the

---

[47] Humboldt, II, 396.
[48] August Wilhelm Schlegel, *Sämmtliche Werke*, ed. Eduard Böcking, 12 vols. (Leipzig: Weidmann, 1846-47), I, 10-11.
[49] A.W. Schlegel, *Sämmtliche Werke*, I, 240.
[50] A.W. Schlegel, *Sämmtliche Werke*, IX, 271.

promptings of the moment. She loses herself in the person portrayed, wrestles with contentious feelings, suffers, grows despondent, is horrified, sinks in exhaustion, takes renewed heart, or is driven to the ultimate decision of desperation; in short, everything whereby tragic poetry moves and shatters our sensibilities she feels to the point of the deception that it is happening to her personally.)

August Wilhelm Schlegel, who, we must remember, was the tutor to her children and her constant companion if not her devoted lover, hastened to add, the saving grace was that she performed classical French tragedies, which meant, that the controls of verse, rhetoric, and prescribed gesture had been built into the very lines of the text.

August Wilhlem's abiding concern for the art of acting is evidenced throughout his *Vorlesungen über dramatische Kunst und Literatur* (Lectures on Dramatic Art and Literature, 1809). In the first of those lectures, originally given in Vienna, he examined the human being's basic psychological predisposition to mimicry and, like so many of his contemporaries, related it to children, who constantly play and make believe. The mythological aspects of performance were then weighed against the historical. In addition to citing Herodotus, August Wilhelm mentioned "die Conteurs, Menestriers und Jongleurs" of the middle ages who performed in public.[51] Not to be excluded from consideration was what was happening during his own lifetime. Consequently he acknowledged the many explorers who were sending back observations of other societies in other climates. Even the aborigines of the South Seas, they had reported, enjoyed a somewhat developed theater in which primitive plays were mounted.

The third lecture is devoted to emphasizing distance among actors. In it, August Wilhelm explained that the ancients' consummate artistry derived from their employment of masks, saltation, stylized gestures, and modulated voices. Everything was controlled, unlike in contemporary German theater: "Sie wollten lieber an der Lebendigkeit der Darstellung einbüßen als an der Schönheit; wir machen es gerade umgekehrt" (They would rather lose something of the vivacity of the portrayal than of the beauty; we do things exactly the opposite).[52] The explanation August Wilhelm offered for the success of ancient theater was one that was used recurrently in Romantic critical theory: "Da der Dichter zugleich Musiker, meistens auch Schauspieler war, so mußte es zur Vollkommenheit der Ausführung viel beytragen" (The fact that the poet was simultaneously a musician, and, in most instances, also an actor, had to contribute much to the perfection of the performance).[53]

In his eleventh lecture, August Wilhelm scrutinized French acting, both the declamatory style and that advanced by Diderot, whose many shifts in position were, however, not taken into consideration. August Wilhelm considered mimetic cues and other prescriptions inserted into the text by the playwright to be extraneous vis-à-vis the professional actor, who, he claimed, would know from experience, habit, and instinct what a particular role required. Such comments indicate that August Wilhelm believed in limiting the playwright's responsibilities while trusting the ability of the performer to breathe life (*der Hauch*) into the role. French theater was successful, as August Wilhelm explained, because of the rhetorical exactitude as well as the emotional distance of its performers. Audiences in France knew all the pieces by heart. And, so did those who published critiques. Since each and every one was known to be very strict and very demanding, the actors responded in kind.

[51] August Wilhelm Schlegel, *Vorlesungen über dramatische Kunst und Literatur*, ed. Giovanni Vittorio Amoretti, 2 vols. (Bonn and Leipzig: Schroeder, 1923), I, 18.
[52] A.W. Schlegel, *Vorlesungen*, I, 44.
[53] A.W. Schlegel, *Vorlesungen*, I, 46.

English acting, as we read in the thirteenth lecture, had always been quite different. The most facile explanation had to do with their national character, but that was not sufficient for August Wilhelm. He wrote that the lack of scenic effects in Renaissance England contributed to the rapid development of histrionic techniques. He thought Shakespeare was unique because he brought together in perfect harmony the skills of the playwright, the actor, and the stage director.

The fifteenth lecture treats the German theatrical scene. In addition to demonstrating his awareness of the *status quo* and his seemingly genuine compassion for the performers, he once again zeroed in on the subject of acting, strongly advocating distance. And, he did so, despite his suspicion that actors could not help but get carried away. There was just something in their basic psychology that made them the kind of exhibitionists who felt at home in the theater and its milieu. As he wrote,

> Der Schauspieler, bei seinen zweydeutigen Lebensverhältnissen, (die einmal nicht zu ändern sind, weil sie in der Natur der Sache liegen) bedarf einer gewissen leichtsinnigen Begeisterung für seine Kunst, um das Außerordentliche zu leisten.[54]

> (The actor, given his dubious circumstances of life [which cannot even be altered since they are intrinsic to the nature of the business], needs a certain frivolous enthusiasm for his art in order to achieve the extraordinary.)

August Wilhelm's essay, "Über den dramatischen Dialog" (1796), treated many of the issues that his father, Johann Adolf Schlegel (1721-1793), and his uncle, Johann Elias Schlegel (1719-1749), had brought up much earlier in the century. Following in their footsteps, August Wilhelm argued that the very assumption of drama distinguished it from everyday reality. What is improbable, false, or impossible in the real world seems perfectly appropriate in art since it is condensed, re-formed, and cleverly veiled.[55] Consequently, he explained, the artistry of the dialogue was more important than the approximation of nature. If dramas were written in verse, as they should be, he continued, the actors would have to adapt and so would the audiences. The on-going adaptation to metrics would counteract the German proclivity towards naturalism and thereby improve tastes. Lauding the progress that had already been made because of Goethe's efforts in Weimar, he singled out Schiller as the only German playwright capable of producing verse dramas with mass appeal.

August Wilhelm Schlegel attacked the mimetic doctrine even more aggressively in the essay, "Über das Verhältniß der schönen Kunst zur Natur; über Täuschung und Wahrscheinlichkeit; über Stil und Manier" (On the Relationship of Art to Nature; on Illusion and Probability; on Style and Manner). He insisted that there was a logical flaw in the claim that art imitates nature:

> Denn entweder ahmt man die Natur nach, wie man sie vorfindet, so wird sie vielleicht nicht schön ausfallen; oder man bildet sie schön, so ist es keine Nachahmung mehr. Warum sagen sie nicht gleich: Die Kunst soll das Schöne darstellen; und lassen die Natur ganz aus dem Spiele? So wäre man der Quälerei los, daß die Kunsterscheinungen zur Natur in diesem Sinne umgedeutet werden müssen; was nicht ohne die äußerste Gewaltthätigkeit möglich ist.[56]

---

[54] A.W. Schlegel, *Vorlesungen*, II, 306.

[55] August Wilhelm Schlegel, *Kritische Schriften*, 2 parts (Berlin: Reimer, 1828), I, 376. I have treated the elder generation of Schlegels in *Opera in the Development of German Critical Thought* (Princeton: Princeton Univ. Press, 1978), pp. 135-46 and 150-58.

[56] A.W. Schlegel, *Kritische Schriften*, I, 313.

(Either one imitates nature exactly as one finds it, then it will perhaps not turn out beautiful, or one forms it beautifully so that it is no longer an imitation. Why not immediately say, art should portray the beautiful and leave nature out of the game altogether? Then one would be rid of the vexatious obligation to reinterpret the artistic product back into nature in this sense, which is not possible without the uttermost violence.)

He joined his uncle Johann Elias in citing among his examples the less than aesthetic effect produced by life-like wax figures.

The mimetic doctrine was harmful for all artistic endeavors, but, as August Wilhelm stated, "Am meisten Unheil hat dieser Grundsatz in der dramatischen Poesie und in der von ihr abhängigen Schauspielkunst angerichtet" (This principle produced the most damage in dramatic poetry and in that art that depends on it, acting).[57] The actor, he contended, was to pretend to be the character rather than become the character. To support his contention, he cited the ancient example of Parmenon, who gave the audience more pleasure with his imitation of a grunting pig than did the farmer with his real pig. In August Wilhelm's opinion, it was ill-advised, "sich blindlings seinen Anlagen, und einer wilden Begeisterung zu nicht bloß scheinbar, sondern wirklich kunstlosen Ergießungen zu überlassen" (to give in blindly to one's tendencies, and not just seemingly to a wild enthusiasm, but genuinely artless effusions).[58] Empathizing to the extreme of losing control and distance contradicted the very essence of art.

August Wilhelm considered August Friedrich Ferdinand von Kotzebue (1761-1819) one of the worst perpetrators of theatrical naturalism and took him to task in *Ehrenpforte und Triumphbogen für den Theater-Präsidenten von Kotzebue bei seiner gehofften Rückkehr in's Vaterland, Mit Musik* (Gate of Honor and Arc of Triumph for Theater President von Kotzebue upon His Hoped-for Re-entry into the Fatherland, with Music, 1800). Purporting to celebrate Kotzebue's adventures in Russia, especially his triumphant return from banishment to Siberia, it presented a satirical collection of sonnets, epigrams, odes, ballads, a travelogue, and *Kotzebue's Rettung oder der tugendhafte Verbannte, Ein empfindsam-romantisches Schauspiel in zwei Aufzügen* (Kotzebue's Rescue or the Virtuous Exile: A Sentimental-Romantic Play in Two Acts). The play, constructed out of the same techniques Tieck employed in his prologue and upside-down world, pokes fun at the mimetic doctrine and the resultant confusion it caused about aesthetic reality and about acting.

The first act opens with the arrival of the global explorer, La Peyrouse, a Papageno figure whose feathers have been exchanged for oars. Despite his familiarity with all kinds of exotic places, La Peyrouse does not know where on earth he has landed. The prompter, whose box quickly comes to his attention, tells him he is on the German stage. When he states that he wants to get back to the real world, the prompter responds, "Immer verkehrter! Du hast hier die Wirklichkeit viel wirklicher als draußen" (More and more mixed-up! You find the reality here far more real than out there).[59] The prompter, upon learning of Kotzebue's predicament, fears the loss of his job and starts to get carried away by his own histrionics. La Peyrouse comments, "Du bist außer dir," and then he warns, "dein Hang zu edler Schwärmerei führt dich irre" (You are beside yourself; your penchant for noble reverie is leading you astray).[60] After calming down, the prompter explains how the characters of

[57] A.W. Schlegel, *Kritische Schriften*, I, 315.
[58] A.W. Schlegel, *Kritische Schriften*, I, 317. I have taken up the subject of Parmenon in "The Dangers of the New Sensibilities in Eighteenth-Century Acting," p. 96.
[59] A.W. Schlegel, *Sämmtliche Werke*, II, 281.
[60] A.W. Schlegel, *Sämmtliche Werke*, II, 285.

Kotzebue's plays can be located so that they can help liberate their creator. La Peyrouse thinks he still needs to go out into the real world, but the exasperated prompter says:

> Wo hinaus denn? Habe ich dir nicht gesagt, daß du hier alles beisammen hast. Versteh doch. Es heißt ja nur, das Stück spielt da und da, aber sie gehen alle auf Einen Boden vor und sprechen Eine Sprache. Das ist eben die Kunst.[61]

> (Whereto next? Haven'I told you that you have everything together here. Do understand. It only means just that the play takes place there and there, but they all march onto One soil [also=to one garret] and speak One language. That's what art is.)

As a result, La Peyrouse starts knocking at the doors of stage sets to various plays. More and more of Kotzebue's characters come forth to volunteer, and, after marching around the theater twice, they climb back through the prompter's box before the curtain descends.

The second act begins in Siberia as Kotzebue demonstrates his virtue by resisting the advances of Puseltusel, the village leader's libidinous daughter. Her bear dance enraptures him so much, however, that he starts screaming when she gives him a box on the ear. His companion chides him, "Besinn' dich, halte Stand, es ist nur Puseltusel und kein wirklicher Bär" (Get hold of yourself, stand fast, it's only Puseltusel and not an actual bear). Thereupon Kotzebue remarks, "Ach – es ist wahr! – Dieß Kunstwerk hatte eine gar zu starke Täuschung in mir hervorgebracht" (Ah – it's true! – This work of art produced quite too strong an illusion in me).[62] The arrival of a Chinese merchant increases Kotzebue's hope for escape. He suggests putting an acting troupe together in order to introduce German theater to China. The merchant agrees since he – like the keepers of Bedlam and other eighteenth-century madhouses – is certain he can make money displaying such lunatics to his countrymen.

Kotzebue forsakes them all when word of his pardon comes. Upon returning to Russia, he learns that his children, that is, the characters from his plays, successfully appealed to the monarch. The scene then shifts, and, in the manner used by Tieck, "Das Theater stellt das Innere eines schön decorierten Schauspielhauses vor, das sich allmählich mit Zuschauern füllt" (The theater presents the inside of a beautifully decorated playhouse which gradually fills with spectators).[63] The performance of a play by Kotzebue is as boring for the audience as it is for the critics. When it ends, an actor steps forth to announce that it will be repeated the next day with "Kotzebues Rettung" as an epilogue.

Empathy is treated with similarly biting criticism in other pieces included in August Wilhelm Schlegel's *Ehrenpforte und Triumphbogen*. One that stands out for that as well as for its hilarious refrain is "Festgesang deutscher Schauspielerinnen bei Kotzebues Rückkehr" (The Festive Song of German Actresses at Kotzebue's Return). Here is the third stanza:

> Du bist unsrer Herzen Mann,
> Der uns recht errathen kann.
> Reden, Thränen kannst du schreiben,
> Wie wir sie zu Hause treiben,

---

[61] A.W. Schlegel, *Sämmtliche Werke*, II, 286.
[62] A.W. Schlegel, *Sämmtliche Werke*, II, 311.
[63] A.W. Schlegel, *Sämmtliche Werke*, II, 322.

Daß wir bei der Lampen Schein
Glauben, ganz wir selbst zu sein.
Das kann niemand so wie du,
Kotzebue! Kotzebue!
Bubu – bubu – bubu – bu![64]

(You are the man of our hearts
Who can us well divine.
Speeches, tears you can pen,
As we indulge in them at home,
So that we by the lamp light
Believe to be ourselves quite.
No one can do that like you,
Kotzebue! Kotzebue!
Booboo – booboo – booboo – boo!)

Karl Wilhelm Ferdinand Solger (1780-1819) was less given to *ad hominem* jabs, but he was equally opposed to any kind of naturalism in the theater. This philosopher, who was a friend of Tieck's and a great admirer of *Die verkehrte Welt*, regularly recorded his observations of theatrical productions and, in most cases, mentioned the style as well as the quality of acting. His review of a German one used the uneven performance of the actors as a basis for complaining: "Sie spielen nicht eher gut, als bis sie warm werden. Dies ist eine der nachtheiligen Folgen des Naturalisirens auf dem deutschen Theater" (They do not play well until they become warm. This is one of the injurious results of naturalizing on the German stage).[65]

Like so many of his contemporaries, Solger pondered why the German style of acting tended towards empathy and naturalism while the French tended towards distance and artistry. In Paris, as he wrote, "Ich erwartete die andere Hälfte der dramatischen Kunst zu sehen, wovon ich die erste Hälfte in Deutschland gesehen hatte" (I expected to see the other half of dramatic art, that I had seen the first half of in Germany).[66] What he witnessed, he described as being way beyond his expectations. The artistry of the French was so great that "Es ist eine fast übermenschliche Würde darin, die uns beim ersten Anblick mit Ehrfurcht und einer feierlichen Stimmung erfüllt" (There is an almost superhuman dignity in it, which at first glance fills us with reverence and a solemn mood).[67] The actors repeatedly posed for moments at a time in striking attitudes either singly or in groups. And, any human being who aspired to perform in a tragic role there, "der muß willkürlich ganz aus der Natur heraustreten und sich in die künstliche Welt des französischen Tragikers versetzen" (had arbitrarily to step out of nature entirely and transfer himself into the artificial world of the French tragedian).[68]

The drawbacks of the style, Solger had to admit, were numerous. First of all, there was too much "Verschrobenheit" (eccentricity) to do justice to Greek tragedy. Second, there were obvious difficulties with modulation. Even the renowned Talma occasionally lapsed into such stridency that he became too hoarse to be audible for the rest of the performance. Third, Solger insisted in patri-

---

[64] A.W. Schlegel, *Sämmtliche Werke*, II, 328.
[65] Karl Wilhelm Ferdinand Solger, *Nachgelassene Schriften und Briefwechsel*, eds. L. Tieck and Friedrich von Raumer, 2 vols. (Leipzig: Brockhaus, 1826), I, 20.
[66] Solger, *Nachgelassene Schriften*, I, 54.
[67] Solger, *Nachgelassene Schriften*, I, 56.
[68] Solger, *Nachgelassene Schriften*, I, 59.

otic German fashion, the French character was simply not profound enough to delve beneath the surface, that is, to notice anything beyond the diction, the stylized gestures, and the *tableaux vivants*.

The actor was also a major theme in Solger's *Vorlesungen über Aesthetik*. Again and again we read that he conceived of acting as originally a religious phenomenon that gradually became secularized into an art form. Solger focussed on the concept of catharsis, and argued, in a fashion reflecting current shamanistic discoveries, that even Aristotle misunderstood the vast complexities. Solger's explanation was that catharsis was "ein mythischer und religiöser Ausdruck, die Befreiung von einem gewissen zauberhaften Banne, von religiöser Schuld u. dergl. bezeichnend" (a mystical and religious expression, the liberation from a certain magical spell, from religious guilt, and so forth).[69] Then he singled out and stressed the all-important healing aspect. Performance or acting in public was a form of art that "soll von dem Wahnsinn der Leidenschaften heilen durch Mittheilung einer höheren Begeisterung" (should heal from the madness of the passions through communication of a higher enthusiasm).[70]

Solger made a great effort in his lectures to explain the essence of enthusiasm. To sum up, he thought of it as something, "worin das Gemüth des Künstlers in seiner Thätigkeit ganz von der Idee angefüllt ist, so daß er die Idee an die Stelle der Wirklichkeit setzen muß. Die Begeisterung versetzt ihn in eine Täuschung, vermöge deren er die Idee für die wirkliche Welt ansieht" (whereby the artist's sensibility in its activity is entirely filled with the idea so that he has to put the idea in the place of reality. Enthusiasm transposes him into an illusion by virtue of which he regards the idea as the real world).[71] Although such enthusiasm was in itself energetic and lively, Solger thought it could be best described as inducing clarity and tranquillity. In such an enthusiastic state, the artist then destroyed the real world "nicht bloß in sofern sie Schein, sondern in sofern sie selbst Ausdruck der Idee ist" (not merely insofar as it is appearance, but insofar as it itself is expression of the idea).[72] His weapon of destruction was irony. There was, according to Solger, no great art, neither temporal, nor spatial, nor a combination thereof, like theater, without the proper balance of enthusiasm and irony. In Solger's own words, "Eben so sind Begeisterung und Ironie untrennbar, jene als Wahrnehmung der göttlichen Idee in uns, diese als Wahrnehmung unserer Nichtigkeit, des Unterganges der Idee in der Wirklichkeit" (Even thus are inspiration and irony inseparable, the former as perception of the divine idea in us, the latter as perception of our nothingness, of the decline of the idea in reality).[73]

More and more physicians began taking cognizance of the poet-performer as well as the illnesses, accidents, and drug-related problems he so often suffered. For the most part, they agreed with the aesthetic theorists, like Solger, Schlegel, Humboldt, Tieck, and Fernow, that irony or self-awareness could moderate the actor's enthusiasm and keep him from going over the brink permanently. Some physicians went on to explore the possible psychiatric applications of play-acting, enthusiasm, irony, and catharsis, in the hope of bringing mad patients out of the world of their own illusions and back into the real world. In other words, they tried the reverse.

---

[69] Karl Wilhelm Ferdinand Solger, *Vorlesungen über Aesthetik*, ed. K.W.L. Heyse (Leipzig: Brockhaus, 1829), p. 16.
[70] Solger, *Vorlesungen über Aesthetik*, p. 17.
[71] Solger, *Vorlesungen über Aesthetik*, p. 124.
[72] Solger, *Vorlesungen über Aesthetik*, p. 125.
[73] Solger, *Vorlesungen über Aesthetik*, p. 242. See also p. 199.

Johann Christian Reil (1759-1813), a pioneering medical researcher and founder of the court theater in Halle, worked avidly to change public attitudes towards the mentally ill. He advocated not just containing them but healing them and returning them to society for a productive life. Like colleagues in France, England, and Italy, he wanted the mad removed from prisons and poorhouses in order to be sent to therapeutic institutes in rural areas. In *Rhapsodien über die Anwendung der psychischen Curmethode auf Geisteszerrüttungen* (Rhapsodies on the Application of Psychic Healing Methods to Mental Derangements, 1803), he stressed the importance of constructing such institutes with ample space for farming, gardening, and raising animals.

Work and a natural, healthy environment away from a gawking public would not always be sufficient. Depending on the severity of the mental illness, various other remedies could be tried, including those thought to be transmitted immediately to the psyche through the body, like wine, opium, warm baths, electricity, stroking, and sex. Remedies appealing to the imagination were considered useful for types of aberrance that derived from pathological day-dreaming, excessive role-playing, habitual introspection, and constant enthusiasm, whether involving people, politics, or religion. In Reil's opinion, irrational activity was normal as long as the person had enough self-composure and distance to recognize it as such and to stop it. He explained that the human being had

> einen natürlichen Hang, sich in einem geträumten Zustand zu denken und in Beziehung auf denselben das Bewußtseyn seiner wahren Verhältnisse zu verleugnen. Das Kind spielt die Wochenfrau, den Soldaten oder König; wir ergötzen uns an den Fiktionen der Mahler, Dichter und Schauspieler, ja es macht uns selbst in den späteren Jahren des Lebens noch glücklich, uns eine Welt in der Phantasie zu schaffen, in welcher wir eine glänzendere Rolle als in der wirklichen spielen. Allein unsere Besonnenheit weist uns bald in unsere natürlichen Verhältnisse zurück.[74]

> (a natural inclination to think itself into a dreamed state and, taking this as its point of reference, to deny consciousness of its true circumstances. The child plays the woman lying in, the soldier, or the king; we take pleasure in the fictions of the painters, poets, and actors. Indeed, even in the later years of life, it still makes us happy to create in our fancy a world where we play a more splendid role than in the real one. Only our self-possession redirects us back to our natural circumstances.)

In some psychic states, like a nightmare or sleepwalking, Reil thought the person retained partial consciousness because of the organization of the nervous system. Such a person was able to observe himself, reflect upon himself, and even consider whether he was doing all those things while awake or dreaming. Therefore, Reil suggested that works of art could be performed by fully conscious human beings or by mere automatons (*blosse Automaten*). He cited as examples the somnambulists who were able to compose sublime poems and speak in foreign tongues. Then, reflecting the rapid technological advances, he added, "Wir haben Gruppen und Züge des künstlichsten und verwickeltesten Muskelspiels in eine fremde Maschine hineingetragen, die sie mechanisch wiederhallt, wie die Aeols Harfe ihre Gesänge, wenn der Wind in ihre Saiten bläst" (We have registered groups and traits of the most artful and confused muscle play in an alien machine which echoes them mechanically as the aeolian harp does its songs when the wind blows on its strings).[75]

---

[74] Johann Christian Reil, *Rhapsodien über die Anwendung der psychischen Curmethode auf Geisteszerrüttungen* (Halle: Curt, 1803; facsimile reprint, Amsterdam: Bonset, 1968), p. 322. Christa Karoli, *Ideal und Krise enthusiastischen Künstlertums in der deutschen Romantik*, Abhandlungen zur Kunst-, Musik- und Literaturwissenschaft, no. 48 (Bonn: Bouvier, 1968), pp. 38-40 and 106, emphasizes the importance of music without going into contemporary psychiatric writings.

[75] Reil, *Rhapsodien*, p. 97.

Along with his contemporaries, like Tieck, and also his intellectual descendants, like Jakob Moreno (born 1892), Reil firmly believed in the curative power of the performing arts. Music had been used since primordial times and so too had play-acting. Therefore, he recommended an inventory of musical instruments and a fully equipped theater for therapeutic institutes dealing with psychiatric cases. He wrote,

> daß jedes Tollhaus zum Behuf ihrer imposanten Anwendung und zweckmäßigen Zusammenstellung ein für diese Zwecke besonders eingerichtetes, durchaus praktikabeles Theater haben könnte, das mit allen nöthigen Apparaten, Masquen, Maschinerien und Decorationen versehen wäre. Auf demselben müßten die Hausofficianten hinlänglich eingespielt seyn, damit sie jede Rolle eines Richters, Scharfrichters, Arztes, vom Himmel kommender Engel, und aus den Gräbern wiederkehrender Todten, nach den jedesmaligen Bedürfnissen des Kranken, bis zum höchsten Grad der Täuschung vorstellen könnten. Ein solches Theater könnte zu Gefängnissen und Löwengruben, zu Richtplätzen und Operationssälen formirt werden. Auf demselben würden Donquichotte zu Rittern geschlagen, eingebildete Schwangere ihrer Bürde entladen, Narren trepanirt, reuige Sünder von ihren Verbrechen auf eine feierliche Art losgesprochen. Kurz der Arzt würde von demselben und dessen Apparat nach den individuellen Fällen den mannichfaltigsten Gebrauch machen, die Phantasie mit Nachdruck und dem jedesmaligen Zwecke gemäß erregen, die Besonnenheit wecken, entgegengesetzte Leidenschaften hervorrufen, Furcht, Schreck, Staunen, Angst, Seelenruhe u.s.w. erregen und der fixen Idee des Wahnsinns begegnen können.[76]

(that for the sake of their imposing application and purposeful assemblage every madhouse could have a thoroughly practical theater especially arranged for such aims, one outfitted with all the needed apparatuses, masks, machineries, and decorations. Those officiating at the institution would be sufficiently versed in acting in the theater so as to be able to portray, to the highest level of illusion, any role of a judge, executioner, doctor, angels coming from heaven, the dead returning from the grave, according to the needs of the sick person in each instance. Such a theater could be shaped into prisons and lion pits, places of judgment and operation rooms. In the same, Don Quixotes would be dubbed knights, imaginary mothers-to-be relieved of their burden, fools trepanated, rueful sinners absolved of their crimes in a solemn fashion. In short, the physician would be able to make the most varied use of it and its apparatus according to the individual cases, to stimulate the fancy emphatically in line with the particular case, to waken thoughtfulness, summon contrary passions, fear, terror, astonishment, anxiety, peace of soul, etc., and to counter the *idée fixe* of the insanity.)

With imagery moving in exactly the opposite direction of Plato's *Ion*, Reil described theatrical performance as something that would not only comfort the mad but also lead them from the lowliest levels of unconsciousness or consciouslessness upwards through a kind of magnetic chain of spiritual enticements to the complete rehabilitation of their senses and eventually of their reason.

Such scientific attention, coupled with the artistic and the philosophical, served to mold the actor into something extraordinary in the popular mind. The theories about the actor's predisposition, genius, aura, and social importance became as significant as his real-life personage and image. As a result, the cross-currents of thought about actors and their misunderstanding of aesthetic reality, their getting carried away with their roles, their eternally tormented personal lives, and their remarkable ability to soothe if not heal through play-acting were used repeatedly by Romantic poets in just about every genre imaginable.

[76] Reil, *Rhapsodien*, pp. 209-10.

The German Romantic poet who stands out because his sensitivity to such problems matched his artistry in dealing with them is E.T.A. Hoffmann (1776-1822). And, it is to his work that I should like to turn in the concluding pages of this paper. Again and again Hoffmann managed to transpose theories of performance, ranging from the empathy of the shaman to the emotional distance of the marionette, into masterpieces of a kind that was just about unparalleled in literary history.

The idea of curing a sensitive performer's illusion with another illusion is the subject of *Das Sanctus* (The Sanctus). Its heroine is a singer who has become so ill that the physician summoned to her bedside predicts she will never sing again. Her Kapellmeister suggests euthanasia. He wants her to be given opium in increasing amounts so that she can die peacefully rather than by overdosing. A much more optimistic prognosis, however, is offered by the traveling enthusiast, who accepts the blame for her illness, which is actually due to the power of suggestion over her imagination. He had been the one to tell her that she would never sing again if she sneaked out from the choir during their singing of the Sanctus at the Roman Catholic mass. Since she did just that, she became ill. The remedy he suggests is a parallel story with a happy end, presumably from the Spanish, to be told loudly enough so that each word gets through to her in the next room. The story is told; she overhears it; and a seemingly miraculous cure takes place.[77]

In *Don Juan, Eine fabelhafte Begebenheit, die sich mit einem reisenden Enthusiasten zugetragen* (Don Juan, A Fabulous Occurrence that Transpired with a Traveling Enthusiast) Hoffmann zeroed in on a *shamanka* capable of bilocation and a few other things that Herder and his contemporaries marveled at in the explorers' reports. She is a performer in a production of Wolfgang Amadeus Mozart's (1756-91) *Don Giovanni*, which is called the opera of all operas. The traveling enthusiast gets a hotel room which happens to have a door into a box at the adjoining opera house. He avails himself of it, experiences the production and also an unexpected visit from the performer playing Donna Anna: "Die Möglichkeit abzuwägen, wie sie auf dem Theater und in meiner Loge habe zugleich sein können, fiel mir nicht ein" (It did not occur to me to ponder how it could be possible that she was on the stage and in my loge at the same time). His visitor repeatedly tells him that he, who is himself presumably a composer, understands her: "denn ich weiß, daß auch dir das wunderbare, romantische Reich aufgegangen, wo die himmlischen Zauber der Töne wohnen" (for I know that the wondrous romantic realm, where the heavenly magic of the tones dwell, has been revealed also to you).[78] He believes that the emotional receptivity of any given audience is precisely that which guarantees the success of the performance, whether it be magic or music. The audience believes because it wants to believe. In a similar vein, he says that only the artist or shaman can understand others who have been initiated into the secrets: "nur ein romantisches Gemüt kann eingehen in das Romantische: nur der poetisch exaltierte Geist, der mitten im Tempel die Weihe empfing, das verstehen, was der Geweihte in der Begeisterung ausspricht" (only a romantic sensibility can enter into the romantic: only the poetically exalted spirit, who received consecration in the temple's core, can understand what the initiated utters in inspiration).[79] The strange premonition he

---

[77] E.T.A. Hoffmann, *Sämtliche Werke*, ed. Carl Georg von Maassen, III, *Nachtstücke* (Munich and Leipzig: Müller, 1909), pp. 136-56. Heide Eilert, *Theater in der Erzählkunst: Eine Studie zum Werk E.T.A. Hoffmanns*, Studien zur deutschen Literatur, no. 52 (Tübingen: Niemeyer, 1977), pp. 14-15, believes he wanted an illusionistic stage, although she does broaden her interpretation when she mentions the "immer wieder postulierte Suggestivwirkung des Theaters" (again and again postulated suggestive effect of theater), p. 73.
[78] Hoffmann, I, (1908), 94.
[79] Hoffmann, I, 98.

has at the stroke of two in the morning is confirmed the next day when he learns of the performer's death. Bilocation, ventriloquism, legerdemain, music, ecstasy, and psychic rapport are also essential features of *Die Automate* and a host of other Hoffmann writings.[80]

In *Ritter Gluck, Eine Erinnerung aus dem Jahre 1809* (Chevalier Gluck, A Remembrance from 1809), Hoffmann takes up ideas about shamanism that involve the transmigration of souls as well as the use of music, the secret language, to induce a trance allowing entry into the "other" world. It was stimulated, among other things, by Goethe's recent translation (1805) of Diderot's *Le Neveu de Rameau*, a work composed of similar experimentation with shamanistic ideas. The description Hoffmann presents of the strange composer is, in any event, a composite of the totally empathizing performer.[81]

The dangers of artistic empathy are treated in *Der vollkommene Maschinist* (The Compleat Machinist). It is in this work that Hoffmann most clearly articulates his support of distance or irony or anything assuring the retention of self-awareness during a performance:

> Der erste Grundsatz, von dem Sie in allen Ihren Bemühungen ausgehen müssen, ist: Krieg dem Dichter und Musiker – Zerstörung ihrer bösen Absicht, den Zuschauer mit Trugbildern zu umfangen und ihn aus der wirklichen Welt zu treiben. Hieraus folgt, daß in eben dem Grade, als jene Personen alles nur Mögliche anwenden, den Zuschauer vergessen zu lassen, daß er im Theater sei. Sie dagegen durch zweckmäßge Anordnung der Dekorationen und Maschinerien ihn beständig an das Theater erinnern müssen.[82]

> (The first axiom from which you must proceed in all your endeavors is: War on the poet and musician – destruction of their evil intent to snare the spectator with deceptive images and drive him from the real world. The corollary is that, precisely to the degree those persons employ everything possible to make the spectator forget he is in the theater, you in contrast, through purposeful deployment of the scenery and machinery, must constantly remind him of the theater.)

As soon as things seem to be going too far, the curtain should fall or something drastic should happen to the set so as to remind the performers and their audience that it is all make-believe.

The summation of Hoffmann's ideas about the art of performance comes in *Seltsame Leiden eines Theater-Direktors* (The Peculiar Sufferings of a Theater Director, 1819), a revised and enlarged version of "Die Kunstverwandten" (The Ones Related through Art), which had appeared anonymously in *Dramaturgisches Wochenblatt* (Dramaturgical Weekly) two years earlier. It begins with a calm, comfortable, satisfied, meticulously dressed Mr. Brown busily at work on a manuscript while having a rather solitary brunch in the local inn. His peace and quiet end abruptly when Mr. Gray storms in and demands at top voice champagne and oysters. He is the sloppily dressed director of the local stage who is so harried, nervous, and unhappy that he is simply bursting to ventilate his many troubles. Mr. Brown, the director of a traveling troupe that happens to be passing through town, turns out to be quite sympathetic. He offers to listen to Mr. Gray's troubles and to give as much help as he can towards solving them.

---

[80] Hoffmann, VI, *Die Serapions-Brüder, Zweiter Band*, (1912), 98-119. Important in respect to such works is Lee B. Jennings, "Hoffmann's Hauntings: Notes towards a Parapsychological Approach to Literature," *JEGP*, 75 (1976), 559-67.
[81] Hoffmann, I, 15-29. See also von Maassen's discussion following "Signor Formica," VIII (1925), p. 112, and Georg Edgar Sluser, "*Le Neveu de Rameau* and Hoffmann's Johannes Kreisler: Affinities and Influences," *Comparative Literature* 27 (1975), pp. 327-28.
[82] Hoffmann, I, *Kreisleriana*, no. 6, p. 79.

Their dialogue reviews contemporary theatrical problems involving audiences as well as actors. The positions the two speakers represent are essentially those of empathy and distance. The real irony here is that they are the opposite of what one would expect. Mr. Gray, who works with living human beings, disputes the magic of theater and the supersensitivity of performing artists. He thinks they are always faking and they are always fully aware of what they are doing, which he views as a major source of his own problems. Mr. Gray doubts very much that the strain of perform-ing is as great as the performers claim. In his opinion, they are too vain about their position or too lazy to work, so that they use all their tricks and talents to make believe they are sick: "Der führt ein ganzes Arsenal des Todes in der Tasche! Fieber aller Art – Lungensucht – Schwindsucht – Gehir-nentzündung – mit grausigen Anfällen jeder Krankheit wirft er um sich in seltsamen Attesten, [...]" (That one carries a whole arsenal of death in his pocket! Fever of very sort – pneumonia – consump-tion – inflammation of the brain – horrible attacks of every sickness he bandies about in odd certifi-cates, [...]).[83] Consequently he has his theater physician treat them with psychic means rather than physical ones.

Mr. Brown, as we learn at the very end, works with marionettes, yet throughout the dialogue, he is the one to affirm the magical aspects of performance as well as the unusual psychological make-up of the performer. He argues that something happens in theater that upsets the laws of normal probability and turns everything around and upside down. As a result, actors very often do go to pieces, have nervous breakdowns, or lose their minds:

> Ich habe Jünglinge gekannt, heitern Sinns, gesunden freien Verstandes und kräftigen Willens, die von innerm Trieb beseelt sich der Bühne widmeten und bei voller Gesundheit gleich in den besondern Schauspielerwahnsinn verfielen, nachdem sie die verhängnisvollen Bretter betreten hatten.[84]

> (I have known youths of cheerful mind, healthy liberal understanding, and powerful will who, motivated by inner drive, dedicated themselves to the stage and, in complete good health, fell straight-way into the peculiar actor's madness once they had trod the fatal boards.)

Mr. Brown continues by contending that great actors are born and not made. Then he ratifies the idea that they become both the producer and the product of art, much like most of us do in our dreams. In order to succeed, he explains, the actor must divest himself of his own personality so that he can be consumed or filled with the new personality that he is expected to radiate: "Das gänzliche Verleugnen oder vielmehr Vergessen des eignen Ichs ist daher gerade das erste Erfordernis der dar-stellenden Kunst" (The absolute and total denial or rather forgetting of one's own ego is therefore the first requirement of the Thespian art).[85] Actors who only pretend to be empathizing never rise above mediocrity and always cause the kinds of problems facing Mr. Gray. Genuine actors can, Mr. Brown offers as comfort, be directed very easily, if one treats them like children. All the director has to do is remind them again and again that it is all just a play and not real. As Mr. Brown states, "Im Moment des Schaffens mag eben die Begeisterung sich in heiterer Unbefangenheit aufschwin-gen, es ist genug, wenn der Verstand nur die Zügel behält" (Enthusiasm may indeed soar in joyous

---

[83] Hoffmann, IV (1910), 25. M.M. Raraty, "E.T.A. Hoffmann and His Theater," *Hermathena: A Dublin University Review*, 98 (Spring 1964), pp. 53-67, especially p. 58, interprets everything from the point of view of creating an illusion that reduplicates everyday reality.
[84] Hoffmann, IV, 39.
[85] Hoffmann, IV, 41.

ingenuousness during the moment of creating; however, it is enough, if only the rational faculty retains the reins).[86]

However, moderation and discretion are of the utmost importance if the other extreme is also to be avoided. Too much control as well as control that is misplaced can deaden true genius and rob it of its innate ability, "die Fittiche zu regen zum höhern Fluge!" (to stir its pinions to higher flight). After all, they are, indeed, "Söhne Apollos, die des göttlichen Vaters Bogen tragen" (sons of Apollo who carry the divine father's bow).[87] The performer-poet, like any genius, Mr. Brown reiterates, "wirkt auch in den höchsten Graden des Enthusiasmus mit Besonnenheit und Freiheit. Er ist von seinem Gegenstande durchdrungen, emporgehoben, begeistert, aber nicht beherrscht" (operates with presence of mind and freedom even in the highest stages of enthusiasm. He is permeated by his subject, elevated, enthused, but never controlled by it).[88]

One of the truly memorable masterpieces that Hoffmann created out of the ideas from this theoretical debate is *Signor Formica, Eine Novelle* (1820). With a truly Mozartian touch, Hoffmann has Salvator Rosa, a painter, actor, multidimensional genius, arrange that two young lovers be united in marriage and, also, that familial happiness result after a suspenseful, yet delightful series of confusing catastrophes. Pasquale Capuzzi, who has fallen in love with his orphaned niece Marianne, refuses to allow her to see her beloved, Antonio Scacciati, a painter of some renown who, however, earns his living as a healer (*Wundarzt*). Antonio enlists the aid of Salvator, whom he has known since healing his wounds from a previous accident. Salvator, who unbeknownst to just about everybody, is also the comedian, Signor Formica, gets Pasquale to attend one of his wildly acclaimed performances.

Knowing just how to appeal to what Hoffmann earlier described as the madness and foolishness inherent in all human beings, Salvator sees to it that Pasquale rekindles the fire of "Theaterlust, die früher in jungen Jahren beinahe ausartete in Wahnsinn" (passion for the theater that in his younger years almost degenerated into madness).[89] He fans the fire further by suggesting that Pasquale's music is so great that it absolutely must have a public performance. The result is a truly mirthful psychodrama at which Pasquale in the audience sees himself or his *Doppelgänger* impersonated on the stage, while the two young lovers make their escape. When Pasquale attempts to wreak vengeance on the youngsters, Salvator creates yet another scenario that teaches him to avoid "zu lebhaften Antheil an dem Schauspiel" (too lively an attachment to the drama).[90] This delightful novella has a happy end, for Marianna and Antonio welcome their poor, benighted, yet so vulnerably human uncle into their home as a surrogate parent.

Hoffmann gives the exact same issues aesthetic form in *Prinzessin Brambilla, Ein Capriccio nach Jakob Callot* (Princess Brambilla, a Capriccio after Jacques Callot, 1821). Again, Italy is the setting, Again, psychodrama is the method. And, again, there is the performing artist who desperately needs to learn about self-awareness, discipline, and irony. The hero, Giglio Fava, is a young, highly impressionable tragedian who deeply loves Giacinta, a very talented, yet down-to-earth seamstress. The local shaman or medicine man (*Ciarlatano* [cf. English, charlatan]) Celionati tries

---

[86] Hoffmann, IV, 49.
[87] Hoffmann, IV, 53.
[88] Hoffmann, IV, 67.
[89] Hoffmann, IV. Horst Daemmerich, *The Shattered Self: E.T.A. Hoffmann's Tragic Vision* (Detroit: Wayne State Univ. Press, 1973), p. 35, contends this work presents a light-hearted view of the artist and consequently dismisses it.
[90] Hoffmann, IV, 101.

to drum up business by advertising the arrival of Prince Chiapperi from Ethiopia, who is coming to have his bad tooth pulled. His incipient love affair with Princess Brambilla constitutes the hoax that Hoffmann uses in order to have his characters restore Giglio to his senses.

If Giglio has long bordered on madness, it is, as everyone knows, because he never played his role, he always played himself. Although the forces representing false tragedy with all its dangers do their best to keep him on their side, the *commedia dell'art* eventually does win out. He dances with the female, so he thinks, who wields the shamanistic tambourine until they both reach what nowadays would be called "disco-high." When he collapses and falls into a kind of hallucinatory trance, so that he thinks he is dreaming, he manages to assert that it is, after all, carnival. And, he realizes that his past behavior was not normal. The local shaman or charlatan, whom he begs not to reveal anything, complies while the faithful nurse comments on what wonderful children they all are.

There are many other examples from the German literary tradition. Among them are Goethe's *Wilhelm Meisters Lehrjahre* (Wilhelm Meister's Apprenticeship, 1795-96), Ludwig Achim von Arnim's (1781-1831) *Hollin's Liebeleben* (Hollin's Love Life, 1802), Jean Paul Friedrich Richter's (1763-1825) treatment of Roquairol in *Titan* (1800-3), the anonymously published *Die Nacht-wachen des Bonaventura* (The Night Watches of Bonaventura, 1805), Wilhelm Hauff's (1802-27) *Othello, Novelle* (1826), Eduard Mörike's (1804-75) depiction of Larken in *Maler Nolten* (Painter Nolten, 1832). Those writers treated the actor either as modifying excessively introspective behavior, or as falling prey to an on-stage accident, or directing the scenario for his own death scene, or gaining revenge against lack of audience support, or shamanizing himself into an early grave. Such varied, yet profound treatment of the performing artist developed into a tradition that expanded into the other arts while accelerating throughout the nineteenth century. It not only came full circle, but it also reached its highpoint with Ruggiero Leoncavallo's (1858-1919) *Pagliacci* (1892) and with Luigi Pirandello's (1867-1936) *Enrico IV* (1922). The latter dramatist had, during his student days in Bonn, become a devotee of German Romanticism.

(German titles and passages translated by *Gerald Gillespie*.)

ULRICH WEISSTEIN

WHAT IS ROMANTIC OPERA? –
TOWARD A MUSICO-LITERARY DEFINITION

> Wie das zeitliche Einschränken [...] hat das sachliche Einschränken [...] etwas Gewaltsames: es ignoriert die Lebensfülle.[1]
>
> (Like the temporal limitation, the limitation in subject matter is somehow contrived; it ignores life's plenitude.)
>
> The Romantic movement made the opera composers specialists because it took its opera more seriously than did the eighteenth century.[2]

I

A collective volume devoted to Romantic drama would be sadly deficient if it failed to consider the kind of multimedia stage work which, as the second motto indicates, became paradigmatic in various countries for various lengths of time during the first half of the nineteenth century. Hence the need for an essay like the present one, an attempt to develop some basic criteria, pinpoint the chief representatives and identify the handful of works that might qualify as paragons of melo-dramatic Romanticism viewed from a supranational vantage point. Throughout, my aim will be methodological rather than historical, although I am not foolish enough to wish to ignore chronology; for to do so would be tantamount to abandoning the justified view of Romanticism as a cultural phenomenon that is as unique as it is *unwiederholbar*, and acknowledging implicitly the existence of a perennial or categorial Romanticism that may surface randomly at any given time or place. (In committing this perspectival error, I would be as penny-wise as the cultural historian who claims, pound-foolishly, that in so far as music is, by definition, a Romantic art, all opera is, at least partly, Romantic.)

Since the Comparative History of Literatures in European Languages, to which this essay and the volume in which it appears belong, is truly international and interdisciplinary,[3] I am honor-bound to focus on the dialectic of indigenous and universal traits which characterizes the Romantic

[1] Werner Braun, *Das Problem der Epochengliederung in der Musik* (Darmstadt: Wissenschaftliche Buchgesellschaft, 1977), p. 39. – All translations in this essay are my own.

[2] Alfred Einstein, *Music in the Romantic Era* (New York: Norton, 1947), p. 103.

[3] The principle of interdisciplinarity was established, at my request, in conjunction with the volume *Expressionism as an International Literary Phenomenon* (Budapest and Paris: Akadémiai Kiadó & Didier, 1973), the first in this series. – A shorter German version of the present study, translated from the original English, appeared in the volume *Einheit in der Vielfalt: Festschrift für Peter Lang zum 60. Geburtstag*, ed. Gisele Quast (Bern: Lang, 1988), pp. 568-88.

age above all ages. Thus we shall find, to no one's surprise, that E.T.A. Hoffmann turned to Carlo Gozzi as a principal source of literary inspiration ("Der Dichter und der Komponist"), that Carl Maria von Weber emulated French opera in *Der Freischütz*, that the "Parisian" Rossini drew on Schiller (*Guillaume Tell*), and that Hector Berlioz availed himself of resources provided by Goethe, Beethoven, and Weber (*Symphonie fantastique*) – not to mention the supposedly neo-Romantic Verdi,[4] who took from Victor Hugo (*Ernani, Rigoletto*) what his native tradition was unable to supply.[5]

One can see that such a dense web of musical, literary, and musico-literary interrelationships is hard to disentangle, and that any sustained effort to dissolve the whole into its parts and reassemble those is likely to require an intense joint effort by representatives of *Musik-* and *Literaturwissenschaft*. I cannot hope to accomplish in a handful of pages what would require a monographic treatment; but perhaps I can measure the vacuum that exists in this respect. As far as I know, no literary scholars or critics have made a move in this direction; and few music historians have tackled the problem systematically. Thus valid solutions are as rare as the proverbial Phoenix, and most authors of books or articles with appropriate titles fail to rise from the ashes of the fire they themselves have set.

Thus, to mention a few recent examples, Palmiro Pinagli's book *Romanticismo di Verdi*[6] offers no explanation whatever of the intended meaning of the key word in its title; and Peter Conrad's controversial *Romantic Opera and Literary Form* – "gepriesen viel und viel gescholten" – is equally opaque in this respect.[7] Wherever we look, labels are loosely attached (as in *Early Romantic Opera*, a series edited by Philip Gossett and Charles Rosen and reproducing the scores of works by Bellini, Donizetti, Rossini, Meyerbeer, and Halévy[8]) or designed to justify the making of strange bedfellows (a in Edward J. Dent's posthumously published Messenger Lectures on *The Rise of Romantic Opera*[9]).

No clearcut sense of what constitutes Romantic Opera emerges from most general surveys of music history, most of which suffer from the handicap of being organized according to composers rather than works. Thus in his widely used and, on the whole, admirable *Music in Western Civilization*[10] Paul Henry Lang treats German Romantic opera – meaning primarily Weber – as a transitional phenomenon in chapter XV ("The Confluence of Classicism and Romanticism"), offers three sections on opera ("The Grand Opera," "Italian Opera," "German Opera" [Marschner and Lortzing]) in chapter XVI, brackets Wagner with Berlioz in chapter XVII ("From Romanticism to Realism"), and handles Verdi alongside Brahms and Bizet in chapter XVIII ("Counter Currents").

---

[4] See chapter XVI of Einstein's book (footnote 2 above), where the bulk of French, German, and Italian operas produced in the second and third quarters of the nineteenth century are dealt with under that label.

[5] For whatever reasons, Verdi seems to have found Alessandro Manzoni's historical tragedies *Il conte die Carmagnola* (1820) and *Adelchi* (1822) unsuitable.

[6] Palmiro Pinagli, *Romanticismo di Verdi* (Florence: Vallecchi, 1967).

[7] Peter Conrad, *Romantic Opera and Literary Form* (Berkeley: Univ. of California Press, 1977).

[8] The series was published by the Garland Press of New York. No explanation for the title is given by the editors.

[9] Edward J. Dent, *The Rise of Romantic Opera*, ed. Winton Dean (Cambridge: Cambridge Univ. Press, 1976). "The purpose of these lectures is to study Romantic opera. The composers whom I select as typical Romantics are Weber and Bellini. You might expect me to talk to you about Donizetti, Wagner, Verdi and perhaps Berlioz; but I may tell you at once that I do not intend to discuss any of these directly at all" (p. 7). In his paper on "The Romantic Spirit in Music," *Proceedings of the Musical Association, 59th Session, 1932-1933* (Leeds: Whitehead & Miller, 1933), pp. 85-95, Dent also identifies Weber as the Romantic composer *par excellence*.

[10] Paul Henry Lang, *Music in Western Civilization* (New York: Norton, 1941).

Historians of opera, too, have largely failed to suggest a distinct, and discernible, pattern. Often they altogether avoid the issue (at least as far as the Table of Contents, the most widely used guide for reading a book, is concerned) by scattering the relevant information. As the respective *indices nominum et rerum* demonstrate, this is true of Donald Grout's standard *A Short History of Opera*,[11] of *The Opera: A History of its Creation and Performance 1600-1941*, a book co-authored by Wallace Brockway and Herbert Weinstock,[12] as well as of the only history of the libretto written in English, Patrick J. Smith's *The Tenth Muse*.[13] The easy way out, which brings no solution, is that preferred by Anna Amalia Abert in her contribution to *Musik in Geschichte und Gegenwart*, where the section on Romantic Opera, so designated, is preceded by a section called "Von den Anfängen bis gegen 1800" and followed by one called "Nachromantische Oper bis zur Gegenwart."[14]

Even where, as in Alfred Einstein's *Music in the Romantic Era*, the focus is entirely on our subject, the distribution of pertinent materials is open to challenge. Thus chapter X ("Romantic Opera") is duly concerned with the German branch but inexplicably concludes with a subsection entitled "Parisian Opera: Meyerbeer." Berlioz is grouped with Mendelssohn, Schumann, Liszt, Brahms, and Bruckner in chapter XI ("Symphonic and Chamber Music"), and Wagner appears, together with Verdi and the Italian *bel-cantists*, in chapter XVI under the heading "Universalism within the National. II: Neo-Romantic Opera." There all of Wagner's and Verdi's works for the musical stage (down to *Parsifal* and *Falstaff*) are sheltered under one umbrella.

Einstein's justification for including Meyerbeer in the chapter on Romantic Opera is paradoxical; for, as he puts it rather gingerly, "The 'Romantic' side of this Parisian opera is revealed primarily in the choice of material" (p. 120), that is to say it is chiefly thematic and, hence, literary.[15] This indicates that Meyerbeer's Romanticism is half-baked, and that there could be, at the other end of the scale, an equally half-baked operatic Romanticism that qualifies solely on account of the inherent musical qualities. We have reached a crucial point in our discussion; for as it turns out, the majority of operas commonly called "Romantic" would seem to be, in one way or the other, impure. Music historians, at any rate, seem to have been agonizingly aware of this dilemma; and Einstein is by no means the only scholar to have pointed to this glaring discrepancy. Thus Paul Henry Lang opines that E.T.A. Hoffmann's *Undine*, thought to be a veritable prototype of the genre, is "romantic in (its) subject matter," while the music is "still in a vein nearer to the classic than to the Romantic";[16] and Grout maintains that in contrast to Bellini's melo-dramatic products, in which "romanticism pervades the music as well," Donizetti's operas "are romantic only in their librettos."[17]

As these observations suggest, the canon of Romantic operas *pur sang* is likely to be small if both literary and musical criteria are applied. Perhaps the only way of settling the issue and obtain-

---

[11] Donald Grout, *A Short History of Opera* (New York: Columbia Univ. Press, 1947).

[12] Wallace Brockway and Herbert Weinstock, *The Opera: A History of its Creation and Performance 1600-1941* (New York; Simon & Schuster, 1941).

[13] Patrick J. Smith, *The Tenth Muse* (New York: Knopf, 1970).

[14] The article appears in volume X of *Musik in Geschichte und Gegenwart* (Kassel: Bärenreiter, 1959), and the relevant section in columns 35-59.

[15] The literary-thematic approach to Romantic opera simply will not do. It would result in vastly enlarging the body of such works, for instance by including most or all of the works discussed by Jerome Mitchell in his book *The Walter Scott Operas* (Tuscaloosa: Univ. of Alabama Press, 1977).

[16] Lang, p. 796.

[17] Grout, p. 341. Paul Henry Lang, on the other hand, states with regard to Bellini and Rossini: "They are not at all the Romantic figures we have known in their literary form, but the music that surrounds them – Italian to the core – is romantic" (*Music in Western Civilization*, p. 834).

ing a halfway satisfactory result is to limit oneself voluntarily to works for the musical stage that are Romantic in a programmatic sense, while staying within a historically viable framework, i.e., approximately the second to fourth decades of the nineteenth century.[18] In order to identify the canonic works, one must scrutinize relevant statements made by composers and librettists with a view toward joint creative endeavors along the suggested lines. I shall do so in the second, pragmatic part of this essay. But the question "Which are the Romantic operas?" cannot be answered until after the one that precedes it, and which furnishes the title of my presentation, – "What is Romantic Opera?" – has been solved.

In order to accomplish this task, I shall have to identify those central features which, at the hub of Romantic aesthetics at large, may enable me to separate the genuine product from those operatic creations which are flawed through compromise with existing traditions and conventions. According to my scheme of values, there are two of these, both compatible with the notion of organicism which, as the evidence suggests, is firmly embedded in Romantic thinking on art. To be specific: the demands I have in mind encompass 1) a merger of composer and playwright, taking the form of *Doppelbegabung* and 2) the unification of text and music (as well the other contributory arts) in the total work of art. It goes without saying that the *Gesamtkunstwerk* envisaged by the proponents of this theory entails the breaking up of the pattern common to both the *Singspiel* and the serious *Nummernoper*, i.e., a more or less regular alternation of spoken dialogue or recitative with detachable arias and ensembles, and its replacement by a more closely woven fabric, the through-composed opera, in which transitions are gradual and the flow of the melo-dramatic action uninterrupted.[19] If these are to be the yardsticks by which the romanticality of an opera is to be measured, Italian works of the *bel canto* type are immediately ruled out, as are the Hugoesque *melodrammi* of Verdi's early middle period. To be sure, Verdi, champion of the *parola scenica*,[20] moved in the direction of the integrated opera; but he did so much later in his career and reached his goal only with *Falstaff*, a work hardly qualifying as Romantic.

Having thus, in a mood of puristic fervor and with one possible exemption still to be discussed (Rossini's *Guillaume Tell*), eliminated Italian opera from the canon, I seem to be rapidly moving toward the conclusion, regrettable in view of the comparative nature of this enterprise, that Romantic opera is, by and large, German opera. Such a conclusion would be premature, however, in so far as the evidence will show that at least one eminently French composer, Hector Berlioz, will figure significantly in my account – not as a composer of works specifically written for the musical stage

---

[18] I personally do not share the defeatism which inheres in Werner Braun's complacent statement (*Das Problem der Epochengliederung in der Musik*, p. 39): "Von den beiden genannten Beispielen für den verallgemeinernden Sprachgebrauch, 'Barock' und 'Romantik,' ist letzteres hier das bessere, weil es nach neuerer allgemeiner Überzeugung keinen romantischen Epochenstil in der Musik gegeben hat und weil demzufolge auch die Grenzen dieser 'Epoche' sehr unterschiedlich gezogen werden." (Of the two examples cited above for the generalizing usage, i.e., "Baroque" and "Romanticism," the latter is more appropriate in so far as, according to a consensus fairly recently arrived at, there is no Romantic period style in music and because, for that very reason, the borderlines of that epoch are drawn in several different ways.) In literature, which precedes music by approximately a decade, the Romantic era, viewed from a supranational perspective, can be said to extend from, roughly, 1795, to, roughly, 1830. Those readers who wish to pursue the latter question are urged to consult *Die europäische Romantik*, ed. Ernst Behler (Frankfurt: Athenäum-Verlag, 1972) and, for the semantic aspect, *"Romantic" and Its Cognates: The European History of a Word*, ed. Hans Eichner (Toronto: Univ. of Toronto Press, 1972).

[19] There are various intermediate stages between the two extreme solutions. Finales, for example, tend to grow in some of Mozart's operas to encompass nearly half an act; and the use of tableaux and "scenes" may enhance the continuity of the melo-dramatic action.

[20] This is a term which frequently surfaces in Verdi's letters to Antonio Ghislanzoni concerning the text of *Aida*. It demonstrates the composer's interest in the correlation between word and tone in a scenographic sense.

but as the author of *symphonies dramatiques* analogous to the *drames symphoniques* conceived and executed by Richard Wagner, his admirer *outre-Rhin*.[21]

At this juncture, and before entering into a discussion of the specifics of Romantic opera, I must raise a theoretical problem that has dogged historiographers of early-nineteenth-century culture: the apparent paradox constituted by the fact that while, on the one hand, music (from Hoffmann to Schopenhauer and beyond[22]) is regarded as the perfect vehicle for expressing soul states and, hence, the condition to which all the other arts aspire, "what unites the various currents that make up the Romantic era," on the other, "is a general literary orientation."[23] The contradiction dissolves if one calls to mind, as a close observer of the scene cannot fail to do, that the Romantic artist, like the Expressionist after him, tended to shy away from pure abstraction and wanted his creations, whether verbal or not, to convey meaning, if only on the emotional and spiritual level, thus conjoining the tangible with the intangible. Another justification for this union of contraries is provided by the Romantics' desire to reconstitute the lost Paradise, that as yet undifferentiated state in which, according to some modern observers,[24] the arts existed in the prelapsarian age. (Kleist, who tackles the question of lost "grace," both in the theological and aesthetic sense, in his essay "Über das Marionettentheater" [1801], unmasks this yearning as utopian.) In so far as the Romantic composers, all the way down to Wagner, clearly exalted the role of music in their operas by assigning it a loftier role, the two conceptions – that of music as the supreme art and that of the need for a *Gesamtkunstwerk* – can be reconciled. Accordingly, the notion which we encounter at the hub of Romantic thinking about opera is equally remote from the two extremes, that is to say, from the unfettered sensuousness advocated by Stendhal, who stresses the insignificance of words in opera by treating the lyrics as mere vehicles for vocal pyrotechnics,[25] and from the programmatic literalism into which Berlioz's symphonic poems deteriorate in the hand of Liszt, Tchaikovsky, and Richard Strauss.[26]

II

In the treatment of my chosen subject, as in any other humanistic pursuit, history, theory and criticism go hand in hand.[27] It is, therefore, my duty to complement the brief theoretical observations on the topic "What is Romantic Opera?" with a somewhat more elaborate attempt to test the qualifica-

---

[21] In the final chapter of his book *La Musique aux temps romantiques* (Paris: Alcan, 1930), Julien Tiersot succinctly states: "Le drame musical de Wagner, c'est donc la continuation normale de la symphonie dramatique de Berlioz." (Wagner's musical drama, then, is the logical continuation of Berlioz's dramatic symphony.)

[22] One need only think of the Symbolists, one of whose principal aims was to bring poetry closer to music. The last line of Verlaine's poem *Art Poétique*, "et tout le reste est littérature" (and all the rest is literature), succinctly defines that goal.

[23] Lang, p. 808. In "Der Dichter und der Komponist," E.T.A. Hoffmann juxtaposes "die unnennbare Wirkung der Instrumentalmusik" with the latter's need, in opera, "ganz in das Leben [zu] treten" and "seine Erscheinungen [zu] ergreifen" (the unnamable effect of instrumental music [...] to enter life fully [... and] cover its entire range).

[24] The Tübingen Romanist Kurt Wais, for example, postulates an initial fusion of the arts in an expanded lecture published under the title *Symbiose der Künste* (Stuttgart: Metzler, 1937).

[25] Relevant passages can be found in his *Vie de Rossini* (Paris: Boulland, 1824).

[26] An interesting discussion of this problem is offered by Jacques Barzun in the chapter "Program Music and the Unicorn" of his book *Berlioz and the Romantic Century* (New York: Columbia Univ. Press, 1969), I, 169-98.

[27] I am referring to the by now classic distinction made by Wellek/Warren in the fourth chapter ("Literary Theory, Criticism, and History") of their *Theory of Literature* (New York: Harcourt Brace, 1949), pp. 29-37.

tion of certain operatic works for admission to the exclusive club with its strict charter. Predictably, I begin my tour of inspection by assessing the role of E.T.A. Hoffmann, whose creative and critical activities in both music and literature uniquely qualify him, true *Doppelbegabung* that he is, to serve both as a model and convenient point of departure. His decisive, though in some ways inconclusive, role was aptly summarized by Friedrich Blume, who notes with apprehension:

> Enttäuschen auch Hoffmanns eigene Kompositionen die Erwartungen, die von seinen ästhetischen Ansichten her an sie zu stellen wären [...] so ist es doch unzweifelhaft E.T.A. Hoffmann gewesen, der den Musikbegriff in der Romantik für Deutschland und von da aus auch für Frankreich geprägt und der das romantische musikalische Denken und Empfinden für ein Jahrhundert entscheidend beeinflußt hat.[28]

> (Even though Hoffmann's compositions disappoint the expectations to be placed on them judging by his aesthetic views [...] there can be no doubt it was he who defined the essence of musical Romanticism for Germany and, by extension, for France, and who decisively influenced Romantic musical thinking and feeling for a century.)

The two works we need to scrutinize, however briefly, are the dialogue "Der Dichter und der Komponist" and the opera *Undine*.

Conceived in 1809 as a "nicht zu lange(r) Aufsatz, der über die Forderungen, die der Komponist an den Dichter einer Oper mit Recht macht, sprechen würde" (an essay of moderate length concerned with the demands which the composer of an opera could justly make of his librettist),[29] "Der Dichter und der Komponist" was written four years later and first published in the *Allgemeine Musikalische Zeitung*.[30] Augmented by a frame, it was subsequently included in the first volume of the collection of novellas and short prose pieces entitled *Die Serapions-Brüder*. Rather than offering a detailed analysis of the piece – still a *desideratum* in spite of Aubrey Garlington's essay[31] – I shall emphasize those features which I have already singled out as being symptomatic for Romantic opera, namely 1) the desired unity of composer and librettist, 2) the notion of the total work of art in which all ingredients are smoothly blended, and 3) the replacement of the "numbers" opera by the through-composed work for the musical stage.

Regarding the *Personalunion* of poet and musician, Ludwig – Hoffmann's spokesman in the dialogue[32] – clearly presents it as desirable but concurrently notes that only in rare instances (and surely not in his own case) will composers have the technical skill and the necessary patience to commit their thoughts to paper in poetically proper, i.e., metrical language. The musician will thus almost invariably turn to the man of letters (in this instance, Ludwig's friend Ferdinand), asking him to furnish the needed text, with the seemingly inevitable result that their collaboration ends in frustration and fails to achieve the envisaged symbiosis. To be sure, the composer may on occasion conceive of his work in one piece, though characteristically in a timeless moment "zwischen Wachen und Schlafen";[33] but the organization of the verbal material, a tedious process at best, would entail

---

[28] Article "Romantik" of *Musik in Geschichte und Gegenwart*, XI, col. 787.

[29] From Hoffmann's letter to the editors of the *Allgemeine Musikalische Zeitung* dated July 1, 1809, as reprinted in *E.T.A. Hoffmanns Briefwechsel*, ed. Hans von Müller and Friedrich Schnapp (Munich: Winkler, 1967), I, 293.

[30] The piece was published in two installments on December 8 and 15, 1813.

[31] Aubrey Garlington, "E.T.A. Hoffmann's 'Der Dichter und der Komponist' and the Creation of German Romantic Opera," *The Musical Quarterly*, 65 (1979), 22-45.

[32] The one-to-one relationship is confirmed by identical wording in Hoffmann's letter to his friend Hitzig dated November 30, 1812 (*Hoffmanns Briefwechsel*, I, 357).

[33] Hoffmann, *Die Serapions-Brüder*, p. 80.

the dissipation of the original model. Consequently, the resulting opera would be a bastard child in whose blood the humors of language and music are unevenly mixed.

As for the relation between words and tones, it is evident that unlike Weber and Wagner, his fellow laborers in the vineyard of Romantic opera, Hoffmann gives preferential treatment to the music. As Ludwig puts it in the opening portion of the dialogue,

> Ja, um noch bestimmter meine innere Überzeugung auszusprechen: in dem Augenblick der musika-lischen Begeisterung würden (dem Komponisten) alle Worte, alle Phrasen ungenügend, matt, erbärm-lich vorkommen und er müsste von seiner Höhe herabsteigen, um in der unteren Region der Worte für das Bedürfnis seiner Existenz betteln zu können. Würde aber hier ihm nicht bald, wie dem eingefan-genen Adler, der Fittich gelähmt werden und er vergebens den Flug zur Sonne versuchen? (p. 81)

> (To express my innermost conviction even more strongly: at the moment of musical inspiration, all words and phrases would seem inadequate, weak and pitiful to the composer, who would have to descend from his height in order to beg for the bare means of existence in the lower realm of words. Would he not, like the captive eagle, find his wings paralyzed as he vainly strove to soar upwards toward the sun?)

He further downplays the significance of the text as a vehicle of expression (or meaning) by stressing, in anticipation of Hofmannsthal,[34] the melo-dramaturgical significance of scene and situation. In his opinion, the composer

> hat es wirklich nötig, ganz vorzüglich bemüht zu sein, die Szenen so zu ordnen, daß der Stoff sich klar und deutlich vor den Augen des Zuschauers entwickele. Beinahe ohne ein Wort zu verstehen, muß der Zuschauer sich aus dem, was er geschehen sieht, einen Begriff von der Handlung machen können. (p. 92)

> (must be doubly careful to arrange the scenes in such a way that the action unfolds clearly and dis-tinctly before the eyes of the beholder. While barely able to comprehend the text, the latter must be in a position to construct the action from the events unfolding on the stage.)

Especially illuminating, because symptomatic of Hoffmann's transitional place in the history of music and opera, are Ludwig's views on the intermixture and patterning of the verbal and musical ingredients. While, on the one hand, the author's fictional *alter ego* nowhere advocates the practice of alternating spoken dialogue and fixed musical numbers, customary in the *Singspiel*,[35] he seems unwilling, on the other, to go much beyond the kind of unification of the elements that is present in *opera seria* in its high tragic mode as exemplified in Gluck's exemplary operas on mythological subjects. Both he and Ferdinand seem to take it for granted that serious operas consist of arias, duets, tercets, and the like, even though they do not find this mode to be fully satisfactory.[36] Hemmed in by convention, they seem to wish to do away with it, one hand taking what the other hand is giving. In actual practice, both Hoffmann and Weber, seasoned conductors steeped in the French repertory, followed the hallowed precedent.

---

[34] I think specifically of Hofmannsthal's preface to *Die ägyptische Helena.*

[35] For Hoffmann's scathing remarks on the kind of *Singspiel* produced by Ditter von Dittersdorf see p. 91 of *Die Sera-pions-Brüder.* His reviews of various exemplars of this genre are found in his *Schriften zur Musik/Nachlese,* ed. Friedrich Schnapp (Munich: Winkler, 1963), *passim.*

[36] Hoffmann's admiration for Gluck, whom in "Der Dichter und der Komponist" he calls "herrlich," is second to that for no other composer, barring Mozart.

If we pursue the comparison between the theoretical notions on Romantic opera conveyed in "Der Dichter und der Komponist" and Hoffmann's "Zauber-Oper" *Undine*,[37] we quickly realize that there are as many discrepancies as there are parallels. Before taking that route, we should call to mind that Hoffmann read Friedrich de la Motte-Fouqué's fairy-tale by that name shortly after its publication in 1811; already in the following year he made plans to use it for an opera. Since, like his double in the dialogue, he did not trust his own skills as a librettist, he asked his friend Hitzig to suggest a suitable collaborator. As it turned out, that collaborator was to be the poet himself; and on August 15, 1812, overjoyed by this prospect, Hoffmann initiated a correspondence by submitting to Fouqué an extended sketch of the projected work, now lost, in which he marked the distribution of musical numbers.[38]

Fouqué completed the libretto in October, 1812, and Hoffmann composed the music between July, 1813, and August, 1814. However, for a variety of reasons the première at the Berlin König-liches Schauspielhaus did not take place until two years later (August 3, 1816). In so far as "Der Dichter und der Komponist" was written while Hoffmann was at work on *Undine* – to be precise: between October 3 and 16, 1813, that is to say after the completion of the music for Act One –, we are justified in treating these works as two sides of a coin, the ideal and the real. For while the dialogue portrays Romantic opera in glowing colors, though not without a dash of skepticism, the completed opus mirrors the need for compromise on several fronts.

First of all, as regards the text, the desirable union of poet and composer failed to materialize – not surprisingly if one considers the strictures imposed in "Der Dichter und der Komponist." Fortunately, in this case Hoffmann, himself a writer of the first rank, managed to enlist the services of the author whose story he had decided to adapt. Although, on the whole, their collaboration seems to have been harmonious, the evidence shows that they did not always see eye to eye. Matters were further complicated by the fact that, as subsequently in Weber's case, the Royal *Intendant*, Count Brühl, proposed additional changes, one of which was made only after Hoffmann's death. One thing is clear: in a number of cases, the composer modified texts submitted by Fouqué or furnished entirely new ones from his own pen.[39] Thus, to a certain degree the text of *Undine* is a joint creation, with most of the credit for the dramaturgy, including the actual distribution of numbers, going to Hoffmann, and most of the credit for the verbal *Gestalt* going to his literary compeer.

Secondly, as I have already noted, Hoffmann's *Undine*, like Weber's *Freischütz*, falls far short of being a through-composed opera. It contains a fair, though not excessive, amount of spoken dia-

---

[37] Hoffmann himself called *Undine* "Zauber-Oper," rather than a "romantische Oper," as if he wanted to indicate, by means of this generic designation, that this was not the paradigm envisaged in "Der Dichter und der Komponist."

[38] Writing to Fouqué on August 15, 1812, Hoffmann observes: "Sie haben, Herr Baron, eine ausführliche Skizze der Oper, wie ich sie mir vorzüglich rücksichts der historischen Fortschreitung denke, verlangt, und nur dieses konnte mich bewegen, die Beylage auszuarbeiten, welche Szene für Szene das Historische, so wie den musikalischen Gang des Stücks nach einzelnen Nummern darlegt" (You have asked me, my dear Baron, to furnish a detailed sketch of the opera such as I envisage it, especially with regard to the plot progression. Only that request could move me to prepare the enclosed outline, which describes, scene by scene, the unfolding of the action, as well as the musical progression of the piece from number to number) (*Hoffmanns Briefwechsel*, I, 347).

[39] His own contributions to the text are included in the volume *Schriften zur Musik/Nachlese*, pp. 814-20, under the heading "Ergänzungen, Abänderungen und Regieanweisungen zu Fouqué's Operntext der *Undine*" (Additions, Modifications and Stage Directions for Fouqué's *Undine* Libretto). More practical considerations speak out of the following passage from a letter to Hitzig dated November 30, 1812: "Ich finde durchaus im Texte nichts zu ändern und nur der gemeinen Bretter und des gemeinen neidischen ärgerlichen Volks wegen, was sich gewöhnlich darauf bewegt, werde ich vielleicht noch eine Arie für die Berthalda wünschen müssen" (I see no reasons for making any changes in the text. Still, solely on account of the wretched stage and the wretched, invidious folk which usually treads it, I would like to request an additional piece for Berthalda) (*Hoffmanns Briefwechsel*, I, 358).

logue and even in its tone (which is serious but popular) seems to corroborate Dent's view that, in spite of all programmatic statements to the contrary, "[German] Romantic opera was derived from comic opera and not from *opera seria*.[40] – Thirdly, and perhaps most glaringly, theory and practice clash on the level of subject matter. For Hoffmann's mouthpiece in "Der Dichter und der Komponist" the preferred Romantic subject is exotic in the most literal sense of the word, that of "having the charm or fascination of the unfamiliar; strangely beautiful, enticing."[41] According to Ludwig, the exotic serves as a channel for the intrusion of the marvellous (*das Wunderbare*) into the world of everyday reality.[42] As an exemplary *Stoff* he cites that of Carlo Gozzi's dramatic fairy-tale *Il Corvo* (The Raven), a detailed outline of whose plot forms part of the dialogue.

Undine, however, while stressing the interplay of natural and supernatural elements within a fairy-tale framework, is essentially an opera of the folk (based on a *Volks-* rather than a *Kunstmärchen*) and, like *Der Freischütz*, with its more ominous overtones, does not exemplify the high fantastic mode.[43] Both operas, it might well be said, smack somewhat of the *Biedermeier*, the most striking operatic incarnation of which is found in the operas of Lortzing, including his *Undine*.[44]

What all these confrontations of theory and practice amount to is an awareness that Hoffmann's vision of Romantic opera was utopian, and that Jean Chantavoine correctly assessed the situation when he stated:

Ainsi se trouve réalisée en partie cette unité que le romanticisme littéraire de Tieck, de Jean-Paul (pour ne pas parler de Hoffmann, qui n'y est pas arrivé dans sa propre *Undine*) envisageait comme le caractère essentiel de l'opéra nouveau. On n'y trouve encore, en effet, ni l'union du librettiste et du compositeur en une seule personne (sauf chez Lortzing, contemporain mais non représentant du romantisme), ni la suppression du dialogue parlé qui subsiste dans *Freischütz*, dans *Obéron*, dans [Marschner's] *Hans Heiling*.[45]

(Thus the unity the German literary Romanticism of Tieck and Jean Paul – not to mention E.T.A. Hoffmann, who did not attain it in his *Undine* – envisaged as the essential character of the new opera was achieved, but only in part. Actually, one finds as yet neither the fusion of librettist and composer in one person (except for [Albert] Lortzing, who was a contemporary but not a representative of Romanticism) nor the suppression of the spoken dialogue, which lives on in *Der Freischütz, Oberon,* and Marschner's *Hans Heiling*.

What goes for Hoffmann, wrongly accused of having written a highly critical review of *Der*

---

[40] Dent, *The Rise of Romantic Opera*, p. 15.

[41] This is the definition offered by Webster's Collegiate Dictionary.

[42] Ludwig distinguishes clearly between what one might call the "high exotic," where the lofty mood is maintained throughout, and what might be called the "low exotic" of the *commedia dell'arte* and the *opera buffa*, where strangeness intrudes into the *Alltagswelt*.

[43] I fully agree with Garlington's conclusion that "Hoffmann's critical speculations remain his major contribution to the efforts of creating German Romantic opera," the "*Undine* was not to be the success, much less the vindication, of his theories that he must have desired," and that the immediate popular success of *Der Freischütz* "appeared to turn German Romantic opera into pathways not consistent with Hoffmann's lofty conceptualization of Romanticism" (Garlington, in *The Musical Quarterly*, p. 42).

[44] Paul Henry Lang has good reasons for calling Lortzing "the embodiment of the German petty bourgeois of the times" (*Music in Western Civilization*, p. 841).

[45] Jean Chantavoine, in Jean Chantavoine & Jean Gaudefroy-Demombynes, *Le Romantisme dans la musique européenne* (Paris: Michel, 1955), p. 102.

Freischütz,[46] goes also for Weber, enthusiastic reviewer of *Undine*.[47] Since Weber is universally recognized as the Grand Master of (German) Romantic Opera, and, in addition, has been widely written about, I do not need to go into detail concerning his role and historical position; nor do I intend to repeat what I have said about *Der Freischütz* in a different context.[48] What is needed is a brief but pithy comparison between his and Hoffmann's melo-dramatrugical theory and practice.

Weber, the melo-dramaturgist, emerges most forcefully in *Tonkünstlers Leben*, those "Fragmente eines Romans" which, written between 1809 and 1820, convey, partly in dialogue form and partly through parodies, his views of and opinions about music both classical and contemporary.[49] The section which most closely corresponds to "Der Dichter und der Komponist" is the fifth chapter, especially the portion dating from 1817 (that is, from the time when Weber was in the early stages of work on *Der Freischütz*). Its key sentence runs as follows:

> Es versteht sich von selbst, daß ich von der Oper spreche, die der Deutsche und Franzose will, einem in sich abgeschlossenen Kunstwerke, wo alle Teile und Beiträge der verwandten und benutzten Künste ineinanderschmelzend verschwinden und auf gewisse Weise eine neue Welt bilden.[50]

> (It is obvious that I am talking of the kind of opera that is congenial to the German and the Frenchman alike, that is to say, an organic, self-sufficient work of art in which the parts and elements contributed by the various arts constitute a new cosmos and lose their proper identity.)

How much importance Weber attached to this credo is shown by the fact that he literally quotes it (omitting "und Franzose") in his review of *Undine*, published that same year. A second source of crucial information about Weber's conception of the *Gesamtkunstwerk*, less familiar than *Tonkünstlers Leben*, is constituted by two conversations with A.C. Lobe which book took place in the early twenties.[51] There Weber elaborates on the characteristic notions of *Hauptelement, Hauptcharakter* and *Haupt(klang)farbe*, techniques and devices aimed at rendering the total work of art more cohesive.

As for Weber's actual practice, illustrated by *Der Freischütz*, that alleged paragon of Romantic opera writ large,[52] it, too, clashes with the theory. Thus, like his fellow composer-conductor, the Dresden *Kapellmeister* did not author his own libretto but engaged the service of the hack writer, Friedrich Kind, with whom he collaborated and on whom he imposed (literally speaking) a fair number of more or less significant changes.[53] Nor is *Der Freischütz* a through-composed opera but a work that is heavily interlarded with prose dialogue, *Melodram* and quasi-recitative (as in the

---

[46] Still cited as his work in some recent books but unmasked by Wolfgang Kron in his study *Die angeblichen "Freischütz"-Kritiken E.T.A. Hoffmanns* (Munich: Huebner, 1957). The text of the reviews in question is reprinted in *"Der Freischütz": Texte, Materialien, Kommentare*, ed. Karl Dietrich Gräwe (Hamburg: Rowohlt, 1981), pp. 104-14.

[47] Reprinted in Weber's *Sämtliche Schriften*, ed. Georg Kaiser (Leipzig: Schuster & Loeffler, 1908), pp. 127-35.

[48] My lecture on the *Freischütz* libretto, delivered at the Fourth McMaster Colloquium on German Literature, has been published in *The Romantic Tradition: German Literature and Music in the Nineteenth Century*, ed. Gerald Chapple, Frederick Hall, and Hans Schulte (Lanham: Univ. Press of America, 1992).

[49] *Tonkünstlers Leben* is included in *Sämtliche Schriften*, pp. 437-503. It has been discussed by Steven P. Scher in *Comparative Literature Studies*, 15 (1978), pp. 30-42, and by Steven Cerf at the above-mentioned symposium.

[50] Weber, *Sämtliche Schriften*, p. 469.

[51] The conversations are reprinted in *"Der Freischütz": Texte, Materialien, Kommentare*, as well as in *Carl Maria von Weber in seinen Schriften und in zeitgenössischen Dokumenten*, ed. Martin Hürlimann (Zurich: Manesse, 1973), pp. 217-50.

[52] *Der Freischütz* appears as a "Romantic opera" both in the *Klavierauszug* and on the title page of the textbook issued for the première of the opera, but not on the *Theaterzettel*.

[53] Including the omission of the opening scenes, these changes are detailed in my contribution to the Fourth McMaster Colloquium.

Wolfsschlucht scene), some of it cut in most performances. It is a *Nummernoper*, each of the sixteen units labelled as such forming an entity by itself. Yet there are instances of closer integration, such as the bracketing of different musical forms in a given number (#13, "Romanze, Rezitativ und Arie"), and signs of greater continuity, such as the fading out of the waltz in #3 and the spilling over of the *Volkslied* in #14.

Weber has further enhanced the flexibility of the melo-dramaturgical scheme by softening the rigid outlines of standard pieces. Thus, in accordance with his notion of "deklamatorisches Anschmiegen" (declamatory snuggling)[54] he has strengthened the expressiveness of Max's "Rezitativ und Arie" (#3, after the waltz) and Agathe's "Szene und Arie" (#8) by alternating moods – in stark contrast to #4 (Kaspar's *Lied*) and #7 (Ännchen's *Ariette*), where the retention of the stereotypical form is justified because we deal with standard patterns in the German tradition. A similar conflict, less clearly resolved, arises with regard to the labeling of the individual numbers which, in the case of Hoffmann's *Undine*, were consistently Italianate. In the piano-vocal score, Weber throughout uses designations like *aria, scena* and *tercetto*; but in the full orchestral score he Germanizes these technical terms (*Arie, Szene, Terzett*), an operation which in some instances (*Romanze, Kavatine*) entails an (intended?) modification of their meaning. Unlike Hoffmann, he juxtaposes such conventional foreign superscriptions with unequivocally German ones (*Walzer, Lied, Volkslied, Jägerchor*), thereby establishing an equilibrium between indigenous and imported features and concurrently demonstrating that his *Freischütz* is part *opera seria* (based on Franco-Italian models as well as harking back to *Fidelio* and the Sarastro strain in Mozart's *Zauberflöte*) and part *Singspiel* and German *Volksoper*.

Without wishing to extend the discussion of Weber's operatic Romanticism unduly, I should like to call attention to Franz Grillparzer's harsh treatment of *Der Freischütz* in a fragmentary review, a parody, a satirical *Avertissement*, and some very serious reflections on the relationship of music and language.[55] The Viennese playwright and would-be librettist for Beethoven[56] castigates that ingratiating piece as a work whose creator has overindulged in the superficial art of tone painting in the vain hope of making the score more natural. Having discussed the aesthetic properties congenial to the two media, Grillparzer concludes the theoretical portion of his essay – the only one to have been written or, at any rate, to have survived – with the following sentences pillorying Weber's attempt to take musical Romanticism to its counterproductive extreme:

> Was folgt aus dem allen, wird man fragen? Soll Musik aufhören, bezeichnend sein zu wollen? Soll sie in der Oper nicht streng dem Text folgen? Soll sie nicht streben, den Verstand zu befriedigen? Es folgt daraus, daß die Musik vor allem streben soll, das zu erreichen, was ihr erreichbar ist; daß sie nicht [...] das aufgeben soll, worin sie allen Redekünsten überlegen ist; daß sie nicht streben müsse, aus Tönen Worte zu machen; daß sie, wie jede Kunst, aufhöre, Kunst zu sein, wenn sie aus der in ihrer Natur gegründeten Form herausgeht. [...] daß so wie der Dichter ein Tor ist, der in seinen Versen den Musiker im Klang erreichen will, ebenso der Musiker ein Verrückter ist, der mit seinen Tönen

---

[54] Weber's formulation as recounted by Lobe (*"Der Freischütz": Texte, Materialien, Kommentare*, p. 158).

[55] All these pieces are reproduced in Grillparzer's *Sämtliche Werke*, ed. Peter Frank and Paul Pörnbacher (Munich: Hanser, 1964), vol. III, "Ausgewählte Briefe, Gespräche, Berichte." The fragmentary review appears on pp. 885-88, the parody (*"Der wilde Jäger*, Romantische Oper") on p. 21, das *Avertissement* on p. 72f., and the serious reflections, under the heading "Über die Oper," on pp. 897-900.

[56] The work in question is *Melusina*, a "Romantische Oper in drei Aufzügen." The text, set to music by Conradin Kreutzer, is reprinted in Grillparzer, I, 1167-1202.

dem Dichter an Bestimmtheit des Ausdrucks es gleich tun will; daß Mozart der größte Tonsetzer ist und Maria Weber – nicht der größte.[57]

(What's the upshot of all this?, people will ask. Should music desist from wanting to designate? Should it follow the text slavishly? Should it strive to satisfy the reason? The upshot is that, most of all, music should strive to attain what is proper to it; that it should not abandon that in which it excels the verbal arts; that it should not attempt to make sounds into words; that, like every art, it ceases to be art as soon as it oversteps its natural boundaries; [...] that, just as the poet who seeks to rival the composer is a fool, so the composer who seeks to equal the poet by trying to express specific ideas is a madman; that Mozart is the greatest composer, and [Carl] Maria [von] Weber is – not the greatest.)

Historically speaking, Grillparzer, in mounting this attack, assumes a puristic stance which in some ways approximates the position defended in "Der Dichter und der Komponist."

While it goes without saying that an essay entitled "What is Romantic Opera?" cannot ignore the art of Richard Wagner without being rightly accused of criminal negligence, the issue at stake in the present context would be muddled if I were to survey that composer's entire output, especially given the fact that Wagner's artistic career extends well beyond the outer limits of European Romanticism conceived in a strict historical sense, making him a contemporary of Brahms rather than Schumann, much less Weber. Thus, with a heavy heart, I must refrain from entering into a discussion of *Tristan und Isolde* (1859), the apogee of that perennial Romanticism to which Chantavoine refers in connection with the Master of Bayreuth.[58] Instead, I shall focus on *Der fliegende Holländer* (1841) as the work which, in more ways than one, brings operatic Romanticism *a la tedesca* to a quintessential climax.

To create the right atmosphere for such a discussion, I should like to remind the reader that Wagner, especially in his twenties and thirties, was an ardent admirer of Hoffmann and Weber (the maker of *Der Freischütz*, not of *Euryanthe* – about which latter he has a few nasty things to say).[59] When a Paris production of Weber's masterpiece was in the offing in 1841 (the *Holländer* year!) he wrote two essays, one in anticipation of the performance and the other, in its wake, as a report to the German public.[60] Describing the opera, in Weber's sense, as "ein vollkommenes, sowohl dem Gedanken als der Form nach in allen seinen Teilen wohlgegliedertes Ganzes" (a whole which, in all its parts, is well articulated both in form and content), he denounced its transformation into Grand Opera. He sounded his note of warning in view, and in spite, of the fact that it was no other than Hector Berlioz, the only French composer likely to stand "auf der Höhe eines solches Versuchs" (capable of tackling such a task) (p. 19), who had been commissioned to adapt the work, supply the mandatory recitatives, and procure the music for the balletic interludes.[61]

Throughout his life, Wagner esteemed E.T.A. Hoffmann, whose work, both creative and critical, he emulated on many occasions.[62] To mention only the most obvious instances of such borrow-

---

[57] Grillparzer, III, 888.

[58] Chantavoine, p. 294.

[59] The critique of *Euryanthe* occupies the better part of a long paragraph in the essay "Die deutsche Oper" (1834), in Wagner, *Gesammelte Schriften* (fn. 60), p. 8f.

[60] "*Der Freischütz*: An das Pariser Publikum" and "*Le Freischutz*: Bericht nach Deutschland" are both reproduced in Wagner's *Gesammelte Schriften*, ed. Julius Kapp (Leipzig: Hesse & Becker, [1914]), VIII, 7-41.

[61] The music for the ballets was taken from various works by Weber and included the famous "Aufforderung zum Tanz."

[62] For a more detailed survey see Linda Siegel's essay "Wagner and the Romanticism of E.T.A. Hoffmann," *The Musical Quarterly*, 51 (1965), 597-613.

ing: taking his clue (or so it would seem) from "Der Dichter und der Komponist," he based one of his early operas, *Die Feen* (1834), on one of Gozzi's dramatic fairy-tales;[63] and shortly after the completion of *Der fliegende Holländer* he furnished, at the request of a hack composer named Dessauer, a detailed scenario based on Hoffmann's "Die Bergwerke zu Falun," a novella which, as Marc Weiner has shown in a recent essay, had an impact on several of his works.[64] Since this was not a labor of love but an *Auftragsarbeit* commissioned on the strength of *Le Vaisseau fantôme* (the text, but not the music), he arranged the material in such a way as to suit operatic convention by subdividing the action into the usual arias, ensembles, and finales.[65] Had he adapted the story for his own use, he would hardly have resorted to this technique; for thus to perpetuate the antiquated *Nummernoper* would have meant a step backwards for one who had embarked on a journey to the *Gesamtkunstwerk*.

Now that the preliminaries, aimed at demonstrating that the young Wagner was an adept of Romanticism and its chief representatives in the field of melo-drama, are out of the way, let us look at *Der fliegende Holländer* as a late bloom of Romantic opera. This is how the work was designated on the playbill issued in connection with its première at the Königlich Sächsisches Hoftheater in Dresden on January 2, 1843. Wagner, who uses the same label in a letter to Schumann dated November 3, 1842, where he refers to the recently completed piece as an opera, "einem ganz anderen Genre, dem rein romantischen [angehörend]" ([belonging] to a totally different genre, the purely Romantic),[66] subsequently applied it to *Tannhäuser* and *Lohengrin* as well, largely, one assumes with reference to their subject. But already in his lengthy "Mitteilung an meine Freunde," composed in 1851, he viewed the whole matter with considerable skepticism. Without repudiating the "Romantic" triad, he states defensively, equating "romantische Oper" with "Grosse Oper,"

Der Richtung, in die ich mich mit der Konzeption des *Fliegenden Holländers* schlug, gehören die beiden ihm folgenden dramatischen Dichtungen, *Tannhäuser* und *Lohengrin*, an. Mir ist der Vorwurf gemacht worden, daß ich mit diesen Arbeiten in die, wie man meint, durch Meyerbeers *Robert der Teufel* überwundene und geschlossene, von mir mit meinen *Rienzi* bereits selbst verlassene Richtung der 'romantischen' Oper *zurück*getreten sei. Für die, welche mir diesen Vorwurf machen, ist die romantische *Oper* natürlich eher vorhanden als die *Opern*, die nach einer konventionell klassifizierenden Annahme 'romantische' genannt werden. Ob ich von einer künstlerisch formellen Absicht aus auf die Konstruktion von 'romantischen' Opern ausging, wird sich herausstellen, wenn ich die Entstehungsgeschichte jener drei Werke genau erzähle.[67]

(The genre which I initiated with the conception of *The Flying Dutchman* also includes my two subsequent operas, *Tannhäuser* and *Lohengrin*. I have been told that with these works I have regressed to the level of the so-called 'romantic' opera which I myself had already left behind with my *Rienzi*, and which found its culmination in Meyerbeer's *Robert le Diable*. In the eyes of those who make this reproach, the *romantic opera* pre-existed operas which, according to the conventional classification,

---

[63] The work on which *Die Feen* was based is *La donna serpente*. Curiously enough, Brahms considered writing an opera on Gozzi's *Il re cervo*, to which Hans Werner Henze turned in his *König Hirsch*.
[64] Marc Weiner, "Richard Wagner's Use of E.T.A. Hoffmann's 'The Mines of Falun'," *Nineteenth Century Music*, 2 (1982), 201-14.
[65] "*Die Bergwerke zu Falun*: Entwurf zu einer Oper in drei Akten" is found in Wagner's *Gesammelte Schriften* (fn. 60 above), VI, 55-67, an English version thereof in the appendix to Weiner's article.
[66] Richard Wagner, *Sämtliche Briefe*, ed. Gertrud Strobel and Werner Wolf (Leipzig: VEB Deutscher Verlag für Musik), II (1970), 170.
[67] Richard Wagner, *Dichtungen und Schriften*, ed. Dieter Borchmeyer (Frankfurt: Insel-Verlag, 1983), VI, 237.

are called "Romantic." Whether, aesthetically speaking, I deliberately meant to create 'romantic' operas will come to light once I describe describe the genesis of these three works.)

In later years he ceased, for tactical reasons, to bestow this weighty epithet on the three works that precede *Der Ring des Nibelungen*.[68] So much for the name of the many-splendored thing that is "romantisch" – and now to its nature, both in the stage of inception and execution. Let us briefly trace the genesis of *Der fliegende Holländer*, so as to demonstrate how Wagner's conception of the work changed due to his growing awareness of the pragmatics of show business. The original outline, a sketch written in French[69] and sold, under some pressure, to the manager of the Paris Opéra, composed by Louis Philippe Dietsch and performed on November 9, 1841 under the title *Le Vaisseau fantôme ou Le Maudit des mers*, "opéra fantastique en deux actes" – was intended as a curtain raiser in which the unity of action was to have been preserved almost in the manner of Greek tragedy. As Wagner states in his autobiography,

> Ich faßte den Stoff [...] für einen einzigen Akt zusammen, wozu mich zunächst der Gegenstand selbst bestimmte, da ich auf diese Weise ihn ohne alles jetzt mich anwidernde Opernbeiwerk auf den einfachen dramatischen Vorgang zwischen den Hauptpersonen zusammengedrängt geben konnte.[70]

> (Due to the kind of subject matter this was, I decided to concentrate the action into a single act since, dispensing with the usual operatic claptrap, which now disgusts me, I was thus able to focus narrowly on the simple dramatic development involving the major characters.)

Wagner never dropped this notion altogether, even though the first plot outline in German indicates a division into three acts that is retained in both "versions" of the score.[71] As the observation contained in a letter to Cäcilie Avenarius "Wir gaben die Oper in drei Aufzügen, so daß sie den ganzen Abend füllte" (We gave the opera in three acts, so that it filled the entire evening)[72] suggests, he regarded the tripartite scheme as artificial and as going against the very grain of his original plan. Indeed, an uninterrupted performance of *Der fliegende Holländer* can be accomplished after minor surgery along the orchestral seams which separate the acts. Productions which treat the work as an "Einakter in drei Aufzügen" have been fairly common in recent years; and some prominent stage directors have cast the action either in the form of Senta's dream (Harry Kupfer in Bayreuth, successfully) or that of the Steuermann (Jean Pierre Ponelle and his assistants in New York, San Francisco, and Chicago, unsuccessfully).[73]

Perceived as Senta's dream, the work has its center of gravity and spiritual, though not factual, point of departure in that character's ballad in the second act, which was one of the first (if not the

---

[68] In letters to Liszt dated November 25, 1850, and February 18, 1851, he still uses the expression "drei romantische Opern"; but a letter to his publishers of August 23, 1851, merely refers to "drei Operndichtungen."

[69] So far unpublished, it will appear in the *Dokumentenband* to *Der fliegende Holländer* in Richard Wagner, *Sämmtliche Werke* (Mainz: B. Schott's Söhne, 1970ff), under the editorship of Charl Dahlhaus.

[70] Richard Wagner, *Mein Leben*, ed. Martin Gregor-Dellin (Munich: List, 1976), p. 193. In a letter to Eugène Scribe (*Sämtliche Briefe*, I, 390), Wagner speaks of a "petit opéra en un acte."

[71] The incomplete prose sketch, dated 1840, was first published in the *Programmheft* of a production of *Der fliegende Holländer* at the Munich Staatsoper in January, 1981, pp. 88-90. The original version of the score was published for the first time in the *Gesamtausgabe* (see fn. 69 above).

[72] Wagner, *Sämtliche Briefe*, II, 204.

[73] As the Chicago production demonstrated, interpreting the opera as the Steuermann's dream is extremely awkward as it necessitates 1) the dreamer's sporadic participation in the dreamt action, and 2) the dreamer's awakening at the end to close the frame.

first) musical number to be written.[74] That Wagner considered this particular piece to constitute the true germ of *Der fliegende Holländer*, which he himself called a "dramatische Ballade,"[75] can be deduced from the following passage in his "Bemerkungen zur Aufführung des *Fliegenden Holländers*" (Remarks concerning the staging of *The Flying Dutchman*, 1852) which seems to justify the oneiric interpretation of the work:

> Die Rolle der Senta wird schwer zu verfehlen sein; nur vor einem habe ich zu warnen: möge das träumerische Wesen nicht im Sinne einer modernen, krankhaften Sentimentalität aufgefaßt werden! Im Gegenteile ist Senta ein ganz kerniges nordisches Mädchen, und selbst in ihrer anscheinenden Sentimentalität ist sie durchaus *naiv*. Gerade nur bei einem ganz naiven Mädchen konnten, umgeben von der ganzen Eigentümlichkeit der nordischen Natur, Eindrücke wie die Ballade vom "fliegenden Holländer" und des Bildes des bleichen Seemannes einen so wunderstarken Hang wie den Trieb zur Erlösung des Verdammten hervorbringen: dieser äußert sich bei ihr als ein kräftiger Wahnsinn, wie er wirklich nur ganz naiven Naturen zu eigen sein kann.[76]

> (The role of Senta is easy to interpret; but there is one thing I must insist on: let her dreamy nature not be understood in the sense of a modern, pathological sentimentality. On the contrary, Senta is an extremely healthy Nordic girl; and even in her apparent sentimentality she is truly naïve. Only in such a girl, surrounded by a characteristically Nordic nature, impressions like those generated by the ballad of the Flying Dutchman and the picture of the pale sailor could produce such a strong desire as her drive to redeem the accursed man. In her case, that desire takes the form of a vigorous madness, such as suits truly naïve persons.)

The dream, which *is* the action of the opera unfolding before our eyes, would thus be triggered by, and revolve around, the "Bildnis eines bleichen Mannes mit dunklem Barte, in schwarzer spanischer Tracht" (the portrait of a pale man with a dark beard, dressed in black Spanish garb) which dominates the setting for Act II; and in the characteristically Romantic interplay between the natural and supernatural sphere the realism of Daland's, Eric's, and Mary's world would be pitted against the fantastic otherworld of the phantom ship and its crew, Senta being the point at which the two spheres intersect.

As regards the unification of the action through the replacement of the *Nummernoper* by the through-composed music drama, Wagner, like Weber before him, has gone only half of the way. For even though in a letter to Ferdinand Heine he claims to have repudiated "den modernen Zu-

---

[74] "Als ich [...] noch hoffte, dieses Sujet für die französische Oper bearbeiten zu dürfen, hatte ich bereits einige lyrische Bestandteile desselben poetisch und musikalisch ausgeführt. [...] Dies waren die Ballade der Senta, das Lied der norwegischen Matrosen und der Spuk-Gesang der Mannschaft des 'Fliegenden Holländers'" (At the time when I still hoped to be able to treat this subject for the (Paris) *Opéra*, I had already executed a few lyrical ingredients of the piece verbally and musically. These were Senta's ballad, the song of the Norwegian sailor and the ghostly chorus of the Flying Dutchman's crew) (Wagner, *Mein Leben*, p. 212).

[75] "Als ich die fertige Arbeit betiteln sollte, hatte ich nicht übel Lust, sie eine 'dramatische Ballade' zu nennen. Bei der endlichen Ausführung der Komposition breitete sich mir das empfangene thematische Bild ganz unwillkürlich als ein vollständiges Gewebe über das ganze Drama aus; ich hatte [...] nur die verschiedenen thematischen Keime, die in der Ballade enthalten waren, nach ihren eigenen Richtungen hin weiter und vollständig zu entwickeln [...]" (When I pondered the title of the completed work, I first thought of calling it a dramatic ballad; for in the course of composing the piece the thematic node quite involuntarily spread like a web over the entire drama, and all that was left for me to do was to develop the various thematic germs contained in the ballad according to the directions suited to them). Quoted from "Eine Mitteilung an meine Freunde" by Dieter Borchmeyer in his contribution ("*Der fliegende Holländer* – eine 'dramatische Ballade'") to the *Programmheft* (cited in fn. 71), p. 16. – Let us remember that it was Goethe who characterized the ballad as the germ (*Keimzelle*) of the three basic literary modes, the lyrical, the epic, and the dramatic.

[76] Wagner, *Gesammelte Schriften*, IX, 51f. Wagner uses "naiv" and "sentimentalisch"in the Schillerian sense, whereas Nietzsche, condemning "Senta-Sentimentalität," obviously does not but introjects the popularized meaning of the term.

schnitt in Arien, Duette, Finales, etc.,"[77] the evidence shows that he did so somewhat halfheartedly by combining various traditional numbers (#4, "Lied, Szene, Ballade und Chor," #6, "Arie, Duett und Terzett," and #8, "Duett, Kavatine und Finale" – to name only the most glaring examples) with the aim of cementing the action and achieving greater continuity. Thus, while making considerable progress in the right direction, he ended by striking a compromise. As Carl Dahlhaus so aptly observes, *Der fliegende Holländer*

> ist keine 'Nummern-', sondern eine 'Szenenoper'. Das Verfahren, einzelne Arien, Duette, Ensemble-sätze und Chöre zu Komplexen zusammenzufassen, statt sie unverbunden nebeneinanderzustellen [...] erstreckt sich (hier) über das ganze Werk, ohne daß jedoch von einem 'durchkomponierten Musik-drama' die Rede sein könnte.[78]

> (is no *numbers* opera but a *scenic* one. The technique of clamping individual arias, duets, ensembles, and choruses together, instead of merely lining them up, here extends to the entire work without there as yet resulting a through-composed drama.)

As I have previously indicated, it would be regrettable if it turned out that the subgenre under consideration happened to be a *typisch deutscher Gegenstand* without any foreign offshoots or equivalents. An effort should, therefore, be made to establish its internationality.

I am, accordingly, well advised to search abroad and look into other national traditions that might be compatible in one way or another. Failing to discover any worthy subjects in England, Russia or Spain, one will turn to Italy and France for corroborating evidence. To begin with the homeland of opera as we know it: since not the faintest hint of a concerted striving for the unified total work of art which I have portrayed as the culmination of Romantic opera, whether in theory or practice, is discernible in Bellini or Donizetti,[79] we would, methodologically speaking, waste our time if we took that much trodden but still hopelessly entangled path.

With the younger Verdi matters are somewhat different in so far as by setting to music two librettos based on plays by the self-confessed arch-Romantic Victor Hugo he would seem to have demonstrated a certain kinship in artistic outlook. On the literary – thematic and stylistic – level, the only one likely to yield results,[80] an explanation, however tentative and general, is provided by David Kimbell in the chapter on *Ernani*: "Verdi abandoned the distinctive Italian kind of Romanticism, the Romanticism of Church and state, in favour of a Romanticism more lurid in hue and more grotesque in form, a Romanticism fundamentally French."[81] That it was precisely this contrast between the sublime and the grotesque, championed in Hugo's "Preface" to *Cromwell* of 1827,

---

[77] Undated letter (early August, 1843) in Wagner, *Sämtliche Briefe*, II, 314.

[78] Carl Dahlhaus, *Richard Wagners Musikdramen* (Velber: Friedrich-Verlag, 1971). From the chapter on *Der fliegende Holländer*, as reprinted in the *Programmheft* (fn. 71), p. 66.

[79] In his massive study of *Donizetti and his Operas* (Cambridge: Cambridge Univ. Press, 1982), William Ashbrook conceives of Romanticism in purely thematic, and literary, terms:"Simply put, the basic demand for Romantic melodrama is that the composer give musical coherence and credibility to an intense plot whose denouement is tragic and inevitable" (p. 497). This will hardly do as a criterion for defining Romantic opera.

[80] In a book which he shrewdly entitles *Verdi in the Age of Italian Romanticism* (Cambridge: Cambridge Univ. Press, 1981), David R. Kimbell states unambiguously that, melo-dramaturgically speaking, Verdi was not "disposed to dispute [...] that opera was [...] a type of drama in which the ongoing action had to be expressed in self-contained, lucidly architected 'numbers'" (p. 624, with regard to *Rigoletto*).

[81] The quotation is drawn from the chapter "Verdi and French Romanticism: *Ernani*" of Kimbell's book (p. 460). Its opening chapter contains a balanced account of artistic and literary life in Italy during the "Romantic" period.

which appealed to Verdi is shown by the following passage from a letter dated December 14, 1850 and addressed to C.D. Marzari, the director of the Teatro Fenice in Venice:

> Putting on the stage a character grossly deformed and absurd, but inwardly passionate and full of love, is precisely what I find the beautiful thing. I chose this subject precisely for these qualities, these original traits, and if they are taken away, I can no longer write music for it. If you tell me that my music can stay the same even with this drama, I reply that I don't understand such reasoning; and I say frankly that whether my music is beautiful or ugly I don't write it by chance, but always try to give it a definite character.[82]

Here, then, is Verdi's artistic credo, echoed in so many letters written, throughout his career, to his librettists. For the rest, Verdi being no theoretician but a man of the theater, who cared little for -isms and was solely concerned with achieving the greatest intrinsic effect – in contrast to Puccini, who preferred the extrinsic effects of melodrama – we can probably take him at his word when he writes, almost three decades later, to Opprandino Arrivabene:

> I shan't talk about music because I no longer remember any. I only know that I've never understood what music of the past and music of the future mean, just as I've never understood in literature the terms classical and romantic [...].[83]

Seen from our, the "Romantic," perspective, the case of Rossini is more promising, not so much in view of his prodigious output of *opere buffe*, culminating in that perennial favorite which is *Il Barbiere di Siviglia*, as with regard to *Guillaume Tell*, his last opera and the crowning glory of the final, Parisian phase of his relatively short career. The potentially "Romantic" nature of Rossini's art had been discerned by Stendhal, the passionate advocate of Romanticism taken in the sense of pure emotionalism, whose *Vie de Rossini*, without so much as breathing the word "romantic," contains a number of passages in which the composer's perspectivism and the atmospheric quality of his works at their best are eulogized, as in the following excerpt from the chapter on *Tancredi*:

> Si l'on veut arriver [...] à l'idée de l'harmonie dans ses rapports avec le chant, je puis dire que Rossini a employé avec succès le grand artifice de Walter Scott. [...] Comme Rossini prépare et soutient ses chants par l'harmonie, de même Walter Scott prépare et soutient ses dialogues et ses récits par des descritipions.[84]

> (If this conception of the relationship between orchestral and vocal music can be made any clearer by analogy, I would suggest that Rossini successfully employs a device invented by Walter Scott. [...] Just as Rossini uses his *orchestral harmony* to prepare the way for and to reinforce his passages of vocal music, so Walter Scott prepares the way for, and reinforces, his passages of dialogue and narrative by means of *description*.)

---

[82] Quoted in English by Kimbell, p. 270. The original text, reproduced in Verdi's *Copialettere*, ed. G. Cesari and A. Luzio (Bologna: Fori, 1913), p. 111, begins as follows: "Io trovo appunto bellissimo rappresentare questo personaggio deforme e ridicolo, ed internamente appassionato e pieno d'amore. Scelsi appunto questo soggetto per tutte queste qualità, e questi tratti originalli; se si tolgono, io non posso più farvi musica."

[83] The letter dates from May 26, 1878. It is quoted in English in *Verdi: The Man in his Letters*, ed. Franz Werfel and Paul Stefan (New York: Fischer, 1942), p. 346.

[84] Stendhal, *Vie de Rossini*, transl. by Richard N. Coe (New York: Criterion Books, 1957), p. 57.

As for *Guillaume Tell*, which is rightly seen as one of the immediate precursors of Grand Opera, it amply rewards an inquiry into its Romantic properties. Since I have tackled that question, among several others, in an earlier paper,[85] I will limit myself to stating that such an ascription could well be justified in terms of the literary and musical, although not necessarily in those of the melo-dramatic, tradition. Based on a play by Schiller, which the latter – author of the "romantische Tragödie" *Die Jungfrau von Orleans* and the "Trauerspiel mit Chören" *Die Braut von Messina*, which parallels the verbal operas of Hugo on a much higher artistic plane – characterized as the upshot of an attempt, "einen romantischen Stoff antik zu behandeln" (to treat a Romantic theme in the ancient manner),[86] *Guillaume Tell* constitutes, musically speaking, a solid link in the chain that extends from Beethoven's Pastoral Symphony by way of *Der Freischütz* to Hector Berlioz, who, in addition to copying the parts of Rossini's score for its publisher, analyzed *Guillaume Tell* in a lengthy essay published in the *Gazette musicale de Paris*.[87]

To be brief: while *Guillaume Tell* satisfies few, if any, of the programmatic conditions attached to the Romantic *Gesamtkunstwerk* – Rossini employed no less than four librettists and created a work that strikes one as being monumental without possessing the virtue of unity-in-diversity[88] – certain portions, especially the universally admired second act, manage superbly to generate a mood and an atmosphere that are reminiscent of *Der Freischütz* and *Der fliegende Holländer* at their best. It most certainly served as a model for the towering genius of French Romantic music, that monstrous exception within the French ambience,[89] whose art E.T.A. Hoffmann (though hardly Weber) would surely have admired. It is to him that we must turn in conclusion, though not in his capacity as an operatic composer in the routine sense. For while works like the opera-oratorio *La Damnation de Faust* and, to a considerably lesser degree, *Les Troyens* (over which the classical spirit of Vergil presides along with the "romantic" genius of Shakespeare) might do to illustrate certain obvious aspects of Berlioz's Romanticism, it is in the *Symphonie fantastique* of 1830, if anywhere, that we shall find a source of satisfaction.

In the same year in which Hugo's *Hernani* had its turbulent première[90] and three years after Delacroix exhibited his monumental "Mort de Sardanapale,"[91] Berlioz, the third member of the triumvirate, composed the piece for which he is most widely known.[92] To use the composer's own

---

[85] "Der Apfel fiel recht weit vom Stamme: Rossinis *Guillaume Tell*, eine musikalische Schweizerreise," read at the *Romanistentag* in October, 1983, and published in the proceedings of the libretto section of that congress: *Oper als Text: Romanistische Beiträge zur Libretto-Forschung*, ed. Albert Gier (Heidelberg: Winter, 1986), 147-84.

[86] This is what, according to Heinrich Voss, Jr., Schiller said at a party in Weimar. The remark is cited in *Dichter über ihre Dichtungen: Friedrich Schiller*, ed. Bodo Lecke (Munich: Heimeran, 1970), II, 462.

[87] The essay appeared in the first volume of that periodical, pp. 326-27, 336-39, 341-43, and 249-51. A complete English version is found in *Source Readings in Music History from Classical Antiquity through the Romantic Era*, selected and annotated by Oliver Strunk (New York: Norton, 1950), pp. 809-26.

[88] Both Berlioz and Verdi (in a letter to Camille Du Locle of December 8, 1869), while greatly admiring the work, were dismayed by its lack of integration.

[89] In his *Le Romanticisme dans la musique européenne*, Chantavoine observes (p. 13): "La conception romantique de la musique n'est pas une conception française; Berlioz est une monstrueuse exception, tout-à-fait isolée dans la tradition musicale française" (The Romantic notion of music is not specifically French; and Berlioz was a monstrous and altogether unique exception within the French national tradition).

[90] Berlioz attended an early performance of the play, though probably not its première.

[91] In 1829 Berlioz wrote a cantata on the subject which earned him the Prix de Rome.

[92] The best general introduction to the Fantastic Symphony in English is that provided in the edition prepared by Edward T. Cone (New York: Norton, 1971), which includes the texts of several versions of the composer's programs. Nicholas Temperley's essay "The *Symphonie fantastique* and its Program" (*Musical Quarterly*, 57 [1971], 593-608) is rather disappointing given the fact that the author is editing the work for the New Berlioz Edition.

description, the Fantastic Symphony belongs to the *"genre instrumental expressif*, [which] is most closely related to Romanticism." As Berlioz puts it, by way of explanation, in the "Aperçu sur la musique classique et la musique romantique," from which the above phrase is culled,

> In the works of Beethoven and Weber a poetic idea is everywhere manifest, but music is wholly in command, with no help from words to give it precise expression: we feel no longer in the theatre, rather a new world opens before us.[93]

This certainly will not do as a justification for the so-styled *Symphonie descriptive de Faust* as which the Goethe enthusiast Berlioz and author of *Huits scènes de Faust* seems originally to have conceived the work.[94] In line with the composer's emerging theory, the symphony ultimately took the shape of a "composition instrumentale d'un genre nouveau" which, initially labeled "Episode d'une vie d'artiste (grande symphonie fantastique en cinq parties)" (instrumental piece of a novel kind [...] episode from the life of an artist (grand fantastic symphony in five parts)),[95] acquired its present title sometime after the composition of the score. What qualifies the Fantastic Symphony as a Romantic "opera" in our sense is, first of all, the unity of composer and librettist (=author of the literary program);[96] but, more important still and epitomizing the trend toward integration on all levels, it is the identity of creator and creature in the unnamed protagonist as whose autobiography the work is presented. While initially Berlioz spoke of his hero's experience as taking place on three different levels – internal in the first movement, external in the second and third, and oneiric in the fourth and fifth – he later changed his "tune" by describing the entire piece as the opium dream of a "jeune musicien d'une sensibilité maladive et d'une imagination ardente" (a young musician with a sickly sensibility and a fiery imagination).[97] More spectacular, because easily apparent and in no need of a programmatic explication, is the introduction of a recurrent melodic phrase embodying the hero's beloved who, being the musical protagonist, is the antagonist of the *drame* which the symphony depicts. Her double function both explains and justifies the use of the term *double idée fixe* which Berlioz attached to this device and which he subsequently modified to *mélodie-aimée* (melody-beloved).[98]

Described in a letter to Humbert Ferrand which contains the first program of what Berlioz then called "mon roman, ou plutôt mon histoire" (my novel or, rather, my history)[99] – designations which are not generic but merely indicate that the work is autobiographical – the *Symphonie fantastique*, patterned after Beethoven's Sixth and therefore, as Robert Schumann puts it in his famous analysis,

---

[93] The quotation, inaccessible to me in the original French, is culled from Barzun's *Berlioz and the Romantic Century*, I, 152. The reference to Weber pertains undoubtedly to *Der Freischütz* (which, like *Fidelio*, Berlioz had recently seen with Wilhelmine Schröder-Devrient in the leading female part), that to Beethoven probably to the Pastoral Symphony.

[94] The designation "symphonie descriptive de Faust" occurs in a letter to Humbert Ferrand dated February 2, 1829. *Correspondance générale d'Hector Berlioz*, ed. Pierre Citron (Paris: Flammarion) I (1972), 232.

[95] The label is supplied in a letter to Humbert Ferrand of April 16, 1830, which offers the first, unpublished program of the symphony. See *Correspondance générale*, I, 319ff.

[96] Like Wagner's *Der fliegende Holländer* which, in the composer's own words, falls short of being "aus einem Guß" (of a piece), the Fantastic Symphony lacks the unity of the creative process in so far as certain portions of the music were derived from earlier compositions by Berlioz.

[97] References throughout this portion of the paper are to the texts of the various programs as reproduced in the appendix to Wolfgang Dömling, *Hector Berlioz: Die symphonisch-dramatischen Werke* (Stuttgart: Reclam, 1979), pp. 143-49.

[98] This term occurs in the third version of the program. See Dömling, p. 149.

[99] The phrase is used in the letter to Humbert Ferrand mentioned in footnote 94.

naturally in five "acts,"[100] was later dubbed a "drame instrumental privé du secours de la parole" and thus in dire need "d'être exposé d'avance" (instrumental drama deprived of all verbal support [...] to be explicated beforehand).[101] As the composer observes in defending the need for verbal support, "le programme suivant doit donc être considéré comme le texte parlé d'un opéra servant à amener des morceaux de musique, dont il motive le caractère et l'expression" (the following program should thus be regarded as the spoken text of an opera aimed at introducing musical numbers whose nature and character it explains).[102] As the Romantic Mendelssohn wrote *chants sans paroles*, so the Romantic Berlioz produced an opera *presque sans paroles*.

After completing a sequel to the *Symphonie fantastique*, an aesthetically deficient and therefore rarely performed monodrama called *Lélio ou Le Retour à la vie* that requires staging, Berlioz changed his mind and downgraded the significance of the program in words that leave little doubt that, however reluctantly, he had abandoned the Romantic perspective, partly, one suspects, in reaction to the blatantly literary though highly poetic program music cultivated by his friend and admirer Liszt:

> Si on exécute la symphonie isolément dans un concert, cette disposition [on the stage] n'est plus néccessaire; on peut même à la rigueur se dispenser de distribuer le programme, en conservant seulement le titre des cinq morceaux; la symphonie (l'auteur l'espère) pouvant offrir en soi un intérêt musical indépendant de toute intention dramatique.[103]

> (When one performs the symphony in the concert hall, that [theatrical] disposition is unnecessary; at a pinch one could even do without the programme while retaining the titles of the five movements; for the symphony by itself – so I hope – offers sufficient musical interest even without the support of an underlying dramatic intention.)

Thus Berlioz, who, in foisting a story upon his instrumental composition, had taken a decisive step beyond the generalized musical program offered by the Pastoral Symphony and had thus single-handedly created his own brand of Romantic opera-for-orchestra, undermined his success by once again drawing a clear line of demarcation between purely instrumental music, on the one hand, and programmatic music on the other. For the Berlioz of 1855 the *Symphonie fantastique* no longer counted as a total work of art as it had originally been conceived, but as counterpart of Beethoven's Sixth.

We have completed our experiment, which was designed to produce examples of Romantic opera in its purest and least adulterated form. After rejecting the thematic approach as well as those definitions which are satisfied with the presence of exclusively literary or exclusively musical qualities alleged to the Romantic, we decided to focus on a view which, programmatically expressed, presupposes a fusion of the contributing arts and calls for the identity of composer and librettist as well as, ideally, the protagonist or perspective. Moving from two opposite poles toward an imagined

---

[100] "Vier Sätze sind ihm zu wenig. Er nimmt, wie zu einem Schauspiel, fünf" (Four movements do not suffice [for him]; he needs five, as is proper to drama). Robert Schumann in his essay "Sinfonie von H. Berlioz," published in several installments in the *Neue Zeitschrift für Musik* (1835) and reprinted in Schumann's *Gesammelte Schriften über Musik und Musiker*, ed. Martin Kreisig (Leipzig: Breitkopf & Härtel, 1914) I, 69-90; quotation on p. 71. An English version of this detailed musical analysis based on Liszt's piano version of the symphony is found in Edward T. Cone's edition (fn. 92).

[101] Dömling, p. 145.

[102] Dömling, p. 145.

[103] Dömling, p. 147. Berlioz called *Lélio* a *mélologue* in 1832 but changed the label to the more familiar *monodrame* in the printed edition of 1855.

center, we singled out two works which, while not altogether perfect paragons, come close enough to being exemplary to deserve some kind of recognition: Wagner's *Der fliegende Holländer* in its incipient balladesque form and Berlioz's *Symphonie fantastique* conceived as an opera without words, both implying the presence of dream structures. In the wake of Romanticism conceived as a historical movement, two works on an even higher level of artistic accomplishment round out the picture: Wagner's *Tristan und Isolde,* heavily weighed down by its philosophical luggage, and Strindberg's *Dream Play,* an orchestrated drama which, profoundly indebted to Wagner though hardly to Berlioz, might well be regarded as the apex of Romantic opera generously defined.

III. AFFINITY, DISSEMINATION, RECEPTION

MARVIN CARLSON

THE ITALIAN ROMANTIC DRAMA IN ITS EUROPEAN CONTEXT

During the Renaissance, England, Spain, and shortly after, France each enjoyed a great period of
theatrical creation. The other areas of Europe whose contribution to the drama has since been of the
most importance – Italy, Germany, Russia, and Scandinavia – developed this genre much later,
during the eighteenth century, and generally speaking, developed it in a much more calculated and
self-conscious way. Not surprisingly they all looked to the French theatre for instruction, not only
because its greatest achievements were more recent, but even more because France in the late
seventeenth and early eighteenth century was a vastly more influential force politically and culturally on the rest of the continent than either England or Spain.

Thus in 1690 the Arcadian Academy was founded in Rome for the express purpose of developing an Italian neoclassic literary tradition modeled on the French. The opera, Italy's major dramatic
genre at this time, was condemned in 1700 by Giovan Crescimbeni, the first president of the
Academy, for its mixture of genres, indifference to Classic rules, and debasement of poetic language, in short for all those qualities later championed by the Romantics. Crescimbeni expressed the
hope that the new century would see the creation in Italy of "true comedy and tragedy" in the
French manner.[1] His program, strategy, and goals almost exactly parallel those of Gottsched and his
circle in Leipzig later in the century, but unhappily he was no more successful than Gottsched in
creating a viable drama which would be both literary and popular. Not until the end of the century,
in the works of Alfieri, did Italy at last achieve such a tragic drama.

Shakespeare, who served so centrally as a counter-model to the French for the Romantic
authors, was during the eighteenth century as unknown and exotic a figure in Italy as he was in
France. Apostolo Zeno, who wrote a music drama called *Ambleto* in 1705, was apparently quite unaware that a major English drama had been written a century before on the same subject. The poet
Antonio Conti, in London between 1715 and 1718, encountered Shakespearian drama there and
probably began his own *Giulio Cesare*, published in 1726. In its preface he mentions "Sasper," as
"the Corneille of the English, only far more irregular," violating the unities of time, place, and
action, and, like all English writers before the enlightened period of Addison, treating "Aristotle's
rules with contempt." Dramas of this sort, Conti suggests, might have been popular if translated into
Italian in the seventeenth century, when Italians, "spoilt by Spanish comedies," would have responded favorably to such crude works.[2]

[1] Giovan Crescimbeni, *La belleza della volgar poesia*, quoted in Robert Freeman, "Opera without Drama," Diss. Princeton 1967, pp. 21-22.
[2] Faenza, 1726, p. 54, quoted in Lacy Collison-Morley, *Shakespeare in Italy* (Stratford: Shakespeare Head Press,
1916), 6-7.

Naturally Conti's own tragedy and his six subsequent original dramas and translations from Voltaire were strictly faithful to French practice. Such was the practice of the Arcadians and their followers, who dominated the Italian literary scene for most of the century. However neither Shakespeare nor the Spanish, despite Conti's condemnation, were completely ignored. Southern Italy in particular, long tied to Spain culturally and politically, continued to be receptive to the works of the Golden Age. Zeno, though ignorant of Shakespeare, borrowed from Moreto and Cervantes. The leading Arcadian tragic author, Metastasio, born in Naples, admired and borrowed liberally from Calderón.

Shakespeare began to attract attention, not surprisingly, when Voltaire began to write about him, for the French writer's authority was as great in eighteenth-century Italy as in his homeland. Francesco Saverio Quadrio's *Della storia e della ragione d'ogni poesia* (On the History and Reasons for All Poetry, 1743) essentially transcribes its ideas directly from Voltaire's *Lettres philosophiques* (1734), calling Shakespeare a "fertile and vigorous genius" whose mind "combined the natural with the sublime" but whose ignorance of the rules of drama made his merits pernicious, since they encouraged subsequent English dramatists to copy both his excellencies and his considerable faults.[3]

Naturally the Arcadians were delighted when Voltaire praised their own work at the expense of the English, corrupted by this unfortunate model. Voltaire's own *Mérope* (1743) was derived from the 1713 tragedy by Scipione Maffei, the most successful of the early eighteenth-century neoclassic experiments, and in its preface Voltaire likened Maffei to Sophocles and ridiculed a recent English tragedy on the same subject. Similarly, the "Dissertation sur la tragédie ancienne et moderne," addressed to the Italian Voltairian Cardinal Quirini and prefaced to *Sémiramis* (1748), lauds the works of Metastasio as the nearest modern art had come to Greek tragedy, both in regard for the rules and in poetic achievement. The same essay contains the famous condemnation of *Hamlet* as a "gross and barbarous piece which would not be supported by the most vile public of France and Italy" and of Shakespeare as an artist in whom nature had combined "whatever one can imagine that is most powerful and good" with "the lowest and most detestable elements of an uninspired grossness."[4]

Thanks to such comments Shakespeare's name began to be known in Italy, though few read him and most critics simply accepted without question the Voltairian vision of the undisciplined, erratic, even gross genius, whose scattered beauties made him a dangerous temptation to naive young playwrights. This is the attitude echoed in the mid-century work of Carlo Goldoni. In 1744 in Pisa he joined an Arcadian society, gaining important support from the Arcadians in his campaign to develop a comedy of literary significance, one which emphasized the author in opposition to the actor-oriented *commedia dell'arte*. The preface to Goldoni's first collection of plays (1750) is buttressed with quotations from Horace and Rapin, though Goldoni also argues for some flexibility in the rules, at least in regard to comedy. "Instruction of the public by diversion and pleasure" should be elevated above any specific precepts of playwriting, and the two "books" studied by the comic dramatist should be the theatre and the world.[5]

Shakespeare is not yet mentioned in this preface, but appears in both preface and text of the 1754 comedy *I Malcontenti*. During the interim Goldoni had become involved in a bitter literary

---

[3] *Della storia*, I, 149, quoted in Collison-Morley, pp. 19-20.
[4] Voltaire, *Oeuvres complètes*, 52 vols. (Paris: Garnier, 1877), IV, 502.
[5] Carlo Goldoni, *Tutte le opere*, 8 vols. (Milan: Mondadori, 1935), I, 771-72.

quarrel with a rival playwright, Pietro Chiari, who disputed his claim as the renovator of Italian comedy. Chiari is parodied in *I Malcontenti* as Grisologo, so openly and sarcastically that the play was banned in Venice. In the second act, Grisologo boasts of being the first Italian dramatist to imitate the English theatre, taking as his example "the celebrated Sachespir." Pressed to describe what he has thus learned, he replies:

> Lo stile mio, che mi renderà singolare al mondo, consiste in una forza di dire vibrato, ampolloso, sonoro, pieno di metafore, di sentenze, di similtudini, colle quali ora m'inalzo alle stelle, ora vo terra terra radendo il suolo. Non mi rendo schiavo della dura legge dell'unità. Unisco il tragico ed il comico insieme; e quando scrivo in versi, m'abbandono intieramente al furore poetico, senza ascoltar la natura che con soverchi scrupoli viene da altri obbedita.[6]

> (My style, which shall make me world famous, consists in the power to speak in a vibrant, ample, sonorous manner, full of metaphors, of similies, of sententiae, which now elevate me among the stars, now bring me to skim into contact with the base earth. I am no slave to the burdensome laws of the unities. I blend tragedy and comedy, and when I write in verse I abandon myself entirely to the poetic fancy, with no regard for nature, which others obey with excessive scruple.)

Somewhat surprisingly, Goldoni's preface, addressed two years later to John Murray, the English Resident in Venice, views Shakespeare in a far more favorable light, as a "model to anyone" desiring to learn playwriting. Here Goldoni claims that Aristotle and his "imitator Horace" with their emphasis on arbitrary rules "have done more harm than good." The English and Spanish should be praised for freeing themselves from such "cramping fetters" and for creating plays which are "reasonable imitations of human actions." Grisologo's error is not in imitating Shakespeare, but in attempting an imitation "without having first thoroughly studied him, and without those principles of nature which are necessary to drama," achieving thus "only a ridiculous caricature."[7]

This pre-Romantic element in Goldoni's thought was long obscured by the dynamics of his more famous quarrel with Carlo Gozzi. Gozzi was a leading member of the Accademia Granellesca, a partially whimsical, partially serious society which was strongly conservative in both politics and letters and which viewed with alarm the steady encroachments of French Encyclopedist philosophy and French fashions into the political and social world of Venice. The attempts of both Goldoni and Chiari to create literary comedy the Granelleschi regarded as subversive and anti-Italian, and Gozzi attacked them both with equal fervor for rejecting the *commedia*, the "particular distinction of the Italian nation," in favor of rhetoric and bombast in the case of Chiari and dullness, crude realism, and obscenity in the case of Goldoni.

In the late 1750s Goldoni and Chiari closed ranks against this common enemy. An aristocratic friend of Goldoni, the Marquis Albergati-Capacelli, who corresponded with Voltaire and supported the Arcadian cause, sent the French author copies of some of Goldoni's plays and information on the literary battle, doubtless hoping to enlist Voltaire's aid. He was successful, since Voltaire, surely unaware of Goldoni's praise for the freedom of Shakespeare and the Spanish, responded with the warmest praise for Goldoni as a "poet of nature" and with a brief poem beginning "In every country those with talent arouse attack" and concluding "To all critics and rivals Nature herself openly con-

---

[6] Goldoni, V, 1059.
[7] Goldoni, V, 1019-20.

fesses, every author has his faults, but Goldoni has painted me."[8] Voltaire also wrote directly to Goldoni, praising him for purifying the Italian stage and rescuing Italy from the Arlequins. Goldoni's work, he suggested, might be subtitled, "Italy freed from the Goths."[9]

These opinions from the leading literary critics of Europe were of course immediately widely distributed in Venice, but if they aided Goldoni's cause with the liberal elements, they correspondingly confirmed the antagonism of the anti-French Granelleschi. Gozzi turned from critical attack to direct literary rivalry, restoring the *commedia* characters to the stage in a fanciful Aristophanic comedy, *L'Amore delle tre melarancie* (The Love of Three Oranges, 1761). Nine similar works followed between 1761 and 1765, drawing attention for the time quite away from the hitherto popular style of Goldoni, who left Venice in 1762 for a position at the Comédie Italienne in Paris and never returned.

Later French and German Romantics tended to regard the Gozzi-Goldoni debate as a precursor of Classic-Romantic confrontations, a much oversimplified interpretation which owes something to the open support of the neoclassic Arcadians and of Voltaire for Goldoni and rather more to the commentaries of Giuseppe Baretti, a member of the Granelleschi and a close friend of the Gozzi family, whose championship of Gozzi, Shakespeare, and the Spanish tended to link these together in his readers' minds as parallel champions of literary freedom. Baretti returned to Venice in 1762 after ten years in England, founding a journal, the *Frusta letteraria* (The Literary Scourge), on the model of the English *Rambler*, in which he assailed the neoclassic Academies, the French, and Goldoni, whom he accused of carelessness in language and crudeness of style. His 1764 review of a recent literary study by Carlo Denina bitterly attacks Denina's assertion that "no nation, ancient or modern, knew the art of literature better than the French writers of the age of Louis XIV." This foolish myth, says Baretti, has led "our Chiaris and our Goldonis to continually bastardize our beautiful language." The rules of the French may be suited to the French, but have little relevance across the channel or beyond the Alps, where one may find "transcendental" artists such as Shakespeare or Ariosto, "whose genius soars beyond the reach of art." A poet like Shakespeare in both comedy and tragedy "surpasses all the Corneilles, Racines, and Molières of Gaul."[10]

The *Frusta letteraria* created so many enemies that it was finally surpressed by the Venetian authorities and Baretti, fearing for his own person, left the city and in 1766 returned to London. There he continued his campaign against French neoclassicism in general and Voltaire in particular. The French author's attacks on Shakespeare and similar irregular drama had entered a new and much more virulent phase in 1764 with the publication of the *Appel à toutes les nations de l'Europe* (Call to All the Nationals of Europe) and the *avertissements* and *dissertations* connected with his edition of *Jules César* and *Héraclius*. Italy and France are portrayed as standing alone against a creeping barbarism most notably represented by champions of the English dramatist. Responding to recent praise of Spanish dramatists for creating works of similar freedom, Voltaire condemns them

---

[8] Voltaire, XL, 426. Letter of 19 June, 1760. In the original:

> En tous pays on se pique
> De molester les talents...
> Aux critiques, aux rivaux,
> La nature a dit sans feinte:
> Tout auteur a ses défauts,
> Mais ce Goldoni m'a peinte."

[9] Voltaire, XL, 560. Letter of 24 September, 1760.
[10] Giuseppe Baretti, *Opere scelte*, 2 vols. (Turin: Unione tipografico-editrice torinese, 1972), I, 242-45.

for their Shakespearian defects – disregard both of rules and of nature and the corruption of tragedy by the introduction of gross buffoonery. He several times quotes Lope de Vega's *New Art of Writing Plays* (*Arte nuevo de hacer comedías*)as evidence that Lope himself acknowledged the inferiority of *his* own drama, which pandered to public taste, to the more regular drama of Italy and France. Thus Lope, a dramatist capable of "correcting" his era, was in fact "subjugated" by it.[11]

Baretti's *Manners and Customs of Italy* (1768) and *Journey from London to Genoa* (1770) challenged all of these assertions. The first cites Voltaire's support of the "crude, vulgar, and linguistically barbarous Goldoni" as evidence of the Frenchman's incompetence in judging Italian literature, while lauding the genius of Gozzi as "the most wonderful, next Shakespeare, that ever any age or country produced."[12] The second calls the contemporary French and English neoclassic drama "the driest and coldest that ever any age produced," and urges Voltaire and his colleagues to study Lope de Vega and Calderón to stimulate their "cold and barren imaginations," and to discover how a natural and powerful drama can be created without all the rules "about which the French make so much noise."[13]

Voltaire's most famous anti-Shakespearian tract, the 1776 *Discours* to the French Academy, stimulated by the recent Le Tourneur translations and their laudatory prefaces, similarly led in turn to Baretti's most important defense of Shakespeare, the 1777 *Discours sur Shakespeare et sur Monsieur de Voltaire*. It is much more an attack on Voltaire, whose illiteracy in both English and French Baretti again seeks to demonstrate, than a defense of Shakespeare, but whenever the essay turns to questions of general literary concern, its Romantic inclination is evident. "Let Aristotle say what he will, I oppose to his authority the experience of Shakespeare, of Lope de Vega, and of many others, who have made us see the contrary."[14]

The *Discours* did not gain the international attention Baretti clearly hoped for it. In England an article on Shakespeare written by an Italian critic in French was regarded at best as a minor literary curiosity. In France Voltaire's reputation was so strong that Baretti's attack, much muted by his editor, went almost unnoticed, or was lightly dismissed for its errors in French. In Italy the response was equally discouraging. The only strong advocate of Baretti's ideas was Gozzi, whose motives were hardly disinterested. After the departure of Goldoni, he began a series of adaptations from Calderón, Cervantes, Moreto, Tirso, and Zorilla, which were an important part of the Venetian theatre scene from 1762 until 1800, defending this undertaking in his *La più lunga lettera di responta* (The Longest Letter of Response, published 1801) in terms reminiscent of Baretti. The fresh approach of these Spanish authors, he writes, can serve "to renew, re-establish, and make fecund our own theatre."[15]

In the now far more influential literary center of Milan Baretti found no such support, but in a letter to a Milanese friend of August, 1778, he seemed resigned to taking a longer view: "You are deceived if you believe that I had hoped my friends in Milan would approve of my debate with M. de Voltaire. I know the present world well enough not to flatter myself in regard to their approval.

---

[11] Voltaire, XXIV, 216.

[12] Baretti, *An Account of the Manners and Customs of Italy*, 2 vols. (London: Davies & Davis, 1768), I, 191.

[13] Baretti, *A Journey from London to Genoa through England, Portugal, Spain, and France*, 3rd ed., 3 vols. (London: Davies, 1770), III, 27, 34.

[14] Baretti, *Opere*, II, 548. In the original: "Qu'Aristote dise ce qu'il veut, j'oppose à son autorité l'expérience de Shakespeare, de Lope de Vega, et de plusieurs autres, qui nous ont fait voir le contraire."

[15] Carlo Gozzi, *Opere edite ed inedite*, 14 vols. (Venice: Zanardi, 1801), XIV, 54.

But I have not written for the present world. I write primarily for the future."[16] The coming Romantic movement in fact vindicated Baretti, but less directly than he deserved. The ideas he championed, as we shall see, had to be reintroduced to Italy a generation later, by French and German theorists. Arcadian influence was still very strong in Italy in the late eighteenth century, especially in the North, and was reinforced at the close of the century by the appearance at last of a tradition of significant modern neoclassic Italian tragedy, beginning with the works of Alfieri and continued by his followers Vincenzo Monti, Ugo Foscolo, and Giovanni Pindemonte.

The Le Tourneur translations of Shakespeare, which aroused Voltaire's wrath, were known to all of these Italian dramatists, and they all expressed warm praise for the English dramatist. Nevertheless in both theory and practice they were far closer to Voltaire than to Baretti, and their success guaranteed the continued influence of neoclassicism in Italy. Alfieri's early tragedies were first written in French, and although his *Vita* lists Shakespeare among those dramatists he most reveres (others are Racine and Aeschylus), he echoes Voltaire in finding a threat in Shakespeare's very attraction: "However much I felt myself drawn toward this author (all of whose defects at the same time I could very well see), I was that much more determined to keep away from him."[17]

Monti in a 1789 preface admits to shedding tears over the adventures of Romeo and Juliet and leaving the theatre "struck with terror and horror by the fury of Hamlet,"[18] and his tragedies contain a variety of Shakespearian echoes – the ghost in *Aristodemo* (1786), parallels to *Othello* in the plot and characters and to *Julius Caesar* in a number of lines in *Galeotto Manfredi* (1788), and the crowd scenes and funeral oration in *Caio Gracco* (1800). Yet when all is said, these elements do not succeed in bringing Monti's plays as a whole much closer to Shakespeare than were the early English-influenced tragedies of Voltaire half a century earlier.

Foscolo rhetorically inquires in a letter of 1809: "Who does not feel his mind broadened and elevated" by reading "the sublime authors" Dante and Shakespeare, yet he goes on to observe: "Who does not see the faults and extravagances" of these same authors.[19] Even when in his *Ricciarda* (1813) he turned from classic settings to a medieval one with faint echoes of *Romeo and Juliet*, Foscolo was careful to remain faithful to all the rules of neoclassicism. Pindemonte's *Elena e Gherardo* (1796) and *Lucio Quinzio Cincinnato* (1804) contained similar Shakespearian echoes in an essentially Alfierian structure. A general liberal philosophy, often strengthened by patriotic fervor, can be found throughout the Alfierian school, and since this political element was strong in Italian Romanticism as well, these neoclassicists were not so firmly rejected by the coming Romantics as were their French counterparts. But in the matters of dramatic structure, genre, and rules, Italian tragedians at the turn of the century at best paralleled the modest neoclassic French reformers like Lemercier and de Jouy.

Only one Alfierian openly broke with this tradition, primarily under the influence of Shakespeare. This was the rather eccentric Count Alessandro Pepoli, who after a series of Arcadian tragedies issued a sort of pre-Romantic manifesto in the *Mercurio d'Italia* in 1796 entitled "On the use-

[16] Baretti, *Epistolario*, 2 vols. (Bari: Laterza, 1936), II, 236. In the original: "Voi v'ingannate, se credete ch'io m'aspettassi di sentire i miei amici milanesi approvare il mio discorsuccio al signor di Voltaire. Conosco il mondo presente quanto basta per non lusingarmi punto della loro approvazione. Ma io non iscrivo tutto quel che scrivo pel mondo presente. Scrivo piuttosta pel futuro."

[17] Vittorio Alfieri, *Vita* (Florence: "La Nuova Italia," 1932), p. 20. In the original: "quanto più mi andava a sangue quell'autore (di cui però benissimo distinguera tutti i difetti), tanto più me ne volli astenere."

[18] Vincenzo Monti, *Opere* (Milan: Ricciardi, 1953), p. 1003.

[19] Ugo Foscolo, *Epistolario*, 8 vols. (Florence: Le Monnier, 1953), III, 148.

fulness, the invention, and the rules of a new type of theatrical composition, called a *'fisedia'"* (*Sull'utilità, sull'invenzione, e sulle regole di un nuovo genere di somponimento teatrale da lui chiamato fisedia*). In the name of Shakespeare and looking to the recent popular success of the sentimental comedy as a "mixed" form, Pepoli proposed seventeen rules for the *fisedia*, which rejected unity of time and place, allowed the use of both kings and peasants, prose and verse, and comic and tragic elements, provided that the former did not take precedence. The only basic rules should be those "followed by all worthwhile plays" – among them "consistency of character, propriety of manners, and clarity of development."[20] A solid theoretical basis for the development of a Romantic theatre was provided by this interesting document, but despite the considerable success of Pepoli's single *fisedia, Ladislo*, in Venice in 1796, his attempt to turn Italian tragedy in a more Shakespearian direction did not bear fruit. The influence of the French tradition, reinforced by a growing interest in Alfieri, proved too strong at this time to overcome.

The political situation contributed in no small measure to this theatrical conservatism. Between 1792 and 1799 the French occupied all of mainland Italy. Briefly driven out by the combined forces of Austria, Russia, and England, they returned and by 1805 were again in control of all of the peninsula north of Tuscany and the Papal States. Alfieri and his followers joined most Italian liberals and intellectuals in welcoming the French as liberators and champions of democracy, an attitude which the politically astute Bonaparte encouraged. Monti became the official Poet Laureate of the new French kingdom of Northern Italy and was appointed head of a panel of judges which after 1809 awarded prizes for the best comedy and tragedy created in the kingdom each year. French neoclassicism was the inevitable model, especially since Napoleon himself was highly conservative in his dramatic taste, and the rigidity of adherence to traditional rules is indicated by the fact that the most likely candidate for the first year's award in tragedy, Arici's *Calleroe*, was disqualified on the grounds that the most restricted unity of place had not been observed – one act showing the interior of a temple, another the exterior.

Thus as the new century opened Italy, especially in the North, was subject to the same forces that gave at this period such powerful support to the decaying neoclassic theatre in France. Moreover Italy possessed in Alfieri what France at this time so notably lacked, a contemporary dramatist still producing significant work in this tradition. Under these circumstances the infusion of Romantic ideas from the relatively remote literatures of England and Germany seemed at this time even more unlikely in Italy than in France, despite a continuing interest in, if not imitation of Shakespeare. This impression, however, proved illusory, for several reasons. One was that Alfieri and his major disciples combined with their neoclassicism an Encyclopedist love of liberty that made them in a critical sense not the opponents but the precursors of the patriotic Romantics who appeared a generation later. When Alfieri found that the French proved as oppressive as the Austrians had been, he turned against them as passionately as he had welcomed their coming. Second, the writings of Mme de Staël, the clearest single influence on the appearance of Romanticism in Italy, were particularly wide-read and influential here because of their author's distinct interest in matters Italian. Finally, after 1815, the Austrian invasion of the peninsula opened Italy to the direct influence of German letters while Romanticism there was still at its height.

Mme de Staël's *De la littérature* appeared in Milan in Italian early in 1803, though of course the Italian literary world could for the most part read her work as easily in French. Her remarks on

---

[20] Peter Müller, *Alessandro Pepoli als Gegenspieler Vittorio Alfieris* (Munich: Fink, 1974), pp. 201-3.

Italian literature are much less extensive and perceptive than those on the Germans and Shakespeare, but her explanations for the weakness of Italian literature surely struck a responsive chord in young liberal authors. Oppressed by their governments and their priests, Italian authors according to Mme de Staël gain release only in self-mockery and a mockery of their oppressors, which is however so lacking in power as to arouse only scorn in these oppressors.[21] Her tour through Italy in 1804-5 resulted in the novel *Corinne*, which considered contemporary Italian theatre in rather more detail, but with little more enthusiasm. Goldoni, given a few kind words earlier, is here found boring and monotonous, Gozzi judged much more original, though equally far from nature, Alfieri austere and stifled in imagination.[22] Again the lack of a national spirit and of political liberty is cited as the cause of the escapism and the inability of modern Italian writers to deal with serious and elevated themes in a successful manner.

Mme de Staël's famous *De l'Allemagne* (On Germany) appeared in Italian translation in 1814, immediately after its publication in Paris. As the capital of Napoleon's Kingdom of Italy, Milan had assumed a position of cultural dominance, and its leading literary journal in 1814, the *Spettatore*, reinforced the effect of de Staël's book by translating articles from its French equivalent, *Le Spectateur*, on the debate aroused in Paris by de Staël's attacks on French Classic ideals. Shorter articles on Goethe and Schiller were also offered, but essentially these were seen through the eyes of contemporary French criticism. Even in its remarks on German literature, Italian criticism followed its traditional imitation of France, but changing political circumstances were soon to bring this long-established orientation to an end.

The defeat of Napoleon and the ensuing Congress of Vienna returned most of Italy to Austrian control and gave fresh impetus to those elements who continued to dream of an Italy free of all foreign domination. Mme de Staël traveled in the peninsula again in late 1815 and early 1816 and her often repeated charges of the corruption of modern Italian literature by an oppressive political system made her a welcome guest in many a revolutionary gathering, a fact which did not go unobserved by the police, who sent regular reports on her travels to Vienna.

In Milan Mme de Staël also met with the more pliable Vincenzo Monti, whose position and privileges had of course ceased with the departure of the French but who was now busily engaged in currying favor with the new Austrian authorities. For the arrival of Emperor Francis I he had composed a celebratory cantata for performance at La Scala and he was now serving on the editorial board for a new journal to be published in Milan, the *Biblioteca Italiana*, which the Austrian authorities hoped to employ to orient the Italian intellectual world away from France and toward Germany. Mme de Staël's political liberalism was of much less concern to Monti than her reputation as a determined enemy of Napoleon and champion of German culture, and he urged her to write for the opening number of the *Biblioteca* an article stressing the usefulness to Italians of the study of German literature.

The result was *Sulla maniera e l'utilità delle traduzioni* (On the Manner and Usefulness of Translations), appearing in January of 1816 and generally considered the beginning of the Romantic movement in Italy. In certain respects it precisely fulfilled Monti's wishes. His own translation of Homer was warmly praised, as were the Shakespearian translations of Schlegel, and Italian authors were indeed urged to look to Germany, as well as to England, for inspiration, but de Staël went

[21] Germaine de Staël, *Oeuvres complètes*, 3 vols. (Geneva: Slatkine, 1967), I, 251.
[22] De Staël, I, 712-14.

further, condemning present Italian literature for its vapidity, its lack of ideas, and its continued "sifting of the dead ashes of the past." England and Germany should be studied not to be imitated, but to lead Italian authors to the creation of a new literature expressive of their own spirit as a people. The appearance of this article stimulated a whole series of arguments in the following months. The pro-French *Spettatore* accused de Staël of carrying on a continuing program of vilification of the Italian people, and disgruntled neoclassicists complained in the *Biblioteca* itself that the Classic Italian tradition still provided sound models for imitation. The statements in support of de Staël tended to appear as separate pamphlets, the most influential of which was the *Lettera semiseria di Crisòstomo* by Giovanni Berchet. In a famous passage, Berchet calls for an end to the "poetry of the dead," imitating Classic models in form and subject, and for its replacement by a "poetry of the living," drawn from the life and culture of the artist and the experiences of contemporary reality. Poetry should express "living nature," and thus be "as much alive as the thing she represents, as free as the thought that springs from it." Among the unnatural limitations on this necessary freedom Berchet cites the unities of time and place and the rigid separation of comedy and tragedy.[23]

In 1817, in the midst of this controversy, appeared an Italian translation of the central work of German Romantic theory, the *Vorlesungen über dramatische Kunst und Literatur* (Lectures on Dramatic Art and Literature) by A.W. Schlegel, who had accompanied Mme de Staël on her Italian tours. The translator, somewhat surprisingly, was a Classicist, Giovanni Gherardini, who seems to have hoped that Schlegel's excesses and low opinion of Goldoni and Alfieri would diminish Italian enthusiasm for the new movement. Indeed Schlegel's observations on Italian literature are among the weakest parts of his lectures. Alfieri he saw only as a minor contributor to neoclassicism, still bound by its restrictions and lacking the musical harmony and delicate emotions of the French. He seemed unaware that the simplicity and directness of Alfieri had its own charm for his countrymen, and far more important, that the passion for liberty that ran through his plays would prove as important for the Italian Romantics as any consideration of form or style. Goldoni is condemned on similar grounds, as following a general French style, but without French wit or richness of invention.

Like Baretti, Schlegel praises Gozzi at Goldoni's expense, but there is nothing surprising or original in this opinion, since German critics had held much the same view for the past twenty years. Gozzi was a discovery not of the German Romantics but of the *Sturm und Drang*. Five volumes of his works, including both *fiabe* and Spanish adaptations, were translated between 1777 and 1779 by August Clemens Werthes, who prefaced the first with a brief account of the Gozzi-Goldoni feud, presenting it as a quarrel between an artist of genius and nature and one of crudeness and artifice, a theme picked up by most reviewers. The *Berliner Literatur und Theater Zeitung* praised the second volume warmly, noting that Gozzi maintained his pre-eminence despite "the intrigues of the Chiaris and Goldonis." After the third volume the reviewer expressed the wish that German dramatists "would read Gozzi immediately after Shakespeare,"[24] an observation perhaps inspired by the translation's claim that Gozzi was "called the Shakespeare of Italy."

In the late nineteenth century Marcus Landau argued that Gozzi's significance was primarily as a spokesman for the political reaction,[25] and subsequent critics, unaware of Gozzi's general vogue

---

[23] Giovanni Berchet, *Opere* (Naples: Rossi, 1972), p. 468.
[24] *Berliner Literatur und Theater Zeitung*, 7 February, 1778, quoted in H.H. Rusack, *Gozzi in Germany* (New York: AMS Press, 1966), p. 27.
[25] Marcus Landau, *Die Comedie im Dienste der Reaktion, Beiträge zur Allgemeinen Literatur*, no. 316 (1881), and *Geschichte der italienischen Literatur* (Berlin: Felber, 1899), pp. 434-46.

in *Sturm und Drang* Germany, have sometimes assumed that it was largely or solely this political conservatism that aroused Goethe's interest in Gozzi, but this seems no more likely than that Goethe was drawn to Shakespeare by the latter's support of the monarchy. In both cases Goethe, seeking new inspiration for the German stage, was exploring the work of dramatists recently discovered and popularized in Germany. Schlegel viewed Gozzi from a more specifically Romantic perspective, seeing in him an "unconscious affinity" with the great masters of the "Romantic" drama, Shakespeare and Calderón.[26] What Gozzi, in rudimentary form, shared with these masters was the idea that fascinated Schlegel – Romantic irony, that ability in the poet to balance tragedy and comedy in such a manner as to rise above his own creation and distance himself and his readers from his created world.

This view of Gozzi was extremely influential among the German Romantics, and in the theatre was most obviously manifested in the fairy tale comedies of Ludwig Tieck, but in Italy the few pages Schlegel devoted to recent Italian drama clearly served more to confirm the neoclassicists in their distrust of contemporary German thought than to provide any inspiration for the Romantics. The latter saw no contemporary relevance in the old Gozzi-Goldoni dispute and were not engaged by such vague and metaphysical concerns as Romantic irony. What inspired them in Schelgel was his detailed and spirited advocacy of Shakespeare and his contempt for the rules of the French stage in general and for the unities in particular.

Clearly such ideas sat well with Alessandro Manzoni, who was at this time writing his first drama, the verse tragedy *Il Conte di Carmagnola*. Manzoni had been exposed to the new ideas earlier than most of his countrymen, during the years 1805 to 1810 which he spent in Paris. There he frequented the salon of Mme de Condorcet, who shared with Mme de Staël a love of Germany and intense dislike for Napoleon. In her circle and that of the historian and critic Fauriel, who remained a life-long friend, Manzoni met Mme de Staël, Schiller's friend Jens Baggesen, and French scholars interested in German culture: Villers, the translator of Kant, and Benjamin Constant, whose version of Schiller's *Wallenstein* appeared near the end of Manzoni's stay in Paris. Back in Italy Manzoni began work on a drama which, he informed Fauriel in a letter of 25 March, 1816, was being written under the influence of "Shakespeare and some things recently written about the theatre" – apparently the de Staël debate of this year. It would strike "a strong blow to the unity of time" and seek a natural poetic speech unlike the "narrow and artificial" rhetorical system of traditional tragedy.[27]

The patriotic echoes aroused by de Staël led the *Biblioteca Italiana* to draw away from Romanticism after this first experience, but a new journal, *Il Conciliatore*, founded in 1818, made itself the major voice of the new movement. Its editor Silvio Pellico had achieved renown as a dramatist with *Francesca da Rimini* (1815), whose passionate language and stirring patriotic passages made it an important precursor of Italian Romanticism. In *Il Conciliatore* Pellico took up the call of Mme de Staël for the study of foreign dramatists and for a theatre of reality focussed on modern concerns rather than upon the sterile conventional plots of neoclassic mythology. He praised Shakespeare's *Othello*, for example, as a work that despite "its multitude of characters and no unity whatever of time or place" still excites compassion and terror by a heroic action and is thus "every whit as true a tragedy as the one that produces these same effects with three characters and all the most revered

---

[26] A.W. Schlegel, *Sämmtliche Werke*, 12 vols. (Leipzig: Weidmann, 1846), V, 365-66.
[27] Alessandro Manzoni, *Lettere*, 3 vols. (Verona: Mondadori, 1970), I, 157-58.

unities."[28] In 1819 Pellico recalled in a letter to his brother how the reading of Schlegel, Shakespeare, and Schiller had "stirred a flame in our hearts and opened more vast horizons."[29]

The other leading *Conciliatore* writer on the drama was Ermes Visconti, who produced one of the best brief summaries of the aims of the new movement in *Idee elementari sulla poesia romantica* (Basic Ideas on Romantic Poetry, 1818) and a sprightly attack on Classic rules in the *Dialogo sulle unità drammatiche di luogo e di tempo* (Dialogue on the Dramatic Unities of Time and Place, 1819). The box at La Scala of one of the leading *Conciliatore* authors, Ludovico di Breme, became the daily gathering place of these authors and a necessary visiting place for foreigners with parallel interests – Schlegel and de Staël, Byron and Hobhouse, and most frequently, the young Henri Beyle, later known as Stendhal. The leading literary journals from England circulated among the group, along with recent Romantically oriented literary studies such as Sismondi's *De la littérature du Midi* (Concerning Southern Literature) and Bouterwek's *Geschichte der Poesie* (History of Poetry), but here, as elsewhere in Europe, the major work for the crystallization of the new ideas in the drama was of course Schlegel's *Vorlesungen*.

Though Byron's work was much admired in Milan, he was more in harmony with the Milan Romantics politically than in terms of literary theory and especially of the drama. He favored respect for the unities and a generally neoclassic approach, and thus found Alfieri and his followers distinctly more interesting than the current Romantic experiments. Doubtless this bias would have appeared in the comments on contemporary Italian literature that Byron originally planned to include in the text or notes of Canto IV of *Childe Harold*, but the poet decided this undertaking was too ambitious, especially in view of his rather brief acquaintance with Italy. He therefore left this part of the *Childe Harold* project to his friend John Hobhouse. Hobhouse was an uneasy as Byron about the solidity of his knowledge of recent literature in Italy, but he undertook the assignment, relying heavily on information and opinions provided him by Ugo Foscolo, who had emigrated to London after the Austrian occupation of Milan in 1816. Foscolo, as an Alfierian neoclassicist, naturally emphasized that tradition, giving much attention to Alfieri, Monti, and himself, and essentially ignoring the younger Romantics, indeed dismissing the entire Classic-Romantic debate as an "idle enquiry."[30] When Hobhouse's *Historical Illustration of the Fourth Canto of Childe Harold* appeared in 1818 the Milan Romantics were furious, and Di Breme wrote lengthy letters of complaint to both Byron and Hobhouse. Foscolo had, however, established himself as an authority on Italian letters in the London literary world and in Whig society and his indifference, if not antagonism to Romantic experiments colored English views of these works for much of the next decade.

At home the *Conciliatore* also faced neoclassic resistance, but its more serious opposition was not literary but political. The journal's continuing interest in progress, patriotism, and liberty proved too threatening for the Austrian authorities and it was suppressed in December of 1819. Nevertheless its ideas, both political and literary, continued to provide inspiration for Italian patriots and authors. Manzoni's *Il Conte di Carmagnola* appeared in 1820, and although Manzoni had not written for the *Conciliatore*, his drama was the most successful attempt so far in Italy to fulfill the ideals there expressed. Its subject was drawn from Italian history, it defied the unities, and its stage was crowded with characters speaking a language strikingly less rhetorical than that of traditional trag-

---

[28] *Conciliatore*, 6 September, 1818, reproduced in Egidio Bellorini, ed., *Discussioni e polemiche sul Romanticismo*, 2 vols. (Bari: Laterza, 1943), I, 408.
[29] Ilario Rinieri, *Della vita e delle opere di S. Pellico*, 3 vols. (Turin: Streglio, 1989-1901), II, 145.
[30] See E.R. Vincent, *Byron, Hobhouse and Foscolo* (Cambridge, MA: Cambridge Univ. Press, 1949).

edy. The *Prefazione* to the play quotes both Schlegel and Aristotle against the unities of time and place and urges that every new composition be judged not on the basis of rules "whose universality and certainty are questionable," but on an understanding of the author's intentions and his success in achieving these.[31] In a letter of 1827 Manzoni says that he learned from Schlegel to regard literary works as "organic and not mechanical in form," so that every composition possessed "its own special nature and reason for existence and thus must be judged by its own rules."[32]

Il Conte di Carmagnola was the first drama of the Italian Romantic period to gain wide attention in Europe, but outside of Italy few reviewers appreciated the particular circumstances in which it was created, the special blend of literary and political concerns that characterized Italian Romanticism in 1820. French, German, and English reviewers each read it in the light of their own attitude toward Romanticism. For the Germans their own Classic-Romantic controversy was already almost a historical phenomenon, and the conflict in Milan was seen essentially as a delayed replay of that controversy. For the French, whose Classic-Romantic battles had scarcely begun, a writer like Manzoni was seen as a potential model or an alien threat, depending upon the critic's theoretical position. For the English, who never became significantly involved in this debate, at least in terms of theatre, the Milanese controversy over rules and artistic freedom seemed a minor literary squabble, a view that the influential Foscolo, who had little love for Romantic literature, strongly encouraged.

The most prestigious of Manzoni's many reviewers was Goethe, who had been following recent literary developments in Milan with keen interest for several years. His article "Classicists and Romantics Engaged in Fierce Struggle in Italy," ("Classiker und Romantiker in Italien, sich heftig bekämpfend"), written in 1818 and published in 1820 in *Über Kunst und Alterthum* (Concerning Art and Antiquity), contained the warmest praise for Manzoni's already published hymns and showed a detailed knowledge of the contemporary Milan literary scene, remarking on the hostility conservative forces had already shown toward the recently founded *Conciliatore*, and praising the "clarity of thought" and "profound knowledge of the ancients and moderns" shown by Visconti in his dialogue on the dramatic unities and other writings.[33] In the same essay Goethe mentions *Carmagnola* as a work in progress, and in 1820, soon after the *Biblioteca Italiana* had dismissed the play as no better than "twenty or thirty such tragedies that appear every year,"[34] Goethe responded in *Über Kunst und Alterthum* with a warm defense and detailed act by act analysis of the work, followed by the observation: "We congratulate the author on his success in breaking with the old rules and in setting himself on a new path with so sure and steady a step that in the future new rules can be derived from his example."[35]

In October of 1820 an article in the *London Quarterly Review* surveyed recent Italian tragedy as illustrated by works of Monti, Foscolo, Pellico, and Manzoni. The influence of Foscolo, directly and indirectly (through Hobhouse, whom the article quotes), is clear. Only a single paragraph is devoted to Manzoni, calling *Il Conte di Carmagnola* a "feeble tragedy," lacking in poetry and gaining so little by its boastful violation of the unities as to convince no one that they need be abandoned.[36] Goethe, who now clearly saw himself as Manzoni's champion, responded in the first 1821

---

[31] Manzoni, *Tutte le opere*, 2 vols. (Florence: Sansoni, 1973), I, 105.

[32] Manzoni, *Carteggio*, 2 vols. (Milan: Hoepli, 1921), II, 359.

[33] J.W. von Goethe, *Werke*, 50 vols. (Stuttgart and Berlin: Cotta, 1902-7), XLI, 211.

[34] Piero Fossi, *"La Lucia" del Manzoni ed altre note critiche* (Florence: Libreria Editrice Fiorentina, 1937), p. 251.

[35] Goethe, *Werke*, XLI, 211. In the original: "So wünschen wir nur noch dem Verfasser Glück daß er, von alten Regeln sich lossagend, auf der neuen Bahn so ernst und ruhig vorgeschritten, dermaßen daß man nach seinem Werke gar wohl wieder neue Regeln bilden kann."

[36] *Quarterly Review*, 24 (October, 1820), p. 87.

issue of *Über Kunst und Alterthum* with a reprinting of this offensive paragraph and a sentence by sentence refutation of it. This essay includes the famous Goethean distinction between the destructive and the productive critic, the former applying blindly to new works already formed rules and expectations, the latter opening himself to the work and attempting to judge it in the light of its own goals and assumptions.[37] The famous "three questions" of good criticsm found here and often attributed to Goethe are in fact Goethe's unacknowledged quotation from the opening paragraph of Manzoni's *Prefazione*: "What is the intent of the author; is this intent reasonable; has the author succeeded in it?"[38]

In a letter of 23 January, 1821, Manzoni thanked Goethe for his support, which he claimed had encouraged him

> a prosequire lietamente in questi studi, un'opera d'ingegno, il mezzo migliore è di fermarsi nella viva e tranquilla contemplazione dell'argomento che si tratta, senza tener conto delle norme convenzionali, e dei desideri per lo più temporanei della maggior parte dei lettori.[39]

> (to proceed in these studies more happily, confirmed in the idea that to produce a work of art, the best method is to consider the subject one wishes to treat through a contemplation that is both lively and relaxed, taking no notice of conventional rules and of the wishes, ephemeral for the most part, of the majority of readers.)

Goethe's warm defense was of course personally satisfying to Manzoni, but beyond that it provided him with a powerful weapon to gain critical acceptance of his work elsewhere, particularly in France. A certain polarization of the Parisian literary world between Classicists and Romantics had already taken place, solidified by the appearance in 1813 of three major Romantic texts, Mme de Staël's *De l'Allemagne*, Schlegel's *Vorlesungen* in French translation, and Sismonde de Sismondi's *De la littérature du Midi*. Sismondi was a member of de Staël's circle, and his work an important complement to its two more famous companions, dealing with Spanish, Italian, Portugese, and Provençal literature in much the same terms as Schlegel dealt with the English and Germans. The Classicist journal *Le Nain jaune* (The Yellow Dwarf) spoke jestingly on 20 December, 1814, of a new "Romantic Confederation," in which Mme de Staël represented England, Holland, Germany, and Switzerland; Schlegel and Kotzebue Russia, Prussia, Austria, and Sweden; and Sismondi Spain, Portugal, and Italy. Their motto was said to be "death to the classics," and their goal the destruction of the purity of the French language by Northern obscurity and Southern bombast. French literature would be pushed beyond its "natural limits" by a forced absorbing of "Ossianic, Gallic, Germanic, Helvetic, Shakespearian, and Gothic" material.[40]

The appearance of Manzoni's play with its iconoclastic *Prefazione* was taken by French Classicists and Romantics alike as clear evidence that Sismondi was correct in viewing Italy along with England and Germany as a source of Romantic inspiration, and the French reviews of the drama reflected this. The most detailed and extensive of these was by Victor Chauvet in the *Lycée Français* of May, 1820. It praised many aspects of the play and even admitted the "novelty and ingenuity" of Manzoni's arguments against the unities, but went on to deplore his unfortunate defense of

---

[37] Goethe, *Werke*, XLI, 345-46.
[38] Manzoni, *Opere*, I, 105.
[39] Manzoni, *Lettere*, I, 223.
[40] René Bray, *Chronologie du Romantisme* (Paris: Boivin, 1932), p. 251.

an "absolutely false system." The unities of time and place, Chauvet insisted, were essential to maintain unity of action and consistency of character, and adherence to these unities was what separated the poet from the historian. Francesco Salfi in the *Revue Encyclopédique* of 18 June, 1820, similarly praised Manzoni's arguments but not his conclusions. His preface gathers "all the best arguments the Romantics have made against the unities of time and place" and "is developed with an analysis of such rigor that one would be almost tempted to share his opinion" were it not for the fact that "so far the facts do not sufficiently accord with the theory." Thus Salfi also found Manzoni intelligent but misguided. He was, however, one of the few critics outside Italy to recognize the political dimensions of Manzoni's work, praising his "pure and patriotic morality" and the "national spirit," that should gain him the sympathy of "all true Italians."[41]

Manzoni, living in Paris when these reviews appeared, began a lengthy reply, directed primarily at Chauvet, but returned to Italy with it still not completed. Back in Milan he wrote to his friend Fauriel, who was working on a French translation of *Il Conte* and who hoped to publish the response to Chauvet with it, expressing some misgivings about a reply that would necessarily appear so long after the attack. He provided Fauriel with other more accessible material in support of his position: relevant articles from the *Conciliatore*, a brief history of the Classic-Romantic controversy in Milan, and a copy of Goethe's warm review.[42]

Fauriel in fact published in 1823 what was essentially an anthology of Romantic theory and drama, containing his translations of *Il Conte* and of Manzoni's new tragedy, *Adelchi*, the history of Romanticism in Milan, Visconti's dialogue from the *Conciliatore*, Goethe's review, and Manzoni's lengthy reply to Chauvet, the *Lettre à M. C----- sur l'unité de temps et de lieu dans la tragédie* (Letter to Monsieur C----- on the Unity of Time and Place in Tragedy). The impact of this material was distinctly increased by the almost simultaneous appearance of the Italian-oriented Romantic observations of Henry Beyle (Stendhal), who had returned to Paris in 1821 after four years in Milan in close contact with the *Conciliatore* group. When a troupe of English actors attempted to perform Shakespeare in Paris in 1822 they were shouted from the stage by patriotic Frenchmen, a scandal that spurred Stendhal to rework material from two articles he had originally written for the now-suppressed *Conciliatore* and to publish this in Shakespeare's defense in the *Paris Monthly Review of British and Continental Literature*. This article, the first of three collectively known as *Racine et Shakespeare*, appeared the week before Fauriel's collection, and was the first major statement of the new Romantic school in France. The convergence of Fauriel and Stendhal is probably shown most clearly by the fact that the central portion of Stendhal's first article is also a translation of Visconti's *Dialogo* from the *Conciliatore*.

Manzoni's *Lettre*, doubtless recalling Salfi's complaint that his drama was historic rather than poetic, turned this criticism to his advantage, calling the new theatre indeed "historic," but opposing this term not to "poetic" but to "classic," which falsifies historic human experience by arbitrary restrictions. The new drama has the freedom to skip over non-essential material and portray the "true dynamic" of history, which the unities prevent, and to mix "the serious and the burlesque, the touching and the low" as did Shakespeare who "observed this mixture in reality and sought to portray the strong impression it made upon him."[43]

---

[41] *Revue Encyclopédique* 4, cahier 17, 28.
[42] Manzoni, *Carteggio*, I, 497.
[43] Manzoni, *Opere*, II, 1684. The fuller original passage reads: "ce n'est pas la violation de la règle qui l'a entraîné à ce mélange du grave et du burlesque, du touchant et du bas; c'est qu'il avait observé ce mélange dans la réalité, et qu'il voulait rendre la forte impression qu'il en avait reçue."

The appearance of the Stendhal essays and the Fauriel collection contributed significantly to bringing the Classic-Romantic debate, now simmering in the journals, to the forefront of public attention. In a famous address before the Royal Institute on 24 April, 1824 Auger, director of the French Academy, solemnly denounced the "Romantic heresy" as a barbarous foreign movement producing only monsters and extravagant fancies in France. The battle was now clearly joined, and later this same year the *Globe*, the leading Romantic journal of the 1820s, was founded, promising to bring to literary criticism an "independance and truthfulness" reflecting the new spirit emerging in poetry and the drama. Its leading drama critic was Auguste Trognon, who had anticipated Fauriel by publishing a translation in 1822 of *Il Conte di Carmagnola* accompanied by his own preface, praising Manzoni's tragedy as an outstanding example of the new Romantic school, which

> voulant reproduire sur la scène la vie humaine avec tous ses principaux accidents, voulant en quelque sorte revivre l'histoire tout entière, franchit les bornes arbitraires que l'autre s'impose, et ne reconnaît d'autre unité que l'unité d'idée et de conception; d'autre vraisemblance que la vraisemblance morale; d'autre loi, en un mot, que la loi suprême de l'art, la vérité, d'où naît pour chaque sujet sa règle particulière.

> wished to place on stage human life with all its major events, to make history come alive again in its entirety, free from the arbitrary bounds of the other [Classicism] and recognizing no other unity but that of idea and conception, no other verisimilitude than moral verisimilitude, no other law but the supreme law of art, the truth, which creates its own particular law for every subject.[44]

Not surprisingly, Manzoni and his idea of "historical truth" became standard concerns of the *Globe*. A three-part series on the unities (1825-26) was based largely upon his *Lettre*, and later in 1826 his preface to *Il Conte* was reprinted in the journal along with one of the first strongly laudatory critical judgements on the play from Italy, the preface to a new edition of Manzoni's work by Camille Ugoni.[45] The concerns most associated in France with Manzoni – the denial of the traditional unities and the emphasis on history and truth as the touchstones of drama – would of course be powerfully reflected in the first great manifesto of the French Romantic theatre, Hugo's *Préface de Cromwell*, which appeared in 1827.

By the time the Romantic and Classic controversy reached its peak in France, however, it was already being viewed in Italy as a matter of history. It had in fact never been as divisive a struggle there as it proved in France. Though they fought spiritedly for the right to ignore the unities and to take subject matter from non-Classic sources, the Italian Romantics did not, like the French, consider themselves irrevocably opposed to Classicism. They had deep respect for Alfieri, just as Alfieri himself had for Shakespeare, and in fact the most important of them, like Manzoni, did not style themselves Romantics at all, but considered themselves mediators, drawing upon the best elements of both schools. The so-called Romantic dramatists who followed Manzoni, headed by Niccolini and Marenco, made common cause with more strict Classicists to produce the major serious drama of the *Risorgimento*, which subordinated technical concerns to the arousing of national and republican sentiment. The quarrels of Classicists and Romantics were forgotten in the struggle with the common enemies, censorship and political repression.

---

[44] Auguste Trognon, ed., *Chefs d'oeuvre des théâtres étrangers* (Paris: Imprimerie Fain, 1822), I, xvii.
[45] *Le Globe*, 29 June, 1826, p. 81.

JOHN DOWLING

ROMANTIC DRAMA IN THE HISPANIC WORLD:
THE PICTURESQUE MODE

The Iberian and Ibero-American world possesses one of the greatest bodies of dramatic literature that civilization has known. The affirmation is to be taken both quantitatively and qualitatively, whether we think of the drama of Spain alone or include the literature of all those people who speak the Portuguese language of Gil Vicente and Camões and the Spanish language of Lope de Vega and Cervantes; and in our times Catalan and Galician must not be omitted. It is an uneven dramatic literature, to be sure, but those who know it do not doubt that Ibero-Americans have consistently maintained a dramatic view of life and death and literature, and they have favored the genre that best translated their view into art.

An historian of the Spanish theater, Emilio Cotarelo y Mori, writing at the beginning of this century, emphasized the richness and abundance of that theater, whether the critic studies leading figures and works or delves into the byways of theater and drama. Cotarelo explains:

> Y es porque en España no es el teatro una sencilla manifestación literaria, más o menos copiosa e interesante, sino la síntesis y compendio de la vida mental de todo un pueblo. Allí se encuentran condensados sus creencias religiosas, sus pensamientos filosóficos, sus ideales artísticos, sus costumbres, sus tradiciones y leyendas, su historia y, en suma, todo lo que de característico y genial pueda tener la raza habitadora de la Península.[1]

> (For in Spain the theater is not simply a literary phenomenon, more or less abundant and interesting [in a given period], but rather the synthesis and compendium of the psychological life of a whole people. In it are to be found epitomized their religious beliefs, their philosophical thoughts, their artistic ideals, their customs, their traditions and legends, their history, and in short, everything characteristic of the natural temperament of the race that inhabits the Iberian peninsula.)

At times the drama of the Hispanic world has been remarkably unified. In other periods, geographical areas have followed different paths. One of the earliest and greatest of Hispanic dramatists, Gil Vicente (1465?-1536?) wrote one play in Spanish, another in Portuguese, and still another in both languages. The *comedias* of Sor Juana Inés de la Cruz (1651-95), known in America as the Tenth Muse, are scarcely distinguishable from those of her Peninsular contemporaries although she herself never left the Valley of Mexico where she was born. In Lima, seat of the viceroyalty of Peru, the plays of Pedro de Peralta Barneuvo (1663-1743) – to mention only the best-known writer – extended Calderonian drama into New World theater well into the eighteenth century. On the other hand, unifying elements are more difficult to distinguish during the Romantic period. It is the pur-

---

[1] Emilio Cotarelo y Mori, *Bibliografía de las controversias sobre la licitud del teatro en España* (Madrid: Est. Tip. de la "Rev. de Archivos, Bibl. y Museos," 1907), p. 7.

pose of this essay to propose that the picturesque mode that prevailed in the theater during the Romantic years provided such a unifying force and that it enabled Spanish drama, and particularly Peninsular drama, to achieve an international dimension.

Whatever the direction of Hispanic drama, the standard against which it is measured is the *comedia* that flourished for about a century from the 1590s and then declined. Lope de Vega created it, and Calderón de la Barca enshrined it. Afterward, the eighteenth-century neoclassicists expended their energies laying to rest the descendants of the Calderonian *comedia*. The *comedia* was a fast-moving play – comic or tragic or both – in which action, verse, music, and eventually spectacle seemed to overpower character and ideas. Yet the *comedia* gave international literature the archetypal Don Juan; it gave international comedy the typical liar (in Ruiz de Alarcón's *La verdad sospechosa* [Suspicious Truth]), the typical hypocrite (in Tirso de Molina's *Marta la piadosa* [Pious Martha]), the typical dandy (in Moreto's *El lindo don Diego* [Dandy Diego]).

In Spain the *comedia* was a powerful ideological vehicle, for it propagated in art the concepts of the Counter-Reformation as southern Europe conceived them. The mighty *autos sacramentales*, which set forth allegorically the Roman Catholic meaning of the Eucharist, presented outright propaganda. Less obtrusive but nevertheless just below the surface in the *comedia* lies the whole range of Counter-Reformation ideology. But that ideology did not prevail beyond the Pyrenees. Even Roman Catholic writers of France attenuated what they found there. In Protestant England the *comedia* provided dramatists with a rich vein of "Spanish plots" that they freely mined during the restoration of the London stage after the fury of Puritan reform had spent itself.[2] But English dramatists took the plots and let the ideas go. In Spain itself, eighteenth-century neoclassic writers – notably the Moratíns, father and son – joined the currents of secularization and devoted themselves to the interment of Calderón. Many of them then lived to see German critics in alliance with early Spanish Romantics undertake his resuscitation.

One interpretation of Spanish Romanticism has emphasized the revival of Golden Age literature. It is but one of many approaches, and it is less successful than others with respect to drama. If we make detailed comparisons of particular aspects of dramatic works, we arrive at contradictory results. Although the *comedia* had been a strong force in the propagation of Counter-Reformation ideology, romantic drama carries little intellectual weight; ideas are the least important aspect of a Spanish Romantic play. The fate that pursues the Duke of Rivas's Don Alvaro is presented on a lower intellectual plane than is the free will that Tirso de Molina's Enrico exercises in *El condenado por desconfiado* (Damned for Mistrust, 1625 or 1626?). In *El burlador de Sevilla* (The Trickster of Seville, 1619 or 1620?) Tirso's Don Juan is condemned because he defies the laws of God and man; Zorrilla's protagonist in *Don Juan Tenorio* (Ladykiller Don Juan, 1844) is saved by a pure love.

In plot the Golden Age *comedia* and the Romantic drama are technically a distance apart, because the neoclassicists had greatly influenced the structure of Romantic drama. In the complicated action of a typical *comedia de capa y espada* several sets of lovers fall in and out of love. Some Romantic plots do hark back to those of seventeenth-century plays. An example is the entangled intrigue of Juan Eugenio Hartzenbusch's *Los amantes de Teruel* (The Lovers of Teruel, 1837). By contrast, the plot of the Duke of Rivas's *Don Alvaro* (1834) is neatly neoclassical. In a sense, the author has even observed a unity of time; although time is measured in years in *Don Alvaro*, it is as

[2] John Loftis, *The Spanish Plays of Neoclassical England* (New Haven and London: Yale Univ. Press, 1978).

carefully plotted as are the hours of the day in Moratín's rigorously neoclassical *El sí de las niñas* (The Maidens' Consent, 1806).[3] Zorrilla's *Don Juan Tenorio* is written in two parts and a total of seven acts. Yet the carefully plotted complications, the rising tension, and the climaxes of each act and of the play as a whole are more sophisticated than the disjointed episodes that Tirso de Molina and Andrés de Claramonte used to advance the action in *El burlador de Sevilla*.[4]

The language of the *comedia* was rich in conceits, and it was notable for the great variety of versification. The powerful effect of metrics gave it a distinction unequalled in any other national theater, and the variety of meters made translation a problem rarely surmounted even to this day. Romantic drama eschewed Baroque metaphor; it was generally straightforward, for neoclassicism had intervened and left its mark. Romanticism made one significant departure in the matter of language. A *comedia* was always written in a variety of verse. The use of verse persisted in the eighteenth century, but the variety of metrics was vastly reduced, because neoclassic authors preferred simple assonant ballad rhyme, which is typical of the Spanish language and very near to prose. Yet out of thousands, only three significant plays were written exclusively in prose before the Romantic period.[5] The Romantics did something creative: not only did they employ a variety of metrical forms; they mixed prose and verse. When Mesonero Romanos satirized a Romantic play, he said ironically that it was written "en diferentes prosas y versos."[6] In mixing verse and prose, the Spanish Romantics achieved a parallel with lyric opera: verse corresponded to lyric passages while prose corresponded to recitative. For this reason, Antonio García Gutiérrez's *El trovador* (The Troubadour, 1836) moved easily from a Spanish stage play to a Verdi opera.

It is clear that in several respects Romantic drama developed characteristics that distinguished it from the *comedia*. However, I believe that the concept of spectacle offers a more accurate approach to Romantic drama in the Hispanic world. The visual aspects of the theater had already been exploited by Calderón, whose operatic productions slightly preceded or overlapped with the performance on the London stage of Dryden's great spectacles. In nineteenth-century Spanish literature, Romanticism is contemporaneous with *costumbrismo*, a movement that is defined as the depiction of manners, customs, places, and social types of a particular city or region. Indeed, the *costumbrista* essay, called a *cuadro*, or picture, became a leading genre.[7] I shall, however, set aside detailed considerations of *costumbrismo*, viewing it as but one aspect of a picturesque mode that prevailed in Europe over a period of about a century. My intention is to show that the development of the picturesque mode in Spain is related to both the theatrical and the visual arts, although it is not associated with landscape architecture as it was in England. It is my further contention that in

---

[3] John Dowling, "Time in *Don Alvaro*," *Romance Notes*, 18 (1977-78), 355-61.

[4] It is now thought that Tirso de Molina, that is, Gabriel Téllez (1583?-1648), was the author of a play entitled *Tan largo me lo fiáis* (between 1612 and 1616?) and that the actor Andrés de Claramonte re-worked it and performed it under the title *El burlador de Sevilla* (1619 or 1620?). A good summary of the scholarship on the subject was made by Gerald E. Wade in his edition of Tirso de Molina, *El burlador de Sevilla y convidado de piedra* (New York: Scribner's Sons, 1969), pp. 3-16.

[5] I set aside the *Celestina*, sometimes classified as a dialogued novel, which has on occasion been successfully adapted for the stage; I also set apart the prose *entremeses* of Cervantes, which belonged to a genre that otherwise used verse. The three plays that I refer to are Gaspar Melchor de Jovellanos's sentimental drama *El delincuente honrado* (1773) and two comedies by Leandro Fernández de Moratín, *La comedia nueva* (1792) and *El sí de las niñas* (1806). The subject was treated by S. Griswold Morley, "The Curious Phenomenon of Spanish Verse Drama," *Bulletin Hispanique*, 50 (1948), 445-62.

[6] Ramón de Mesonero Romanos, "El romanticismo y los románticos," in *Escenas matritenses* in *Obras*, ed. Carlos Seco Serrano, Biblioteca de Autores Españoles, no. 200, (Madrid: Atlas, 1967), II, 65.

[7] Useful are the introduction and the texts of E. Correa Calderón, *Costumbristas españoles*, 2 vols. (Madrid: Aguilar, 1950). He presents *costumbrismo* using both narrow and broad definitions, but he focuses on it as a Spanish phenomenon and does not consider it within a European context.

the Hispanic world the picturesque became a principal mode or style in which the Romantic spirit and Romantic ideology manifested themselves, especially in drama.

At the beginning of the eighteenth century Joseph Addison initiated in *The Spectator* a discussion of aesthetics which was to have portentous results in the course of the Romantic movement.[8] Following Addison, Edmund Burke and other essayists advanced their concepts of the beautiful and the sublime: the beautiful was pleasing, attractive, smooth, and gentle; the sublime was obscure, vast, infinite, terrifying, or delightfully horrible.[9] Spaniards of the eighteenth century were susceptible to the sublime. Gaspar Melchor de Jovellanos, when he crossed the pass between Vitoria and Burgos, before entering the Castilian plain, wrote in his diary of the great stones of Pancorbo, "de sublime y hórrida vista" (of sublime and horrid appearance).[10] In the course of the century, British sensibility detected another quality, distinct from the beautiful and the sublime, which the Reverend William Gilpin called "picturesque beauty."[11] From the beginning it was associated in England with landscape painting and landscape gardening. In the hundred years or so that the picturesque mode held sway, British eyes converted landscapes into pictures and pictures into landscapes.[12] Those who wrote on the subject, such as William Payne Knight and Uvedale Price, found picturesque beauty in rough and shaggy objects, in high coloring, in sudden variation, and in abrupt irregularity.[13] Picturesque vision meant to them the ability to see nature with a painter's eye.

Knight discovered the origin of the mode among the Italians. The polyhistor Francesco Redi (1626-98) – physician, biologist, and linguist – used the word *pittoresco* meaning "after the manner of painters."[14] He must have been thinking of the tempestuous Salvator Rosa (1615-73), a painter and writer whose words and canvases portrayed, as Ernest Wilkins has said, "the wilder aspects of nature and of human nature – forests, craggy mountains, rocky shores, storms, ruins, bandits, battles, and scenes of human tragedy."[15] English aristocrats who carried Rosa's paintings back to England brought the word and the mode together.

In Spain, the use of the word *pintoresco* and the picturesque mode developed independently of the British usage, although both doubtless had a common source in the Italian. The Cordoban painter Antonio Palomino (1653-1726) defined *pintoresco* in the first volume of his *Museo pictó-*

[8] Addison's eleven papers on "the pleasures of the imagination" appeared in *The Spectator*, Nos. 411-21, June 21-July 3, 1712. Walter John Hipple, Jr., devotes to Addison the first chapter of *The Beautiful, the Sublime, and the Picturesque in Eighteenth-Century British Aesthetic Theory* (Carbondale: Southern Illinois Univ. Press, 1957), pp. 13-24.

[9] Edmund Burke, *A Philosophical Enquiry into the Origin of our Ideas of the Sublime and the Beautiful*, ed. James T. Boulton (London: Routledge & Kegan Paul, 1958; reprint, Notre Dame, Ind.: Univ. of Notre Dame Press, 1968). Burke's discussion of the sublime is in Part I, Section VII, pp. 39-40. The first edition was dated 1757.

[10] Gaspar Melchor de Jovellanos, *Diarios* in *Obras*, ed. Miguel Artola, B.A.E., no. 85 (Madrid: Ediciones Atlas, 1956), III, 43.

[11] William Gilpin, *Three Essays: On Picturesque Beauty; On Picturesque Travel; and On Sketching Landscape: to which Is Added a Poem, On Landscape Painting* (London: Printed for R. Blamire, 1792). For a discussion of Gilpin's contribution, see Hipple, *The Beautiful, the Sublime, and the Picturesque*, pp. 192-201.

[12] I have followed in particular the work by Christopher Hussey, *The Picturesque: Studies in a Point of View*, (Hamden, Conn.: Archon Books, 1967). The first edition was published in 1927.

[13] Two works by Richard Payne Knight are considered especially significant: *The Landscape, A Didactic Poem. In Three Books. Addressed to Uvedale Price, Esq.*, 2nd ed. (London: Bulmer for G. Nicol, 1795) (the first edition was dated 1794); and *An Analytical Inquiry into the Principles of Taste* (London: Printed for T. Payne and J. White by Mercier, 1805). Important works by Uvedale Price are: *An Essay on the Picturesque as compared with the Sublime and the Beautiful; and on the Use of Studying Pictures for the Purpose of Improving Real Landscape* (London: J. Robson, 1794); and *A Dialogue on the Distinct Characters of the Picturesque and the Beautiful* (Hereford: Walker for J. Robson, 1801). Further bibliography may be found in Hussey and in Hipple.

[14] Knight, *An Analytical Inquiry*, p. 143.

[15] Ernest Hatch Wilkins, *A History of Italian Literature*, rev. Thomas G. Bergin (Cambridge, Mass.: Harvard Univ. Press, 1974), p. 320.

rico y escala óptica: "Cosa, que está pintada con buen manejo" (Something that is painted with great skill); or, in Latin, "*Benè manipulata*" (Well turned). He used the word in the prologue to the second volume and in the title of the third volume, which was devoted to the lives of Spanish painters: *El Parnaso español pintoresco laureado con las vidas de los pintores y estatuarios eminentes españoles.*[16] The compilers of the *Diccionario* called "de autoridades" (based on authorities) cited Palomino when they defined the adjective (V, 277; 1737): "Lo que toca o pertenece a la Pintura o a los Pintores" (That which deals with or pertains to painting or painters), a meaning similar to that of Francesco Redi. One century later, in the Academy dictionary of 1837, the definition (p. 581) has been modified to an adjective "que se aplica a las cosas que presentan una imagen agradable, deliciosa y digna de ser pintada" (that is applied to things that present an agreeable, delightful image worthy of being painted). In our own day the eighteenth edition (1956) preserves the 1837 meaning; it also gives a second figurative meaning (p. 1029): "Dícese del lenguaje, estilo, etc., con que se pintan viva y animadamente las cosas" (It is applied to the language, style, etc., with which things are portrayed in a lively animated way). The nineteenth edition (1970) adds a third definition, also figurative (p. 1028): "Estrafalario, chocante" (Flamboyant, shocking).

None of these definitions seems to be derived from paintings such as those of Salvator Rosa. In the Spanish context, however, they are revealing. The 1837 definition is especially interesting, because one year before Ramón de Mesonero Romanos had begun to publish the *Semanario Pintoresco Español*, a magazine that used pictures to illustrate the essays called *cuadros de costumbres*. It was a successor to *El Artista*, another illustrated magazine on which both writers and artists had collaborated from 1834 to 1836. The weekly issues of the *Semanario Pintoresco Español* devoted columns to theater reviews and frequently published pictures that illustrated the plays being reviewed. As we leaf through the pages of these magazines, as we walk through galleries of nineteenth-century Spanish paintings, or as we see Romantic plays performed, we perceive that Spaniards of the middle third of the nineteenth century had come to see the stage scene as a picture, a *cuadro*, and to see a picture as if it were a stage scene.

I believe that the change in Spanish vision began with the development of playhouse architecture in the eighteenth century. The old Spanish *corrales* had a stage that projected out into the audience. They had no roof, and the spectator witnessed a scene that was undefined around the edges. In small towns, plays were presented in the open air on platforms with the standing audience gathered about. Furthermore, the scenes in *comedias* were often peripatetic. By that I mean, for example, that a scene may begin on the outskirts of a city and next the characters find themselves before a house in the middle of a city. The clues are in the dialogue and the passing scene is imagined by the spectators. Italianate theater architecture, adopted first in the Buen Retiro theater and then, during the eighteenth century, in public theaters such as the Teatro del Príncipe, introduced the proscenium arch. When the curtain rose or was opened, the spectator saw a picture.

We find evidence of this changed vision in stage directions. The *acotaciones* (stage directions) in Golden Age plays, if they are found at all, are brief and usually deal with the entrance or exit of actors. By contrast, Ramón de la Cruz (1731-94) revolutionized stage directions in such *sainetes* (one-act farces) as *La Pradera de San Isidro* (The Meadows of San Isidro). The first scene of the

---

[16] Antonio Palomino de Castro y Velasco, *El museo pictórico y escala óptica: Tomo I, Theórica de la pintura* [...]; *Tomo Segundo, Práctica de la pintura* [...]; *Tomo Tercero, El Parnaso español pintoresco laureado* [...], 3 vols. in 2, (Madrid: de Bedmar, 1715-24). The definition is contained in the "Indice de términos," vol. I, after p. 306. Palomino calls the word an adjective although he uses *cosa* in the Spanish definition. The prologue of vol. II is without pagination.

play takes place in a *salón corto*, that is, a space just behind the main curtain, that represents, in this case, a room in a private house. When the actors exit, another curtain opens upon the hermitage of San Isidro. Goya did two paintings of San Isidro on the saint's feast day, May 15 in 1788. In the one the viewer has his back to the Manzanares River and looks toward the hermitage. In the other his back is toward the hermitage and he faces the scene on the banks of the river with Madrid in the distance.[17] Cruz imagines the spectator facing the hermitage but at a distance so that his eyes encompass elements of both the Goya scenes. He uses 375 words to describe what he expects the stage designer and the actors to lay before the eyes of the audience.

This minutely described scene is eminently picturesque: two couples are picnicking with their burro and their baby; other couples are dancing; one man is making a picnic salad while another is ogling the girls.[18] The backdrop gives a distant perspective. These instructions are intended for the director, the scene designer, and the actors; the picturesque results are to be communicated visually to the audience. We find nothing like this in the Spanish theater before the time of Cruz. By the 1830s, however, the picturesque had become a common mode of expression in the Spanish theater.

The Duke of Rivas's *Don Alvaro, o La fuerza del sino* (Don Alvaro, or The Power of Fate, 1834), which illustrates many aspects of Spanish Romanticism, is also exemplary in this respect. Rivas was a painter, and for each of the settings of the play he describes a picturesque scene. *Jornada Primera* (First Episode, i.e., Act I) begins with these directions for a setting on the banks of the Guadalquivir River in Seville:

> El teatro representa la entrada del antiguo puente de barcas de Triana, el que estará practicable a la derecha. En primer término, al mismo lado, un aguaducho o barraca de tablas y lonas, con un letrero que diga: AGUA DE TOMARES. Dentro habrá un mostrador rústico con cuatro grandes cántaros, macetas de flores, vasos, un anafre con una cafetera de hoja de lata y una bandeja con azucarillos. Delante del aguaducho habrá bancos de pino. Al fondo se descubrirá de lejos parte del arrabal de Triana, la huerta de los Remedios con sus altos cipreses, el río y varios barcos en él, con flámulas y gallardetes. A la izquierda se verá en lontananza la Alameda. Varios habitantes de Sevilla cruzarán en todas direcciones durante la escena. El cielo demostrará el ponerse el sol en una tarde de julio, y al descorrerse el telón aparecerán: el TIO PACO detrás del mostrador en mangas de camisa; el OFICIAL, bebiendo un vaso de agua y de pie; PRECIOSILLA, a su lado templando una guitarra; el MAJO y los DOS HABITANTES DE SEVILLA sentados en los bancos.[19]

> (The scene shows the entrance to the old pontoon bridge to Triana, which leads offstage to the right. In the foreground, on the same side, a refreshment stand or booth made of boards and canvas with a sign that reads: TOMARES WATER. Inside the stand there is a rustic counter with four large pitchers, several flower pots, glasses, a burner with a tin coffee pot, and a tray with sugar wafers. In front of the stand there are pine benches. In the distant background, can be seen part of the Triana district,

---

[17] Francisco de Goya, *La ermita de San Isidro el día de la fiesta* (Prado no. 2783); and *La Pradera de San Isidro* (Prado no. 750). Reproductions: Richard Schickel, *The World of Goya: 1746-1828* (New York: Time-Life Books, [1968]), pp. 17-19; José Gudiol, *Goya, 1746-1828: Biography, Analytical Study and Catalogue of His Paintings* (Barcelona: Ediciones Polígrafa, 1971), I, Nos. 252 and 253, p. 262, II, figs. 357-61; Pierre Gassier and Juliet Wilson, *The Life and Complete Work of Francisco Goya*, 2nd ed. (New York: Harrison House, 1981), Nos. 272, 273, pp. 66-67, 98.

[18] Ramón de la Cruz, *Sainetes de Don Ramón de la Cruz en su mayoría inéditas*, ed. Emilio Cotarelo y Mori, Nueva Biblioteca de Autores Españoles, 23 (Madrid: Bailly-Balliere, 1915), I, 313.

[19] Ángel de Saavedra, Duque de Rivas, *Don Alvaro, o La fuerza del sino*, in Lewis E. Brett, ed., *Nineteenth Century Spanish Plays* (New York: Appleton-Century Company, 1935), Act I, Sc. 1, pp. 61-62. Russell P. Sebold, "Introducción" to Tomás de Iriarte, *El señorito mimado. La señorita malcriada* (Madrid: Clásicos Castalia, 1978), pp. 72-73, notes the similarity between the opening *cuadro* of the second play (produced 1791) and that of *Don Alvaro*.

the Remedios gardens with tall cypresses, the river, and in it several barks with pennants and streamers. On the left can be seen the Alameda in the distance. Several inhabitants of Seville are crossing in all directions during the scene. The sky depicts a sunset on a July afternoon, and as the curtain parts we see: UNCLE PACO *in shirtsleeves behind the counter; an* OFFICER, *standing at the counter and drinking a glass of water; beside him [the gypsy]* PRECIOSILLA *tuning a guitar; the* YOUNG BUCK *and* TWO INHABITANTS OF SEVILLE *seated on benches.)*

Each setting in the play has similar picturesque qualities. Notable is the one at the beginning of the fifth act. The *acotación* itself is brief:

El teatro representa lo interior del claustro bajo del convento de los Angeles, que debe ser una galería mezquina, alrededor de un patiecillo con naranjos, adelfas y jazmines. A la izquierda se verá la portería; a la derecha la escalera [...].[20]

(The scene shows the interior of the lower cloister of Los Angeles convent, which should be a miserable gallery surrounding a small courtyard with orange trees, oleanders, and jasmine. At the left is the porter's lodge; on the right is the stairway [...].)

As Father Melitón distributes soup to the beggars, we witness the picturesque in action. The scene seems to animate Leonardo Alenza's painting *La sopa boba* (Sponger's Soup);[21] or, more probably, the painting illustrates Rivas's scene:

HERMANO MELITON	Vamos, silencio y orden, que no están en ningún figón.
MUJER	Padre, ¡a mí, a mí!
VIEJO	¿Cuántas raciones quiere Marica?
COJO	Ya le han dado tres, y no es regular ...
HERMANO MELITON	Callen, y sean humildes, que me duele la cabeza.
MANCO	Marica ha tomado tres raciones.
MUJER	Y aun voy a tomar cuatro, que tengo seis chiquillos.
HERMANO MELITON	¿Y por qué tienes seis chiquillos? ... Sea su alma.
MUJER	Porque me los ha dado Dios.
HERMANO MELITON	Sí ... Dios ... Dios ... No los tendría si se pasara las noches, como yo, rezando el rosario, o dándose disciplina.
PADRE GUARDIAN (*Con gravedad.*)	¡Hermano Melitón! ... ¡Hermano Melitón! ... ¡Válgame Dios!
HERMANO MELITON	Padre nuestro, si estos desarrapados tienen una fecundidad que asombra.[22]

(BROTHER MELITON	Come on, be quiet, and get in line. You're not eating in a tavern.
WOMAN	Father, gimme some, gimme some.
OLD MAN	How many servings does Mary want?
LAME MAN	They've given her three already, and it's not right.
BROTHER MELITON	Be quiet and show some humility, because I have a headache.
MAIMED MAN	Mary's got three servings.
WOMAN	And I'm going to get four more, because I have six kids.

---

[20] Rivas, V.i, p. 109.

[21] Leonardo Alenza (1807-45), *La sopa boba* (also called *La sopa del convento*), Museo Lázaro Galdeano, Madrid. Reproductions: *Historia del arte español*, vol. 48: *La pintura española del siglo XIX* (Madrid: Hiares Editorial, n.d.), pp. 7-8, slide no. 10; *Historia de la pintura*, vol. 10: Víctor Nieto Alcaide, *Romanticismo y realismo* (Madrid: Editorial Magisterio Español, 1973), p. 17, slide no. 37.

[22] Rivas, V.i, p. 109.

BROTHER MELITON   And why do you have six kids? Bless your soul.
WOMAN   Because God gave them to me.
BROTHER MELITON   Yes. God .... God ... You wouldn't have them if you spent your nights the
   way I do, praying with your rosary or castigating yourself.
FATHER WARDEN (*Circumspectly.*) Brother Melitón! Brother Melitón! For Heaven's sake!
BROTHER MELITON   Father, these ragged beggars are astonishingly prolific.)

The Duke of Rivas's scene could be a *cuadro de costumbres*. Changed to a prose description
with dialogue and with a black and white version of Alenza's painting, it could have appeared in the
pages of Mesonero Romanos's *Semanario Pintoresco Español*. Indeed, in the *Semanario* we find
illustrations of the Romantic theater that remind us forcefully that they are pictures of pictures, for
the scene is shown within the proscenium arch. Many of these illustrations are of historical plays.
The pages of the *Semanario* and the galleries of nineteenth-century paintings suggest a symbiosis
between historical drama and historical painting. The final scene of Hartzenbusch's *Los amantes de
Teruel* (1837) could have inspired Antonio Muñoz Degrain's painting of the same scene (1884); or,
put another way, the painting could illustrate the last scene of the play.[23]

The great Romantic dramas of Spain were produced in a period of fifteen years between the
première of Francisco Martínez de la Rosa's *La conjuración de Venecia* in 1834 and the performance of José Zorrilla's *Traidor, inconfeso y mártir* (Traitor Unshriven and Martyred) in 1849.
Some have enjoyed a vigorous life up to our own day on the stages of the Hispanic world. The most
notable is Zorrilla's *Don Juan Tenorio*. Yet the rest of the Ibero-American world did not enjoy such
a degree of creativity as did Madrid. The norm elsewhere was comedy. In Brazil, for example, the
comedies of Martins Pena (1815-48) were the usual stuff, while Gonçalves de Magalhães's tragedy
Antônio José (1838) was the anomaly. In Portugal a notable exception to the usual comic fare was
Almeida-Garrett's *Um auto de Gil Vicente* (1838).

For the sake of illustration, I wish to pursue briefly my theme of the picturesque in a single
comedy by an admirer of Moratín, the Mexican-born Manuel Eduardo de Gorostiza. *Contigo pan y
cebolla* (Bread and Onions with You) was produced in both Madrid and in Mexico City in 1833,
and for a hundred years it was one of the most popular comedies for amateur performance in the
Spanish-speaking world. In this spoof of the Romantic pose, Matilde de Lara has read *Paul et Vir-
ginie, Atala*, and so many other Romantic novels that she expects life to imitate art. The bourgeois
setting – as befits the theme – has one picturesque element, itself a painting. Hanging on the wall of
the middle-class parlor is a reproduction of *The Burial of Atala* (1808) by the French painter Anne-
Louis Girodet de Roucy-Trioson (1767-1824).[24] Before Matilde elopes with her sweetheart – her
father, by the way, is delighted with the match – she kneels devoutly before the picturesque painting
as if it were a family altar dedicated to the Virgin Mary.

The picturesque mode of the brief Romantic period left its mark on dramatic structure for many
years thereafter. Let me return to the *sainetes* of Ramón de la Cruz. The typical *sainete* has a structure that is based on two *cuadros*, although Cruz did not use the term. For example, in *La Pradera
de San Isidro*, the first *cuadro* is a room, a restricted area; then the second *cuadro* opens a larger

---

[23] Antonio Muñoz Degrain (1841-1924), *Los amantes de Teruel*, Museo del Prado, Colección de Arte del Siglo XIX.
Reproduction: *Literatura española en imágenes*, vol. 21: Leonardo Romero, *Prosa y teatro románticos* (Madrid: Editorial La
Muralla, 1973), pp. 28-29, slide no. 40.
[24] Reproduction in Marcel Brion, *Art of the Romantic Era* (New York: Praeger, [1966]), p. 137.

vista to our eyes: the hermitage and the vast meadow in front of it. The pattern may be reversed in another *sainete* such as in *La presumida burlada* (The Vain Woman Outwitted).[25] The first *cuadro* is a street in Madrid while the second is a room in a private home. The effect may be likened to the use of a zoom lens on a camera.

Between the time of Ramón de la Cruz and the Romantic period, the neoclassic mode established unity of place as a norm. *Don Alvaro*, with its fifteen changes of setting, broke the pattern. Rivas divided his play into *jornadas* – he could as well have called them *actos* – and *escenas*. These divisions correspond respectively to the action (or plot elements) and to the entrances and exits of characters. The fifteen changes of setting correspond to what, later in the century, became known as *cuadros*. *Jornada Primera* has two *cuadros*, each consisting of four scenes. Rivas follows Cruz's pattern of moving from the panorama – the scene on the bank of the Guadalquivir River – to the closed space, the bedroom of Doña Leonor. *Jornada Segunda* also has two *cuadros*, the first consisting of two and the second of six scenes. Here, Rivas follows the other Cruz pattern: he moves from the closed space – a room in the tavern at Hornachuelos – to the panoramic scene in front of the Convento de los Angeles. With *Jornada Tercera* the pace of setting change becomes vertiginous as does the plot. There are four *cuadros* made up of nine scenes. *Jornada Cuarta* has three *cuadros* with seven scenes; and *Jornada Quinta* has four *cuadros* with eleven scenes.

Although Rivas did not use the word *cuadro*, he clearly had it in mind as a way of dividing up drama. This method becomes strikingly evident in the nineteenth-century *zarzuela*, or operetta. We may take as typical Ricardo de la Vega's *De Getafe al paraíso* (From Getafe to Paradise, 1883).[26] It is divided into two acts whose function is related to the plot. The total *zarzuela* is divided into five *cuadros*, two in Act I and three in Act II; and they correspond to five changes of setting. A *cuadro* is divided into several scenes according to the coming and going of the characters. Each of Vega's *cuadros* has its own title whereas in *Don Alvaro* the titles corresponded to the *jornadas*. In short, the picturesque mode has become an integral part of the dramatic structure.

The development is reflected in Academy dictionaries. That of 1837 has two definitions of *cuadro* (p. 215) that are important for my purpose: 1) "Cualquier lienzo, lámina o cosa semejante de pintura" (Any canvas, picture, or object similar to a painting); and 2) "El marco solo, sea de pintura, ventana u otra cualquiera cosa" (The frame alone, whether of a painting, window, or any other thing). Recent editions (e.g., 20th, 1984, I, 402) give a definition (p. 384) which is clearly the result of a process that began with Ramón de la Cruz and was developed by the Duke of Rivas and his nineteenth-century followers:

> Cada una de las partes en que se dividen los actos de ciertos poemas dramáticos modernos, las cuales son a manera de actos breves. Cada una de estas partes pide cambio de escena, que en la representación teatral suele hacerse a vista del público, o bajando por un instante el telón de boca, para que de una a otra no haya intervalo.

> (Each one of the parts into which the acts of certain modern dramatic scripts are divided, which are similar to brief acts. Each one of these parts requires a change of scenery, which during the theatrical performance is normally done in full view of the audience, or else by lowering briefly the main curtain, so that there is no interval between one part and the other.)

[25] Cruz, I, 487-93.
[26] Ricardo de la Vega, *De Getafe al paraíso, o La familia del tío Maroma*, in *El género chico (Antología de textos completos)*, ed. Antonio Valencia (Madrid: Taurus, 1962), pp. 49-98. The music is by Francisco Asenjo Barbieri. The première was at the Teatro Variedades, January 2, 1883.

If we look at the continuum of Hispanic theater from the eighteenth century to our own time, the direct line appears to be from the neoclassic comedy of Moratín through his followers such as Gorostiza, the individualistic Bretón de los Herreros, the expert and facile Ventura de la Vega, and then to the so-called *alta comedia* with its elevated moral tone and un-comic plots. Romantic drama thus appears as a detour from the main line of development in the Hispanic theater. Yet in large measure because of this short-lived movement, Spanish Romantic drama attained by way of the opera an international dimension such as Hispanic drama has seldom enjoyed, and it was a primary influence on the *zarzuela* that flourished from the mid-nineteenth century through the 1920s. I believe that the picturesque qualities of Romantic drama gave it the strength to exert this widespread influence.

I do not suppose, of course, that the picturesque is the unique mode of nineteenth-century Spanish Romantic drama. William Gilpin in an introductory letter to his essay *On Picturesque Beauty* wrote to William Lock in 1792: "I think, my dear sir, we picturesque people are a little misunderstood with regard to our *general intention*. I have several times been surprised at finding us represented as supposing *all beauty* to consist in *picturesque beauty* – and the face of nature to be examined *only by the rules of painting*." He goes on to assert: "We everywhere make a distinction between scenes that are *beautiful* and *amusing*, and scenes that are *picturesque*. We examine and admire both."[27]

Spanish Romantics envisioned the world of their imagination as if through the proscenium arch of a theater or as if it were painted on great canvases. The picturesque mode is but one approach that we may take toward an appreciation of the art of the Romantics. In Spain, it has the advantage of integrating the parallel currents of Romanticism and *costumbrismo*.

Three of the greatest Spanish Romantic plays provided libretti for operas. Verdi's librettists created *La forza del destino* from Rivas's *Don Alvaro*, and *Il trovatore* and *Simone Boccanegra* from plays by García Gutiérrez. The lyric qualities of these plays were important for their adaptation for opera. But opera is the genre that encompasses all the arts, and therefore, *a fortiori*, also the visual arts. The picturesque qualities that Rivas and García Gutiérrez wrote into their texts and their stage directions appealed to an age when scenic design rivaled the other arts in the creation of a total aesthetic experience for the theater.

---

[27] Gilpin, pp. i-ii.

Harold B. Segel

POLISH ROMANTIC DRAMA IN PERSPECTIVE

Polish Romantic drama occupies what those who study it believe to be a unique place in the history of the European Romantic movement. Once properly understood, this uniqueness may in turn enhance the credibility of the claim that the Polish may in fact be the most vital of the European Romantic theatrical traditions. If the claim is advanced as a matter of course by specialists in Polish literature who have a firsthand knowledge of the material, it must undoubtedly raise eyebrows among those who have little or no knowledge of Polish Romantic drama or the circumstances in which it arose. While regrettable, such scepticism is understandable, even on the part of Western comparatists who only rarely take the trouble to include anything East European in their field of vision. The Polish language is not widely studied in the West, Polish history and culture – despite the interest stimulated by the political events of the 1980s and early 1990s – are little known and only a few of the plays of the Polish Romantics have been translated into Western languages.[1] Compounding the problem of access is the fact that almost all the important Polish Romantic drama was written in verse, in Polish meters for which Western prosodic equivalents are hard to find. Without the participation of poets in the translation process, the inevitable results are philologically accurate but usually flat prose translations in which only meaning is conveyed or verse versions which either violate both the form and the content of the original or fail the crucial test or readability in the target language.

In the face of such obstacles, the inattention to Polish Romantic drama in the West is pardonable. Sad to say, however, until good translations become available or Western comparatists make the effort to break out of the parochial confines within which Western comparative literary scholarship usually labors, the situation will remain the same. The crucial, and at the same time problematic, role of the comparatist in extending the frontiers of knowledge and shaping attitudes is exemplified by two relatively recent comparative studies of European Romanticism in which East European phenomena for a change are not ignored. H.G. Schenk's well-known *The Mind of the European Romantics*, published in 1966 and reissued as a paperback in 1979, does make an effort, albeit in a very limited way, to include Polish developments in a thematic analysis of the characteristic features of European Romanticism. In a short chapter on "National Messianism" (pp. 187-94), Schenk strikes an apologetic note at the outset when he declares that "Polish Romanticism has hitherto hardly been touched upon in this study."[2] But he is then quick to assert that Polish developments may have sufficient merit or uniqueness to warrant their inclusion in any comparative study.

---

[1] For the only collection of Polish Romantic plays currently available in English, see Harold B. Segel, trans. and ed., *Polish Romantic Drama* (Ithaca and London: Cornell Univ. Press, 1977).
[2] H.G. Schenk, *The Mind of the European Romantics* (1966; rpt. Oxford, New York: Oxford Univ. Press, 1979), p. 187.

"Yet it is undeniable that Poland contributed more than its share to the European Romantic symposium."[3] The significant Polish contribution, from Schenk's point of view, came in the area of national messianism which he identifies as a "highly questionable but peculiarly Romantic concept."[4] Schenk's focus is almost entirely on the greatest of Polish Romantics, Adam Mickiewicz (1798-1855). While his treatment of the very complex issue of Polish Romantic messianism, as embodied above all in Mickiewicz's career, suffers from superficiality, his willingness to use Polish material to examine a facet of Romanticism particularly well developed in the Polish tradition and especially in the drama is much to his credit. The same can be said for his remarks about one of the most important (and accessible) Polish Romantic plays. *Nieboska komedia* (The Undivine Comedy, 1834) by Count Zygmunt Krasiński (1812-59), in his chapter "Forebodings and Nostalgia for the Past." Again, as in the case of national messianism, Polish phenomena are introduced as examples of extremism – messianic national self-congratulation in one case, apocalyptic apprehension about social and political upheaval in the other. But however minimal or distorted the treatment, the very inclusion of the Polish as something of more than marginal possible relevance advances the cause of comparative scholarship.

The distortion and imbalance that can arise from a comparatist's reliance on quantative translation availability and secondary literature in his native language are manifest in Charles Dédéyan's survey *Le Drame romantique en Europe* (1982). By way of broadening coverage of the development of Romantic drama in Europe so that it will not be confined only to Western Europe, Dédéyan adds an entire chapter on Russia to those on France, England, Germany, Italy, and Spain and includes Russian material in most of his thematic chapters ("Situation de la tragédie, décadence en renouveau," "Shakespeare sur le Continent," "La Tragédie et la Drame préromantique," "Les Théoriciens du drame romantique," and "Le Théâtre tragique et romantique de tendance sur le Continent"). By completely ignoring Poland in his survey and implying the existence of a Russian Romantic drama of sufficient weight to warrant inclusion in a broad comparative survey, Dédéyan does the field no small injustice. Important and illuminating Polish developments are totally overlooked while a much weaker Russian Romantic drama is given a representation out of proportion to its actual achievements and to its status relative to both the West European and the Polish.[5] Dédéyan's complete reliance on abundant French translations and French-language scholarship for his chapter on Russia strengthens the argument advanced earlier that good will and occasional articles are no substitute for more translations – despite the difficulties – if Polish drama is ever to be acknowledged as among the more interesting and even unusual in Europe during the Romantic period.

One of the very first problems that arises in any study of Polish Romantic drama also has to do with terminology. We speak of Polish Romantic drama and not of Polish Romantic theater, for example, because the plays subsumed under the rubric of Polish Romantic drama were not written with foreseeable theatrical production in mind, a fate they shared, for different reasons, with plays by Alfred de Musset and Georg Büchner. We also cannot speak of the Romantic drama of *Poland*, since the partitions of the late eighteenth century ended the existence of an independent Polish state until 1919 and Romantic drama written in the Polish language was almost wholly the creation of political émigrés most of whom had settled in France.

---

[3] Schenk, p. 187.
[4] Schenk, p. 187.
[5] Charles Dédéyan, *Le Drame romantique en Europe* (Paris: Société d'Édition d'Enseignement Supérieur, 1982), pp. 321-47 ("Le Drame romantique en Russie").

Just as an alternate Poland began to emerge within communist Poland in 1980-81 in the form of the workers' movement known as Solidarity, so too did an alternate Poland arise in the emigration which followed the suppression of the first major attempt by the Poles to regain their independence by force of arms in the nineteenth century, the November Insurrection of 1830. The "Great Emigration" as it is known in Polish historiography derived its greatness from the large number of people who flocked westward in the wake of the collapse of the Insurrection and from the presence in the ranks of the émigrés of such luminaries of Polish culture as the historian Joachim Lelewel (1786-1861) and the poets Adam Mickiewicz, Juliusz Słowacki (1809-49), and Cyprian Kamil Norwid (1821-83). And if Count Zygmunt Krasiński as the son of a Polish general who remained loyal to the Russian Tsar had no need to relocate in the West after the debacle of 1830-31, he identified with the Great Emigration spiritually and chose to publish his most important works there anonymously.

The émigrés created in effect a new Poland in the West after the Insurrection. Since most were concentrated in France, Paris became a Polish capital as well and the logical center of Polish émigré publication, a role it was to assume again after World War II. Although other centers of Polish emigration arose in London, Geneva, Rome and Constantinople, Paris was by far the most vital politically and culturally. As strange as it may seem at first, France was almost as much the home of Polish Romanticism as it was of the French. When a professorship of Slavic literatures was established at the Collège de France in 1840 – in part the result of the impact of the Polish emigration on the French consciousness – the poet Mickiewicz was the first appointee. His lectures there from 1840 to 1844 brought out many of the leading lights of French culture and society, among them an enthralled George Sand, who may have been the first Western admirer of Polish Romantic drama, and Lamennais, whose *Paroles d'un croyant* (1834) has long been thought to bear the influence of Mickiewicz's *Books of the Polish Nation and Pilgrimage* (1832).

If the Polish émigrés were able to maintain publishing offices, found a library (still in existence), and open schools, their priorities denied resources, however, to any significant theatrical enterprise. This should not be too surprising in view of the history of failed émigré foreign-language theaters in general. That this situation did not in and of itself discourage the writing of drama among the émigré poets offers some evidence, I believe, of the strength of the dramatic impulse among Romantic writers who were above all poets and for whom the cultivation of dramatic form could exist independent of performance. Yet the fact remains that a significant body of Polish Romantic drama did arise in conditions of emigration inhospitable to theatrical production; indeed it had to wait until the early twentieth century for stage mounting to be undertaken.

The parallel here with Georg Büchner's fate in the theater is inescapable. Like almost all Polish Romantic drama, *Dantons Tod* and *Woyzeck* began their theatrical history only in this century. But there are also other parallels with Büchner. The very structure of the major plays – *Dantons Tod* in the case of Büchner, Mickiewicz's *Dziady, Część trzecia* (Forefathers, Part III, 1832), Słowacki's *Kordian* (1834), and Krasiński's *The Undivine Comedy* among the Poles – as well as the absence of a nineteenth-century staging tradition resulted in a variety of technically and ideologically interpretive productions of considerable influence on both dramatic and theatrical developments in Germany and Poland, respectively.

While considering parallels, however interesting, we also have to take note of differences. Büchner's subversion of history, his treatment of revolution, his vision of man, and the idiosyncrasies of his play structure, especially in *Dantons Tod*, precluded the possibility of stage production in Büchner's own age and throughout the nineteenth century. However there were theaters, in the physical sense, in which Büchner's works could have been performed had society and the theatrical establishment been less inimicable. But no such theaters existed for the Poles. The Great Emigration in the West lacked them while in partitioned Poland, where theaters of course existed, a stern censorship regarded most émigré publications as suspect and in any case would hardly have approved for production plays that indicted the Russians of a campaign of cultural genocide against the Poles (Mickiewicz's *Forefathers*), depicted a conspiracy to assassinate the Tsar (Słowacki's *Kordian*), or portrayed a successful popular revolution against the established order, even if that revolution yields to a vision of Christ triumphant (Krasiński's *The Undivine Comedy*).

Another distinction must also be kept in mind. Büchner, like Musset in France, was the odd man out among his fellow dramatists and the theatrical neglect of him until the twentieth century was certainly not characteristic of German Romantic drama as a whole. In the case of the Poles, on the other hand, virtually the entire corpus of Romantic plays reached the stage only in the twentieth century.

Once the plays of the Polish Romantics began appearing on stage, in large measure because of shifts in the winds of art and politics, then the process of adaptation to the demands of scenic realization was initiated, as in the case of Büchner. The problems, and results, in both instances were similar. With Mickiewicz's *Forefathers* – actually a four-part drama written in two very different stages in the poet's life (1822-23, 1832) – the key question demanding resolution was whether to attempt to combine into a single performance the first three essentially undramatic parts, one of which exists only in fragmentary form, and the far more significant and innovative Part III, as the last part came to be called, or to reduce the first three parts to a theatrical prefix to Part III, or to forget about the first three parts entirely. Staging *Forefathers, Part III* by itself also posed certain challenges particularly with the respect to the play's alternation of dramatic dialogue and long narrative passages, the concluding "Digression" which consists of yet another half dozen narrative poems, and a soliloquized mystical transport (the "Great Improvisation") extremely demanding of an actor's skill.

Słowcki's *Kordian*, on one level a polemic with the ideology of Polish messianism as elaborated in Mickiewicz's *Forefathers*, provided no less a challenge. How were the play's supernatural elements, large cast of characters, and lengthy monologues to be handled? And what about the stage direction calling at one point for 10,000 devils to descend onto the stage? With some of Słowacki's later plays as, for example, *Fantazy* (ca. 1843), a putdown of sham Romantic posturing written in a period of mystic involvement when the poet was strongly interested in Calderón, there were textual questions to be settled since the play was discovered posthumously in not quite finished form.

Krasiński's remarkably precocious dramatic inquiry into the dynamics of history and revolution, *The Undivine Comedy*, must surely rank among the most difficult of Romantic dramas to bring to the stage, as much for the introductions to the four parts into which the play is divided and which seem clearly intended for narration or reading, as for its supernatural elements, anti-Semitism (crypto-Jews seek world domination by supporting revolutions), and poetic prose style. And as for Cyprian Kamil Norwid, whose late Romantic plays began appearing on Polish stages only after World War II, there are problems of scenic translation yet to be addressed.

Despite similarities with the theatrical history and reception of Büchner's plays in Germany, certain factors set Polish Romantic drama apart from the rest of the European, including the Russian.

The first distinguishing feature of the Polish tradition has already been mentioned, namely the creation of the Romantic drama within the context of a mass political emigration. Furthermore, the overwhelming majority of Polish Romantic plays in one way or another, directly or obliquely, develop their thematics out of the experience of emigration and the failed insurrection from which it ushered. Whatever their apparent subjects which in their national self-concern are easily mistaken for parochial, the plays use the calamities of late eighteenth- and early nineteenth-century Poland as a springboard for inquiry into universal questions of liberty, human dignity, the morality of political power, the responsibilities of leadership, the existence of God, the dynamics of revolution, the role of the artist (the poet) in society, and the meaning of history. Born of insurrection, the plays seethe with the spirit of revolt both secular and metaphysical, in content and form, and in this respect represent the most stunning embodiment of the revolutionary ethos of the entire European Romantic movement.

The second major distinguishing feature of the Polish Romantic drama is that none of it was professionally performed before the late nineteenth and early twentieth centuries. When production began to be undertaken, on the initiative above all of the turn-of-the-century poet and dramatist Stanisław Wyspiański's version of Mickiewicz's *Forefathers* in Cracow on October 31, 1901, staging the drama of the Romantic émigré tradition soon acquired the status of the litmus test that confirmed the genius of a director, stage designer, or actor. It has remained that way to the very present with each new theatrical generation exploring its own interpretations and conceptualizations.

What began with Wyspiański has been continued by the leading figures of the twentieth-century Polish theater: Leon Schiller (1887-1954), whose production of *Forefathers* in Lwów in 1932 as a great national mystery play can be compared in impact to the Reinhardt staging of *Dantons Tod* at the Deutsches Theater in December 1916; Juliusz Osterwa (1885-1947), a co-founder of the Warsaw Reduta Theater; Aleksander Bardini, who directed the first post-World War II production of *Forefathers* in 1955; Erwin Axer, who reintroduced Słowacki's *Kordian* at the National Theater in Warsaw in 1956; Kazimierz Dejmek, whose production of *Forefathers* at the National Theater in late 1967 touched off demonstrations of an underlying political nature resulting in the banning of the play in January 1968; and such more recent and highly individualistic interpreters of the Romantic drama on the Polish stage as the late director of the Old Theater (Stary Teatr) in Cracow, Konrad Swinarski (who incidentally directed a highly acclaimed production of *Woyzeck* in Cologne in 1967), Jerzy Grotowski, whose early production of Słowacki's very personal version of Calderón's *El príncipe constante* served as one of the most effective vehicles of his ideas on acting eventually set forth in his book *The Poor Theater*, and Adam Hanuszkiewicz, whose modernized production of Słowacki's fairy-tale-like *Balladyna* created a sensation at the National Theater in 1975 and who in February 1976 introduced a theatrical triptych of his own conception based on the life of Mickiewicz but incorporating yet a new version of *Forefathers* as its central part.

In the absence of a classical Polish dramatic tradition before the Romantic era, in the absence, that is, of anything even remotely resembling the tradition of Shakespeare in England, Molière, Corneille, and Racine in France, Lope de Vega and Calderón in Spain, or Goethe and Schiller in Germany, the Romantic drama has in fact become the classical Polish dramatic tradition. Moreover, the circumstances in which it arose and finally reached the stage have only served to strengthen the association. Here, of course, the Büchner analogy breaks down completely, and the temptation to seek out a parallel in Russia is similarly doomed. The Romantic achievement in Russian drama is less

impressive than that of Poland, to say nothing of Germany. Leaving aside for the moment the greatness of Gogol's comic gifts and the matter of how Gogol relates to Romanticism, Russian Romantic
drama consists in the main of a handful of plays: Pushkin's co-called little tragedies (*The Stone
Guest, Mozart and Salieri, The Covetous Knight*) and the imperfect neo-Shakespearean *Boris Godunov*, Lermontov's highly melodramatic *Masquerade*, Küchelbecker's three-part Byronic verse
drama *Izhorsky*, and, only in part, Griboedov's excellent comedy *Woe from Wit*. Like other European Romantic plays, especially costume dramas – Hugo's *Hernani, Le Roi s'amuse*, and *Lucrèce
Borgia* – *Boris Godunov* has survived primarily as opera. No highly innovative, avant-garde, self-
regenerating twentieth-century tradition of Romantic play production – apart from Vsevold Meyerhold's acclaimed stagings of *Woe from Wit* and *Masquerade* in the late teens and twenties – has
developed in Russia comparable either to the German or to the Polish.

The last important factor setting Polish Romantic drama apart from the rest of the European is
the political. When the Great Emigration took shape in the West following the defeat of the Insurrection of 1830, hopes ran high that a return to a liberated Poland would be possible in the lifetime
of the Emigration. The subsequent failure of émigré political initiatives as well as the spreading
fragmentation of the community as a whole created an environment favorable to the assumption by
poets of a type of spiritual leadership. Circumstances were ripe, in other words, for the realization of
impulses inherent in the Romantic ethos: the view of the hero as the shaper of history, in a Carly-
lean sense, the belief in the privileged endowment of the poet, and the vatic imperative among poets
needing for fulfillment only the proper concatenation of events. The collapse of the November
Insurrection, the settlement of thousands of émigrés in the West, and the breakdown of a cohesive
political program prepared among the Poles just such a fertile field for Romantic aspirations.

Poets hastened to fill the vacuum left by a bankrupt political leadership and soon elaborated a
unique, to a certain extent self-congratulatory, and perhaps also aberrant émigré ideology according
to which – reduced to its simplest terms – Poland was a messiah nation martyred through the partitions and the defeat of the November Insurrection for the holy purpose of leading a lapsed Europe
back to the path of Christian virtue. The Emigration was, therefore, the vanguard of the great Polish
Christian nation transplanted in the West the better to realize its divine destinity. Polish émigré
literature, but above all Polish émigré drama, became the principal expression of this outlook, an
outlook developed into an ideology and even into a mystic philosophy.

Its principal exponent in the drama was Mickiewicz whose *Forefathers, Part III* demands consideration as one of the unique achievements of European Romantic drama. Inspired by the medieval mystery play and the Romantic enthusiasm for the folk rather than by classical Greek tragedy
or Shakespeare, as Romantics elsewhere, Mickiewicz interwove folkore, recent Polish history, and
the supernatural to create a modern mystery play on the theme of Poland's martyrdom and eventual
resurrection. Modern readers (or viewers, as the case may be) may find the subject difficult to relate
to in its intense preoccupation with Polish destiny, but George Sand was able to grasp its universal
character when she declared in 1839 that since the days of the Old Testament Prophets nobody had
presented with such dramatic impact an event of such significance as the downfall of a nation.[6]

Those familiar with Polish history know the antecedents to the messianism of Polish émigré
Romanticism which was elaborated with such conviction by Mickiewicz, Krasiński (more in his

---

[6] George Sand, "Essai sur le drame fantastique," *Revue des Deux Mondes* (December 1, 1839), p. 627. Sand's essay,
dealing with Goethe, Byron, and Mickiewicz, treats of *Forefathers, Part III* on pp. 625-45, under the title of "Konrad," and
includes lengthy quotes from the play in French translation.

poetry than in his plays), the philosophers Józef Hoene-Wroński (1776-1853), Bronisław Trentow-ski (1808-69), and August Cieszkowski (1814-94), and the mystagogue Andrzej Towiański (1799-1878) who for a time was a decidedly influential force in the Great Emigration, especially among its poets.[7] The important Polish contribution to the defeat of the Turks during the siege of Vienna in 1683 (the tricentennial of which was celebrated with much fanfare in Poland and Austria in 1983) was regarded by Poles as a fulfillment of their nation's messianic destiny to save European Chris-tendom from the infidel hordes which threatened it in the sixteenth and seventeenth centuries. Furthermore, pride in the "golden freedom" of the Polish nobility, which had effectively trans-formed the Polish Commonwealth of the sixteenth to eighteenth centuries into a "gentry democ-racy," provided additional underpinnings to the sense of Polish specialness when compared to other European nations and enhanced the idea of messianic investiture.

The messianism of the Polish émigré Romantics clearly relates to an earlier tradition, yet derives from different sources. The psychological trauma of the unprecedented partitions and the accompanying loss of national pride and dignity, followed by the failure of Napoleon to make good his promises to the Poles in return for their aid in his campaigns, above all against Russia, and then finally the suppression of the November Insurrection of 1830 and the Great Emigration created a climate favorable to the growth of an ideology, indeed even philosophy, which could offer comfort-ing explanations of such calamities. Through messianism, the Poles could turn defeat into victory; their losses in the political and military arenas were compensated for by a spiritual triumph which elevated them to the nation equivalent of Jesus Christ. In Europe, and perhaps throughout the Chris-tian world, Poland would fulfill a mission analogous to that of Jesus among men. Martyrdom would achieve redemption and finally salvation and just as in Christian thought Jesus' sacrifice promised universal human salvation, Polish émigré messianism held forth a similar hope for Christian Europe: the sacrifice of Poland would lead inevitably to the redemption of a Christendom that had abandoned Christian principles out of greed and pettiness. The partitions themselves acquired sym-bolic significance as the measure of Christian Europe's fall from grace. If all of this seems like hubris and an extreme act of national self-congratulation, the emergence of messianism as a major current in the post-insurrectionary Great Emigration has to be seen as a response to deep psycholog-ical and emotional needs.

The compatibility of this messianism and the Romantic movement as a whole must also be taken into account. Viewing himself as a supernaturally gifted individual endowed with a vision denied ordinary mortals, the Romantic poet comfortably assumed the mantle of seer. Given the absence of effective political leadership in the Emigration, it was by no means unusual to find poets attempting to fill the gap by offering a spiritual guidance and leadership which in the circumstances of the Emigration seemed more important than the political. The articulation of a messianic ideol-ogy by poets as a way of achieving unity among the émigrés and giving their lives hope and mean-ing was as much a Romantic act as it was anything explainable by reference to the specifics of Polish history and culture.

Much the same can be said of the mystic content of Polish Romantic literature and, in particu-lar, the plays of Mickiewicz (*Forefathers, Part III*) and Słowacki (*Ksiądz Marek*, Father Marek, and *Sen srebrny Salomei*, The Sliver Dream of Salomea, both written in 1843). Enthusiasm for the

---

[7] For an excellent study, in English, of Polish messianism in philosophy and literature, see Andrzej Walicki, *Philos-ophy and Romantic Nationalism: The Case of Poland* (Oxford: Oxford Univ. Press, 1982).

mystic and mystic activity, whether individual or group, flowed naturally from the Romantic *Welt-anschauung* and Romantic occultism. What distinguishes the Polish from related manifestations elsewhere in Europe was the political situation. Among the Poles, mysticism assumed two distinct aspects: 1) it became an integral component of messianic deliverance (to be worthy of their mission and destiny the Poles had to achieve a high level of spiritual and moral self-perfection which encouraged the diffusion of mystic practices), and 2) it served as a method of inquiry into the "meaning" or "meanings" of the Polish calamities of the late eighteenth and early nineteenth centuries.

These remarks about the place of messianic-mystic thought in the development of Polish Romantic writing may create the impression that the great Polish Romantic poets spoke with a single voice. This was anything but the case. The factionalism that opened deep fissures in the émigré community and lent ever greater urgency to the achievement of unity had its parallel in literature as well. Mickiewicz's immense prestige as the *wieszcz* (vates, seer) of Polish Romanticism naturally enhanced the appeal of a messianism ardently advanced by Zygmunt Krasiński, a lesser talent whose affiliation with the Emigration was tenuous anyway, and by respected philosophers (especially Hoene-Wroński) whose writings were clearly not for mass consumption. The apparently spellbinding public appearances of the enigmatic Andrzej Towiański who preached to Polish audiences from the steps of Notre Dame in Paris (before his expulsion from France) also did much to further the movement.

The widespread popular appeal of messianism did not, however, inhibit criticism and the consideration of alternatives at least on the intellectual level. For all his advocacy of the messianic doctrine in his poetry, Krasiński conceptualized a different vision in one of the most outstanding of Polish Romantic dramas, *The Undivine Comedy*. Inspired by the French and Polish uprisings of 1830 as well as possibly by the Russian Decembrist revolt of 1825, Krasiński applied Hegelian thought to social and political transformation in Europe in his own time. But the inevitable collapse of the old order of aristocracy and privilege before the onslaught of revolution and democratic egalitarianism could not result in the triumph of the latter which Krasiński, a devout Catholic, despised for its godless materialism. The final victory had to be Christ's and in the play's final scene the appearance of Jesus in the sky over the battlefield and the dying words of the revolutionary leader, Pankracy, echoing Julian the Apostate's "Galilee, vicisti!" (Galilean, you have conquered) convey the millennial vision of a reunion in the love of Christian brotherhood of all men.

The sharpest rebuke to what may be called mainstream Polish émigré messianism came from Słowacki in his play *Kordian*. The name of the titular hero, an anagram of the Konrad of *Forefathers, Part III*, already hints at a polemical response to Mickiewicz's drama. With his subject the failure of a conspiracy to assassinate the Russian Tsar during a state visit to Warsaw, Słowacki sought to show through the figure of Kordian the failure or Romanticism itself. Kordian's desire to act alone, the vision of the self as avenging angel, the intoxication with gesture and image, and the ultimate collapse of the will collectively represented to Słowacki a Romantic malady which negated the possibility of effective revolutionary action. Thus, the failure of Kordian to carry through the assassination of the Tsar was the failure of the entire Romantic generation of Poland of which the November Insurrection was the quintessential expression. Kordian was thus conceived as a repudiation of Mickiewicz's Promethean avenger who as a poet-mystic alone was empowered to wage battle with God in the name of universal justice. In *Kordian* as well as in his biblical prose poem *Anhelli* (1839) Słowacki argued that the generation of 1830, as a Romantic generation, was as incapable of national deliverance as it was of effecting a successful revolution. Closer in this respect to Krasiński's thinking in *The Undivine Comedy*, Słowacki believed that only within the context of a great upheaval – one not limited jut to the Poles – could any redressing of Poland's plight occur. But unlike Krasiński, Słowacki placed his hopes for a final victory in a new social and political world order rather than in a Second Coming. That Słowacki later fell under the sway of Towiański's mystic "circle," and, indeed, wrote some of his most intriguing later dramas in the period of his deepest involvement in mystic thought alters the picture but slightly. If mysticism seemed for a time a way out of personal and collective frustration, Słowacki remained a member of the "circle" only a relatively short period of time, broke with it decisively, and never significantly assimilated the messianic national self-righteousness of its teaching.

The waning of the Romantic hegemony and of the Great Emigration as a dynamic force in Polish political and cultural life shifted the momentum for change back to partitioned Poland. The immediate catalyst was the disastrous January Insurrection of 1863. Its brutal suppression by the Russians and the tendency within Poland to view the uprising as yet another failure of Romantic delusion accelerated the ascendancy of a Positivist philosophy profoundly inimical to Romantic politics and Romantic literature.

As belief in the efficacy of revolution soured and emphasis came to be placed instead on a preparation for eventual independence by gradualist means, a systematic assault on virtually every aspect and vestige of Romanticism was waged. That is still another reason for the long delay in bringing the plays of the Romantic poets to the stage. The atmosphere in Poland in the 1860s, '70s, and early '80s was far too inhospitable. When the political climate, above all in the Austrian partition, improved in the late nineteenth century and – of no less consequence – changes in literary sensibility also occurred, a fresh perspective on the weighty Romantic legacy became possible perhaps for the first time during the century. No additional stimuli were really needed, but the psychological impact of approaching centenary commemorations, beginning with the Franco-Polish alliance in the time of Napoleon, ought to be taken into account. History had already become too vital a part of the Polish psyche to allow an era as momentous for the Poles as the Romantic to recede to the far reaches of national consciousness.

Responding to perceived affinities with the Romantic movement and able to assess, or reassess, the whole strange episode of the Great Emigration and its literary monuments from the vantage point of the turn of the century, Polish artists of the period made both the Emigration and Romanticism major concerns. In their many works dealing with, or inspired by, Romantic themes (for example, the cycle of plays on the November Insurrection by Stanisław Wyspiański) their assimilation of the Romantic legacy was anything but uncritical. Indeed it could not be otherwise in view of the extent to which the outlook of turn-of-the-century artists had been shaped by Positivism. However, despite the avowed hostility of the Positivists toward Romanticism, the importance of the Romantic heritage was beyond denial for it went to the very heart of national self-perception and purpose. The writers of "Young Poland," as this period in the history of Polish art is called on the model of "Young Germany" or "Young Scandinavia," opened up a dialogue on the Polish past and Polish destiny with their Romantic predecessors which has been kept alive in Polish literature and thought down to the present.

The establishment in World War I of Jósef Piłsudski's "legions" patterned after the "legions" of Polish émigré volunteers organized by General Dąbrowski in northern Italy in the 1790s at the outset of the Polish alliance with Napoleon, the rebirth of an independent Polish state in 1919, the dominance of that state in the interwar period by the personality and politics of Marshal Piłsudski, World War II and the Holocaust, and the subsequent changes in Polish society and culture to our own time, including the birth and suppression of the Solidarity movement of 1980-81, have all worked to strengthen rather than diminish the vitality and validity of that dialogue. And this in turn has re-enforced the viability of the Romantic tradition on the Polish stage as well as, to be sure, in the Polish consciousness.

As the greatest expression, the embodiment, in fact, of the spirit of nineteenth-century émigré Romanticism, the Romantic drama would naturally serve as the frame of reference within which any dialogue with the Romantic past and the insurrectionary mystico-messianic legacy of émigré Romantic thought would take place. It was to prevent that dialogue from being resumed that the Polish communist regime prohibited stagings of Mickiewicz's *Forefathers, Part III* for some ten years after World War II and it was, in fact, only in 1955 – two years after the death of Stalin – that the first postwar production was mounted. The reaction of the audience on that very special opening night was movingly recorded by Jan Kott who was there at the time:

> The production of Mickiewicz's *Forefathers' Eve* [by which title the work is also known in English] was the most important event in the Polish theatre for ten years. We all felt this on the first night in the tightly packed auditorium of the Teatr Polski. The greatness of poetry and the presence of poetry are not one and the same thing [...].
>
> At the first night of *Forefathers' Eve* people cried – in the orchestra as well as in the balcony. Government ministers were crying, the hands of the technical crew were shaking, the cloakroom attendants were wiping their eyes. *Forefathers' Eve* moved and shocked and became the subject of discussions going on long into the night. I know of no other drama in the whole of world literature that could move an audience after a hundred and twenty-five years as *Forefathers' Eve* did. *Forefathers' Eve* stuck home with greater force than any play written since the war, in its historical aspect as well as in its contemporary relevance.
>
> Time did not consume the play's modern spirit, and it still haunts us today. There is dynamite in *Forefathers' Eve*, and it exploded on the first night.[8]

When *Forefathers* again demonstrated its great capacity to touch sensitive chords in Polish audiences in the tense political climate of 1967-68, the play was placed once more under a ban.

Since Romanticism and Polish national aspirations came together nowhere more powerfully than in the drama, it stands to reason that, in the later dialogue about Poland's past and future opened up by the great émigré Romantic poets, drama would assume a pivotal role. The trend began with Stanisław Wyspiański whose large dramatic output includes plays on virtually every major event and figure of Polish Romanticism from the November Insurrection itself (*Warszawianka*, The Varsovienne, 1898, *Noc listopadowa*, November Night, 1904) to the revolutionary historian Joachim Lelewel (*Lelewel*, 1899) and the ill-fated legion Mickiewicz organized in Italy in 1846 in the hope of leading it into battle against the Austrians during the "Spring of Nations" (*Legion*, 1900). In *Wesele* (The Wedding, 1901), the greatest of his plays, the failure of an uprising to materialize is attributed to Poland's lack of preparedness for national regeneration and its enslavement by myth. In one of his most powerful and enigmatic dramatic works, *Wyzwolenie* (Deliverance, 1903),

---

[8] Jan Kott, *Theatre Notebook, 1947-1967*, trans. Boleslaw Taborski (Garden City, NY: Doubleday, 1968), pp. 50-51.

the myth to which the deliverance (or liberation) of the title refers is that of Poetry in the sense of vatic leadership associated with the figure of Mickiewicz.

Insurrection and revolution, though not specifically identified as Polish, was also an abiding concern of the engrossing if sometimes puzzling early twentieth-century visionary and occultist novelist and dramatist Tadeusz Miciński (1873-1918) whose "rediscovery" has come only in the last thirty years. The apocalyptic note struck by Miciński in his most powerful drama of revolution, *Kniaz Patiomkin* (1906), based on the same episode that inspired the early Soviet film maker Sergei Eisenstein's world-famous *Battleship Potemkin,* also resounded in the plays of another even more highly regarded representative of the twentieth-century pre-World War II Polish avant-garde, Stanisław Ignacy Witkiewicz (1885-1939).[9] Like Miciński, whom he acknowledged as a mentor and with whom he shared certain expressionistic-surrealistic stylistic inclinations as well as an apocalyptic view of the world, Witkiewicz also explored the dynamics of revolution in such plays as *Bezimienno dzieło* (The Anonymous Work, 1921) and especially his more naturalistic *Szewcy* (The Shoemakers, 1934). In his highly effective one-act *Nowe wyzwolenie* (The New Deliverance, 1920) Witkiewicz not only extended the thematics of Polish Romanticism but added his voice to the internal debate of Polish drama over the Romantic legacy begun by Wyspiański and his "Young Poland" contemporaries. Consciously alluding to Wyspiański's *Deliverance,* Witkiewicz's *The New Deliverance* transmogrifies Wyspiański's self-doubting hero Konrad (based, of course, on the central character of Mickiewicz's *Forefathers, Part III*) – who must first rid himself of the tyranny of the Romantic past before being able to fulfill himself as a national liberator – into the grotesquely ineffectual Florian Snakesnout who passively submits to his own destruction. In keeping with his catastrophist Spenglerian view of the world, Witkiewicz projected Wyspiański's negative judgment of the Poland of his own time as unripe for liberation onto a broader plane in which the Europe of the pseudoliberal bourgeoisie lacks the resolve not only to liberate itself from the burden of the past but also to oppose the totalitarianism bent on crushing it. As to the shape and nature of that new totalitarian world order whose imminence filled him with dread, Witkiewicz drew chilling visions in his plays *Oni* (They, 1920), and *Gyubal Wahazar, czyli Na przełęczach bezsensu* (Gyubal Wahazar, or Along the Cliffs of the Absurd, 1921).

Witkiewicz's bleak prophesies of the future, unrelieved by the promise of messianic deliverance or the hope of an East-West, Catholic-Orthodox, Russian-Polish pan-Slavic symbiosis as advocated by Miciński, were fulfilled beyond even his darkest imagination by the events of World War II and its aftermath in Poland. The reality of totalitarian power in the postwar period from the consolidation of a Soviet-backed communist regime in the late 1940s down to the suppression in December 1981 of the most recent expression of the Polish desire for true independence and democratic freedoms – the Solidarity movement – provided a new impetus to the continuation of the debate over the Romantic past. Several of the most resonant postwar plays reflect the moral and philosophical interest of contemporary Polish literature in general in the dynamics of power, plays such as *Imiona władzy* (Names of Power, 1957) by Jerzy Broszkiewicz (born 1922), *Król IV* (King IV, 1963), with its elements of parody of Słowacki's *Kordian* as well as Shakespeare's *Hamlet,* by Stanisław Grochowiak (1934-76), and *Striptease* (1961), *Testarium* (The Prophets, 1967), and especially *Tango* (1964) by the major Polish dramatist of the postwar period, Sławomir Mrożek (born

---

[9] For a good study of Witkiewicz in English, with particular attention to his plays, see Daniel Gerould, *Witkacy: Stanisław Ignacy Witkiewicz as an Imaginative Writer* (Seattle and London: Univ. of Washington Press, 1981).

1930). How contemporary Polish drama ocasionally operates ironically even with motifs derived from earlier drama related to the debate with Romanticism is spledidly illustrated by *Tango*, a play about rebellion that ends with a grimly ironic dance intended beyond any doubt to trigger association with the somnambulent dance presided over by a fiddle-playing mulch at the end of Wyspiań-skis's *The Wedding*.

The antipathy of most post-World War II Polish drama to the myths and ideals bequeathed by the Romantic past often expresses itself in ironic association, as in Mrożek's *Tango*, or in parody of Romantic characters and plays, as suggested by Grochowiak's *King IV*.[10] Mrożek himself had addressed the issue of Romanticism directly in his play *Indyk* (The Turkey, 1960) in which humor derives from a pastiche of recognizable Romantic themes, while in the slightly later *Śmierć porucznika* (The Death of a Lieutenant, 1962), a similar technique was used to demonstrate the harmfulness of inculcating school children with Romantic values through the traditional teaching of Romanticism in Polish schools. One of Poland's greatest twentieth-century writers, Witold Gombrowicz (1905-69), most of whose life was spent in emigration, based one of his best works for the stage, *Operetta* (1966), on a parody principally of Krasiński's *The Undivine Comedy*. The play incorporates as well a puppet-like somnambulistic dance of aristocrats at a masked ball patently modeled on the finale of Wyspiański's *The Wedding*. Romantic echoes and reminiscences similarly appear in the grim absurdist plays of the highly regarded poet and playwright Tadeusz Różewicz (born 1921). Eschewing traditional value systems and cultures as irrelevant, indeed meaningless in the light of the events of World War II, Różewicz used the loose "open form" drama of the Romantics in one of his most important plays, *Kartoteka* (The Card Index, 1968), to portray the metamorphosis of a wartime Romantic hero into the postwar antihero who is uncertain of his own identity, can no longer act, and whose life is reduced to a daily routine of minimal physical actions necessary for survival.

Poland's political situation after World War II – the imposition of a Communist government lacking legitimacy and the periodic outbreaks of popular discontent from 1956 through 1981 aimed at making the regime more responsive to demands for greater honesty and efficiency – lent new meaning to Polish feelings of impermanence and unreality. Exile and emigration again became realities of Polish life. In the tragicomedy *Ślub* (The Marriage, 1946), the first postwar play by Witold Gombrowicz who left Poland on a trip to Argentina shortly before the German invasion in September 1939 and was never to return, the absurdist dream of a Polish soldier serving in France during the war is used to make the point that the only Poland to which return is possible is the unreal Poland of dream experience. France is again the setting in Mrożek's *Emigranci* (Emigrants, 1974), one of his few more conventionally structured plays in which a dialogue about Poland between two émigrés, one an intellectual, the other a worker, becomes a pretext for an analysis of the extent to which the Romantic tradition shaped the attitudes of the former and at the same time was responsible for a division of Polish society which must be overcome if a sense of reality and national purpose is ever to be achieved. Loss of country again figures in Mrożek's absurdist *Ambasador* (The Ambassador, 1982) where the envoy of a Western democracy in a totalitarian state learns at a certain point that his government no longer exists although his enemy is willing to maintain the fiction that it does for the sake of ideological competition.

---

[10] On postwar Polish drama and the Romantic legacy, see also Rochelle Stone, "Romanticism and Postwar Polish Drama: Continuity and Deviation," Henrik Birnbaum and Thomas Eekman, eds., *Fiction and Drama in Eastern and Southeastern Europe: Evolution and Experiment in the Postwar Period* (Columbus, Ohio: Slavica, 1980), pp. 379-414.

That contemporary Polish dramatists are willing to directly confront the Romantic legacy is plainly evidenced in a play such as *Rzecz listopadowa* (The November Matter, 1968), the first and most popular play by Ernest Bryll (born 1934). Its very form announcing its Romantic lineage (short loosely related scenes in verse), the play creates a frame of reference out of emotionally charged national and literary associations – the November Insurrection, All Souls' Day (the holiest day of the Polish calendar when the entire country flocks to graveyards to remember its dead and the setting, significantly, of Mickiewicz's *Forefathers*), and yet another symbolic dance of people as lifeless dolls – for the purpose of castigating those who play roles in a kind of Romantic unreality unmindful of the fact that beneath the pavements on which they posture a vast cemetery of men and aspirations lies buried. Bryll's bitter conclusion is that Polish and Western experience contrast so sharply because the Poles' sense of desolation over their history, over the perception of Poland as a great cemetery, is compounded by their inability to make foreigners, above all Westerners, understand it as they do.

Quite apart from the correlation between Polish political history and the continued relevance of the Polish Romantic dramatic tradition, there is also an important artistic dimension to the vitality of the Romantic drama in the Polish theater. Created in an environment affording virtually no possibility of stage production and hence free of the restraints on form imposed by prevailing theatrical techniques and traditions, the Romantic drama became a laboratory of experimentation. It is no exaggeration to say that hardly an aspect of modern Polish play technique or theatrical production was not in some way adumbrated or prefigured by it. The best known of the plays – *Forefathers, Part III, Kordian, The Undivine Comedy* – are monumental in conception and design and easily reconciled with the theatrical impulses of the turn of the century, including the renewed interest in spectacle, mass, and open-air theater. Structurally loose and open-ended, all three plays bring Georg Büchner's works to mind but are richer in dramatic action. In all three, moreover, the integral presence of the supernatural establishes the metaphysical dimensions of their authors' concerns and forms an important link between the drama of the Polish Romantics and the neo-Romantic and visionary plays of such early twentieth-century Polish dramatists as Stanisław Wyspiański and Tadeusz Miciński.

The externalization and corporealization of inner states, as in *Kordian*, for example, when the titular character stands poised to assassinate the Russian Tsar, anticipate later experiments with psychodrama and monodrama (especially by the Russian "theatricalist" Nikolay Yevreinov). The madhouse scenes, also in *Kordian*, hint at both surrealism and the absurd and lead directly to the important interwar avant-garde drama of that boldest of modern Polish playwrights, Stanisław Ignacy Witkiewicz (compare, for example, his play *Wariat i zakonnica*, The Madman and the Nun, 1923). The great ball scene in *Forefathers, Part III* handsomely embodies the Wagnerian idea of the *Gesamtkunstwerk* and assumes additional interest as a device of social and political satire. The direct influence, in both respects, on Wyspiański's *The Wedding* is easily established notwithstanding the play's indebtedness to the Polish tradition of Nativity puppet theater known as *szopka*. Mysticism, a deep current in Polish émigré thought and writing, figures prominently in Mickiewicz's *Forefathers, Part III* and Słowacki's works of the 1840s (above all *Father Marek, The Silver Dream of Salomea*, and the adaptation of Calderón's *The Constant Prince*), at once illuminating a vital facet of the intellectual and spiritual life of the Polish Great Emigration and the Romantic movement in general. That such plays could appeal to the occult and supernatural interests especially of artists of the turn of the century (for example, Miciński) should come as no surprise.

This essay had three goals at the outset two of which, hopefully, it has achieved. The first was to trace the rise of Polish Romantic drama and to define its specific character. The second was to elucidate the reasons for its considerable importance within the Polish cultural context and then to demonstrate by way of proof its profound impact on Polish drama and theater from the late nineteenth century down to the present. The third goal, which may yet require some vigorous persuasion if conventional views are to be altered, was to argue on the basis of its continuing vitality as both cultural phenomenon and artistic catalyst that compared to other European traditions of Romantic drama the Polish is the most vital and at the same time unique. From the comparative perspective, what ought to be regarded as the most noteworthy aspect of Polish Romantic drama is its sometimes penetrating inquiry into fundamental elements of Romantic art and outlook, above all the interpenetration of art, artist, society, and cosmic mystery. Born of rebellion and revolution, like Romanticism itself, the major plays, each in a different way, raise questions about revolution and are themselves revolutionary. As such, they represent the European Romantic tradition in the drama most thoroughly shaped by the dynamics of the Romantic movement itself. If they do not succeed handsomely in translation because of the language and verse of the original texts, and do occasionally require some initiation, the modest effort demanded seems worth it if we are ever to understand the full range of Romantic experience in the drama.

ALEXANDER GERSHKOVICH

RUSSIAN ROMANTIC DRAMA: THE CASE OF GRIBOEDOV[1]

I

The fate of Romantic drama in Russia took shape in an unusual manner. Its highest achievements, *Gore ot Uma* (Woe from Wit) and *Boris Godunov*, inspired by the new Romantic poetics, were not classified as Romantic plays in Russian criticism even though Griboedov spoke of his comedy as a "stage poem," and Pushkin of his *Boris* as a "true Romantic tragedy."[2] On the other hand, standard literary history, without any particular regret, assigned artistically weaker plays such as the pathetic tragedies of Ryleyev and Küchelbecker and the pseudo-patriotic melodramas of N. Kukolnik and N. Polevoy, to the Romantic School. Such a view has suited the purpose of "official" twentieth-century criticism to prove the immutable realistic nature of Russian art, its originality and separateness from the Western literary process.[3] The impression was created that the ideas of Romanticism, having come from the West, were pathogenic for Russia, did not deeply affect Russian drama, and did not strike root in Russian soil in a pure form. As anomalies of "secondary" poets, these ideas supposedly did not apply to the "shaft-horses" of Russian literature, from Griboedov to Gogol, pulling the main cart of national drama.

But the development of Russian drama from Griboedov to Chekhov, and even further to M. Bulgakov, cannot be adequately understood without taking account of the beneficial influence of Romanticism. First, it is important to establish what the Russians understood about Romanticism. The closest understanding was formulated by the leader of Russian critical thought, V. Belinsky (1811-48), who from a philosophical viewpoint looked at Romanticism as one natural characteristic not only of art but of the human spirit, as "the concealed life of the heart," – "where the human being is, there also is Romanticism."[4] From a historical/literary vantage, he found Romanticism

---

[1] This essay was begun in Moscow and completed in Boston. The author is grateful to Tracy Rich for translating the original Russian draft into English. The first English version has been revised by Gerald Gillespie. Unless otherwise noted, emphasis in quotations have been added.

[2] A.S. Pushkin, *Polnoe Sobranie Sochinenie v Desvati Tomakh* (Complete Collection of Compositions in 10 volumes) (Leningrad: Nauka, 1978), VII, 52. Pushkin also called *Boris Godunov* a Romantic tragedy in a letter to P.A. Vyazensky (X, 146) and in other places in his correspondence.

[3] This point of view finds even more complete expression in the works of the official commentator of Russian classics in the Soviet period, Academician D.D. Blagoy. During more than half a century, from the 1920s to the 1980s he tried to "round off" and at the same time to distort the authentic picture of Russian literature's contradictory development which characterizes his two-volume composite work, *Ot Kantemira do Nashikh Dney* (From Kantemir to Our Days) (Moscow: Hudozhestvennaya Literatura, 1979).

[4] V.G. Belinsky, *Sobranie Sochinenie v Trekh Tomakh* (Collection of Compositions in Three Volumes) (Moscow: OGIZ, 1948), III, 217. The Soviet editor considers it necessary to add the following commentary here: "However, the social essence of Romanticism slips away from Belinsky; therefore, the design of Romanticism's development carries a still too formal-logical character. However, with all the inadequacies thrown at us, Belinsky's concept [...] was the first attempt to examine Romanticism in a historical context as a whole complex of problems interconnected by a deep inner unity" (III, 872). See also the valuable research of Donald Fanger in *Dostoevsky and Romantic Realism* (Cambridge, Mass.: Harvard Univ. Press, 1967).

among ancient Greeks (Euripides), in the East, and the Middle Ages. In the nineteenth century, however, it had been born completely transformed as "an organic unity of all the moments of the Romanticism which had been developed in the history of humanity."[5] On this basis, Belinsky considered that "Romanticism is not the property or belonging of any one country or epoch: it is an eternal side of nature and of the human spirit – it didn't die after the Middle Ages, but rather only underwent a transformation."[6]

Analyzing the newest Romanticism from an aesthetic point of view, Belinsky calls it, "a war with a deathly imitation of the assertive form" of Classicism and "a striving for freedom and originality of form."[7] In another place (in an article about Griboedov) he sums up his idea even more succinctly: "*Classical* art has a complete and harmonious *balance between idea and form*, and Romantic (art) placed idea over form."[8] Finally, Belinsky adheres to the opinion that Russian experience, in contrast to that of the West which vainly tried to revive the Romanticism of the Middle Ages artificially, represents an organic process of development. Russia "did not have her own Middle Ages," and therefore, her literature could not possess an original Romanticism. However, since "without Romanticism poetry is the same as a body without a soul," when Russia joined the life of Europe, and felt the influence of the intellectual movements which were arising, Russian literature was not able *not* to give birth to Romanticism. This occurred, however, without those complexes of anachronisms which the West had experienced. Of all the Western Romanticists, Belinsky especially singled out Byron, who, like Prometheus, inflicted the mortal blow on this useless attempt to revive the old and became the herald of the new Romanticism, Romanticism which was also close to Russian aspirations.[9]

Belinsky was essentially correct in seeing that Russian Romanticism, especially in the area of drama, although born out of the battle with Classicism, did inherit much from the preceding literary schools, selecting building-materials from them. In this sense it is possible to understand Belinsky's ironic observation about "the Romantic classics" of Russian literature (he referred here to second-rate artists such as N. Kukolnik and N. Polevoy) which, in essence, are representative of the "eclectic reconciliation of Classicism with Romanticism, in which a little something is held over from Classicism and something is taken from Romanticism."[10] This is an old song with new words, that is, Classical absurdities in new Romantic clothing take place when the poet, calling himself a Romantic and an opponent of Classicism, as if it were a criminal offense, is actually continuing to look on the subject from without and not from within. Therefore, says Belinsky, it only seems to the poet that he is nimbly running forward, while he is actually turning in the same place, going around himself in circles. In contrast, because Belinsky considered Griboedov and Pushkin authentic representatives of the new Romantic direction in Russian drama and poetry, he explored the nature of Romanticism in large theoretical essays devoted to their work.

In the 1820s Russian drama took a striking leap. At the beginning of the century it was still in imitative apprenticeship to Western classicist modes, with rudiments of the Enlightenment and Sen-

---

[5] Belinsky, II, 232.
[6] Belinsky, II, 245.
[7] Belinsky, II, 176.
[8] Belinsky, I, 461 and 466.
[9] Belinsky, III, 225-236
[10] Belinsky, I, 463.

timentalism. In the genre of tragedy, the pompous V.A. Ozerov (1769-1816) was still in complete favor, with subjects taken from Greek, Roman, medieval Western, and Russian history (*Oedipus in Athens*, 1804, *Fingal*, 1805, and *Dimitry Donskoy*, 1807). In enlightened comedy, the mocking fabulist I. Krylov (1768-1844) wrote the edifying *Fashionable Store* (1806) and *Lessons for the Daughters* (1807). In vaudeville, the light-minded M.N. Zagoskin (1789-1852) enjoyed success by showing *The Provincial in the Capital* (1817) and in reverse, the metropolitan resident in a village in *Bagatonov, or the Surprise to Himself* (1821). Comedies of manners, usually remakes of French plays, were written by the "anti-sentimentalists," N.A. Zhander, N.I. Khmelnitsky, and A.A. Shakhovskoy. These were all close friends of Griboedov who, at the beginning, was often a co-author of these playwrights.

Russian drama was just barely unfurling its sticky light-green leaves. Suddenly, in the atmosphere of the Pre-Decembrist storm it was as if an electric spark discharged: *Gore ot Uma* (1823-24) and *Boris Godunov* (1825) – unsurpassed examples of Russian comedy and tragedy up until that time – appeared on the scene one right after the other. Unexpected and innovative in design, deeply national in their character, humanist in content, they immediately raised Russian drama to an unprecedented artistic and public level, placing it in European ranks alongside the best of world Romantic drama. Attentive Western observers immediately took note, and thus the first complete edition of *Gore ot Uma* appeared not in Russian but in a German translation by Karl von Knorring in Revel in 1831, while the first deeply objective, scholarly analysis of *Boris Godunov* was done by the German scholar Varnhagen von Ense. "We will be still more surprised at the dramatic strength of the genius Pushkin, if we take into consideration the slender means by which the poet reached his goals," he wrote in 1843 from Leipzig.[11] He valued *Gore ot Uma* highly as did the first English translator and populizer, Nicholas Benardaky who in 1857 wrote that Griboedov's talent was "more closely akin to Juvenal than to Molière," and that the character Chatsky, with his biting irony, is a result of heart and sensitivity and not cold calculation.[12] More recently, although still stipulating some measure of Classicism, I. Sőtér has reaffirmed the connection of *Gore ot Uma*, along with early Pushkin, to the flowering of Romanticism in Russia; and the same view has been put forth by J. Bonamour in his fundamental work on Griboedov.[13]

It was more difficult for Russian Romantic drama to gain recognition in its homeland. It was forbidden and distorted by the censors. None of the authors of the above-mentioned plays ever did see their works on stage, and Griboedov and Lermontov did not even live to see their work published. The critics brought humiliating fire down upon them, having become acquainted with them through notes passing from hand to hand. Nevertheless, they became known to the public and exerted a deep and growing influence on all of Russian culture, still important in our time. In the Soviet era, the officially sanctioned approach to art narrowed the understanding of Romanticism to such an extent that not only the early Pushkin, all of Griboedov, and the early Gogol did not fit in, but even Lermontov's *Masquerade* – a work Romantic to the core. In the two-volume *History of Romanticism in Russian Literature* (1979), *Gore ot Uma* is not even referred to, as if Griboedov

[11] K.A. Varnhagen von Ense, *Denkwürdigkeiten und vermischte Schriften*, (Leipzig: Brockhaus, 1843), V, 592-635.

[12] A.S. Griboedov, *Gore ot Ouma*, trans. by Nicholas Benardaky (London: Simpkin, Marshall & Co., 1857), pp. i-iv. Further references to this edition are enclosed in the text in parentheses after the symbol G.

[13] István Sőtér, "A romantika Elötörténete és Korszákolása," in *Az Europa Romantika* (Moscow: Nauka, 1973), pp. 79-80. Jean Bonamour, *A.S. Griboedov et la vie littéraire de son temps* (Paris: Presses Universitaires de France, 1965).

never existed.[14] On the other hand, it examines in detail young Belinsky's scholarly composition *Dmitry Kalinin* which is of marginal significance.

The swift development of Russian drama at the beginning of the nineteenth century began in an atmosphere of spiritual ascent in Russian culture after the victory over Napoleon in 1812. It was accompanied by the crossing and interlacings of the most heterogenous artistic currents. Russian drama, thanks to its backwardness in relation to the West's development, in a short ten years transversed a path on which Western European theater spent a century. Thus the accelerated development of a national culture let to the birth of works of mixed stylistic form. "Classicist by form, drama inscribes a sentimental spirit; sentimental poetry assimilates Romantic motifs; the Enlightenment grows into revolutionary Romanticism; sentimentalism yields realistic fruit. It is not difficult for a historian of literature and drama to become entangled in this mixture of artistic ideas and tendencies. It [the mixture] came into existence because [...] the Russian artistic idea, trying on the one hand to remain in national traditions, at the same time hurried to master all the newness which had arisen in the West [...],"[15] the Soviet theoretician, Anikst, has justifiably written.

This process was also rather typical for other Eastern European countries which were experiencing their own national renaissance. The interdependency of various artistic styles was inherent in Polish, Hungarian, and Czech drama of the age of Romanticism.[16] Far from being eclectic, this mixture of styles in all its specificity contained an inner logic; it paralleled the search for a national drama, answering to the spirit and needs of its people.

II

Gore ot Uma clearly reflected this search. Its author, Alexander Sergeevich Griboedov (1795-1829), was one of the mysterious figures of Russian and world literature. He stepped into history as a literary man focused single-mindedly on one idea, a creator of one masterpiece. Griboedov's life and work exhibit the fate of a fiery dreamer in "a country of eternal snows," who having established his remarkable abilities by serving falsely chosen goals, recognizes this too late.[17] An individualist by nature, Griboedov's lofty poetic spirit was interwoven with contradictions. Hating slavery more than anything, especially slavery of the spirit ("According to my times and taste/ I hate the word slave"), Griboedov, perhaps more than other poets of his time, was a slave of the society in which

    [14] A.S. Kurilov, ed. in chief, *Istoria Romantizam v Russkoi Literature* (History of Romanticism in Russian Literature) (Moscow: Nauka, 1979). Prepared by the Gorky Institute of World Literature of the USSR Academy of Sciences.
    [15] A. Anikst, *Istoria Uchenii o Drame. Teoria Drami v Rossii ot Pushkina do Chekhova* (History of Studies on Drama. Theory of Drama in Russia from Pushkin to Chekhov) (Moscow: Nauka, 1972), p. 10. See also the brilliant essay of Roman Jakobson, "Pushkin in a Realistic Light," in *Pushkin and His Sculptural Myth* (The Hague and Paris: Mouton, 1975), p. 63.
    [16] A.A. Gershkovich, "Teatr i natsional'naya Kul'tura (k postanovke problemi)" (Theater and National Culture [Relating to the Statement of the Problem]), in *Teatr v National'noy Kul'ture Stan Tsentral'noy i Ugovostochnoy Evropi XVIII-XIX vv* (Theater in the National Culture of Central and South-Eastern European Countries of the XVIII-XIX centuries) (Moscow: Nauka, 1976), pp. 7-25. Also in French: "Le Théâtre Est-Européen à la charnière des Lumières et du Romantisme," *Neohelicon*, 3, Nos. 3-4 (1975), 51-67.
    [17] Near the end of his life he confessed to his closest friend, Begichev (in a letter dated December 9, 1826, from Tiflis), "Will I ever not be dependent on people? Dependency on family, secondly on service, thirdly on life's goals which I created for myself, and perhaps I will defy fate. Poetry! I love her without memory, passionately, but is love alone enough to bring fame to oneself? [...] Who of us respects singers sincerely inspired, in that land where dignity is valued in direct relationships to the number of medals and enslaved serfs. *It's torture to be a fiery dreamer* in a land of eternal snows." V. Orlov, ed., *Griboedov: Sochinenia* (Griboedov: Compositions) (Leningrad: Hudozhestvennaya Literatura, 1940), p. 534.

he lived. He "made a career," despite his inner convictions and dream to "be independent of people," and despised himself for this, having a foreboding that it would end badly. Thus into Russian literature was born the type of the implacable Chatsky – the first Romantic hero of Russian drama – no doubt based on the author himself.

Griboedov was a descendant of an old, noble family, rich, and one of the most educated people in Russia and Europe at the beginning of the new age, having studied with Göttingen Professors I.T. Booulet, B. Ion, and Schletzer Junior. He spoke many European languages fluently, reading and translating Shakespeare, Goethe, and Shiller. He knew Latin and Greek, Persian, Arabic, and Turkish. Graduating with ease simultaneously in philology, law, physics and mathematics from Moscow University, he was awarded the title of Doctor of Law. He was an excellent pianist and a composer of sentimental romances. He participated in the War of 1812 against Napoleon. He was a member of the Freemason Lodges in Moscow and Saint Petersburg; mixed in higher circles, had friendships with Decembrists; was involved in the uprising of 1825, but was pardoned by the Tsar; was acquainted with the disgraced Pushkin and close to the gendarme informer Fadey Bulgarin, to whom fell the trouble of publishing *Gore ot Uma*. And finally, Griboedov became an official of "the diplomatic unit" of the Russian colonial army in Transcaucasia and progressed as a specialist in the assimilation of subjected territories of the Eastern peoples. He became a bearer of the Order of Lev and of the Sun, second degree, and of Saint Ann with diamonds. Subsequently, by royal decree, he was named state advisor and Ambassador Plenipotentiary of the Russian Empire in Persia, where he was killed by Shi'ite fanatics in Teheran during the destruction of the Russian embassy on January 30, 1829, at thirty-four years of age.

The discord between dream and reality, subjective desires and objective circumstances, in the final analysis, between word and deed, became the main theme of Griboedov's creative work. His lyrical "I" continually strives to overcome this contradiction in the only sphere where it is still possible to be relatively independent of outer circumstances – in the sphere of art. His work wonderfully illustrates the idea of Madame de Staël, whose works were well known in Russian: "In our days, a poet must forfeit both his hopes and faith to intelligence; only then can his philosophical mind make a large impression [...] In the age in which we live, melancholia represents the authentic source of talent."[18] Griboedov's poetic credo was expressed in the free translation of the "Prologue in the Theater" from the first part of Goethe's *Faust*. He took up this translation immediately upon the completion of *Gore ot Uma* in 1824, or even possibly while still working on the play. In any case, Griboedov's exposition of Goethe appeared as an aesthetic prologue in the almanac *Arctic Star* in 1825, long before the publication of his comedy.

The relationship of Griboedov to Goethe is known to us through his conversation with the Decembrist A. Bestuzhev.[19] Goethe's dramatic poem drew Griboedov's attention to the idea of the inevitability of compromise, not only in life but in art as well, and to the age-old conflict between high poetic intention and the earthbound needs of "the masses," in the form of didactic discussion

---

[18] *Literaturnie Manifesti Zapadnoevropeyskikh Romantikov* (Literary Manifestos of Western European Romantics) (Moscow: Nauka, 1980), p. 382. From the original French of de Staël, *De la littérature considérée dans ses rapports avec les institutions sociales* (1800). Concerning sources of de Staël's literary theory, see R. Wellek, *A History of Modern Criticism: The Romantic Age* (New Haven and London: Yale Univ. Press, 1955), p. 220.

[19] A. Bestuzhev (Marlinsky), *Znakomstvo moë s Grivoedovim* (My Acquaintance with Griboedov) (Otechestvennie Zapiski, 1860), CXXXII, 635. "You called them both (Goethe and Byron) great, and in relation just to them this is fair, but between the two of them all superiority in greatness must be assigned to Goethe – who with his own idea explains all of humanity; Byron, with all sorts of diverse thoughts, a single person."

between the sober-minded Theater Director and the immeasureably ardent Poet. Griboedov, however, changes the outcome completely in Chatsky's accusatory speeches:

> No, no, his Poet rejects the Director's reason,
> Go away, go look for others to serve you.

Characteristically, Griboedov also enriches Goethe's theatrical crowd with new personages, with an openly Russian character:

> Here villains gaze around in the darkness
> To lie in wait for a word and ruin with a denunciation.
>   (G. 356-60)

Pushkin was more honest and consistent on this score. Literally during the same days that Griboedov was working on the "Prologue," Pushkin turned to the same Goethean theme of the "poet" and "the multitudes" – evidence of how acute this problem was in Russian literature – and wrote his famous "Conversation between the Bookseller and the Poet" along with the first chapter of *Eugene Onegin*, in which the distinctive preface not unlike Goethe's appeared (1825). He solves the worrisome problem of the relationship of art and life through open compromise between the Bookseller and the Poet, in the words of the Bookseller:

> Позвольте просто вам сказать:
> Не продается вдохновенье,
> Но можно рукопись продать. [20]

> (Let me simply say to you:
> Inspiration is not sold
> But to sell a manuscript
> possible.)

In response to this mercenary declaration, Pushkin's Poet, in contrast to Griboedov's Poet, does not explode with righteous indignation, but rather answers completely reasonably and accomodatingly, in low prose – as if emphasizing the reality of what is going on: "Вы совершенно правы. Вот вам моя рукопись. Условимся." (You are absolutely correct. Here you are – my manuscript. Let's settle it.) This dual relationship of creative work is the key theme of Russian Romantic drama. The difference in the positions of Griboedov and Pushkin, on the surface, nonetheless turns out to be purely outward, declarative. Actually through all of his writing, Griboedov confirmed Pushkin's concept of Russian art – the inevitability of compromise between the high calling of the artist, as the Romantics understood him, and lowly Russian everyday reality.

III

The project *Gore ot Uma* was conceived by Griboedov at the turning point of his life, after the scandalous duel of 1818 when he abandoned Moscow with a train of high-society aspersions behind

---

[20] Pushkin, II, 179.

him. His hasty exit from Moscow with the Russian diplomatic mission to Persia was more like an escape from a society which he thoroughly knew, loved, and hated. He left for the East against his will, with an evil foreboding. Henceforth, his life would be made up of continual "leavings," and "crossings."[21] Yet the reason for his break from Moscow society was rooted more deeply. The results of the Patriotic War of 1812, in which Griboedov took part first-hand, were disappointing in the end. The unusual rise of patriotism, especially among the noble army officers, who had become accustomed to Western freedom, changed to general apathy. "The expectations, that the fall of slavery follows in answer to the exploits of the people, were not realized."[22] In 1812, heroes were replaced by people indifferent to everything, except their own careers. A "female regime" was established; "wives" acquired power, and this reverberated throughout the whole societal organism. Former gallant commanders became ladies' pages at balls. In this deathly pause during the last years of the "liberal" Alexander I's reign, the sole rational word heard in the worldly drawing room was: "Ах! боже мой! что станет говорить/ Княгиня Марья Алексевна!" (Oh my God! What is the Princess going to say!)[23] This ironic remark by Famusov concluded Griboedov's comedy. Not only did it contain the comedy's main idea, the mainspring of the plot; it is reasonable to suggest that *Gore ot Uma* as the author first conceived it, grew out of this kernel. Two incomplete drafts of letters by Griboedov to unknown people have survived written in November 1820 from Tavriz. In one of them, marked 1:00 a.m., Griboedov writes about a dream he had which resembles, just like two peas in a pod, the atmosphere of Famusov's Moscow in Acts III and IV of *Gore ot Uma*. The hero of this dream was Griboedov himself, who finds himself at a ball and is made to vow that he will write "something or other." Even the remark with which Griboedov's acquaintances meet him is given in detailed description. Unmistakably the actors of his future comedy, meeting Chatsky upon entering the hall, repeat this remark nearly word for word.[24]

We can understand Griboedov's method as a dramatist modifying his Romanticism to accord with the Realism of the day if we distinguish the original version of *Gore ot Uma*, which apparently pleased the Romantic Küchelbecker so much, from the final edition. The author himself unequivocally pointed out this difference in his notes as he was preparing it for publication in 1824-25:

---

[21] In 1820, describing his life in the East, he noted that "and here my wits are in shock." Speaking ironically of Moscow life, he grieved over it with all the passion of a Romantic nature ("Gone is happiness, I am not writing poetry [...],") and he called his departure "political banishment." Griboedov, p. 481.

[22] U. Tinyanov, *Pushkin i ego Sovremenniki* (Pushkin and His Contemporaries) (Moscow: Nauka, 1969), p. 359.

[23] Orlov, ed., p. 133. Of several English translations, we prefer that by Joshua Cooper in his book, *Four Russian Plays* (New York: Penguin Books, 1982), p. 210.

[24] In the dream: "Is that really you, Alexander Sergeevich? How you've changed! It's impossible to recognize you." Griboedov, pp. 487-88. In the play (III.v): "Ah, Alexander Andreich, is it you? – Is it possible three years have changed me as much?" Griboedov, p. 86.

Three years is exactly the time period which separates Griboedov's departure/escape from Moscow and the beginning of work on the play. His friend, a witness to the creation of *Gore ot Uma* and its first audience, the Romantic poet Küchelbecker, came to Tiflis from Western Europe. He left evidence that Griboedov read him "each separate scene immediately after it had been written." V.K. Küchelbecker, "Dnevnik, 1833" (Diary, 1833), in *Puteshestvie, Dnevnik, Stat'i* (Travels, Diary, Articles) (Leningrad: Nauka, 1979), p. 227. He certifies, in addition, that the poet did not intend to write simple portraits, as the contemporary critics thought: "His wonderful soul," writes Küchelbecker, "was higher than such trifles." However, he takes note of the critics, "qui se sent galeux qu'il se gratte." Küchelbecker, 227-28. The French saying which Küchelbecker uses means "The cat knows whose meat he ate." Küchelbecker here defends Griboedov from the unjust attacks of the critics on *Gore ot Uma* in conjunction with the publication of a short excerpt in the almanac *Russkaya Taliya* in 1825. He suggested that M. Dmitriev, the writer of the criticisms, be tried in a court of honor for "the perfidious praises to the lucky portrait" in Griboedov's comedy, which Küchelbecker considered a conscious distortion of the author's intention.

The first inscription of this *stage poem*, as it was born inside of me, was much greater and of *higher* meaning than now, in the vain apparel in which *I was compelled* to clothe it. The childish pleasure of listening to my poems in the theater [...] forced me to *spoil* my creation, as much as possible [...]. And besides, there are so many customs and conditions, not in the least connected with the aesthetic side of creation, with which *it is necessary to conform* [...]. There is a genre of theory (on which many pride themselves) that art is to please her [the public], that is, to create stupidity. (G. 400)

From this acknowledgement it obviously follows that in its original conception, the comedy was a "purely" Romantic drama. The compromise with ruling tastes or deliberate "ruining" of the play lasted a few years, right up to the summer of 1824 when Griboedov wrote to his closest friend, S.I. Begichev:

I am cutting it down, changing the whole business to rubbish, so that in many places my dramatic pictures' bright colors have completely faded. I get angry and put back that which I have just crossed out so that it seems, that for my work there is no end [...]. (G. 498)

Begichev was asked not to share the first version with anyone but to burn it if he thought it was necessary; for "it is as imperfect as it is impure," wrote Griboedov. The author aimed at achieving a plot of maximum transparency and simplicity (at the last minute he put in the domestic scene, "Sofia with a Candle") and unifying the poem. In June 1824 he already was writing to Begichev, "I have changed more than 80 lines; now it is as smooth as glass."

But Griboedov had little success in "ruining" his comedy, no matter how hard he tried. His aspiration "to conform" to the customs and conventions of the public of those times, "not connected with the aesthetic side of creation," even became strangely useful to the play. Having been freed from the grip of Classicist rules, Griboedov was inspired as he worked, and the further he got the more he was satisfied with what he was doing: "an alive, quick thing, recalling the final version of the comedy, the verses poured out in sparks." In the same letter to Begichev, he reports on the success of the readings of the comedy in Petersburg ("Eight readings, no I miscounted – twelve [...] I pound, make noise, there is no end to delight, curiosity") and admits that "in many places he improvises and experiences passion for a new invention, a new theory, a change of place and occupation, people and unusual pursuits." (G. 498-99)

The main reproach against Griboedov which was presented by his friend Katenin, was precisely his abandonment of rules, in favor of the game of imagination: "Talent rather than art." Griboedov answered his friend's criticism, completely in the spirit of Romanticism, "The most complimentary praise [is that] Art exists only *to be subordinate to talent* [...]." Griboedov clearly rejcted the Classicist era:

The one [...] who had more ability to please with schoolish requirements, conditions, habits, grandmotherly traditions, than with one's own creative strength – is not an artist – let him throw away his palette and brush, his knife or pen – out the window. (G. 511)

Nevertheless, he opted for the path of compromise: "I know that any craft has its ruses." As an experienced diplomat, he attached great meaning to these ruses, calling them in Latin, *nudae difficiles* (difficult trifles). Now his task was a combination of Romantic design and Realistic analysis unusual for Russian literature. "There is no action in it!" an exasperated critic raged indignantly.

"The scenes are strung together arbitrarily," said even well-wishing friends – professionals. Griboedov did not dispute all this; he did not strive for obvious scene connections according to the rules of French drama, but to excite curiosity.[25]

The reproach that *Gore ot Uma* lacked action was answered by the like-minded Küchelbecker:

> I will not begin to insist that this is unjust, although it would not be difficult to prove that there is more action or movement in this comedy [i.e., inner action, movement of the soul in the hero's development], than in the majority of those comedies in which all the entertainment is built into the plot. In *Gore ot Uma*, precisely the whole plot is made up of the opposition of Chatsky to the other characters [...].[26]

Later, Küchelbecker gives a shining formula of the inner, heartfelt conflict of Romantic drama:

> Take Chatsky, the given characteristics; they are considered together and show what kind of meeting there will be, without fail, of these antipodes – and only. This is very simple, but in all this simplicity is newness, bravery, greater than that poetic consideration which they didn't understand.[27]

Griboedov actually preserved two of the Classical unities: time and place. The evolution of his hero, from the moment when he arrives at his beloved's after a three-year separation, and up until the final break from her and the escape from Moscow, fits strictly into twenty-four hours, from morning to midnight. The place of action is as strictly bounded in the drawing room of the rich Moscovite, Famusov. But the absence of unity of action, the creation of an exceptionally Romantic hero and the new kind of dramatic conflict veer from Classicism. The play's action, beginning with a trivial lover's intrigue, shifts grounds in the third act, when his beloved's fiasco becomes evident to Chatsky. The main action commences, for which the play really was written – the single-handed combat of Chatsky against society, hateful to him with its stagnation and hypocrisy.

This seeming inner contraction in the play evoked surprise and censure in many contemporaries.[28] What especially annoyed Belinsky was Chatsky's reasonableness and coldness in expressing living sentiments: when the hero finds out the bitter truth, that he is not loved, instead of leaving quietly, he begins "to rage against all of society" and uses the time "to read a few homilies." About what happens later in the play Belinsky did not even care to write, for him the play was already exhausted with the love intrigue, "And so, the comedy has no wholeness, since it has no idea." Nonetheless, Belinsky grasped at the significant negative definition: "The opposition of an intelligent and deep person against the society in which he lives" cannot form the positive idea of Russian drama. If the Famusovs were hated by Chatsky, why should they meet together? Let them look for their own circle, reasons the great critic and comes to an odd conclusion: "Society is *always righter and higher* than the private person, and the private individual is real and not a phan-

---

[25] The more "outside" of the West that the events are, as he explained his principles, the more they entice curiosity: "I write for those like myself – when by the first scene I am already guessing the tenth, I am filled with yawns and then I run from the theater." (G. 498)

[26] Küchelbecker, p. 228.

[27] Küchelbecker, p. 228.

[28] Even Pushkin, the admired master of convoluted love intrigues, was sorry that "the whole comedy did not revolve around it; it seems Griboedov didn't want it – his will." (Pushkin, X, 97.) Belinsky expressed it still more categorically. Chatsky for him was, in general, "a silly character" as a 'lover.' All the words expressing his feelings for Sofia are so ordinary, in order not to utter banalities!" (Belinsky, I, 508.) It is necessary to admit Belinsky had a point.

tom only to the degree that he is expressed by society."[29] On this basis Belinsky announces further that because Chatsky as a personality expresses no one besides himself, he is foolish, like "an image without a face," like a "'phantom,' like something imaginary and unreal."[30] Here we have arrived at the core of the play itself – at the problem of the Romantic hero in Russian drama, and the theme of the Russian treatment of individualism. Chatsky is antitheatical not only according to the utilitarian view of Belinsky, but even to the ideas of Decembrist aesthetics, to which Griboedov was close at one time.

IV

The idea of the free individual was common to Russian and Western European literature of the 1820s. The vogue for Byron in Russia was as great as in the West. However, the Russian ideal of the person under an authoritarian regime did not really accord with the understanding of the personality's value which had been developed in the generally more liberal West. It has been noted long ago, that the process of the individual's development in Russia took place under conditions completely different from those in the West.[31] In Russia, from the time of Peter, and with a few interruptions during the intervals of liberalism under Alexander I and Alexander II, social development was accompanied by far-reaching enslavement of personality, by an attack on its sovereignty, by the subordination of the private person to public or state interests. The famous Russian historian S.M. Solov'ev said that Nicholas I wanted to behead all those who rose above the average – to make them all equal.

It is significant that the Decembrists, though having supported personal freedom, also demonstrated the destructiveness of the philosophy of individualism. Their ideal was "a saintly offering of oneself for the common good of the people," and the higher manifestation of personal freedom was in service to the commonweal.[32] During the same years and months that Griboedov was creating his character Chatsky in Tiflis, completely different requirements for the ideal Russian hero were heard in bitter arguments about the meaning of art in Saint Petersburg. On June 13, 1821, in the main headquarters of literary free thought, in the unrestricted society of amateurs of Russian literature, the Romantic poet N. Gnedich delivered a famous speech in which he rejected the ideal person as put forward in German and English Romanticism.[33] Having Byron in mind, Gnedich condemned the individualistic character of his poetry and philosophy:

---

[29] Belinsky, I, 508.

[30] Belinsky, I, 515.

[31] Recently the Hungarian scholar Erzsebet Köves offered an interesting comparison between the Western and Russian paths of development in the first half of the nineteenth century in his book *Kelet és Nyugat* (Budapest: Magvetö, 1983).

[32] Cf. passim Richard Pipes, *Russia under the Old Regime* (London: Weidenfeld & Nicolson, 1977); ch. 1, pp. 20-30 in Adam B. Ulam, *In the Name of the People* (New York: Viking Press, 1977); James H. Billington, *The Ikon and the Axe: An Interpretive History of Russian Culture* (New York: Vintage Books, 1970).

[33] Russian Romantics of the Decembrist doctrine placed the problem of the Romantic hero in antiquity and far from the contemporary Slavic/historical material on the abstract/heroic plane, rejecting "the useless" Byronesque individualism. "It is more necessary to overmeasure, that is, to exaggerate the greatness of a person than to belittle him," demanded the same N. Gnedich, inviting Russian literature to exhibit "a saintly offering of the self for the good of the people." *Dekabristi i Ikh Vremya* (Decembrists and Their Time) (Moscow and Leningrad: Nauka, 1951), p. 134. Serious Soviet scholars, e.g., G.P. Makogonenko and E.N. Kupreyanova, with their valuable book *National'noe Soveobrazie Russkoy Literaturi* (National Distinctiveness of Russian Literature) (Leningrad: Nauka, 1976), expound on Gnedich's view but without giving it its full value.

Shunning, like a cold wall, the society of those who are like-minded, a person sees himself – a cheer-
less spectacle! – alone in the world and the world for him alone.[34]

He argued further that individualism destroys the person, implants disdain towards society, leads to
egotism and spiritual emptiness of the soul. This was said at the time when Byron, having been torn
from English society and having given free rein to his individualism, joined the Italian Carbonari
movement and participated in the liberation battle of the Greek peoples.

In contrast, Griboedov was basing on Byron not only the features of his hero Chatsky's world
outlook, but also the main conflict in the plot, Sofia's invention of Chatsky's craziness.[35]

The Decembrist theory, finding expression in the dramas of Ryleev, Küchelbecker, and others,
in essence, controverted European Romanticism with its cult of inner, individual, "egotistic" life.
Taken to the extreme, this theory, as the American historian of Russian culture, Richard Pipes, justly observed, began to work against itself:

> The quarrel [...] was not over aesthetics but over the freedom of the creative artist – and, ultimately,
> that of every human being – to be himself. The radical intelligentsia [...] began to develop a service
> mentality of its own. The belief that literature and art [...] had a primary responsibility to society
> became axiomatic in Russian left-wing circles.[36]

One long-range result was the lifelessness of literature, its subordination to openly propagandistic
goals.

Griboedov's different road for Russian literature turned out to be impracticable under Russian
conditions. The image of Chatsky is the first and – alas! – right up to the present the only effective
and consistent portrait of individualism in Russian literature on a European scale. It is an image not
so much of a hero as of a Romantic anti-hero in Russian life, *not the rule*, but an *exception*. Proud,
smart, caustic, open, unprotected, detesting lies and hypocrisy, Chatsky finds himself in a state of
war with everyone. He has no allies; he is "a lone soldier in the field," and hence much closer to the
Romantic hero of Western literature than even to the Russian Onegin and Pechorin. Goncharov has
written about Chatsky that he was a full head higher than those who also had once shone as a
fashionable idea, though like a stylish suit. But "Onegin and Pechorin turned out to be unfit for the
matter, for the active role, although both vaguely understood that all around them had been reduced
to ashes."[37] Despising the emptiness of life, the festive lordliness, these "progressive personalities,"
as Goncharov judges, yielded to it. Their general dissatisfaction did not keep them from playing the
dandy, "to shine," to flirt, and Pechorin, in addition, to be wretched in his laziness and melancholy.
Despising both society and and themselves in society, they adapted to life in it. In this resided both
their Russianness and their typicalness.

Chatsky, in contrast, does not wish to be reconciled with anything, does not wish to pretend,

---

[34] Gnedich, pp. 133-34.

[35] Based on the story of Lord Byron, which was making itself heard in the West and in Russia. Byron was blamed for
his wife's mental illness, which served as a reason for his break from society and his running away from England. "As he
himself says, he had to fight alone against all," wrote the Russian press in the 1820s. *Sin Otechestva* (Son of the Fatherland),
1822, no. 21, p. 24. For more details on Byron and Griboedov, see U. Tinyanov's article "Suzhet *Gore ot Uma*" (The Plot of
Gore ot Uma) in *Pushkin i ego Sovremenniki*, pp. 347-379.

[36] Pipes, pp. 279-80. In Russian translation: *Rossia pri Starom Rezhime* (Cambridge, Mass.: Harvard Univ. Press,
1980), pp. 374-75.

[37] I.A. Goncharov, *Million Terzanii (Kriticheskii Etud)* (A Million Agonies – A Critical Study), cited from *Gore ot
Uma* (Moscow: Pravda, 1980), p. 110.

does not wish to look "like everyone else." The only time that he does pretend in the play – in the scene of the resolute explanation with Sofia (III.i), he considers it his duty to play a part – "Just for this once I am going to pretend." Chatsky appears happy, energetic, witty, self-confident, deeply sensitive, open to the whole world, similar to Hamlet before the meeting with the ghost of his father. He craves activity; he is full of optimistic hopes. He jokes, entertains. His enthusiasm, lifting the soul a little, his rare gift of eloquence a result of constant work on his ideas and spiritual development. And if such "related souls" in society are, in fact, non-existent? If each of your jokes is met as a flaw? If your mockery of peoples obvious defects, of stupidity, self-conceit, emptiness, and laziness is assessed as "a snake's bite?" If your indignation at human baseness, cajolery, hypocrisy meets society's response, "Oh my God, is he a Carbonaro?" If you are deceived by a loved woman and want to have it out with her and she lets a rumor out that "you are not in your right senses" which is snatched up by everyone? And then they are already shunning you like they would a madman? Then how should you act?

Having drunk the cup of agony to the bottom, not finding in a single soul, the "sympathy of the living," at first, Chatsky more and more loses self-control. Disappointingly, it turns out that there are too many antagonists – the whole Moscow world. He feels that the battle in isolation has exhausted him. But, he doesn't give up. Experiencing "a million agonies," squeezing his chest, he becomes jaundiced, nagging, immeasurably irritable and, boiling with rage, continues to expose the lie, flinging himself on everyone and everything indiscriminately, passing a merciless sentence on Moscow before abandoning her forever:

> I've no more dreams, the scales have fallen from my eyes.
> Now it would do no harm to take them all in turn –
> Daughter and father,
> And the brainless lover,
> And the whole world, and pour upon them
> All of my bitterness, all my frustration.
> Who was I with? Where did Fate cast me up?
> Tormentors, all of them; Cursing and persecuting,
> [...]
> You all with one accord declared that I was mad –
> And you were right! A man could go through fire unharmed,
> If he could spend a single day with you,
> Breathe the same air as you.
> And keep his reason.
> Out, out from Moscow! Now, no more I'll ride this way;
> I am off, I'm running, I'm not looking back,
> I've gone to search the world,
> To find some niche where outraged sense can shelter! –
> My carriage! Get my carriage![38]

---

[38] Griboedov, p. 147. In the first edition of *Gore ot Uma*, this second to last line was different: "Where there is a cosy corner both for reason and sense." In our view it expresses the main idea of the comedy more exactly (which in its original version was titled "Gore Umu" (Tragedy to the Reason). The accepted, smoothed over version, "Where for the insulted one there is a corner for sense," puts the accent on the lover's intrigue and relates, in our opinion, to the corrections in the text which in Griboedov's own words, "spoiled" the comedy and made it poorer. Here the remarks of the American translator J. Cooper are appropriate. In the latest edition of his translation (*Four Russian Plays [...]*, p. 213), he suggests to compare this line with the words of Alceste in Molière's *Le Misanthrope* (V.iv): "Et chercher sur la terre un endroit écarté Où d'estre homme d'honneur on ait la libérté." Although Cooper (who titled his translation of "Gore ot Uma," *Chatsky*) follows the Russian text exactly, his remark that Chatsky, like Alceste, promotes consideration of "reason" strengthens our supposition.

In Chatsky's last monologue we find, in essence, a model for the whole play. The monologue actually brings to mind a gryphon – that fantastic winged being with a lion's body and eagle's head – with which Griboedov compared his comedy, emphasizing two beginnings in it, the real and ideal, from which latter alone appears a "wonderful, ideal nature, higher than is visible to us."[39] From another perspective, in the monologue is reflected a completely realistic, even emphatically common everyday background, upon recognition of which occurs "the sobering" of the hero – he finds a concrete world of sinister old women and men, grown decrepit over made-up things, nonsense, in the poisoned air of the Moscow *beau monde*.

Griboedov's picture of Moscow is dominated by the Romantic image of Chatsky's coach, the real emblem of the daily life of the city's nobility, and simultaneously, the symbol of the wandering, searching, eternal dissatisfaction of the suffering and staggering hero. Chatsky's coach, as theatrical metaphor, suggests rushing off somewhere, not finding one's destiny in Russia. Not in vain was this image of Griboedov's snatched up afterwards with such lyrical strength by N.V. Gogol. In the final part of the first volume of *Dead Souls*, he transforms the *kibitka* (a hooded cart) of his arch-Realistic hero Chichikov into an unexpected Romantic symbol of all of Russian life:

> Eh, thou troika, thou that art a bird! Who conceived thee? Methinks it is only among a spirited fold that thou couldst have come into being [...] Whither art thou soaring away to, then, Russia? Give me thy answer! But Russia gives none [...] all things on earth fly past and, eyeing it askance, all the other peoples and nations stand aside and give it the right of way.[40]

(Translated from the Russian by *Tracy Rich*.)

---

[39] I am citing from the innovative work of I. Medvedev, *A.S. Griboedov: Gore ot Uma*, (Moscow: Hudozhestvennaya Literatura, 1971), p. 71, which presents a rare analysis of the elements of Romanticism in Griboedov's work. The author comes to the conclusion, in this work, that in *Gore ot Uma*, developing a new poetics, "Griboedov masterfully carried out [...] the inner fused unification of two styles: Romantic and Classical" (p. 68).

[40] Nikolai Gogol, *Dead Souls*, trans. B. Guerney, introd. by René Wellek (New York: Rinehart, 1948), pp. 303-4.

HANA VOISINE-JECHOVA

ROMANTICISM IN GENRES OF DRAMA IN BOHEMIA

The comparatist always finds himself facing supplementary difficulties when he attempts to study those literatures whose development differs noticeably from the phenomena considered as dominant in cultures of wide diffusion. In addition, the study of dramatic genres poses particular problems. What is involved is a protean creation (one sole play inspires multiple stagings, the text, even by virtue of its destination, lends itself to innumerable modifications); its originality is "flexible," less respected and less insisted upon than originality in other literary genres, and that, to boot, at the beginning of the last century. There is, in effect, a common theatrical repertory, differentiated according to the type of public envisaged and according to the cultural function of the spectacle rather than its belonging to one or another national literature. This situation is most evident in literatures which were are searching for their voice in the chorus of European cultures during the Romantic period, as is the case for Czech literature. The analysis of a national theater under these circumstances becomes, to some extent, the study of translations and adaptations of foreign works. And finally, we have only a fragmentary documentation at our disposal. Manuscripts which did not attract much attention are lost; only some second hand bits of information indicate their existence and reception on the part of the public.

In Bohemia, an additional problem aggravates these difficulties. In the first half of the last century there was a very complex symbiosis between Czech and German theatrical life in Prague and even elsewhere, and this was reflected as much in the realization of shows as in the composition of dramatic works. The actors themselves, Czech and German, played (and sang) in productions in the German language and in the Czech language. One even finds bilingual plays. Among these *Čech a Němec* (The Czech and the German, 1816) by J.N. Štěpánek deserves special mention, as it has survived down to the twentieth century in the repertory of Czech theater. One set of the actors in it performs in German, another set performs in Czech, thus transmitting the linguistically mixed atmosphere of Bohemia at the time. To be sure, Carl Maria von Weber was involved in German opera in Prague and he is justifiably considered one of the creators of the German national opera. Nonetheless, he was in contact with the Czech milieu, his work was translated and performed in Czech for the Czech public, and it contributed to introducing certain Romantic procedures in Czech stagings and even in Czech original theatrical creations, above all in those by the composer František Skroup (1801-62).

To simplify things, one could say that Czech literature has only one great Romantic who is a "true" poet, K.H. Mácha (1810-36), some imitations of his work, such as V.B. Nebeký's (1818-82), several poets of popular inspiration who in certain instances came close to a Romantic mode of expression that was specifically Slavic, and many authors who combined a didactic Classicism with a moderate Romanticism, or indeed Sentimentalism. How then, under these circumstances, should dramatic production be studied?

One could say that, with the exception of some dramatic fragments, Romantic drama in Bohemia failed to experience a flowering analogous to that in other literatures where Romanticism manifested itself with vigor and under several forms, as for example in the case of Victor Hugo's dramatic work, or as is well-known, under another form, in Polish literature of the 1830s and 1840s. Beyond that, we could bring our reflections to an end.

All the same, the postulate of Romantic drama did exist in Bohemia. The most eminent literary theoretician Josef Jungmann (1773-1847), who himself oscillates between Classicism and Romanticism, speaks in his work *Slovenost* (On Literature, 1820, 2nd aug. ed. 1846) of the Romantic genres of drama, especially of Romantic tragedy (section 51) which he considers to be one of the peaks of literary creativity. Several dramatists of the times (above all V. Klicpera, 1792-1859) sought to create a tragedy of this kind whose existence would prove that Czech literature had reached the level of the most advanced European literatures. In effect, these authors combine elements of the *Schicksalstragödie* with representations of "Romantic" heroes, torn, hesitant, and lost from the start through their incapacity to decide and act. Such plays, which found scant favorable response from the public of those times and are forgotten today, nevertheless testify to certain Romantic aspirations in Czech dramaturgy and to the difficulties that their intellectual supporters, open to foreign inspiration, encountered among the patriotic public who belonged to the large popular or semi-popular strata, rather than to any social elite.

Another Romantic feature, very important for the development of the aesthetic conscience of the age, was exhibited foremost not in the characters of the dramatic text, but in its staging, its visualization through "Romantic" scenery. The Gothic vaults of a prison, the fortresses perched on rocky heights, disquieting forests, the moon's pale glimmer, flashes of lightning and thunder, all this was part of the usual repertory of the era's stage productions, and it is thence that they penetrated into the lyric poetry of which Mácha's work *Máj* furnishes the most eloquent example.

In principle, it is necessary to take account of the co-existence of Classicizing and Romantic tendencies at the beginning of the nineteenth century in Czech literature, as well as elsewhere in all other literatures under differing forms. It is not at all appropriate to speak solely about Romantic elements in literary production, without mentioning how they are interlaced with elements of a "non-Romantic" character. Yet in proceeding in this fashion, our survey would cease to be devoted to Romanticism in the dramatic genres of Bohemia; it would become a summary of the era's entire dramatic creation in Bohemia, in which some aspects could be interpreted as "Romantic," but within a rather broad definition, that is not lacking in ambiguity. Besides, is it possible to reduce dramatic production in Bohemia during the era in question exclusively to the co-existence of Classicizing and Romantic elements? Or would it be necessary to take into consideration yet other components that cannot easily be classified as pertaining to a literary current or movement, or that are even difficult to grasp because of their inchoate popular character and because of their, in the strict sense of the word, more didactic and entertaining than aesthetic function? We incline toward this second hypothesis which renders our task yet more complicated, that is to say, the investigation of Romanticism within drama as a cluster of genres in Bohemia.

At the same time, we should take account of the fact that, from the end of the eighteenth to the second half of the nineteenth centuries, several generations of Czechs without doubt were anxious to create a great national theater, even though what resulted from their aspirations was rather disappointing. One does not find a great Classic or Romantic theater in Bohemia. It is only with the opera, starting in the second half of the nineteenth century, and with certain experimental pieces for theater, cabaret, and ironic or absurd fairy-tale shows, that Czech dramatic production asserts itself on an international level. In analyzing Romantic drama, we will be induced, then, to explore not only the character of works edited in those times, but also their failures, erroneous undertakings, and inadequate efforts.

Our labors can succeed only by recourse to a compromise. Even while trying to bring the Romantic characteristics of Czech dramatic creation into evidence, we shall be obliged to demonstrate their conflation, indeed their confrontations with other aesthetic and cultural tendencies.

It is difficult to establish a periodization of literary phenomena, the character of which would be marked by respect for clearly defined aesthetic criteria. In the case of polymorphous and polyvalent creations, to which the dramatic production we are going to examine seems to belong, these difficulties become almost insurmountable. For practical reasons, we propose to limit our observations to the period starting from the second decade and finishing in the sixth decade of the nineteenth century. The first date corresponds to Josef Jungmann's definition of the aesthetic criteria which several writers attempted to apply in their writings. It also applies to the publication of the first literary works which attained an internationally recognized level after the cultural weakening that occurred in Bohemia as a consequence of the Thirty Years' War. (I refer to the *Královédvorský Manuscript*, "discovered" in 1817, and the *Manuscript* of *Zelená Hora*, which emerged in 1818.) The second date corresponds to the temporary choking-off of Czech national hopes through Austrian absolutism under Bach, which set in after Prince Schwarzenberg's death on April 5, 1852.[1]

This period is, however, far from being homogeneous. In the dramatic genres, one finds a complex and multiple development of forms and of literary contents, ranging from a naïve and chivalric Romanticism either toward a sentimental or pathetic declamatory style, or toward visions of horror and crime that taint the marvelous, the fantastic, and the exceptional. All the same, as we have just said, this movement is not the only one leaving its mark on theatrical production in Bohemia. Alongside the "Romantic" characteristics (which manifest themselves elsewhere under several aspects and definitions) there were yet other tendencies which led to the introduction of a certain moderate, entertaining, humoristic, or didactic "Realism" and combined in several forms with "Romantic" elements.

By way of summary, one could say that as of the end of the eighteenth century, Czech theatre generated two distinct forms: chivalric plays, often presented as "historical" and designated explicitly as "Romantic"; and scenes from daily life, transcriptions and/or critiques of banal events which tended to evolve in the direction of "Realist" representation of personages and ordinary intrigues.

Scholarly investigations usually address only this first type of dramatic production leaving the second aside. However, since one of the characteristic traits of Romantic theater is the mutual contamination of the sublime and the grotesque, we are obliged to mention the fact that the quotidian – which easily acquired grotesque characteristics in confrontation with fantastic or pathetic elements – was firmly anchored in theatrical consciousness in Bohemia and penetrated abundantly into all sorts of dramatic productions. Yet the result of this was not a concentrated Romantic vision, amal-

---

[1] Alexander Bach, Minister of Justice, Minister of Interior in Austria from 1849-59; he sought to surpress liberal and patriotic tendencies under the monarchy.

gamating the sublime and the grotesque, but a mosaic of procedures that destroy the aesthetic unity of the work. Given the primary role of scenery and stage effects, works of this genre offered an exterior visualization of juxtaposed Romantic elements rather than a Romantic vision, at once exterior and interior, of contradictions inherent in human destiny.

Czech dramatic genres of the time had only a slight chance of being represented on the professional stage, they had to be satisfied with being preformed in the private theaters that were active during a rather limited period and without institutional stability in various places, most particularly in Prague. The dramatists depended above all on amateur actors, and they also had to pay attention to the marionnette theater which, in the case of Matěj Kopecký (1775-1847), played an important role in the development of a taste for spectacles, most especially in the countryside.

Of course, acquaintance with certain works of Schiller and Shakespeare went back a rather long time, and the latter was even cited as one of the models of the Czech dramatists, as well as of Schiller. (The translations of *Macbeth* and the *Räuber*, by K.I. Thám, were published in book form in 1786.) All the same, the most often translated, adapted, and performed authors in the first two decades of the nineteenth century were Heinrich Cuno, Johann Heinrich Zschokke, and August Kotzebue. The Czech works of "chivalric Romanticism" are constructed after the model of these second-rate authors, rather than after the great models of European Romantic drama.

Among the numerous playwrights, one can distinguish two dramatic authors at the beginning of the nineteenth century who, to be sure, are not Romantic in all their works, but have made use of certain motifs and procedures which one can associate with this movement. I refer to Jan Nepomuk Štěpánek (1783-1844) and Václav Kliment Klicpera (1792-1859). These two authors excelled more in the comic genres, little affected by Romanticism, than in the serious, chivalric, and/or historical genres, where Baroque pathos in plot and language combined with the Romantic taste for the marvelous and mysterious.

An historical subject-matter, however, did not guarantee a Romantic conception of the storyline. In evoking the celebrated past and the moral and martial qualities of their ancestors, the writers actually very often expressed an eloquent but moderate patriotism, in accordance with the taste of enlightened rationalism, that had nothing in common with the harrowing visions of a Romantic patriotism that later found its masterly expression in Polish Romantic dramas, but also in the works of K.H. Mácha. Certain "Romantic" traits appeared first in naïve and traditional plays which are historical only in appearance. Schematic conflicts were situated in the scenery of a vague and inconsistent past; an innocent young girl is menaced by a scoundrel, but at the last moment her faithful lover arrives to save her, and the criminal is punished. Štěpánek created such a chivalric piece (in Czech "rytířna") in his drama *Jaroslav a Blažena aneb Hrad Kunětice* (J. and B. or the Castle of Kunetice, 1816). Klicpera proceeded in an analogous fashion in his work *Blaník* (written in 1813, staged in 1816), and one could cite several further examples.

In principle, this type of play conflates two series of bipolarities: a) on the moral plane (confrontation between perfect knights and accomplished malefactors, one clearly distinct from the other); and b) on the social plane (noble personages and their servants who represent the common people). The characters of the heroes are schematic, set, not susceptible to change during the unfolding of the story. The action is based on external conflicts, resulting from accidental circumstances rather than a profound logic of human relations. The language is figurative to a high degree, often characterized as "artificial," and considered sometimes as one of the reasons for the failure of these plays in the short or long term. One must bear in mind that in Bohemia at this time, and most especially in certain dramatic works, there was conflation between Baroque taste, still contemporary at the end of the eighteenth century and even at the start of the nineteenth century, and Romantic taste, which made its inroads on the one hand through the interest in popular poetry and on the other through the discovery of the models of European Romanticism (above all, Shakespeare).

Dramatists and critics were aiming at the creation of a great poetic tragedy in the Romantic taste, or rather, moving close to certain aesthetic tendencies of Romanticism, without thereby completely abandoning the poetics of Classicism. It is in the framework of these efforts that one should situate the one-act play *Bratrovrah* by J.N. Štěpánek (The Fratricide, published in book form in 1821; accompanied by the music of F. Skroup, it was performed in the theater in 1831). The same year that Byron published his mystery *Cain*, the Czech dramatist, independently of the English poet, evoked the same biblical characters and thus tried to achieve the genre considered as the summit of dramatic creation – a religious drama. The hero of Štěpánek is no longer univocal and monolithic. In choosing a personage who could serve as a model for Romantic heroes, marked by a metaphysical culpability and inwardly torn, the Czech dramatist treats, in effect, the series of Romantic characters who are double personalities, who vacillate, and are tortured by doubts. But in the staging of his play it seems that this aspect was not yet brought out. The actor who played the principal role, Grau, was renowned for his portrayal of criminals and malefactors, but he probably eliminated the problematic character of Cain, in an interpretation that followed the pattern of a traditional villain.

More ambitious yet is Klicpera's tragedy in verse, *Soběslav, selský kníže* (S., The Peasant Prince, written in 1824, published in book form in 1826, but not represented on stage until 1839). The work bears witness to the conflation of the chivalric "old Romanticism" with a "modern Romanticism," marked by the influence of Shakespeare. As in *Hamlet*, the dead father's ghost appears here to the orphan son to put him on guard; the tragic action is interrupted by an interlude introducing the chit-chat of two Prague citizens. Set at the dawn of the history of the Czech house of the Przemyslides, the story is concentrated around an impassioned and torn "Romantic" hero, who inevitably precipitates his own fall. Although highly appreciated by the critics of the period and considered down to our day as an important step in Czech dramatic creativity as "chivalric Romanticism" evolved toward a "modern Romanticism," Klicpera's tragedy nonetheless has not enjoyed the success of his comedies and his farces. It served as reading material gratifying young poets in their exalted musings, rather than fulfilling any genuine dramatic function.

Other dramatic works, conceived according to the criteria of *Schicksalstragödie* and/or marked by the interest in Romanticism as an exalting vision of the exceptional destiny of individuals, were received by the public in the same fashion. Though they were admired by critics, and appreciated as a Romantic form of dramatic literature, they failed to become part of a permanent repertory.

The ambition of creating a great poetic drama that would satisfy the taste for Shakespeare and Schiller went hand in hand with the interest in historical, or rather mythic, subjects. Thus Josef Linda (1789-1834) evoked a legendary event of the thirteenth century in the play *Jaroslav Sternberg v boji proti Tatarům* (J.S. in the Combat against the Tartars, published in 1823). The author was long considered one of the "falsifiers" of the *Manuscripts* of *Dvůr Králové* and of *Zelená Hora*. He was a poet of undoubted qualities but did not possess a dramatic vein. His play contains grand declamations in a style overloaded with poetic tropes and figures rather than presenting an action. Rejected by Czech critics of the time, it never made it to the stage. Happier in this regard is the drama by Jan Erazim Vocel (1803-71), *Harfa* (The Harp, published in 1825, performed on the stage in 1837). Even in this piece, the story of which is situated in the ninth century, elements of a *Schicksalstragödie* are combined with procedures characteristic of chivalric drama, without resulting in a truly dramatic vision.

The other attempts to introduce a *Schicksalstragödie* in Bohemia did not enjoy any greater success. Thus, Klicpera's *Rod Svojanovský* (Family S., published in 1821), which J.N. Štěpánek had introduced in 1832 on the boards of the Theater of the Estates (The Nostitz Theater) as a manifestation of the noble dramatic genre in the Czech language, was hardly a memorable affair and was doomed to be quickly forgotten. And even the play most appreciated by criticism of the age, František Turinsky's (1797-1852) *Angelina* enjoyed success as a poetic work, undeniably enriching Czech literature, but not as a dramatic creation in the true sense of the word. Published in book form in 1821, this drama's première took place as late as 1897 at the National Theater in Prague. It seems, in effect, that the great timeless visions of human conflicts and passions scarcely attracted Czech dramatists, not only in the first decades of the nineteenth century, but throughout the history of Czech dramaturgy right down to the present. Czech literature seems marked, rather, by its interest in the concrete, in what is defined historically and socially and results in a certain sense from external conditions.[2]

Romantic elements appeared not only in the tragedy, or in serious drama with an elevated subject, but equally in some plays with plots drawn from the everyday life of the common people. Set in the ordinary present and thus without distance in time or in space which favored the introduction of a Romantic optic, these plays combined most often an idyllic or lachrymose Sentimentalism with humorous passages, with jokes, or even a not-very-naughty satire. This type of dramatic production could be regarded as "Biedermeier" rather than as "Classic" or "Romantic," if one wanted at any cost to attribute a label to it indicating attachment to a literary current. The free structure of works of this genre, which were composed, in reality, of a mosaic of images, of dialogues, and of fragmentary or incidental little stories, permitted the introduction of almost independent motifs, some of which belonged to the Romantic repertory. Thus in Klicpera's comedy, *Belouši* (written in 1816, produced in 1818, and published in 1821) there appeared the bizarre character of a foolish beggar, mystic and simple in spirit, who can be interpreted as a survival of Baroque motifs, but also as a Romantic hero, visionary and ineffectual at the same time. In any case, he had little in common with the play's main plot which was inspired, according to the author's testimony, by Plautus' *Amphitryon*; and in the stage adaptation, probably carried out by J.N. Štěpánek, this role was simply suppressed. The hero fallen out of his social class, surrounded by mystery, and announcing truths which exceed the logical reasoning of ordinary people is represented in yet further plays, often "alongside the principal plot." His most famous incarnation is the character of Mares in *Fidlovačka* (Spring Festival, performed in 1834) by J.K. Tyl (1808-56), which J. Skroup set to music. The song which the blind violinist sings at a popular Prague festival, "Kde domov můj?" (Where is My Fatherland?) has, in fact, become the Czech national anthem which is still sung on solemn official occasions.

Interest in the theater was still growing in the 1830s and 40s. It was no longer identified with the provinces, as was still the case in the first decades of the nineteenth century in certain elite

---

[2] See *Dějiny českého divadla*, II, ed. František Černý and Vladimír Procházka (Prague: Academia, Nakladatelství Ceskoslovenské Akademie Věd, 1969), pp. 138-39.

circles, but almost all the writers of renown, whom one habitually considers as "Romantics," tried to distinguish themselves either as dramatists, or as theatrical critics, or even as actors. All the same, this enthusiasm did not bring about spectacular results. The most ambitious projects remained incomplete, unknown to the public, and at times even conceived in a manner unacceptable to the spectator of the times. Thus K.H. Mácha, himself active as an amateur actor, contemplated writing a cycle of historical dramas in the spirit of Shakespeare, yet there are only a few fragments of this in his manuscripts. J.J. Langer's (1806-46) drama, *Marinka Záleská* (1831), evoking the conflict of an exceptional individual with his insensitive entourage in the Romantic taste, likewise remained unfinished.

The Romantic plays of Europe were admired by the Czech poets, but they were perceived as elevated reading, without thought being given to staging them. In the thirties Mácha was enthusiastic about the dramas of Juliusz Słowacki, but the Polish poet had to wait more than a half-century even in his own county before his plays were performed – and his Czech admirer cited him in order to introduce his own visions and poetic concepts, without stressing the dramatic genre of his model. Other Slavic works, above all Russian and Polish, which began to make inroads with the Czech public, as well as some plays from the European repertory (usually through German translations or adaptations), often suffered the same fate.

On stage, it was above all Nestroy who attracted attention, though interest in Kotzebue remained strong. From the French repertory, only one play by Eugène Scribe, *Le treizième manteau*, was performed in 1834 in Štěpánek's adaptation that followed the German adaptation by K.L. Blum. The first play by Victor Hugo put on in Czech was the translation of the German adaptation of his novel, *Notre-Dame de Paris* (The Hunchback of Notre Dame, in November 1848). It was only two years later that the Czech theater turned towards his dramatic work, properly so called, by staging his *Ruy Blas* (titled "The Queen and Her Lover" in the Czech version).

Most in favor, then, were the farces, comedies, and vaudevilles representing the life of craftsmen and merchants in lowly and traditional plots. These plays were performed in Prague or even in other cities of Bohemia or Moravia where amateur companies and even some professional actors were propagating Czech theater, they gave prominence to local color, the respect for which can be considered as one of the characteristics among Romantic tendencies although it signals at the same time an orientation toward literary realism.

While the first phase of Czech drama in the Romantic period witnessed a coexistence of Baroque, Classicizing, and Romantic elements, the second seems marked above all by the coalescence of realistic and Romantic characteristics. The evolution of taste and of aesthetic procedures is nonetheless slow and hesitant. The preferred genre in the theater of the thirties and even forties was, in fact, the *Märchendrama*, the dramatization of fairy tales familiar to dramatists and spectators alike.

At the beginning of the previous century, theoreticians, collectors, and imitators of popular poetry played a very important role in all Slavic literatures. In this context, procedures of the traditional and fixed genre of *Märchendrama* (or *Zauberspiel*) conflated readily with the poetic vision of popular fantasy. In Bohemia, this process was of a particular importance. The great picturesque spectacles with dazzling scenic effects were increasingly influenced by the imagination of the popular audience. The heroes were no longer knights represented according to schematic literary models, but peasants, craftsmen, minor village artists (above all musicians), and women of the people. Being based on two trends in Romantic inspiration (*Zauberspiel* and interest in folklore), these plays at the same time introduced aspects of realism which appear both in the dramatic text itself and in stage directions. This involved using types of simple persons, characterized in precise fashion with picturesque details, and associating the mainsprings of the plot with their lives (the aspirations of man in a bourgeois society).

The best known example of this genre is J.K. Tyl's *Strakonický dudák* (The Bagpipe Player of Strakonice, staged for the first time in 1847). Here the supernatural world is combined with scenes from popular everyday life. The timeless subject of a mother's sacrifice and of the love which surmounts all obstacles is accompanied by motifs which translate the concrete situation of the simple folk in Bohemia in the author's own times. Švanda, the bagpipe player, is the son of a fairy. He is dissatisfied with his humble station and goes in search of happiness – money – in the world. The motif of economic emigration, which was beginning to disturb the society, is translated into a fairytale vision: the exotic milieux that the Czech musician visits and the intervention of beneficent and maleficent supernatural forces provide opportunity for a picturesque spectacle in the taste of popular festivals. Saved by the sacrifice of his mother and by the faithful love of his girlfriend Dorotka, Švanda returns to the beloved in order to appreciate simple happiness there, more precious than money. Through the idyllic conclusion, the play is associated with numerous Czech narratives of the times, usually considered "Romantic," in which conflicts end in reconciliation and emphasis on simple happiness in honorable and humble conditions. The masterpiece of Czech prose, *Babička* (Grandmother, 1855) by Božena Němcová (1820-62) follows the same pattern.

Rather than presenting a dramatic action in the true sense of the word, Tyl's play is composed by juxtaposition of picturesque scenes. The songs and dances (in popular costumes) contribute palpably to its impact on the public. (The play, performed with success down to the present, has been translated into several languages and has twice been adapted for the screen.) The play is interspersed with songs that are almost independent (they are at times sung in front of the curtain) and contain commentaries on extra-literary questions of the day rather than on the play's plot. This type of spectacle, very much in favor in Bohemia, seems to enjoy success right to the present. In any case, it was widely used in the "Liberated Theater" of Voskovec and Werich in the nineteen thirties.

Still other dramatists were trying themselves out in this genre, combining foreign models with autochtonous popular inspiration. Very popular have been the Czech and Moravian adaptations of Adolf Bäuerle's *Aline oder Wien in einem anderen Welttheile* (Aline, or Vienna on Another Continent), introduced in Prague by J.N. Štěpánek and in Brno in 1839 by Karel Ruber. It served widely as a model for Czech dramatists, including J.K. Tyl. In 1847, Klicpera created a dramatic fairy tale, *Česká Meluzína* (The Czech Melusina), and Tyl himself composed several more plays of this kind, of which *Tvrdohlavá žena* (A Stubborn Woman, 1849), *Jiříkovo vidění* (Georgie's Vision, 1849), and *Lesní panna* (The Wood Nymph, 1850) merit mention.

Tyl was indeed the representative dramatist of the times. Equally active in other literary genres (above all tales), he was an actor, producer, translator, adaptor, and author. He composed some fifty original plays and adaptations for the theater and was officially considered to be a "dramatic poet."[3] His choice of subjects and aesthetic procedures can be interpreted as typical tendencies in the Czech theater of the times, or at least characteristic of some of these tendencies which predominated in the atmosphere of the 1840s in one group of the Czech elite.

Tyl actually stands out in those already established genres that had attracted several Czech

---

[3] *Dějiny českého divadla*, II, 312.

dramatists. Alongside the "Märchendrama," he cultivated on the one hand farce and "scenes from daily life," and on the other hand historical drama. Tyl's dramatic work is didactic. Like some of his predecessors, he is attempting to educate the people through theater, to inculcate moral, patriotic, and social ideals. The aspect of entertainment is more clearly subordinated to ideological concerns in his case than in the case of dramatists of the preceding age. Several of his plays extol simple, modest, and poor people. In their willingness to sacrifice themselves and to forgive, they come into conflict with rich, insensitive people who are culpable but sometimes repent. True happiness consists in relationships of love and understanding which, however, are almost always threatened by lust for money and power. Most of Tyl's "scenes of life" are based on this simple, explicit, and in principle non-problematic bipolarity. They interpret contrasts and conflicts springing from external conditions, from social inequality and injustice; they only rarely express inner contradictions born from the unimaginable complexity of human conscience. Among the most popular of these plays are *Paní Marjánka, matka pluku* (Madame M., Mother of the Regiment, produced for the first time in 1845), *Pražský flamendr* (A Profligate of Prague, produced for the first time in 1846), and *Palicova dcera* (The Incendiary's Daughter, first performed in 1847).

Historical subjects are of a capital importance in all literary genres; their patriotic didacticism is a characteristic of Czech cultural efforts. In drama, their function is more accentuated than elsewhere. Alongside fictional characters placed arbitrarily in the historical past, the dramatists attempted – already as of the end of the eighteenth century – to introduce real historical personages whose actions could serve as a model and awaken national pride. In the 1830s and above all in the agitated atmosphere of the 1840s, this tendency solidified and even became dominant. There was a pronounced predilection to make the glorious and tragic events of the Hussite movement come alive again upon the stage. Several dramatists created plays about Jan Žižka, King Wenceslas the Fourth, and above all Jan Hus. Some of these works are not genuine dramas, but "Tableaux vivants." Thus in 1848, to hail the Constitution, Czech theater put on a great scenic tableau, *Jan Žižka z Trocnova*; it was introduced by a poem of J.K. Tyl, which the author himself recited. The visual aspect and the solemn declamation transmitting the writer's ideas prevailed over the dramatic action itself even in proper dramatic works. Such is the case of Tyl's *Jan Hus* (1848), a play highly appreciated and considered representative down to our days. In pathetic and moving verse, the dramatist transcribed and visualized that chapter of Czech history which the patriotic public, attracted by democratic ideals, venerated as the most precious heritage of the national past. As the poet Jan Neruda (1834-81) later confirmed, it was the spectators who by their enthusiastic reception lent that work its value and its dramatic dimensions.

If the Hussite epoch was more in favor, above all in the atmosphere of the Springtime of the Peoples, playwrights readily handled subjects drawn from other epochs. Czech authors were turning rather infrequently towards the past of foreign countries, and even Greek and Roman antiquity scarcely attracted the dramatists. Turinsky's poetic tragedy *Virginia*, conceived in the taste of *Schicksalstragödie* and evoking the struggles between Romans and Samnites in the third century B.C., was never produced. It was published in book form in 1841.

More often, the historical subjects drawn from the national past served to express theological concepts of the present, or to introduce "Romantic" characters, indeed to emphasize "Romantic" situations. Tyl leans towards the first possibility. His play *Krvavé křtiny aneb Drahomíra a její synové* (The Bloody Baptism, or D. and Her Sons, first performed in 1849) uses medieval conflicts to illustrate the irreconcilable antagonism of Czechs and Germans; – this was a widespread idea in

Czech society of the time; it controls František Palacky's view of the Czech people's history. The second conception dear to writers of the 1840s, the struggle for social justice, was expressed in his drama *Krvavý soud aneb Kutnohorští havíři* (The Bloody Judgement, or the Miners of Kutná Hora, presented for the first time in 1848), in which, using the example of a miners' strike in the fifteenth century, the author comments, in fact, on social agitation in his own day.

Another conception of historical drama appeared in the work of Josef Jiří Kolár (1812-96). As an actor, Kolár impersonated on the Czech stage as well as on the German stage of Prague, in the taste of pathetic Romanticism, exceptional persons who are stirred by great passions and find themselves in bloody conflict with the surrounding world. Through his play-acting on stage as well as his translations of Schiller and Goethe and his original dramas, he contributed to the creation of the grand style Czech theater. Like several dramatists of his day, he too was inspired by the "most glorious" period of Czech history and wrote a drama about Žižka (*Žižkova smrt*, Žižkova's Death, 1850). But information about the past of the country and ideological exhortation in his work did not have the same clarity as in Tyl's. This is particularly evident in the verse tragedy *Monica* (first staged in 1846), and in *Magelóna* (first staged in 1852), which exhibit the passions of uncommon individuals against the historical backdrop, and represent the irreparable acts of treason, crime, and vengeance in an atmosphere of enigma and mystery.

Kolár was not alone in emphasizing grand gestures, violent actions, and untamable passions. F.B. Mikovec (1826-62) carried off a success in 1848 with a tragedy composed according to the same fashion, *Záhuba rodu Přemyslovského* (The Extermination of the House of the Przemyslides). This type of theater did not really develop in Bohemia. The play *Kocan Ratiborský* (published in book form in 1847) by J.V. Frič (1829-90), which evokes a supreme act of vengeance, has not even been produced on stage.

In conclusion there is abundant evidence that Romantic elements entered Czech drama in the second decade of the nineteenth century; but they combined with other elements taken up from a moderate Classicism or a sentimental and didactic Realism. The Romantic characteristics seem more evident in works that had mediocre success with the public or even were not produced on stage, than in the plays then in favor. The grand Romantic drama, featuring exceptional individuals and conflicts and passions beyond the common, was not produced except by J.J. Kolár at the end of the forties when, in the international context, pathetic Romanticism was already giving way to other forms of dramatic vision and representation. Kolár's dramas, which moreover widely imitated foreign models, have scarcely survived the test of time.

One could nonetheless say that Czech dramatic genres belong to a specific sort of Romanticism in which the convergence of idyllic, popular, and didactic traits also permits the introduction of fairy-tale visions and pathetic declamations. Seen in this light, the plays of the time were expressing the same tendencies as the lyric and epic genres in Czech literature.

However that may be, this hesitant and polymorphous theater has played a very important role in the formation of modern Czech culture. Its ambiguous position in the European context testifies to the complexity of the Czech situation in the age when the tradition of literature "for the people" was combining with Romantic impulses coming from abroad and with a native "Romanticism" – a moderate Romanticism, distinguished by its admiration for popular song and for folkloric and ethnographic studies which were attractive to scholars as well as to Czech poets and prose writers.

(Translated from the French by *Gerald Gillespie*.)

MIHÁLY SZEGEDY-MASZÁK

ROMANTIC DRAMA IN HUNGARY

1. Historical Tragedies

There are at least two possible ways of approaching Romantic drama in Hungary: one can either characterize the vigorous theatrical life of the early nineteenth century, doing justice to the great number of plays written by Hungarian authors, or concentrate on those works which may be regarded as important artistic achievements and original contributions to Romantic drama in general. The first method would be justified by the fact that Romanticism was the first artistic and literary movement to inspire a comprehensive profligacy of dramatic writing in Hungarian. Yet as an overall treatment of the output of Hungarian playwrights may be out of place in an international context, our attention here will focus primarily on generally acclaimed masterpieces, taking it for granted that some historical background is a necessary precondition for their valid interpretation.

Although Hungarian writers hardly produced any dramatic works of great aesthetic value before 1800, Hungarian Romanticism was much indebted to earlier theatrical traditions. When writing *Csongor and Tünde*, for example, Vörösmarty drew not only upon folktales and romances of the *bella istoria* type, written by such sixteenth-century poets as Albert Gergei, but also upon moralities which together with mysteries had been performed in Hungary as in other parts of medieval Europe. Furthermore, the strong intellectual character of both Vörösmarty's play and the *chef-d'oeuvre* of Madách, *The Tragedy of Man*, may owe something to the tradition of religious play-writing initiated by Protestants in the sixteenth century and carried on by Jesuits and Piarists over the next two centuries.

In any case, it would be wrong to assume that Hungarian drama did not develop before the advent of Romanticism. Bálint Balassi (1554-94), the most outstanding poet of the Hungarian Renaissance composed a pastoral play before any major secular drama was written in England. This in itself suggests that drama had a strong if uneven tradition before the Romantics emerged and wrote superlative works of art for the stage.

There are two main reasons for the quantitative changes brought about by Romanticism: the vogue of the national past and the construction of permanent theatres for the bourgeois middle class. Although some Protestant writers of the sixteenth century had taken an interest in national characteristics, the international spirit of Classicism was not favourable to works stressing the *couleur locale* of Hungary. Besides, until the later eighteenth century there was much uncertainty about the origin of the "Magyar" language. When in 1770 Nepomuk János Sajnovics, a Jesuit scholar, pointed out that his native tongue belonged to the group of Finno-Ugrian languages, the discovery had a profound impact on public opinion: Hungarians became aware of their linguistic isolation in a continent largely populated by peoples speaking Indo-European languages.

This awareness, together with the Enlighted despotism of Maria Theresa and Joseph II, may have contributed to the revival of nationalism. A significant change of emphasis can be felt if we compare two plays written by György Bessenyei (1747-1811), a leading figure of the Hungarian Enlightenment. The first of these two works, *Ágis tragédiája* (The Tragedy of Agis, 1772), is about the ambiguities of *absolutisme éclairé*, much in the spirit of Voltaire. The somewhat later comedy *A filozófus* (The Philosopher, 1777) has a Hungarian squire among its characters whose resistance to international progress and love of local traditions clearly show the Hungarian writers' dilemma at the end of the eighteenth century.

Should Hungarians imitate more civilized nations or should they preserve their own customs and ways of living? Nationalists cited Montesquieu who once visited Hungary and argued that the same form of government was not valid for all nations, or Rousseau who had more understanding for the special needs of the Polish nation than Voltaire or Diderot. To see whether the past revealed any values worth preserving, one had to rediscover national history, and the theatre was well suited to that purpose. Bessenyei himself turned to Hungarian history for the subjects of his later plays, and the growing popularity of Shakespeare, as well as the influence of German literature, inspired playwrights to search for the inner logic of Hungarian history.

While in the eighteenth century most plays were performed in schools or in the private theatres of aristocratic families, from the turn of the century companies toured the country and permanent theatres were opened in the larger cities. At first, most of the new theatrical institutions had to face financial and professional difficulties, but they produced more and more plays originally written in Hungarian and worked for an audience incomparably larger than the theatre of the Eszterházys, who commissioned the best actors of Europe, but did not show interest in plays written in Hungarian.

Within a few decades travelling companies and permanent theatres created a wide-spread interest in dramatic genres. In 1815 Gábor Döbrentei, the editor of the periodical *Erdélyi Múzeum*, organized a competition calling for a historical drama to mark the opening of the National Theatre in Kolozsvár, the largest city in Transylvania (a region that, after Hungary lost World War I, was given to Romania). József Katona (1791-1830), a law student who took a passionate interest both in literature and history, submitted his five-act play written in 1813-14, based on the story of Bánk, as related by Antonio Bonfini in *Rerum Ungaricanum Decades Quattuor et Dimidia* (1487-96), a work commissioned by the Hungarian king Matthias I. The result of competition was not announced until 1818. The first prize was not given to any of the plays submitted, and Katona's work was not even listed among those deserving praise. The author rewrote the text and published it in 1820, but his disillusionment was serious enough to put an end to his short career as a playwright. As was the case with some other works of striking originality, the public was not prepared to understand it until some years after its author's death. Its first performance was held in Kassa (a large city today in the South-East of Slovakia) in 1833, and János Arany (1817-1882), the great post-Romantic poet, was the first serious critic to recognize its artistic merits.

In view of the extreme brevity of his literary career, Katona developed very quickly as an artist. His uneven but interesting lyrics, marked by a cult of sensibility, show him to be an experimenter with the language of violent emotions. Tormented by a hopeless love for a leading actress, Róza Széppataki, he shared the life of a travelling company. Translating and adapting German plays as well as acting under a pseudonym, he acquired first-hand knowledge of theatrical conventions. The more experience he gained, the more original his writing became. *Jeruzsálem pusztulása* (The Fall of Jerusalem, 1814), his penultimate play, contained some powerful lines, and in *Bánk bán* he created a work far superior not only to anything he had previously written himself, but also to all the historical dramas produced by Hungarian Romanticism.

The delayed recognition of this play requires some explanation. The first decades of the nineteenth century saw a far-reaching and systematic language reform in Hungary, launched by Ferenc Kazinczy (1759-1831), an important prose writer, a minor poet, a translator of dramatic works by Shakespeare, Molière, Metastasio, Lessing, Goethe, and Schiller, and an extremely energetic organizer of literary life. To replace Latin terms widely and frequently used by earlier writers, a great number of new words were coined, sometimes with the help of non-existent stems and suffixes. Throughout the country intellectuals were encouraged to enlarge their vocabulary. Many of the neologisms were later integrated into standard usage; others became obsolete after a few decades.

In the 1840s a strong reaction set in. The natural ease of the spoken language became the model for a new generation led by János Kriza (1811-75), who discovered the Hungarian ballads sung in Transylvania, János Erdélyi (1814-68), an important theoretician of folklore, Sándor Petőfi (1823-49) and János Arany, the two major poets of the mid-nineteenth century, who set themselves the task of purifying poetic diction. In the light of this change in public taste, many literary works written in the first decades of the century seemed outdated, and the reputation of *Bánk bán* rose because it was free of neologisms.

Katona disregarded the language reform and abstained from coining new words. As a result, the vocabulary of *Bánk bán* is much more limited than that of most literary works composed in Hungary in the early nineteenth century. And yet Katona was an innovator of poetic language: for him, syntactic dislocation and fragmentation, together with metaphor and wordplay, constituted the basic elements of dramatic diction. Aiming to find adequate expression for passionate emotions and spiritual conflicts, he often created an impression of syntactic disorder.

Katona's artistic intention becomes especially clear if we compare his play, named after the nobleman Bánk, to other dramatic treatments of the same subject, i.e., the assassination of the wife of the Hungarian king Andrew II in 1213. George Lillo, as the very title of his *Elmerick or Justice Triumphant* (performed posthumously in 1740) suggests, eliminated the conflict by justifying violence. Almost the same could be said of Franz Grillparzer's undoubtedly superior *Ein treuer Diener seines Herrn* (1828).

The structure and meaning of Katona's tragedy are far more complex. Andrew II must go abroad, because his wife Gertrude is ambitious and has urged him to conquer another country. Patriotic nobles led by Petur, a man characterized by violent outbursts and an almost total lack of self-control, decide to oppose the German-born queen, who has too much influence on her husband and makes the country serve purposes alien to its own interests. The conflict is not only between foreigners and natives, but also between central power and feudal anarchy. Bánk must face a dilemma: he is at once the most powerful of the barons, but also the representative of royal authority in the monarch's absence. When Tiborc, a serf, comes to visit Bánk to complain about the heavy taxes peasants must pay towards the upkeep of Gertrude's court, he shows pity and even sympathy, while being aware that the fate of a country cannot be identified with that of the poor. He learns, however, that the foreign exploiters of the country have also brought him personal humiliation: Gertrude's younger brother Otto has seduced his wife Melinda by using drugs to overcome her resistance. Seeing that shame has driven her mad, and believing, not without good reason, that Otto must have been encouraged by Gertrude, he charges the latter with nepotism and corruption, and when the queen fails to show any respect for the dignity of his office, he stabs her. No sooner is the deed done than he realizes that the punishment he has administered is out of proportion with the guilt. He is further humiliated when, immediately prior to being executed by soldiers, Petur, whose conspiracy against the court has been crushed, curses him as a murderer. The king returns to take revenge, but understands that as a ruler he must blame his wife for her abuse of power. Because of this, he can only make Bánk responsible as a private man. He is just about to do this when Tiborc arrives and informs Bánk of Melinda's assassination by murderers hired by Otto. Recognizing the justice is beyond his power, the king decides not to punish Bánk.

Even such a sketchy plot summary may suggest that a wide range of mental states is presented in the play. Unlike much Romantic verse drama, *Bánk bán* is fee of monotony. Each of the characters speaks a highly idiosyncratic language, and tension is often heightened by clashes between individual styles. The dialogues between the insane Melinda and her bitter husband, the desperate Tiborc and his seemingly absent-minded lord, the angry Bánk and the haughty Gertrude, are examples of a lack of understanding on both sides which is due as much to widely different states of mind and value systems as to different idioms.

Even minor characters are highly individualized in their speech. Biberach, a vagrant knight who first assists Otto for financial reward, but later informs Bánk about Melinda's shame out of contempt for Otto and for the world as a whole, speaks a sophisticated intellectual jargon, full of twists and ambiguities. His complete negation of all values may remind one of Solger's or Kierkegaard's definition of irony, and his whole character is reminiscent of the demonic *humour noir* of Beddoes. Stabbed by Otto, his life seems to have been pointless, in keeping with his view that death is not tragic, only ridiculous, because there are no higher values which could give meaning to the life of any human individual.

If compared to Katona's masterpiece, most historical tragedies written in Hungarian at the beginning of the nineteenth century seem to be excessively melodramatic. This is even true of the works of Károly Kisfaludy (1788-1830), the leader of the first generation of Hungarian Romantic writers. The youngest brother of the important lyric poet Sándor Kisfaludy (1772-1844) – who himself wrote for the stage – showed a keen interest in a variety of genres, ranging from the elegy to comic narrative in prose. He even tried his hand at the visual arts and became the earliest of Romantic landscape painters in Hungary. His first play, *A tatárok Magyarországban* (Tartars in Hungary, written in 1800 but not performed until 1819), is full of bombastic rhetoric, as he himself admits in an epigram composed in 1826.

More interesting is *Stibor vajda* (Voivode Stibor, 1819), a four-act verse drama about Hungary in the early fifteenth century. While in the earlier work conflict is limited to a hostility between the Tartars invading thirteenth-century Hungary and the defenders of their country, the interrelation in the later play between different conflicts creates more dramatic tension.

To understand the nature of that interrelation one must be familiar with the historical background of the events referred to by the characters. The Hungarian nobility led by Kont, Voivode of Transylvania, rebel against the absolutism of Sigismond, who is both King of Hungary and the ruler of the Holy Roman Empire. The king, a member of the Luxemburg dynasty and so a foreigner, succeeds in defeating the conspirators, thanks to the financial and military assistance given him by Stibor, a Pole. Kont is executed and Stibor inherits his title, thus becoming the most powerful of the barons, second only to the monarch. The implication may be that the cause of social progress is at variance with that of national independence. Their conflict is further complicated by psychological factors: Rajnald, Stibor's only son, falls in love with Gunda, the daughter of a poor serf who has been killed by the soldiers of Stibor.

As in *Bánk bán*, the play focuses on abuse of power. Although Kisfaludy's play lacks the close-knit structure of Katona's work, it is more than a didactic parable, because of the complexity of the hero's character. Rich and brave, he is "partly a man, partly a devil," an example of a sublime egotist. His view of the world relies on the assumption that there is no higher value than human will. Because he is not afraid of any human being, he is convinced that no one can defeat him. In a sense he is one of the Satanic heroes created by Romantic poets who have lost their belief in super-natural justice. Ostensibly, he is given punishment when a snake bites him and makes him blind while he is asleep, yet his character retains a sort of sublimity until the very end of the play when, having lost his sight, he commits suicide. His view of existence is not invalidated: even the closure suggests that there are only natural forces at play in the universe.

In sharp contrast to *Bánk bán*, most of Kisfaludy's plays were written for immediate consumption. Their success was huge at the time of their composition, but proved to be ephemeral. This is true even of his comedies from *A kérők* (The Suitors, 1817-19) to *Csalódások* (Disappointments, 1828). Amusing and fresh as these plays written in prose may be, they do not show much improvement in dramatic technique upon such earlier works as the unfinished *A méla Tempefői* (The Dreamy Tempefői, 1793) or *Az özvegy Karnyóné s a két szeleburdiak* (The Widow of Mr. Karnyó and the Two Rascals, 1799), both by Mihály Csokonai Vitéz (1773-1805), a major poet of the cult of sensibility. They are hardly more than sets of caricatures loosely knit together. There is only one aspect of Kisfaludy's comedies which affords them unquestionable historical interest: by contrasting an older generation, which observes generally accepted rules of conduct, with younger people whose ideals are emphatically individual and subjective, they signal a major shift of emphasis in the value system of the age.

2. Lyrical Drama and Fairy Tale

Turning from the works of Kisfaludy to those of those of Mihály Vörösmarty (1800-55), we leave the realm of uneven works of local interest for that of major poetry of international stature. A tireless experimenter in poetic diction, Vörösmarty extended the semantic possibilities of the Hungarian language by creating highly original metaphors and a characteristically Romantic syntax, full of dislocations and fragmentations, and composed some powerful lyric poems expressing a tragic sense of being on a cosmic scale in a visionary yet condensed style. Although the epic poems and historical verse tragedies which he was compelled to write by social demand are remembered chiefly for their lyrical character, it cannot be denied that his verse occasionally shows great dramatic strength. His earlier plays, such as *Salamon király* (King Solomon, 1827), *Hábador* (1827), or *A bujdosók* (The Fugitives, 1830) are lyrical tragedies revealing a profound understanding of Shakespeare, whose *Julius Ceaser* (1840) and *King Lear* (1853) he later translated with great skill. Yet his verse proved to be too poetic for contemporary Hungarian audiences; and so in the 1830s he tried to write more popular plays, influenced to a certain degree by French Romanticism. By the mid-40s, however, he was forced to realize that he had missed his goal – his heavily metaphoric writing was at variance with the melodramatic plot of pseudo-historical tragedies such as *Vérnász* (Blood Wedding, 1834) or *Marót bán* (1838) – and he abandoned writing for the stage.

In his time Vörösmarty the dramatist was respected rather than liked. Although the National Theatre of Pest was opened with a short piece he had written for the occasion, *Árpád ébredése* (The Awakening of Árpád, 1837), none of his longer dramatic works could hold the stage. There is only one remarkable exception, *Csongor és Tünde* (Csongor and Tünde, 1829-31), a mixture of dramatic fairy tale and *Menschheitsdichtung*, composed between the two creative phases mentioned above. György Lukács – who had a very uneven knowledge of Hungarian culture and dismissed many of its products as provincial – called this work the most original piece of dramatic writing composed in nineteenth-century Hungary, in his second book *A modern dráma fejlődésének története* (The Development of Modern Drama, 1911). What is more, he suggested that Vörösmarty's play may have been written with a new type of theatre in mind. There may be a measure of truth in this remark, for *Csongor and Tünde* has none of the shortcomings of many Romantic verse dramas and seems to foreshadow the Symbolistic works of Ibsen.

Csongor is a disillusioned wanderer who has travelled the whole world over, unable to find the subject of his dreams. At the end of his wanderings, he meets Mirigy, the elder sister of Time, who is chained to a tree in the middle of the garden which is the property of Csongor's old parents. At night apples grow on this tree of life, but they always disappear before daylight comes. Mirigy tells Csongor about Tünde, the fairy who had planted the tree. She is identical with the subject of his dreams, the old witch argues, and she collects the fruits of the tree at night. In exchange for this information, Mirigy asks Csongor to let her free.

To explain the success *Csongor and Tünde* had with innovative theatrical artists, both in the Symbolist and subsequent periods, we must have recourse to the interrelations and sometimes even clashes between different semantic strata in the text. In many cases the same incident can be taken in a literal as well as a metaphoric sense. Csongor's aim is to find what he has seen in his dreams. This abstract ideal is impersonated by Tünde on the concrete level of action. He hides under the leaves of the magic tree, waiting for Tünde to arrive, but she is late, and he falls asleep. When the fairy appears, accompanied by her maidservant Ilma, she awakens him, but their meeting is cut short by Mirigy cutting off a lock of Tünde's hair from behind, thus casting a spell over her and forcing her to leave Csongor. While this episode may remind one of the more concrete material of fairy tales, the next one has an ambiguity hardly found in oral culture. When the hero desperately asks Ilma where he should search for his lover, Tünde's companion indicates that the middle of three roads meeting on a plain will guide him to his goal. Compelled to continue his wandering, Csongor arrives at the crossroads, only to find that each of them seems to be a middle road. This may be the first hint to suggest that the play is about the loss of purpose in human existence.

Travellers approach from all three directions, propagating values that contradict each other. The Merchant speaks about material wealth, the Prince is a man of authority and power, and the Scholar has come to the conclusion that though he is unable to understand the world, his lack of knowledge is superior to all kinds of self-assurance. Csongor's reaction to these interpretations of human existence is characteristic of Romanticism. The Merchant's basic value is self-reliance. In his view production becomes, as it were, the law of life. Spiritual ambition is hardened into material effort. Such Puritanism fosters welfare, but also selfishness. Vörösmarty seems to support a kind of anti-capitalism which many Romantics professed, yet he does not share the illusions of some of his contemporaries about the Middle Ages. This becomes clear when the message of the Prince is also dismissed, because power is viewed as resulting in an inexorable process which leads to destruction. As to the arguments of the Scholar, they are presented as having more validity, yet even his scale of values is rejected on the ground that it does not give creative imagination its due. The untenability of three conflicting interpretations of human existence awakens the suspicion in the hero that all such interpretations may be false.

After his encounter with the three wanderers, Csongor undergoes further trials. First he meets Balga, a simple peasant in love with Ilma, who offers devastating comments on Csongor's idealism. Then he makes the acquaintance of three goblins who are quarrelling over an invisible mantle, a running sandal, and a whip. Csongor steals the goblins' inheritance, hoping that by means of these magic instruments he can leave the prosaic world he inhabits and reach the fairyland in which Tünde resides, but this episode turns out to be just another trap for the hero.

The distance increases between a chaotic existence, afflicted with a basic contradiction between appearance and reality, and a dreamworld which knows no ambiguity of values. After he has been distracted by a whore, Csongor realizes that all his efforts to meet his ideal have failed. A long time must have passed since his meeting with the wanderers, because now he can hardly recognize them. The Merchant has lost all his wealth in the free competition he used to praise. He is a lame and penniless beggar, deserted by everybody. No less destitute is the Prince, having been dethroned by his people, and even the Scholar is unhappy, tormented by the paradox that a man cannot both live and think, caught between his disbelief in God and his inability to accept mortality.

Simultaneously with Csongor's encounter with the wanderers, Tünde and Ilma find themselves in a desert and have to listen to the monologue of Night. This is the climax of the play. Having lost his belief in transcendence, the poet made Night assert the omnipotence of nothingness surrounding man. Later on Tünde and Ilma catch sight of Csongor's garden, but they can scarcely recognize it, because it has been transformed into a wilderness. Mirigy is digging up the tree of life planted by Tünde.

Whether the closing scene that follows is an organic part of the whole, or an indication of some compromise the poet had to make with his audience is a matter of controversy. Mihály Babits, an outstanding poet of the early twentieth century, was probably the first to ask this question, in a seminal essay on the later Vörösmarty (*A férfi Vörösmarty*) published in 1911. According to Babits the closure was not an integral part of the structure, a position I myself adopted in my essays on nineteenth-century Hungarian poetry, written in the 1970s. It can hardly be denied that on the level of action the happy ending seems to be a kind of *deus ex machina* device: the goblins decide to change sides and capture Mirigy. The magic tree is transformed into a palace, and the lovers are united. It is equally true, however, that while the stylistic complexity of the earlier scenes – a variety of poetic idioms ranging from the tragic sublimity of the monologue of Night to the vulgar dialect used by Balga or the grotesque nonsense poetry spoken by the goblins – is replaced by a uniform style, this final narrowing of scope is in keeping with the circular structure of Vörösmarty's lyrical drama. The closure echoes the airy style of the beginning, taking us back from the tragic aspects of human existence to the dreamworld of fairytales.

3. Lyrical Drama and Encyclopaedic Form

When trying to give some explanation for the delay in the success of *Bánk bán*, I referred to a reaction against the excesses of the language reform. That reaction set in just after the composition of *Csongor and Tünde*. A new generation gained ground in the intellectual life of the country. Notwithstanding their respect and even admiration for the sublimity of Vörösmarty's diction, the younger poets made an effort to bridge the gap between spoken and written language, rural and urban culture. Petőfi and Arany wrote lyric and narrative poems in a more popular style, works which were accepted as masterpieces by everybody but the worst snobs, but no talent of comparable originality emerged among dramatists. The new genre, a variant of the Viennese *Volksstück*, introduced by Ede Szigligeti (1814-78), was hardly more than a form of popular entertainment, a kind of musical *Lebensbild*, supplying the uneducated with the clichés of Romanticism: superficial *couleur locale*, stereotype representation of the Hungarian *Puszta*, operetta-like, sentimental imitation of peasant life, and mannered stylization of inauthentic floklore. It might even be suggested that Szigligeti's plays from *A szökött katona* (The Deserter, 1843) to *A cigány* (The Gipsy, 1853), and *A lelenc* (The Foundling, 1863) initiated one of the worst traditions of Hungarian culture, a tradition which survived into our century in operettas, films, and all forms of *Kitsch*.

It is against this background that the *chef-d'oeuvre* of Imre Madách (1823-64) should be appraised. After the Hungarian revolution was repressed by the army of the Russian tzar in 1849, some Hungarian intellectuals regarded all forms of superficial patriotism as not only cheap but also harmful. Laying the blame (not without reason) upon certain Liberal governments (England's, for example), they came to the conclusion that Europe failed to understand the revolution led by Kossuth, because the Western world had a superficial and inauthentic image of Hungary, based upon the impression that the provinciality of Hungarian culture made upon foreigners. None of these intellectuals went as far as Madách, who considered patriotism almost irreconcilable with artistic creation: "Patriotism can be the subject of poetry only with us, who are struggling for our very existence; no great poet has ever resorted to it," he wrote in one of his notebooks.[1] Undoubtedly, the formulation of this promise does not belong to his early years, but was rather a conclusion he arrived at after Lord Palmerston, the Prime Minister of the most Liberal of all nations, asked the Austrian Emperor to crush the Hungarian revolution as quickly as possible. In the pre-revolutionary decade, Madách himself wrote historical tragedies about medieval Hungary – *Nápolyi Endre* (Andrew of Naples), *Mária királynő* (Queen Mary), and *Csák végnapjai* (The Last Days of Csák) – whereas in the post-revolutionary period his chief aim became to give some interpretation of human history as a whole, having realized that the idea of national character, a concept at the basis of most historical tragedies written in the first half of the nineteenth century, was invalidated by Positivist science.[2]

In one respect Madách's somewhat far-fetched conclusion seems to have been justified: his most important work has been translated into more languages than any other piece of Hungarian lit-

---

[1] *Összes müvei* (Collected Works), ed. with an Introduction and notes by Gábor Halász (Budapest: Révail, 1942), II, 752. Cf. his similar remarks: "Patriotism could be a poetic principle only with Hungarians, for the reason that other nations have no idea of the struggle involving existence and non-existence" (p. 751). "Other nations do not know of conditions like those in the political life of Hungary. We are in a constant struggle for our life, in one cage with the beast which is ready to devour us at the next moment. If they are fighting, their goal is no more than a change from good to better" (p. 762).

[2] "What is national character? – Bad habits." (*Collected Works*, II, 757.)

erature. Furthermore, despite the fact that all the translations are inaccurate and unpoetical (with the possible exception of Jean Rousselot's French version), *Az ember tragédiája* (The Tragedy of Man, 1859-60) has attracted the attention of many important writers, from Maxim Gorky to James Joyce and Virginia Woolf.[3]

The great variety of interpretations this drama has enjoyed may indicate that its influence has been the result not only of its general subject matter but also of the ambiguities of the text. Some of these derive from the way Biblical material is treated by the poet. The first speech of the Lord in the opening scene suggests a Deist conception of God. The created universe is compared to a machine just completed. The wheels go round, and the Creator may rest, for ages may pass before one spoke will need repair. Yet this static interpretation of the universe is immediately challenged by Lucifer, the spirit of negation. The Lord could not have created anything without his support, he argues; and so he must have his share. This claim appears to be justified, because the Lord gives Lucifer two trees, having doomed them first.

Lucifer is further characterized in the next scene, which portrays the story of the Fall. His view of existence echoes that of Schopenhauer: time has no direction, it is no more than eternal recurrence. Individuals may be different, but the roles played by them are the same. Man must have knowledge, because it enables him to choose; thus it brings maturity.

Some interpreters of *The Tragedy* claim that Adam and Lucifer are the heroes of the play, and their dialogues reflect a dilemma with which Madách had to struggle in the post-revolutionary decade: Adam's values are those of a Romantic Liberal, whereas Lucifer's mistrust of generalizations, value-judgements, normative statements, and teleology may remind one of Positivist reasoning. Scene 3 – in which Adam is presented as living outside of Eden in a godless universe, and Lucifer's interpretation of time is further elaborated by his arguments that the present has no duration and thus no existence, and that the universe is constantly created and destroyed by forces which work in silence and secrecy – undoubtedly supports such an interpretation.

After three introductory scenes, the main body of the text offers us samples from human history. Adam is anxious to know the fate of his race, and Lucifer gives him a chance to have a vision of the future through a long dream consisting of eleven episodes.

The first of these is one of the best parts of the work, as far as the sheer quality of the writing is concerned. An unfinished pyramid, symbolizing human ambition, is seen in the background. Its creator, the Pharaoh, is a Romantic Titan, a man who has became a god unto himself. Apparently he has more power than God, but he is tormented by solitude. Eve, the wife of a dying slave, teaches him to hear his people's anguish. The Pharaoh renounces his power and liberates the people.

At this point comes the ironic twist so characteristic of the writing of Madách. The crowd has an everlasting longing for a master, Lucifer argues, and it will certainly look for a new tyrant before long. What we see does not contradict Lucifer's argument. Adam cannot help admitting that he has wasted too much time in an aimless attempt to transform man. Although Eve suggests that they could find happiness in private life, Adam finds her horizon very limited and asks Lucifer to lead him to new adventures.

The Egyptian scene enacts a vision of interpreted design. Adam is presented as an example of

---

[3] See József Waldapfel, *Gorkij és Madách* (Budapest: Akadémiai Kiadó, 1958), and Attila Faj, "Probable Byzantine and Hungarian models of *Ulysses* and *Finnegans Wake*," *Arcadia*, 3 (1968), 48-72. One of the English translations of Madách's play (by C.P. Sanger, himself a member of the Bloomsbury circle) was published by The Hogarth Press in 1933.

the egotistic sublime, whereas Lucifer is a commentator who is able to philosophize and can unveil the ontological preconceptions underlying what others say. For him truth is never given; its mode of existence is not eternity. In his interpretation, being is understandable only as projected upon the horizon of temporality. What he seems to suggest by the vision of the pyramid covered by dust and sand is that being must be interpreted by way of time. How then does time show itself? What is the truth-character of time? Such are the questions asked by him, and his focus is on something very different from the common sense of time which we have, "use," spend, read from the clock and which we perceive as presence, as an infinite and linear sequence of "nows." Lucifer views life from the perspective of being-toward-death. That is why some interpreters draw a parallel between Madách's conception of being and Existentialism.

The author of *The Tragedy* was a well-read man, and he drew upon various sources when writing his masterpiece. Himself a Roman Catholic, his close friends were Protestants, and his approach to Genesis was influenced by Milton and the Satanic readers of *Paradise Lost*. The symbol of the unfinished pyramid echoes *Childe Harold's Pilgrimage*, and the picture of Greek Democracy in the next scene may have been inspired by Shakespeare's presentation of the crowd in *Julius Caesar* as well as by Tocqueville's ideas on American society. Adam's reincarnation, Miltiades, the brave soldier, is sentenced to death by the people whose city he has just saved from the enemy. The focus is on his disillusionment; what he calls the majestic people proves to be a mob selling its vote. Questions asked previously are answered here, thus creating a sense of continuity, yet the first two parts of Adam's dream are also contrasted: the lyric monologues and symbolism of the previous scene are replaced by dialogues of powerful theatrical intensity.

If the example of Athens has shown that the general mood of the people can be manipulated in a democracy and man does not need freedom, the next scene presents Adam with an antidote. All values are contested, including the life of the individual. Nihilism prevails in Rome until the city is menaced by a pestilence. Unable to continue to live in an atmosphere of total disillusionment, Adam craves for some guiding principle. Remembering those few who have been crucified for their belief in universal brotherhood and in the liberation of the individual, he listens to Peter the Apostle, who speaks of the arrival of a new faith.

Soon, however, he must learn a bitter lesson. History seems to justify Lucifer's scepticism: the poor want no brotherhood once they have become rich, and the same Christianity which appears as a healthy reaction against the relativism prevailing in Rome will turn into a new form of tyranny in medieval Byzantium.

At this point one could assume that the message of the play rests on the underlying idea that all principles lead to disaster once they have been put into practice, but the following scenes show this to be a gross simplification.

The presentation of sensuality in Rome may be one of the less successful sections of *The Tragedy*. Taken as a whole, the sixth scene resembles *A kegyenc* (The Favourite, 1861), the only play by Count László Teleki (1811-61), an outstanding Liberal statesman, without having any of the more profound intellectual implications of the earlier play. Chance stands for the loss of teleology in both works, but in *The Favourite* the presentation of gambling is subordinated to a devastating vision of the total absence of meaningful human relations. In the opening scene Valentinianus Caesar, the hero of Teleki's Romantic parable, drinks a health to a monkey, thus suggesting the deterioration of understanding and the impossibility of human communication in a society without communal values. As compared to this portrayal of the Roman Empire, the interpretation of decadence in Madách's work seems to be more conventional.

Something similar could be said about the second half of the next part, the love scene between Tancred, just returning from a Crusade, and Isaura, a nun from a convent. Still, the first half of Scene 7 is crucial to the understanding of the ideological aspect of the meaning of the work as a whole. Christianity has triumphed but only at a heavy cost: words are contradicted by deeds. Appearance is in conflict with reality; the soul has departed and only the carcass of the ideal survives. The rights of the individual are denied; those who depart from the officially sanctioned and institutionalized interpretations are persecuted.

Once fully institutionalized, the movement becomes self-destructive. Heretics are executed in Constantinople. The conflict between the advocates of "homoousion" and of "homoiousion" is presented as a ridiculous hair-splitting debate. Like John Stuart Mill, one of the most influential Western thinkers in Hungary in the post-revolutionary years, Madách seems to have shared Hegel's condemnation of Byzantine society. One could argue that in *The Tragedy* this unfavourable judgement is made by Lucifer, and he falsifies evidence in order to convince Adam that all ideas deteriorate once they have triumphed, but this possibility is ruled out by the fact that Adam is forced to endorse Lucifer's conclusion by his own experience. Mill was an agnostic; in this sense his total condemnation of Byzantine Christianity was quite understandable. In the case of Madách, however, a similar value-judgement begs for some kind of explanation. In his essay *Madách tragédiája* ("The Tragedy of Man* by Madách"), first published in 1955, the Marxist philosopher György Lukács argued that the question whether Jesus was man or God had lost its relevance for the author of *The Tragedy*, and so the message of the work could not be reconciled with Christianity.

Such an interpretation, however, must be discarded as irrelevant. Lukács seems to have overlooked a crucial passage in the final scene of the play. After reaching the conclusion that history is meaningless, Adam intends to commit suicide, but he is stopped by Eve, who tells him that she feels she will become a mother. Lucifer warns her that the child was conceived in sin and would bring only misery to the Earth but her response is that God has the power to create somebody who can bring redemption from both sin and misery.

In other words, it would be an exaggeration to maintain that some kind of Positivist lack of faith is asserted in *The Tragedy*. In Constantinople Adam learns how to question the legitimacy of any power which claims to render justice in the name of any ideology. Lucifer vainly tries to convince him that the abuse of power should be seen from a comic rather than a tragic perspective, Adam feels desperate that ideals have died for him.

Exhausted, he tries to seek relief in taking rest in an age marked by indifference, but he cannot find happiness in passivity. Re-incarnate as Kepler, he looks for new interpretations of the world. While for others existence is governed by a a stable hierarchy, he identifies higher spiritual rank with curiosity and an inclination to question the legitimacy of existing laws and to see a contradiction between *de facto* and *de jure* authority. Ideas may change, but their total absence results in boredom, a form of existence that knows neither aims nor struggles. That is why Kepler yearns for excitement in life.

And now follows one of the most brilliantly paradoxical scenes, a dream within a dream, a kind of *mise-en-abyme*, a variation upon the themes of earlier parts. Like Miltiades, Danton subordinates his individual interests to a common cause, but the movement becomes a destructive force, and those who have power are alienated from the people. In his solitude Danton makes a desperate attempt to understand his opponents, the aristocrats, but communication between people with different beliefs seems impossible. The revolution is transformed into inquisition. Even the guillotine has ears.

The Paris scene is similar to a mirror in so far as it brings together all the basic motifs of *The Tragedy*. Eve has two incarnations; as a marquise she is sublime and idealized, as a woman from the mob she is vulgar and grotesque. Ironically, in retrospect, after its fall, the old aristocracy seems to have a superiority over the class that has been oppressed for such a long time, but this conclusion proves to be superficial if we compare the Paris scene and the one that follows. Danton seems to be a kind of arch-liberal, who hates the ruling class but tolerates all individuals. The crowd cannot understand his attitude; and so he too, is sentenced to death by the Sovereign People he has served. One would expect a sense of disillusion on the part of the hero, but when awakened by Lucifer, Kepler calls his dream magnificent. Violence as such, it seems, is not rejected in *The Tragedy*, because in the tenth scene Kepler strongly condemns rules which protect long established power relations and reaffirms his belief that the false virtues of habit make man forget how to walk upon his feet and to exercise his mind.

Yet the next scene, a huge and well constructed *danse macabre*, gives another twist to the argument. Adam has grown older and no longer plays an active role in the action. A London Fair symbolizes free competition, the democracy of capitalist society, characterized by unlimited private property, free enterprise, and the freedom of the stronger to overcome the weaker by following market rules. The anachronistic class barriers of feudalism have crumbled down, superstitions are left behind, and people are led by the assumption that wealth brings happiness. Hope of gain is regarded as the most important incentive to productivity, and many of those who rebelled against capitalism in their youth will endorse possessive individualism in their later life. Each citizen is governed by what he considers to be his vital interest, and thus society seems to be a mere collection of self-interested individuals in perpetual conflict with each other, because they are infinite consumers whose only desire is their own private benefit.

There is a little doubt that the London scene was inspired by the ideas of Bentham, whose works were widely read in Hungary at the time Madách studied in Pest. *Hitel* (Credit, 1830), the second and most influential book by count István Széchenyi (1791-1860), had exerted a profound influence on all the intellectuals of Madách's generation. It contained both a summary and an implicit but also radical critique of Benthamism. Following the lead of Széchenyi, Madách, relied upon the Romantic interpretation of capitalism when presenting workers who reject mechanical civilization and students who detest the prosaic urban life. In the London scene Adam's disappointment is unquestionable: the French Revolution has led to a utilitarianism which kills not only religious faith, but also belief and creative imagination. What is more, it makes people cruel. If the only thing that matters is personal greed, individuals seek power over each other and their main wish is to exploit others.

Since anarchy has brought a dog-fight for a bone, instead of liberty, the only antidote to this chaotic yet ruthless world Adam can think of is some kind of centralized community controlled by science and guided by reason. When his ideal is realized in the form of a phalanstery, it proves to be even more destructive than the world of competition. Utilitarianism is pushed one stage further, material welfare being the only guiding principle. Individuality is repressed by division of labour.

Life is ruled by excessively centralized plans, egalitarianism implies standardization, history is reduced to a heap of preconceptions, and the legitimacy of art is denied together with the rights of the individual. All that is left is "solid mediocrity"; the age no longer requires genius. The symbolic figures of Plato, Luther, and Michelangelo are reduced to the size of average men.

As some other Hungarian intellectuals of his generation, Madách was familiar with the works of such Socialist theoreticians as Saint-Simon and Fourier. Inspired by his readings, he created a negative Utopia, a vision of a totalitarian state in which the network of such traditional communities as nation and family is replaced by the ideal of official truth. The state presented in the twelfth scene of *The Tragedy* seems to act from benevolent motives, but if one looks behind the rhetoric, the sole purpose of the methods of the aged man who embodies authority is to prevent people from using whatever may have been left of their freedom. Madách's phalanstery is behavioristic; it does not care what people may think.

The conclusion reached by Adam at the end of this scene is that although free market and central planning seem to represent opposite poles, they behave alike: both deny self-developmental freedom. Although the leader of the phalanstery preaches equality, what he forces upon people is uniformity. Madách's Liberalism was similar to the conception of freedom formulated by John Stuart Mill: he regarded liberty as the equal, effective freedom for all to develop their capacities.

As he finds no society in which the individual is judged by the extent to which he has realized his capabilities, Adam looks for freedom in space. By now an aged man, he flies with Lucifer, leaving the Earth behind. It is dusk, turning gradually to night. Adam has lost all sense of direction. He cannot get over the sense that life is not worth living if one has no goal in view. He has learned to accept mortality, but cannot do without some meaningful occupation.

Asking Lucifer to show him the end of human history, he is taken back to the Earth. Lucifer lives up to his principle, and deprives Adam of his last illusion. The last human beings are Eskimo-like creatures living in a region that once belonged to the tropical zone. Adam understands that traditional forms of energy have been used up and that scientists have failed to find appropriate substitutes. Life is doomed to a slow death.

The fourteenth scene, which prophesies an end to all life on earth, clearly indicates that Madách viewed himself as a latecomer who lived in an Alexandrian age characterized by self-irony, incapacity for action, parodistic deformity, and an awareness that its twilight mood would eventually turn into a grotesque deterioration of the human race. Adam has become a broken old man. Leaning on his stick, he is a symbol of spiritual decline. Science has been defeated and noble deeds, ambitions have disappeared. Creative efforts are obliterated by material needs, and man is reduced to the status of animals.

This gloomy perspective makes Adam cry out in despair, and his long dream comes to an end. We are taken back to the landscape of the third scene. Adam cannot forget his dream and decides to save mankind from future sufferings by committing suicide, but Eve tells him that she is expecting a baby. Thus, Adam's conclusion is refuted by Eve's supra-historical unwisdom.

"Das Ewig-Weibliche/ Zieht uns hinan" (The eternal womanly draws us upward). These words from the "Chorus mysticus," ending the second part of Goethe's *Faust* and sung at the conclusion of *Eine Faust-Symphonie* (1854), one of the major works by Madách's compatriot Ferenc Liszt, may have been in the Hungarian poet's mind when writing the last scene of his lyrical drama. Yet the closure of *The Tragedy of Man* also foreshadows Nietzsche's reflections on the disadvantages of history for life. Adam's obsession with history has led to the paralysis of personality, a loss of self-respect, and the belief in the old age of mankind.

The hero's last words reaffirm his despair over the slow passing away of his race, a nightmare vision he is unable to forget. The Lord tries to comfort him, but the point he makes does not seem to be very strong. When affirming the value of struggle, he relies on a principle which Adam himself tried to assert before it became invalidated by the vision of the end of life on the Earth. If this is so, it is possible to suggest that *The Tragedy of Man* disqualifies any theological interpretation of human existence. It is no wonder, then, that some critics have characterized the message of the play as non-Christian.

Still, in view of certain other passages in the final scene, such a conclusion may seem to be somewhat simplified. When Lucifer reminds Eve that her child has been conceived in sin, she affirms her belief in God's freedom to create a child to bring salvation. The allusion to the Messiah is made more important by the angelic choir calling eternal grace the most fundamental characteristic of the Lord.

Madách's interpretation of God may owe something to a distinction drawn by Kant, a philosopher whose works were fairly well-known in the years following 1837, when Madách began to study at the University of Pest. In his essay *Der einzig mögliche Beweisgrund zu einer Demonstration des Daseins Gottes* (The Sole Possible Argument for a Demonstration of God's Existence, 1763) Kant defined existence (*Dasein*) as absolute position, whereas in the *Kritik der reinen Vernunft* (Critique of Pure Reason, 1781) he seemed to identify being (*Sein*) with "mere position." Although Madách was not a systematic thinker, what *The Tragedy of Man* suggests is that existence might be regarded as belonging to God's essence, whereas being as "mere position" is a characteristic of man. In any case, the end of the play seems to be in harmony with the conclusion Kant reached in his *Critique of Pure Reason*: the whole of our knowledge finally ends in unanalyzable concepts.

Besides the ability to struggle, two other values are mentioned by the Lord in his final speech. Poetry and music are called curative forces, reminding us that the conflict between the historical sense and the creative imagination is a leading motif in *The Tragedy of Man*. Historicizing is presented as the activity of the old age of mankind, a malady against which art is the only medicine. In an age of Positivistic science Madách affirmed man's right to forget, and tried to conduct our gaze away from culture (equated with becoming) to art (regarded as the eternal and stable).

One of the reasons for the disagreements among critics about the message of the Hungarian poet's lyrical drama may be that several alternative conclusions are left unreconciled in the final scene. This open ending may also have something to do with the success of the work. At any rate, it is in keeping with the structure of the text. The fifteen scenes constituting the surface structure are subordinated to a deeper thematic structure, the dialogue of Adam and Lucifer being a projection of an inner debate between the teleology of Romantic Liberalism and the cyclical view of existence, held by some Positivists. To present this dialogue, Madách resorted to the device of the double (*Doppelgänger*), used by many Romantics. The relation between Adam and Lucifer is somewhat similar to that of Deianeira and Jolé, or Forgách and Palizsnay, in *Férfi és nő* (Man and Woman) and *Queen Mary*, plays which Madách wrote in the early 1840s.

A comparison of *The Tragedy of Man* with the poet's earlier works may reveal his double intention when composing his most ambitious work: while keeping the general framework of a

Romantic genre, he also wished to move beyond some of its limitations. Heracles in *Man and Woman*, Palizsnay in *Queen Mary*, Csák in *The Last Days of Csák*, or Lucifer in the Biblical poem *A nő teremtése* (The Creation of Woman, c. 1855), are all Romantic rebels guided by emotion, whereas the Lucifer of *The Tragedy* is a highly intellectual descendant of Romantic rebels; his Satanism is more akin to that of Baudelaire and Lautréamont than to that of earlier poets. He has a cyclic conception of life, yet his irony is mixed with pathos. The lyrical character of the drama is manifest in his somewhat uneasy, reluctant laughter at the end of most of the historical scenes which prove him right. He foresees Adam's failures, but registers them with a wry smile. He finds no satisfaction in his knowledge that Adam's teleological claims are mistaken, because he seems to be aware that the commentator is as much part of an interpreted design as the hero.

Although one could say that an intellectual monologue projected into dialogue is the most essential part of *The Tragedy*, it would be misleading to underestimate the contribution of Eve and the Lord to the ambiguities of the play. It is true that in some passages Eve seems to have none of the complexities of the two protagonists. Ready to accept the truth of Lucifer or the Lord, she lives in an eternal present. In Constantinople she is no more than a nun who observes the rules of her convent, in Prague she is selfish and empty-headed, in Paris her lack of personality is emphasized by the fact that she appears in two roles: first as the sister of an average *marquis*, then as a ruthless woman of the people, and in the last scene but one she is reduced to a mere caricature of herself. On the other hand, there are crucial moments when she is able to exert a decisive influence on the outcome of the events. In Paradise she has a deeper understanding of the intricacies of the relation of man to God, in London her faith resists mortality, and in the final scene she is the one who can foresee the advent of the Messiah.

No less riddled with contradictions is the character of the Lord. A Jesuit author has accused Madách of irreligious views.[4] This is obviously an exaggeration, but, as already suggested, it is undeniable that certain passages of *The Tragedy* cannot be reconciled with Christianity without some difficulty. On the basis of his first words, János Arany, the great poet and first critic of Madách, called the Lord "complacent like a craftsman,"[5] and indeed in the first scene the Creator seems to be not only passive, but even alienated from his Creation. Furthermore, the opening lines of the Choir of Angels may strike us with their ambiguity:

> Our part but His Great shadow on us thrown,
> Praise Him who in His boundless mercy grants us
> A measure of that light which is His own.[6]

This metaphoric ambiguity is further strengthened by another contradiction when the text swerves from Genesis: the Lord gives two trees to Lucifer but forbids anyone to touch the fruit of immortality: "he who eats thereof shall die." The Arian Milton and his Satanic interpreters may have inspired Madách to stress this ambiguity, especially in Scene 2, when Eve summarizes man's relation to God in the following way:

---

[4] Jakob Overmans, "Die Weltanschauung in Madách's Tragödie des Menschen," *Stimmen aus Maria-Laach*, 80 (1911), 14-28.
[5] *Az ember tragédiája*, a critical edition by Vilmos Tolnai, 2nd ed. (Budapest: Magyar Tudományos Társulatok Sajtóvállalata, 1924), p. 2.
[6] *The Tragedy of Man*, translated by J.C.W. Horne (Budapest: Corvina Press, 1963).

Why should he punish? For if he hath fixed
The way that he would have us follow, so
He hath ordained it, that no sinful lure
Should draw us otherwhere; why hath he set
The path athwart a giddy yawning gulf
To doom us to destruction? If likewise,
Sin hath a place in the eternal plan,
As storm amid the days of sunlit warmth,
Who would the angry storm more guilty deem
Than the life-giving brightness of the sun?[7]

Has Adam any chance to resist his fall? Lucifer says no, and the Lord does not care to contradict him. Adam cannot reconcile himself to his fate, and Lucifer's joy is mixed with sadness. Both of them defy the Lord. Surrounded by Calvinist friends, living in an age when the fate of Hungary was determined by external forces and the intellectual climate by Positivism, Madách dramatized a polemic consciousness. The line of argument underlying the dialogue between Adam and Lucifer follows a sequence of four statements:

1. my existence must have a purpose;
2. I cannot see this purpose;
3. it must have been set by somebody/something mightier than me;
4. to learn that purpose I have to find this mightier force.

Madách's conception of history is somewhat akin to that of Ranke, who started his career as a disciple of Hegel and moved toward Positivism. This German historian, widely read in Hungary in the middle of the nineteenth century, compared the history of ideas to a sequence of theses and antitheses. He also claimed that the spirit of denial was an inalienable attribute of God.[8] In *The Tragedy of Man* Lucifer's role is that of ironic denial, without which new historical reality cannot be apprehended. In the historical scenes Lucifer not only becomes the *Doppelgänger* of Adam, but also grows into a humanized instrument of a God who is absent from history. Such an overlapping in the heroes is further evidence of the lyrical character of the play. For Adam it is easier to follow Lucifer's arguments than the Lord's advice, because Lucifer stays with him through all his adventures and cannot help guiding him in his search for an answer to his questions, while God punishes him for a deed the significance of which he is permitted to see only after committing it. The two protagonists are brought together precisely because not only Adam, but occasionally even Lucifer, is tormented by the aloofness of the Lord.[9]

---

[7] Cf. *Paradise Lost*, III, 98-99:

  [...] I made him just and right,
  Sufficient to have stood, though free to fall.

Madách might have read Milton in German translation. See the biography of the poet by his nephew, Károly Balogh, *Madách: Az ember és a költő* (Budapest: Dr. Vajna György és társa, 1934), p. 82.

[8] Leopold von Ranke, *Deutsche Geschichte im Zeitalter der Reformation* (1839-40), in: *Meisterwerke* (Munich and Leipzig: Duncker & Humblot, 1915), I, 81.

[9] It is interesting to note that God is presented as inhumanly aloof in some of the poet's earlier lyrics:

  Where God rules over death and winter
  Holy monotony sets in for ever. (*Télen* – In Winter.)

Most interpreters have laid emphasis on the discrepancy between the ten historical scenes and the rest of the play. Explicitly or implicitly they missed a homogeneous organizing principle in *The Tragedy* as a whole. This must be considered the result of a rather superficial analysis confined to the level of action. On a deeper level the episodic plot is subordinated to a structural sequence following a strict inner logic that can be detected from the opening Choir of the Angels to the final words of the Lord. The thematic structure of the work is based on a sequence of disjunctions which is in sharp contrast to the ideal of a homogeneous paradise, the memory of which accompanies Adam and Eve throughout history. The disjunctions result in the falling apart of previous unities and the irreconcilable contradiction between the parts. The historical scenes show human culture – in the widest sense of the word – unable to reach a synthesis.

Right after the beginning of the drama, the disunion of God and the universe, relatively independent from the moment it has been completed, is already taking place, followed by the separation of God and man in Paradise. In Scene 3 Adam is forced to leave his original surroundings, and becomes a wanderer in exile.[10] Scene 4 and 5 (Egypt and Athens) present the conflict between the masses and the individual from both sides, in Scene 6 (Rome) the unity of existential freedom and material welfare disintegrates, while in Constantinople Adam abandons his previous ideal, losing his trust in religion. In the Kepler scenes man and culture, *de facto* power and *de jure* authority become estranged; Scenes 9 (Paris), 11 (London), and 12 (Phalanstery) show stages in the disintegration of end and means. In the vision of a capitalism based on free competition and in the satirical utopia of a perfectly planned and utilitarian society, the continuity of the past with the present is lost; this anti-historicism, together with the disappearance of individual rights may indicate a Romantic rejection of the ideas of Auguste Comte. In the Phalanstery scene, analysis and synthesis, biological and moral, international and national values are in conflict, and the former effaces the latter. In some respects Madách almost foreshadows Nietzsche's objections to Positivism: not only by his cult of the individual, which both he and Nietzsche inherit from Romanticism, but also also by his claim that activity is inseparable from contemplation. In fact, the negative utopia of Scene 12 is more akin to the picture of the utilitarian society presented in *Martin Chuzzlewit, Hard Times,* the works of Tocqueville and Matthew Arnold, or the interpretation of American society given in the 329th aphorism of *Die fröhliche Wissenschaft* than to Fourier's idea of a *phalanstère*. In Scenes 13 and 14, nature and society, quantity and quality, surface and depth are brought into opposition, and in each case the latter is obliterated by the former.

In short, the structure of *The Tragedy* may be compared to a regressive sequence. The last stages in this sequence indicate that Madách foresaw the threat of technocracy at a time when he could have no first-hand experience of its influence in his own country, and when some Positivist thinkers, living in the most highly developed capitalist societies, were unaware of such a danger. The Hungarian poet attacks mediocrity and uniformity and considers artistic creativity a possible antidote. Like several other Romantics, he regards music as the highest form of artistic creation, and in the best parts of his play he attempts to imitate the organic unity of musical form. An example of a gradually developed symbol can be drawn from Lucifer's speech on mortality in Scene 4:

---

[10] When writing the first scenes, Madách could rely on his earlier lyrics, in which Nature without Man (*Isten keze, ember keze* – God's Hand, Man's Hand) and childhood (*Hazaérkezéskor* – Homecoming, *Gyermekeimhez* – To My Children) often symbolized the harmony of an undivided world as well as the unity of the inside and the outside, whereas the wanderer in exile stood for man's alienation from his surroundings (*Önvád* – Self-reproach).

> Didst thou not feel a gentle, cooling breeze
> That swept across thy face and then flew on?
> A little wave of dust doth mark its flight,
> That mounts a few short inches in a year,
> And some few cubits in a thousand years;
> Yet a few thousand years shall overwhelm
> The pyramids, and thy great name shall be
> Buried beneath a barrier of sand.
> Jackals shall in thy pleasure gardens howl,
> And, in the desert, dwell a servile race.
> And all this no raging storm shall bring to pass,
> No shuddering upheaval of the earth,
> Only a little breeze that gently plays!!

In passages like this a symbol is created in which abstract idea and concrete language, signified and signifier form an indissoluble unity, with threads connecting the unfolding symbol so organically to preceding and subsequent passages that the boundaries of the symbolic unit are hardly discernible. This is especially worthy of consideration in view of the great aphoristic skill Madách shows in the notebooks. The originality of the style of *The Tragedy* is partly due to a tension between aphoristic statements and gradually unfolding symbols. The structural function of the latter may remind one of the role of Wagner's "infinite melodies." Besides their encyclopaedic bent, this may be another similarity between the art of Madách and that of Wagner, another late Romantic struggling with Positivism.

This similarity, however, may exist only on a vary abstract level, and should not be overestimated, for the interpretation of existence given in the Wagnerian musical dramas is radically different from that suggested by *The Tragedy*. Madách does not seem to believe in any of Wagner's alternative values: ecstasy (*Tristan*), a greed for power (*Der Ring des Nibelungen*), or redemption (*Der fliegende Holländer, Tannhäuser, Lohengrin, Parsifal*). There is evidence to suggest that the Hungarian poet may have struggled with the idea of a universe empty of values. In some of his short poems autumn symbolized a gradual loss of values (*Őszi ének* – Autumn Song, *Sárga lomb* – Yellow Leaves), and the speaker of *Ifjan haljak meg* (Let Me Die Young) is a sailor who throws all his possessions into the sea, until he himself gets immersed. Yet when composing his *chef-d'oeuvre*, Madách did not go as far as suggesting nihilism. The contradictions of the final scene mentioned earlier indicate that, while raising the most troubling issues of his age, the Hungarian poet gave no definitive solution to any of them.

It should not be forgotten that this is the only work of Madách which has an open ending. Of the two other plays dating from his best creative period, *A civilizátor* (The Civilizer, 1859), a satirical comedy, has a melodramatic happy ending, while *Mózes* (Moses, 1861) affirms teleology through suffering. Although both are interesting minor works, it is quite possible that the much greater success of *The Tragedy of Man* is inseparable from its inconclusiveness, the tensions it creates between different and sometimes even antagonistic conceptions of human existence. What is more, the fact that Christian, Romantic, and Positivistic interpretations of *The Tragedy of Man* are almost equally valid may indicate that Madách's play marks the end of a period in Hungarian literature.

Most scholars view this lyrical drama as the last significant work of Romanticism, a kind of summing up of what has gone before. A few years after its completion important and sudden social changes started in the country, and a new generation of writers appeared on the literary scene. In 1867 a compromise was made between Austria and Hungary, and the establishment of a dual monarchy led to the rapid industrialization of the eastern half of the Habsburg Empire. Budapest became one of the large cities of the Continent. Positivism gained ground, and its vogue inspired young playwrights to portray the daily life of bourgeois or working class families under the influence of social determinism. The continuity with the past was lost. Romantic dramas were found too sophisticated, vague, or poetical for the stage. Naturalism became a dominant trend, bringing an entirely new conception of theatre, and inspired writers to compose plays that were radically different from Romantic dramas. Not until the turn of the century, the period of *Sezession* or *Jugendstil* in the decorative arts and Symbolism in literature, was Romantic drama re-valued, but by that time it was no longer regarded as a living tradition but as belonging to a past that had come to an end before the modern age of industrial civilization began.

GEORGE BISZTRAY

ROMANTIC TRENDS IN SCANDINAVIAN DRAMA[1]

The sociocultural frame of eighteenth-century Scandinavia[2] was similar to the dominating European one. Sweden and Denmark were absolute monarchies, and the latter also ruled Norway. Both monarchies were still mourning their lost glory of the previous centuries. As elsewhere, the taste of the royal court was strongly influenced by French Classicism which did, indeed, shape the dramatic production of the best Northern playwrights of the century, notably the Norwegian-born Danes Ludvig Holberg and Johan Herman Wessel.

As in a number of other European countries, the theater grew from a form of court entertainment to a matter of social concern and an important institution polishing the native language as well as boosting national consciousness. In 1712 a theater was established in Copenhagen Castle, but by 1748 also the Royal Danish Theater was founded to entertain the citizens of the capital. In Sweden, the playhouse of Drottningholm Castle was first established in the seventeen-forties, then was rebuilt in its present shape in 1766 following a devastating fire. Two decades later, the wider public of Stockholm, too, got its theater: the Royal Dramatic Theater. Musical performances were at least as popular as plays, especially in Sweden where the Royal Opera (opened in 1773) rose to cultic significance under King Gustav III (1771-92). Norway, on the other hand, was held in a disadvantaged position: its intellectuals and artists studied in Copenhagen, and Oslo (then called Christiania) was an insignificant, provincial merchant town. Until as late as the mid-nineteenth century, there was neither a Norwegian national theater nor national drama. Consequently, references to the Norwegian Romantic drama will appear only in the conclusion of this paper where the aftermath of Romanticism is considered.

In spite of the seemingly unshakable Classicism, we find traces of a fermentation. One of these was the increasingly narcissistic preoccupation with role-playing, the mask, and pretensions. As important as the theater was for Diderot and Goethe, King Gustav III of Sweden also asserted that life was a big artistic illusion.[3] Himself a talented playwright and author of several opera librettos, he was so infatuated with the stage that this attitude caused considerable dissatisfaction among his politicians. Ironically in tune with the murder of Gustav III in his beloved Opera at a masquerade-ball, the king's excessive preoccupation with roles and identities foreshadowed a more conscious utilization of Romantic irony in nineteenth-century Scandinavian literature.

---

[1] The research for this paper was facilitated by a grant from the Humanities and Social Sciences Committee of the University of Toronto.

[2] The term Scandinavia is utilized as defined by the American Board of Geographic Names, meaning Denmark, Norway, and Sweden.

[3] As a Swedish literary historian observed, "in Gustav III we find a slight trace of romanticism, and for this kind of tendency the operas and carrousels [i.e., spectacles] were more appropriate means of manifestation than was French classical tragedy" (Henrik Schück and Karl Warburg, *Illustrerad svensk litteraturhistoria* [Stockholm: Rabén & Sjögren, 1926-49], IV, 452).

Another influence, that of the cult of sensibility, also arrived in Scandinavia during the later eighteenth century. Sentimentalism mixed with a Herderian interest in folk art and culture influenced Johannes Ewald's musical play *Fiskerne* (The Fishermen, 1779). The mixed genres of the Rococo (mostly musical plays) and the mixing of tragic and comic elements (as in certain plays of Gustav III)[4] are also pre-Romantic characteristics, as is the perfection of theater machinery to create complex and bedazzling spectacles. For instance, for the performance of Ewald's *Fishermen* stage manager Christoffer Nielsen designed a moving sea of waves in motion which, according to contemporary accounts, created a perfect illusion.[5]

Along with these pre-Romantic trends, the cult of Shakespeare was evolving and was soon opposed to the tyranny of French Classicism. Shakespeare was introduced to Denmark by the Schleswigean H.W. Gerstenberg (1737-1823) who repeatedly praised him in the influential *Schleswiger Literaturbriefe* which he edited in Copenhagen between 1766-68 and in 1770. Awareness of Shakespeare had died out after the initial introduction of his plays by wandering English actors at the end of the sixteenth century. Thus, so far as modern reception is concerned, Shakespeare was first performed in Scandinavia in Norrköping, Sweden, where *Romeo and Juliet* was staged in 1776.[6]

The spreading of Romantic tendencies is also observable in new trends in the translation and performance of foreign authors. In 1791 the actor-director Didrik Gabriel Björn (1757-1810) translated into Swedish Kotzebue's *Menschenhaß und Reue* (it was staged subsequently) – a tear-jerker which, however, greatly influenced the sentimental sensibility of the Romantics. After 1791, Kotzebue became one of the most popular foreign playwrights on the Scandinavian stage, and in general, the new, "German" taste was winning a quick victory. Such "Gothic" thematic elements as medieval castles, graveyards, hidden grottos, secret orders, witchcraft, wild nature, and the like were organic parts of Gustav III's posthumous *Den svartsjuke neapolitanaren* (The Jealous Neapolitan, performed in 1793); of the Swedish Anders Fredrik Skjöldebrand's (1757-1834) *Herman von Unna*, an adaptation from German; and of the Danish Johannes Ewald's *Balders Død* (Balder's Death, 1773).

After the turn of the century Romanticism made its breakthrough in Scandinavia, first in Denmark where its figurehead Adam Oehlenschläger (1779-1850) became a brilliant and versatile poet; next in Sweden where several groups and individuals represented the movement. While discussing Scandinavian Romanticism, we should keep in mind that both Denmark and Sweden were influenced by German Romanticism as strongly as they had earlier been influenced by French Classicism. One can definitely find certain analogies between Danish and Swedish Romanticism but it is futile to search for significant interactions: the fountainhead of inspiration was contemporary German literature for both countries.

As it happened, Oehlenschläger was not only the first truly prominent figure of Scandinavian Romanticism – he was also a playwright. For all his Romantic zeal, he introduced a self-critical perspective as well, already in his first published play, *Sanct-Hansaften Spil* (Midsummer Night's Play, 1802). Although rather a book-drama than a conveniently performable one, this play manifested Romantic irony for the first time in Scandinavian literature. The combined influence of Goethe's

---

[4] Schück and Warburg, IV, 490.
[5] Cf. Frederick J. Marker and Lise-Lone Marker, *The Scandinavian Theatre* (Oxford: Blackwell, 1975), pp. 104-5.
[6] F. Marker and L.-L. Marker, p. 109.

Das Jahrmarktsfest zu Plunderweilern, Tieck's *Prinz Zerbino,* and Shakespeare's *A Midsummer Night's Dream* is readily evident in this playful, dramatized cavalcade.

Oehlenschläger's next play, *Aladdin* (1805), is also rather restricted to reading, mostly because of its size (almost 300 printed pages), its extremely kaleidoscopic structure, and its fifty *dramatis personae* plus several ambitious choirs and mass scenes – which, however, did not hinder its being staged in different adaptations. *Aladdin* is a program drama, a declaration of the rights and responsibilities of the Romantic genius, and as such, an elaboration of Oehlenschläger's poem "Guldhornene" (The Golden Horns, 1802) which is regarded as a manifesto of Northern Romanticism. The play asserts that the chosen ones can occasionally transgress the social and ethical limitations imposed on man, yet they should not only find luck (in Aladdin's case the magic lamp, later the love of women and the people) but should also learn how to keep and deserve their luck. The play *Aladdin* won the appreciation not only of Oehlenschläger's contemporaries but also of such great later Scandinavians as Søren Kierkegaard and Henrik Ibsen as an incarnation of the cult of the artist and the dreamer.

Between 1805 and 1807, Oehlenschläger travelled in Germany and France, meeting virtually all important figures of his time: Arnim, Fichte, the Schlegel brothers, Schleiermacher, Mme de Staël, Tieck, Voss, Zacharias Werner, Wieland, and last but not least Goethe himself, who dedicated his autograph "dem Dichter des Aladdin." From Halle, Oehlenschläger sent back to Denmark in 1806 *Hakon Jarl,* his most impeccable drama which shows Schiller's influence in its preoccupation with ethics, but manifests even more clearly the impact of organic historicism. The heathen Earl Hakon remains the central tragic hero throughout the whole drama and embodies the Romantic idea of the greatness of the vanishing past. At the same time, the challenging force, Christianity represented by the returning pretender Olaf Trygvason, has not only ethical superiority over Hakon and his decaying epoch but also appears as the new, victorious idea which outgrows the vanishing pagan past. It should not be forgotten that in quite a few manifestations of the Northern mentality, Christianity stands for the South as well as for anything foreign and forcibly imposed on good old Scandinavia. Oehlenschläger spells out, however, that the North joined Europe precisely by resigning from the worshipping of its local Germanic gods. This is an indicator of the universalist idea in Romanticism (that is, one form of *Universalromantik*); while another thesis, that the old, established order outlived itself and had to yield to a new system, is an organic idea. In the North, where even the Enlightenment cherished the pre-Christian past, Oehlenschläger dared to pose the dichotomy of pagan and Christian as a matter of either/or, and dared to choose the wider community, Europe. In his later years, he did not appreciate at all N.F.S. Grundtvig's ethnocentric cultural nationalism, an attempt at a synthesis which emphasized the assimilation of Christianity to the surviving local pagan tradition and proclaimed once again the "decadence" of the South and the "noble values" of the North.

Aside from historical philosophy, *Hakon Jarl* was also a play of masterful dramatic skills, inviting effective performances such as its very Romantically staged première in 1808.

Whereas Scandinavian pre-Romanticism manifested elements of Romantic thought as well as dramatic technique, Oehlenschläger's plays touched on the essence of Romanticism, which was a new attitude of the individual toward existence. The cult of the genius, sensibility, a holistic, organic, and individualistic perception of life, and the release of naive fantasy are elements of all three plays mentioned. Perhaps this is why their Romantic character is so profound and yet spontaneous, which creates an enchanting effect.

Oehlenschläger also enjoyed diversity, however, and the number of the plays he wrote (over a dozen) gave him opportunity to create in different styles and moods. Consequently, some of his dramas, like *Balder hin Gode* (Balder the Good, 1806) and *Axel og Valborg* (1808), are exercises in different aspects of neoclassicism (or "Classicistic Romanticism"). Especially his numerous late dramas are, however, rather documents for literary history than living parts of the Danish dramatic tradition.

Considering his achievement as a whole, there is no doubt that Denmark had no other Romantic playwright comparable to Oehlenschläger – in fact, it is questionable whether Northern Romanticism (including pre- and post-Romanticism) can boast a more significant representative. Literary history has noted the Shakespearean plays (*Mithridat*, 1812, *Blanca*, 1815) of Bernhard Severin Ingemann (1789-1862), and the cosmopolitan and exotic book-dramas of Johannes Carsten Hauch (1790-1872) – yet, the originality and élan demonstrated by Oehlenschläger increasingly became manneristic in their works. Even more obvious was the same trend in late Romanticism, called *romantisme* ("romanticizing") in Danish literary terminology as opposed to *romantik*. This mode of writing emphasized a variation of Biedermeier sentimentalism and respected the public's need for entertainment, thereby paving the way to the technically faultless intrigue-dramas in the manner of Sardou and Scribe.

The great figure of post-Romanticism, Hans Christian Andersen (1805-75) himself wrote dramas, of which *Mulatten* (The Mulatto, 1840) is relatively the most "romanticizing" (on Martinique, the love of a French countess saves the life of a noble Mulatto who is facing enslavement and cruel death at the hands of a revengeful planter); while literary history considers other plays, such as *Kjaerlighed paa Nicolai Taarn* (Love on Nicolai Tower, 1829) as parodies of the Romantic tragedy of fate. This is a period of ironizing over Romanticism itself, of doing away with its excesses in favor or Realism. Such self-deprecating use of Romantic techniques of presentation reminds one of Heine's reaction to German Romantic literature. In *Love on Nicolai Tower*, for instance, a cruel father, watchman of a city tower, wants to force his daughter to marry one of his elderly colleagues while she loves a taylor's apprentice. When she resists, the father threatens her thus: "I'll immure you alive behind the walls of a seamstress' workshop!"[7] Under the conditions of a well-regulated bourgeois existence, Romantic phrases and mythological clichés pronounced by the characters sound comic; and a struggle for the recovery of the "kidnapped" daughter appears as an unheroic brawl between members of the watchmen's and taylors' guilds.

The Danish master of this period is Johan Ludvig Heiberg (1791-1860). The first time he made hilarious fun of the Romantic preoccupation with illusions and their denial of solid identities was in his *Julespøg og Nytaarstøyer* (Christmas Jests and New Year's Tricks, 1816), a work analogous to Oehlenschläger's *Midsummer Night's Play* in its theme, but resembling rather Tieck's *Der gestiefelte Kater* (Puss-in-Boots) in its technique and philosophy. This drama, centered around festivities of the winter solstice in Copenhagen (while Oehlenschläger's shows those at the time of the summer solstice) puts reality in a three-dimensional kaleidoscopic box. These dimensions, taken one by one, look quite fixed and realistic – when considered in their mutual relations, however, they create an impression of utter relativism. When somebody cries "Fire!" – is there a real fire? And is the spectator just invited up to the stage, or is another person who has remained on the floor, the

---

[7] "Jeg skal Dig lade levende indmure/ Hos een af Byens Modehandlerinder!" (H.C. Andersen, *Samlede Skrifter* [Copenhagen: Reidzel, 1876-79], IX, 6.)

"real" fire captain whose duty should be the verification of the warning? The problem is, of course, that both figures claim to be the real authority. This playing with identities and roles goes on and on, bringing home the message of a certain world outlook which no longer takes Romanticism "seriously," yet at the same time never bores us, thanks to Heiberg's lifelong interest in stage effects and techniques.

As one of the most prolific Danish stage authors who wrote dozens of plays, Heiberg later fell under the spell of Scribe and his school of the *pièce bien faite*; henceforth his individual style gained expression mostly in vaudeville-plays. A brilliant manifestation of his *romantisme*, that is, his post-Romantic ideas and technique, is *Elverhøy* (Elves's Hill, 1828), written for a royal wedding and traditionally performed on such occasions ever since. The juxtaposition of Danish folklore and superstitions with a sophisticated court milieu is but the frame: love intrigues, changelings, a buried piece of jewelry which is needed to solve a secret, are some typical elements of the plot. Yet Enlightenment and earthly justice, represented by the court of Christian IV, come out as powers dominating over the surreal folkloric world of elves and other magic creatures. Romanticism is once again defeated by its own means. It is worth noting that many of H.C. Andersen's fairy tales also end in this ironic nostalgia for an irrevocable fairy dream.

Unlike in Denmark, there was no single figurehead of Swedish Romanticism. Instead, the movement centered around two ideological groups. One was the so-called *Auroraförbundet* (Aurora Society; regularly met between 1807 and 1810), whose spiritual leader, Per Daniel (Amadeus) Atterbom (1790-1855) inscribed the cult of fantasy and intuition on their banner. The Society published two periodicals, one in Stockholm (*Polyfem*, 1809-12), the other in the university town Uppsala (*Phosphoros*, 1810-13, continued under other titles until 1832). The title of the latter lent the popular name *fosforisterna* (Phosphorists) to this faction of the Swedish Romantic movement.

Another assembly was the *Götiska Förbundet* (Gothic Society, 1811, inactive after 1824, dissolved 1844), whose members were later called "Goths." This society emphasized the organic view of history, mythology, and folklore. Its prominent figures were Esaias Tegnér and Erik Gustav Geijer, who belong among the most significant Swedish Romantics. At the same time, we can write off this variation of the "organized" Romantic movement for the purpose of the present discussion since the Goths did not write plays and even their historicism had surprisingly little impact on Swedish Romantic drama.

Finally, a third, uncommitted, solitary and decadent figure of Swedish Romanticism was Erik Johan Stagnelius (1793-1823) who, like Atterbom, contributed some significant and typical plays.

Fågel blå (Bluebird), Atterbom's first but unfinished Romantic play which he started writing in 1811 and worked on until his death, is based on an Indian as well as Celtic motif (a prince is turned into a bird by his evil stepmother) – a motif which Atterbom found in French sources. Southern exoticism (the scene is Cyprus), the power of love, mysticism, metaphysical longing are some of the leitmotifs. Also, it is a program declaration of Romanticism. "Isn't poetry the real nature, driving force and mother of matter, the proto-form of all shapes?" exclaims Deolätus, one of the characters, in exaltation.[8] Heroes characterized as "materialistic" come out in bad shape when compared with the "idealists."

---

[8] "Och är ej dikten den egentliga/ Naturen? Ej materiens liv och moder?/ Ej alla formers odelbara urform?" (P.D.A. Atterbom, *Samlade dikter* [Örebro: Lindh, 1858], III, 55.)

Even more allegorical and ideologically biased is Atterbom's magnum opus, *Lycksalighetens ö* (The Island of Bliss), which he wrote between 1821 and 1827. The size of this book drama is certainly impressive, and so is the manifest ambition driving the author: to create a universal vision of Romantic existence. Its hero is the young Northern fairy-tale king Astolf whose longing for love and happiness guides him down South to find his dreams "realized" on an island, in the arms of the superhuman, beautiful fairy queen Felicia. After a while, the sense of duty awakens in the Romantic Odysseus and he returns to his country only to find it transformed into a "Hyperborean Republic" governed by the mob, demagogues, and dangerous liberal ideas. "Rather death!" thinks the noble but slightly conservative king and returns to his fantasy island where he indeed dies in Felicia's arms. On the one hand, details of the whole drama manifest a great formal talent, a masterful command of the Swedish poetic language, and a richness of fantasy unknown in Swedish literature before. On the other hand, the work is unproportioned, overdecorated, without the least claim to any psychological plausibility. At its worst, it is also downright reactionary: with due respect to aesthetic values, no reader can miss recognizing that the target of Atterbom's criticism was not an utopian Northern republic but the basic principles of any modern democracy. Here, Platonism (which especially Swedish literary historians regard as the fundamental characteristic of their Romanticism)[9] definitely acquires political significance. But, as the literary scholar Carl Santesson pointed out, there was plenty of direct German Romantic influence on Atterbom when he wrote *The Island of Bliss*[10] such as the example of Tieck's *Die verkehrte Welt* (The Land of Upsidedown).

Considering that Atterbom started his literary activity around 1809, it is hardly surprising that his most significant drama, as a late-comer in the 1820s, bore certain symptomatic ailments of European Romanticism after Napoleon's defeat. His contemporary, Stagnelius, can be regarded as a representative of the decadent rather than the socially retrogressive elements of Romanticism. An insecure, introverted, ugly young man of excessive eroticism, and probably also an opium addict, Stagnelius wrote eleven plays of different lengths, plus two dramatic fragments. His most celebrated allegorical poetic drama is *Bacchanterna eller fanatisme* (The Bacchants, or Fanaticism, 1822), in which he actually intended to follow the Classic norms of artistic creation. The unities, the closing action, the Greek mythological subject (The Orpheus motif) are here only deceptive devices, however: the underlying ideology is esoteric Christianity. There is a clear analogy between the death of Orpheus and that of Christ. It is obvious from the play that Swedenborgian mysticism made a strong impact on Stagnelius. Besides religious mysticism, preoccupation with the transcendental and with the survival of the soul after death provides little opportunity for more clearly identifiable or conventional Romantic elements to appear in the play. Elsewhere the situation may differ, of course: such as in *Riddartornet* (The Knights' Tower), in which drama the unfaithful wife of a German general is sitting in a medieval dungeon and her daughter is working on a plot to help her escape. Stagnelius also made attempts to fuse Classicism, Romanticism, and Nordic mythology or historicism, as for instance in *Sigurd Ring* (1816-17) and *Wisbur* (1818).

Considering Atterbom, Stagnelius, but also the minor representatives of Swedish Romantic drama, one can realize that this period produced mainly plays for reading but not for the stage. Also, Swedish Romantic plays were largely allegorical and transcendental, with long tirades but little

---

[9] Cf. esp. Albert Nilsson, *Svensk romantik: den platonska strömningen* (Lund: Gleerup, 1924), on Atterbom: pp. 232ff.; Sven Stolpe, *Den svenska romantiken från Atterbom till Runeberg* (Stockholm: Askild & Kärnekull, 1977), p. 15.
[10] Cf. Carl Santesson, "Tysk kalenderlyrik i 'Lycksalighetens ö' och nyromantiska tidningsförbindelser," *Samlaren*, 46 (1925), 169-93; "Tiecks prosa och 'Lycksalighetens ö'," *Samlaren*, 47 (1926), pp. 109-27.

spectacle or, especially, action suited for the stage. As if he had felt these paradoxes, Carl Jonas Love Almqvist (1793-1866), an Uppsala graduate from the generation of Atterbom and the Phosphorists, made some belated attempts at writing stage-worthy Romantic dramas. He, however, himself represented the Swedish paradox. His most interesting quasi-dramatic work, *Amorina*, was itself a book drama finished by 1822 but not published until 1839. His two dramas from the thirties which are more suited for the stage – *Ramido Marinesco*, 1834, and *Signora Luna*, 1835 – were, on the other hand, rather belated, "romanticizing" plays whose elementary device to gain the spectators' attention was Southern exoticism (as in Andersen's *Mulatoo*).

The thematic leitmotifs of all three works are a family curse, the unknown identity of several characters, and, as a result of these two, incest between brothers and sisters, and indirect or direct murdering of kinsfolk. The rest is variation on these themes, with ample additional romanticizing effects added: vampirism and the rejection of bourgeois "common sense" in *Amorina*, a mysterious monk and a poisoned picture in *Ramido Marinesco*, interracial love in *Signora Luna*. *Ramido Marinesco* also deserves attention for its innovative handling of an international tradition. The hero is, namely, Don Juan's only son (from Donna Bianca) who, when sent from Majorca to Valencia by his ambitious mother to make his fortune, instead keeps falling in love with young ladies who turn out to be his half-sisters from his overproductive father. The mood of the drama is by no means comic, however; finally the embittered Don Ramido dies, with the indirect assistance of his father who, disguised as a monk, is seeking penitence by calling upon himself the hatred of those who once loved him.

The relative formal novelty of *Amorina* in Scandinavian literature lies in the fact that most of the text[11] consists of dramatized monologues and dialogues, that is, direct speech.[12] At the same time, the links between the dramatized parts are epic and novelistic: although they also provide descriptions of the upcoming or changing scenes as if they were stage directions, they contain the reflections and comments of an omniscient narrator. Such narrative episodes occur only at the beginning and end of the chapters, however, which strengthens the impression that one is reading a book drama. And yet, in spite of the pseudo-dramatic form, the whole work falls at least as close to the novel as to the drama. Although it is conceivably adaptable to the stage, it can be most appropriately called a "dialogue novel."

Yet, it is especially in the novelistic *Amorina* that we find a striking example of Almqvist's attempt to create a *Gesamtkunstwerk*. Almqvist called his consistent experiments with the synthesis of epic and drama during the 1830s the "poetic fugue," as he regarded the fugue as a synthesis of the whole musical art. This view coincides with Friedrich Schlegel's definition of the novel as a synthetic genre.[13] Similarly rooted in Schlegelian aesthetics is Almqvist's view that the receptor of the literary work should participate in the creative process by developing his own interpretation of the characters, problems, and events represented in the artistic product. Although Almqvist provided this contribution to the theory of the open literary form in an essay primarily related to the reading process,[14] it can be applied to his own quasi-drama *Amorina* and to his two plays, particularly

---

[11] 90%, in Bertil Romberg's estimate (in his monograph *Carl Jonas Love Almqvist* [Boston: Twayne, 1977], p. 39).

[12] Cross-breeding the novel and the drama is not unknown in European literature, the first such work in modern times being the Spanish Renaissance work *La Celestina* by an unknown author. One cannot discard the possibility of a more direct impact on European Romanticism of Diderot's *Jaques le fataliste*.

[13] Romberg, pp. 34-40, 72-74.

[14] "Om två slags skrivsätt" (On Two Ways of Writing, 1835), *Samlade Skrifter* (Stockholm: Bonnier, 1921), VII, 211-15. (This is a fragment of a longer essay entitled "Dialog om sättet att sluta stycken," Dialogue on How to Finish Pieces.)

Ramido Marinesco. Needless to say, the Schlegelian idea that Almqvist also subscribed to was a predecessor of Brecht's view of the active role of the spectators, as well as of the "aesthetics of reception."

Everything considered, Almqvist is the culmination of the paradoxical development of the Swedish Romantic drama. His most successful attempt at playwriting turned out a novel rather than a drama. He was a belated Romantic, rather than a "romanticizer." Finally, his two undoubtedly stageable plays are sound but by no means significant, let alone outstanding literary pieces.

Facing this Swedish paradox, one can naturally find several "excuses." Perhaps the "heavy" Romantic dramas were written exclusively for the "theater of the mind," to use a Romantic metaphor for the visualizing capacity of the human psyche. Taking a more socio-historical standpoint, one may argue that the Swedish book-dramas (which they in the last analysis really are and as such possess significant artistic qualities) were exercises in the potentials of the Romantic mode of writing. They were intended to assert the presence of Romantic ideology in the North by their sheer existence. By all means, they have a place in literary history – but, do they belong in the history of the theater? Historians of literature surely cannot ignore this question entirely.

The difference in the development of Romantic drama between Denmark and Sweden is quite striking, especially if we consider the Renaissance of Swedish poetry during the same period which, in its turn, was probably both more significant and voluminous than that in Denmark. Only more synthetic and thorough modern studies in Scandinavian Romanticism could answer the question why the same movement achieved excellence in different genres among the quite similar socio-political conditions of neighbor countries. Such studies are by and large missing, however. Not only has no full-size study ever been written about the Scandinavian Romantic drama, but the whole Northern Romanticism has been treated with considerable shyness by Scandinavian literary histories after World War II. Romantic plays did not fare better on the stage during recent decades.[15] It is somewhat easier to understand this attitude in Sweden than in Denmark whose Romantic period inspired a number of fairly typical dramas and even produced a truly outstanding playwright: Oehlenschläger.

In the last analysis it is probably true, however, that not so much the dramatic achievements of Scandinavian Romanticism in their own right but rather their impact on the more modern Northern masters of the stage constituted the real significance of this genre-period for world drama. Henrik Ibsen (1828-1906) grew out of the belated Norwegian national Romanticism, a movement which gained strength only after the eighteen-thirties and was at least as significant politically as it was artistically. There is nothing new about the claim that most of Ibsen's early dramas and folkloric plays (such as *Kjaempehøien*, The Warrior's Barrow, 1850; *Sancthansnaten*, St. John's Eve, 1852; *Fru Inger til Østeraad*, Lady Inger of Østraat, 1855; *Gildet paa Solhoug*, The Feast at Solhaug, 1856; *Olof Liljekrans*, 1857; *Haermaendene paa Helgeland*, The Vikings at Helgeland, 1858) are Romantic in their initial inspiration, philosophy, and style. Less generally shared is the view that the Romantic trend never completely disappeared from Ibsen's plays in any one period of his activity. It was not until 1982 that Errol Durbach devoted a whole book-size study to Ibsen's Romanticism.[16] Durbach found three elements of Romanticism in Ibsen's plays: National (or historical) Roman-

---

[15] Cf. H. Topsøe-Jensen's "Indledning" to C. Hostrup, *Komedier og digte* (Copenhagen: Det Danske Forlag, 1954), pp. 5-11.
[16] Durbach, *"Ibsen the Romantic": Analogues of Paradise in the Later Plays* (Athens, Ga: Univ. of Georgia Press, 1982).

ticism, "Fairy Tale" (that is, folkloric) Romanticism, and "Neo-Romanticism," that is, psychological Romanticism. What makes Durbach's study especially interesting is that he also pointed out the difference between the fundamentally Romantic and the ironically Romantic in Ibsen's plays.

As Romantic heroes in general, Ibsen's dramatic protagonists are in search of the absolute, which, however, may be an obsession, even a deadly one. This search is described basically in a serious, emphatic way in *Brand* (1866), *Et dukkehjem* (A Doll's House, 1879), *En folkefiende* (An Enemy of the People, 1882), *Hedda Gabler* (1890), or *Bygmester Solness* (The Master Builder, 1892); whereas it receives ironic treatment in *Peer Gynt* (1867), *Gengangere* (Ghosts, 1881), *Vildanden* (The Wild Duck, 1884), and *John Gabriel Borkman* (1896). It was especially in *Peer Gynt* that Ibsen created a most brilliant, retrospective dramatic exposition of Romanticism. Peer Gynt, who is clearly an anti-hero and as such a travesty of the Romantic hero cult, is a man without identity. Ibsen shows the shallowness of his character through overused yet recognizably Romantic situations and encounters, thereby creating an illusion of Romanticism while destroying the essence of Romanticism.

What Ibsen de-romanticized in *Peer Gynt* relatively early were the clichés of Norwegian "National Romanticism," which consisted of convenient and complacent amalgams of historicism and folklore. He never gave up, however, the quest for the ideals that Kierkegaard, Hegel, and later Nietzsche represented in his eyes. The ascending consciousness of the hero as he progresses through the stages of his quest, the condemnation of the stagnation and finitude that philistinism stood for, are frequent and familiar motives of Ibsen's dramas. So is the revolt against the confines of bourgeois morals and values: Hedda Gabler's aesthetic resistance, Boletta Wangel's yearning to "get away" (in *Fruen fra havet*, The Lady from the Sea, 1888), are just a few examples. Again, revolt may challenge death, whose symbol is the avalanche in *Brand*, an early play, and the same symbol occurs in Ibsen's last drama, *Naar vi døde vaagner* (When We Dead Awaken, 1899). Recognizable Romantic dichotomies are the clash of illusion and reality (or, the aesthetic and the ethical), the artist's dilemma (the choice between "calling" and popular expectation, between art and life) – hardly any of Ibsen's dramas lack these motives. Even the realization that lying to oneself may be necessary to keep the individual alive (the famous thesis of *livsløgn*, or life-lie) as it occurs in *Vildanden*, *Bygmester Solness*, or *John Gabriel Borkman*, shows an ironic affirmation of the dualism of existence.

It was, of course, only the shallow and overused spectacles of Romanticism, and not the essential philosophy, that Ibsen rejected. While he discarded the banal folkloric elements – the trolls, fairies in *Peer Gynt*, nay, the main character himself, a semi-mythological figure of the folk tales – he kept subtly using the more symbolic, complex motives. Just to mention one example: Ellida Wangel (in *Fruen fra havet*) is both the girl of the Norwegian folk songs (which Ibsen himself collected in the summer of 1862 and 1863) whom the trolls claim and, at least in part, also a realistic reincarnation of H.C. Andersen's Little Mermaid: the girl who left the sea and could not find her place since.

There are also Romantic traits in the staging that Ibsen envisioned for his plays. Especially the Shakespearean changes of the scenes, the dialectics of inside and outside settings is striking, particularly in his early (*Brand, Peer Gynt*) and quite late (*Naar vi døde vaagner*) dramas. But the purely imaginary dimensions of place, which are present both physically and symbolically in such plays as *Brand, Naar vi døde vaagner* (verticality: high - low) and *Fruen fra havet* (horizontality: closed -

open), penetrate even plays which take place entirely inside, in an elusively Classical-Naturalist interior. In *Vildanden* and *John Gabriel Borkman* we find the opposites of upstairs-downstairs; in *Et dukkehjem*, those of the closed and open. Finally, no matter how general and overused the term "Romantic setting" may be, the Norwegian summer night with the glimmering fjord and the silhouette of the mountains in the background, the glory of the highland plateaus, provide convincing evidence that nature spontaneously triggers Romantic feelings in Norway.

The attempt to define the Romantic trait is much more difficult in the oeuvre of August Strindberg (1849-1912), the other great nineteenth-century Scandinavian playwright, Ibsen's younger contemporary and rival. No doubt those features of modern drama which we associate with its twentieth-century development (Expressionism, Theater of the Absurd) are already clearly identifiable in Strindberg's plays.

All this cannot make one forget that in his autobiographical novel series, *The Son of a Servant*, Strindberg called his alter ego, Johan, a "half-breed Romantic" who, "as a transitional species possessed the characteristics of both a Romantic and a naturalist. [...] This dualism of his nature was the key to his personality and his authorship."[17] It was not only on the basis of such confessional elements but also on the evidence of Strindberg's art that twentieth-century criticism has cautiously but consistently discussed certain Romantic elements in Strindberg: his often Platonic dualism, his Rousseauism, his strong attachment (despite occasional vitriolic outbursts to the opposite) to Schiller, Schopenhauer, Kierkegaard, Ibsen, and Nietzsche, and the Faustian and Shakespearean traces in his dramas. Especially three plays have been regarded as particularly reminiscent of the Romantic: *Gillets hemlighet* (The Secret of the Guild, 1880), *Lycko-Pers resa* (Lucky Per's Journey, 1883), and *Herr Bengts hustru* (Herr Bengt's Wife, 1882). Strindberg's thorough academic biographer, Martin Lamm, discussed these three together as a short Romantic period in the author's dramatic oeuvre;[18] while a recent critic mentioned *Lycko-Pers resa* as an example of the Romantic drama showing indisputable parallels with Tieck's, Raimund's, Goethe's, Oehlenschläger's, and Atterbom's oeuvre, and with Ibsen's *Peer Gynt*.[19]

While the Romantic element is, indeed, more circumscribed in Strindberg's works than in Ibsen's, its occasionally significant presence is nevertheless evident. The *Gesamtkunstwerk* was one of his aesthetic ideals, and he was quite specific about the artistic motives accompanying and explaining his plays, e.g.: Chopin in *Pelikanen* (The Pelican, 1907) and *Stora landsvägen* (The Great Highway, 1909), pieces from Haydn to introduce each act of *Påsk* (Easter, 1901). Strindberg called Beethoven's Sonata 17, opus 31, no. 2 "The Ghost Sonata" and named a play after it (*Spöksonaten*, 1907). At the end of this play, Böcklin's painting "The Island of the Dead" emerges in the background. Also vaudeville elements, these eclectic and ironic products of the late Romantic stage, ap-

[17] "en halvblodsromantiker [...] som övergångsformation behöll han båda artkaraktärerna av romantiker och naturalist [...]. Denna dobbelnatur var nyckeln till hans personlighet och till hans författeri." *Tjänstekvinnans son: i röda rummet. Samlade Skrifter* (Stockholm: Bonnier, 1920-21), XIX, 140.
[18] Martin Lamm, *August Strindberg* (Stockholm: Bonnier, 1948), pp. 82-88.
[19] Richard Bark, *Strindbergs drömspelteknik i drama och teater* (Lund: Studentlitteratur, 1981), p. 48. Cf. also Bark's general assessment of Strindberg's dream plays in the appendix "Summary in English": "Many scholars share the view that Strindberg wrote for a stage which did not exist. Nothing can be more wrong. He wrote for a stage which had existed before the breakthrough of Realism and Naturalism: the stage from the Baroque and the fairytale play of the Romantic period" (p. 213).

pear in *Lycko-Pers resa*, but perhaps even more significantly in *Himmelrikets nycklar* (The Keys of Heaven, 1892), in which several Shakespearean (Hamlet, Romeo and Juliet, Othello and Desdemona) and folkloric (Tom Thumb, Cinderella) characters, as well as Don Quixote and Sancho Panza make bitter fun of the absurdities of existence in many set pieces within the dramatic sequence. This mockery of the Classics reminds one especially of Oehlenschläger. This reminiscence grows even stronger upon reading *Gillets hemlighet* in which Sten, the idealist, becomes the master builder of Uppsala cathedral, while Jacques, the traditionalist who only imitates the masonic technique inherited from his father without putting faith and soul in it, suffers defeat. The analogy with such "sons of fortune" as Aladdin, and with the Romantic philosophy of *Sanct-Hansaften spil*, is striking.

In *Lycko-Pers resa*, but also in *Svanehvit* (Swanwhite, 1901), and *Himmelrikets nycklar*, the folklore and fairy-tale elements provide philosophical and structural evidence of the Romantic impact. *Svanehvit* itself resembles a widely known folkloric motif, the heroine being an innocent young girl who endures many tribulations from her cruel stepmother. The lover's kiss which brings a young dead person back to life in the same play is as charmingly familiar as the Christmas setting which serves as a frame (in the first and last act) to *Lycko-Pers resa*; this holiday functions similarly as in H.C. Andersen's, Dickens's, and E.T.A. Hoffmann's respective tales – even the rat characters appear, as in Hoffmann's *Nußknacker und Mausekönig*. Wishes coming true play as much a role positively in the fairy world of the dramas as curses do in a negative way. No matter how violently Strindberg repeatedly lashed out at Ibsen, the ironic handling of fairy-tale motifs in *Himmelrikets nycklar* is quite similar to certain scenes in *Peer Gynt*, notably the one in the Dovre Hall of the trolls. Transformations, changed identities are frequent. Finally, what Durbach called "psychological Romanticism" in Ibsen, namely, the utilization of dreams and the unconscious, is also present. This question actually takes us far beyond Strindberg's plays: in his whole work, in his notoriously contradictory views of women, there is a Romantic element of the Janus-face of human existence, of the male opposition to, but also his paradoxical acceptance of, the Goethean *Ewigweibliche*.

Ibsen and Strindberg had little impact on, or contact with, contemporary Scandinavian playwrights. The late nineteenth-century Neo-Romantic generation of the three Northern countries cultivated genres other than drama. Among the turn-of-century Symbolist and Neo-Romantic European playwrights, however, both men had their parallels in Hauptmann, Hofmannsthal, Maeterlinck, Oscar Wilde, and others. Thus, indirectly and paradoxically, the distinct and once thriving but by now mostly forgotten Scandinavian Romantic drama contributed to world literature immensely by shaping the career of some of the greatest masters of modern world drama.

RICHARD PLANT

FROM DARK INTO LIGHT:
NINETEENTH-CENTURY ROMANTIC DRAMA IN ENGLISH-CANADA

As to the assurance given that a paper on a native Canadian Romantic drama will be presented, this is simply not possible because such a drama exists neither in French nor in English for the period under consideration [the nineteenth century].[1]

The anonymous author of those words might take exception to this paper, which proposes to survey nineteenth-century Romantic drama in English-Canada, on the grounds that it is airy and insubstantial, to which I must respond by asking what else could be expected of an essay written about something which does not exist? Yet I need not be so cavalier and dismissive. The anonymous opinion joins many other misconceptions about English-Canadian drama which recent scholarship is dispelling.

What is strange, however, is that this view could have been formed at all. The general impression among commentators until two decades ago was that a poetic drama, filled with Romantic conventions and spirit, had been the predominant dramatic mode of nineteenth-century English-Canada. In the *Oxford Companion to Canadian History and Literature*, the standard literary reference until it was superseded in 1983 by the *Oxford Companion to Canadian Literature*, poetic dramas, all but two possessing significant Romantic characteristics, made up the entire "Drama in English" entry for the eighteenth and nineteenth centuries. When in his 1963 article, "Playwrights in a Vacuum," Michael Tait wrote about "English-Canadian Drama in the Nineteenth Century," he discussed only a number of these same poetic dramas as if nothing else existed, although he acknowledged the century as the "most energetic popular theatre Canada has ever enjoyed."[2] In actuality, approximately one-tenth of the published plays in English before 1900 were Romantic dramas or poetic dramas with strong Romantic tendencies. And this drama has inspired a sizeable body of critical commentary, including recent work re-introducing lesser-known writers, such as Eliza Cushing, Sarah Anne Curzon, John Hunter-Duvar and Thomas Bush.[3] In that light, the anonymous opinion quoted above offers a change of perspective, but it reminds me of Dr. Johnson's answer to the lady asking how a particular definition came to appear in his dictionary: "Sheer ignorance, madam."

---

[1] The anonymous comment is by an individual who, on behalf of the Social Sciences and Humanities Research Council of Canada, assessed the proposal submitted for the International Symposium on Romantic Drama, 16/17 October 1981 at the University of Alberta, Edmonton, Canada.

[2] Michael Tait, "Playwrights in a Vacuum," in *Dramatists in Canada*, ed. William New (Vancouver: Univ. of British Columbia Press, 1972), pp. 13-26; reprinted from *Canadian Literature*, 16, (Spring 1963).

[3] Among the most engaging of recent studies offering analysis of works which I refer to as Romantic are articles by Heather Jones: "Feminism and Nationalism in Domestic Melodrama: Gender, Genre, and Canadian Identity," *Essays in Theatre,* 8, no. 1 (November 1989), 5-14, and and the forthcoming "Main Course or Mere Confection: Gender Issues in Historical and Dramatic Representations of Laura Secord," (*Canadian Literature*).

There are upon us, however, changes in thinking about nineteenth-century Canadian drama, as is shown by the recent *Oxford Companion to Canadian Theatre* (1989) where poetic drama is given little generic attention but set within its theatrical and literary contexts. Since Michael Tait in 1963 stated of Charles Heavysege, author of *Saul* and *Count Filippo*, "The absence of any facilities for the production of native plays once induced him to try his luck in the United States,"[4] we have learned of many nineteenth-century productions of indigenous plays--and continue to learn of more. Patrick B. O'Neill estimates he has seen some 5000 titles of Canadian plays in various copyright registers. While this does not indicate that they were staged, it does give a sense of the body of Canadian drama created over the century, and allows us to situate Romantic drama in a broader perspective. As early as 1816 in Saint John, New Brunswick, for instance, audiences were entertained by *The Sailor's Return; or Jack's Cure for the Hystericks* written by a "youth in St. John."[5] Even Toronto, comparatively late in introducing Canadian plays to its stage, saw *Fiddle, Faddle and Foozle* by 1853.[6] By the time Heavysege published the first edition of *Saul* (1857), Montreal, where the monograph was printed, had over a half-century of English-language theatre, to say nothing of francophone activity – which was also available to anglophones. Admittedly the nature of the live theatre might have driven some authors away from drama entirely, or to a theatre of the mind and print. We know that inferior buildings and equipment, many second-rate performers and often immoral or rowdy behaviour associated with theatre companies or their patrons disturbed people of a delicate or lofty sensibility. For example, there is a hint of a deliberate avoidance of the crass reality of the theatre in John Hunter-Duvar's "Preface" to *De Roberval* when he writes: "It is unnecessary to add that the drama is not written for the stage."[7] But American theatres were much the same as their Canadian counterparts, so it is unlikely that such a consideration played a major role in Heavysege's case.

Exactly how accessible Canadian theatres were to the writers of Romantic drama is a question with a complex answer having as much to do with the nature of Romantic drama itself and the artist's own aspirations and attitudes as the presence of theatres. It seems a larger question than the paper at hand can answer satisfactorily; nonetheless, we can rest assured that Canadian dramatists, even poetic dramatists, did not write in the vacuum as Michael Tait argued was the case. Charles Mair, for example, author of *Tecumseh*, wrote to his friend George Denison, that *Tecumseh* might be a "good acting play [...] for it is full of striking situations – I may live to see it on the boards in Toronto yet."[8] Given then that Canadian authors could choose the nature and form of their drama while aware of an active theatre, both in and outside the country, what would encourage them in the direction of a Romantic mode? If I may move into more speculative argument for a moment, I shall try to sketch at least part of an answer.

There is another misconception floating about which fixes English-Canadians into a dispassionate temperament, one antithetical to Romantic flights of fancy. This might help our anonymous critic explain the supposed dearth of Romantic drama. But from a twentieth-century point of view, English-Canadians appear to have had an affinity for the Romantic. In fact, a strong argument could

---

[4] Tait, in W. New, ed., p. 17.
[5] Mary Elizabeth Smith, *Too Soon the Curtain Fell* (Fredericton: Brunswick Press, 1981), p. 21.
[6] Patrick B. O'Neill's "*Fiddle, Faddle and Foozle*: The First Stage Production of a Canadian Play in Toronto," *Canadian Drama*, 3 (1977), 20-22, discusses the play written by George Simcoe Lee staged in Toronto in April 1853.
[7] John Hunter-Duvar, *De Roberval* (Saint John: McMillen, 1888), "Preface."
[8] Charles Mair, letter to George T. Denison, 21 March 1885. Held at the National Archives of Canada, Ottawa.

be advanced that the essential sensibility of nineteenth-century Canadians was Romantic, the expression of a yearning spirit in conflict with the various restraints on its fulfilment and troubled by guilt from past transgressions. And this sensibility might explain the generally-acknowledged Romantic vein running through nineteenth-century poetry and fiction. Early in the century, for instance, we find John Richardson's important novels, *Wacousta* and *The Canadian Brothers*; the century ends on Gilbert Parker's *Seats of the Mighty* and William Kirby's *The Golden Dog*. In the intervening years is a host of novels of equally Romantic character. It is worth noting, as well, that *Wacousta* and *Seats of the Mighty* were adapted for the popular stage.

Consider for a moment, then, that many of those who settled the country were in their prosaic way fulfilling a Romantic notion: the quest for truth and freedom in a natural world untouched by corrupting European civilization. Moreover, their presence in Canada often had its share of individual revolt since many who came, including several of our dramatists, did so to escape confining social, political, religious, moral or economic conditions in the old world. Many people born here felt a similar need to break out of corrupt, oppressive regimes. The so-called "rebellions" of William Lyon Mackenzie and Louis-Joseph Papineau in 1837, and of Louis Riel in 1869 and 1885 might be seen in that light. It was only fitting that the land which they inhabited was seen as one of great natural beauty, a feature often celebrated in drama; for example, Sarah Anne Curzon had Laura Secord, the heroine in a drama of the same name, pause on her arduous journey carrying the truth to General Fitzgibbon about an impending Yankee attack. As she rests she "contemplates the scene":

> O this is beautiful! Here I could lie –
> Were earth a myth and all her trials nought –
> And dream soft nothings all a summer's day.
> In this fair glade were surely celebrate
> The nuptials of the year: and for her gift,
> Fair Flora, lightly loitering on the wing
> Of Zephyrus, tossed all her corbel out,
> Filling the air with bloom.
> From yonder copse,
> With kindling eye and hasty step, emerged
> The gladsome Spring, with leafy honours crowned,
> His following a troop of skipping lambs:
> And o'er yon hill, blushing for joy, approached
> His happy bride, on billowy odours borne,
> And every painted wing in tendance bent.
> Procession beautiful! Yet she how fair! –
> The lovely Summer, in her robes of blue....[9]

Further textual indications suggest a Canada even more deeply and fundamentally Romantic than first appears. In a scene shortly after the lines just cited, Laura Secord, now tired and fearful, pauses in another spot in the forest:

---

[9] Sarah Anne Curzon, *Laura Secord, the Heroine of 1812: A Drama and Other Poems* (Toronto: Robinson, 1887), pp. 39-40.

> Gloomy, indeed, and weird, and oh, so lone!
> In such a spot and hour the mind takes on
> Moody imaginings, the body shrinks as 'twere,
> And all the being sinks into a sea
> Of deariness [sic] and doubt and death.
> *The call of the death-bird [owl] is heard.*[10]

At the same time as the country's magnificence charmed the eye, its natural beauty could be seen to harbour a terrifying, dark side which came to be reflected in literature as an extension of the individual's own dark self. And we are aware that Canadians of the time were constantly having to deal with their darker selves in terms of a feeling of guilt inherent in their puritan heritage. In reality, beautiful Canada proved dangerous, powerful, and often fatal. As a result, Canadians might have had a need to see heroic figures challenging great forces and hear them expressing lofty sentiments, confirming that a world could at least be imagined in which those caught in powerful tensions struggled toward rewards and the atonement of their sins. In this light, given the existence of a Canadian dramatic muse, it seems only reasonable that Canada should have a drama which grappled with Romantic issues providing an imaginative expression of the Romantic tensions.

And indeed, some nineteen published plays, with another handful known but unpublished, demonstrate that Romantic drama was written in Canada. Although only two appeared after 1795 and before 1843, dates sometimes taken to mark the age of Romantic drama,[11] the body of texts illustrates a preponderance of characteristics integral to the form. The situation is simply that Romantic dramas, some possibly influenced by a Transcendentalist philosophy, flourished later in Canada than elsewhere.

There is another change of thinking which may be upon us concerning Romantic drama in Canada. Twentieth-century scholarship has normally spoken unfavourably of the form, partly as a result of the present century's natural rejection of its parents, so to speak. Simply put, Romantic drama fell out of fashion except as a whipping boy. Michael Tait says of Charles Mair's *Tecumseh*:

> The gravest fault is the utter lack of unity. Three main conflicts are introduced (the Indians vs. the Americans; the Americans vs. the British; Tecumseh vs. his brother), together with a variety of satirical and romantic episodes. None of these elements is properly integrated with the others, and the result is a lively chaos. In his eagerness to translate a maximum volume of Canadian history into Canadian literature, Mair simply ignores the problem of form.[12]

There are tell-tale words here. Tait cites "romantic episodes," but refuses to acknowledge the Romanticist's desire for freedom from the "properly integrated." He criticizes "lively chaos" when it more rightly might be seen as one of the Romanticist's aims. I am reminded here of Schlegel's comment in the *Dialogue on Poetry*: "The highest beauty, indeed the highest order, is yet only that of chaos." For the early (or, in German terms, high) Romantic Schlegel, and many of the later Romantics, this ontological chaos was an "inexhaustible fund of life which is constantly developing

---

[10] Curzon, p. 47.
[11] Among the works which suggest these dates is Richard Fletcher's *English Romantic Drama 1795 to 1843* (New York: Exposition Press, 1966).
[12] Tait, in W. New, ed., pp. 17-18.

itself in nature, in matchless but evergrowing beauty."[13] Mair does not ignore the matter of form; he may have different models in mind than Tait allows: the likes of Schiller, Byron, and the Shakespeare of Stendhal. While it is difficult to disagree with Tait's overall assessment of these dramas – "[...] although unsuccessful in their entirety, a few of them show a degree of skill, poetic if not dramatic, in isolated sections [... and] they reflect in an oblique and singular way, the temper of the period"[14] – one is conscious of his chastizing a horse for not being a camel. The result is that aspects of the dramas are ignored or misread.

In essence, it is time for a re-examination of nineteenth-century Romantic drama in Canada in a perspective admitting that a more complex set of circumstances was present when the dramas were written. This new perspective must also take more account of the past century's cultural attitudes and modes of thought. In so doing we should come closer to understanding not only the worth of the dramas but to bridging the gap between those in the nineteenth-century who admired works such as Heavysege's *Saul* and their outright condemnation in our own age. This latter point is no better illustrated than by a passage, again, from Michael Tait's important article:

> It was this work [*Saul*] which received, after its first edition in 1857, such extravagant praise from Coventry Patmore whose account of it appeared in the *North British Review*. Patmore found it "exceedingly artistic, akin to Shakespeare in its characterization and scope." Emerson in a letter referred to its "high merits"; Longfellow is reported to have called Heavysege the "greatest dramatist since Shakespeare." The critics were reinforced by the politicians. Sir John A. Macdonald wrote to the author in 1865: "I read 'Saul' when it first appeared with equal pride and pleasure [...] and as a Canadian I felt proud of our first drama." The level of his contemporary reputation may be gauged by a scene from Mr. Robertson Davies' *Leaven of Malice* in which it is suggested a study of the collected works of Heavysege represents the last ludicrous infirmity of the academic mind.[15]

My hope is that in addition to giving an indication of the nature of Canadian Romantic drama, this essay will help move us toward a thorough and sympathetic study of the form.

If arriving at an understanding of what constitutes Romantic drama in other countries is difficult, the problems in Canada are compounded, sometimes by the simplest detail. Take for instance the fact that before 1867 Canada did not really exist. Can we refer to drama composed before Confederation as Canadian? To see the ramifications of this I would like to turn to Robert Rogers's *Ponteach, or the Savages of America*, an eighteenth-century heroic drama whose essence is Romantic. It was published in London, England in 1766 and is noted in Reginald Watters's *Checklist of Canadian Literature 1628 to 1960*, an early, formative bibliographic source. Some people consider the play to be the first significant Canadian drama published in English, and it has been influential on later Canadian dramatists: there is a marked similarity, that seems to have gone unnoticed, between *Ponteach* and Charles Mair's *Tecumseh*; Robertson Davies has written *Ponteach and the Green Man*, an ingenious if not altogether successful play built around the enactment of scenes from Rogers's original.

But American literature has laid the more obvious claim to *Ponteach*. It appears in Montrose Moses's *Representative Plays by American Dramatists* (vol. 1), and its author, who fought at Pon-

---

[13] Friedrich Schlegel, *Dialogue of Poetry and Literary Aphorisms*, trans. by Ernst Behler and Roman Struc (University Park: Pennsylvania State Univ. Press, 1968), p. 53 (passage slightly modified).
[14] Tait, in W. New, ed., p. 13.
[15] Tait, in W. New, ed., p. 14.

tiac's siege of Detroit, receives a lengthy entry in the *Dictionary of American Biography*. Yet, Rogers hardly held American sentiments, even though he was born in what is now geographically the United States. In his tumultuous career as a British Army officer, he first gained recognition as the leader of "Rogers's Rangers" in bloody campaigns against the French in the 1750s and 1760s. His New England birthplace was insufficient to make him acceptable to American revolutionaries when the War of Independence broke out, especially when his pro-British leaning became evident in a second troop called the "Queen's Rangers." As John R. Cuneo states: "[...] his name conjured up visions of silent, grim giants, appearing out of the darkness and swooping down, Indian fashion, on a town with tomahawk and torch."[16] After the Seven Years War, he was imprisoned in Montreal and tried on a vague charge of treason against the British Crown. Although acquitted, he lost command of Fort Michilimackinac and was subsequently viewed with suspicion by the British. He was divorced from his wife, spent time in debtor's prison in America, England, and Halifax, and died poor in England in 1795, an image of the Romantic outcast.

While I would not go so far as to claim *Ponteach* as fully a Canadian drama, I shall suggest that it is in the unclear area of writing emanating from British North America (as distinct from the United States) and exhibiting sentiments consistent with those that became the foundation of English-Canadian life. That the play has influenced later Canadian authors and can be seen as a root of Romantic drama, and that Rogers spent a good deal of time in Canada, albeit some in jail, might help strengthen the bond with our literature. But the most important consideration remains the spirit in which Rogers handles his drama, its themes and attitudes.

The play presents the Romantic tale of Pontiac's battle against the encroaching White European "civilization," a story of the corruption of innately good people by evil invaders. Pontiac's Indians are being cheated and murdered by English traders, and treated inhumanely by disreputable English soldiers led by the corrupt Colonel Cockum, Captain Frisk, and three Governors, Sharp, Gripe, and Catchum. In retaliation, Pontiac and his confederate tribes plan to attack the English. But first they need to gain the help of the Mohawks, which Philip, Pontiac's bastard son, arranges through the love of Monelia, daughter of the Mohawk Chief, for Chekitan, Pontiac's legitimate heir. The dissembling Philip's real plan is to gain revenge on his half-brother for a former injury, and to secure control over Pontiac's empire. The war commences and in it the evil traders and English soldiers are punished. Philip kills Monelia, blaming the English, but Torax, her brother, reveals the truth. Chekitan, consumed by passion, kills Philip, then in remorse for his deed and the death of Monelia, he stabs himself leaving Pontiac childless and desolate. At the same time, the Chiefs of the other tribes have quietly made peace with the honourable English reinforcements. In the last lines of the play, Pontiac, his plans defeated and his sons destroyed, courageously resolves to escape,

> And wait a Respite from this Storm of Woe;
> Beget more Sons, fresh Troops collect and arm
> And other Schemes of future Greatness form;
> Britons may boast, the Gods may have their Will,
> Ponteach I am, and shall be Ponteach still.[17]

---

[16] James R. Cuneo, *Robert Rogers of the Rangers* (New York: Oxford, 1959), p. 270.
[17] Robert Rogers, *Ponteach or the Savages of America*, in *Representative Plays by American Dramatists*, ed. Montrose J. Moses (New York: Dutton, 1918), I, 208.

Characteristic of later English-Canadian Romantic drama, *Ponteach* is written loosely after the "Shakespearean" fashion using five acts of blank verse complete with pensive soliloquies and other "Elizabethan" traits. It contains an echo of *Macbeth* in the plight of the wife and family of one of the evil traders at the hands of the Indians, and of *King Lear* in the kingdomless, childless state of the noble Pontiac at the end of the play:

> Where will this rough, rude Storm of Ruin end?
> [...]
>   My Sons, my Name is gone;
> My Hopes all blasted, my Delights all fled;
> Nothing remains but an afflicted King.
> That might be pitied by Earth's basest Wretch.
> [...]
> Ye that would see a pitious wretched King,
> Look on a Father griev'd and curs'd like me;
> Look on a King whose Sons have fled like mine![18]

There is even a familiar ring from *The Duchess of Malfi* in "Ponteach I am, and shall be Ponteach still."

Alongside these literary borrowings are indications that *Ponteach* owes a debt to the live stage. In contrast to some Canadian dramas in the nineteenth century, *Ponteach* makes no outrageous demands of the theatre. I think here of stage directions like that the end of Heavysege's *Saul*: "The Philistine cavalry sweep across the scene and carry off the corpse of Saul."[19] Instead, the action is comparatively efficient and concrete; it moves quickly, and large scenes, such as the Indian-British battles, are not requested on stage. In fact, with careful handling, *Ponteach* could likely have been presented in the theatre of its time, although as far as is known, it never was. (It has been in recent times.)

This mix of stage and literary conventions is characteristic of nineteenth-century Canadian Romantic drama, testifying to a desire among Canadian authors, including some seemingly closet dramatists, to have their work considered in a theatre. Even Heavysege had visions of a stage production of the six-act, 10,000-line *Saul*, which Charlotte Cushman apparently considered. In fairness to the author, I should note that he went about creating a shortened version, and that Cushman had the good fortune to die before the production could take place.

Like Robert Rogers in *Ponteach*, many Canadian Romantic dramatists chose their subjects from indigenous sources, often with a nationalist purpose or at least an unconscious desire to explore Canadian themes. John Hunter-Duvar wrote *De Roberval* in 1888 dramatizing the attempt by Sieur de Roberval to establish a French colony at Quebec in the 1840s. Like *Ponteach* the play has enormous scope, chronicling De Roberval's wars with the Indians, his search for a route to China, and his love for Ohnawa, a wise and comely Indian maiden who dies saving him from an Indian ambush. With an irony that points out De Roberval's own inner conflict, the play also contains the Romantic tale of De Roberval's niece, whose love for a commoner causes the aristocratic nobleman to abandon the two lovers on an island in the St. Lawrence. Wilfred Campbell published

---

[18] Rogers, p. 206.
[19] Charles Heavysege, *Saul*, in *Saul and Selected Poems*, ed. Sandra Dwja (Toronto/Buffalo: Univ. of Toronto Press, 1976), p. 328.

Daulac in 1898, an account of Daulac's thwarted love and his historic defence of the Long Sault. Campbell writes that the play is meant to "depict the ultimate triumph of the fate of an unsuspecting innocence over the wiles and plots of a clever and scheming malice, and to show that the final heroic deed was but the natural outcome of an unusually noble nature in the personality of Daulac."[20] A patriotic Charles Mair in 1886 pitted the noble Chief Tecumseh, in the drama of the same name, against his evil brother, The Prophet (echoes of Ponteach and Philip), and the Americans. By far the most interesting character in this play is Lefroy, a White man fled from England to live with the Indians. Unlike Wacousta, the exiled British army officer who lives with Pontiac in John Richardson's novel, Lefroy does not become a suicidal monster of vengeance. Rather, he represents an ironically naive vision of freedom possible only in a world untroubled by what he calls the "mis-rule of kings" or the seemingly radical republicanism of the United States. In his study of Charles Mair, Norman Shrive offers a description of Lefroy which draws attention to some of the openly Romantic aspects of the play. Noting that Mair calls Lefroy "a poet-artist enamoured of Indian life and in love with Iena [Tecumseh's niece]," Shrive writes:

> [...] this young English expatriate, who wanders in and out of the woods searching for love and serenity has a psychological complexity quite lacking in his fellow *dramatis personae*. He is a Byronic figure, the melancholy poet on a quest, but transplanted from a corrupt Europe to an about-to-be-corrupted Canadian wilderness. Like Tecumseh, he deplores "the sordid town that here may rise," yet sees no solution in clearly defined boundaries for different races....
> [...] At first, Mair intended "to kill Lefroy" in the fifth act, "to get him out of an unhappy world" [...] but instead [...] when Lefroy goes forth to battle, Iena dresses as an Indian boy so that she can follow him in disguise. At a critical moment she springs from "behind a large sugar maple," intercepts an American bullet, "and is shot dead." So Lefroy is left as "but a shell,/ A husk, an empty case, or anything/ That may be kicked around the world."[21]

Although the use of indigenous subject matter for Romantic dramas was more evident toward the end of the nineteenth century, non-Canadian topics appeared throughout. The same John Hunter-Duvar who wrote *De Roberval* also wrote *The Enamorado*, an equally sprawling drama in which a renowned Spanish soldier-poet, Mazias, falls in love with an alluring, dark-haired woman, who marries another man. Mazias's uncontrollable passion drives him to seek her out; they declare their love, but the ensuing hours result only in a great deal of blood-letting.[22] Whereas, *The Enamorado* is set in fifteenth-century Spain, Wilfred Campbell's *Hildebrand* is about Pope Gregory VII and takes place in Rome. Campbell reprinted *Hildebrand*, along with *Daulac, Mordred* and *Morning*, in 1908 in a volume entitled *Poetical Tragedies of Wilfred Campbell*. In its preface he wrote about his choice of topics:

> The four tragedies included in this volume are widely separated in their subject-matter. It is a far call from Arthur of the Round Table, of ancient Celtic Britain, to Daulac, of the French Canadas, and they each are seemingly separated from the fortunes of the great Pope Gregory; yet these plays are included in one volume because they deal with those eternal problems of the human soul which all of the world's thinkers have had at heart.[23]

[20] Wilfred W. Campbell, *Daulac*, in *Poetical Tragedies of Wildred Campbell* (Toronto: Briggs, 1908), p. 127.
[21] Norman Shrive, "Poets and Patriotism," in *Dramatists in Canada*, ed. William New (Vancouver: Univ. of British Columbia Press, 1972), p. 34.
[22] John Hunter-Duvar, *The Enamorado* (Summerside, P.E.I.: Grave, 1879).
[23] Campbell, p. 5.

A similar concern for "those eternal problems of the human soul" may have been what drew Eliza Cushing in 1838 to the biblical tale of Esther for a drama of the same name. In it we see Esther, the beautiful, virtuous Jewish Queen to the Persian Ahasueras save her people from the evil machinations of Haman.[24] In *The Fatal Ring*, among the most Romantic of all nineteenth-century Canadian dramas, and one of its most engaging, Cushing focusses on another beautiful, virtuous woman, Estelle, the wife of the Count de Chateaubriand. Estelle is drawn to the royal court where, despite her virtue and through her openness to suggestion, she eventually falls prey to the passionate advances of King Francis. Her anguished husband wreaks havoc at discovering his wife's behaviour, allowing us to form a conclusion that moral and sexual transgressions ultimately lead to an agony of body and soul.

Before leaving the matter of choice of subject, one more play bears at least brief mention. Thomas Bush's *Santiago* (1866) is centred around an occurrence in South America where an earthquake frightened the parishioners in a church. Because the doors hinged inward and the terrified people crushed toward them, hundreds perished in the fire when they could not get out. Bush uses this as an apocalyptic climax when he dramatizes the vengeance of Vampries, a mysterious stranger with supernatural powers, on a group of corrupt Roman Catholic priests and their idolatrous congregation. While I would not term *Santiago* Romantic drama, the play does show us a world in need of redemption which has been corrupted by an institutionalized arm of civilization. In Vampries we see an especially dark and enigmatic personification of retributive justice who is described as an associate of Lucifer.

As one can judge from the subjects themselves, settings vary in location and presentation. But they all share a tendency toward the exotic, the sublime, gothic or otherwise distant locale. *Santiago* is set in South American mountains, described as a "storm-ridden realm" and marked by features such as "sepulchres of stone," "vacant chasms" and "mouldy skeleton[s] [...] hacked by ravenous beasts;/ Hewn by fell murder."[25] It is, in short, a fictive, microcosmic hell standing for the evil everyday world. *The Fatal Ring* opens in "an apartment in the Castle of the Count de Chateaubriand, in Britanny. The Baron de Leoncourt reclining in a fauteuil."[26] Before it ends, we have been in the Castle gardens, the Count's Paris home, the Louvre, a huntsman's lodge in the Bois de Boulogne, and the palace at Fontainebleau. (Clearly Curzon's imagination was unfettered by geographical boundaries.) Even Canadian settings were given a touch of the unusual. In *The Count's Bride*, a play resembling *Die Räuber* in many ways, George Washington Johnson set the action incongruously amid a gothic wilderness of the mountains of Hamilton, Ontario – in reality, a 200-foot rock escarpment still euphemistically referred to by Hamiltonians as "the mountain." Johnson writes that his purpose is to show "though justice for a time delay/ It sleepeth not, but will a vengeance pay." He goes on to state that "To show virtue liveth in our day,/ The plot is laid in Hamilton in Canada."[27] But it is a Hamilton none of us would recognize. Charles Mair through the lips of Lefroy in *Tecumseh* creates a vision of an idyllic Canada. The passage is a revealing and exemplary one from which I would like to quote at length:

---

[24] Eliza Cushing, *Esther, a Scared Drama; with Judith, a Poem* (Boston: Dowe, 1840).
[25] Thomas Bush, *Santiago*, in *Canada's Lost Plays. Volume One: The Nineteenth Century*, eds. Richard Plant and Anton Wagner (Toronto: Canadian Theatre Review Pubications, 1979), p. 26.
[26] Eliza Cushing, *The Fatal Ring*, in *Women Pioneers. Volume Two: Canada's Lost Plays*, ed. Anton Wagner (Toronto: Canadian Theatre Review Publications, 1979), p. 26.
[27] George Washington Johnson, *The Count's Bride*, in *Maple Leaves* (Hamilton: the author, 1864), p. 41.

Enter Lefroy, carrying his rifle, and examining a knot of wild flowers.

> This region is as lavish of its flowers
> As Heaven of its primrose blooms by night.
> This is the Arum which within its root
> Folds life and death; and this the Prince's Pine,
> Fadeless as love and truth – the fairest form
> That ever sun-shower washed with sudden rain.
> This golden cradle is the Moccasin Flower,
> Wherein the Indian hunter sees his hound;
> And this dark chalice is the Pitcher-Plant,
> Stored with the water of forgetfulness.
> Whoever drinks of it, whose heart is pure,
> Will sleep for aye 'neath foodful asphodel,
> And dream of endless love. I need it not!
> It is the hour of meeting [...]
> [...]
> And Iena has never failed till now
> To meet me here! What keeps her? Can it be
> The Prophet? Ah, that villain has a thought,
> Undreamt of by his simple followers,
> Dark in his soul as midnight! If – but no –
> He fears her though he hates!
>   What shall I do?
> Rehearse to the listening woods, or ask these oaks
> What thoughts they have, what knowledge of the past?
> They dwarf me with their greatness, but shall come
> A meaner and a mightier than they,
> And cut them down. Yet rather would I dwell
> With them, with wildness and its stealthy forms –
> Yea, rather with wild men, wild beasts and birds,
> Than in the sordid town that here may rise.
> For here I am a part of Nature's self,
> And not divorced from her like men who plod
> The weary streets of care in search of gain.
> And here I feel the friendship of the earth:
> Not the soft cloying tenderness of hand
> Which fain would satiate the hungry soul
> With household honey-combs and parloured sweets,
> But the strong friendship of primeval things –
> The rugged kindness of a giant heart,
> And love that lasts.[28]

Among the aspects evident in the passage is an indication of the nature of the characterization found in Canadian Romantic drama. Although many of the secondary and minor roles are thin stereotypes, the central figures often provide engaging complexity. Just as Lefroy is caught between the "sordid town" and "Nature's self," Estelle in *The Fatal Ring* is tricked from her country home to

---

[28] Charles Mair, *Tecumseh, A Drama and Canadian Poems* (Toronto: Radisson Society, 1926), pp. 91-22.

the "glittering court" where "Ambition, pleasure, power are shining lures,/ Too strong for women's weakness to resist."[29] But Eliza Cushing adds layers to this framework. If we look beyond Estelle as the male paradigm of womanly beauty and virtue, we discover her pulsing heart and a "touch of high ambition."[30] Her husband's misogynist uncle warns of "her youthful soul/ Impassioned as it is";[31] she is herself aware of "my passion's fault."[32] Up to the time the action of the play begins, she has controlled these inner powers:

> I yield perforce, –
> For such is woman's lot, doomed to renounce
> Each cherished wish, each generous impulse crush,
> That is at war with man's supremacy – [33]

When at court, by nature she does not resist the alluring King Francis, and is destroyed in the resulting turmoil, a woman devastated by the collision of her inner desires and the inhibiting structures, decidedly patriarchal, around her. But even the married King Francis, outwardly a villain, might be seen to offer another side to his character. He engenders a note of sympathy from us as we come to recognize that his inner self boils with passion also confined by the social and political framework – his roles as King and husband whose marriage was enforced, for politic reasons, ironically by his Machiavellian mother.

Charles Heavysege's portrayal of Saul also reveals an entrapped and troubled spirit at odds with the moral world around him. I am indebted to Sandra Djwa for an unusually sympathetic view of the character when she writes that the drama

> portrays powerfully the predicament of the tormented soul in a world of order and universal degree, a world governed, as it was to the Elizabethans, by an Old Testament God. When Saul, like Prometheus, rejects this order, he takes on the attributes of the Romantic hero. Ultimately, however, Heavysege views Saul's offence as Shakespeare did that of Macbeth, as an offence against degree. The eloquence of the drama develops from Saul's questioning of the moral order (a questioning suggestive of Byron's Lucifer from *Cain*, 1821) and from the tragic spectacle of Saul's fall into destruction.[34]

On the surface, Saul appears to be brought down by a Lucifer-like pride, but the play presents character in a more Romantic fashion having to do with preying psychological demons. Saul's darker self is reflected in Malzah, an "Evil Spirit from the Lord," who, as Djwa says, "resonates with the deeper psychological implications of the recognition of the doppleganger [...] 'the latent treachery in us all'."[35]

In their respective plays, both Pontiac and Tecumseh are depicted as typically-Romantic noble savages touched, and then destroyed, by White civilization. But in each case, the downfall is engineered through the collusion of a blood relative. Tecumseh is felled by the machinations of his brother, the Prophet, in some ways a sinister *alter ego* who has been corrupted by the Americans.

---

[29] Cushing, *Fatal Ring*, p. 28.
[30] Cushing, *Fatal Ring*, p. 37.
[31] Cushing, *Fatal Ring*, p. 37.
[32] Cushing, *Fatal Ring*, p. 28.
[33] Cushing, *Fatal Ring*, p. 36.
[34] Cushing, *Fatal Ring*, p. 34.
[35] Sandra Djwa, ed., *Saul and Selected Poems*, p. x.

Ponteach's bastard son, Philip, significantly given a "civilized," White name, seems a manifestation of Ponteach's own unbridled passion returned from former years to haunt him. It is worth noting, incidentally, that there are bastards other than Philip in Canadian Romantic drama; for example, Wilfred Campbell's *Mordred* is about King Arthur's deformed bastard son. Their unhappy fate, like that of the White who turns Indian (Lefroy, Wacousta) or the Indian turned White (Philip, The Prophet), as well as White-Indian couples in love (De Roberval/Ohnawa, Lefroy/Iena), seems an ominous reflection of the collision of a natural world with the "civilized" – a reflection of Canada itself.

For a comment on form, I can profitably turn to Wilfred Campbell again, who wrote that:

> The author makes no apology for the form of these plays. Like other writers, he has his own literary ideals, and with the great mass of the sane British peoples, believes that Shakespeare is still the great dramatic poet of the modern world.[36]

Many Canadian dramatists must have shared his view. Almost without exception, the Romantic dramas employed an episodic structure which often interwove more than one plot through three or five acts, as Michael Tait observed of Mair's *Tecumseh*. On the one hand, this can be seen simply as an emulation of Shakespeare. But, on the other hand, in the second half of the century, when almost all of the Canadian dramas were written, it also reflects the later-Victorian mind's coming to grips with the interpenetrating surface and subterranean psychological forces newly perceived to be at work in an apparently increasingly complicated world. The effect created was a sense of ominous inter-relationships that mirrored a world losing its solid centre of traditional laws and beliefs.

As we glimpsed in the selections from *Ponteach* and *Tecumseh*, the authors generally chose language aimed toward high style, diction perceived as elevated enough to serve as an appropriate, worthy vehicle for the "eternal problems of the human soul." They borrowed freely, often directly, from Shakespeare, as well as from Milton, Byron and Tennyson, to name some of the most frequent sources. (This matter of imitation has proved a problematic one for twentieth-century critics. Our age's high regard for originality and novelty has led critics toward an insensitive analysis leaving out the effect deliberately sought and achieved by the borrowing of nineteenth-century authors.) Familiar echoes sounded from selected words or phrases embedded in blank verse (there were few prose dramas) which owed its existence to the author's own creative imagination. In most cases, that resulted in something conventional and undistinguished by either great strength or glaring weakness. Of course there were exceptions, most of an unfortunate nature. But Eliza Cushing proves to have been a more satisfying poet than most. If sometimes overburdened by imagery, her dialogue is nonetheless speakable, resonant, and often highly effective. Charles Mair's verse and language were those of a minor poet, graced with the occasional speech of considerable rhetorical power, particularly when he celebrated the natural scene. This is equally true of Wilfred Campbell, whose landscape poems have attracted critical attention. But there is a lot of ponderous and sentimental verbiage in his work as well. Thomas Bush, too, displays rhetorical skill in some parts of *Santiago*, but he also writes passages so muddled by philosophical meanderings that they are incomprehensible. All too often Charles Heavysege's invention – which furnishes some elaborate and occasionally some apt imagery – lets him down, as it does when in *Saul* he speaks of the dawn "in the east fermenting."[37] In that case, the reader would probably be happier to have him borrow "Lo,

---

[36] Sandra Djwa, ed., pp. xxi-xxii.
[37] Campbell, p. 5.

the rosy-fingered morn," which he actually does in another instance.[38] Heavysege also has Saul, amid the heat of his eastern Mediterranean setting, urge his soldiers to "follow me and be the ball/ Tiny at first, that shall, like one of snow/ Gather in rolling."[39]

Canadian Romantic drama clearly has its share of ill-chosen similes, metaphors, and verse patterns. Yet, the overall quality of its language and verse is not greatly inferior to that of the mass of Romantic drama in England or the United States. In fact, that statement can be made concerning other aspects of the Canadian works. To be sure, there are no Canadian artists of the talent and stature of Byron or Shelley, or plays with the strength even of Boker's *Francesca da Rimini*. But the nature of Canadian experience created an allotment of individuals, either real or imaginary, who were at odds because their natural feelings and actions were confined by social, political, religious or moral boundaries – within or outside themselves. Their souls, shaped by English-Canada's strong puritan complex, were tortured by an almost indefinable guilt which heightened the tension between the characteristic Romantic polarities. The hero's quest to resolve this tension (all too often handled in strictly moral terms by the authors) was mirrored in the sprawling form of the dramas: multiple plot structures, excessive language, exotic locations. Indeed, such a drama did exist in nineteenth-century Canada. It has not been treated well or thoroughly, but it is time it should be.

[38] Heavysege, p. 99.
[39] Heavysege, p. 24.

DINNAH PLADOTT

NINETEENTH-CENTURY AMERICAN DRAMA: A ROMANTIC QUEST

The term "Romantic Drama" conjures up a very definite image when one is concerned with European theater. It means the ushering in of a new type of drama, which revolts against all that the so-called Classic theater holds dear. In form, it rejects the long-cherished notion of the three unities in favor of a looser, more flexible construction. The enthusiasm with which Shakespeare is discussed by such Romantic figures as Schiller, Schlegel, Goethe, Wagner, or Hugo testifies to their sense of liberation in the dramatic form which no longer heeds the strict demands of plot construction.[1]

In terms of content, on the other hand, one may borrow August W. Schlegel's description of Goethe's novel *The Sorrows of Young Werther* (1774), to sum up Romantic drama as "a declaration of the rights of feelings in opposition to the tyranny of social relations."[2] From the *Sturm und Drang* (Storm and Stress) movement of the latter half of the eighteenth century, to the height of Romantic drama in de middle of the nineteenth century, we witness a continuous celebration of the individual as a subjective but autonomous unit, whose emotional and spiritual claims are in conflict with the repressive demands of social and familial organizations. The specific materials may, and often do, take the form of Romance as described by Saintsbury:

> The absence of central plot, and the prolongation rather than evolution of the story; the intermixture of the supernatural; the presence and indeed prominence of love affairs; the juxtaposition of tragic and almost farcical incident; the variety of adventures arranged rather in the fashion of a panorama than otherwise [...].[3]

---

[1] See, for example, the translation of Shakespeare by Friedrich and August Wilhelm Schlegel, who in 1798 founded the *Athenaeum* as a primary Romantic forum for ideas; c.f., A.W. Schlegel, *Course of Lectures on Dramatic Art and Literature* (1811), trans. John Black; rev. ed. A.J.W. Morrison, 1848 (rpt. New York: AMS Press, 1965). Compare with Goethe's remarks: "The pieces of Shakespeare deviate, as far as possible, from the unities of time and place; but they are comprehensible – nothing more so – and on this account, the Greeks could have found no faults in them." (1825; cited in Barret H. Clark, ed. *European Theories of Drama* [New York: Crown, 1918; rev. 1965], p. 272). Similar sentiments are found in Goethe's 1813 essay *Shakespeare Ad Infinitum*, cited in *Theater and Drama in the Making*, ed. John Gassner and Ralph G. Allen (Boston: Houghton Mifflin, 1964), pp. 485-94. Even more explicit are Coleridge's remarks, which celebrate Shakespeare's deviations from Classical norms as a revolution and a development in dramatic effectivity: "there are greater advantages in this; – a greater assimilation to nature, a greater scope of power, more truths, and more feelings [...] allowed a freedom from the laws of unity of place and unity of time, the observance of which must either confine the drama to as few subjects as may be counted on the fingers, or involve gross improbabilites, far more striking than the violation would have caused. [...] On the Greek plan a man could more easily be a poet than a dramatist; upon our plan more easily a dramatist than a poet." (Clark, ed., p. 413. See also *Coleridge's Writings on Shakespeare*, ed. Terence Hawkes, [New York: Capricorn, 1959], pp. 66-68, 83-88.) A more complex view of Shakespeare's strength and weakness as a "modern" dramatist appears in Richard Wagner's *Opera and Drama*, cited in *Wagner on Music and Drama*, ed. Albert Goldman and Evert Sprinchorn (New York: Dutton, 1964). If we conjoin these various sentiments with Hugo's in the "Preface" to *Cromwell* (Gassner and Allen, eds., pp. 530-40), Shakespeare's function as the model for the Romantic ideals of dramatic freedom becomes clear.

[2] Quoted in Mordecai Gorelic, *New Theaters for Old* (New York: Samuel French, 1945), p. 106.

[3] Gorelic, p. 106.

However, as Tom Driver has noted, both Romantic structuration and Romantic contents still take two distinct avenues, depending on the playwright's conception of the term "history." One attitude to history views the past as the store of lost experiences of greatness, courage and nobility. The Wagnerian interest in German folk myths, Ibsen's utilization of Norwegian folkloristic symbolism, or the Romantic poets' fascination with the Greek mythological figures (cf., Shelley's *Prometheus Unbound*), all exemplify the attempt to replenish and regenerate the fragmented present with the aid of myths that link the present to its organic past. On the other hand, another view of history perceives the moment as a primary unit in a continuous process, and attempts to explore all the ramifications of the present moment in order to grasp the meaning of experience as a whole. Driver calls the first approach "Romanticism of the dream," and labels the second "Romanticism of the here and now."[4]

Romanticism and the American Dream

American drama of the nineteenth century is habitually considered aesthetically inferior, provincial, and devoid of interest. Yet a closer scrutiny of the dramas themselves, and of the general patterns of their transformations, suggests that a revaluation is in order. First, if one considers the theater performance, rather than the written script or drama,[5] as the object under consideration, the American theater and the developments it manifests during the nineteenth century indicate a parallel, rather than an inferior, relationship to their European siblings. Secondly, as our discussion will demonstrate, in the American theater the Romantic attempt to fashion new and more flexible dramatic forms, and the Romantic emphases in matters of dramatic contents, are inseparable. The celebration of the individual's right to defy the oppressive burden of tyranny in all its forms finds an analogue in the progressive determination of the American dramatists and actors-producers to avoid all slavish imitation of European dramatic models. Hence even the admiration for Shakespeare's greatness, which is the topic of countless lectures, essays, and public addresses,[6] becomes tinged with increasing defiance as the century unfolds.

[4] Tom F. Driver, *Romantic Quest and Modern Query* (New York: Delacorte, 1979), p. 15.

[5] Gorelic, p. 49, notes the changing function and the relative position and importance of the written drama in the theater system during different periods of theater history. (Compare R. Southern, *The Seven Ages of the Theatre* [London: Faber and Faber, 1962].) Due to the prominent role of the actor and the actor-producer in shaping the American theater, and due to the unremunerative position of the playwright until the passage of an initial, semi-adequate copyright law in 1856 (see Arthur Hobson Quinn, *A History of the American Drama. Vol. I: From the Beginning to the Civil War* [New York: Croft, 1949], pp. 184, 369-70), performance and written drama must both be considered as we attempt to describe and analyze the theater at that period.

[6] From an early journal entry in 1822 on, Ralph Waldo Emerson repeatedly expressed an almost hyperbolic admiration for Shakespeare. In 1864 he honored the three hundredth anniversary of the birthday of "the first poet of the world" by a glowing speech at the Saturday Club. In 1835 Emerson dedicated two lectures to Shakespeare, one treating him as a poet of imaginative, philosophic, and practical excellence and energy; the second focusing on the microstructure of rhythm, language, and character in the plays. *Shakespeare; or, The Poet* which was first published in *Representative Men* (1850), originated in a lecture given in 1848 at Exeter Hall, London. One characteristic passage illustrates Emerson's assessment of Shakespeare's role and dimensions:

> It took a century to make [Shakespeare's genius] suspected; and not until two centuries had passed, after his death, did any criticism which we think adequate begin to appear. It was not possible to write the history of Shakespeare until now; for he is the father of German literature; it was with the introduction of Shakespeare into German, by Lessing, and the translation of his works by Wieland and Schlegel, that the rapid burst of German literature was most intimately connected. It was not until the nineteenth century, whose speculative genius is a sort of living Hamlet, that the tragedy of Hamlet could find such wondering readers. Now, literature, philosophy

This desire for a native American dramatic voice ultimately shapes both the theatrical exploration of the "Romanticism of the dream" and that of the "Romanticism of the here and now."

The Dream of a Romanticized Past

As we look at the theater performances attended by American crowds during the nineteenth century, we perceive that here, as in Europe, the Romantic dramatization of history is very much in evidence. From John Howard Payne's *Brutus* (1818), through Mordecai Emmanuel Noah's *The Fall of Athens* (1822), Frances Wright's *Altorf* (1819), Robert Montgomery Bird's *The Gladiator* (1831), *Pelopidas* (1828), *Oralloossa* (1832), or *The Broker of Bogota* (1834), Nathaniel Parker Willis's *Tortesa the Usurer* (1839), and George Henry Boker's *Francesca da Rimini* (1853), to name only a few, American dramas were divorced by their authors from the American scene through temporal and spatial distance. Placed side by side with the performance of the famous actor Junius Brutus Booth in the title role of David Paul Brown's *Sertorius* (1830), or with the 1841 performance of another famous actor, Edwin Forrest, in Robert I. Conrad's *Jack Cade* (1835), a single common denominator immediately demands attention: these productions dramatize repeatedly a heritage of Romantic values in past actions which are placed as a model of integrity and valor before the present audience.

Moreover, the conflict between the defiant individual, who rejects the oppression of tyrannical institutions even at the price of his life, and the powers that crush and destroy him, is the central leitmotif in all these plays, regardless of their specific, and exotic, settings. Thus *Caius Marius* deals with the revolt of the Roman populace against the stifling rule of the oligarchy; *Pelopidas* celebrates the rebellion of the Thebans against Sparta; *The Gladiator* depicts the repudiation of slavery by the men led by Spartacus; *Oralloossa* conjures the similarly bold uprising of the Indians in South America against their Spanish oppressors; *Sertorius* celebrates the revolt of Spain against the Roman conquest; and *Jack Cade* depicts the rebellion of the common populace against the stranglehold of the English nobles.

Furthermore, a close look at the plays reveals the Romantic concern with delineating and evoking in full splendor the magnificent character of the individual rebels. John Howard Payne's *Brutus* (1818) is a case in point. The figure of Brutus, the patriot, commands attention as he responds to the

and thought are Shakespearized. His mind is the horizon beyond which, at present, we do not see. Our ears are educated to music by his rhythm. Coleridge and Goethe are the only critics who have expressed our conviction with any adequate fidelity: but there is in all cultivated minds a silent appreciation of his superlative power and beauty which, like Christianity, qualifies the period. (Cited in Eric C. Carlson, ed., *Emerson's Literary Criticism* [Lincoln: Univ. of Nebraska Press, 1979], p. 171.)

In 1850, Melville published in the *New York Literary World* a review of Hawthorne, "Hawthorne and his Mosses," in which he spoke eloquently of Shakespeare's true achievement in portraying "the sane madness of vital truth." Yet even when he praises Shakespeare for his greatness, Melville insists on American literary equality with the English bard. In an ironic inversion of an 1820 comment by an English critic, disparaging American literature, drama, and art, Melville asserts: "The day will come when you will say, who reads a book by an Englishman that is modern? The great mistake seems to be, that even with those Americans who look forward to the coming of a literary genius among us, they somehow fancy that he will come in the costume of Queen Elizabeth's day [... w]hereas great geniuses are part of the times." Melville's mixture of reverence and rebellion is typical among the major thinkers in America at the time. Henry David Thoreau, in *Walden*, places Shakespeare among the "altitudos" of high excellence; but he also expresses doubt about the ability of English literature to match the vitality and power of the emergent American writers, since "so long a civilization must have banished [wildness and spontaneity] from it [...]. It will only be heard in America." For a full discussion of Shakespeare's reflection in the eyes of nineteenth-century American thinkers, see Esther Cloudman Dunn, *Shakespeare in America* (New York: Blom, 1968), pp. 249-83.

tyranny and corruption of the Tarquins. His valiant and cunning reaction to the rape of Lucrece leads to the founding of the Republic and to his election as Consul along with Valerius. The tragedy of this father who must consequently condemn his own son for treason is therefore all the more poignant. As we compare Payne's play to the five extant dramas written on this subject, including Voltaire's 1730 *Brutus*, his achievement is thrown into relief. Payne demonstrates a skill in characterization as well as in the construction of an effective tragic plot. Quinn comments: "The born playwright and actor combined plays which had either had little success on the stage or had even been denied representation into one of the most successful and long-lived tragedies of the nineteenth century, which was played as long as there were great Romantic tragedians to play it."[7]

An examination of nineteenth-century accounts of the theater, such as F.C. Wemyss's *Twenty-six Years of the Life of an Actor and Manager*, illustrates the impact of the above-mentioned plays, many of which were equally striking in language, plotting, and characterization.[8] American drama begins, quite early in the century, to manifest the essentially Romantic concern with the autonomous state of individual conscience, and with rebellion as a redeeming rather than a damning action. This phenomenon is not rooted merely in the receptivity to new European trends and influences.[9] Instead of the American theater being a servile imitator of European models, it appears rather that what Driver calls "the Romanticism of the dream" took root on the American stage because the Romantic values were congenial to the American native situation. In 1847, in reviewing *The Gladiator*, Walt Whitman reiterates the implications of the ancient story for the present situation by exclaiming: "This play is as full of 'Abolitionism' as an egg is of meat [...]. Running o'er with sentiments of liberty – with eloquent disclaimers of the right of the Romans to hold human beings in bondage – it is a play calculated to make the hearts of the masses swell responsively to all those nobler manlier aspirations on behalf of mortal freedom."[10] Whitman's position is corroborated clearly by the playwright Frances Wright in her preface to *Altorf* (1819), where she links her belief in the primacy of individual liberty to her faith in the future of the theater in a Romantically inclined America:

> I cannot help believing that this country will some day revive the sinking honour of the drama. It is I
> believe generally felt by the public of Great Britain as of America, that the dignity of English Tragedy
> has now degenerated into pantomime; and that rapid movements, stage tricks and fine scenery have
> filled the space of poetry, character, and passion. The construction as well as the management of the

---

[7] Quinn, I, 172. Quinn reports that when *Brutus* was first performed in the British Drury Lane Theater on December 3, 1818 it became an immediate success: "the British public was thronging to the Drury Lane to see one of the most successful tragedies written in English in the nineteenth century" (p. 170). Its success was equally immediate in France and the United States.

[8] Wemyss observes, for example, about the climactic second act of Bird's *The Gladiator*: "Accustomed as an actor is to striking scenes, I was taken by surprise at the effect produced at the closing of the second Act. The rising of the Gladiators in the arena, and the disposition of the characters as the Act drop fell, I do not believe was ever surpassed in any theater in the world." F.C. Wemyss, *Twenty-six Years of the Life of an Actor and Manager*, 2 vols. (New York: Burgess, Stringer and Co., 1847), I, 94.

[9] See, for example, Quinn's account of the interpenetration of European and American drama, where European dramas were brought to America in translation or adaptation, while American dramas were in their turn exported to Europe. As Quinn describes it: "Kean took *Brutus* to Paris in 1827, and it may well have had an effect upon Hugo and his school" (p. 187).

[10] Quoted in *The American Theater as Seen by Its Critics 1752-1934*, ed. Montrose J. Moses and John Mason Brown (New York: Norton, 1934), p. 69. It is, by the way, instructive to compare Whitman's dismissal of Shakespeare to the European Romantic idolization of the Bard. In Whitman's view, Shakespeare "stands entirely for the mighty esthetic sceptres of the past, not for the spiritual and democratic, the sceptres of the future" (p. 67). The American desire to be independent of British influence, which will be discussed below, pierces through this evaluation.

London Theaters perhaps present insurmountable obstacles to any who might there ambition to correct the fashion of the stage. No such difficulties exist here. But this is not all: America is the land of liberty. Here is the country where Truth may lift her voice without fear; – where the words of Freedom may not only be read in the closet, but heard from the stage [...] there is not such a stage in England from which the dramatist might breathe the sentiments of enlightened patriotism and republican liberty. In America alone might such a stage be formed; a stage that should be, like that of Greece, a school of virtue; – where all that is noble in sentiment, generous and heroic in action should speak to the hearts of free people, and inspire each rising generation with all the better and nobler feelings of human nature.[11]

The Present Reality – Explored and Glorified

When we turn to what Driver calls "Romanticism of the here and now," the developments in American drama are even more marked by Romantic ideas and values.[12]

As the slowly developing American nation struggles to define its present experience, it undertakes the supremely Romantic task of discovering an individual voice and an original expression. The most famous clarion call on this topic has been sounded by R.W. Emerson in his 1837 essay *The American Scholar*: "We have listened too long to the courtly muses of Europe." This call is reiterated in his 1844 essay *The Poet*: "We have yet had no genius in America, with tyrannous eye, which knew the value of our incomparable materials, and saw, in the barbarism and materialism of the times, another carnaval of the same gods whose picture he so much admires in Homer." Similar, and equally enthusiastic calls for an American – and dramatic – literature were expressed, however, already in 1825. "There is no other country," exclaims the critic and journalist George P. Morris in the influential *The New York Mirror*, "whose records present more abundant matter, more various character, or more interesting scenes and events for dramatic exhibition or general exaltation."[13] Piercing through these exhortations is the Romantic belief in the organic form, where the container and the thing contained are related by natural and internal affinity, rather than by externally

---

[11] Quoted in Quinn, p. 195.

[12] Richard Moody, *America Takes the Stage: Romanticism in American Drama and Theater 1750-1900* (Bloomington: Indiana Univ. Press, 1959), pp. 179, 181; Barnard Hewitt, *Theater U.S.A.* (New York: McGraw-Hill, 1959), *passim.* Romantic ideas are in the air, so to speak. Moody (p. 8) notes that in 1835, for example, the *Western Messenger* was treating all the English Romantic poets. Between 1840 and 1844, the *Dial* gave American readers a first-hand knowledge of the German literature and philosophy, while American writers and painters sampled abroad, and brought back with them, the Romantic notions of England, France, Germany, Italy, and Spain. Emerson's discussion of Shakespeare, quoted above, is an illustration of this process.

[13] R.W. Emerson, in Carlson, ed., pp. 42; 24, 28, 36, 96-97; George P. Morris, *The New York Mirror*, October 15, 1825. Morris expresses the hope that "the honest prejudices of ruder or less enlightened times" would not impede "the efforts of the republic in her generous and intellectual contest with the civilized states of Europe." He concludes in criticizing the failure of American audiences to recognize and support the budding efforts of such native writers as Samuel Woodworth in *The Forest Rose, or American Farmer*.

The same fervor informs the nativist pride of such inferior dramatist as Samuel Benjamin H. Judah, who subtitles his 1821 *The Battle of Lexington* "A National Comedy, Founded on the Opening of the Revolution," and who asserts the plays of a national character based on the Revolution "should be the first and most desirable subject for an American dramatist." (Printed as *A Tale of Lexington* [New York: Dramatic Repository, 1823]; Readex Microprint, 1952, of a copy held by Harvard Univ. Library.) Cf. the three articles which appeared in the *American Quarterly Review*: "American Drama," 1 (June 1827), pp. 331-57; "Dramatic Literature," 8 (September 1830), pp. 331-57; "Dunlap's American Theater," 12 (December 1832), pp. 509-531. The articles deplore most what the writer sees as a lack of a contemporary American dramatist of real genius, but also provide an interesting panoramic view of the American theater and of the powers that shape and misshape it. Finally, they reflect the renewed faith in the theater as a forum for intellectual ideas and ideals.

imposed, artificial, and foreign rules. In fashioning a national dramatic literature, one is implicitly replacing an imitative, artificial discipline in favor of an organic method. Moreover, one rediscovers the theater as a forum for intellectual ideas and ideals. Thus Fenimore Cooper, whose *Leather-stocking* novels did much to naturalize Romantic notions in American literature, is one of the most vocal critics calling for a national and independent literature and drama, imbued with social consciousness. His 1838 Preface to *Home as Found*, for example, asserts that an American "useful stage can exist," with American playwrights independent enough "to delineate the faults of society."

In 1845, Edgar Allan Poe, in two reviews of Anna Cora Mowatt's *Fashion*, expresses a similar preference for original American drama. In the first review he criticizes what he sees as Mowatt's indiscriminating imitation of *The School for Scandal*. A week later, he withdraws his criticism, since he no longer believes, "upon reflection, that her entire thesis is not an original one." What most delights Poe, however, is his belated realization that in *Fashion* one can see, as he puts it, "a revival of the American drama," which is really the emergence of a native American dramatic voice.[14]

Rousseauesque Heritage

The preceding discussion sheds light on an interesting tendency in the American theater. "Romanticism of the here and now" leads European dramatist to ironic formulations, which culminate in realistic and naturalistic critiques of their society.[15] In America the situation is different. The seminal influence here, overshadowing all other Romantic concepts, is the influence of Jean-Jacques Rousseau. Rousseau's 1749 prize-winning essay exploded the notion that the development of the arts and the sciences constituted an improvement of the human condition. Instead, it suggested that civilization and culture contribute to the corruption of man. "Let men learn for once that nature would have preserved them from a science as a mother snatches a dangerous weapon form the hands of a child," said Rousseau. He gave the example of the "savages of America" as illustration of his notion of the "natural man," better known as "the noble savage," preferring their "natural mode of government" even to "the laws of Plato." The dream he shared with Chateaubriand – the dream of "an American wilderness peopled with a host of nature's noblemen living the perfect life" – was enthusiastically absorbed by American writers.[16]

With the exception of Moody, those who have noted Rousseau's influence on American literature, have overlooked its similar effect in the theater. And even Moody does not recognize that a consistent and universal pattern informs the apparently heterogeneous and dissimilar dramas written by native Americans on native subjects. Yet a significant, and Romantic, pattern does emerge. The

---

[14] Moses and Brown, eds., pp. 59-66.

[15] Driver, pp. 15, 36-44.

[16] Jean-Jacques Rousseau, *Discours sur les arts et sur les sciences*, in *Social Contract and Other Discourses*, trans. and ed. by G.D.H. Cole (London: Dent, n.d.; Everyman's Library, no. 660), pp. 139, 135. Cf., Moody, *America Takes the Stage*, p. 80.

The debt of American culture to Romanticism is discussed in Vernon Louis Parrington, *The Romantic Revolution in America 1800-1860* (New York: Harcourt Brace, 1927). The Romantic literary pattern is discussed in Leo Marx, *The Machine in the Garden: Technology and the Pastoral Ideal in America* (London: Oxford Univ. Press, 1964; rpt. 1972). Compare and contrast with the discussion of the European developments in Erich Auerbach, *Figura: Scenes from the Drama of European Literature* (New York: Meridian, 1959).

characteristic Romantic perception is what Driver calls "the chiaroscuro" vision;[17] i.e., the tendency to perceive reality in terms of dialectical pairs. As Victor Hugo defines this tendency in the "Preface" to *Cromwell*:

> the modern muse [...] will realize that the ugly exists beside the beautiful, the unshapely beside the graceful, the grotesque on the reverse of the sublime, evil with good, darkness with light [...] it is of the fruitful union of the grotesque and sublime types that modern genius is born – so complex, so diverse in its forms, so inexhaustible in its creation; and therein directly opposed to the uniform simplicity of the genius of the ancients.[18]

Hugo's insistence on the *modern* marriage of the sublime and the grotesque is gradually but increasingly translated by the nineteenth-century American dramatists into the tension between two antipodes. On the one hand we find the "evil" pole which represents the forces of technology, civilization, and culture, and these are viewed as agents of rapacity, aggression, repression, and emotional stultification. By contrast, the "good" pole manifest the natural condition, which may, sometimes, be lacking in the fine graces of culture and education, but which is the locus of inborn instinctual and emotional liberty. The specific representation of these poles varies, but the opposition remains constant.

Moody suggests six categories under his "native themes and characters" in *America Takes the Stage*. A brief discussion of several groups should provide ample illustration for the fact that all these categories manifest the pattern of opposition between the antithetical value systems.

The Indian Plays

Most "Indian Plays" document the confrontation between the White settlers, who have come to colonize the American continent, and the Indian inhabitants of the land. Although they often base their plots on historical or semi-historical incidents (cf., the story of Pocahontas and the American Captain she has saved), the *dramatis personae* are painted with bold, broad strokes.

John Augustus Stone's *Metamora, or The Last of the Wampanoags* (1830), relies on the Shakespearean technique of weaving plot and sub-plot which counterpoint as the action progresses. The main plot consists of the growing suspicion and hostility which drive Sir Arthur Vaughn, Master Errington (the Chief of Staff), and Captain Church, to renege on their solemn treaty with the Indian chief, Metamora. The sub-plot consists of the attempts of the scoundrel Fitzarnold to extort from Master Mordaunt the hand of his fair daughter, Oceana, despite the latter's firm devotion to the orphan Walter. The first plot hinges on the libellous duplicity of the self-righteous White leaders, who have corrupted the Indian traitor, Sasamond, and turned him against his benefactor, Metamora. The sub-plot unravels with the unmasking of the equally false, equally devious Fitzarnold, and with the discovery that Walter is really Sir Arthur Vaughn's son. Moreover, a negative analogy obtains as well between the two strands. The steadfast Romantic love of Oceana and Walter finds its parallel in the equally faithful and gallant love between Metamora and his wife Namehokee. But whereas Metamora tragically loses both Namehokee and their son, Oceana and Walter

---

[17] Driver, p. 2.
[18] Clark, ed., pp. 357-58.

find fulfillment for their hopes; and whereas Metamora is able to save Oceana from the panther's attack at the beginning of the play, Oceana and Walter's combined efforts are incapable of saving Metamora's life at the play's conclusion. There is no Shakespearean reconciliation here between the antithetical poles of nature and society.

The abyss separating them is thrown into relief in this play. In speech as well as in action, Metamora is the absolute antithesis of the White settlers. They condemn him with harsh words, both as a potential source of physical danger, but also as the representative of an alien, anti-rational scale of values: a member of "this heathen race, who spite of reason and the word revealed, continue hardened in their devious ways, and make the chosen tremble."[19] Reprimanded for having given shelter to "a banished man," Metamora answers in his characteristically poetic idiom:

> If my rarest enemy had crept unarmed into my wigwam and his heart was sore, I would not have driven him from my fire nor forbidden him to lie down upon my mat. Why then should the Wampanoag shut out the man of peace when he came with tears in his eyes and his limbs torn by the sharp thorns of the thicket? Your great book, you say, tells you to give good gifts to the stranger and deal kindly with him whose heart is sad; the Wampanoag needs no such counselor, for the Great Spirit has with his own fingers written it upon his heart. (*Metamora*, II.iii, in Moody 213)

It is interesting to read this passage in the light of Derrida's discussion of metaphoric and literal forms of inscription in Rousseau's *Essay on the Origin of Languages*. Rousseau, claims Derrida, believes that the natural principles do not need the mediation of writing in order to move and affect the individual in his pristine human state. "The natural law, the gentle voice of pity, is not only uttered by maternal solicitude, it is inscribed in our hearts by God." This metaphoric inscription, "natural writing, the writing of the heart," is opposed by Rousseau to literal writing, "the writing of reason," explains Derrida. Consequently, in Rousseau's view, "one would have to reread all the texts describing culture as the corruption of nature." It is hardly surprising, therefore, that Metamora, whose untrammelled communion with nature is one of his most striking features, aligns himself here with the metaphoric *natural writing, the writing of the heart*, inscribed by *the fingers of the Great Spirit*; and that he consigns the literal writing of *the great book* to the role of the superfluous, if not outright insidious and corrupting: *the writing of reason*.[20]

The sheltering of the poor man, we soon discover, is just another parallel, recalling the initial hospitality with which the Indians had welcomed the White settlers when they have arrived. As Metamora eloquently puts it, "the red man took you as a little child and opened the door of his wigwam. The keen blast of the north howled in the leafless wood, but the Indian covered you with his broad right hand and put it back. Your little ones smiled when they heard the loud voice of the storm, for our fires were warm and the Indian was the white man's friend" (*Metamora* II.iii, in

---

[19] Richard Moody, ed., *Dramas of the Early American Theater 1750-1909* (Cleveland, Ohio: Cleveland World Publishing Co., 1966), p. 212. (Henceforth, references to this anthology will be run-on in the text in parentheses after the abbreviation Moody.)

[20] See Jacques Derrida, *Of Grammatology*, trans. G.C. Spivak (Baltimore: John Hopkins Univ. Press, 1974; rpt. 1982), pp. 174, 180. Derrida's reference is to Jean-Jacques Rousseau, *Essay on the Origin of Language*.

The opening stage directions already indicate Metamora's place amidst raw nature: "A wild, picturesque scene; high craggy rocks in distance; dark pine trees, etc. Rocks cross stage, with platform cross behind." (*Metamora*, I.i, in Moody, 206.) It is likewise in the midst of sleep in the very lap of nature, "by the seaside, in the eyes of the moon," that Metamora dreams of the visionary voice that warns him of the impending danger. Finally the whole of nature cries in unison with the endangered Metamora: "The high hills sent back the echo, and rock, hill and ocean, earth and air opened their giant throats and cried with me" (*Metamora*, III.ii, in Moody 215).

Moody 213). The Whites, hitherto so outraged by Metamora's scorn for "the word," respond to this unwelcome reminder of their unpaid debt of gratitude with the curt "such words are needless now." Clearly, these Englishmen have not yet read their Rousseau:

> It is then certain that compassion [*pitié*] is a natural feeling, which, by moderating the violence of love of self in each individual, contributes to the preservation of the whole species. It is this compassion which hurries us *without reflection* to the relief of those who are in distress [...] in spite of all their morality, men would have never been better than monsters, had no nature bestowed on them a sense of compassion [*pitié*] to aid their reason.[21]

If Metamora's instinctive and unrestricted affinity with nature makes him unresponsive to the products of culture and of rational *reflection* – "the word," "reason," and "the book" – the result clearly discredits his opponents rather than himself. In Rousseau's terms, the Whites represent the emotional degeneration and atrophy which attend the operation of *reason* and *reflection*. But even to the least sophisticated member of the thronging audiences which made this play one of the most popular in American theater history, the Whites are still clearly presented as the spokesmen of un-natural deviousness, duplicity, obtuseness, and cold-hearted self-interest. Their pompous arrogance is thrown into relief by the graciousness, loyalty, love for kin, honesty, dignity, and courage of Metamora.

It is significant that among the Whites, Metamora's stature as "the grandest model of a mighty man" is recognized only by Oceana and Walter. The young lovers must, similarly, defy the oppressive inhumanity of the English, albeit in the form of parental and societal prohibitions (*Metamora*, I.i, in Moody 207). It is as if only those whose youth and impetuous love redeem them from the corrupting effect of conventions and social norms, can recognize in Metamora a fellow human being, deserving both admiration and sympathy. They are consequently the only Whites who acknowledge the tragic plight of the Indian individual and of his people (*Metamora*, III.iii-iv, in Moody 216, 217).

The difference between Metamora and such glorious, tragic, rebellious figures as Spartacus, lies in the fact that the Indian has been endowed, in addition to his natural nobility and courage, with the emotional spontaneity and the reliable intuitive perception absent in any European figure. Thus his recurrent dreams provide him with a store of warnings and information unavailable to the rationalist Whites. His awareness of emotional states and his responses to such phenomena, moreover, suggest even to the pre-Freudian audience an individual in a natural, uncontaminated state; one whose passionate spirit has not yet been completely subjugated by the overdomineering intellect and reason.

Moody notes in his introduction to the play that the representation of the Indian as "the 'noble savage'" permeates the "some seventy-five Indian dramas written during the nineteenth century" (Moody 203). The enormous popular success accorded to *Metamora* and to such excellent Indian plays as John Nelson Berker's *The Indian Princess, or La Belle Sauvage* (1808) and George Washington Parker Custis's *Pocahontas* (1830), testifies to the enthusiasm with which Americans embraced this new dramatic incarnation of the Romantic hero.

---

[21] Jean-Jacques Rousseau, cited in *On the Origin of Language*, trans. John H. Moran and Alexander Gode (New York: Ungar, 1966), pp. 183-84 (italics added).

The Yankee Plays

The fascinating theater phenomenon presented by the development of the stage Yankee and Yankee plays has received a book-length treatment.[22] The roots of the Yankee figure run deep into popular lore.[23] The earliest, most famous stage Yankee appears in Royall (William Clark) Tyler's 1787 comedy, *The Contrast*, which is the first comedy written by an American to be produced in America. The serious impact of this rowdy comedy is underscored by its description in Halline's Introduction as "in its own sphere a spiritual Declaration of Independence" because it is "the first dramatic presentation of the concept of America cultural self-sufficiency."[24]

The Contrast contributes to the store of American stage models the dramatization of a comic, but philosophically charged, contrast between the natural and the culturally acquired. The first is represented by the innately positive, independent thinking of the Yankee Jonathan. The second is represented by the artificial mannerisms and insincere professed emotions of those whose character has been corrupted by the desire to ape the "civilized" British example, most notably the Chester-fieldian conduct of British socialites. Jonathan reflects the Romantic criteria of the play by his pref-erence for the idyllic happiness of rural poverty over the dubious contentment of sophistication and wealth: "If this is the way with you city ladies, give me twenty acres of rock, the Bible, the cow, and Tabitha, and a little peaceful bundling" (*The Contrast*, III.i., in Halline 28).

The Contrast has had a long-lasting influence on American drama, as Hodge's book makes clear. The figure of the Yankee provided Americans with a symbol of national character around whom they could weave their emergent national literature. Moreover, *The Contrast* provided a viable theatrical model for a variety of disparate dramatic forms retaining the same comic, and even satiric, tension between the opposite poles. A case in point is Anna Cora Mowatt's *Fashion* (1845), an excellent comedy of manners *cum* social satire. The play revolves around the social-climbing family, the Tiffanys, who attempt to ingratiate themselves into what they consider the *beau monde* of contemporary New York. Their grappling with such two-timing double-dealers as the false Count Jollimaître and Millinette, Snobson, and T. Tennyson Twinkle, provide the kernel of the action. The denouement of the play revolves around the unmasking of the villains, and the revelation of the true identity of the gentle and honest governess, Gertrude (who has been maligned throughout the play), as the granddaughter of a rustic millionaire.

The Yankee figure in that play is fittingly called Adam Trueman, and he is indeed a true man. Measured against his rustic simplicity and honesty, the sham and hypocrisy into which the parvenu Tiffany family has descended, are all the more striking. Furthermore, in Trueman's final judgment

---

[22] Francis Hodge, *Yankee Theater: The Image of America on the Stage 1825-1850* (Austin: Univ. of Texas Press, 1964). This book provides an additional testimony to the enormous shaping power exerted on the American theater by actors and actors-producers, as opposed to the playwrights whose work these men commissioned and supported, or rejected when they saw fit to do so.

See also Daniel F. Haven, *The Columbian Muse of Comedy: The Development of Native Tradition in Early American Social Comedy 1787-1845* (Carbondale and Edwardsville: Southern Illinois Univ. Press, 1973), pp. 8-51.

[23] In Constance Rourke, *American Humor: A Study of the National Character* (New York: Harcourt, 1931), Chapter I, we find a humorous delineation of the genesis and development of the legendary figure as an accretion of folk lore "from the South, from the West, even from new England." He could be found in Western almanacs, joke books, and the popular media. Jennette Tandy, *Crackerbox Philosophers in American Humor and Satire* (New York: Columbia Univ. Press, 1925), p. 2, concurs. She points out that since the Revolution, the figure of the comic countryman, Brother Jonathan, "wandered through doggerel, anecdote, and stage caricature. For forty years he clumped around in the lowest reaches of literature."

[24] Allan Gates Halline, *American Plays* (New York: American Books, 1935), pp. 5-6. (Henceforth, references to this anthology will be run-on in the text in parentheses after the abbreviation Halline.)

we discover that two systems of oppositions underlie both *The Contrast* and *Fashion*. First, the American example of unfettered thinking and vigorous feeling is juxtaposed with the European examples of emotional aridity, effeteness, and frivolous dandyism, the by-products of cultural and social advances. Secondly, as the pastoral idyll of rural life is identified with the truly American values, the city becomes associated with the corrupting effects of culture, technology, and sophistication. Hence Trueman sentences the Tiffanys to a redemptive exile from the urban blight, which will simultaneously return them to their native American roots:

> You must sell your house and all these gew-gaws, and bundle your wife and daughter off to the country. There let them learn economy, true independence, and home virtues, instead of foreign follies [...] let moderation, in the future, be your counselor, sand let *honesty* be your confidential clerk. (*Fashion*, V, in Moody 346)

Mowatt is working within a rapidly growing tradition. In fact, as early as 1825 Samuel Woodworth, in *The Forest Rose; or, American Farmers*, combines the native themes of a "pastoral opera" with the portrayal of another stage Yankee, Jonathan Ploughboy. The result was "one of the most popular American plays before the Civil War."[25] The Romantic bias of the play in favor of idealized rusticity is most clearly evident in the lyrics (in dialect) set to John Davies's music:

> Ye fair, who seek a splendid lot
>   Behold content, a richer prize
> Within the humblest ploughman's cot,
>   That rank and pride dispise.
> And palace or cot, whatever your lot,
>   The farmer your table supplies, my dear,
>   The farmer your table supplies.
>
> CHORUS
>
> For lords of the soil, and fed by your toil
>   American farmers are blest, my boys,
>   American farmers are blest.

The play revolves around the separation and the reconciliation of lovers, and the unmasking of the licentious, villainous rake. But the comedy reasserts in the process the value of the farm over the city, and of native American values over imported British ones. Love – Harriet's for William, Blandford's for Lydia – which has been set aside in the city in favor of empty class and "culture" distinctions, finally triumphs in the pastoral natural habitat of Miller's farm. And the unscrupulous, conniving English fop, Bellamy, is driven off in disgrace as a direct result of Jonathan's curious blend of integrity, common sense, and native wit. Bellamy plans to abduct and dishonor Harriet. Rather than aid Bellamy in his ugly machinations, for a good sum of money, Jonathan decides "to keep the purse instead of the promise." He turns the tables on the rake, so that the would-be cheater is himself cheated.

---

[25] Ima Honaker Herron, *The Small Town in American Drama* (Dallas, Texas: Southern Methodist American Press, 1969), p. 48. In fact, notes Herron, in Jonathan Ploughboy, Woodworth created "the first stage Yankee who attained anything like general popularity or length of days" (p. 49).

This victory is only the latest in a series of verbal and witty skirmishes between Jonathan and Bellamy, in which the uneducated native American humor and humanity triumph over the 'highly civilized' British complacency and amoral attitudes. Thus, beneath the habitual trappings of Romantic comedy, one rediscovers the opposition between the home virtues of the representatives of American farming – William, Harriet, Miller – who embody honesty, social egalitarianism, and moral uprightness; and the corrupting effects of urban culture, whether in the social snobbism of the Blandfords, or in the vanity, effeteness, and lack of moral rigor of the Briton Bellamy. Describing the tortured history of this highly humorous and exceedingly popular "pastoral comedy," as it was reshaped by succeeding and diverse actors, Hodge concludes with an observation about the Joshua Silsbee version produced in 1850 in London: "the villainy of the city types in this version is even more sharply focused to contrast vividly with the virtues and industry of William and Jonathan as country types."[26]

The same theme, now translated into the view that nature has been mangled and vanquished by the disruptive forces of social organization and advanced mechanization, is sounded in 1830, in Dunlap's *A Trip to the Niagara*. The critique of the spreading urban blight, one of the most lasting leitmotifs of American drama to this day, is explicitly expressed by the figure of John Bull as he takes on the Yankee role of Jonathan:

> But these curst creetures [New Yorkers] have spoilt all that. What with their turnpike roads, and canals, they have gone, like tarnal fools that they are, and put towns and villages, gardens and orchards, and sich common things, where the woods and wild beasts and Indians and rattlesnakes ought to have been.[27]

The Frontier Plays

Nothing so lends itself to a Romantic treatment as the adventurous existence of the frontiersmen, spearheading the progressive westward movement of the American nation. American literature, in the hands of Cooper, Bret Harte, and Mark Twain, tended to emphasize the freedom of movement, the absence of discipline, and the colorfulness of daily life enjoyed by the frontiersmen, minimizing the real hardships they experienced. American drama followed suit. Moreover, it adapted the tension between the two poles to the needs of the frontier drama, increasingly contrasting the unpolished and untamed nature of the frontiersman with the constricting repression of East Coast culture and mores. A typical example is Frank Hitchcock Murdock's *Davy Crockett* (1872), which exemplifies the affinity of the expanding American frontier to Romantic treatment.[28] In some ways, Davy resembles such popular figures as Rip van Winkle, the American Everyman, grappling with

---

[26] Hodge, pp. 56, 249. *The Forest Rose* was originally printed by Chattam Garden, New York, 1825; it is available in a 1954 Readex microprint, copy held by the University of Pennsylvania.

[27] William Dunlap, *A Trip to the Niagara: or Travelers in America* (New York: Clayton, 1830), p. 43. It is interesting to compare these sentiments to Cooper's attempt to reconcile in *The Pioneers* (1823) and *The Prairie* (1827) the same dichotomy between the natural liberty, offered by the wild and virgin land, and the constraining order of civilization. It is also instructive to consider the treatment of the City-Country antinomy in such twentieth-century plays as *Death of a Salesman*.

[28] As Louis Mumford has said, the pioneering "westering" "was an experimental investigation of Nature, Solitude, The Primitive Life." *The Golden Day: A Study in American Literature and Culture* (New York: Norton, 1926), p. 56.

"fact and fancy; youth and age; love and hatred; loss and gain; mirth and sadness."[29] But Davy Crockett is above all the model of the "noble frontiersman"; "rough-mannered but gentle in feeling; brave but shy and unassuming; the man without education but endowed with incomparable prowess and a great store of emotion and affection; above all, capable of great sacrifices for love. In short, 'nature's nobleman'."[30]

Initially, the natural gifts, the innate harmonic relationship with nature, do not receive their due appreciation in the world depicted by the play. Confronted with his childhood companion, Eleanor, who is passing through the area after she has tasted of the pleasures of civilized society, Davy exclaims: "I ain't fit to breathe the same air with you. You are scholarly and dainty, and what am I, nothing but an ignorant backwoodsman, fit only for the forests and the fields where I'm myself hand in hand with nature and her teachings, knowing no better."[31] But the play's action serves to throw into relief Davy's truly heroic stature. Scott's "Ballad of Young Lochinvar," which Eleanor reads to Davy, highlights his role in the play as the Romantic Knight who would save the damsel in distress. Moreover, the plot operates to underscore the gap between the ineptitude and moral corruption of the civilized East Coast people, and the spiritual as well as physical integrity and stamina of the frontiersman. Davy is not merely in tune with nature, and thus capable of rescuing the freezing Eleanor from the snow as well as from the howling, ravenous wolves that besiege their log cabin. He is also courageous and decisive enough to save his beloved from the manipulative, money-grubbing clutches of her false suitor, Neil Crampton, and his Machiavellian uncle, Oscar Crampton. After the adventure in the wolf-ridden icy snow, Eleanor is not yet free of the Eastern value system. She recognizes Davy's "noble self – your loyalty, your unselfish devotion, [...] the greatness of your heart." But although she avows that "rugged and simple but still pre-eminent, you stand a man," she also concludes sorrowfully: "but the world divides us. We must part here, and both must learn to forget" (p. 135). Only after the flight from the Cramptons does she realize that Davy and the Cramptons represent two irreconcilable ways of life, and makes her choice by marrying Davy in defiance of conventional procedure. The choice between an unadulterated, natural, and native humanity, and a debased sophistication, is similar to the one imposed by Adam Trueman on the Tiffanys in *Fashion*. Yet, as Hewitt puts it, "The United States had grown old enough and big enough so that the conflict between East and West could replace the conflict between America and England."[32] Davy's role as a variant of the Rousseauesque Romantic hero, "nature's nobleman," explains the phenomenon described by Moody: "no semimythical or mythical frontier hero received such an elaborate and complete literary record [...]. Daniel Boone, [...] Paul Bunyan [...], and Mike Fink [...] – although the legends of all three were endless – never achieved in literature and on the stage the heroic stature destined for Davy Crockett."[33]

It is of great interest to contrast the popularity of *Davy Crockett* with the uneasy reception American audiences accorded to Augustin Daly's *Horizon* (1871). On the face of it, Daly's five-act play extends and illuminates the antinomy between the socially organized, cultured East, and the free-spirited West. The oppressive principles of the former are rejected outright in favor of the more

[29] William Winter, *The Life and Art of Joseph Jefferson* (London: Macmillan, 1894), p. 180.
[30] Hewitt, p. 223.
[31] Frank H. Murdoch, *Davy Crockett*, in *American's Lost Plays*, ed. Eugene R. Page (Princeton: Princeton Univ. Press, 1941), IV, 133.
[32] Hewitt, p. 226.
[33] Moody, *America Takes the Stage*, pp. 179, 181.

egalitarian and human priorities of the latter. The frontiersmen claim explicitly that the West institutes its proceedings according to natural principles. As the character Sundown Rowse insists,

> we are here proceeding according to law. Not the musty statutes of effete systems and oligarchies of
> the old world, but the natural law implanted in the bosoms of man since our common ancestors were
> washed, wrung out, and hung up to dry by the universal flood. (*Horizon*, I, in Halline 356)

The contrast between Eastern gentility and artificiality and the rough-edged frontier vitality is
also operative in the love story of Loder and Med, the girl who has been brought west by her shift-
less father. Loder protects Med after her father's murder, and in the process he sheds most of his
negative links to the "John Oakhurst type of gentlemanly gambler" which Daly borrowed from Bret
Harte.[34] Thus his stature as the typical heroic frontiersman becomes enhanced and crystallized.
However, unlike Davy, Loder remains locked in his perception of Med as the frail "White Flower of
the Plains," who is his social superior. He relinquishes her to her aristocratic lover, the West
Pointer Alleyn Van Dorf, in a moving scene which eschews both melodrama and purple rhetoric in
favor of dignified and restrained eloquence.[35]

Daly's refusal to provide the love story with the customary happy end is of double significance.
First, it presents a deviation from the popular melodramatic devices for the unravelling of the plot,
in which the hero invariably gets his beloved heroine at the end of the drama. Second, it suggests
that, in contradistinction to the author of *Davy Crockett*, Daly does not subscribe unquestioningly
and unequivocally to the belief in the superiority of the frontiersman over the highly educated
Easterner.

This moderation is of a piece with his other realistic modifications of romanticized elements.
Much of the satiric humor of the play deflates such notions as that of the "noble savage." The Indian
Chief Wannemucka, described as "civilized Indian and 'Untutored Savage',," is a master poker
player. Sundown's objection – "Who'd have thought of this romantic injun sporting a deck and
offering to play poker? [...] That knocks the romance" – is answered satirically by Loder:

> That's civilization my friend! When the noble savage was in his native state, he went for the hair of
> your head. Now he is in the midst of civilization, he carries the weapons of enlightenment [a greasy
> pack of cards] and goes for the money in your pocket. (*Horizon*, II, in Moody 352)

Similarly, Rogue's Rest, as its name attests, shows the wear and tear which accompany the independence from traditional legal authority. The "blacklegs, horse-thieves, and other alibis and aliases"
have overrun it (*Horizon*, II, in Moody 348). In fact, the play's incidents span the kidnapping of
Sundown and Columbia Rowse and the Widow by the Indians, and their last-minute, hair-raising
rescue; and episodes dealing with the minority rights of Cephas, the hymn-singing Negro, and the
Heathen Chinee (sic). These illustrate Daly's view that the frontiersman's existence, where everyone lives "just as they do in romances," has its price.

In short, Daly presents the frontier life with a blend of Romanticism and realism. He retains the
original antinomy between the opposite poles, but undercuts its Romantic fervor with the use of

---

[34] Herron, p. 137.
[35] Quinn, for example, commends the scene "which for simplicity of language and restraint of passion goes far to
establish Daly's claim to be the first of the modern realists in American playwriting." *A History of American Drama*, Vol. II:
From the Civil War to the Present Day (New York: Croft, 1927; 1936; 1964), Part I, p. 14.

humor and realistic satire. The ironic result may have been too *avant-garde* for his contemporary audience.[36] But the pattern in which frontier ruggedness and rough nobility are contrasted with Eastern artificiality and sham spiritual patina persists throughout the Frontier Plays, and beyond them into twentieth-century drama.[37]

Conclusion

The pattern which we have been tracing is too insistent – both in the categories we have discussed, and in those unexamined in the restricted space alotted to us[38] – to escape comment. It calls for a reconsideration not only of the prevalent critical denigration of American dramas written and produced before the 1920s, but of the very concept "Romantic drama." Whereas European playwrights passed beyond the obsession with individual character – a direction already apparent in plays the

[36] See, for example, Herron's assessment of Daly's "bold departure" from "the glorification of the West" as the source of his cold reception (*The Small Town*, p. 136). Moody, on the other hand, emphasizes Daly's link to the past operations of the antithetical pattern: "In Daly's play frontier coarseness was contrasted with Eastern artificiality, just as New England Yankee bluntness has been contrasted with urban blandness" (p. 178).

[37] See, for example, William Vaughn Moody's twentieth-century treatment of the theme in *The Great Divide* (1906). For extensive discussions of Frontier Plays, see Moody, *America Takes the Stage*, pp. 168-86; Herron, *The Small Town in American Drama*, pp. 107-76; Arthur Hobson Quinn, *A History of the American Drama*, II, Part I, pp. 105-24.

[38] A representative of the category Moody terms "The War Plays" is William Dunlap's *André* (1798). This dramatization of an incident in the Revolutionary War follows, quite naturally, the pattern in which Americans and Englishmen are made to represent opposite scales of values. The Americans are the rebellious, heroic individuals who defy the oppressive and tyrannical intentions of the English Crown in the name of egalitarian and libertarian ideals. (*André*, Act I, in *Six Early American Plays 1798-1890*, ed. William Goyle and Harvey G. Damaser [Columbus, Ohio: Merrill, 1968], pp. 12, 13, 14, 15, 16.) Moreover, they are gallant and honorable freedom fighters, whereas the Britons are mercenary and murderous thugs (Act I, p. 14, 16; II, p. 22; III, p. 26; V, p. 43). There is, however, novelty in the consistent manner in which the conflict between the claims of the emotions and the claims of reason is brought into the foreground. The warm inclination to pity, empathy, and love for one's fellowmen is constantly made to clash with the cold demands for rational control of mind over feelings, with the result that even the patriotic loyal sentiments are stretched to the breaking point (see Act II, p. 21; III, p. 27; IV, p. 33). In one of the most ardent clashes, Bland answers M'donald's call for rational and moral restraint:

> Cold-blooded reasoners, such as thee, would blast
> All warm affection; asunder sever
> Every social tie of humanized man.
> Curst be thy sophisms, cunningly contriv'd
> The cunning coldness of thy heart to cover. (IV, p. 34)

The passage recalls Rousseau's preference for natural *pitié* over unnatural *réflection* and its reasoned morality. In dramatizing the conflict between the two, *André* has set the model for future "war plays." These plays repeatedly focus on the resulting struggle between the opposing allegiances, transcribed as passion and duty, or private and patriotic loyalties (see Moody, *America Takes the Stage*, pp. 143, 147, 157, 160, 163, 167, 168). As the revolt of the common man against oppression is progressively taken for granted, it becomes a mere backdrop for the central emotional conflict.

It is also significant that the only British individual who is credited with the grandeur and natural humanity of courage and compassion – André, whose life the grateful Bland is trying to save – turns out to have been himself the victim of oppression and authoritarian double-dealing. His love for Honora has been thwarted by her father, who has shamelessly maligned and cheated him. As André terms it, this is the well-known theme depicting the heartless despotism of parental rule:

> The woes of youthful hearts, by the cold hand
> Of frosty age, arm'd with parental power,
> Asunder torn. (IV, p. 36)

The critic, however, recognizes the similarity between André's sympathetic portrait, and the sympathetic portraits of Oceana and Walter in *Metamora*. In both cases, it seems as if the passage from the pole representing the unnatural, oppressive, and anti-libertarian forces to the pole representing instinctual, emotional, and spiritual freedom, is reserved for those who have themselves been purified and scorched by the oppressive pressures of societal and familial tyranny. In *André* as well as in *Metamora*, the exception of the suffering lovers only reaffirms the abyss which separates the antipodean poles.

French term "pre-Romantic," and the German term Storm and Stress – to new concerns in the nineteenth century such as the drama of a visionary world theater, American drama of the same period retained the earlier inward-directed Romantic focus. The unique and individual American universe, and the dream of an equally unique and individual American dramatic voice, remain the focal points. Consequently, throughout the nineteenth century, American drama and theater struggle to embody Romantic ideas and ideals. But by the same token, playwrights and actors-producers, actively as well as unconsciously, seek independence from European dramatic models. They progressively evolve a national drama which shapes specifically American materials according to a specific American Romantic pattern. The American protagonist is neither the highly reflective Byronic hero, undergoing the drama of consciousness, nor the severely limited, nearly inarticulate victim figure of *Woyzeck*; but a version of Rousseau's "noble savage," the unintellectual "nature's nobleman," functioning in an increasingly civilized and corrupted universe.

Furthermore, the American version of "Romanticism of the here and now" diverges both from its European counterpart and from the "Romanticism of the dream." The contrast it draws between nature and society, or between the sublime ideal society and the grotesque real world, does not present the "Other" as an elusive ideal: it does not place the local scene in the slot reserved for the degenerate, debased "real society." Instead, the American scene – wholly or in part, depending on the play – is depicted as pertaining to the sublime pole, insofar as it approximates, or is closely linked to, the natural, ideal society. Hence American society is represented as superior and preferable to the repressive and repulsive European social organization; and parts of the American panoramic spectrum, such as the idealized rural settlements or the Western regions, retain the attributes of natural idyllic existence even when others, such as urban life or the cultivated East Coast, increasingly take on the coloring of cultural and technological contamination. The Edenic, bi-polar Rousseauesque view of America has such a strong hold on the imagination of American dramatists, in fact, that it is still manifest in today's dramas. Many of Sam Shepard's plays, for example, can only be appreciated as an attempt to deconstruct this mythic American dream once and for all.

On the other hand, the concern with social justice cuts across a wide spectrum of dramatic types: it is not excluded from purely entertaining dramas or melodramas; nor is it restricted, in the European manner, either to ironic tragedy or to social comedy. We can only speculate here, but these phenomena may account for the late appearance of Realism in the nineteenth-century theater, and for the rarity of true Naturalism on the American stage at any time. As we have seen, the opposition between a just and an unjust order – between a human and humane scale of values, and a dehumanized and debased value system – lies at the very foundation of the American plays by virtue of the Rousseauesque pattern which informs them. The result is a theater celebrating Romantic ideals though the very antinomial structure which serves as its "deep structure."

EMILIO CARILLA

THE ROMANTIC THEATER IN HISPANIC AMERICA

Introduction

The study of Hispanic American Theater of the nineteenth century does not by necessity impose the obligation of passing its colonial forerunners in review. There is, as is easily ascertained, no firm continuity, nor are there notable aesthetic coincidences. Nonetheless, it seems to me that a brief overview of colonial theater can illustrate, beyond moments of transition, some elements that indeed are related. And in the final instance such a synthesis casts light on the possibility of establishing, however schematically, a picture of previous linkages, within the lines appropriate to an artistic phenomenon as peculiar as the theatrical spectacle. This is, then, the principal motive which justifies (or attempts to justify) this introduction.

Although colonial dramatic literature does not excel the lyric from the sixteenth to the eighteenth centuries, there can be no doubt that it is the literary genre that is next in abundance and prominence. And to these traits we should add the special political, social, religious, and linguistic connotations stemming from its formation. The upshot of all the above is, in effect, that colonial theater (once again, theater as "literary spectacle") is one of the definitive cultural manifestations of Hispano-American letters during the period. In addition, it makes sense that over such an extended passage of time the cultural trajectory offers diverse alternatives; in part, as a reflection of the Peninsular trajectory, but not less, as an echo or response of the actual human world producing it, with the particular resonance of the political-religious values that regulate colonial life.

My purpose is not to adorn the colonial theater with an artistic brilliance that it certainly did not have, but to present it within a visible continuum and, above all, with a character of its own that is not seen, or little seen, in the other literary manifestations of the colonies. I refer to the presence of the main indigenous tongues that on occasion constitute the exclusive content of a work and at times part of a mixed content. If we take into account the fact that Hispano-American colonial letters are in overwhelming proportion the product of whites, it is valid to gauge how this trait fits, even though it reveals a design that frankly aspires to conciliate politico-social, religious, and cultural interests.

Without exaggerating identities, it seems to me apposite to establish here some resemblances with phenomena in the plastic arts, especially with the traces that the indigenous race (as the expression goes) managed to leave in stone, wood, and cloth. That possibility was open within set limits and derived from the "new society" from which such art came.

The chronological development of the theater in the three colonial centuries shows us various lines – fundamentally two – that, without being totally separate (an impossibility), are I believe, obviously dominant. First there is an eminently religious line in the service of evangelization; by reason of its content and aims it responds less to the changes and styles of the epoch. It is represented by a group of works that permit the total or partial inclusion of indigenous languages. It is thus the line offering a majority of anonymous works. Its repertory encompasses above all the genre of *autos*, in Spanish, or as mentioned, with alteration of Spanish and indigenous tongues. It is predictably Spanish and Nahuatl or Spanish and Quechuan. Its essential character of religious indoctrination does not rest only on the contents; it is also conspicuously at its apogee, in parallel with the political process, throughout the sixteenth century and at the beginning of the seventeenth, an abundance afterwards attenuated.

Second, there is a gaudier line with greater freedom of themes, religious and profane, more closely tied to the styles of the epoch and to the models indicated by the great Peninsular authors. It is exemplified by some of the most important names in colonial letters. It comprehends works written in Spanish, although this does not exclude certain exceptions (such as "El Lunarejo" [Moles] and some others). In this line, but in a special category, it is necessary to include a work like *Ollanta* or *Ollantai* which is recognized today as a drama that seems to reconcile indigenous races and sentiments, on the one hand, and Spanish theatrical structure on the other.

Having defined the two directions which to me seem essential, I note that the picture would be incomplete without the inclusion of a third line which we can consider as intermediate. I include here – and underline their special place – Spanish *comedias* by famous authors (such as Lope de Vega and Calderón) translated into indigenous languages. As we shall see, it was their special condition as translations which helped grant such dramas their status.

There would remain lastly the very small group constituted by "purely" indigenous works which we can legitimately consider to be pre-Hispanic phenomena, such as occurs, for example, in the case of *Rabinal Achí*, a work in the Quiché language. Unfortunately, numerous testimonies of that past have been lost.

And without trying to augment the groups artificially I believe I can add – at the other chronological extreme, almost on the eve of the Revolution – short plays that are strongly local, such as glimpses of the gaucho theater on the Río de la Plata. The evidence is scarce, but announces what is to come and what even in its poverty wears sufficient individuality to warrant being kept in this account.

The bibliography of Hispanic American dramatic literature demonstrates a series of outstanding names in the colonial era. With no intention of exhausting this list, I include authors such as Fernán Gonzáles de Eslava, Cristóbal de Llerena, Juan Pérez Ramírez, Juan de la Cueva (tangentially), Alarcón (with the well-known reservations), Juan del Valle Caviedes, Juan de Espinosa Medrano ("El Lunarejo"), Gabriel Centeno de Osma, Juan de Guevara, Sor Juana Inés de la Cruz, Pedro Alejandrino de Peralta Barnuevo, Count de la Granja, Eusebio Vela, Jerónimo de Monforte y Vera, Antonio Fuentes del Arco, Fray Francisco del Castillo ("El Ciego de la Merced," The Blind Man of Mercy), Santiago de Pita, Pablo de Olavido, Cayetano Cabrera Quintero, José Agustín de Castro, Manuel José de Lavardén, and others. In certain cases their relative survival rests more on their lyrical than on their dramatic productions.

On the whole these authors reproduce, or rather contribute to supporting the recognized social and literary picture. Initially, European Spaniards who have taken up residence in America predominate; later on, authors born in the New World assert themselves. The certainty that a dramatic work existed does not always – and more so in those times – mean the certainty it was produced. (In this regard we may summarize numerous tributes which the authors jealously guarded or left among their manuscripts and which have resuscitated scholarship in the nineteenth and twentieth centuries.)

The locale suited for theatrical functions, in principle, was also lacking. To be sure, this presented no obstacle to religious productions which, as the record shows, took place in colleges, courtyards, squares, and streets, and replicated in America, with some lag, the itinerary of European medieval theater. In reality, the physical body of the stable theaters was solidified in the course of the eighteenth century, the cities Mexico and Lima being always, as one might guess, the site of advance. Cities like Puebla (The Old Coliseum or Corral of Comedies), Buenos Aires (with its Teatro de la Ranchería), and Montevideo followed later. For their part, Bogotá and Santiago de Chile arrived at this point almost on the eve of the Revolutions of Independence...

It is premature to speak of the formation of a theater audience in those centuries such as the Iberian metropolis boasted; or aside from spectacles that were more directly tied to religious festivities and purposes; or, with time, to select academies and limited gatherings. All the same, the linkage which we can establish between the public and the stable theaters of the eighteenth century (not very "stable") is the best index of a slow but visible growth. The theater public of those centuries appears quite inferior to the character of the frequent literary contests that customarily accompanied the religious festivities and imparted movement and color to the ordinarily quiet life in the colonies.

With the first years of the nineteenth century we are already entering a new epoch determined by abrupt social and political changes, and no less by appreciable aesthetic changes that certainly include the theater. A bit further on, we enter the first phase of Romanticism...

Romantic Theater

Almost nothing survives of the Romantic theater of Hispanic America. There is no lack of dramatic authors, it is true, but in proportion, they appear in a smaller number than those cultivating other genres and do not specialize in drama only. The scant value of Romantic drama perhaps maintains a relationship to its cultural proportions. To a lesser extent, the stimulus of the theater was lacking. A dramatist often writes thinking about the production, the scenery, the public. The book is the occasional vehicle of his work, but – then as now – the performance has always been the aim of every dramatic work. Paradoxically, there were playhouses in the Romantic epoch; not many, but they existed. What happened was that this theater lived on fixed names and works, in particular on translated works; so that the quality of the work itself was enhanced by the prestige of the foreign author, whether in plays by Spanish authors, or in translated plays. Let us also add the political vicissitudes of the epoch, which had direct repercussions within social life, at whose core the theater lives and works. This instability did not eradicate the enthusiasm for the theater, but limited it, and in parallel, severely limited the concerns of dramatic authors.

Playhouses did exist in Hispanic America, built in consonance with the difficulties to which the newborn countries were liable, first in the Wars of Independence, and afterwards in the Civil Wars. Sometimes they were modest buildings set up in old dwellings that were transformed to serve this purpose; most times they were buildings expressly constructed to be theaters. Some of the best buildings were found among those which were still being constructed at the end of the colonial epoch. The most important theaters were the following: in Mexico, the Iturbide and National Theaters constructed by the Guatemalan Francisco Arbeu, and the Hidalgo Theater;[1] in San Juan, Puerto Rico, the Municipal Theater;[2] in La Habana, the Coliseum, constructed at the end of the eighteenth century,[3] the Prince and the Liceum; in Caracas, the Public Coliseum;[4] the theater of Bogotá; in Guayaquil, the Olmedo Theater; in Lima, the Principal Theater and the Varieties;[5] in Valparaiso, the Comic Theater and the Café of Commerce; in Santiago de Chile, the Municipal Theater and the Provisional Theater, of Mercier;[6] in Montevideo, the Playhouse (Casa de Comedias),[7] and in Buenos Aires, the Provisional Coliseum – later called the Argentine Theater –, the Theater of Victory, the Alegría Theater, the Columbus Theater (primitive)... Besides, the value which the circus had as a foundation for the theater in certain regions (above all, in Argentina and Mexico) as the century advanced, should not be forgotten. This was particularly true in reference to the Gaucho theater in the Argentine, which found the circus environment appropriate (Juan Moreira is the example par excellence).

Limitations of every kind as regards facilities did not prevent notable American actors from stamping their names upon the heterogeneous works which they represented. Spanish actors did not disappear; in many regions, they remained an overwhelming majority, but the presence of Creole actors (above all, good actors) initiated a period which has greater significance than is commonly assigned to it. In the Río de la Plata and Chile, such is the meaning which the unusual prestige of Juan José de los Santos Casacuberta[8] and Trinidad Guevara[9] enjoyed. In Mexico, the work of the actress Merced Morales was so famous her death took on the dimensions of national mourning.[10]

Disregarding their nationality, the following were distinguished actors: Merced Morales, Antonio Castro, Soledad Cordero, Juan Martínez and the Spaniard Eduardo González; in Cuba, Hermosilla (director and afterwards actor) and Prieto; in Columbia, the comics Villalba, Torres, Gallar-

---

[1] Cf. Armando de María y Campos, *Entre cómicos de ayer* (Mexico: Editorial "Arriba el Telón", 1949).

[2] Cf. Emilio J. Pasarelli, *Orígines y desarrollo de la afición teatral en Puerto Rico* (San Juan de Puerto Rico: Editorial Universitaria, 1951), p. 68.

[3] The *Coliseo* in La Havana was a true theater and did not take second place to the better theaters in Spain. (See José Juan Arrom, *Historia de la literatura dramática cubana* (New Haven: Yale Univ. Press, 1944), pp. 12-15.)

[4] Cf. José Juan Arrom, "Documentos relativos al teatro colonial de Venezuela," in the *Boletín de estudios de teatro* (Buenos Aires), 15 (1946), 211. In Caracas, the so-called Teatro del Maderero (Carpenter's Theater) was described in a picturesque form by Nicanor Bolet Peraza.

[5] The Teatro Principal was first built in the eighteenth century; the Teatro de Variedades, in the middle of the nineteenth century. (See Manuel Moncloa y Covarrubias, *Diccionario teatral del Perú* [Lima: Badiola y Berrio, 1905], p. 120.)

[6] "The theater at that time was a center of real social activity [...] and all were demanding that in Santiago and Valparaiso there be erected buildings adequate to the importance of this element of civilization and progress." J.V. Lastarria, *Recuerdos literarios* (Santiago de Chile: Libreria de M. Servat, 1885) p. 185.

[7] The exiled Argentinian reformer and educator (later President of Argentina), Domingo Faustino Sarmiento, refers without doubt to this theater in one of the first letters of his *Viajes* (Voyages): "In a miserable theater, they give miserable productions in Spanish, Italian, French, like the *Archivo* of Buenos Aires. In these days there was performed an original rhapsody which tries to paint one of the horrible scenes of the Mazorca." Sarmiento, *Viajes* (Buenos Aires: Vaccaro, 1922), p. 86. Clearly Sarmiento is referring to productions during the "Sitio de Montevideo." (Cf. also Lauro Ayestarán, "La Casa de Comedias," in the *Boletín de estudios de teatro* [Buenos Aires], 2, no. 5, [1944], pp. 3-8.)

[8] In Chile, Sarmiento noted the attraction which Casacuberta exercised on the spectators: "The attention of the public is fixed on the protagonist. The play, the decorations, the rest of the actors are in shadow, are mere incidentals; the words, the movements, the diverse and varied intonations of the actor form the foundation [...]." Sarmiento, *Obras*, (Santiago de Chile: Imprenta Gutenberg, 1885), II, 97. On Casacuberta, see the monograph by María Antonia Oyuela, *Juan [Aurelio] Casacuberta* (Buenos Aires: Imprenta de la Universidad, 1937).

[9] See Arturo Capdevila, *La Trinidad Guevara y su tiempo* (Buenos Aires: Kraft, 1951). On Casacuberta and la Trinidad Guevara, see also Raúl H. Castagnino, *El teatro de Buenos Aires durante la época de Rosas* (1830-52) (Buenos Aires: Academia Argentina de Letras, 1989).

[10] Cf. Armando de María y Campos, pp. 143-45.

do, Dolores Alegre, the husband and wife Belaval, Emilio Segura, Iglesias, Robreño and the Armentas[11] (I imagine that a good part of these were Spaniards); in Chile, aside from Casacuberta and la Guevara, the Fedriani, Cáceres, Jiménez, Toribia Miranda, the two Samaniego sisters,[12] and the Velardes (famous was Toribia Miranda of Lima, a beautiful woman and a gifted actress,[13] who performed with Casacuberta); in the Río de la Plata, Francisco Cáceres, Joaquín Culebras, Antonia and Dominga Montes de Oca, Antonio González, the Spanish company of Francisco Torres y Fragoso, Juan Antonio Viera, Rosquellas, Matilde de la Rosa, Alvara García, Matilde Díez, Tula Castro, Hernán Cortés, almost all Spaniards (naturally, at the head of all these, Casacuberta and la Guevara).

There were also impresarios who are remembered for various reasons. In Mexico, the well-known author Manuel Eduardo Gorostiza was an impresario; in the Río de la Plata, the Argentine Pedro Lacasa was, in reality, better known for his political hustling and bustling (secretary of Lavalle, first; afterwards, attached to Rosas) than for his involvement with the theater as an author and impresario.

Juan Bautista Alberdi, who did some dabbling in drama, pointed out in one of his newspaper articles in *La Moda* (Fashion), that a sign of the Argentine theater was the nationality of the interpreters:

> One of the conditions, furthermore, of the nationality of the theater is the nationality of its actors, who ought to find themselves penetrated by the spirit of the people whose ideas and passions they are to express on the boards [...].[14]

Without accepting the last part – very vague and "Romantic" in style – , it is not possible to discuss the degree of truth it contains. (We certainly include the dramatic work itself within the "spirit of the people.") Actors like Casacuberta and Merced Morales and actresses like la Guevara, la Cordero, and la Miranda had significance as pioneers... These nineteenth century actors took their place by the side of the Spanish actors who were the majority. And some attained such prestige that they suffered the problem, frequent then as now, of being assigned made-to-order works or ephemeral works accommodated to the histrionic virtues of the manager of the company, as occurred in the case of Casacuberta and the blood-and-thunder melodramas by Ducange. Furthermore, there were actors who built an extensive, addicted audience that frequently went to see the actor more than the work he happened to be performing.

Positively, there remained an evident histrionic quality above and beyond the heterogeneous elements of the repertory; that is to say, that repertory which imparted a stamp to the theater of the middle of the last century. Thus we arrive at the almost paradoxical fact that the original dramatic

---

[11] Cf. the liberal politician and newspaperman (later President of Columbia), Rafael Núñez, "Románticos y decadentes," in *Los mejores artículos políticos* (Bogotá: Editorial Minerva, 1936), p. 154; S. Camacho Roldán, "Gregorio Gutiérrez González," in *Poetas y críticos de América*, ed. Claudio Santos González (Paris: Garnier, 1912), pp. 299-300.

[12] See Lastarria, p. 185.

[13] See Eugenio Pereira Salas, "El teatro, la música y el arte en el movimiento intelectual de 1842," in the *Boletín de la Academia Chilena de la Historia* (Santiago de Chile), no. 45 (1951), XVIII, 27.

[14] Alberdi, in an article titled "Teatro," in *La Moda* (Buenos Aires), November 25, 1837. J.A. de Diego observed that, in the second half of the century, retrogressing in certain respects to the situation of the Colonies, Argentinian works were put on by Spanish ("and even Italian") companies. See J.A. de Diego, "Camilla Quiroga," in the journal *Comentario* (Buenos Aires), 56, (1967), pp. 53-54. And Arrom, an outstanding Cuban critic of our days, concurs with Alberdi when, describing the vicissitudes of the theater in Cuba during the Romantic period, he attributes its irregular movements to the lack of Cuban actors. Nor does he overlook the relation between actors and work. (See José Juan Arrom, *En torno a la historia de la literatura dramática cubana*, pp. 20-21).

production of the time has been forgotten without regrets, whereas the memory of famous actors such as the Argentine Casacuberta, without equivalent among the American actors of the nineteenth century,[15] has endured and even grown.

The available works in the Hispanic American repertory were plays by Spanish authors, and even more plays translated from the French; alongside these, and very sporadically, American works, or works by local indigenous authors. Thus the list of works produced in Hispanic America includes works by Alexandre Dumas (*Antony, Catherine Howard, La Tour de Nesle, Henri III et sa cour*), by Victor Hugo (*Ruy Blas, Hernani, Angelo, tyran de Padue, Le Roi s'amuse, Marie Tudor, Marion Delorme*), by Larra (as much in the original as in translations or arrangements: *Macías, Don Juan de Austria* [arrangement], *No más mostrador* [arrangement], *Un desafío* [translation], *El arte de conspirar* [arrangement]), by García Gutiérrez (*El trovador*),[16] by Ventura de la Vega (*El hombre de mundo, La muerte de César*), by Zorilla (*El zapatero y el rey, Don Juan Tenorio*), by Bretón de los Herreros (*Muérete y verás, Marcela o a ¿cuál de los tres?, Un tercero en discordia, A Madrid me vuelvo*), by Hartzenbusch (*Los amantes de Teruel*), by Scribe (*Le Vieux de vingt-cinq ans,* translated by Ventura de la Vega; *Una cadena, El enemigo íntimo, El arte de conspirar,* translated by Larra), by Ducange (*Les sept étapes du crime, Le Joueur, La Vengeance, Quinze Ans ou les effets de la perversion*).[17] As the century advanced, the Spanish dramatist Francisco Camprodón enjoyed great prestige, above all through his works *Flor de un día* and *Espinas de una flor*. This is the testimony which Lucio Vicente López has left us of the première of the latter:

> *Flor de un día* was adopted by all the theaters of Latin America [... And further on:] Thou, who hast made an entire continent weep from Vera Cruz to Buenos Aires![18]

Also played were works by Shakespeare (*Othello, Romeo and Juliet, The Merchant of Venice, Hamlet, King Lear*), by Schiller (*Maria Stuart, Wilhelm Tell*), by Martínez de la Rosa (*Abén Humeya*), by Quintana (*El duque de Viseo*), by Moratín (*El sí de las niñas*), by Ramón de la Cruz... To be sure, the Shakespeare who was initially known was not the true Shakespeare (or at least, one

---

[15] There is a quite immature article by Bartolomé Mitre, titled "Reflexiones sobre el teatro," published in *El Defensor de las leyes* (Montevideo, July 20, 1837), with material of scant profit, which makes reference to the actors: "The comedian, in order to be that, must be some gentleman, must be deeply acquainted with all the sciences, and principally with history, must have frequented good society, have refined, elegant manners, and a perfect knowledge of fencing. Another of the essential qualities of an actor is to have a good grip on his language (and even others) [...]." Clearly what is involved is not a manual for the courtier or for the perfect man of society, but some "reflection" about the comedian... His other comments (stage, works) have greater value. Mitre's words seem directly copied from texts of the Spanish Golden Age. With the essential difference that the latter take the author and not the actor as their reference: "The poet has to treat vigorously of everything and say everything, for he is a painter of all that happens in the world [...]." (Luis Alfonso de Carvallo, *Cisne de Apolo* (Medina del Campo: Iuan Godínez de Millis, 1602]). "The poet not only has to know all the sciences or at least the principal ones among them, but has to have the greatest experience in the things which occur on Earth and at sea [...]." (Lope de Vega, *La Arcadia* [Madrid: Luis Sanchez], 1598), Book III).

[16] The poet and politician Rafael Núñez speaks enthusiastically of his success in Columbia and other places: "There has not been in this century a literary work with a more rapid, ardent, and popular resonance [...]." (Núñez, p. 158.) On June 9, 1938, a Spanish Romantic drama, *El trovador*, by García Gutiérrez, was performed in Buenos Aires and became the work most often staged during the Rosas period. Cf. Raúl H. Castagnino, "El romanticismo en el teatro porteño (1830-52)," in the review *Lyra* (Buenos Aires), Nos. 174-76 (1959).

[17] Ducange belongs on the lowest rung of a theater that did not rise much; he was something like a "serialized story" on stage. He had considerable success in spite of the fact that Sarmiento already called him "the indigestible Ducange." (See Norberto Pinilla, *La polémica del Romanticismo in 1842* (Buenos Aires: Editorial Americalee, 1943), p. 95.) On Ducange and his theater, see Arturo Berenguer Carisomo, "La obra en que la muerte sorprendió a Casacuberta," in the *Boletín de estudios de teatro* (Buenos Aires) 26 (1949), pp. 50-54.

[18] L.V. López, *La gran aldea* (1884; rpt. Buenos Aires: Editorial Universitaria de Buenos Aires, 1961), p. 46.

known by way of direct translation). He was, instead, Shakespeare as arranged by the Frenchman Ducis. Finally, some works of Lope de Vega, Calderón, and Moreto were played – Lope, above all, in the arrangements by Cándido María Trigueros (equivalent to Ducis, in the case of Shakespeare). Here is a judgement by Paul Groussac:

> La nommée *Niña boba*, dont le sous-titre pouvait être: *ou le couteau à Jeannot*, est le resemblage de Lope par un Grimaud, appelé Trigueros, qui l'a ramenée aux trois unités, qui l'a déformée, mutilée à merci, et, chose plus odieuse, refondue et récrite en grande partie [...].[19]

In addition, many works were put on without the names of the authors, or with the simple mention "translated from the French," works which often awakened doubt and equivocation through the coincidence of their titles and themes.[20]

The public did not skimp in its attendance if we measure by the conditions of the times, and was stronger than is often supposed. In no other manner can we explain the presence of a theater in that age, centered in the most important cities as a means of security. The Peruvian historian José de la Riva Agüero, in his work *Carácter de la literatura del Perú Independiente*, blames the absence or scarceness of the theater in Peru on the lack of production and public:

> There is neither one nor the other in towns that have no more than colonial somnolence for their heritage, and which do not attain even the relative social advance that the dramatic genre requires.[21]

This assertion seems somewhat unfair to me. There was a public: the productions prove that, but for various reasons, a dramatic tradition of high quality did not manage to arise or sustain itself in the colonies (more precisely, in the two most important territories, Mexico and Peru).

During the nineteenth century, a certain regularity was achieved in the production of new works and this was accomplished through the favor of a public who permitted the establishment of spectacles, more or less adequate halls, impresarios, actors..., even if no national "author" appeared. Finally, there were some few newspapers or bulletins concerned with the theater movement, doubtless as a consequence of audience interest.[22] This was more important than is generally recognized. A tradition was started at that time reaching to our days. It was successful especially because of a public which upheld the productions in spite of the instability which characterized American political life during the nineteenth century. We should not forget that theater is the space where an art lives, or where particular art lives, but which also – above all at that time – constitutes a center for

---

[19] P. Groussac, "Le drame espagnol" in *Une énigme littéraire* (Paris: Picard, 1903), p. 214.

[20] Thus, for example, Sarmiento referred to a drama entitled *Cromwell* ("drama translated from the French") which was not, he said, either that by Victor Hugo, nor that by Emilio Souvestre, nor that by Félix Piat. (See Sarmiento, *Obras*, II, 113.)

[21] Approvingly quoted by Unamuno in *Algunas consideraciones sobre la literatura hispanoamericana* (Buenos Aires: Espasa-Calpe, 1947), pp. 78-79. Menéndez y Pelayo, for his part, explains the scarcity and mediocrity of theater in America as a consequence of the lack "of a complex state of affective relations and of technical conditions, which it is impossible to produce artificially in recently originating peoples and in new societies." And he adds: "At most, one may be able to arrive at attempts to imitate like those by Pardo and Milanés, and at farce or at superficial and exaggerated representation of popular customs, as we see in the Peruvian Segura." (*Antología de poetas hispanoamericanos* [Madrid: Tip. de la "Revista de Archivos", 1927], I, xi-xii.) In spite of such learned words – and relying on the same Menéndez y Pelayo – let us recognize that it is debatable to speak about "recently originating peoples" and "new societies" in referring to the emergent Hispano-American countries of the nineteenth century.

[22] Cf. Armando de María y Campos, pp. 118-24; Pedro Henríquez Ureña, *Historia de la cultura en la América Hispánica* (Mexico: Fondo de Cultura Económica, 1947), p. 93.

social gathering for which in the course of time there will be no substitute. The chronicles of the productions are collected in the newspapers of the age. The description of the public, fashions, enumeration of persons and personalities in the hall often has as great a place as the production itself.

In *El ideal de un calavera* the Chilean novelist Alberto Blest Gana describes a humble Santiago theater in the Calle de Carmen, and uses it in his fiction for some descriptive scenes:

> On the great highway of human progress, the popular theaters of Santiago have only managed to take their baby steps, inasmuch as they are now that which they were in the epoch of the present history for the delight of the democratic classes. Then, as befell those days, the representation of religious plays [autos sacramentales] was preferred, which, copied from the Spanish theaters by the same actors or by the impresarios of their companies, after two editions, underwent such rare linguistic metamorphoses that, if their authors had been resuscitated, they would not have been able to recognize them. Add to this the alterations which were made in the plan in order to adapt their *dramatis personae* to those who were supposed to represent them; the essentially *popular* pronunciation of various of the actors; the poverty of the locale and extreme poverty of the decorations and costumes, and an idea may be had of the production, which some of the principal personages were going to attend, whom the reader knows [...].[23]

Certainly not all Hispanic American theaters had this emaciated profile which in Blest Gana touches the limits of caricature, even though there were many like them. The "principal" theater of Mexico was more important, but the testimony of Frances Erskine Inglis, Countess Calderón de la Barca, writing in her book *Life in Mexico* (1843) about the period from 1839 to 1843, is not much more encouraging:

> What a theater! Dark, filthy, filled with bad smells: wretchedly illuminated, the corridors which lead to the boxes, of the sort that in passing through them one fears treading on another person's corns. The actors, by their style. The leading lady, a favorite of the public, not badly dressed, enjoys a great reputation for her honorable conduct; but she is of straw, totally of straw, and won't stop being so, not even in the most tragic scenes. I am certain that when the production comes to an end, she will not have disarranged the slightest fold in her gown. She has, besides, this singular mania of arching her mouth, as if smiling, and at the same time she knits the space between her brows with tears in her eyes; one might say that she's trying to characterize a day in spring. I would enjoy hearing her sing: "I spoke a smile to a tear."
>
> There were no interruptions for applause, and half of the boxes were empty, so that it seemed that the throng occupying the others only yielded to the force of habit, and by reason of this being the sole nocturnal diversion. The prompter spoke so robustly that, just as [...] the events to come project

---

[23] Alberto Blest Gana, *El ideal de un calavera* (Paris: Bouret, 1893), II, 72. Sarmiento has left us a more or less Burlesque analysis of the elements which constitute the theater and production (First, Orchestra; Second, Dramatic Composition; Third, Execution; and Fourth, Theatrical Apparatus), related to "El teatro de Santiago a fines de 1842," in *El Progreso* (Santiago), November 15, 1842. See, in addition, "El teatro durante el año 1841," in *El Mercurio* (Valparaíso), February 11, 1842.

Alberdi, too, describes a production in the then-new "Teatro de la Victoria" of Buenos Aires. The description begins with the exterior building, continues with the hall ("an immense birdcage"), the ladies' gallery, the decorations, the curtain (overloaded with designs and colors), and culminates with the references to a work being staged (*L'Angèle*, by Victor Hugo). Of course, this is Alberdi's satire "Figarillo" (Little Figaro). See Alberdi, "Figarillo en Montevideo," in *Obras completas* (Buenos Aires: Imp. de "La Tribuna Nacional", 1886), I, 366-71.

Many years later, in *La gran aldea*, Lucio V. López will describe at a distance a production of a drama by Camprodón, *Flor de un dia*, in the Teatro de la Victoria, by the García Delgado company. (See López, ch. 8.)

their shadow in advance, he announced every word confidentially to the public before it officially left the lips of the actors. The whole of the pit was smoking. The galleries were smoking. The boxes were smoking, and the prompter [...].[24]

In spite of what Blest Gana gives us to understand, there is no doubt that Romantic playwrights took special care in scenic design. Peón y Contreras provides a minute description of the decor for the first act of *La hija del rey*:

> Street decoration. To the right of the spectator, the side of the convent of Jesús María, with a tall grille in the foreground and next to it a little further, the entrance of the concierge, with staircase. The wall of this side is to run diagonally to the back, hugging the street, with the result that the public can distinguish the person who speaks from the grille. On this side and in the back, a street intersects. To the left of the spectator, another street intersects; in the foreground, in one of its most visible corners, will be the niche with an image weakly illuminated by a small lamp. It is night.[25]

The Romantic author was also inclined to schemes using complicated and spectacular stage tricks related to set works and situations: earthquakes, torrents, snow, exotic landscapes... As regards care for the flow of simple scenes, we see the following stage direction in a comedy by Felipe Pardo y Aliaga (which mixes Classic and Romantic traits):

> In this entire scene, the actresses, seated around the proscenium, should accompany the dialogue with very animated action, and with frequent guffaws at the part relative to the criticism of the Marquesa's function. (*Frutos de la educación*, Act III, scene iii)[26]

Even granted that not all Spanish-American dramatists were as meticulous as the Bogotá writer José Peregrino Sanmiguel, the beginning of a "double drama for reading and production" (?) may serve as a pattern:

> Before the curtain is raised, a tempest is heard let loose. It diminishes by degrees, and at the signal the curtain rises. The obscure scenery, invaded by strange figures which move in distinct directions. They talk to one another in secret. And books, newspapers, and a variety of objects are shown with great mystery. Others, like shadows, pass rapidly, making menacing grimaces at the pit and boxes. Steps are heard of a person who treads heavily and with spurs and arms. The phantasms begin to flee, and

---

[24] Countess Calderón de la Barca, *La vida en México*, trans. into Spanish by Enrique Martínez Sobral (Mexico: Viuda de C. Bouret, 1920), seventh letter; cited by Armando de María y Campos, pp. 68-69.

[25] See *Cuatro siglos de literatura mexicana*, ed. Ermilo Abreu Gómez (Mexico: Editorial Leyenda, 1946), p. 297. This complicated scenography also extended – a sign of the age – to productions of old Spanish works whose fantastic subject-matter required complex stage tricks. In Buenos Aires, the Spanish director and actor Francisco Torres put some of these works on stage (*Pata de cabra, Los polvos de la Madre Celestina*) they gained wide acceptance by the public. See R. Rosenblat and A. Blanco Amores, "Diez años de actividad teatral en Buenos Aires, 1852-1862," in *Cursos y conferencias* (Buenos Aires), 31 (1947) p. 159.

[26] See *Biblioteca de Cultura Peruana*, first series, no. 9, p. 193. In another comedy of manners, the Columbian José María Samper indicated: "The same decoration from the first act, without the previous furniture. It is supposed that don Pascacio's house looks over the town square, and that his neighbors are at public festivities. Now and then mandolins, cries, and popular songs will be heard, and at times lights and people will be seen at a distance through the curtain. Doña Petrona appears to be overseeing the arrangement of the hall for a masked ball; all the furniture will be different and remains grotesquely mixed. On the wall and in the middle there will be a few lamps of unequal size with tallow candles." José María Samper, introduction to Act Two of *Un alcalde a la antigua y dos primos a la moderna* (Bogotá: Editorial Minerva, 1936), p. 115.

the night appears with this shield-bearer. The knight, lifting his visor and looking in all directions and in impressive attitude, says with mettle [...].[27]

The authors' recommendations were followed with greater or lesser fidelity. Where they really placed particular care and exhibited unsuspected fervor was in the costumes, especially in historical dramas. Often the costumes had to serve for historical events rather distant in time, but the gowns and boots of various colors, the movements of the plumes, the flashing of the swords, pleased the audience. There were works, then (because no other explanation fits), which attained success solely through the ingenuity of the stage machinery or the color of the clothes.

The Hispanic American theater did not engender many works of merit either then or later.[28] Nonetheless, it is fitting to keep in mind a few names of the colonial period: González de Eslava, Ruiz de Alarcón, Sor Juana Inés de la Cruz, Caviedes, Peralta Barnuevo, Fray Francisco del Castillo, Juan Augustín de Castro, Vela; and the fragmentary, localized brilliance of the Buenos Aires and Mexican theater of the nineteenth century. Romantic works belong to a few well-defined groups: historical dramas, dramas about contemporary affairs, and, to a lesser extent, comedies. By their abundance, historical plays are the characteristic genre of the moment. One of the fundamental battles of European Romanticism had already taken place around these dramas. (Suffice it to mention as an illustration the première of *Hernani*, the productions of Alexandre Dumas, or finally, the significance which the prologues of dramatic works often had: Hugo, Manzoni.) This vogue of historical drama passed to America in two clear cycles: that of European history, and that of Colonial affairs. In the first case, the plot and themes unfold in the Middle Ages and Renaissance, save for a few works which take place in Antiquity. (Examples: in Columbia, Manuel María Madiedo, *Coriolano*, and *Lucrecia*; in Cuba, Gertrudis Gómez de Avellaneda, *Saúl* and *Baltasar*, and Joaquín Lorenzo Luaces, *Aristodemo*; in Peru, Clemente Althaus, *Antíoco*.)

One of the first dramatists at the time, if not the first, was the Dominican Francisco Javier Foxá. He wrote *Don Pedro de Castilla* (1836), *El templario* (1838), and *Enrique VIII* (1839). Foxá spent a great part of his life in La Habana and developed his literary work there. According to the Cuban critic Aurelio Mitjans, the memory of the première of *Don Pedro de Castilla* remains in the annals of the Cuban theater. Foxá was crowned and his work had unprecedented success. The critic compared it to the triumphant night for *El trovador*, in Madrid.[29] In Cuba, José Jacinto Milanés's work *El conde Alarcos* and Gertrudis Gómez de Avellaneda's *Munio Alfonso* also entered the record; in Santa Domingo, Félix María del Valle (*El último Abencerraje*, a dramatization of the story by Chateaubriand). In Mexico, Fernando Calderón wrote historical dramas (*El torneo, Ana Bolena, Herman o La vuelta del cruzado*); likewise Manuel Nicolás Corpancho (*El poeta cruzado*,

---

[27] José Peregrino Sanmiguel, in *El granate granadino americano y católico* (Santa Fé de Bogotá, 1862). The author is cited as an example of extravagance by Ezequiel Uricoechea, in a letter to Rufino J. Cuervo, of 1878. The text which I have reproduced corresponds to a note by Mario Germán Romero. (See Uricoechea, Cuervo, M.A. Caro, *Epistolario* (Bogotá: Instituto Caro y Cuervo, 1976), pp. 272-73.

[28] Let's take, for example, what happened in Bolivia, where, according to the critic Enrique Finot, sixty dramatic works were registered in the course of forty years (curiously, more dramatic works than novels). The fact is symptomatic, touching Bolivian literature. See E. Finot, *Historia de la literatura boliviana* (Mexico: Librería de Porrúa Hermanos, 1943), p. 178. Of course, the artistic level and the survivability of this dramatic production was not of any great account.

[29] *Don Pedro de Castilla*, "a drama fervently applauded in the Teatro Príncipe, much to the liking of Palma and Suzarte, who continued to crown it ostentatiously that night, with indescribable enthusiasm; celebrated in Cuba, as was the première of *El trovador* in Madrid as the date of a tumultuous theatrical happening never before seen." Aurelio Mitjans, *Historia de la literatura cubana* (Madrid: Editorial-América, 1918) p. 194.

El templario) in Peru; Salvador Sanfuentes (*Juana de Nápoles*) in Chile; José Caicedo Rojas (*Miguel de Cervantes*) in Columbia; José Mármol (*El cruzado*) and Claudio Mamerto Cuenca (*Muza*, not completed) in Argentina. The best dramatic works of Gertrudis Gómez de Avellaneda – which are those we have cited – were written and performed in Spain. But her ties to her homeland were more insistent than those of other Americans who lived in Spain and completely forgot America. She was already famous when she returned for a time to Cuba, where her works were produced, too, and became as well-known.

The drama on colonial affairs starts with Ignacio Rodríguez Galván, who filled in Mexico a role similar to that of Foxá in Cuba. Rodríguez Galván wrote *Muñoz, Visitador de México* (1838) and *El privado del virrey* (1841), and José Peón y Contreras authored *La hija del rey* (1876), *Hasta el cielo* (1876), *El conde de Peñalva* (1877), *El capitán Pedreñales* (1879).[30] Other colonial dramas by American playwrights include: Lucio V. Mansilla, *Atar Gull* (1855);[31] Luis Benjamín Cisneros, *Alfredo el sevillano* (1856); Miguel García Fernández, *La novia del hereje*, a theatricalization of the novel by Vicente Fidel López (1861); G. Gutiérrez de Piñeres, *El oidor* (1865); L. María Pérez, *El corsario negro*; Carolina Freyre de Jaimes, *Blanca de Silva* (1879). A third less numerous group of plays refers to the epoch of the Conquest. Into that category fit *Cora o Los hijos del Sol* (1844), by the Venezuelan Rafael Agostini; *Un amor de Hernán Cortés*, by Peón y Contreras (1876); *Lucia Miranda*, by the Argentine Ortega; *Huáscar y Atahualpa* and *Atahualpa y Pizzaro*, by José David Berrios, a Bolivian; *Atahualpa* (1869), by José Pol, a Bolivian. A fourth group focussed on the age of Independence and were noted for dramatic exultation over revolutionary deeds and men, akin to contemporary lyric tributes. Into this category fit Alberdi, *La Revolución de Mayo* (not completed); Reyes Ortiz, *Las lanzas*; Nataniel Aguirre, *Represalia de héroes* – all patriotic dramas centered around the political theme.[32] Lastly, there are the works whose events develop in the day of the writer and whose sentimental tendency and melodramatic tone characterize Romantic drama in general. Examples: Peón y Contreras, *Gabriela* (1890) and *Soledad* (1892); José T. de Cuéllar, *Deberes y sacrificios*; José Mármol, *El poeta* (1842); Rosa Guerra, *Clemencia* (1856); Félix Reyes Ortiz, *Odio y amor...*

The gaucho theater falls within this restricted orbit. In its beginnings as a spectacle, it is a product of the conjunction of a special scenario, the Creole circus, and of a popularly rooted theme, the gaucho. Eduardo Gutiérrez's drama *Juan Moreira* provides the fundamental proposition, more important for what it announces than for its intrinsic value. Actually, as we witness in greater amplitude in the novel, the passage to the theater of the persecuted, of the "Romantic" bandit, is realized here through the gaucho's particular character.[33]

---

[30] See Ermilo Abreu Gómez, "Un aspecto del teatro romántico," in *Contemporáneos* (Mexico) 30-31 (1930), pp. 246-47.

[31] This is a juvenile work of Mansilla, an author who never sparkled in the theater. The action takes place in Pernambuco at the end of the seventeenth century, and the protagonist is a Negro slave whom passion impels to engage in true butchery. A poor work (see the edition published in Buenos Aires, 1926), like almost all those cited here. Here is the statement of the author: "[...] I was saying, I wrote my drama *Atar Gull o Una venganza africana* in forty-eight hours; a drama which was not Romantic in its results, although it was of this genre [...]." Lucio V. Mansilla, *Mis memorias* (Paris: Garnier Hermanos, 1904; rpt. Buenos Aires: Librería Hachette, 1955), p. 155.

[32] Bartolomé Mitre's drama *Cuatro épocas*, written in Montevideo in 1840 (see the edition published in Buenos Aires, 1927) also belongs in this series, although the subject matter occurred in the epoch in which the author was writing.

[33] As Raúl H. Castagnino cogently observed, "the transformation of the delinquent into the novel-like hero by Eduardo Gutiérrez is an echo of low Romanticism [...]." See R.H. Castagnino, *Sociología del teatro argentino* (Buenos Aires: Editorial Nova, 1963), p. 117.

In view of the abundance of historical dramas, above all those treating happenings exotic or distant in time, some critics recommended closer, more familiar subject-matter. Thus, Alberdi, in pointing out the failure of Mármol's *El cruzado*, attributed it to the theme selected:

> [...] for societies like those of America, the erudite and historical drama is totally inadequate, and much more so if the history which suggests nourishment for it is from the other hemisphere and times which are far distant from our own. The society in which we live, that is American society with its traditions, uses, characteristics, passions, and peculiar interests, will be the material from which the author of *El cruzado* should take his inspirations in the future.[34]

Obviously, it was not a question of themes, but of creative ability. But faced by the profusion of European themes, Alberdi was right in recommending themes which could be felt as one's own in the Americas. Finally, within European theater, works like *Antony* by Alexandre Dumas, which the publics of Hispanic America enjoyed so much, also provided a guideline as to what would constitute a contemporary event translated to the stage (although, curiously, one of the characters of this work defends historical drama as more apt for exhibiting the shock of passions).

Commonly, the Romantic distinguished between the intrigue, terror, and death, which he projected backwards in time and developed by way of the historical drama, and the game of ingenuity with a certain air of "costumbrismo" (depiction of contemporary customs) which unfolds in the comedy. Death is accustomed to win the field in drama. It is almost always the obligatory finale, although there are anticipations well in advance and chains of relationships prevail. The characters are superficial and the situations do not spring from within but from the movement of the action: a violent, tense action of limited ploys, but efficacious ploys from the dramatic point of view. The passions overflow and acquire a ready reflection – commonly an exaggerated reflection, in the emphasis of the actors. Evidently, the distinctive traits of Hispano-American Romantic drama are violence and emphasis.

Smiles, mischief, and complicated stories dominate in comedy. There is certainly no attempt to reproduce "tragedy and comedy" in the classic manner, but to divide them with less rigor; this is true above all in the ample range which the term "drama" connotes, into which comic or picturesque elements are able to enter, giving an idea of the variety and at the same time the unity of human nature.

Finally, Romantic drama in Hispanic America does not make any discoveries in relationship to European Romantic drama, the absorbing model. The work *Muñoz, Visitador de México* by Rodríguez Galván, begins thus (we easily imagine how it ends):

(Muñoz, sentado en el sitial)
>   Agitación y pesar,
>   y martirios furibundos,
>   me atormentan iracundos
>   sin dejarme respirar.
>   ¡Que no pueda yo encontrar
>   el reposo que deseo!...
>   Triste estuve en el paseo
>   y en la actualidad lo estoy...

---

[34] Alberdi, *Obras selectas* (Buenos Aires: Librería "La Faculdad" de J. Roldán, 1920), II, 359-68.

Por donde quiera que voy
Fantasmas y espectros veo...

(Muñoz, seated on the dais)

(Agitation and sorrow,
and martyrdoms of rage,
wrathful, torment me,
without letting me breathe.
Why cannot I find
The rest that I desire!...
I was sad in the past
and am so in the present...
wherever I go,
I see phantasms and spectres...)

With respect to external form, and consonant with known models, the Hispanic-American drama has had recourse to verse much more frequently than to prose. In spite of what Stendahl had recommended in his treatise *Racine et Shakespeare*[35] verse is notoriously the preferred vehicle. For all that, Alberdi writes dramatic works in prose (*La Revolución de Mayo, El gigante Amapolas*), although in Alberdi the dramatic production seems to be something occasional, or rather as a variant activity by the polemicist and political writer. (Also, we think, verse was outside of his orbit: the redaction of *El Edén*, a work written in collaboration with Juan María Gutiérrez, only confirms this.) The Mexican Peón y Contreras wrote works in verse and works in prose. The majority, and the best-known, he wrote in verse, but he has some in prose (*Doña Leonor de Sarabia, Gabriela, Por la Patria*). No clear division exists but it is evident that almost always the prose corresponds to a contemporary happening.

In 1846 (we are not going to ascertain the date with complete exactitude), Sarmiento was writing:

This drama cannot be in verse because verse is never able to express the passions with their true language, without study, without visible dressing-up, as the rhymes by assonance and consonance are; and against the known rules, modern comedy or drama is an *action*, a happening in prose. Victor Hugo, the first poet of the age, obeying this new inversion of the rules, has written his best dramas in prose, like Dumas, like all, because they cannot evade it, although from time to time, compositions in verse reappear. [...].[36]

In Mexico, already in 1860, Antonio Cisneros Cámera was maintaining that the theatrical work ought to be written in prose and that asides and monologues should be eliminated at the same time

---

[35] Stendahl, *Racine et Shakespeare* (Paris: Larrire, 1952), p. 45. In contrast, Alfred de Vigny *Lettre à Lord... sur la soirée du 24 octobre 1829 et sur un système dramatique*) and Victor Hugo ("Preface" to *Cromwell*) defended verse in the theater, although Hugo does not completely eliminate prose, such as he took upon himself to demonstrate concretely in some dramatic works. Already in the eighteenth century, the then-famous La Motte, a declared Classicist, endeavored to impose tragedy in prose. See his work *Oedipe*. For his part, Flaubert did not appear to be very much in agreement with Stendahl's theory, when citing from a paragraph of his work *De l'amour* in *Bouvard et Pécuchet*. Cf. G. Flaubert, *Bouvard et Pécuchet* (Paris: Denoel, 1966), II, 187.

[36] Sarmiento, *Viajes*, II, 39-40. It is not quite exact that the superior dramatic works by Hugo are in prose: *Hernani, Ruy Blas*, and *Les Burgraves* are works in verse, and beyond doubt, the best of the middle theater of Hugo. Besides, the beginnings of Hugo proper can be recalled in the "Preface" to *Cromwell*.

in order to achieve a greater closeness to the live reality.[37] But this differentiation of historical subjects, in verse, and contemporary, in prose, remained far from being commonplace. There remains finally, and it is a reflection of the age, dramatic work in both prose and verse. Such work overflows the limits of polymetrics and exhibits in prose a new element in the gradation of passions, stage business, and expression. Bartolomé Mitre wrote his drama *Cuatro épocas* (1840) in this manner, perhaps based on the close memory of *Don Alvaro*, by the Duke of Rivas.

The comedy customarily termed Romantic is in reality a comedy halfway Romantic. In any case, it is comedy of the Romantic epoch. If theater par excellence of the age encased itself almost exclusively in historical drama, the typical comedy that was then seen with greater frequency was by preference a "costumbrista" comedy, in the middle of the road – not even that – between Classicism and Romanticism. Evidently, the separation between neo-Classical comedy and Romantic comedy is relative. At least, in the line which I am pointing out. Hence Manuel Ascensio Segura would underline as a literary ideal the work directed to "correct the customs, the abuses, the excesses with which, to its misfortune, our soul finds itself plagued."[38] This is explainable in great measure in terms of the easily recognizable origin of these comedies: In effect, the bases tended to be Moratinian comedy (above all, *El sí de las niñas*). All the same, this situation changes almost not at all in relation to the Spanish comedy of the age (Bréton de los Herreros, López de Ayala).[39]

It is curious but three Americans residing in Europe came to achieve some prominence in comedy: Gorostiza, Pardo y Aliaga, and Ventura de la Vega. The three belonged to the middle of the road between Classicism and Romanticism, and two of them (Gorostiza and Pardo) returned to their countries, Mexico and Peru, in order to continue their work there, and gained notoriety through the influence they enjoyed among the young dramatists of the age.[40] Let us add to Gorostiza and Pardo the name of the Peruvian Manuel Ascensio Segura, and we shall have the most memorable group of Hispanic American comedy of those times.

Manuel Eduadro de Gorostiza (1789-1851), born in Veracruz, moved at an early age to Spain and there began his literary career. He returned to Mexico when his homeland sought its independence, and he occupied important public posts in his land. Also of importance is that he continued his dramatic labors within the Moratinian line, to which he brought, without doubt, a popular and efficacious wit.[41] Among his best remembered works, one encounters *Indulgencia para todos* (1818), *Las costumbres de antaño, Don Dieguito*,[42] *Contigo pan y cebolla*, all written in

---

[37] Cited by E. Abreu Gómez, in *Un aspecto del teatro romántico*, pp. 224-25.

[38] Cited by Jorge Cornejo Polar, *Sobre Segura* (Arequipa: Universidad Nacional de San Agustín, 1970), p. 69. Also see Antonio Cornejo Polar, prologue to Clorinda Matto de Turner, *Indole* (Lima: Instituto Nacional de Cultura, 1974), p. 8.

[39] The adjective *moratiniano* in Carilla's text refers to the eighteenth-century playwright Leandro Fernández de Moratín, who was born in Madrid in 1760, and died in Paris in 1828. As a partisan of the French cause, he was exiled when Fernando VII returned to Spain. He was credited with restoring Spanish theater and, because he took Molière as his model, was sometimes called "the Spanish Molière." Leandro's father Nicolás (1737-80), one of the most fervent imitators of French neo-Classical doctrines, was noted especially for his tragedies *Hormesinda, Lucrecia*, and *Guzmán el Bueno*, and his finest comedy, *Petimetra*, as well as for his lyrical and epical works. (G.G.)

[40] The Columbian José Manuel Marroquín included Bretón de los Herreros among writers worthy of being imitated, and said: "The study of his comedies is above all to be recommended for those who dedicate themselves to comic poetry." See *Retórica y poética* (Bogotá: Editorial Minerva, 1935), pp. 151-52.

[41] See Pedro Henríquez Ureña, "El teatro de la América Española en la época colonial," in the *Boletín de estudios de teatro* (Buenos Aires), 27 (1949), p. 181.

[42] *Don Dieguito* and *Contigo pan y cebolla* were produced in Buenos Aires in the years 1835 and 1836, respectively. Mariano G. Bosch, *Historia del teatro en Buenos Aires* (Buenos Aires: Est. Tip. El Comercio, 1910), pp. 245-46, from whom I take the dates, attributes the second to "M.E. de Gorostiaga," an error that remained in the *Indice cronológico de datos* of that work, prepared some years ago by Manuel Artacho (Buenos Aires, 1940), p. 376.

Spain;[43] and in Mexico, *La madrina, La hija del payaso, Estela, o el padre y la hija*.[44]

Felipe Pardo y Aliaga and Manuel Ascensio Segura fit comfortably within a Peruvian (or rather, Lima) tradition, which had acquired a distinct stamp in the colonial era. I refer to its propensity to jest and satire. Pardo y Aliaga (1806-68) is the aristocrat by family, education, and character, who avails himself of the pen in order to mock personages and situations which he considers grotesque, or not in accord with his thought and ideals. In him, ingenuity and sharpness of wit are but forms of his social condition, with great affinity to the new state of America. Works: *Don Leocadio, Aniversario de Ayacucho, Frutos de la educación* (1829), *Una huérfana en Chorrillos* (1833). A conservative mind, Pardo y Aliaga seems more inclined to the Classic than to the Romantic. Patricio de la Escosura in a first study considered him a Classicist; in a second, a Romantic.[45] The truth is that his situation is one that little aided the true direction of Romantic theater, although his name cannot be omitted in this age.

Manuel Ascensio Segura (1805-71) reveals a less cultivated grace, less "aristocratic" than that of Pardo y Aliaga. Segura was of humble origin, and his life had much of Bohemia about it. Therefore, he has not been considered as a representative of "Creole grace" insofar as he reflects popular life through his characters with greater assurance and freedom. Works: *El sargento Canuto* (1839), *La saya y el manto* (1842), *La moza mala* (1845), *Nadie me la pega* (1855), *Ño Catita* (1856),[46] *Un jugete* (1858), *Las tres viudas o El lance de Amancaes* (1862).

Certainly, we are not dealing with extraordinary works; simply – within the given scarcity of original work by Hispano-American talents of the age – comedies of agile movement and communicative grace, above all those aimed at the Lima public. Typical entanglements, contrasts, caricaturesque personages, satire on mores... give the tone to all this productivity.

[43] The edition of *Teatro escogido* (2 vols. [Brussels: En casa de Tarlier, 1825]) by Manuel Eduardo de Gorostiza, "Mexican citizen," includes – the date indicates this – works written in Spain. A review of that collection was published in *El Repertorio Americano* (London), 3 (1827), pp. 78-93. In the same manner, the works by Gorostiza which Leandro Fernández de Moratín cites in the *Catálogo de piezas dramáticas publicas en España desde el principio del siglo XVIII hasta la época presente* (1825) (in *Origines del teatro español* [Paris: Garnier Hermanos, 1883], p. 493) correspond to his first period. Apropos Moratín, it is worthwhile remembering a just eulogy of Gorostiza by A. Alcalá Galiano: "Taken all together, it is necessary to place him below Moratín, but closer to him than the rest of the authors of contemporary comedies [...]." Antonio Alcalà Galiano, *Literatura española siglo XIX de Moratín a Rivas* (originally 1834, trans. V. Lloréns; rpt. Madrid: Alianza Editorial, 1969), pp. 116-17. For his part, Menéndez y Pelayo considered him a "poet of true comic talent." And he also said: "Don Manuel Eduardo de Gorostiza belongs to Mexico, not only by his birth, but also by his public life, posterior to 1824, when he entered into the service of his homeland, already constituted as an independent nation; but he scarcely belongs by his literary work, considering the fact that with a sole exception, all his comedies were staged in Madrid and written for a Spanish listenership, without the poet's American nationality shining through in any part [...]." (Menéndez y Pelayo, I, c-ci.)

[44] Recently the Mexican critic Armando de María y Campos has done notes on various manuscripts of Gorostiza, among them some reflections titled *Del primitivo teatro español* and a biography of the famous actor Máiquez. (See "Obra inédita de Manuel Eduardo de Gorostiza," in *Cuadernos Americanos* (Mexico), 15, no. 5 (1956), pp. 149-78). The manuscripts correspond to his years in Spain and reveal neo-Classicistic ideals. They are interesting nonetheless to the extent they show a new epoch immediately preceding Romanticism.

Lota M. Spell, in turn, in a later study, points out diverse errors in the study by María y Campos (thus also in an edition of Gorostiza done by the critics). See L.M. Spell, "Notes on Gorostiza," the *Hispanic American Historical Review* (Durham), 38, no. 2 (1958), pp. 256-59.

I shall say, finally, that upon Gorostiza's passing, Montalvo busied himself as a translator. It is not frank praise, but it stands out from the epoch: "Gorostiza does not lower his lance in Flanders, but passes [...]." [The colloquial expression *poner una pica en Flandres* means to perform a great feat, achieve a triumph. G.G.] "El Buscapié," in *Siete tratados* (Buenos Aires, 1944), p. 529. I make clear that, among other more or less free versions, Gorostiza made an arrangement of Lessing's *Emilia Galotti*, following the French translation.

[45] See the article "Costumbristas y satíricos," in *Biblioteca de Cultura Peruana* (Paris: Deselées, de Brouwer, 1938), I, 99-101.

[46] "That admirable comedy, whose paternity the great Molière would not disdain," says Ricardo Palma with more than amiable judgement. See "La bohemia de mi tiempo," in *Tradiciones peruanas completas*, p. 1,304.

Less widely known than the foregoing, the Columbian José María Samper also cultivated "costumbrista" theater and achieved a certain success in his homeland (see *Un alcalde a la antigua y dos primos a la moderna*, "comedy of national customs" in two acts and in verse).[47] A little-known and curious coincidence affecting the success of Samper's comedies in Columbia has to do with the fact that earlier on Jorge Isaacs elaborated *María* as a comedy and, with hindsight, considering the advice of José María Vergara y Vergara, gave it the form of a novel. To be sure, we know neither the initial comedy nor its contents (in case its date is exact), nor the true import of its denomination as "comedy."[48] In Mexico, Vicente Riva Palacio (more known as a novelist) wrote various comedies in collaboration with Juan M. Mateos (*Borrascas de un sobretodo*, and *Odio hereditario*, both 1861, and others which he included in *Las liras hermanas*, 1871), comedies and verse which, so far as I imagine, did not distinguish themselves in a major way. Fernando Calderón also wrote comedies in Mexico (*A ninguna de las tres*). In Cuba, José Jacinto Milanés, famous for *El conde Alarcos*, wrote various comedies (*A buen hambre no hay pan duro*, *Ojo a la finca*, *Una intriga paternal*, the last lost). In Argentina, Claudio Mamerto Cuenca, one of the few writers who remained in Buenos Aires during Rosas's tyranny, cultivated the theater and left us two works: a comedy, *Don Tadeo* (comedy of manners in five acts and in verse), and an incomplete historical drama, *Muza*. The comedy, which ought to be able to make itself felt, does not offer greater merits. It makes frequent allusions to the new state of America, to its elders and to its youths, to Spain and to Argentina. The finale does not let up preaching the moral:

> Ya sois libres, ahora, pues,
>   *¡conquistad el pensamiento!*
>
> (You have your freedom, so now,
>   Conquer thought!)[49]

Naturally satire is not only present but dominates in the comedies cited. This is no obstacle to our distinguishing, within such a panorama, political satires as a group apart. Even though there were not many possibilities, the gasping political life of the epoch which is reflected as such in the literary products, also affected dramatic works. Hence some, not many, satirical comedies were born, constituted around the political situation as a core. Juan Bautista Alberdi's *El gigante Amapolas* is of this type.

In the comedy, verse and prose tended to be, so far as the number of works goes, in greater equilibrium than in the serious drama. The balance was weighted, without doubt, by the sphere of manners, and the smooth satire, without forgetting Spanish examples of the age.

---

[47] Cf. Samper, *Un alcalde a la antigua* (Bogotá: Editorial Minerva, 1936).

[48] According to the statement by J.M. Saavedra Galindo. See *Otros cuentistas* in the series *Biblioteca Aldeana de Colombia* (Bogotá: Editorial Minerva, 1936), p. 6. A parallel fact: Zorrilla de San Martín wrote a primitive *Tabaré* as a dramatic work in 1877. The work was not published nor produced. See Aída Cometta Manzoni, *El indio en la poesía de América Española* (Buenos Aires: Torres, 1939), pp. 193-94.

Finally, there is the note that Montalvo wrote five dramatic works, not intended for production, gathered in *El libro de las passiones* (La Habana: Cultural, 1935).

[49] Cf. Claudio M. Cuenca, *Obras poéticas* (Buenos Aires: Imprenta Argentina de El Nacional, 1860), II, 246.

Conclusion

The Hispanic American dramatic works of the Romantic age were rarely produced and have come down to us as evidence of a moment and of the theater and not as an unassailable bastion of literary value. Perhaps the comedies succeeded in being represented with greater frequency by virtue of their subject matter and the direct character of these works. This cannot be imputed as a fault of the public, given the fact that the public was in existence and did attend the productions of European (Spanish or translated non-Spanish) works. The list of works put on stage constitutes our best document. Let's recall here, although it falls somewhat outside our area, that the famous Brazillian novelist and dramatist Alencar made echo, not without bitter irony, of this preference for foreign works in his nation, too.[50]

The best defense of the Hispanic American theater of the age possibly has the character of a paltry consolation. This is the fact that neither did the European works survive (those which were preferred by reason of the prestige of their authors or their origin) with that much greater frequency than those which were written in the New World, although there remains a somewhat more positive balance. This finding does not escape being a relative defense, but it serves, if not to justify the Hispanic American theater, to square accounts for the moment.

Drawing things together, the conclusion one reaches after traversing these dry lands of Romantic theater in Hispanic America can be reduced to verifications that are not very inspiring, although indubitable. Knowledge of Romantic drama and appraisal of it as less than mediocre make it more interesting to the history of manners than to the history of literature, more significant for the evolution of external aspects (actors, scenography, public, architecture) than for an indispensable core of productions, that is, for dramatic works. But in any event, it is a sector which must not be overlooked in the panorama of the age.

(Translated from the Spanish by *Gerald Gillespie*.)

---

[50] Words uttered in the prologue of his work *O jesuita*, cited by Leo Kirschenbaum, in the article "Teatro," in Rubens Borba de Moraes and William Berrien, *Manual bibliográfico de estudos brasileiros* (Rio de Janeiro: Gráfica Editora Souza, 1949), p. 728.

IV. THE ROMANTIC LEGACY

GERALD GILLESPIE

CLASSIC VISION IN THE ROMANTIC AGE:
GOETHE'S RECONSTITUTION OF EUROPEAN DRAMA IN *FAUST II*

I

Goethe sensed that the completed *Faust II* was too advanced for his times when, at the end of his own life in 1832, he sealed up the manuscript, its "serious jests," for posterity. Appreciation of the extraordinary modernity of the entire Faust play in its final form has flourished in recent decades with the renascence of interest in the poetic power and structural complexity of Part II. I shall attempt to suggest here, in abbreviation, the consonance between the dramatic tendency of the ensemble *Faust, eine Tragödie* and its resolution in the symbolic outcome of Part II. One of Goethe's major contributions to the evolution of dramatic form was that he converted into a primary subject-matter of his work the inherent challenge he faced in seeking to embody his classic vision in the Romantic age. Even though Goethe interacted with Romantic artists and savants and enjoyed cordial relations with many across Europe, he carefully distanced himself from all aspects of the Romantic movement which seemed to exhibit modern "sickness." Thus it is one of Goethe's remarkable achievements that his *Faust, eine Tragödie* – among other things – not only rendered a critique of the situation of modern consciousness already deeply affected by Romanticism, but that his play outstripped in boldness the most experimental Romantic dramas. *Faust, eine Tragödie* indeed has remained since 1832, and probably will yet long remain, the monumental turning-point, challenge, and standard in world drama.

Part I of *Faust* is itself remarkable for more than its dynamics and organicism which derive to a considerable degree from the breakthrough of Storm-and-Stress techniques in Goethe's playwriting of the 1770s. While Goethe, in the course of revising, obviously could have pulled the play *Faust* more toward neoclassical norms such as he had mastered in *Iphigenie auf Tauris* in the 1780s, he chose instead to keep the rapidly shifting variety of settings, and the mixture of fixed and free verse forms plus prose, without any formal division into acts. Historical criticism has tended to think first of all about the appropriateness of a Storm-and-Stress structure to the combination of materials in Part I: the "Gothic" and folkloric backgrounds, the clash of medieval ways and newer Renaissance impulses, the story of Faust's hubris and crime, the sentimental martyrdom of Margarete, imaginative and also ironically distanced penetration into demonic realms, etc. Yet in response to Goethe's publication of the *Fragment* (1790), predecessor to Part I (1808), key early Romantic writers already formulated the idea that the *Faust* play was inherently a symbolic drama. Friedrich Schlegel saw it as potentially superseding *Hamlet* in this regard, and Schelling intuited it would have to move toward expressive heights like Dante's *Divine Comedy* if completed.[1] During the twentieth

---

[1] Friedrich Schlegel, "Über das Studium der griechischen Poesie," in *Schriften zur Literatur*, ed. by Wolfdietrich Rasch (Munich: DTV, 1972), pp. 121ff. Friedrich Schelling, *Gesammelte Werke* (1859), I.v. pp. 731ff.

century, in the wake of the Symbolist movement, attention has increasingly been paid to the fact that from its inception Goethe's treatment of the boundary-line situation of *Faust I* and *II*, where many ages overlap, sparkled with poetological sophistication. That is, not just Part II, but already Part I constantly invites us to consider the dramatic action in generic terms and thereby involves us in the play's deeper reflections on the philosophy of history.

For example, not very far into the opening scene "Night" in Part I, when Faust has just faced the terrifying Earth-Spirit, the intrusion by Faust's famulus Wagner provides comic relief. This all-too-human would-be-humanist has rushed from bed thinking his master might be reading something profitable for a student of rhetoric, "a Greek tragedy" (line 525).[2] Faust's scathing remarks can scarcely dampen Wagner's obtuse pride in his own "critical aspirations" (560), his Renaissance enthusiasm to get back to the sources. By ironic indirection Goethe broaches crucial issues indeed first raised by the Renaissance and restated afterwards as a problematic of development: above all, our awareness of the gulf separating us from what was thought to be the primary moment of creativity in archaic Greece, and from nature. Faust's pained reaction, condemning the shallow present and its virtually extinguished sense of that glory, also voices the concerns of the later eighteenth century. Unmistakable in the magus's scornful references to the distorting "mirror" of intellect, "pompous historical drama," and "puppet" plays is the bias which Storm-and-Stress eagerly took over from Lessing. In no. 17 of the seminal *Briefe, die neueste Literatur betreffend* (Letters Concerning the Newest Literature, February 16, 1759), for instance, Lessing had condemned both the confused *Haupt- und Staatsaktionen* (High and State Actions) in the commercial theater of the German past and French neoclassical obsession with rules, had posited the qualitative affinity of Sophocles and Shakespeare, and had suggested that the native Faust story possessed Shakespearean potential.

Goethe lets these wholly retrospective, anachronistic terms stand in 1832 both as polysemous elements indicative of the multiple time-layers in his finished *Faust* and as innuendo about the glaring inadequacies of the contemporary *Zeitgeist*:

> Mein Freund, die Zeiten der Vergangenheit
> Sind uns ein Buch mit sieben Siegeln.
> Was ihr den Geist der Zeiten heißt,
> Das ist im Grund der Herren eigner Geist,
> In dem die Zeiten sich bespiegeln.
> Da ists denn wahrlich oft ein Jammer!
> Man läuft euch bei dem ersten Blick davon:
> Ein Kehrichtfaß und eine Rumpelkammer,
> Und höchstens eine Haupt- und Staatsaktion
> Mit trefflichen pragmatischen Maximen,
> Wie sie den Puppen wohl im Munde ziemen!
> (lines 575-85)

> (To us the times of yore, it is decreed,
> Are like a book by seven seals protected;
> The so-called spirit of the age, you'll find,

___
[2] Citations from *Faust, eine Tragödie*, indicated by traditional verse numeration in parentheses, follow Ernst Beutler's commentated edition of *Die Faustdichtungen*, vol. V of the Artemis *Gedenkausgabe der Werke, Briefe und Gespräche* (Zürich: Artemis, 1950). English versions will be marked with the initials WA whenever taken from the translation by Walter Arndt in the very useful Norton Critical Edition, *Faust: A Tragedy* (New York: Norton, 1976), edited and commentated by Cyrus Hamlin and containing appended materials on backgrounds, sources, and critical opinion.

In truth is but the gentlemen's own mind
In which the ages are reflected.
And there you're apt to face a scene of gloom!
One glance is quite enough to make you stagger:
A refuse barrel or a lumber-room,
At best a stiff bombastic masque aswagger
With such sagaciously pragmatic saws
As might come fitly from a puppet's jaws.)
                    (WA lines 575-85)

Faust's keen Renaissance awareness of the distinction between meaningful, creative time, on the one hand, and history as mere habit, somnolence, and decadence, on the other, not only befits the portrayal of intellectual tumult in the waning Middle Ages and sixteenth century. Goethe here exploits the scholar's dissatisfaction to give us a more direct signal about the self-sustaining ironic tension in the play between that contemporary reality which appears firmly established as the historical lot in any age and that ideal toward which vital human aspirations ever tend. Faust's critique, echoing as if out of the Renaissance, implicates the audience in their own relation to the present and to those various pasts haunting the present (e.g., the more recent Storm and Stress, more distant Renaissance, remote Antiquity). Moreover, restless and skeptical Faust keeps us attuned to events *as theater*, for instance, in his resistance to the "magic business" (2337) and "damned puppets" (2393) of the scene "Witches' Kitchen," although – in an ironic twist – he soon enough succumbs like a parodic Tamino to the "heavenly image" in the "magic mirror" (2433f.). As Jane Brown has shown, the constant allusion to theatricality in Part I, which continues the world-theater thematics established in the Prologues, is one of several tools Goethe uses to shape a non-Aristotelian, illusion-breaking drama.[3]

The part of Mephisto, too, inherently reminds us we are witnessing a drama. Mephisto openly displays his theatrical skills in donning Faust's robes to interview the disciple in the scene "Study" and remains the deliberate meddlesome actor throughout Part I. He is undisputed master of the show in riotous scenes such as "Auerbach's Tavern," "Witches' Kitchen," and "Walpurgis Night." Typical of Mephisto's complicated role is the way (4189ff.) he openly connects the "enchantment" in the grisly vision of a beheaded Margarete both to the ancient Perseus myth and to the banal nineteenth-century reality of seduction in Vienna's fashionable Prater Park – references obviously outside the hypothetical time zones of the plot, and thus ironic breaks in the theatrical illusion. In romanesque terms, this moment proves to be a spectral preview as well. In a similar vein, as the frenzy of Walpurgis Night peaks, Mephisto sarcastically delights in the "actual theater" inserted into the black sabbath for comic relief, the separately titled "Walpurgis Night's Dream or the Golden Wedding of Oberon and Titania: Intermezzo" (4223-298). Surely devils cannot be that boring for Mephisto by comparison? This ironic alternative to the expected climax in a triumphant arrival of Satan on the Blocksberg further blurs the boundary separating the dramatic fiction about the German "past" on stage from ordinary contemporary life, the normal world in which, often just as an escape, we go to various plays.

For an audience around 1810, it is an ambiguous compliment to be offered reminiscences of one of the favorite Shakespearean fantasies of the Romantic age. In the process of commanding our

[3] I agree extensively with the general reading of the play and its self-reflectiveness by Jane K. Brown, *Goethe's "Faust": The German Tragedy* (Ithaca and London: Cornell Univ. Press, 1986).

attention, the segment "Intermezzo," overseen by a "Theater Master" and literally orchestrated, specifically comments on the processes at work in the play *Faust*. If we dig below the surface, we face a complex provocation: the challenge of relating the strife and resolution of Shakespeare's multi-levelled comedy *A Midsummer Night's Dream* to the meaning of the depicted commotion of natural forces in the pagan-Christian festival. And at the same time, we puzzle over a satire on the failings and inadequacy of Goethe's contemporary society, – fashions and schools, poetry, philosophy, politics, speaking in their disparate voices. Nonetheless, as the illusion dissipates, Ariel (appropriated, of course, from Shakespeare's *The Tempest*) points in the final direction of the entire play – a direction that Part II will reaffirm: "Upwards to the mount of roses!" (4394). That is, the somewhat obscure allegorical-musical masque, "Walpurgis Night's Dream," dizzyingly constitutes a play within a play within a play, an illusion at least to the third power. In this respect, at such a juncture, *Faust* rivals the contemporary genre of fantastic satires launched by Tieck's *Die verkehrte Welt* (The Land of Upsidedown, 1797).[4]

In Part I, the resolution of the opening scene "Night" occurs at dawn on Easter. Goethe handles the themes of rebirth and redemption in terms of ultimate theater; he invokes sacred rite itself to convey what will be restated at the conclusion of Part II. For the non-Christian Goethe, the Christian tropes serve to signify the nature of a miracle that has happened and happens in particular ways at special junctures of history and life and can happen anytime, once we grasp the hieroglyph. Moreover, within the entirety of the completed *Faust, a Tragedy*, all of Part I, like Part II, is conditioned by being triply framed by the "Dedication," "Prelude in the Theater," and "Prologue in Heaven." As we enter the play, each layer of the outer framework in turn progressively modifies our experience of the next and thus our participation in the openly acknowledged illusion. This is not mimesis, and Faust clearly is not to be regarded as a sentimental protagonist. One of the first themes is that of authorial submission to the mysterious purpose that manifests itself. After an interruption of two decades since the last major efforts on the play, the dramatist engages in a profoundly personal taking of bearings in historical time in the "Dedication." Here Goethe subjects himself and the evolution of his own work to the higher perspective that should govern also our witnessing of a vision. Next we hear or read the less personal (earlier composed) "Prelude in the Theater." The fictional contemporaries, the "Director," "Dramatic Poet," and "Merry Person" of the troupe, who are preparing a production of *Faust* at some unspecified German theater, discuss the poetological and social dimensions of drama in a way familiar in the preludes and internalized self-reflection of Renaissance and Baroque dramaturgy. Such framing was still used by urbane eighteenth-century playwrights such as Marivaux (e.g., in *L'Ile des Esclaves*, 1727), before Tieck exploited the tradition as a major structuring device for Romantic fantastic comedy that ironically violated the rules of rational mimesis (e.g., in *Der gestiefelte Kater*, Puss-in-Boots, 1797).

The Director's closing words in the "Prelude" invite us as if into the spaces of a resuscitated Renaissance and Baroque *theatrum mundi*. The celestial-earthly-infernal levels thereof are then revealed axially in timeless copresence in the urbane "Prologue in Heaven." The setting of this highest theater, as in Shakespeare, Masen, or Calderón, is the traditional feudal court. In contrast to the solemn hymn which God's highest officers, the archangels, intone praising the splendor and har-

---

[4] On the waves of Romantic fantastic comedy, see Gerald Gillespie, "Young Tieck and the Romantic Breakthrough," *Theater Three*, no. 4 (Spring 1988), 31-44, and "Romantic Irony and Modern Anti-Theater," in *Romantic Irony*, ed. Frederick Garber (Budapest: Akadémiai Kiadó; Atlantic Highlands, N.J.: Humanities Press, 1988), pp. 322-42.

mony of the cosmos as their ruler's domain, Mephisto speaks in a motley mixture of colloquialisms like a court jester, denigrating humanity. Goethe expects us to associate Mephisto's wager against the representative man Faust with the testing of Job by Satan. The Lord's superiority clearly subsumes the powers of the "spirits of negation" as agents of His mysterious purpose. (Only disinherited modern minds would bother to question that, for Goethe, archetypal, rather than doctrinaire, proposition.) Through the Lord's final words in the "Prologue," addressed to the angels (344-49), the poet Goethe invites us to share the transcendental perspective of symbolic drama and be "sons of God":

> Doch ihr, die echten Göttersöhne,
> Erfreut euch der lebendig-reichen Schöne!
> Das Werdende, das ewig wirkt und lebt,
> Umfaß euch mit der Liebe holden Schranken,
> Und was in schwankender Erscheinung schwebt,
> Befestiget mit dauernden Gedanken!
> >   (344-49)

> (But you, true scions of the godly race,
> Rejoice you in the font of living grace!
> By ever active, ever live creation
> In love's enchanting fetters be you caught,
> And that which sways in wavering revelation,
> May you compact it with enduring thought.)
> >   (WA 344-49)

Although Goethe was not at all aiming to implement the pronouncements of Romantic theoreticians, the Lord's words here suggest a poetic process of envisioning and they encourage the creative participation by the audience in the hovering vision. Elizabeth Starr sums up our awareness, in the ending twentieth century, that *Faust* offers innumerable "metaphors for the operation and nature of literary creation," but she stresses that "the creative mind which *Faust* depicts is [...] not so much that of a poet as that of a reader" for whom "the trip [is] its own reward," once the reader embarks in response to "the play's invitation to extravagantly multiple readings."[5] By a slight shift of perspective, this view is readily compatible with Jane Brown's analysis that "In *Faust* Goethe follows Shakespeare in declaring the independence of art from simple connections to social or concrete reality," and that the questing authorial mind, not any one fixed protagonal mask worn by Faust, is the governing spirit: "Prospero's power is coterminous with and equivalent to the power of the playwright; it exists only so long as it is limited to the sphere of the play itself."[6] The Janus-faced relationship of "author"/"reader" is well-suited to a work which, as Harry Levin says, seems to be based on slipping from one mythologeme to another, and discovering their linkages through conflation, in a grand tour of the whole mythological repertory from antiquity to modernity.[7]

These insights are not particularly "modern" insofar as Goethe already has formulated them and transmitted them in the idiom of his time, and we are actually not dependent on more recent

---

[5] Elizabeth Starr, "Illusion and Reality in Goethe's *Faust*: A Reader's Reflections," in *Faust through Four Centuries: Retrospect and Analysis – Vierhundert Jahre Faust: Rückblick und Analyse*, ed. by Peter Boerner and Sidney Johnson (Tübingen: Niemeyer, 1989), pp. 137ff.

[6] Jane K. Brown, "The Prosperous Wonder Worker: Faust in the Renaissance," in Boerner & Johnson, eds., p. 62.

[7] Harry Levin, "A Faustian Typology," in Boerner & Johnson, eds., pp. 1-12.

theory for a critical grasp of them. It is just as useful to think of the Lord's pronouncement as fitting in broad terms with Friedrich Schlegel's idea of a higher, benign Romantic irony. True, the Goethean version differs in emphasizing the importance of human engagement with reality, too; however, it shares a sense of process or "becoming," and identifies the binding principle ("love") that infuses a poetry which, as Schlegel says, "in each of its representations represent[s] itself, too, and simultaneously in every part [is] poetry and poetry of poetry."[8] This kind of imagination does not evade recognition of the actual limits within which humanity strives. The total structure of *Faust* accomplishes as transcendental poetry the goal set for philosophy in Schlegel's distinction: "Transcendental is what is, must be, and can be above: transcendent is what will upward and cannot or ought not rise. It would be blasphemy and nonsense to believe mankind could overstep its goal, overleap its forces [...]."[9] The numerous chiasmi in the *Faust* play express this simultaneity of the actual and the ideal, their reciprocity and tension. For example, in the descent from Heaven just before the curtain rises on Part I, Mephisto seems to have the last word for the meanwhile; but even he succumbs to the forces of love in the scene "Entombment" (11604-843) at the conclusion of Part II, and his discordant voice is absent from the seraphic epilogue scene "Mountain Gorges" (11844-12111). The repeated acts of descent into historical strife and existential crisis in the play are balanced by the removal to special realms of poetic imagination in Part II and by the final poetic ascent toward Heaven.

This spiritual levitation begins through contemplation of the feminine archetype. The famous final statement by the "Chorus Mysticus" is simultaneously an ultimate gathering of the play into pure meditation, and a dissolving away of the vision – as in Baroque *theatrum mundi* and Hindu symbolic drama. *Faust* ends in a gently ironic celebration of the pain of our separation from life and of our actual human condition. The eight lines of the "Chorus Mysticus" exhibit formally the sacred number associated with the Virgin Mary; pair by pair, each two lines embody through oxymoron or antinomy the dualism inherent in the "impossible" predication that becomes utterance:

> Alles Vergängliche
> Ist nur ein Gleichnis;
> Das Unzulängliche,
> Hier wird's Ereignis;
> Das Unbeschreibliche,
> Hier ist's getan;
> Das Ewigweibliche
> Zieht uns hinan.
>   (12104-111)
>
> (All in transition
> Is but reflection;
> What is deficient
> Here becomes action;
> Human discernment

---

[8] "[...] in jeder ihrer Darstellungen sich selbst mit darstell[t], und überall zugleich Poesie und Poesie der Poesie [ist]." Rasch, ed., p. 50.

[9] "Transzendental ist, was in der Höhe ist, sein soll und kann: transzendent ist, was in die Höhe will und nicht kann oder nicht soll. Es wäre Lästerung und Unsinn zu glauben, die Menschheit könne ihren Zweck überschreiten, ihre Kräfte überspringen [...]." Rasch, ed., p. 69.

Here is passed by;
Woman Eternal
Draw us on high.)
        (WA 12104-111):

To the phrase "Alles Vergängliche" (everything transitory) there momentarily still clings a reminder of our insubstantial human condition, as the great Baroque playwrights have examined its virtual nothingness. But the fuller proposition, "Alles Vergängliche ist nur ein Gleichnis" (Everything transient is merely metaphor), initiates a transformation of the troubling vestigial thought of limitation. The first sentence becomes triune iteration by the addition of two negations ("the insufficient," "the indescribable") that are converted into "event" and "deed." These three stages yield the fourth and confirming statement, and the work's "open" closure: "The Eternal Feminine draws us upward." The four whole sentences merge in an absolute parataxis unexcelled in all of literature. The quasi-ecphrastic essence of this vision embodied in a quadrature of abstractions manifests the completion of the cosmic process and echoes and answers Faust's fourfold brooding on the Gospel in the scene "Study" in Part I. Prominently embedded in the outcome of the fourth sentence, and thus mysteriously affirmed, momentarily reunited, is the intersubjective first-person plural "us": "Das Ewigweibliche/ Zieht *uns* hinan" (my emphasis). Jointly involved as poet and reader, "we" are furthermore an affected "object" that interacts with the other "subject" attracting us. The logic of a mysterious reciprocity tells us we are seeking that which attracts us.

                                    II

The temptation to impose some neat symmetry between Parts I and II of *Faust, eine Tragödie* because of the correspondances, balancings, and echoes in Part II finally must be resisted.[10] The formal relationship is, rather, roughly like that between Parts I and II of Cervantes's novel *Don Quixote*, where each part distinctly has its own internal structure and the second part not only repotentiates the themes of the first part to a yet more startling level of self-reflection but attains a definitive coda applicable to the whole work and the ensemble of its ironic framing devices.[11] Thus the Faust play's second coda in the scene "Mountain Gorges" – by reaffirming the rebirth thematics at the opening of Part II in "Charming Landscape" – simultaneously restates the protagonist's awakening on Easter morn in the opening scene of Part I, "Night," and answers the tragic separation of Margarete and Faust in the "Dungeon" coda of Part I. But the lyrically intense "Charming Landscape" – in which Mephisto is momentarily absent just as he will disappear at the end in "Mountain Gorges" – already signals an even bolder shift into a new kind of symbolic drama. Readers who are too comfortably familiar with the Gothic and Christian atmosphere of *Faust I* and not attentive to

[10] The formalistic argument of intricately complex balances and correspondences between Parts I and II ("the continuous fabric of theme, motif, symbol, with its patterns of repetition and variation, [...] the structural principle of the interlude, [...] the architectonic relationship of monodrama and polydrama, [...] the succession of symbolic prototypes [...] understood [in] the context of the whole") is pressed furthest by Harold Jantz, "Patterns and Structures in *Faust*," *Modern Language Notes*, 83 (1968), 359-87.
[11] The view that, with the ensemble of prologues, Parts I and II together form an organic unity consisting of five successive great thematic sections, and that the "open," post-Storm-and-Stress "'barbaric construction'" is fundamentally "epic" and thus capable of subsuming the generic and stylistic variety, is advanced forcefully by Rudolf Eppelsheimer, *Goethes "Faust": Das Drama im Doppelreich* (Stuttgart: Verlag Freies Geistesleben, 1982).

the ironic context may react with dismay or even shock to Faust's recovery after his misdeeds. If we expect some Christian punishment or expiation, we may resist accepting the evolved standards that Part II imposes on Part I; or as many artists have in fact done, we may consciously revise Goethe's *Faust* and rechristianize the story as one of damnable hubris.

However, this flies in the face of the overture "Charming Landscape" which, as its title hints, is first and foremost about a primal trope (and the paradigmatic discovery embodied therein) that haunts mankind. Or, understood from the perspective of "Mountain Gorges," this overture is a scene that reenacts the *Urtrope* and reformulates it in our retrospective state of modern exile from the originary experience: our discovery that spirit can only be mediated, not directly confronted. Through Faust we are to reexperience the awesome glory veiled in the poetic heritage of the *locus amoenus*: the paradisal moment of dawn, of springtime, of transfiguring light and energy. Goethe reinvokes the majesty of larger nature and the great chain of being (learned from poets such as Klopstock), integrates these ultimate dimensions of the eighteenth-century sublime with the cosmic magic of Renaissance-Baroque *teatro del mundo* (learned from Shakespeare, Calderón, and others), and (with the ancient mythological references surviving into modernity) gives us a foretaste of the rediscovery of the ancient sense of being in the world that occurs in Part II.

As Faust turns away from the blinding sun to "gaze back upon our homely planet" (4713), witnesses the waterfall, favorite Goethean image of the flow of divine energy in individuation, and grasps the light in its "colorful refraction" (4727), the poet demonstrates the movement of the human mind into reflective thought. Fundamental to the structure and meaning of Part II, this precondition for ennobling the primordial drive for experience and understanding is already implicit in our heritage, i.e., in the poetic shaping of the trope. Hence we cannot legitimately apply old-fashioned criteria of verisimilitude in characterization and dramatic action to the five-act structure of Part II.[12] Nor can we say that Part II asserts a "right" Classical view that overturns a "wrong" Romantic view in Part I ("*romantic*" either in the broader sense of Western culture after the collapse of antiquity, or in the narrower sense as the self-styled movement during Goethe's lifetime).

Rather, the classical outline for drama, as this was reintroduced by the Renaissance, in large measure stands here for the processes and overarching rhythm of the reborn genre, a genre regained at the epochal turning-point when the legendary Faust lived. Within that outline we observe there is, paradoxically but not accidentally, less "verisimilar" unity of character and action than in the externally "irregular," organicistic Part I. For Part II is classical vision as recaptured, almost miraculously, in the Romantic age, in the mode and under the conditions of reflection that (as Goethe noted internally in the play as well as elsewhere) sometimes seemed to threaten self-disintegration for European artists and profound cultural rupture.[13] Yet perhaps no other dramatic work in the entire European repertory after antiquity is so daring and plenteous in its evocation of ancient lore as *Faust II*. How, then, given Goethe's constitutional antipathy for the tragic, are we to comprehend the playwright's powerful sense of life, his vivid classical recollections, and the startling apotheosis for a transgressor as *tragedy*, the term he chose?

---

[12] In an excellent broad-gauged essay on "*Faust. Der Tragödie zweiter Teil*," in the Reclam collection *Goethes Dramen: Neue Interpretationen* (Stuttgart: Reclam, 1980), pp. 281-312, Victor Lange stresses the extraordinary literariness of Part II and the way Goethe's enormous learning is mobilized to create an "astonishing universe" rather than a mere plot.

[13] In *Goethe's "Faust": The German Tragedy*, Brown has stressed the distinction "visionary" drama in the tradition of world-theater as against "illusionist" drama in the Aristotelian, rationalist mode, Goethe's closeness to the Miltonic variety of classicism as against the French (p. 80), but his reversal of Rousseau and critique of Protestantism (p. 83) within a larger schema that incorporates appreciation of great poetic insights from the Catholic world (e.g., Dante, Calderón).

The answer is foreshadowed in the scenes of Act I, when Faust reenters the realm of "history," not particular history but representative history, set in the court of the Holy Roman Empire consonant with the original chapbook, thus "history" which has been made generic, poeticized, and standing in contrast to the generic, poeticized "nature" of "Charming Landscape." It is as if everything about the mainsprings of social and political power that Goethe could extrapolate from Shakespeare's Histories and other plays is compressed into a symbolic action modelled on Calderón's *La vida es sueño*. However, when Goethe concentrated on Acts I and II in the years 1827 to 1830 in relationship to the Helena materials, he expanded upon their overt theatricality in a way hardly thinkable prior to Romanticism.

Scholarship today agrees in broad outline, if not in every detail, with Wilhelm Emrich's view that Goethe's final reshaping of the Helena interlude was, paradoxically, in critical opposition to Romanticism as an inadequate, misleading modernity.[14] In Act III, Helena – the essence of beauty and art, symbol of timeless classical culture and man's creative powers – is brought back into the Christian world. In the encounter between Helena and Faust, who ostensibly is a savant living on the border between the Middle Ages and the Renaissance, the transition from classical meter to rhyme occurs on stage, or the emergence of our early modern prosodies; and Euphorion, the offspring of their union, represents both the exuberant spirit of poetry and the birth of Romanticism, in the wider sense of everything postclassical as well as of the contemporary movement from which Goethe distances himself, its charms and dangers:

> Thus this Helena act, which retraces three thousand years of European development in a symbolic flash, represents the reconciliation of classical and Christian culture. It stands for Goethe's own classicism, in which Christianity and antiquity are fused in miraculous unity.[15]

Before turning to the thematics of reconciliation in Act III, however, it is instructive to consider the approach toward this climax; because, as Katharina Mommsen has shown, Helena is to be understood in this dramatic fiction not as an actual incarnation, but as a phantom, a cultural memory, who is bodied forth by dream, in a poetic recollection.[16]

The scenes of Acts I and II set at the imperial court consist almost wholly of depicted stagings of plays and entertainments. In "Imperial Residence," the intruder Mephisto immediately assumes the role of a riddling jester and he also prompts the speeches of the astrologer, while the venal, incompetent officials brood about the dangerous state of the realm. Mephisto soon tempts them with the supreme jest, promises of illusory wealth based on paper money. The emperor impatiently wants to escape to the carnival festivities, an Italianate-Elizabethan masque which is elaborately staged in the scene "Spacious Hall" under the Herald as master of ceremonies. Various kinds of Northern poets shuffle wordlessly by with telltale attributes, but clearly lack the power to infuse sufficient spirit into their world. They give way to the speaking ancient figures of the Graces, the Fates, and

---

[14] Wilhelm Emrich, "Das Rätsel der *Faust-II*-Dichtung," in *Geist und Widergeist* (Frankfurt a. M., 1965), pp. 211-35; English version reprinted in the Arndt-Hamlin edition under the title "The Enigma of *Faust, Part II*: A Tentative Solution," pp. 585-603. For a basic analysis of Part II, also consult Emrich's *Die Symbolik von "Faust II": Sinn und Vorformen* (1943; 3rd ed. Frankfurt a. M. and Bonn: Athenäum Verlag, 1964).

[15] Emrich, in Arndt-Hamlin, ed., p. 600.

[16] Mommsen has elaborated this thesis in three important books, to which the present essay is indebted: *Goethe und 1001 Nacht* (1960; 2nd. ed., Frankfurt a. M.: Suhrkamp, 1981), especially pp. 185-290; and *Natur- und Fabelreich in "Faust II"* (Berlin: De Gruyter, 1968); *Goethe und die arabische Welt* (Frankfurt a. M.: Insel Verlag, 1988).

the Furies; then come allegorized fear, hope, intelligence; until the main "hero" Plutus (the disguised Faust), the god of wealth, arrives with the "treasure" in a chariot pulled by dragons and steered by a Boy Charioteer who represents poetry. When the crowd grows disorderly, grabbing for the magic lucre, and Mephisto shapes it into a threatening phallus, Plutus takes over control from the shocked Herald and, in a surprise twist, he introduces a raucous troupe of fawns, satyrs, gnomes, giants, and nymphs who praise the great Pan (Emperor). As the new master of ceremonies, Plutus first allows the wild sprites and the watching court to be engulfed in illusory flames and then releases them from the mad spell.

The structure and details of the masque reflect the problematics of Act I: the search for meaning and sources of creative vitality, and the ambivalence of illusion. As Jane Brown has shown, Goethe's constellation of core figures recapitulates the Ariel-Prospero-Caliban relationships probed in Shakespeare's *Tempest*.[17] In counterbalance to Part I, this archetypal positioning of the mature magician-poet suits the new role which Faust assumes by now figuring as Plutus or – in Emrich's words – "the supra-individual, timeless, superior, objective type of man [...] organically anchored in nature and sleep," and disposed to witness and reveal "the eternal fundamental manifestations of existence."[18]

The magic and illusion which dominate the happenings in Act I appear to be inspired, at least in part, by Oriental story-telling, most notably the *1001 Nights*, according to Mommsen. In the next scene, "Pleasure Garden," the Emperor explicitly praises the art of Faust, the unmasked Plutus, and declares Mephisto to be "straight from the *Arabian Nights* [...] as inventive as Scheherezade" (6032f.). Ulrich Maché, too, has pointed out the private symbol of the turban, mysteriously associated with Faust as Plutus or the poet divinely rich, in the great masque (5565) – an emblem hinting at the Oriental proclivities of the older Hatem-Goethe of the *West-östlicher Divan* (West-East Divan, 1819).[19] In such open clues we glimpse an invitingly "hidden" layer of reference undergirding the more apparent, intricately conflated ancient, medieval, and Renaissance allusions. Maché emphasizes the accord between the portrayal of Faust's new role as a sometimes poet in Part II and Goethe's own sovereign freedom to choose motifs appropriate to an allegorical progression. Hence the opening scene of Act I, "Charming Landscape," resonates with gentle irony as a preparatory announcement of the poetic decision to occupy the *locus amoenus* out of time. In an operatic transformation of the stage in Act III, we will remove from the Gothic castle to the Virgilian soul-landscape of Arcadia for the climax of the episode. Indeed, as Mommsen stresses, this Arcadia is actually in a fairytale realm, located in a magical grotto. We confirm this from Mephisto-Phorkyas' report of the wedding of Faust and Helena (9574ff.).[20]

If not only the episodes at the Emperor's court, but also Faust's way toward Helen and his wooing of her are modelled, often rather closely, on passages Goethe found in Oriental literature as well as on the European tradition, how does this authorial playfulness affect the nature of his "tragic" purpose? The title hero's assumption of the Plutus mask can be read as signaling a higher integration of his personality and the emergence of the poetic as a new experiential goal; moreover,

---

[17] Brown, "The Prosperous Wonder Worker," in Boerner & Johnson, eds., passim.

[18] Emrich, in Arndt-Hamlin, ed., pp. 587ff.

[19] Ulrich Maché, "Goethes Faust als Plutus und Dichter," *Jahrbuch des Freien Deutschen Hochstifts* (1975), pp. 184ff.

[20] See especially pp. 53-62 of the ch. "Der Helena-Akt" in Mommsen's *Natur- und Fabelreich in "Faust II."* In a ch. on "Goethes 'Helena'" (pp. 1-43) in *Esoterik bei Goethe* (Tübingen: Niemeyer, 1980), Joseph Strelka explores in fascinating detail the mystagogic complexity of this symbolic figure as a fusion of ancient Greco-Egyptian, neo-Platonic, gnostic, Christian, Sufi, alchemical, theosophical, Baroque, and Romantic elements.

since the action is often explicitly called a *play* in Part II, we sense the larger shift from subjective impulse, based on self-assertion, toward objectivity, based on comprehension. It is a necessary paradox that – on the authorial plane – imagination enables this kind of objectivity. *Faust I* indeed takes place in outline as if it is a story of tragic will, and by and large in *Faust I* the older Goethe avoids meddling too often in the particular truth of that mode of Faustian striving while we are observing it. Part II, in contrast, not only lends substance to the personal, social, historical, cultural, poetological, and metaphysical dimensions suggested by the introductory "Dedication," "Prelude in the Theater," and "Prologue in Heaven" introducing Part I; but as the resolving sequel, Part II conditions, supersedes, and stands in intensifying polarity as a mirror to the experience of Part I.

Herman Meyer rightly sees in Part II, Act I, in the remarks by spectators and humorous comments by Mephisto, who is supervising the dim-lit show of the botched conjuration of Helen in the scene "Hall of Chivalry," something "akin to 'romantic irony'."[21] Goethe's irony everywhere specifically joins the thematics of doubleness and theater. When Mephisto puts the paper money with the Emperor's replicated signature into circulation in the scene "Pleasure Garden," this counterfeiting of real money duplicates socially Faust's individual pact with the devil and represents the erosion of "the relation of word to sense, of text to substance, of medium to essence." It also raises the question: how reliable is the theatrical medium in which Helena will soon be embodied? In the scene "Dark Gallery," nonetheless, we detect a serious counter-movement to this tug toward dissolution in seductive fantasies. As newly appointed master of the revels, Faust is eager to conjure Helen and Paris for the Emperor to see. Mephisto first disparagingly worries about trifling with such alien pagan phantoms, but then "like the mystagogue in chief" (6249) Mephisto dispatches Faust, armed with a "key" (6258) as Hermetic wand, on the far more important, deeper mythological journey into boundless cosmic vacancy, to the Mothers. Faust's "descent" (through a stage trap door) parallels the many visits by heroes to another realm. Most especially it recalls that of Aeneas who in Book IV of Virgil's *Aeneid* ambiguously returns to the world through the gate of ivory.

Thematically, this mythological-psychological-cosmological trip by Faust to where all formed being emerges, to "Formation, transformation, The eternal mind's eternal recreation" (6287f.), resembles the penetration into the trinitarian mysteries of generation out of the primordially virginal feminine, such as is sung in Canto X, "The Marvels," of Giambattista Marino's Baroque cosmic epic *Adone*. The trip – initially to somewhere still out of our sight in the ordinary theater space of the 1800s – prepares us for what poetry at last enables us to visualize: Faust's later mythological journeying into fabled archaic realms and his quest for a psychic cure in Act II. But ambiguously, in the transitional scene "Brightly Lit Ballrooms," while Faust's daring search is invisibly underway, Mephisto clearly is in charge of the show.

In the rapidly following scene "Hall of Chivalry," Mephisto "prompts" the court's perception of the life-images which Faust, who hovers into view, craves to materialize as a "bold magician" (6436) – Goethe's original term was "bold poet." It goes without saying that the onlooking ladies of the Renaissance court are ecstatic over conjured Paris, the men over Helen. Faust is intoxicated by his new "priesthood" (6491), i.e., poetry. Falling into frenzied adoration – "out of part" (6501), so Mephisto rebukes from his prompter's box – Faust causes the magic show to explode by presuming to rescue and possess Helena "doubly" (6557), that is, to bring back as real what exists only as a

[21] Herman Meyer, *Diese sehr ernsten Scherze* (Heidelberg: Stiehm, 1970); English excerpt in Arndt-Hamlin, ed., pp. 603-15.

wraith of history. Even while whetting our appetite with the conjuration, Act I demonstrates the wrong way to regain Helen. Faust tries to embrace her ghost passionately, a lapse into his old character; supreme beauty, however, cannot be seized by force. Besides, as Mommsen argues, Helena is a fusion of mythic creatures old and new, Eastern and Western, not a sentimental *dramatis persona*. Such a reconstructed mythologeme perfectly suits Romantic as well as Goethean requirements.

The daring contrast actually staged in Act II is that Faust is first shown dreaming and then he realizes the Helen myth symbolically as a poetic recollection that unfolds before our eyes. We enter, as it were, voyeuristically into his dream. In Act II's opening scene "Gothic Chamber," Mephisto reveals Faust to be asleep and takes pleasure in sporting again with the learned world they have left so far behind, a world where Doctor Wagner has meanwhile risen to be the ruling authority and new-fashioned arrogant younger studentdom (modelled on the Storm-and-Stress/Romantic generations) struts. In the scene set in the alchemical "Laboratory" (6819ff.), a creature quite unlike Mephisto, though he also emerges out of the fog-shrouded medieval North, the incubated Renaissance brainchild Homuculus proves capable of seeing the vision that vies for birth in the mind of the bereft Northern European. It is a Faust love-sick for antiquity who dreams the myth of Leda and the Swan, the engendering of Helena. Although on one level Mephisto manages the enchantment, on another level Homunculus must drag the reluctant demon off southeastward to the strangeness of archaic Greece. Goethe lets us witness the subplot, the story of the intermediary figure Homunculus, who serves as a reminder of the distance gained in the drama from the more outwardly striving intellect of the North, a force which heedlessly plunged into experience in Part I, but now is ill as a consequence of incomplete development and the perils of reflection.

The title of the sequence of scenes, "Classical Walpurgis Night," is an ironic inversion corresponding to the bizarre involvement of Northern figures in the ancient South, seen on stage. This sequence turns the tables, since ordinarily the South is contained as a cultural notion "in the North," by virtue of European historical destiny. Faust is allowed to walk back into his own dream, while Homunculus guides Mephisto into its contents. In the scary tenebrae of the "Pharsalian Fields," on the upper Peneios, Mephisto gropes comically amidst Egypto-Grecian monsters, the gryphons, sphinxes, and sirens. These are preclassical manifestations of aspects of the archetypal feminine; later the arrival of Galatea will confirm the glorious classical moment. In the measure that the character Faust deals in illusions and dreams in Part II of his "Tragedy," he gravitates toward saying "yes" to his world, in contrast to the "no" of the restless philosopher of Part I. With the "Classical Walpurgis Night," we reach the very soil of poetry, a realm Faust will "seriously and thoroughly research" (7079). The episode ostentates an anachronistic title that links the ages.

Correspondingly, Mephisto assumes new functions in Part II marking him as the non- or anti-classical principle. This counterforce was present at the dawn of time and is both pre- and post-classical in historical-developmental terms, from Goethe's modern perspective. For example, in the mask of Phorkyas which Mephisto assumes as protective cover in Act II and retains in Act III, the modern devil can sense and grudgingly appreciate deep patterns in all human experience, including the archaic layer beneath Greek civilization. Whereas he mocked Faust's feelings in Part I, now he defends "romantic" attitudes in Part II. Both linear recapitulation and parallelism occur: our whole perception of evil changes with the shift from the Christian North to the pagan South, and this change occurs in conjunction with the subdrama of Homunculus. He is at first artificial, a perceiving intellect, but merely spiritual potential that lacks organic connection; but contact with the an-

cient Greek sense of vitality and beauty galvanizes his desire for full incarnation – a moment symbolized in his erotic surrender to the radiance of Galatea ("Inlets of the Aegean Sea," 8424-487).

Whether they be "dreams" or "memories" (7275), the "incomparable shapes" which Faust
glimpses on the lower Peneois (7250ff.) are witnessed lyrically in a way that anticipates the self-ref-
erential Modernist imagination of Mallarmé in "L'Après-midi d'un faune" and of Yeats in "Leda
and the Swan." As Faust rides on the back of the wise teacher, the centaur Chiron, he can put ardent
questions about mythological figures immediately to a representative of that lost world. Faust openly mythologizes within his own dream *while* he is dreaming it. Recognizing his dire sickness, carefully admonishing him about his weaknesses, and hinting at the tragic outcome for any short-lived
attempt to repossess the lost past, Chiron ultimately brings Faust to Manto, the priestess who
presides at Apollo's temple and can conduct him deeper to beg Persephone's intercession as did
Orpheus. By making Manto into a daughter of the healer Aesculapius (son of Apollo), instead of the
seer Tereisias, Goethe in effect invents and combines his own mythic elements and thereby proves
his own point about poetic freedom – and, we could add, also happens to realize the Romantic aspiration of "neomythic" creation.

Like a hero in a magical fairytale, Faust has progressed past many threats and seductions in his
quest. Meanwhile the scene reverts to the upper Peneios (7495ff.) and continues to shift rapidly in a
way that today we would associate with such cinematic techniques as cross-cutting. Of course,
Goethe built these pulsations up imaginatively out of the resources of the Baroque illusionistic
theater and Oriental fantasy. The mythological creatures and divinities talk about their own world
and contend in a complex flux of rhythms that prepare for the major revelation in the scene "Rocky
Inlets of the Aegean Sea." The archaic landscape of Greek myth and of the earliest cosmological
theorizing comes into view with lyrical intensity. Yet, ironically, Mephisto, growing ever more
accustomed to things ancient, wanders back into sight in Faust's dream, commenting, comparing
things to his North, acting as interlocutor for the rival thinkers Thales, the pre-Socratic speculator
(who holds the Neptunist view of geological change and evolution), and Anaxagoras, the "materialist" philosopher (who holds the Vulcanist view). "Old Chaos' beloved son" (8027), Mephisto, can
momentarily disappear by discovering his own hermaphroditic kinship to the Phorcyads, and it
exactly suits his theatrical proclivities to adopt the grotesque one eye and tooth the three sisters
must share. Mommsen also argues convincingly that this is another instance where Goethe spins an
underground network of connections. Through the Phorcyads, Mephisto is obliquely associated with
the Perseus role, which he expressly pointed to in the "Walpurgis Night" of Part I when he called
the beheaded Gretchen a "magic image, [...] lifeless, an idol" (4190).[22] He must now secretly
retrieve dead Helena from pagan Hades which, like Dante, Goethe treats as analoguous to Christian
Hell.

Just as complicated in Act II is the contrastive parallelism between the story of Faust and the
subplot of Homunculus.[23] A clairvoyant entelechy not yet encumbured and darkened by incarnation,
Homunculus expresses the urge toward participation in the realm of contingency, and his pathway
countervails that of Faust who exits from the human form and regains clarity in "Mountain Gorges."
Homunculus' characteristic flame motif (masculine element) and transformation are associated with

---

[22] See especially the ch. "Mephistopheles als neuer Perseus" in Mommsen, *Natur- und Fabelreich*, p. 159-67.
[23] Eppelsheimer treats the structural principle of doubleness in Goethe's *Faust* as integral to a modern "mystery play."
Into its wonders the poet-magician, as a mature mediator, expressly draws the spectators (p. 57).

Eros. Important is that he is ready to reject the opportunity to rule over pygmies and other primitive beings on the upper Peneios and is attracted toward becoming a human being in the mode of Greek humanity. His most important guide, Proteus, demonstrates all meaningful transformations up the evolutionary scale (8237ff.). In the triumphant Aegean Sea episode, which Goethe depicts with all the radiance of the most inspired Renaissance painters of such mythological subjects, Homunculus becomes organic in marrying the waters (feminine element) upon sight of beauteous Galatea, who rides Aphrodite's shell throne as her representative.

This neo-Platonic epiphany gathers the multiple threads of mythological complexes (e.g., the Pygmalion story) cultivated by Renaissance poets and passed down to the eighteenth century. On one level, the movement and devotion of Homunculus to Galatea and Nature parallels that of Faust to Helena and Art – if we regard these as two interlaced explorations of antiquity. On another level, however, the wayfaring of Homunculus within *Faust, eine Tragödie* is a play-within-a-play with ironic double import. For it ends in a glorious celebration in counterpoint to Faust's tragedy, the tragedy of being in the human condition. And it demonstrates the greater truth of Nature, as against Art; yet this truth, too, paradoxically is being revealed through Art. At the same time, the progress of Homunculus, moving past lower aspects of being (e.g., the Kabiri and Telchinen) toward the full incarnation of Nature witnessed in Galatea, presages the turning of Faust's entelechy toward the supreme archetype embodied at the end of the play in the Queen of Heaven.[24] This paean to the restored synthesis of the four elements in Act II, brought about by Homunculus' baptism-wedding, anticipates the fourfold "Chorus Mysticus" of Act V.

III

If we accept that in Acts I through III of Part II, Goethe accommodated a wealth of ancient and Christian motifs to patterns he found in the stories told by Scheherazade, this departure into the poetically liberating realm of Oriental fable accomplished brilliantly in practice, not just in theory, what many Romantics were suggesting: the creation of a self-reflexive drama in which the normal boundaries of the theater would be dissolved by poetic imagination. When the persistent search for buried treasure is fulfilled, the paired Faust and Homunculus arrive in two contrasted encounters at perception of the priceless essence of Greece. The play arrives at classical vision. The climax of the Helena sequence of Acts I through III results in an ascension to "High Mountains," as the opening scene of Act IV is named. Faust emerges in Act IV as "cured" by the encounter. But Act IV then brings many lessons and recognitions in the field of representative history. As on stage the "empire" disintegrates from within, we witness how all realms dependent on illusions must collapse.

Acts IV and V appear to take place in the turbulent Renaissance-Reformation past, but they also allude to the actual disorders and dislocations of the Napoleonic era and its aftermath, and as Mommsen has so thoroughly demonstrated, *Faust II*, especially in the grim lessons of Act IV, con-

---

[24] For a more detailed examination of the arrival at the Apollonian stage of development in the evolution out of the mythological into the historical age, celebrated in the Aegean Sea episode, consult Alan P. Cottrell, "The Sun of Apollo: Reflections Prompted by Goethe's Telchines of Rhodes," in *Herkommen und Erneuerung: Essays für Oskar Seidlin*, ed. Gerald Gillespie and Edgar Lohner (Tübingen: Niemeyer, 1976), pp. 93-102. Also the chs. "Homunculus' Weg zum naturhaften Sein," "Homunculus und Helena," and "Die 'Klassische Walpurgisnacht' der 3. Teil der *Italienischen Reise*," in Mommsen, *Natur- und Fabelreich*, pp. 168-235.

stitutes Goethe's political testament.[25] As Brown has shown, the parodic allusions to Milton and Byron in the opening of Act IV underscore that here we are in the fallen realm of Christian culture, far removed from the classical ideal.[26] Faust now appears to function in a demythologized nature whose loss of its ancient magic has been brought about by the "modern" enlightened scientific mind. Faust will still, symbolically, try to manage his world and will commit grave offenses in so trying in Act V, before the reconfirmation of the ascension of his entelechy. The fore-enactment of ascension occurs meanwhile in the opening of Act IV, when borne aloft by the garments of the vanished wraith Helena, Faust perceives the cloudlike metamorphosing allure of the feminine and remembers the dawn of that attraction in Gretchen.[27] His words anticipate the message of the "Chorus Mysticus":

> Täuscht mich ein entzückend Bild
> Als jugenderstes, längstentbehrtes höchstes Gut?
> Des tiefsten Herzens frühste Schätze quellen auf:
> Aurorens Liebe, leichten Schwung bezeichnets mir,
> Den schnellempfundnen, ersten, kaum verstandnen Blick,
> Der, festgehalten, überglänzte jeden Schatz.
> Wie Seelenschönheit steigert sich die holde Form,
> Löst sich nicht auf, erhebt sich in den Äther hin
> Und zieht das Beste meines Innern mit sich fort.
> (10058-10066)

> (Am I deceived by an enchanting shape,
> As of long-lost, most cherished boon of earliest youth?
> The inmost heart's primordial treasures rise again,
> Aurora's love, winged impetus it means to me,
> The swiftly felt, first, scarcely comprehended glance,
> That, caught and held, outglittered any gem.
> Like beauty of the soul, the lovely image is enhanced
> And, undissolving, wafts aloft into the ether,
> Drawing away with it the best my soul contains.)
> (WA 10058-10066)

This entrance into the denouement and catastrophe of Part II immediately reasserts that what we are witnessing is symbolic drama and that we, too, must rise to the new level attained through the trials and rites of passage in the search for Helena.

Faust instructs Helena in speaking in verse (9365ff.) in the scene "Inner Courtyard of a Castle" of Act III, because – on the allegorical plane – the "ancient" will return in whatever form "modern"

[25] See G.C.L. Schuchard, "Julirevolution, St. Simonismus und die Faustpartien von 1831," *Zeitschrift fur deutsche Philologie*, 60 (1935), 240-74, 362-84; and "Fausts 'Vorschau' im Lichte von Schillers ästhetischen Briefen," *Journal of English and Germanic Philology*, 48 (1949), 533-42. Katharina Mommsen, "*Faust II* als politisches Vermächtnis des Staatsmannes Goethe," *Jahrbuch des Freien deutschen Hochstifts* (1989), 1-36, meticulously identifies the motifs in the play behind which Goethe veiled his own experiences and insights as a statesman and politician, including the conflicts surrounding his friendship with Carl August and his disappointments in the baleful failures of this ruler.
[26] Brown, *Goethe's "Faust": The German Tragedy*, pp. 216-30.
[27] Strelka points to the subtle distinction between the higher "veil" of Helena as divine Beauty and Sophia, on which Faust floats upward, and the ordinary exuvia of poetry manifested in his son Euphorion (p. 25).

human nature imposes in its reshaping of the past. The story of Euphorion, the son of Faust and Helena, in "Arcadia" is a poetic fairytale clearly removed from any semblance of ordinary dramatic mimesis, openly conflating the myths of Hermes and Icarus, and allegorizing the foibles and excesses of Romanticism. Euphorion's parabolic flight and plunge exhibit the lack of moderation inherited from Faust. Faust, a modern Paris and Orpheus, cannot keep the conditions imposed by Persephone, and so the idyll on a fragile, circumscribed poetic territory is disrupted by his bound-less craving for happiness. When Helena and Euphorion vanish back into the underworld, left behind are the emblems of poetic work in the form of their garments and the lyre. This allegorized self-unmasking of the poet as an earthbound magician is an important step, because its positive meaning resides in the accomplished poetic work which ultimately does raise the poet. The con-struction of cultural memory also qualitatively alters our world, even though we are returned to the grim actuality of history (then and now) when the vision dissolves.

This motif of spiritual elevation has recurred over the centuries. The medieval mystics knew the mountain top as the apex of the soul where it met the godhead; and the father of modern poetry, Petrarch, and others since have been on the high mountain where Faust finds himself momentarily at the start of Act IV. In the poem "Ad Divam Virginem in silva quietus," Germany's great Latin lyricist of the late Renaissance, Jacob Balde, specifically felt the presence of the divine feminine at the summit where there reigns the beatific peace heard later in Goethe's poem "Über allen Gipfeln." In Acts IV and V we come down from the summit temporarily with Faust into the perils of histori-cal and existential reality. The portrayal of internecine warfare springing from wrong policy and moral weakness, too, is a familiar subject-matter inherited from Renaissance and Baroque drama that lives on into Modernism. By typological reduction of plays like Calderón's *La vida es sueño*, Alfred Jarry's *Ubu roi* pushes the genre into the realm of the absurd, while Hofmannsthal's *Der Turm* maintains the somber moral tone.

Goethe already distinctly annouces his purpose, in the climax of Act III. It is to allow this play to ascend to celestial precincts. Yet despite the daring invocation of the highest Catholic symbol, the Virgin Mother, Goethe's "tragedy" scarcely resembles a traditional Christian miracle play; and although Faust acts in a terrestial show under the Lord's aegis, Goethe's authorial irony outstrips the Calderonian model revered by the Romantics. The operatic and liturgical traits of Faust's "apo-theosis" are unabashedly a distillation of multiple traditions in Western literary, musical, and plastic art, presented in joyful openness by a benign poetic mind. The aura of the older Shakespeare glows in these sacramental trappings and in the firm but gentle consciousness of the playwright as magi-cian. This synthesis which reinstates so much – for example, the vision of Dante in the *Paradiso* – more than satisfies the loftiest requirements of Romantic irony.

If a central subject of *Faust II* is the recovery of a vital Classicism, we may characterize Goethe as grappling, like his eighteenth-century predecessors Winckelmann and Wieland, with a dream that Nietzsche reformulated in the later nineteenth century. But, unlike Nietzsche, Goethe is not diminished by acrimony or incomprehension of the feminine. Rather, in Goethe, we observe a turn-ing away from the dissatisfactions of Christianity to an idealization of Greek civilization and to a liberating mode of Oriental fantasy, but distanced from Romanticism proper. The conception of *Faust II* may well have been tempered by Goethe's sense of a favorite Indian play, Kalidasa's *Sha-kuntala*. By the start of the nineteenth century this work was celebrated throughout Western Europe as in India as an epitome of Hindu symbolic drama for the way it moves onto heights where mortals encounter the divine. *Shakuntala* achieves the most prized sentiment or *santa rasa*, a feeling of peace, serenity, and oneness, a transcendental, ineffable joy.[28] Hindu aesthetics, as codified by Bharata, defined the highest drama as "the imitation or representation of conditions or situations," so as to reestablish the harmony of the eight fundamental sentiments, not to purge the spectators.[29] Goethe may have welcomed such hints on circumventing undesirable implications of the Aristotelian teleological imperative in Western drama and of the Judaeo-Christian moral choices which determine the tragic or damned as against the happy or saved condition. As Lal states, "In the Hindu worldview [of *Shakuntala*], the chief sin being ignorance, *rasa* became a form of enlightenment through participation in esthetic ritual."

The Romantic canonization of the great Baroque playwrights created a bridge for reaching nineteenth-century contemporaries through symbolic drama. The delayed reception of Schopenhauer's seminal treatise *The World as Will and Idea* helped to reconfirm respect for symbolic, as against realistic, works in the later nineteenth century. Schopenhauer's ranking of tragedy as the supreme form in which the mind rises above the life-force or "will" and experiences sympathy with all life, and his assertion of a degree of spiritual affinity with Hindu and Buddhistic wisdom on the part of Shakespeare and Calderón, were to reinforce this tendency after Goethe's death. Goethe was independently attracted toward a drama of ultimate reconciliation, as we can see in a fairly late reflection, his "Gleaning on Aristotle's *Poetics*," published in 1827 in his journal *Kunst und Altertum* (Art and Antiquity), reinterpreting the perennial question what is meant by catharsis in terms of atonement, expiation, and reconciliation rather than pity. Aristotle, writes Goethe, "understands by catharis this reconciliatory rounding off which actually is required of all drama, indeed even of all poetic works." In Goethe's view, the larger pattern of the Greek trilogy serves this very purpose, and *Oedipus at Colonus* exemplifies the highest kind of "catharisis" when the wretched criminal "nonetheless at last, still expiating, and yet reconciled, a tutelary spirit who dispenses blessings to a land and merits his own worship by sacrifices, is uplifted as kindred to the gods."[30]

It is not far-fetched to think of a resemblance to Oedipus being translated from the grove of the Furies outside Athens, when we observe how in approaching death the blinded Faust, too, despite his transgressions, acquires vatic stature and enters into a numinous realm. This is not a primary identification, but a general kinship with threatened blind fools who plumb the depths of human nature; for example, Lear. Goethe indeed felt a repugnance for the gloomy archaic vestiges of the Oedipus story that made it unsuitable for his purposes. Goethe did not have to search far afield from his own predilections to find an analogy for the movement of the Sophoclean trilogy from fateful error, over a curse against life, toward a vatic promise and blessing, and the moral healing exempli-

---

[28] Without the benefit of knowing Mommsen's work (which should be applied as corrective), Ekbert Faas argues the spiritual affinities and broad resemblances in "*Faust* and *Sancontola*," *Comparative Literature*, 31 (1979), 367-91.

[29] On the principles of Sanskrit dramaturgy, see P. Lal, *Great Sanskrit Plays in New English Transcreations* (New York: New Directions, 1964), general Introduction (pp. xi-xx) and Preface to *Shakuntula* (pp. 3-10).

[30] Goethe, "Nachlese zu Aristoteles' Poetik," Berliner Ausgabe, XVIII, pp. 121-25. The two more immediately relevant passages read: "[Aristoteles] versteht unter Katharsis diese aussöhnende Abrundung, welche eigentlich von allem Drama, ja sogar von allen poetischen Werken gefordert wird." "Ferner bemerken wir, daß die Griechen ihre Trilogie zu solchem Zwecke benutzt: denn es gibt wohl keine höhere Katharsis als *Der Ödipus von Colonus*, wo ein halbschuldiger Verbrecher, ein Mann, der durch dämonische Konstitution, durch eine düstere Heftigkeit seines Daseins, gerade bei der Großheit seines Charakters, durch immerfort übereilte Tatausübung den ewig unerforschlichen, unbegreiflich folgerechten Gewalten in die Hände rennt, sich selbst und die seinigen in das tiefste, unherstellbarste Elend stürzt und doch zuletzt noch aussöhnend ausgesöhnt und zum Verwandten der Götter, als segnender Schutzgeist eines Landes eines eignen Opferdienstes wert, erhoben wird."

fied in the daughter Antigone. In the ensemble of Parts I and II, as well as internally in Part II, Goethe may well be recapitulating a pattern readily noticed in Shakespeare's later works, once we regard them as an interconnected series of efforts.[31] In *Cymbeline, The Winter's Tale,* and *The Tempest,* we see the sweet hope of forgiveness and acceptance, the sacramental rectification of wrong done, the healing of a divorce from the feminine, the reconcilement effected through the daughter or granddaughter. It is not necessary to confirm this speculation in order to grasp how the total play *Faust* moves from its predominantly masculine, action-oriented opening moment of Part I to its predominantly feminine, contemplative outcome at the end of Part II.

Hans Eichner has emphasized that, in Goethe's writings after settling in Weimar, the poet tended to portray the mode of action as male and the mode of purity as female (e.g., in the figures Iphigenie, Natalie, Ottilie, and Makarie). Hence Eichner regards the miracle at the end of *Faust* to be, in artistic terms, indeed a miracle: Goethe unifies the Virgin and Mother through his magisterial reappreciation of the Catholic archetype Mary.[32] Emrich characterizes the ending as a reversion to the Christian idea of "grace," divine aid. However, if we respect Goethe's post-Christian thinking, in his case the miracle of a rebirth of classical being can be linked directly to his approbation of the feminine – as a "yes" to the tragic conditions which *are* the conditions of life.

Such a conclusion does not conflict with the view that *Faust* is "a tragedy of the will to will" or that the play, as such, in Benjamin Bennett's formulation, "reminds of the essay 'Shakespeare und kein Ende'," where Goethe directly associated "the concept of will with the idea of a union of classical and Romantic." In this sense *Faust* "is an attempt to out Shakespeare," to be more modern than Shakespeare in the tragic understanding of man's will to will.[33] Eudo Mason earlier linked Goethe's view of Shakespeare in 1771 to his invention of the contrast in *Faust I* between the sign of the "Makrokosmos" (contemplative vision, acceptance of the whole, etc.) and that of the "Erdgeist" (activity, individual will, direct participation in a messy natural world).[34] The will leads to transgression; however, Goethe's representative experiencer, Faust, does not exit in revulsion over the real hurt in existence, as the trauma of Part I might make us expect. Instead, the symbolic Faust progresses toward that other aspect of his own being as a creature of life. In the miracle of the feminine through which life is channeled, he finds life, including the life of the spirit, its eternally potential rebirth.

A century separates the "yes" spoken in *Faust* and Goethe's capacity to behold all of myth as in a single moment from the "yes" spoken in *Ulysses* and the capacity reclaimed by Joyce in a

---

[31] Double, triple, or multiple involution of artistic rivalries within a work is a common phenomenon in modernism, but rather than inventing it, the modernists found this kind of reception as a structural feature in certain of their crucial antecedents. In an essay entitled "Afterthoughts of Hamlet: Goethe's Wilhelm, Joyce's Stephen" (in *Comparative Literary History as Discourse: In Honor of Anna Balakian,* ed. Mario Valdés, Daniel Javitch, and A. Owen Aldridge [Berne, New York, Frankfurt a.M., Paris: Lang, 1992], pp. 285-301), I have examined the case of Joyce's reception of Shakespeare (in part) via Goethe as an earlier receptor. Goethe anticipated Joyce in being able to incorporate a perceived lifetime pattern of Shakespeare's development in *Wilhelm Meisters Lehrjahre* as a thematic guide for interpreting the life pattern of Wilhelm. This grand outline was attractive enough to capture the attention of Joyce, who conflated the Goethean insights with other later attempts, such as Mallarmé's and Freud's, to correlate Shakespeare's life and works. It only stands to reason that Goethe could and would have woven elements of a presumed pattern pertaining to deeper truths of human development into the career of his symbolic protagonist Faust.

[32] Hans Eichner, "The Eternal Feminine: An Aspect of Goethe's Ethics," *Transactions of the Royal Society of Canada,* series 4, vol. 9 (1971), 235-44; in Arndt-Hamlin, ed., pp. 615-24.

[33] Benjamin Bennett, "The Classical, the Romantic, and the Tragic in Part Two of Goethe's *Faust,*" *Studies in Romanticism,* 19 (1980), pp. 549-50.

[34] Eudo C. Mason, "The Erdgeist and Mephisto," in *Goethe's "Faust": Its Genesis and Purport* (Berkeley: Univ. of California Press, 1967), pp. 119-65; excerpt in Arndt-Hamlin, ed., pp. 484-504.

modernist love-hate relationship with Christian civilization. Because of intervening writers like the dramatists Krasiński, Madách, and Ibsen and humoristic-encyclopedic novelists like Joyce and Mann, the daunting complexities of Goethe no longer seem so unfamiliar. But the new scope for dramatic literature that Goethe demonstrated still seems overwhelming, insofar as by its concrete example *Faust* exhibited how a play could be opened generically to become an all-embracing kind of superdiscourse.[35] In a later chaper, Martin Esslin examines the appearance of attempts to achieve such "cosmic" inclusiveness. Habent sua fata libelli: To the extent that the reception of *Faust* made its structure into an international phenomenon characteristic of Romanticism, Goethe belongs as a coopted member in the supreme Romantic pantheon.

---

[35] In its radical positing of itself as fiction, Goethe's *Faust* (although not cited as an example) fits Paul de Man's notion of a special kind of "romantic" consciousness; that is, "literature, [...] the only form of language free from the fallacy of unmediated expression. [...] The self-reflecting mirror-effect by means of which a work of fiction asserts, by its very existence, its separation from empirical reality, its divergence, as a sign, from a meaning that depends for its existence on the constitutive activity of this sign, characterizes the work of literature in its essence." (*Blindness and Insight: Essays in the Rhetoric of Contemporary Criticism* [New York: Oxford Univ. Press, 1971], pp. 17ff.) In a review-article, "'Du ahnungsloser Engel, Du!'! Some Current Views of Goethe's *Faust*," *German Life and Letters*, 36 (1982-83), 116-47, Nicholas Boyle poses, without venturing to answer, the "immense" question: "[...] how did it come about that the [essentially elitist] intellectual world of the founders of modern Anglo-American literature was so closely parallel to the intellectual world of classical and romantic Weimar and Jena, of which those very modernists knew, and wished to know, so little?" (p. 133). One part of the answer, that the Symbolist writers and critics served as an important bridge, was already apparent from monographic studies such as Werner Vordtriede's *Novalis und die französischen Symbolisten* (Stuttgart: Metzler, 1963).

VIRGIL NEMOIANU

ROMANTIC IRONY AND BIEDERMEIER TRAGICOMEDY

In the decades after the Congress of Vienna, tragicomedy experienced a revival. This in itself is a significant fact, since there are only two other periods in Western literature in which tragicomedy is frequent. One of them is the Baroque period (the end of the sixteenth and the beginning of the seventeenth century) particularly in England, but also elsewhere. The other is the twentieth century, particularly after World War II (Beckett, Ionesco, Dürrenmatt, and others are all devotees of tragicomedy). The third period is the later phase of Romanticism. However, this fact is often ignored or overlooked. Van Tieghem and other historians of European Romanticism do not even mention it; they tend to place tragicomic works under the headings of poetic and lyrical comedy, or satire, or historical drama.

I want to list some of the more prominent works relevant to the tragicomic experience, to analyze briefly some examples taken from the works of Musset, Büchner, and Słowacki, and then to offer two explanations. One is that in my opinion the correct background for an understanding of this flowering of tragicomedy is the decline of Romantic irony, the feeling that its possibilities were exhausted and its claims too large – this I would like to call the secularization of irony. The second is that in itself the contemporary growth of tragicomedy was connected with a number of other literary and sociocultural phenomena, in short, that it was a fitting expression of the European Biedermeier, the later phase of European Romanticism.

I

Although the theoretical strictures of Neoclassicism in Europe during the later seventeenth century and the eighteenth century banned generic mixtures, they were not too faithfully adhered to. There was always a folk theater that made free with the rules, and the advent of the bourgeois drama and the *comédie larmoyante* strengthened it. Goldoni and the *commedia dell'arte* provided an alternative to the tradition of Neoclassicism. The memory of Shakespeare and of his Jacobean contemporaries never entirely faded in England and, indeed, the Shakespearean revival of the last third of the eighteenth century affected not only England, but much of the Continent. It gave considerable encouragement to those who felt in need of an authority for the mixture of tragic and comic features or for other departures from Neoclassic rules. Finally there was embedded in the Enlightenment itself an ironic and parodic strain which, from Pope to Voltaire to Wieland, provided ammunition for tragicomic experimentation.

Nevertheless, all these separate phenomena can be said to be variables relating to an invariant or constant hub, namely the body of Neoclassical doctrine with its philosophical underpinnings.

Their meaning and their sociocultural weight is modified contextually by the presence of a firm referential level. Once the philosophical change of an emerging Romantic idealism and the cultural changes that accompanied the crumbling of the old order removed that level, all kinds of experimentation acquired a different significance. Less noticed by literary historians, but significant nevertheless, were the various experiments in tragicomedy from the 1780s to the 1820s. Some of these deserve attention, although I will not attempt anything like a complete presentation, but merely suggest the pervasiveness of the phenomenon.

One of the first to experiment with generic combinations was Nepomucène Lemercier (1771-1840) who got in trouble with the censorship of many successive regimes. His *Plaute, ou comédie latine* (Plautus, a Latin Comedy, 1808) is just a mildly irreverent picture of the Latin classic, but Lemercier found it necessary to strengthen his defenses by a prologue in verse in which Mercure and Thalie converse, as well as by a preface in prose containing a discussion between himself and a critic. In this dialog Lemercier suggests that he is struggling to achieve a fusion of genres. In a note attached to *Christophe Colomb* (1809) Lemercier complains of the "difficulté qui se trouve à unir le comique au pathétique" (difficulty in combining comic elements with pathos). The play itself is not successful, and one must assume that Lemercier and his audience found a source of laughter in the tension between the greatness of Columbus's achievement and the sweaty efforts and anxieties that accompanied the preparation for the expedition.

Lemercier was rather proud of having initiated the "comédie historique."[1] In *Richelieu, ou la journée des dupes* (?1804) the Cardinal is shown eavesdropping behind closed doors, the bungling plot of France's high nobility is frustrated by the accidental interference of an innocent commoner, and King Louis is shown whining for guidance and terrified by his own lack of decisive opinions. The most successful experiment in this manner was *Pinto, ou la journée d'une conspiration* published a little earlier, in 1798. The earlier editions described it variously as "drama" and "comedy"; the play presents the revolt which in 1640 liberated Portugal from 60 years of Spanish rule. Pinto Ribeiro, the chief administrator of the affairs of the duke of Bragança (who became king of Portugal upon the happy outcome of the conspiratorial movement) is shown to have been, like Beaumarchais's Figaro, the clever moving force behind the high figures of church and nobility. Although Lemercier deleted the death of Vasconcellos, the Spanish ministerial agent, from Act V in later versions of the play, there is no question that a historical act of grave import is shown to be determined and controlled by random facts and droll occurrences, thus producing comic effects.[2]

We are not sure whether Victor Hugo's later sonorous proclamation of the rights of tragicomic mixture was actually influenced by the reading of Lemercier, but it certainly was facilitated by the existence of his works and those of others.[3] After the "Preface" to *Cromwell* the dispute was openly aired in France, but even before its publication, different kinds and proportions of generic mixture were becoming more frequent outside France.

---

[1] However, this demystifying manner has among its possible predecessors works as varied as those of Plautus, Molière (*Amphitryon*), Corneille (*Nicomède*), Rotrou, and others. Scribe, Bernard Shaw, and Anouilh are among the later masters of this subgenre.

[2] Perhaps the most intriguing work of this prolific and bizarre author is *La Panhypocrisiade, ou le spectacle infernal du seizième siècle* (An Epic on Universal Hypocrisy, or the Hellish Image of the Sixteenth Century, 1819), which is described by Lemercier himself as an epic comedy in 16 cantos; it may have been inspired by Milton, but it is in many ways (not least through the images of dark anarchy gaining universal power which conclude it) close to Pope's *Dunciad*. This work confirms that Lemercier was constantly preoccupied with the tragicomic as a problem, irrespective of the medium.

[3] "Preface" to *Cromwell* in Victor Hugo, *Oeuvres complètes* (Paris: Hetzel & Quantin, 1881), I, 17, 23, 49, 69.

Thus Kleist's *Prinz Friedrich von Homburg* contains more than a touch of the comic and of irony in the frame of a grave action; his *Der zerbrochene Krug* (The Broken Ewer) is a moody and somewhat heavy comedy in the tradition of Shakespeare's *Measure for Measure*; and, like Molière, Kleist wrote an *Amphytrion*. The plays of Tieck with their emphasis on the absurd burlesque imply and sometimes explicitly posit a reversal of the tragic and the serious. The Dane Adam Oehlenschläger (1770-1850) wrote a dramatization of the Aladdin material (1805) in which under the veneer of the fairytale the serious and the amusing intermingle freely. The German popular theater of the day, like its French counterpart, chose to look at the action from a vantage point which minimized the distance between the tragic and the comic. The works of Wilhelm Iffland (1759-1814) for instance can be shown to be based upon the teachings of Lessing, Diderot, and Mercier, thoroughly adapted for the consumption of a wider audience.[4] Kotzebue (1761-1819) chose in his plays, for which *Menschenhaß und Reue* (Misanthropy and Regret, 1790) might stand as a prototype, a rather constant combination of sentimentality, sensationalism, and laughter. In Kotzebue, Iffland, and others the tragic and the comic are toned down until they become quite easily compatible. Christian Dietrich Grabbe (1801-36) probably learned from all these techniques and used them with more aesthetic sophistication. In his historical plays such as *Hannibal* (1835) or *Napoleon* (1831) he resorts to many of the demystifying or even ironic techniques that he had found already in use by the time he started writing, while his *Aschenbrödel* (Cinderella, 1835) applies a similar approach in the frame of the fairy-story. *Don Juan und Faust* (1829) is read by many specialists as a consummate tragicomedy with its tension between the erotic and the intellectual,[5] between the earthbound and physical manner of the one hero, and the spiritual aspirations of the other. I would argue that *Scherz, Satire, Ironie und tiefere Bedeutung* (Joking, Satire, Irony, and Deeper Meaning, 1822) is the most successful embodiment of laughter in despair: comic corrosiveness slides by degrees into tragedy.

Grillparzer also often displays his attraction to tragicomedy. His most famous comedy *Weh dem, der lügt* (Liar, Beware, 1838) was unsuccessful on the stage precisely because it was weighted with melancholy wisdom. The fairy-land atmosphere of *Melusina* (1833) and *Der Traum, ein Leben* (Dream as Life, 1840) has many touches of the tragicomic. One of Grillparzer's earliest dramatic exercises was his somewhat free translation of *Il Corvo* (The Crow, 1814) by Count Carlo Gozzi (1720-1806). The importance of Gozzi as a supplier of methods and themes for the Romantic dramatists cannot be emphasized enough. Schiller thought him the equal of Shakespeare; Tieck and Grabbe acknowledged his influence; Büchner chose him as a tutelary deity for one of his plays. In Austria his manner of writing was continued by Ferdinand Raimund (1790-1836). The old Viennese popular theater, as it developed in the later eighteenth century, was to a great extent an attempt to adapt local peasant traditions to the flexible structures of the *commedia dell'arte*.[6] Although Raimund's main concern was with the opposition between reality and illusion, serious and grotesque oppositions also appear in his plays. Thus in *Der Diamant des Geisterkönigs* (The Diamond of the Ghost-King, 1824) the serious and sentimental quest of Eduard, son of the magician Zephises, is doubled by that of his comic servant Florian Waschblau; additionally some of his adventures are comic rather than serious (he is at one point transformed into a poodle). All of

---

[4] Karl Heinz Klingenberg, *Iffland und Kotzebue als Dramatiker* (Weimar: Arion, 1962), pp. 27, 35, 42.
[5] Karl Guthke, *Geschichte und Poetik der deutschen Tragikömodie* (Göttingen: Vandenhoeck & Rupprecht, 1961).
[6] See e.g. John Michalski, *Ferdinand Raimund* (New York: Twayne, 1968), pp. 20-22.

Raimund's plays have a happy ending, but in each of them this ending is brought about through the intercession of an arbitrary superior power. Despair and humor work together in them: the fairy-tale hero is first modified with many comic and earthy features, but soon we find him in grave, desperate or allegorically ruinous situations. The return to comedy is *willed* by the author.[7] In England tragicomic experimentation was fairly frequent in a variety of media. Perhaps the most characteristic work in drama was Thomas Lowell Beddoes's *Death's Jest-Book or the Fool's Tragedy* (published in 1850, but written mostly between 1825-28). The subject of the play is in its structure pure Gothic sensationalism, but the treatment and the language are comic "for it is the loss of humor, of imagination, of the ridiculous that Beddoes laments more than the fact of death itself."[8]

This brief reminder of the variety of tragicomedy and ironic elements in the dramas of the early nineteenth century could be easily enriched. It will be more useful, however, to examine in some detail three important figures of the period after 1815 – Alfred de Musset (1810-57), Juliusz Słowacki (1809-49) and Georg Büchner (1813-37) and on this basis draw some general theoretical conclusions.

II

Most of the plays of Musset are based on the aesthetic experimentation with harmony and trouble; he tries out, against each other, the possible relationships of serenity and tragedy, without fully tightening them into a tragicomic conflict. For instance, one recurrent pattern indicates that conjugal bliss, harmony and order are to be achieved only through intrigue and confusion and by fully taking advantage of the intricate dialectics of appearance and reality. This can be seen in *Louison* (1849), *Un caprice* (A Whim, 1832), *Il ne faut jurer de rien* (Never Fully Trust, 1836), also to some extent in *La Coupe et les lèvres* (The Goblet and the Lips, 1831), and elsewhere. Other and more ambitious plays, such as *Lorenzaccio* (1834), *La Nuit vénitienne* (1830), or *Bettine* (1851), seem to have a hovering focus: the possibilities of achieving good through evil, the desire to avoid being ridiculous even if the price is tragedy, the awareness of one's formal status through other characters – are basic concerns. Such themes and structures might be said to be the primary material for tragicomedy, or its accompanying and inchoate forms. However, two of Musset's main plays can be fully described as tragicomedies: *Les Caprices de Marianne* (1833) and *On ne badine pas avec l'amour* (Don't Toy with Love, 1834). In both of them a typical comic situation leads finally to tragedy. Marianne, the wife of Claudio, a solemn and boring magistrate, is – in the first of these two plays – courted by the helpless, shy, and sentimental Célio. Her cousin Octave, an adventurous, high-spirited, elegant, and ironic rake, mocks the pair, consents to act as an intermediary, encourages them, and is finally on

---

[7] See the detailed analysis of Laurence Hardding, *The Dramatic Art of Ferdinand Raimund and Johann Nestroy* (The Hague: Mouton, 1974), pp. 52-65. He also refers to Guthke (see note 5).

[8] Marilyn Gaull, "Romanticism Theater," *The Wordsworth Circle*, 14 (1983), 262. Many passages in Beddoes's play are strikingly similar to those of Grabbe's *Scherz, Satire, Ironie und tiefere Bedeutung*, or Büchner's *Leonce und Lena* which he ignored, I believe: "O world, world! The gods and fairies left thee, for thou wert too wise [...]." Gaull emphasizes the importance of popular melodrama in that age, as does Peter Brooks in talking of Pixérécourt and similar French authors in *The Melodramatic Imagination* (New Haven: Yale Univ. Press, 1976), pp. 24-68. The layer of dramatic material discussed by Gaull and Brooks corresponds approximately to the writings of Gozzi and Goldoni in Italy, as well as to the Viennese theater and the Kotzebue-Iffland school. In other words Biedermeier tragicomedy, no less than Romantic irony used as a basic strategy the heightening of a level of raw material that had subsisted throughout most of the eighteenth century in a humbler and less visible position.

the point of supplanting Célio in the heart of Marianne. But Claudio, driven to mad jealousy, hires assassins, and Célio is caught in a deadly ambush to which his friends send him unwittingly. Octave, broken-hearted, abandons Marianne, leaving behind his whole youth, his adventures and his dissipation. As the title shows, the main motivating element is Marianne's change of attitude (and, we must conclude, her shifting standard of value) during the play – from pious propriety to sulky vengefulness and finally to full love. But the tragic outcome could not take place if she were not simultaneously faced with an equally unstable partner: Célio and Octave are parts of one and the same character (Lorenzaccio cut in two, as E. Gans suggests).[9] Octave is expression without content, Célio content with no expression.

Structurally, we may speak here of the comic searching for a tragic possibility – by trial and error, as it were – and finally finding it. In *Les Caprices de Marianne* the mobility of comedy turns into the conflictual rigidity of tragedy. Célio is a fairly stable character; his values are sublime love, unyielding honor, passion, faith. As long as he is isolated with these anti- and supra-social values, he can do neither good nor harm; it is only when Marianne in her erratic search for a convenient stance *adopts* the same values (though their *object* is different) that a tragic situation is created – because confrontation turns into conflict.

This point will be illustrated by a look at *On ne badine pas avec l'amour*. Perdican, the son of a baron, wants to marry Camille, his cousin; he is a sprightly and engaging scapegrace who is looking for domestic harmony and stability. Camille is, like Marianne, in search of an identification with a set of values: should she return for good to the convent? should she devote her life to the predictabilities of a pre-arranged marriage? or will she be able to experience total loss of self in a consuming love? Most of the play is taken up with the changing positions of the two main characters towards each other, along with some marginal influences of other characters. Finally, Perdican draws humble Rosette into an affair; she dies or commits suicide when Camille is reunited with Perdican; Camille leaves Perdican for good. Rosette is the exact counterpart of Célio: the carrier of values such as absolute love, faithfulness, honor, purity. The moment Camille's search has reached its object, i. e., the moment she has invested her interior energy in values that are similar to those of Rosette – tragic conflict strikes with lightning speed. At this point mobility turns into rigidity. The situation differs from that of *Caprices* because the desired object (Perdican) is fairly well defined and stationary. But the morality of the structure is the same in both cases: the extremes of passion and idealistic devotion are tolerable only in isolation; the moment they "connect," the moment they tend to create alternative societies, the moment they are converted into reality, tragedy ensues.

III

Dramatic strategies and problematics strikingly similar to those of Musset can be encountered in the writings of Juliusz Słowacki. In *Mazeppa* it is interesting to notice first the choice of material. Pushkin was interested in the shattering dilemmas of an ageing yet insecure hero (*Poltawa*). Hugo and Byron were eager to investigate the psychological horrors of the young courtier's deathly cavalcade, bound to the back of a galloping steed: strong colors and sensationalism, but also a heralding

---

[9] Eric Gans, *Musset et le "drame tragique"* (Paris: Corti, 1974), p. 169. See also Herbert Gochberg, *Stage of Dreams: The Dramatic Art of Alfred de Musset (1828-1834)* (Geneva: Droz, 1967), p. 146.

of future greatness. They chose therefore out of Mazeppa's biography not the episodes of his maturity, when the *hetman* of the Cossacks was demonstrating his masterly political and military ability by juggling between the seventeenth-century Russians, Swedes, Turks, and Poles, but rather the episode in which the leader, as a young and unruly page at the Polish King's court was punished for his misbehavior. Słowacki, closest in space to the hero and perhaps most likely to admire him, ignored all this and wrote a play on the hero before he becomes a hero, that is a play on Mazeppa as a young page, on the lusty King Jan Casimir, on an elderly Voivod and his pure wife, and on their high-strung stepson Zbigniew. The conclusion is tragic or at least melodramatic: the Voivod plunges a dagger into his own heart, after his much tortured wife and her adoring stepson have lost their own lives; the philandering Jan Casimir finally decides to act as a true ruler; Mazeppa is tied to a horse and whipped away into the steppe. But what ends in melodrama had begun as highly ambiguous comedy. The old husband jealously guarding a much younger wife eagerly pursued by courtier bucks, the instigating Madame Castellan Robroncka, in middle-age between coquettishness and lechery, the elegant bantering of a jocular, pert, ironic Mazeppa – all the trappings are here. Mazeppa is Protean; at one point he courts Amelia by taking on the cynical mask of the utter nihilist who jests because he will not believe in anything, the next moment he is ready to play Leporello to the King's Don Juan (II.ii). But already by the end of the first act when the young man cuts his own hand to save Jan Casimir's honor we have intimations of change. These hints of things to come have been linked all along with the glum and intense Zbigniew, the third wooer of Amelia, who might be said to stand like Esmeralda in *Notre-Dame de Paris* in the eye of the hurricane, an emblem of some absolute natural balance. Zbigniew, as we get to understand him, is Mazeppa's other side: they are united like Octave and Célio.[10] The key explanatory scene is to be found in Act II when the duel between the two young men is followed by passionate reconciliation. Mazeppa maintains the distance of a lucid though mild amusement on this occasion, while Zbigniew reveals his common denominator with his new-found "brother": nihilism and pessimism.

From this point on the action veers wildly between macabre, comic, and serious melodrama. The Voivod hardens into a murderous maniac, the King pushes his jocular irresponsibility to treacherous cynicism, Amelia's schizoid tendencies reach the point of no return. Słowacki's intention may have been merely to delineate how a budding hero reacted to some traumatic and opposing pressures and how he coped with them. What the play demonstrates in fact is something rather different. It is the explosive potential of comic conflict. Mazeppa comes in all seriousness and with no ulterior motive to Amelia's room to give her fair warning. He finds himself trapped here by the bumbling and fuming old husband – a comic scene. His good intentions combined with those of Amelia and Zbigniew (the seekers of the absolute), lead him to the tragic and horrifying situation of being walled-in in the alcove where he had sought refuge. The return of the King brings back comedy, honor is relative, error reigns in human life, and even the Voivod – a Corneillean hero in a hysterical mode – enhances the zaniness. The suicide of Zbigniew and the revelation of his love for Amelia will, in turn, crush the old husband and his comic potential.

Apparently *Mazeppa* is a comedy that ends in tragedy. But Słowacki introduces an additional and decisive ambiguity. The survivor is the comic character, the signet of openness and indiffer-

---

[10] Mazeppa occasionally acts and talks like Zbigniew. Juliusz Słowacki, *Mazeppa*, trans. by Marion Moore Coleman (Cheshire, Conn.: Cherry Hill Books, 1960), p. 9. See Juliusz Słowacki, *Dziela Wybrane*, ed. Julian Krzyzanowski (Wroclaw and Warsaw: Zaklad Narodowy Im. Ossolinskich, 1974), IV, 277-78.

ence. Those who perish represent the "old world" of fixed values. Cynicism and the fluidity of the real world are vindicated; Mazeppa can embark on his heroic adventure because he has rid himself of illusions. Rigidity is self-defeating. Purification appears in the guise of freedom from morality, in energy and high aspiration.

Fantazy is not too different from *Mazeppa* in its ultimate outcome, but much more explicit in admitting cultural morphology as its reference system; also much more explicit in the self-reflection of the characters on their tragicomic situation. Fantazy declares: "The devil himself is playing a comedy with me [...] and the saddest at that,"[11] or "My mocking tones were the last pain of my soul" (p. 306), or "Just see what jesters Poland produces; they can amuse you to the death" (p. 308); while his pedestrian friend and famulus Rzecznicki observes: "I had no idea, you see, whether a wedding or a funeral would result from the enterprise" (p. 290), and even flighty Idalia cautions: "You'll be left to play a comedy in the graveyard" (p. 296).[12]

As to the "morphocultural" level of reference, it seems to be our chief help in understanding an otherwise confusing and obscure play. The characters are grouped in three tiers. In the back there is the gross rationalism and materialist common sense of Rzecznicki and Count Respekt, accompanied by the conventional idyllic posturing of such as the Countess who wants to transform the estate into a large pastoral *tableau vivant* (I.iv) with little peasants weaving baskets, fishing nets and goatherds, and Ukrainian folk songs by the waterfall. In the front we have the tragic group of the patriot hero Jan, the passionate and faithful Diana, and the enigmatic, self-sacrificing Russian major. These are characters emerging from a past that is not remote, but that many would like to see buried and forgotten. They act out the drama of idealism, purity, and vision in the midst of an embarrassed and often unsympathetic audience. Nevertheless they offer suffering and fulfillment in an absolute form. In between there is a third, central group, represented chiefly by the title hero, Count Fantazy Dafnicki, and Countess Idalia. They stand for the ironic hopelessness and nihilistic elegance of an age that was grasping for substitutes for the lost absolute of Romanticism. They provide a self-conscious, mocking, and elaborate imitation of Romantic processes staged for the needs of a stodgy and insensitive audience. The stridence, the fantasy, and the pert cynicism of their antics is due partly to a desperate loss of ideals, but also to the need to impress rather gross eyes and ears. At the same time their connective function is positive. In Act V, Fantazy calls Rzecznicki "this famulus of mine" (p. 308);[13] at the same time both he and Idalia admire and "emulate" Jan and Diana.

In Act I the scene is set up for a farcical demonstration. Fantazy, already preceded by his "Romantic" (low-Romantic) reputation as a melancholy Mediterranean traveller and feverish letter writer, perhaps even mystic and poet, returns to Poland for a largely prearranged marriage of convenience. But very soon two complementary disasters are revealed. One of them is "the return of the dead" – Jan the martyred hero is able to emerge briefly from Siberian exile and Diana does not hesitate to choose authenticity over the arabesques of imagination. The other is Fantazy himself who is engaged in a perpetual negation of his own reality, in doubt and self-deprecation. Fantazy is described by the author, and understands himself as a creature of instability, built out of contradic-

---

[11] Juliusz Słowacki, *Fantazy*, in *Polish Romantic Drama*, ed. Harold Segel (Ithaca: Cornell Univ. Press, 1977), p. 263. Hereafter references parenthetically in the text. For the original see *Dzieła*, IV, 384 in Act I, scene 13, ll. 412-13.
[12] Słowacki, *Dzieła*, IV, 463 in Act V, scene 1, ll. 9-10 and, respectively, IV, 466 in ll. 77-78 and earlier IV, 431 in Act III, scene 8, ll. 361-62 and IV, 443 in Act IV, scene 2, ll. 84.85.
[13] Słowacki, *Dzieła*, IV, 465 in Act V, scene 1, ll. 60-61.

tions that are held together, for a while only, by loud gestures and histrionics. He aspires to the pure Romantic experience of totality but does not ignore his own inability to achieve it, and his cold, sometimes mean fury at the world is a mirror-image of self-contempt. He is ready to fall in love with Diana as soon as she rejects him (I.14.15), even though a few minutes earlier he had proclaimed with ringing pathos: "she's the kind of person who needs wounds. Her lips are made for the drinking of poison" (p. 264). Idalia displays a mixture of fantastic aspiration and cynical self-mockery.

The difference between this pair and the foreground circle around Jan is best seen in comparing their language. Jan may often use the same high register as Fantazy, for instance, throughout his conversation with Stella (II.ii): "the seven stars bound together that you showed me once, my golden astronomer [...] above the terrible image of frozen misery – of an extinguished life, of a snowy hell" (p. 270). But there is, as the reader is never allowed to forget, an iron solidarity between these words and his action, indeed his whole life. More than the others, Idalia recognizes this. In II.iii after Jan's lonely song, she slips easily into the role of Biedermeier passive spectator to high-Romantic substantial action. Indeed, she proclaims: "With the masters gone, the lackeys are dressing themselves in their clothes and conducting romances in their places" (p. 279),[14] which is clearly a statement about the basic terms of life, not about a particular society. Her sophisticated self-conscious discourse is seen as madness by a puzzled Jan; pure verbalism is beyond his ken. The opposition comes to a head in the rapid alterations of life and death, ridiculous and earnest, that mark with their speedy, hysterical rhythm the last scenes of Act IV and the beginning of Act V. After Diana's true feelings become public knowledge, Fantazy and Idalia act out in the graveyard an incoherent scene of despair, sardonic laughter and suicide, which, needless to say, will be unconsummated. The scene will be swept aside unceremoniously by the intrusion of a higher reality: the actual sacrificial death of the Russian major which ties a bond between Diana and Jan.

Fantazy is thus a very odd comedy – its comic quality is the outcome of the conflict between Romanticism and Biedermeier, between genuine tragedy and mock-despair. Respekt, Rzecznicki, and others are butts and victims of this transcendent joke. And is the link between Jan and Diana, invoked by the poet seemingly as the beginning of Eden, one of exemplary perfection? Is it not more likely to result in the foundation of a further variant of Biedermeier socializing, spectacularly unhappy in the Siberian snows or in lukewarm, country-squire coziness? Thus, as in *Mazeppa*, the apparent victory of a tragic sense of life seems idle; the Major has exploded the redeemed society through his death. For instance, at least within the framework of the play, Romantic irony would have been based upon the coexistence of this society and the girl's parents. The interposition of a relativizing middle level must obstruct decisively such ironic wholeness. Moreover, Fantazy will now have the field to himself, precisely because he has remained in the twilight area of tragicomedy. The characters keep using theatrical imagery and asking (with almost detached curiosity) about the outcome of their own tangled affairs. The answer, in the spirit of late-Romantic tragicomedy, is, clearly, more questioning and an enduring painful openness.

---

[14] Słowacki, *Dziela*, IV, 387 in Act I, scene 13, ll. 466 and, respectively IV, 397 in Act II, scene 2, ll. 68-71 and IV, 403 in Act II, scene 3, ll. 233-35.

IV

Musset's and Słowacki's contemporary, Büchner, resorts to many analogous strategies. His "serious" plays, *Woyzeck* (1836) and *Dantons Tod* (Danton's Death, 1835), contain their share of jocular references, and particularly of sarcastic and grotesque touches. *Woyzeck*, the tragedy of seediness, is spiced with heavy doses of earthy obscenity, as in the exchanges of the non-commissioned officers on Marie, as well as in the catty, lust-filled clash of Marie and Margreth over the good graces of the drum major. These and other scenes go beyond the general tragic irony of the play. In *Dantons Tod* such touches are even more frequent. Jocular frivolity establishes a distance between man and his fate, or life and death, and relativizes both.

The reverse is true in *Leonce and Lena* (1836). Sadness and the tragic are superadded elements which change the general frivolity and merriment into a threatening world picture, or to put it otherwise, relativize the comic. The most accurate description of Büchner's purposes in *Leonce and Lena* is that he directs his irony against Romantic Irony. Even the choice of the main character's name is suggestive. It is a pun upon the name of Büchner's own highly serious hero who embodies Romantic aspiration (Lenz), it reminds us forcefully of Brentano's *Ponce de Leon*, and as Majut has shown, confirms the usage of the name in works such as Mme de Staël's *Delphine*, Mme Cottin's *Isola Bella* (German translation 1833), and Grillparzer's *Weh dem, der lügt* (the cook boy Leon), and later George Sand's *Tévérino*. (Majut concisely defines Leonce as "die biedermeierliche Form des problematischen Menschen," the Biedermeier variant of an ambiguity-riddled man.)[15]

Ludwig Büttner graphically shows the opposition between Schlegel and Büchner in terms of their attitude towards leisure. The former talks about the creativity and nobility of leisure, and the power of imagination. Leisure is called in *Lucinde* "die Lebensluft der Unschuld und der Begeisterung" (the very life's breath of any innocence and passion). Büchner refuses such (high-)Romantic aspirations and perceptions – for him leisure is emptiness, imagination is an idle, wildly titillating toy.[16] Not only Leonce, but the other characters also are tired, they move slowly, often recline. They have stylized, languidly foppish gestures.[17] Leisure is for them not primarily the space of freedom and creation, but the symbolic preparation for death. Leonce is a Mussetian character, whom one might expect to encounter in Pushkin too.[18] His skepticism and boredom are designed to hide sensitivity, yearning and aspiration, even a touch of despair. Leonce's drama is real, in spite of its ridicule. At every point his fantasy flies off on a tangent, and (almost) breaks away from the body of his existence; Leonce barely manages to hold on to his social environment. (Therefore, in my opinion, those who seek satirical implications in the play are bound to be disappointed.) Leonce fears conformity more than anything, but precisely by fleeing it, falls into it (the conventional marriage). This is the best explanation of the famous exchange between the two young people towards the end of the

[15] Rudolf Majut, *Studien um Büchner* (Berlin: Ebering, 1932), p. 70.

[16] Ludwig Büttner, *Büchners Bild vom Menschen* (Nürnberg: Hans Carl, 1967), pp. 105-6.

[17] Liciano Zagari, *Georg Büchner e la ricerca dello stile dramatico* (Torino: Edizioni dell'Albero, 1956), p. 126.

[18] The influence of Musset is generally admitted by the leading commentators. See Herbert Lindenberger, *Georg Büchner* (Carbondale: Southern Illinois Univ. Press, 1964), pp. 58-59, 65, or Karl Viëtor, *Georg Büchner: Politik, Dichtung, Wissenschaft* (Bern: Francke, 1949), p. 187. More specialized investigations in Maurice Gravier, "Georg Büchner et Alfred de Musset," *Orbis litterarum*, 9 (1954), 29-44, and Henri Plard, "A propos de *Leonce und Lena*: Musset et Büchner," *Études Germaniques*, 9 (1954), 26-36. The earliest works to have pointed to this connection were apparently those of Heinz Lipman, *Georg Büchner und die Romantik* (München: Hueber, 1923), and Armin Renker, *Georg Büchner und das Lustspiel der Romantik* (Berlin: Ebering, 1924), pp. 96-108.

play: L., "Ich bin betrogen." L., "Ich bin betrogen." L., "O Zufall!" L., "O Vorsehung!" (L., "I have been duped." L., "I have been duped." L., "Oh, random chance!" L., "Oh, noble providence!")[19] It is arguable that a Leonce who would not have run away would have had a better chance to achieve some genuinely Romantic aims. At any rate, the ending is highly ambiguous, and many questions remain open. Has Leonce indeed given in to conformist pressures? Is he now tamed? Has he decided that fantasy can be secret, that it can be accomodated in a miniature framework, by small places and things?

We can understand the full weight of such questions only if we admit that the ironic treatment of irony must inevitably give birth to a tragic dimension in literature. As Büttner correctly observes: "Das idyllische Ländchen und die biedermeierlich behagliche Gartenlaube stehen auf dunklem unfestem Grund" (the idyllic little country and cozy and comfortable middleclass garden arbor rest upon dark and unstable foundations).[20] Those who ignore the tragicomic mixture do so at their own risk: they have to over-emphasize the light satirical touches into heavy criticism and protest, or else they could not explain the earnestness that often seems to breathe out of so light and playful an action. Even the insights of some able critics are thus distorted.[21] Viëtor is much more judicious and his opinions may provide the most reliable starting point for a discussion of the tragicomic in *Leonce and Lena*. He concludes: "Die Melancholie in dieser Komödie ist von der Art, die auch in Büchners beiden Trauerspielen erscheint" (This comedy is melancholy in just the same way as Büchner's two tragedies are),[22] after a colorful enumeration of the play's ingredients, which would certainly fit *Measure for Measure*. Viëtor is also impressed by cruelty, misanthropy, "Welthaß," and the deadly earnestness of many rejoinders (p. 176). Leonce's exclamation, "[...] ich bin so jung und die Welt ist so alt [...]" (I am so young, and the world is so old) – followed by the expressionistic anxiety of her words, "Die Erde hat sich ängstlich zusammengeschmieget wie ein Kind" and "über ihre Wiege schreiten die Gespenster" (Like a child, our earth is huddled with fear [and] Ghosts are stepping over its crib) in Act II, scene 2 – [23] catches very exactly the pervasive fear which neutralizes effectively the merriment and jocularity of the action. Viëtor touches only slightly upon what is left: ambiguity, the lack of substance of the characters symbolizing the hovering intellectual and social uncertainties of the age, boredom as the mother of melancholy.

More radically it can be claimed that conversely, boredom is the outcome of melancholy or, more precisely, of despair. The arguments for reading Büchner's play as the irony of Romantic irony are compelling. They include, as mentioned, the figure of Leonce (the pale, impotent, skeptical verson of Danton or Lenz); they include the figure of König Peter who, like Teuffelsdröckh, relativizes Romantic idealistic philosophy, in fact, by resorting to the metaphor of clothes (in I.ii, he

---

[19] Georg Büchner, *Gesammelte Werke*, ed. K. Edschmid (München: Desch, 1948), p. 200.

[20] Büttner, p. 41.

[21] Hans Mayer, *Georg Büchner und seine Zeit* (1946; rpt. Wiesbaden: Limes, 1959), pp. 399-440; and, in a very heavy-handed way, Gerhard Jancke, *Georg Büchner: Genese und Aktualität seines Werkes* (Kronberg: Scriptor, 1975), pp. 253-270 who reduces *Leonce und Lena* to a drama of protest leading to a "paranoide Utopie." To a lesser extent this is the problem with the view of Henry J. Schmidt, *Satire, Caricature, and Perspectivism in the Works of Georg Büchner* (The Hague: Mouton, 1970). Similarly, Maurice Benn, *The Drama of Revolt. A Critical Study of Georg Büchner* (Cambridge: Cambridge Univ. Press, 1976), p. 162, complains: "for Büchner reality is essentially tragic. Consequently, in tragedy he can be fully realistic. In comedy not so." Though the tragicomic is thus conjured away, Benn nevertheless speaks repeatedly of a modification and reduction of reality, and thus admits, I think, that the gap between tragic and comic is often narrowed considerably.

[22] Viëtor, p. 174.

[23] Büchner, p. 189.

runs around the room naked to illustrate the *Ding-an-sich*); they include Valerio's mockery of Romantic communion with nature in the opening scene: "Ich werde mich indessen in das Gras legen und meine Nase oben zwischen den Halmen herausblühen lassen und romantische Empfindungen beziehen" (Meanwhile I will lie down in the grass, I will let my nose sprout out among the blades and will engage in Romantic emotion);[24] they include the openness of the ending. But we must not overlook the converse perspective, from which the play is a tragedy without the tragic release of a catastrophe. The almost panic feeling of generalized fear pervading the play is part of this syndrome. It grips not only the sensitive, but even König Peter, and in fact the whole of nature and society (Lena, Rosette, even Valerio). The death wish remains just yearning, as in the case of Fantazy. The love encounters between Leonce and Lena have a strange somnambulistic quality, with many references to impending death. Valerio, who is often interpreted as the simple man of soul and common sense, should be understood instead as a destructive, careless pragmatist. His language is similar to that of Leonce in extravagance and cynical word-choice; but he has deliberately eliminated the touches of hope, the occasional softness and delicacy. Looked at closely, Valerio turns into the grinning figure of coming modernity. His final tirade is more than an irony, it is a brutal threat against the distraught attempts of Leonce to build a thin web of protective illusion around his life. Beyond even Valerio's questioning is the radical questioning of the characters' validity and right to existence by Büchner himself. Leonce tells his companion (I.iii): "Mensch, du bist nichts als ein schlechtes Wortspiel. Du hast weder Vater noch Mutter, sondern die fünf Vokale haben dich miteinander erzeugt" (Man, you are nothing but a bad pun. You have neither father, nor mother – you are the offspring of intercourse among the five vowels); only to receive the answer: "Und Sie, Prinz, sind ein Buch ohne Buchstaben, mit nichts als Gedankenstrichen" (You, prince, are a book with no letters in it, just hyphens).[25] Whereas Grabbe's Mordax was retreating into his verbality in order to escape death or punishment, here the characters recognize their own deficient reality in the fullness of their "life" – an additional token of tragedy. But even this verbal reality is problematic. As Jürgen Schröder has shown quite convincingly, the language of the play must be related all the time to nothingness. It is not self-sustaining, but rather an attempt to fill a void,[26] to shut out the silence. In other words, the characters are not only sucked back into the purely fictional level of textuality, they are further diminished by the relativization of the text itself. A tragic ending would have restored some dignity, some finality to their existence. The denial of a tragic ending means that Leonce and Lena are fixed in eternal ambiguity and uncertainty. The illusions they express in the final scene are not only a whistling in the dark, they are consciously expressed as illusions and as concessions of defeat. Tragedy eludes them, and that signifies that existence itself eludes them. But that in itself is their greatest tragedy, precisely because they are not really the type of puppet figures that Grabbe had staged.[27] There is, indeed, a certain animosity between Grabbe and his characters: he tries to humiliate them and to indicate their inferiority by making public the author's manipulative rights and powers. By contrast Büchner humanizes even his most puppet-like characters, and thus they escape him after a point, taking on a life of their own.

---

[24] Büchner, p. 172.
[25] Büchner, p. 182.
[26] Jürgen Schröder, *Georg Büchner's "Leonce und Lena": Eine verkehrte Komödie* (München: Fink, 1966), p. 199, 53.
[27] I disagree with Mario Carlo Abutille, *Angst und Zynismus bei Georg Büchner* (Bern: Francke, 1969), pp. 87-88.

V

The whole edifice of this later Romantic tragicomedy seems thus to have as its premise a certain distrust in Romantic irony. Irony is a part of the high-Romantic model and is closely associated with other key concepts, such as organicism, dialectics, lyrical intensity, melancholy – there is mutual dependence between them and they overlap; dialectical and ironic tensions cannot be imagined without one another; prophecy and irony, opposite as they are, may collaborate.[28] Friedrich Schlegel takes irony seriously and he thinks philosophy must be its foundation; he also speaks of it as the agility of the ontological fullness of chaos. Schelling mantains that irony is the basis of objectivity. For Solger, irony is self-consciousness and hence a negation which props up the affirmation contained in an aesthetic text. The angry rebuttals of Hegel and Kierkegaard were soon to undermine this confidence.[29] The irony of Heine or Byron in its turn had nilhilistic overtones. They and many of their contemporaries are bitter and debunking; they do not use irony for the kind, open-ended world-unification that their predecessors had tried. Romantic irony at its highest is found theatrically in *Faust*, despite Goethe's grumblings at his Romantic contemporaries, as Gillespie has shown in the preceding chapter. It is found in Kleist's *Prinz von Homburg*, and in the plays of Tieck; this irony often seems to forgo comic effects.

The loss of the fusionary ideal (that is, irony as an organic and dialectical tool intended to disclose and grasp all the sides of a complex reality) is first seen in the proliferation of the grotesque in literature after 1815. It is not as if the grotesque had been unknown before, but it seems to me that the defiant insistence of so many writers on grotesque figures and situations changes its weight and meaning. I do not want to join here the long and acrimonious battle of the concepts between those who want to find a demonic component in it, and those who, on the contrary, see a peaceful neutralizing in Peacock, Hugo, Hoffmann, Gogol, Büchner, or Grabbe. In fact I find it more practical to accept some of the older theorists, such as Hegel, or the more technical Wilhelm Michel, who confine themselves to emphasizing duality and contradiction, distortion and lack of balance in their definitions. These seem to me to be the direct outcome of an ironic worldview subjected to additional centrifugal pressures. The center is thus lost and the way is open to a literary situation in which the parts that had been held together by their very opposition (irony) will now find themselves in mere juxtaposition. This is tragicomedy, a mode in which parataxis is the morphological principle. Essentially I claim that the burst of tragicomic production is the result of a kind of Romantic "decline," not in artistic quality, but in the very principle of Romanticism.

What I mean is that the principle of maximum expansion and regeneration, which according to Abrams and to other scholars is the foundation of the Romantic model, is by necessity transitory and has to be followed by adaptation, or by relativity, or by disapppointment. The lofty visionary claims of the early figures of high Romanticism, of Blake in his prophetic works, of Wordsworth in the *Prelude*, of Novalis in the *Hymns* and in *Ofterdingen*, the intensities of the early Schelling and of Hölderlin, and, I would add, the absolute political utopianism of Saint-Just, for instance, cannot

---

[28] Michael Cooke, *Acts of Inclusion* (New Haven: Yale Univ. Press, 1979), pp. 21, XIII. Frederick Garber, *The Autonomy of the Self from Richardson to Huysmans* (Princeton, N.J.: Princeton Univ. Press, 1982), pp. 92-121.
[29] See for a broader discussion: Helmut Prang, *Die romantische Ironie* (Darmstadt: Wissenschaftliche Buchgesellschaft, 1972); Ingrid Strohschneider-Kohrs, *Die romantische Ironie in Theorie und Gestaltung* (1960; rpt. Tübingen: Niemeyer, 1977); Beda Allemann, *Ironie und Dichtung* (1956; rpt. Pfullingen: Neske, 1969); Ernst Behler, *Klassische Ironie, romantische Ironie, tragische Ironie* (Darmstadt: Wissenschaftliche Buchgesellschaft, 1972).

be maintained at the same level. It does not represent a feasible or practical solution for an audience or for a social group of any size. Irony, an integral part of the Romantic visionary project, undergoes the same changes as other components: it is in fact symptomatic of the dynamics of Romanticism as a whole.

Biedermeier Romanticism in Germany and its equivalents in other European literatures is tantamount to a taming of Romantic energy, and sometimes even to a peculiar kind of debasing. It tries to secularize high Romanticism and put it to work for specific purposes, sometimes of social change, sometimes of national renewal, sometimes of personal gratification or small-group serenity. Another strategy of retreat is to relativize the Romantic model; this is usually a reduction in size or a kind of sectionalization. Thus irony itself can be treated ironically. While this sometimes leads to pure comedy, it often leads to a tragic ending. The juxtaposition of tragic and comic situations and characters is part of this general Biedermeier process. This is not merely a matter of conflict between an ideal and reality (a state of affairs that is, after all, always with us), but of some more specific conditions. The mixture of stylistic levels, recognized by Auerbach and others as conducive to tragicomic literature is certainly consistent with the anxious reach for a new stability and the class mobility brought about by events in the generation preceding 1815.[30]

In the plays of Musset and in some of those of his contemporaries, the repeated transformation of the comic into the tragic illustrates the impossibility of organizing the world coherently according to a high-Romantic scheme in which even irony had an ordering role. Biedermeier drama acknowledges a dramatic world with a random distribution of frivolous and serious elements, therefore basically a comic world. Tragedy will grow out of the tendency to see these elements organized in an intelligible fashion and according to high values. Paradoxically, the type of insecurity expressed in Musset's plays is for him (and for his readers) a kind of security; it offers protection from the cosmos-shattering consistency of Romanticism. The cynical and frivolous overtones are really "soothing" – the essence of life is a random succession of serious or comic elements; we have to restrict our expectations and actions, we have to avoid the hybris of large-scale systems. The redeeming power of Romantic irony turns into the ultimately resigned tragicomedy of European Biedermeier life.

---

[30] See Virgil Nemoianu, *The Taming of Romanticism: European Literature and the Age of Biedermeier* (Cambridge, Mass.: Harvard Univ. Press, 1984). A more detailed discussion of the problems of tragicomedy and of their sociocultural background can be found in chapters I and V. Several sections of the present essay represent the original shorter version of the corresponding passages in the book.

MARTIN ESSLIN

ROMANTIC COSMIC DRAMA

Est ergo subiectum totius operis, literaliter tantum accepti, status animarum post mortem simpliciter sumptus. Nam de illo et circa illum totius operis versatur processus. Si vero accipiatur opus allegorice, subiectum est homo prout merendo et demerendo per arbitrii libertatem iustitiae praemiandi et puniendi obnoxius est.[1]

(The subject of the whole work, then, taken merely in its literal sense, is simply the state of souls after death. The course of the whole work derives from and revolves around that. But if the whole work is taken allegorically, its subject is our liability to be rewarded or punished by justice according to our exercise of our freedom of will.)

And justify the ways of God to men.[2]

So schreitet in dem engen Bretterhaus
Den ganzen Kreis der Schöpfung aus
Und wandelt mit bedächt'ger Schnelle
Vom Himmel durch die Welt zur Hölle.[3]

(So on this narrow house's boards as space
Creation's fullest circle start to pace,
And walk with leisured speed your spell
From Heaven through the World to Hell.)

I

To compress into the narrow ambit of the boards of a stage the whole arc of creation, surely, is the most ambitious of all objectives a playwright can set himself: to encompass in the sweep of his work the whole gamut, physical, historical and moral, of Man's life and of his world; to produce, in fact, a "summa" of human experience and wisdom – a truly "cosmic" drama. Yet that, precisely, is what Goethe proclaimed as his ambition when he composed his "Vorspiel auf dem Theater" (Prelude in the Theater). It was only gradually, over a period of several decades that Goethe's *Faust* developed into such an undertaking, a peak of achievement, that, later, many poets tried to emulate or even to surpass.

The *Urfaust*, composed between 1773 and 1774 did not yet pursue that ambition, although the character of Faust, the passionate seeker after knowledge, already contained the potential of grow-

---

[1] Dante, excerpt from section 8 of "Letter to Can Grande della Scala" (1319).
[2] Milton, *Paradise Lost*, I, 26.
[3] Goethe, "Vorspiel auf dem Theater," lines 239-42.

ing into an archetype of modern Western man relentlessly assaulting the frontiers of the unknown, even at the peril of his soul.

It was almost twenty years later that Goethe added the two prologues, "Vorspiel auf dem Theater" and "Prolog im Himmel" which clearly elevated the work to the level of a "cosmic drama." These sections of the play, probably composed between 1797 and 1801, were published as parts of *Faust: Eine Tragödie* in the eighth volume of Goethe's works in 1808. Yet at this time the cosmic "vom Himmel durch die Welt zur Hölle" could still be understood as referring merely to the play's range from the opening in heaven to Faust's obvious damnation as the destroyer of Gretchen in the final scene.

The plan to extend the play beyond that rather parochial compass into a microcosm of human life, human knowledge and human history arose much later. It emerged with the publication of the Helena-episode in 1827 under the highly significant title "Helena: Klassisch-romantische Phantas-magorie." For here Goethe, who had hitherto tended to repudiate the concept of Romanticism, open-ly acknowledged that the work, as it now seemed to be developing, would at least share some of the characteristics of the Romantic sensibility. And, indeed, the mixture of styles and approaches, the fusion of medieval, Baroque and contemporary ingredients, the coexistence, within one work, of tragic, comic, parodistic, and ironic elements and allusions, stamps the great two-part tragedy in its final form, which Goethe readied for publication shortly before his death in 1832, with the unmis-takable imprint of Romanticism.

The success of Goethe's *Faust*, its acknowledged status as one of the major masterpieces of world literature, which it acquired soon after it first appeared, inspired many imitators and emulators. But the impulse towards such a type of work accorded well with the general synthetising and system-building tendencies of the period, indeed with the spirit of Romanticism itself. A long-ing for wholeness, a repudiation of the arid rationalism and pragmatism of the Enlightenment, a deep nostalgia for the Middle Ages when the whole of Christendom had been united by a single, comprehensive faith and world view, was, after all, the dominant impulse of the Romantic Move-ment. In philosophy this expressed itself in the building of systems of thought: Kant, Hegel, Scho-penhauer, even Marx, are examples of this striving towards a comprehensive world view that could replace the deeply satisfying catholicity of of the *Summa Theologica* of Aquinas. And if Dante had so triumphantly succeeded in giving that all-encompassing philosophy a literary form, it was only natural that the poets of the Romantic age should strive to do likewise in relation to the philosophi-cal systems of their own time.

II

Goethe's *Faust*, as the work grew throughout its creator's lifetime, clearly embodied this impulse, albeit at first subconscioulsy, as the organic outgrowth of his education and intellectual interests combined with his natural bent towards universality and synthesis: the Book of Job, that primordial "cosmic drama," the chapbook and puppet play of Dr. Faustus, but also the preoccupation with epic poetry and myth under the influence of Herder, all these played their part in the genesis of a work that would ultimately deal with the basic questions of man's fate and existence. So also did memories not only of Dante's great poem but also of Milton's *Paradise Lost* and of Klopstock's

Der Messias (published in instalments between 1751 and 1773), that grandiose attempt to surpass Milton by retelling the story of Christ's martyrdom and resurrection in twenty massive cantos of hexameters. In these epic poems man's existential situation is depicted as being in the centre of a cosmic drama of the forces of Heaven and Hell contending for his soul.

The same contention in dramatic form was the subject matter of the spectacular tradition of Baroque drama, and its antecedents in the Spanish *auto sacramental* and German Jesuit school drama in Latin, of which Jacob Bidermann's *Cenodoxus, sive Doctor Parisiensis* (1602) is perhaps the best-known and most characteristic example. In this play Heaven and Hell as well as Earth are represented on stage. The great doctor Cenodoxus (i.e., emptily learned) suffers from the mortal sin of self-love, personified on stage by Philautia; he is protected by his guardian angel Cenodoxophylax, and admonished by Conscientia. Cenodoxus is the Renaissance scholar who believes that man, not God, is the measure of all things – as such he is very close to the position of Faustus in Marlowe's almost contemporary play. During his funeral the corpse miraculously comes to life and cries out that he is accused. We see him appear before a heavenly tribunal of angels and saints, presided by Christ Himself, and condemned to eternal damnation. The Devil, Panurgus, exults:

> Captus es; meus es; eris;
> Nec esse desines.[4]
>
> (You're my prisoner, you're mine,
> Will never cease to be mine.)

This type of Jesuit school drama came to be ever more elaborately staged in the Catholic parts of Counter-Reformation Europe and merged with the tradition of the Italian Baroque machine opera, highly popular in Vienna. This was the origin of a rich tradition of Austrian folk-theatre, the *Zaubermärchen* ("magical fairytale"), a form of serio-comic cosmic drama, rich in demons and angels contending for the soul and well-being of humans. The best-known of these, immortalised by Mozart's music, is Emmanuel Schikaneder's *Die Zauberflöte* which Goethe not only knew and loved, but to which he wrote a sequel.

And, of course, behind all such cosmic plays lies the the topos of the world as a stage and the stage as a world of which Calderón's auto *El gran teatro del mundo* is perhaps the greatest example, the topos that was inscribed over the entrance to Shakespeare's Globe Theatre: "totus mundus agit histrionem." And, finally, the mystery plays of the Middle Ages themselves with their arc that stretched from the Fall of Man to the Last Judgement, and the moralities like "Everyman," in which vices and virtues dispute the salvation of an archetypal human being, certainly also must be regarded as "cosmic dramas."

III

The "cosmic drama" of the Romantics thus can look back on a venerable tradition. Yet it departs from that tradition and its great model achievements in ways that are highly characteristic. Above all, the religious and moralistic intent of works like the *Divina Commedia, Paradise Lost*, or the

---

[4] Bidermann, *Cenodoxus*, ed. D.G. Dyer, Edinburgh Bilingual Library, 9 (Austin: Univ. of Texas Press, 1974), p. 184.

Spanish *autos* and medieval mystery and morality plays is here reversed: the hero displays just that independence of spirit and belief in his own autonomy, personal fulfilment as his ultimate objective, for which Cenodoxus and Faustus were sentenced to eternal damnation. Moreover, the hero's personal fate is not only heightened to a metaphor of the condition of modern Man himself, it also becomes the vantage point from which the whole of humanity's existential situation and history can be surveyed in a highly compressed yet comprehensive shape.

The conclusion to be drawn from this synoptic and synthetic view of man's position in the world tends to be that, whatever the cosmic forces involved in shaping his fate, ultimately it is not to an external moral law that he has to be true, but to his own inner voice. Even Byron's Cain, deeply repentant for having killed his brother, voices his conviction that ultimately

> That which I am, I am; I did not seek
> For life, nor did I make myself; but could I
> With my own death redeem him from the dust –
> And why not so? Let him return to day,
> And I lie ghastly! So shall be restored
> By God the life to him he loved; and taken
> From me a being I ne'er loved to bear.[5]

Marlowe's Faustus and Bidermann's Cenodoxus were condemned to Hell; Goethe's Faust is redeemed because, although he sinned, he never ceased from striving for self-fulfilment and a deeper insight into the workings of the universe.

This individual struggle for existential autonomy, however, is always seen proceeding against the backdrop of history, as the parallel process of mankind's struggle for higher self-awareness and a continuous striving to transcend its own condition. This overwhelming and wholly new type of historical sense is one of the prime characteristics of the Romantic movement: Hegel, Marx, Bachofen, Michelet, Mommsen, Ranke, Macauley are as much reprentatives of the Romantic sensibility as Shelley, Musset, Hugo, Novalis, Hölderlin, or the Goethe who wrote *Faust*.

In France this tendency to combine an exploration of the individual hero's fate with a synoptic view of history found expression in a number of grandiose projects for the creation of epic poems that would, in fact, mirror the whole of human history, the "poème d'humanité" as it has been christened. It was Lamartine who conceived a grandiose plan for a sequence of narrative poems that would encompass the whole history of mankind. Only the first and last parts of this project were completed. *La Chute d'un ange*, published 1838, describes the descent of an angel, Cédar to human life because he has fallen in love with a beautiful maiden. When, after many adventures among giants, his wife and children die, Cédar kills himself by jumping into the flames of their funeral pyre. An angel of the Lord collects his ashes and foretells him that he will have to redeem himself by nine future incarnations at different periods of human history.

The last, and tenth, part of this epic poem, *Jocelyn*, which Lamartine had published two years earlier (1836), takes the story of the fallen angel, who clearly symbolises fallen Man, to the poet's present: the period during and after the French Revolution. Destined to be a priest, he falls in love, but must renounce all hope of consummating his passion when he is ordered by the Bishop of

[5] Byron, *Cain*, III.i.510-16.

Grenoble, who has been sentenced to the guillotine, to accept ordination so that he can administer him the last rites. He reaches spiritual redemption by devoting the rest of his life to helping the sick and plague-stricken.

Lamartine's plan was highly ambitious, yet it remained uncompleted. Victor Hugo's *La Légende des Siècles* of which the first part was published in 1859 did reach completion when further volumes appeared in 1877 and 1883. But this vast composition of poems which covers the course of human history from the creation to a visionary glimpse into the the the next, the twentieth century, merely was to form the central part of a triptych, between *La Fin de Satan* and *Dieu*.

Lamartine's and Hugo's "poèmes d'humanité" have, at times, been brought into relation with the dramatic poems that, in the wake of Goethe's *Faust*, have tried to encompass all of human experience, the gamut of the human condition.[6]

Madách's *The Tragedy of Man*, one of the most interesting of the "cosmic dramas" that fall within the purview of this paper has, in fact, been brought into the ambit of the "poème d'humanité" and, being a bold synoptic view of history, it certainly has a good deal in common with Lamartine's and Hugo's subject matter. Yet, it seems to me, its salient characteristic is precisely the dramatic form and its very close relationship to Goethe's *Faust*. And, indeed, it can be argued that the most important feature of the works under discussion within the framework of Romanticism and its characteristic contribution to the evolution of the modern sensibility, is precisely the shift from the epic poem to drama as the main vehicle for the highest ambitions of poetry.

IV

It is no coincidence that this shift occured mainly in the German-speaking world and in those countries of Central and Eastern Europe that were most closely influenced by German culture: throughout the eighteenth century the rebirth and rise of German nationalism had been closely linked with attempts to create a great national dramatic literature and a national theatre. From Bodmer and Breitinger to Gottsched and Lessing it was assumed to be axiomatic that any claim to being a great, independent nation must be buttressed by a national language that had produced a great literature. And as the other great nation states, France, Spain, and England had their Racine and Molière, their Calderón and Lope de Vega, and, above all, their Shakespeare; and as Aristotle had declared tragedy to be the highest form of poetry, this struggle for a national identity and political unity became closely linked with the effort to create a great dramatic literature. Goethe and Schiller had finally achieved that objective. Goethe's *Faust* seemed to crown it – a dramatic poem that encompassed the whole of man's striving and destiny, more universal in its scope than *Phèdre* or *La vida es sueño* and even *Lear* or *Hamlet*.

The nationalistic movements in countries like Poland, Hungary, Croatia, Slovenia, Bohemia and Moravia, Rumania, and Serbia took their cue from Germany. In those countries Romanticism itself became almost synonymous with the struggle for national identity. The creation of a National Theatre became a harbinger of political independence, long before that goal itself could be

---

[6] See Dieter P. Lotze, "Madách's *Tragedy of Man* and the Tradition of the 'Poème d'humanité' in European Literature," *Neohelicon*, 6, no. 1 (1978).

achieved. Hence in these countries and in these languages the striving to create a major national dramatic literature assumed paramount importance, while in some of the longer-established national states the epic poem still maintained its primacy which it yielded, only gradually, to its prose successor, the novel.

Moreover, the dramatic form, with its dialogic structure and greater conciseness through the elimination of the lengthy descriptive passages that had always been the glory of the epic poem, was well suited to the authors' aim to compress a vast, multifarious subject matter in the most economical compass. Goethe's *Faust*, admittedly, appeared as a "Lesedrama" rather than as a play suitable for performance, yet being in dialogue it succeeded in covering its universal subject in a swift-moving sweep, capable of a variety of styles unmmatched in any other form: philosophical dialogues, ribald comedy scenes, a wide variety of metres in rhymed and unrhymed verse, short, sharp scenes in prose ("Trüber Tag" and "Nacht, offen Feld"), veritable revues of satirical cameos as in the "Walpurgisnachtstraum" – all these in the first part of the tragedy, and an even wider variety in part two – testify to the flexibility and economy of the genre. Such intermingling of styles, moreover, is one of the hallmarks of the Romantic sensibility. The "cosmic drama" thus became a kind of apex of the ambitions of Romantic poets of the period.

V

One of the earliest – and most remarkable – emulators of Goethe's *Faust* was Zygmunt Krasiński (1812-59) whose *Nieboska komedia* (The Undivine – or Nondivine – Comedy) was completed by November 1833 and published, anonymously, in Paris in 1835.

That Krasiński knew Goethe's *Faust* is beyond doubt. On 4 April 1833 he wrote to his friend Henry Reeve, whom he met while both were studying at the University of Geneva:

> La fin de *Faust* me prouve que Goethe a véritablement été un grand poète, plus grand que Byron lui-même; car considérez *Manfred, Cain, Marino Faliero*, etc. etc., et vous verrez partout la perdition couronnant l'oeuvre. En cela, Byron n'est qu'une approximation dans la poésie de l'univers. Il n'a pas compris le tout; or Goethe a compris l'univers, la lutte du bien et du mal, et a fait triompher le bien. Et pourtant, dans la forme, Goethe est encore de l'école du dix-huitième siècle. Il a eu tel jour où Goethe a pris Diderot pour modèle; c'est bien étrange que cet homme ait vaincu à la fin le monde et la pompe de Satan! C'est aussi une grande idée que Faust devenant aveugle. Mais cela devait être. Il avait tout épuisé sur la terre. Il avait tout épuisé dans l'enfer. Théorie et pratique, tout était fini pour lui.[7]

This young man of twenty-one thus was fully aware of the universal nature of Goethe's work: regarding Goethe as a follower of Diderot, which is to say a man of the eighteenth-century Enlightenment, he was astonished to find him giving his *Faust* a mystical, Dantesque ending. As a self-conscious Romantic he could hardly believe that Goethe too had turned in this direction. In fact, in concluding his own "cosmic tragedy," Krasiński, if anything, proved himself far more darkly pessimistic than Goethe.

---

[7] *Correspondance de Sigismond Krasiński et de Henry Reeve*, ed. J. Kallenbach (Paris: Delagrave, 1902), II, 43.

Zygmunt Krasiński was the scion of an old Polish aristocratic family. He was born in Paris on 19 February 1812, while his father, General Count Wincenty Krasiński, was serving in Napoleon's army. After the fall of Napoleon, the general, a fervent Polish patriot but a realist aware of the hopelessness of insurrection, opted for compliance with the Tsarist rule in Poland. This was the cause of deep inner conflicts in his son, who was an equally dedicated patriot, and loved and understood his father, but had to confront the hostility of his fellow students at Warsaw University who regarded him as the son of a traitor. On the day of the funeral of a nationalist hero, when all the students decided to attend, and to boycott classes at the university, the general ordered his son to go to his usual lectures. He was the only one present and later became the target of bitter attacks from his fellow-students. The general sent him to continue his studies abroad, at Geneva, and later at Paris, Vienna, and Rome.

There can be little doubt that these traumatic experiences hastened the maturing of the young man, who had, from his earliest boyhood, been a prodigy of intelligence and learning, having been admitted to the university at the age of fifteen. This may be the explanation for the truly astonishing depth of his *Nieboska komedia*, a phenomenon comparable only with the achievement of Georg Büchner or the young Mozart.

The *Undivine Comedy*, a dramatic poem in prose, is in four parts (acts), each of which is preceded by a lengthy passage of narration; guardian angels and evil spirits enter the action, very much in the tradition of Baroque theatre. The play's subject matter is no less than an exploration of modern, creative man's personal and political destiny.

The hero of the play, Count Henry (referred to on the left margin of the page where the character speaking is indicated merely generically as "the Bridegroom" in the first scene, and as "Mąż," "the Man," thereafter) is an aristocrat of immense ambition, a poet who begins life in the passionate pursuit of the ideal, perfection in everything. The play opens with his wedding to a young woman he deeply loves. But soon after the marriage he is appalled by the triviality of daily life:

Od dnia ślubu mojego spatem snem odretwialych, snem żarłoków, snem fabrykanta Niemca przy żonie Niemce.[8]

(Since my wedding day I have slept the sleep of the torpid, the sleep of gluttons, the sleep of a German manufacturer alongside his German wife.)[9]

A beautiful maiden, who, to him, embodies the spirit of ideal poetic love seduces him away from home shortly before the christening of his son. His wife, deeply distressed by his absence at the ceremony, and aware that his desertion was due to the absence of poetry – as he conceived it – from their relationship, vows that the child must become a poet, otherwise she will curse him. As the child grows up he does become a poet but has to pay for his gift by going blind. In vain pursuit of his poetic ideal Henry finally sees the phantom that seduced him as what it really is, a hideous skeleton, an evil spirit. He returns home, but it is too late: his wife has gone mad (like Ophelia and Gretchen) and soon dies.

---

[8] Zygmunt Krasiński, *Dzieła Literackie*, ed. Pawel Hertz, 3 vols. (Warsaw: Państwowy Institut Wydawniczy, 1973), I, 331.

[9] The translation cited is by Harold B. Segel, *Polish Romantic Drama* (Ithaca and London: Cornell Univ. Press, 1977), p. 182.

This action, the maturing of the hero through a personal traumatic experience, his shedding of youthful illusions and false ideals, occupies the first two parts of the play. The third and fourth parts (corresponding in fact to the Second Part of *Faust*) show us Count Henry in his public persona, as a statesman occupied with the task of saving civilisation. A vast revolutionary army is besieging the strongholds of aristocratic rule: the revolution threatens the traditional, Christian way of life, upheld by the aristocracy, guardian of values, protector of the ignorant masses. This revolutionary army is led by a fanatic of power, Pankracy (Pancras, Greek for "all-ruler") who, in the narrative opening part three, is described as follows:

[...] – czoło wysokie, przestronne, włosa jednego na czaszce nie masz, wszystkie wypadly, strącone myslami – skora przyschła do czaszki, do liców, żółtawo się wcina pomiędzy kośce i muszkuły – a od skroni broda czarna wieńcem twarz opasuje – nigdy krwi, nigdy zmiennej barwy na licach – oczy niewzruszone, wlepione w słuchaczy – chwili jednej zwątpienia, pomieszania nie dojrzeć; [...] (Hertz, ed., p. 362)

(His forehead is high and broad, his head without a single hair on it, all fallen from thought. His skin has dried to the skull, to the cheeks, yellowishly sinking in between the bones and muscles and, from the temples down, a black beard surrounds the face like a wreath. Never blood, never a change of color in the cheeks – eyes unmoved, fixed intently upon those listening to him – betraying not a single moment of doubt or confusion.) (Segel, ed., p. 203)

The resemblance of this demonic revolutionary leader to Lenin seems uncanny. Pancracy is, in fact, one of the great characters of modern drama, a secularised Mephistopheles (Mephisto himself also makes a brief appearance in the play, claiming to be a ventriloquist to divert Count Henry from recognising the true voice of his guardian angel) (Segel, ed., p. 197; Hertz, ed., p. 354).

Pankracy is the first archetype in modern literature of the totalitarian dictator, of formidable intelligence and dedication, ruthlessly in pursuit of power as an end in itself. Pankracy wants to meet his adversary, Count Henry, who has become the leader of the aristocratic party. He sends a henchman, a converted Jew, who has joined the revolutionaries from his desire to destroy Christian civilisation (there is a strong, typically Polish aristocratic anti-semitism in Krasiński) to arrange a meeting between them. Count Henry, in turn, forces the convert to take him, in disguise, to the camp of the revolutionaries. This leads to a sequence of scenes that can be seen as a secularised Walpurgis Night. Here Count Henry encounters the club of lackeys who want to murder their masters; free women, at war against husbands, and freely distributing their love to those who now acknowledge their rights; artisans and factory workers mobilising against their employers; peasants rising against landowners; terrorists bent on murder, who are taking part in a solemn ritual, during which their daggers are blessed; an apocalyptic procession of the impending destruction of the established order.

In a long and brilliantly conceived debate that takes place in the hall of Count Henry's castle with the portraits of his ancestors looking down, Pankracy and Henry confront each other with arguments for and against the traditional values and the role of the aristocracy in an hierarchically ordered society. Henry rejects the anarchic views of his adversary but recognises in him the harbinger of an inevitable future. His faith in the possibility of victory for his side has been deeply shaken:

Tyś młodszym szatana. [...] Daremne marzenia – kto ich dopełni? – Adam skonał na pustyni – my nie wrócim do raju. [...] Postep, szczęcie rodu ludzkiego – i ja kiedyś wierzyłem – ot! macie, weżcie głowę moją, byleby... Stało się. – Przed stoma laty, przed dwoma wiekami [...] (Herts, ed., p. 392)

(You are Satan's younger brother. [...] Vain dreams, who shall fulfill them? Adam perished in the wilderness; we shall not return to Paradise. [...] Progress, the happiness of the human race – I once believed in them. There you are, take my head just so long as... It's done.) (Segel, ed., pp. 229-30)

In part four the aristocracy is at its last stronghold, the Castle of the Holy Trinity. Henry is apalled by the stupidity, selfishness and dissension among the ranks of his fellow-nobles. When his blind son, the poet, is killed by a stray bullet, he despairs and throws himself from the ramparts.

The revolutionaries take over, they guillotine the surviving aristocrats. Pankracy has reached the peak of human power. With his henchman, Leonard, the practical revolutionary whose character foreshadows features of Stalin, he surveys the scene. But Pankracy, the man of superior intellect, deep down, realises the futility of mere physical power. In the clouds he begins to see the sign of the Cross, surrounded by blinding light:

PANKRACY: Dai mi choć odrobinę ciemności! –
LEONARD: O mistrzu mój! –
PANKRACY: Ciemności – ciemności! –
LEONARD: Hej! obywatele! – hej! bracia – demokraty, na pomoc! – Hej! ratunku – pomocy – ratunku! –
PANKRACY: *Galilaee, vicisti*! (*Stacza się w objęcia Leonarda i kona.*)
(Hertz, ed., p. 417)

PANCRAS: Give me at least a particle of darkness!
LEONARD: O my master!
PANCRAS: Darkness, darkness!
LEONARD: Citizens! Brethren! Democrats! Help! To the rescue! Help! Help!
PANCRAS: *Galilaee, vicisti*! (*He staggers into Leonard's arms and dies.*)
(Segel. ed., p. 247)

And with that reminder of the dying words of Julian the Apostate the play ends.

Here, then, the Faustian hero, Henry, is not redeemed, he perishes in despair at his own inability to stop the destruction of civilisation – his kind of civilisation – in the face of the onrush of the barbarism of a new age. It is Pankracy, the incarnated Satan, who dies, at least proclaiming the victory of the spiritual principle, even if unredeemed still. And Leonard remains in control of the world, wielder of supreme power over a barbarised mankind. It is a dark conclusion, staggering in its prophetic modernity.

The basic Faustian structure is preserved by Krasiński: the tragedy of the countess, caused by the naive idealism of her adolescent husband, corresponds to the Gretchen tragedy; Henry's struggle against the revolutionaries to the political-philosophical subject matter of the second part of Goethe's tragedy. Yet Krasiński has, as it were, shifted the pattern onto a far more directly realistic social and topical plane. The impact of the revolutionary upheavals of 1830 and 1832 in France is clearly discernible, but so also is a typically Polish fear of the threat of Eastern, non-Catholic barbarians (including Jews who pretend to be converted to Christianity while plotting its downfall and desecrating its symbols).

But the play is more than merely a tract for the times. The confrontation between traditional values and the rise of a new world that rejects them has, here, been raised to the level of a general metaphor for the underlying pattern of the process of history itself, in fact, for the thesis that history is a sequence of class struggles, a continuous confrontation between hierarchical order and egalitarian chaos. Pankracy, the victor in this struggle, dies when he realises that the overthrow of a society based on a hierarchic value system leaves no more than a vacuum, empty power. (A point, incidentally, also made more than a century later by another outstanding Polish playwright, Sławomir Mrożek, in *Tango*).

In the first two parts Henry's painful realisation that the pursuit of the absolute, an ideal of love and pure poetic emotion, is not only vain but destructive of real love, is analogous to Faust's destruction of Gretchen for similar motives. Faust does not marry Gretchen because he cannot conceive of settling down and giving up his quest for the absolute. In that sense both plays are basically "Bildungsromane" – the Gretchen tragedy corresponding to the *Lehrjahre* of Wilhelm Meister; the second part of *Faust*, and the philosophical-political section of *The Undivine Comedy*, to the *Wanderjahre*. There is a close correspondence here also to Kierkegaard's *Stages on Life's Way* (1845), with the pursuit of the ideal love representing the "aesthetic" phase, the realisation of man's responsibility to family and polity, the "ethical" phase; the final, in Count Henry's case ultimately elusive, phase being the "religious" stage, the leap into spiritual commitment of the highest order. Yet this ultimate highest plane not being reached, but merely implied by its tragic absence, even more powerfully suggests the need for such a consummation of human upward striving. Krasiński's play, first published at the beginning of 1835, remained unperformed for almost seventy years. It was first staged in Cracow on 29 November 1902. Its startling and original title may well have played its part in suggesting the title of another form of "cosmic" fiction (the legitimate successor of the epic poems of a previous age), Balzac's *La Comédie Humaine*. There is an impressive body of evidence that Balzac may have been aware of Krasiński's play through his relationship with Mme Hanska and thus the Polish colony in Paris, as well as through his acquaintance with Krasiński's English bosom friend, Henry Reeve.[10]

Lord Byron had died before the second part of Goethe's *Faust* appeared. His Faustian dramas thus are based on his knowledge of part one alone. In *Manfred* (1817) he elaborated the idea of the intrepid seeker after knowledge at the risk of his own soul; *Cain* introduced the satanic principle in the cosmic setting of the world on the morrow of creation and, in a stupendous second act, took the hero into the "the abyss of space" and "Hades," a truly Dantesque conception; in the fragment "The Deformed Transformed" ("founded," as the preliminary advertisement acknowledges, "[...] partly on the *Faust* of the great Goethe"), Byron approached both the problem of human identity and of the process of history.

There is a "cosmic drama" that combines the Faustian concept of the wager between the Lord and the Devil, a view of the primal scenes of the Fall of Man closely akin to Milton and Byron's *Cain*, and a synoptic view of the whole of human history: it is one of the most daring and least known works of the nineteenth century, Imre Madách's *Az ember tragédiája* (The Tragedy of Man, 1859-60).

Imre Madách (1823-64) was a Hungarian country gentleman, participated in the Hungarian uprising against Austrian rule in 1848-49, spent some time in prison, and played some part in parlia-

---

[10] This evidence is discussed by Wladislaw Folkierski in a paper "The History of Two Titles: The *Undivine Comedy* and the *Comédie Humaine*," in *Zygmunt Krasiński, Romantic Universalist: An International Tribute*, ed. W. Lednicki (New York: Polish Institute of Arts and Sciences, 1964).

mentary politics. *The Tragedy of Man* was first published in 1862, but had to wait for its first performance till 1883. The strong direct influence of Goethe's *Faust* is only too manifest. The play
opens with a Prologue in Heaven, choruses of angels praising the beauties of the world which has
just been created, the appearance of Lucifer who challenges the Lord about the obedience of Man.
Additional features of Goethe's *Faust* are discernible throughout the play: the Spirit of the Earth
plays an important part analogous to that of Erdgeist in *Faust*; there is a "Schülerszene" in which
Lucifer satirises human knowledge; a scientist who is constructing an "homunculus"; and many
other parallels. Yet the general concept behind the play is wholly original and of great clarity and
elegance of execution. The opening scene in Heaven is followed by Lucifer's seduction of Eve and
Adam's and Eve's expulsion from Paradise. In scene three, East of Eden, Adam questions Lucifer
about the future of mankind and Lucifer agrees to let him have a glimpse into it. The subsequent
eleven scenes show us Adam's dream of human history. In each of these Adam, Eve and Lucifer
appear in different shapes.

In ancient Egypt Adam is a Pharao for whom untold millions of slaves labor, Eve is the wife of
one of the slaves who dies; Adam/Pharao falls in love with her and, another Ekhnaton, resolves to
introduce greater freedom. In classical Athens, democracy is the ruling principle; Adam has become
the hero Miltiades, who, having saved his country is envied by lesser men and, as democracy is the
rule of the mediocre, banished as a reward for his heroic labors. In imperial Rome Adam has become a sensualist, his life an endless orgy; but his complacency is shaken by an encounter with the
plague. The apostle Peter shows him and his mistress Julia (Eve) another path to salvation – Christianity.

But in scene seven, Adam, now Tancred, the leader of a crusade, witnesses the rape and pillage
of Constantinople by the Christian crusaders who have no pity for their fellow Christians; while the
Byzantines themselves are burning other fellow-Christians as heretics for the sake of a mere iota.
Adam/Tancred falls in love with Isaura/Eve whom he has saved from rape, but she has been
pledged to become a nun, Christianity has frustrated the consummation of their love.

The play shifts from the Middle Ages to the Renaissance. We are in Prague at the court of the
Emperor Rudolf. Adam is now Kepler, the great scientist, who is, however, employed by the supers-
titious sovereign as his astrologer and must waste his time with drawing up horoscopes for money.
His wife, Eve, is discontented with their poverty, she is flirting with some shallow courtier, who is
enticing her to a secret tryst in the garden at night. There follows a dream within a dream: Adam/
Kepler, the frustrated scientist, dreams of the results of a wholly secularised, enlightened ideology;
he sees the French Revolution, himself as Danton. Among the aristocrats going to the guillotine is
Eve, he falls in love with her, wants to save her, but she prefers death to life in a society ruled by
terror. Soon after, Danton himself is led to execution, accompanied by the wild jubilation of the
maenad-like *tricoteuses*; among the most violent of these he recognises Eve – another aspect of the
nature of woman. Kepler awakes, and in scene ten we are back in Prague. Eve has indignantly
refused her secret suitor's suggestion that she should poison her husband. Lucifer impersonates
Kepler with a student in an echo of the "Schülerszene" in *Faust*. Kepler turns from theory to practice, from science to technology.

In the next scene we are in the world that was contemporary with Madách, the world shaped by
technology, steam, the industrial revolution – a Dickensian London. The crowds surge through this
highly animated metropolis – here Madách has adopted the structure of the "Osterspaziergang" of

Faust. A puppetteer presents his play; it is the story of Adam and Eve and the fall of man. The social problem of industrialisation is introduced when a poor man who has become a thief is led past to execution. Adam – for the first time no longer a historical character, but merely a traveller passing through – falls in love with Eve, a rich merchant's daughter. At first he is rejected when he accosts her (as Faust does Gretchen); Lucifer spreads the rumour that Adam is vastly wealthy and soon has Eve's mother, another Marthe Schwerdtlein, on his side. But when it turns out that Lucifer's wealth is false, Adam and Lucifer have to withdraw. Night falls as Lucifer and Adam watch from the battlements how all the varied characters of this teeming London scene descend into their graves in a modern Dance of Death, each summing up the futility of his life in a short couplet. The mercantile, industrial, capitalistic society has not brought spiritual peace, only emptiness.

But human history must continue: in the next scene (the twelfth) we are in Madách's future, the world of socialism. Madách did not model this world on the teachings of Marx, but on those of the French social philosopher Charles Fourier (1772-1837). Adam and Lucifer are visitors in one of the phalansteries on which Fourier based his scheme of a totally egalitarian and scientifically organised society. All individuality has here been eradicated. The visitors are received by a scientist who shows them a museum of extinct life-forms. All animals not directly useful to man have been exterminated. The chemist is trying to create life in the laboratory. As evening comes, the workers' batallions return from the factories and fields. There is a roll-call of those to be punished for bad work. The workers have no names, only numbers. But Lucifer points out to Adam that the one who is punished for being too dreamy would, in other epochs, have been Plato; the one who was bored by carving the legs of chairs, Michelangelo; the one who was too quarrelsome and passionate, Cassius, the archetypal revolutionary and freedom fighter. Eve appears; she is a mother who refuses to have her child taken from her, as all education in the phalanstery is scientifically conducted outside the family. Adam offers to marry her, but the scientist does not approve him. He and Lucifer have to withdraw in haste. In the thirteenth scene Adam, horrified by the turn of events, has been taken into outer space by Lucifer. He wants to abandon the earth, but the Spirit of the Earth shows him – as he did Faust in Goethe's play – that man is tied to his planet.

The last scene of Adam's dream shows him the end of human history. The sun has cooled, the earth has become a vast icy waste, inhabited by an Eskimo and his wife (Eve), who are the last human beings alive. Man has reverted to primitivism, his God is his food, the seal. The Eskimo, who looks upon his visitors as superior beings, has only one gift of hospitality to offer them – his wife, Eve. Adam recoils in horror. The last scene shows Adam waking from his dream. He is in despair about what he has been shown. History is a senseless tale, told by an idiot. Adam decides to end it all by committing suicide and stopping the course of history. But as he prepares to throw himself from the rock, Eve comes and tells him that she is pregnant. Mankind's destiny cannot be stopped anymore. The gates of Heaven open and the Lord appears in all his glory. Adam asks the Lord the ultimate question: is this to be Man's destiny? The Lord leaves the answer open. Indeed, it is the uncertainty of the future, the freedom of Man's will, his ability to transcend the harshness of reality by poetry and love that should provide Man with the strength to endure. And Lucifer, the negative spirit of rationality and doubt has his own part to play in this scheme of things. The play closes with the Lord's final message: "Mondottam ember: küzdj' és bizva bizzál" (I told you, Man: fight on in confidence!).

VI

There is one remarkable feature that *The Undivine Comedy* and *The Tragedy of Man* have in common. In spite of the involvement of supernatural powers, angels and devils, good and evil spirits, and the appearance of the Saviour in one, God Himself in the other play, the debate about Man's striving remains on an entirely secular level. Whereas Dante and even Goethe in *Faust* still invoke the idea of an immortal after-existence in Paradise or Hell, Krasiński and Madách completely neglect this side of the metaphysical problem. Their regard is entirely fixed on History as the arena of man's destiny. At the end of the *Tragedy of Man* when the angels sing of the glory of Man's destiny which consists in fulfiling the divine plan, Adam's reaction is:

> Gyanitom én is, és fogom követni.
> Csak az a vég! – csak azt tudnám feledni! –
>
> (I can grasp it too, and shall follow it.
> But that conclusion! – if only I could forget it! –)

There is no mention of the just sitting at the right hand of God in Paradise. Nor is there any hint of a reward in an afterlife for Count Henry or Pankracy in Krasiński's play, which inspite of its championship of Christian civilisation remains true to its title as an *undivine* comedy.

History – "die Weltgeschichte ist das Weltgericht," in Hegel's phrase – has taken the place of the Last Judgement and ultimate justification of Man. Both Madách and Krasiński are obviously influenced by Hegelian ideas. This is particularly clear in the case of Madách who uses a dialectical scheme for the evolution of Adam's (mankind's) quest of the ideal way of life and social organisation. Both Madách and Krasiński see the next step in the evolutionary process as the coming of an egalitarian mass society. Pankracy's and Leonard's revolutionary armies are anarchic, but the implication that a reign of power for power's sake would result in an egalitarian mob-dictatorship is very clearly present. Madách, by adopting the ideas of Fourierist socialism as the scheme of the future, presents such a society in a horrifyingly concrete vision: human society has become an antheap or beehive of identical, de-individualised workers. Here Krasiński and Madách are far more pessimistic than Hegel who put his trust in the dialectical process leading to the gradual emergence of higher and higher stages and the ultimate manifestation of the "Weltgeist" in its purest form.

Goethe, Krasiński, and Madách are also typical representatives of their period in their view of the role of woman, as a foil of man, designed to draw out his higher emotions through his need to cherish and protect her, the nurturing mother of his children, rather than an intellectual equal and partner. "Das ewig Weibliche/ zieht uns hinan" directly continues Dante's view of pure love as the driving force of the universe, with the female principle more important than the intellectual or social individuality of any particular female person.

It is significant that the same idea also dominates the two "cosmic dramas" of Henrik Ibsen, *Brand* (1865) and *Peer Gynt* (1867). Like Krasiński's Count Henry, Brand destroys his wife and child by an excessive devotion to an abstract ideal. Like Faust and Madách's Adam, Peer Gynt is redeemed (perhaps) by the love a pure woman, Solveig, whose faith survives his having deserted and betrayed her, as Faust betrayed Gretchen. Like *Faust* and *The Undivine Comedy, Peer Gynt* also follows the structural scheme of a first part involving the hero's personal and emotional evolution from adolescence to a mature identity, with a second part showing him active in the social and political world before he confronts his inevitable end, his judgement day. And in Ibsen's scheme of things, too, history has taken the place of an immortal afterlife. The Button-Moulder in *Peer Gynt* who has to decide whether to reuse the material Peer was made of or to let him survive as a memory in mankind's storehouse of fulfilled individuals, clearly represents Hegel's "Weltgericht" – history, mankind's collective memory. The criterion here, as in Goethe's *Faust*, as in Madách's *Tragedy of Man* is whether the individual has transcended himself in striving to fulfill God's, or History's, plan. "Wer immer strebend sich bemüht, den können wir erlösen" is the formula by which Faust is redeemed; Adam is advised to struggle and be confident, in the face of the overwhelming evidence that the universe is absurd; Peer Gynt can be redeemed only if he can prove that he was not merely "sufficient to himself," i.e., that he did not remain complacently self-satisfied with his petty sensual satisfactions, the life style of the Trolls.

If the nineteenth century was the century of a belief in the relentless progress of mankind, the "cosmic dramas," that emerged as the products of literary Romanticism, diverged from the spirit of the century. They were darkly pessimistic about the benefits of positivism, scientific rationalism, technology, and industrialisation. While searching for a firm value system, they failed to find anything more solid than the relentless judgement of human history, than the gospel of striving in the face of almost certain failure.

VII

No-one expressed this view more directly than the author of what must be regarded as one of the most ambitious of all "cosmic dramas," Richard Wagner in his tetralogy *Der Ring des Nibelungen*.

Abandoning the Christian framework within which Goethe, Krasiński, Madách and even Ibsen placed their work, Wagner entered the mythical world of the *Edda* and the *Nibelungenlied* to fashion his dark vision of the failure of the Gods as well as Man to transcend the tragic cycle of greed, vainglorious ambition and lust for power. To the Fall of Man, in Byron's *Cain* or Madách's survey of human history, the internecine quarrels and petty ambitions in Krasiński's play, there correspond in Wagner's mythical universe the initial failure of the Gods to avoid becoming bound to the forces of a demonic nether world, and the subsequent tragic weakness of the human hero, Siegfried, who though destined to redeem the Gods' mistakes through the founding of a race of supermen, betrays his beloved, the fallen Walkyrie, Brünhilde, destined to be his mate, by winning her for the cowardly Gunter. And so eventually the whole fabric of the universe crumbles in the downfall of the Gods of Walhall.

By shifting the action onto a plane outside the recognisable confines of human events, into an "Urzeit" beyond history, Wagner hoped to raise his supreme drama onto a truly "cosmic" level, to create a true "mythos" for a post-Christian world, a new kind of religious mystery, to be absorbed at set times in the framework of a quasi-religious festival, akin to that for which the great Greek tragedies were written. Some of this atmosphere still clings to performances of the *Ring*-cycle to this day; but the pseudo-religious impulse has been watered down to a mere aesthetic, or pseudo-aesthetic, experience, from which the ideological and philosophic dimension has almost wholly evaporated. It was Bernard Shaw, a fervent supporter of Wagner's musical genius, who was the first to recognise that, in fact, the *Ring* was far from being an eternal myth, but rather an allegorical image of the pursuit of power, and self-inflicted doom in an industrialised society.

VIII

This series of examples highlights the great difficulty, the near impossibility, of creating the truly universal, "cosmic" work of literature, that could embody truly "eternal" human truths. The "cosmic dramas" of the period between 1800 and 1870 are an expression of the spirit of their times, or even merely of some tendencies within the complex ideological currents of the period, in the same manner in which their models, Dante's *Commedia* and Milton's *Paradise Lost* and *Regained*, were perfect expressions respectively of Thomist philosophy and of Puritan religious concepts. This in no way diminishes their importance and achievement, even the prophetic quality of certain aspects of their analysis of tendencies of their period which have only fully manifested themselves much later, in our own time.

The impulse towards the creation of a work of art that could synthetise the experience of a lifetime, enfold a whole world, has, by now, largely shifted from drama to the novel and from a "cosmic" or mythic to a social, historical, and psychological plane. Tolstoy's *War and Peace* is an example of a work of art that attempts to synthetise a basic insight into the workings of the historical process; Joyce's *Ulysses* and *Finnegans Wake* attempts a synthesis of human consciousness, the waking and dreaming, of an entire culture, and, on the level of the collective unconscious of the dreamer, of the recurring historical process – not the linear dialectic of Hegel, but the eternal cyclical recurrence of Giambattista Vico.

As far as drama is concerned, Thomas Hardy's "Lesedrama," *The Dynasts* (1904-6), attempted to do for the British side of the Napoleonic wars what Tolstoy had accomplished in his novel. Here history unrolls against a chorus of supernatural voices, the spirits of the years, spirits ironic and sinister, spirits of the pities, recording angels, and a host of cosmic observers and commentators.

Most attempts at such "cosmic" fiction tend to great length, trying to encompass a totality of experience in a vast synthetic structure. It could be argued that one of the most successful attempts to compress the whole of human experience into a dramatic fiction, and thus a "cosmic drama" – whether Romantic or not might be left open – is a work that pursued the opposite course, analytic compression rather than comprehensive synthesis. Beckett's *Waiting for Godot* does, in fact, approach the same subject matter as Goethe or Madách, the question of man's position in the universe, the problem of what he should do with his life. But here the problem is reduced to its barest essentials; history is present in the background, because waiting is concerned with Time, and history is Man in Time; and the question posed is whether active striving, in the Faustian sense, is the solution, or whether it is contemplative resignation. Here the endless expanse of historic time is compressed into two short acts, which, by being structurally identical, suggest endless extension into the future; and the vast variety of human types is subsumed in no more than four archetypal characters. It could be argued that *Waiting for Godot* (1953) is a late example of Romantic "cosmic" drama. It is still using a Christian imagery, it is full of Romantic irony, grotesque gargoyles, and it is equally far removed from the realism of psychological drama, or the serenity of classical tragedy. Surrealism with which it has much in common can be regarded as a late offspring of the Romantic sensibility. Perhaps, then, this might be the last of the Romantic "cosmic dramas."

GERALD GILLESPIE

THE PAST IS PROLOGUE:
THE ROMANTIC HERITAGE IN DRAMATIC LITERATURE

The general reputation of Romantic drama as inherently failed because unplayable no longer holds up to scrutiny. The essays in this volume challenge critics who still extrapolate such a view from a limited span of years or from an apparent dearth of successful productions or few survivals lasting into today's repertory in any single national literature. A closer look at the details in the bigger picture yields a quite different understanding of the effects created by Romantic drama across Europe. Not only was Romantic drama important in the shaping of national consciousness in countries in Western and Eastern Europe; in the case of Polish literature, it was also foundational for the modern drama. And in certain nations such as France and Denmark a good number of Romantic plays in fact entered the repertory, some maintaining a hold down to the present. The relative ease of acceptance of certain Romantic plays can be attributed in part to their being less daring in any departures from the rationalist and sentimental codes of the Enlightenment period (e.g., Musset's *On ne badine pas avec l'amour*, Don't Joke with Love), or to their capturing those particular qualities of romance and pageantry that were closer to popular tastes (e.g., Hugo's *Ruy Blas*). In contrast, more precocious plays, notably in Germany in the earliest phases of Romanticism (e.g., Tieck's *Der gestiefelte Kater*, Puss-in-Boots), may not have gained instant or wide acclaim by the public. Nonetheless, they demonstrably influenced later generations of writers throughout Europe. A preeminent case is that of Goethe's *Faust I* and *II*, the single most influential work in Europe since Shakespeare's plays.

Not only has the sense of what can be put on the stage shifted significantly over the past two centuries, but one of the primary Romantic ideas – that of a theater of the mind not limited by the stage apparatus or older conventions – has recurred under various guises. The most recent has been the period of Absurdist drama after World War II to the present. In fact, modes of drama unthinkable without the conceptual renewal that occurred in Romantic drama have gradually imbedded themselves in all the literatures in European languages and reached beyond to other areas of the world. Part One of the present volume pays special attention to the important relation between renewal and innovation. In the nineteenth century, Romanticism was an important force stimulating appreciation of older nonclassical dramaturgy (Shakespeare, Calderón, Webster, et al.) and newer generic experimentation (e.g., Wagnerian "music drama"). Concomitant with the gradual spread and recycling of Romantic ideas of drama in the twentieth century has been the development of new imaginative media (film, television) that were especially compatible with the Romantic heritage.

Revisions of the Canon

As Furst and Burwick show in their essays in Part One, deep paradigm shifts in dramatic theory and practice manifested themselves in a series of waves appearing earliest in the German territories.

Furst argues convincingly that German Storm and Stress with its adulation of Shakespeare provided the foundation for the creative surge by the German Romantics in the 1790s, whereas French cultural patriotism, absorption in the Revolution, and a much later start in translating the difficult English texts delayed the comparable reception of the foreign "barbarian of genius" until the 1820s and 1830s in France. As in Italy, there was no extensive Gallic "pre-Romantic" phase for the drama because of tenacious clinging to the neoclassical model; yet, curiously, the relative lack of concrete knowledge of the Shakespearean texts amid the broader public fostered his myth in France once the general Romantic momentum had built in the period of Guizot, Stendhal, Hugo, and Vigny. Under Part Two, Lefevere illuminates this same clash of rival French and German poetics from the double perspective of a comparative history of reception and of the contending cultural codes involved in translation. In the longer run, he confirms, the stylistic and structural metamorphosis in French drama was proportionate to French resistance to Shakespeare. This prominent case of cultural triangulation (Britain-France-Germany) underscores the significance of textual sharing as a major factor in shaping epochal distinctions in Europe.

The new wave of enthusiasm for Shakespeare in his own country was no less important than his rising fame abroad as a factor promoting the general reception of Romantic dramaturgy. The evolution of staging and performance in the English theater over the first half of the nineteenth century and the careers of many notable English actors after Garrick, such as Kemble, Kean, and Macready, were intimately intertwined with the persistent deepening of appreciation of Shakespeare in his homeland. Just as the new efforts associated with enacting his works conditioned the atmosphere of the contemporary Romantic theater, so too British criticism, through heightened interest in Shakespeare, steadily gained qualities of interpretation that sped up the processes of sharing Romanticism with Europe.

The disruptive effect of the prolonged Franco-British political conflict of the Revolutionary and Napoleonic period masks a more significant reason for erosion of the prestige of French drama in Britain. A special rapport between German and English literary development was already flourishing in the second half of the eighteenth century. From Shaftesbury onward, a range of homegrown eighteenth-century English ideas of nature and the sublime as legitimately irregular – for example, at midcentury, Burke's *A Philosophical Inquiry into the Origins of Our Ideas of the Sublime and Beautiful* (1756) and Young's *Conjectures on Original Composition* (1759) – were compatible with German organicist thought such as Herder espoused. Lessing's *Hamburgische Dramaturgie* helped Coleridge arrive at agreement with the view of Romantic theorists like Jean Paul and A.W. Schlegel that Shakespeare's drama offered an open, organic form which was a welcome alternative to the closed neoclassical model of the French. Coleridge approved of Shakespeare's mixing of comedy and tragedy, poetry and prose, and contrastive moods and figures, on the grounds that thereby he preserved the power of creative imagination and gave authentic expression to the fullness of life in its actual variety. Coleridge's friend Lamb emphasized that in comedy, too, what mattered was the creation of an engaging higher reality on stage through the power of the imagination, not a replication of the confining real world (*On the Artificial Comedy of the Last Century*, 1822). For Lamb, the play sphere transcended reality, converting even the ugly and bizarre into aesthetic material. We can detect general affinities to aspects of Coleridge and Lamb in Hugo's formulation of the idea of drama as a total artwork that unifies the sublime and grotesque in the "Preface" to *Cromwell* (1827).

In the London of the early decades of the nineteenth century, material of Storm-and-Stress character and German Romanticism were not clearly distinguished; thus, for example, Schiller's plays *Kabale und Liebe*, *Die Räuber*, and *Wilhelm Tell* were rewritten with stronger Romantic accents in the process of belated adaptation for the stage. English openness to foreign music, too, facilitated wider public acceptance of German Romanticism. Weber's operas *Der Freischütz* and *Oberon* were a success in London in 1824, as were German productions of Beethoven's *Fidelio* and Mozart's *Zauberflöte* and *Don Giovanni* a decade later. Gradualism in the English shift from late eighteenth-century to Romantic tastes helps explain in part the position of the liberal Byron within the Romantic movement. On the one hand, asserting his own identity as a playwright, Byron sought to be programmatically anti-Shakespearean; on the other hand, in his *Manfred* (1817), by adapting Goethe's *Faust I* to suit his own image of the cursed rebel and fatal man, he was a perfect representative of the kind of poet who could bridge the Shakespeare-oriented Storm and Stress and Romanticism proper. Hazlitt, the most important English Romantic critic, was intensely fascinated by Goethe's and Schiller's plays (of the Storm-and-Stress and *Klassik* decades) in their own right as expressions of the historical will of the age. He recognized in their dramaturgy, which he thought exhibited a tendency toward the exposition of speculative ideas, an epochal assertion of German cultural character rooted in a particular past. Just as the English drama with its pronounced "Gothic" streak represented an evolutionary growth, so likewise the German drama was not subject to criticism according to artificial norms derived from another tradition. In an essay on "Wit and Humour" introducing his *Lectures on the English Comic Writers* (1819), Hazlitt demonstrates general atunement with the constellation of Romantic ideas and tastes represented by the Schegels and Jean Paul. Going beyond organicist thought, he stresses in "laughter, the ludicrous, the ridiculous," ascending levels of a self-reflexive, critical principle: "humour [...] the growth of nature and accident; wit [...] the product of art and fancy."

As noted, Furst's essay directs our attention to the important fact that Germany experienced its own distinct period of Classicism (*Klassik*) in the drama from the 1780s to 1810, but one that followed the powerful indigenous pre-Romantic movement called Storm and Stress (after Klinger's play *Sturm und Drang* in 1776) and that overlapped with high Romanticism. In a book focussed on such Classicism in its own right, Bennett has examined in some detail the ways in which, from Lessing over Goethe to Kleist, German drama developed an internal self-reflexiveness as an instrument of cultural consciousness. In Bennett's view, which unjustly relegates the drama of high and late Romanticism (i.e., Tieck to Büchner) to secondary importance as a channel, this innovative streak is rooted in the peculiar fortunes of German Classicism.[1] Be that as it may, Howarth too stresses in his essay in our volume that the German picture clearly contrasts with the French. The French began echoing an older anticlassical vocabulary of approbation of irregularity, nature, freedom, truth, and feeling in the drama with greatest fervor at a juncture when England and Germany were already passing through late Romanticism. In the European context, France's particular reception of Shakespeare promoted the telescoping together of a style and language like those in Storm and Stress with traits of a delayed Romanticism. In his book *The Taming of Romanticism*, Nemoianu has added the important reminder, however, that France lived through its own unique national form of "high Romantic" drama as the series of spellbinding, and sometimes horrific, moments played out in the

---

[1] Benjamin Bennett, *Modern Drama and German Classicism: Renaissance from Lessing to Brecht* (Ithaca and London: Cornell Univ. Press, 1979).

actual Revolution.[2] Discussing irony and the interrelated sublime and grotesque in *Die Vorschule der Aesthetik* (Preschooling in Aesthetics, 1804), Jean Paul Richter made this very point about the theatrical quality of history as it had unfolded in real history in France. For decades to come, Romantic writers and their successors saw the logic of treating figures of the Revolutionary age as Romantic protagonists.

Burwick examines the contrast of world views underlying the paradigm shift in the drama that occurred toward 1800 in Germany, but was slowed or absorbed by public events in France and would not be fully embraced or implemented until significantly later in many nations for a variety of reasons. He reminds us of the deeper roots of an idealist position in England that would predispose English writers to a Romantic outlook with many points of contact with German literature, including the accommodation of organicist thinking. He points to Gallic spiritual affinities in the development of a sense of the radical primacy of the subject, an epochal trend which, as in England and Germany, ultimately militated against objective mimesis or "rational illusion" and for a new code of imagination. Not "reality," but the human mind becomes the focal object of dramatic representation; and plot reveals, rather than conceals, the playwright's efforts at illusion-making, into which the audience is invited as participant. The play realm involves something not ontically present, a "meontic" fiction. Burwick illustrates the powerful appeal of this newer "meontic" paradigm in a variety of expressions including Kleist's *Amphytrion* (1807), Byron's *Sardanapalus* (1821), Shelley's *Charles I* (1821), and Hugo's *Cromwell* (1827).

In essence, the French theater public could not be weaned from its neoclassical expectations until artists and critics first in some way reconstructed the alternative dramatic values that had made their appearance in the late sixteenth and early seventeenth century, but had steadily been submerged and excluded from the privileged center after the establishment of the Academy under Richelieu. From the 1820s onward, Shakespeare served as a main bypass to that lost world for the French Romantics, but even after Shakespeare was pressed into service, half a century elapsed before French criticism, with the advent of Symbolism, started paying serious closer attention again to their own nation's literary ties to Golden Age writing. The thematics and structuring principles of a "theater of the world" found in Lope de Vega and Calderón had flourished in works by the young Corneille, Rotrou, and Tristan L'Hermite; they still surfaced in such eminent playwrights as Molière (*L'Impromptu de Versailles*, 1663) and Marivaux (*L'Ile des esclaves*, 1725).

German seventeenth-century dramaturgy from Bidermann over Gryphius and Lohenstein to Weise had remained closer to the spirit of the Spanish and French Baroque and of the English post-Elizabethans. But, in Germany too, it was Shakespeare – aided and abetted by the example of Milton in the epic – who served to reconnect native German drama to the challenging subject-matters and imaginative power of the Baroque period from which rationalist and religious bourgeois critics of the early eighteenth century (e.g., Gottsched and Bodmer) had turned away out of the desire to create a reassuring moral ethos. The desire for reform led the Germans, too, first to a rejection of the darker insights, the alleged philosophic perversity, and stylistic "excesses" of their own seventeenth-century authors. A leading signal of reconsideration was the essay *Vergleichung Shakespeares und Andreas Gryphs* (A Comparison of Shakespeare and Andreas Gryphius, 1741) by the playwright J.E. Schlegel, uncle of the famous Romantic critics, suggesting some deeper affinity

---

[2] Virgil Nemoianu, *The Taming of Romanticism: European Literature and the Age of Biedermeier* (Cambridge: Harvard Univ. Press, 1984), especially pp. 105-19.

between the ancient Greek and the British and German Baroque tragedy. When Lessing tipped the balance of critical opinion in the mid-eighteenth century against francophile neoclassicism, the Germans were already poised to find in Shakespeare a channel to an uncensored, more complex vision. Goethe's Shakespearean "history" of social transformation in the tumultuous Reformation era, *Goetz von Berlichingen von der eisernen Hand* (Götz of Berlichingen of the Iron Hand, 1773), was the first great achievement breaking a new pathway.

The range of potential connections appeared in the symptomatic playwright Tieck in the late 1790s.[3] Among other things a lifelong adulator and a major translator of Shakespeare, editor of Kleist and Novalis, translator of *Don Quixote*, and founder of the Romantic fantastic comedy, Tieck also brought out the first anthology including German Baroque tragedy in the nineteenth century. His *Deutsches Theater* (1817), with plays from Sachs to Gryphius, complemented his *Altenglisches Theater* (1811), as a demonstration of authentic art rooted in a folk. Besides using elements from Shakespeare for "Gothic" effects in some early works, Tieck appreciated the Jacobean and Caroline tragedians of England in whose works were antedated the somber vision and profound moral shock of high Romantic tragedies such as Shelley's *The Cenci* (1819). At the same time, as the founder of German Romantic "fantastic comedy," Tieck drew, in his *Die verkehrte Welt* (The Land of Upside-down, 1798), upon the Baroque and eighteenth-century comic genre which combined sprightly poetological satire with the twinned topoi of a topsy-turvy world and a world-theater. Tieck's early comedies exhibited a bold reception of a variety of influences – Aristophanes, Sachs, Shakespeare, Weise, Gozzi, Lessing, Goethe, and more.

The reawakened fascination for their own great poetry of the late Renaissance no doubt was, as Hilt suggests in his essay, initially an impediment to broader English enthusiasm for Spanish Golden Age drama. The great Calderón enjoyed only a *succès d'estime* through efforts such as Shelley's. Another reason that should be cited was the ready absorption of Spanish literature, especially prose narratives, in England from the end of the sixteenth century onward, establishing earlier taste trends and saturation that perhaps blocked any surge of further imports; by the later eighteenth century *Don Juan* was a stock figure on the English puppet stage, and Sterne counted Rabelais and Cervantes as his "masters." But A.W. Schlegel's promotion of Spanish drama and of Calderón in particular as "one of the fathers of modern poetry next to Shakespeare and Dante" found fertile ground in the first decade of the nineteenth century in Germany. Goethe's staging of *La devoción de la Cruz* in a German version (*Andacht zum Kreuze*) in Weimar in 1802 was the needed strong signal; translations of Golden Age works and eventually productions of them increased. Tieck again pointed the way by incorporating the characteristic motifs and lyrical variation of a Calderonian *auto sacramental* in the Prologue to his influential Romantic mystery play *Kaiser Oktavian* (1804). By the 1830s, Calderón's *La vida es sueño* (Life is a Dream) and *El príncipe constante* (The Constant Prince) had enjoyed enough performances to enter the German canon of high literature. To playwrights such as Eichendorff and Grillparzer who were the immediate heirs of high Romanticism, Golden Age drama was one of the unshakable pillars in the temple of the human spirit. Especially Schopenhauer's inclusion of Calderón with Shakespeare and the ancient Greek tragedians among the highest manifestations of the transcendence by art over captivity to the "will" proved seminal in the second half of the nineteenth century. The delayed reception of Schopenhauer's

---

[3] For a fuller treatment of the plays between 1795 and 1800, consult Gerald Gillespie, "Young Tieck and the Romantic Breakthrough," *Theater Three*, no. 4 (Spring 1988), 31-44.

masterwork, *Die Welt als Wille und Vorstellung* (The World as Will and Representation, 1818), had the effect of making the Romantic canon freshly attractive to Symbolist poets and of conveying Romantic ideas by way of Wagner and Nietzsche to Modernism.

Even though the intensity of the Calderonian cult subsided on their side of the Rhine, the German Romantics, by having developed Spain into the epitome of a pre-Enlightenment land of romance, meanwhile reinforced budding Gallic opinion in this regard. Drawing initially on A.W. Schlegel, French critics began to see the Spanish *comedia* as a repository of colorful romance and an example of freedom from artificial rules, and in the 1820s the first serious attempts at original plays in the Spanish mode were capped by Hugo's celebrated *Hernani* (1830), while Mérimée's short plays entitled *Théâtre de Clara Gazul, comédienne espagnole* (1825) already could reflect ironically on the new vogue. The Iberian materials were soon caught in the strong pull toward the grotesque, pageantry, and melodrama in France – in the European context, tendencies characteristic of late Romanticism. Hugo's famous "Preface" to *Cromwell* (1827), propounding an epical model for drama as a kind of *Gesamtkunstwerk* that could encompass all aspects of existence from the "sublime" to the "grotesque," also reflected this new "Hispanized" view of the connection between drama and romance. Furthermore, as Schmeling argues in his essay, the "Preface" exhibits the Romantic aspiration for a neomythological capacity to represent history as a divine spectacle or play in its totality. The Romantic philosopher Schelling explicitly linked the idea of man's involvement as player in a co-authorship of the drama of humanity to the general Romantic subjective desire for identity with the universe.

In identifying "play thematics" as central to the Romantic breakthrough, Schmeling takes up the German term *Spiel* which, because it covers a very broad semantic field, was particularly suited to express the metaphoricity and conceptualization behind the new sensibility. At least two terms, "play" and "game," are required in English to suggest the allusive range. In a recent book on play concepts, Mihai Spariosu corroborates the crucial role of the term *Spiel* for German Idealism and the age of subjectivism. It is found both in the new philosophy set forth by Kant and in Schiller's aesthetic vision of man who is distinct through his "play-drive."[4] In a virtually simultaneous book, Burwick stresses the ways that Romantic drama worked out the deliberations of philosophy and critical theory by building an acute consciousness of illusion into the fabric of drama.[5] The playing of the mind is a prime matter in the metadrama of Goethe, Coleridge, and Tieck.

Driven by an unceasing yearning to resolve the split between "object" and "subject," the German Romantic poets around 1800 rediscovered the principles of vision and play in the Baroque world theater. In his essay on this topic, Schmeling stresses the ambiguity in Tieck's fantastic comedy that was to become so productive in dramaturgy of the future. On the one hand, Tieck's self-reflexive art illuminated cultural reality critically and satirically; on the other hand, as "potentiated illusion," it had itself as its goal and constituted "'pure' poetry." Approaching this tension in terms of a paradigm shift in the conception of dramatic "illusion" that was in progress at the end of the eighteenth century, Burwick finds its metaphysical roots in pre-Kantian (e.g., Humian) as well as Kantian philosophy. Schmeling notes connecting threads in France and Italy as well as England

---

    [4] Mihai I. Spariosu, *Dionysus Reborn: Play and the Aesthetic Dimension in Modern Philosophical and Scientific Discourse* (Ithaca and London: Cornell Univ. Press, 1989), especially Part I, section 1, "Play and the Aesthetic Turn in German Idealism (Immanuel Kant: Philosophy and/or Play?; Friedrich Schiller: The Play of Reason)."
    [5] Frederick Burwick, *Illusion and the Drama: Critical Theory of the Enlightenment and Romantic Era* (University Park: Pennsylvania State Univ. Press, 1991), passim.

and Germany in a line from the play-within-a-play and rehearsal traditions of the late Renaissance down to the Romantics. Important in Schmeling's eyes is that certain playwrights such as Tieck pushed beyond the eighteenth-century poetological critiques of theatrical art (e.g., satire of trends such as melodrama, jibes at the social and cultural attributes of the audience, etc.) and explored the anti-illusionist implications of a play that is self-reflexive. By problematizing and ironizing the structures of drama and openly playing with them, Tieck explored the strange new realm of an art striving for autonomy, divorcing itself radically from any subordination to institutional, utilitarian, educational, or moral purposes. The self-mirroring of drama in his early plays also tended to disperse and relativize the referentiality of particular contents that tied his fantastic story-lines to historical patterns and events, such as the Revolution. Out of this Tieckian lesson a succeeding generation of playwrights – for example, Büchner and Grabbe – fashioned their own powerful means for juxtaposing existential principles and ideological forces, and for projecting a tragicomic world view.

Romantic use of the "world theater" idea in imaginative and discursive literature contributed in the longer run to the drift from aesthetic idealism to profound pessimism and even historical nihilism; and it helped stimulate the corollary idea of the artist's participation in the creation of a vast world-engirdling intertextuality. These were natural consequences of the Romantic yearning for "totalization" (F. Schlegel's "universal-progressive poetry"). In various segments of the evolving Romantic intertext, we can see two significant forces at work. First, there is the drive to knit together all typologically deducible and historically recorded phenomena of human behavior. This kind of totalization revitalized the older European aspiration to write a "universal history" and contributed many patterns to nineteenth-century historicism. More affected by Romanticism than they were able or willing to admit, positivist and materialist thinkers of the nineteenth and early twentieth centuries sometimes assumed that certain such patterns of a presumed universal history were "scientific" facts. Second, there is the twinned Romantic drive to conflate perceived patterns in modern Europe with all known mythologemes and archetypes (Novalis's idea of a "new mythology"). On the one hand, this aspiration recapitulated the humanist impulse to apply in their own poetic works the metaphysical and psycho-historical patterns thought to underlie the welter of mythology. On the other hand, the Romantic shift toward myth reversed the bias in the Enlightenment drive to convert myths into a form of history; as Coleridge and Novalis proposed, Romanticism should recapture history as a kind of myth-making.

In his comprehensive view of assimilation and adaptation of forms under Part One of this volume, Howarth explains the broader picture of paradigm shifts in relation to the inertial centrality of French neoclassical drama in the eighteenth century. He emphasizes two key breakthroughs: (in agreement with Carlson) the idea of the history play with national subject-matter, reaching from England not only to Germany but to France and Italy; and (in agreement with Furst) the liberating effects of "pre-Romantic" sensibility, especially the example of Storm and Stress in theater, reaching slowly from Germany, but to a large extent displaced by a cruder, popular melodrama in France. Howarth offers us an engaging, fresh assessment of Schiller, seen through a comparatist's eye from the French vantage, as a representative of the fortunate eclecticism that characterized German drama in the period from the French Revolution to 1830. We observe a variable balancing of Classical restraint and pre-Romantic desire for freedom, with genuine forays into Romantic treatment of historical subjects and of dramatic structure, in Schiller's *Die Jungfrau von Orleans: Eine romantische*

Tragödie (The Maid of Orleans: A Romantic Tragedy, 1801). The mixes and swings between the Classical and Romantic in Kleist's plays are scrutinized in the same spirit, and Howarth finds *Käthchen von Heilbronn, oder die Feuerprobe* (Kate of Heilbronn, or Trial by Fire, 1808) and *Prinz Friedrich von Homburg* (1810) to exemplify two kinds of Romanticism: one the highly romanesque idealization of the Middle Ages, the other "the conflict of a complex individual's nature with the demands of law and authority" in the real world. Despite differences of tone, it is Grillparzer above all who, in his judgment, continues with distinction the range represented by Schiller and Kleist.

Underneath the Elizabethan, Jacobean, and Gothic traits of Shelley's *The Cenci* (1819), Howarth finds a still essentially neoclassical approach. In consciously exorcizing Shakespeare's influence, Byron is deemed to create a theater of the mind that seeks to combine a modern Classicism with the Romantic temper. Howarth associates Byron's historical tragedy *Marino Faliero, Doge of Venice* (1820) with treatments of the same story by Delavigne, Dumas, and Vigny in 1829 – that is, considers it to arrive at, but not yet cross over, the Romantic threshold of experimentation with a new poetic language. Howarth concurs with those who hold that this ultimate step was taken by Hugo's *Hernani* in 1830, after being announced in the bolder propositions of the "Preface" to the epical *Cromwell*. Attempts such as Vigny's in *Chatterton* (performed 1835) to create a non-Hugolian "drama of thought" ran into the considerable obstacle posed by the gradual merger between the bourgeois drama and melodrama in France which allowed a popular detour around the great Romantics. In Howarth's scheme, the tragic hero in the new fashion, the sufferer crushed by ennui and the *mal du siècle*, appeared in Büchner's *Dantons Tod* (Danton's Death, 1835), a play ahead of its time as was Musset's *Lorenzaccio* (1834). Looking from the French vantage, he points to Büchner as the significant modernizer of the European "bourgeois tragedy" in his *Woyzeck* (left incomplete at his death in 1837), especially because he contributed to drama "the historical pessimism and the metaphysical despair" of the Romantic *Zeitgeist*.

Howarth is a consistent spokesman of a French-oriented view which sees the juncture of greatest creative activity in the drama of Western Europe around 1830.[6] What other contributors to our volume such as Schmeling bring supplementing and adjusting this view is an awareness of the remarkable surge of experimentation that Tieck engaged in an entire generation earlier, and the importance of Goethe's completion of *Faust* I (1808) and II (1832) in the interval of the opening decades of the century. In broader evolutionary terms, as Nemoianu shows in his essay, drama took a decidedly Romantic turn around 1800 in Germany and the phenomena appearing in France around 1830 can legitimately be regarded as representing a late phase of Romanticism into which was gathered a number of recapitulations of pre-Romantic and early Romantic motifs.

---

[6] This orientation appears, for example, in the brief glossary (pp. 326-28) accompanying Stéphane Michaud's essay "La Parole risquée: L'aventure de la poésie moderne (XIXe-XXe siècles)," as well as in the description of the flow of lyricism in France as against Germany and England (pp. 321-49), in *Précis de littérature comparée*, ed. Pierre Brunel and Yves Chevrel (Paris: Presses Universitaires de France, 1989). The unmistakable importance of the work of major writers such as Nerval at mid-century and the appearance of Baudelaire as an axial figure between European Romanticism and Symbolism lend weight to the thesis that Romanticism in France either (re)emerged belatedly or acquired pronounced rhythms that are associated with "late" Romanticism in Germany and England. Among those making the case is Lilian R. Furst, *Romanticism in Perspective* (London: Macmillan, 1969; New York: Humanities Press, 1970). Still indispensible as a guide to a reasoned periodization of Romanticism (and a model that could be extended to include the literatures of Northern and Eastern Europe and North and South America) is Henry H.H. Remak, "West European Romanticism: Definition and Scope," in *Comparative Literature: Method and Perspective*, ed. Newton P. Stallknecht and Horst Frenz (Carbondale and Edwardsville: Southern Illinois Univ. Press, 1971), pp. 275-311.

Romantic Classicism, Classicistic Romanticism

The several opening essays of the present volume offer insights into the appearance of key innovative attitudes within distinct cultural contexts. The aim is to help scholars deal with confusing discrepancies among the variant national terminologies – that is, to integrate these vocabularies into a
more comprehensive framework applicable to European literature as a whole. At this level, we
begin to perceive artist and audience sharing within a polycentric civilization. Comparatists should
certainly no longer accede to remnant chauvinistic habits of dating significant junctures in a flow of
Romantic currents as if what is at stake is that nations somehow earn merit points for defending an
established set of literary conventions or sponsoring a newer set. By the same token, our cautious
approach to "periodization" must openly acknowledge the artificiality of a comparativistic pan-
European scheme. To construe supposed rough synchronistic correlations of phenomena that cut
across some two dozen languages is to posit useful hypotheses at best.

That is why there is very little profit (outside of the arena of old nation-based cultural rivalries)
either in trying to disentangle the strands of closely related Classicist and Romantic impulses in certain dramaturgies, except in specific works as peakings of one or the other tendency, or in denying
the predominance of one or the other strand for an extended time, or in failing to pay proper attention to notable early exceptions. Howarth reminds us forcefully that neoclassical impulses often co-
existed, and sometimes entered into symbiosis, with more distinctly Romantic impulses. I shall
illustrate by reference to Chénier, Hölderlin, and Niccolini two of the most obvious sources of critical confusion about this historical association. One occurs when artists who appear to be entirely
devoted to a classical subject-matter hit upon Romantic insights through it. Another occurs when
artists who, after a considerable career as neoclassical writers, absorb Romantic substance in their
late work.

Marie-Joseph Chénier's *Oedipe Roi* repaired only part of the damage which, by its inability to
accept the pre-Christian religious experience of fate, Voltaire's influential *Oedipe* (première in
1718) had "inflicted" on Sophocles.[7] But Chénier's *Oedipe mourant* (1785), later titled *Oedipe à
Colonne*, endeavored to restore most features of the original Greek tragedy and its aura of sacred
mystery. The protagonist was allowed to assert his role as a sacrificial victim placed beyond
remorse or fear and associated with the numinous realm of fate. Chénier's complete Oedipal tragedies (published posthumously in 1818) aimed to convey a sense of Greek drama on the Parisian
stage such as it might have been played in ancient Athens, with the choral parts, which most contemporary French critics could not accept. In effect, his purist devotion was beginning to push
beyond the known French neoclassical territory. Meanwhile Chénier's national and ancient historical tragedies, such as *Charles IX* (1788) and *Timoleon* (1794), reflected the issues of freedom, tolerance, and republican virtue that gripped the Revolutionary period. (Marie-Joseph escaped the fate of
his brother, the poet André Chénier, executed during the Terror.) In his choice of dramatic subjects
and his aesthetic approach he shared much with his Italian contemporary Alfieri who, in turn,
demonstrated affinities to the Storm-and-Stress and classicist traits in the playwright Schiller.
Despite his low opinion of German drama as this had been imported into France before 1800,
Chénier in *Philippe II* (1801) exhibits lyrical accents that are influenced by Schiller's *Don Carlos*

---

[7] See the Introduction to *Oedipus the King* (pp. 131-53) in *Sophocles: The Three Theban Plays*, trans. by Robert
Fagles, introd. by Bernard Knox (Harmondsworth: Penguin, 1984).

(1787) and pull his work away from the more austere form of Alfieri's yet earlier *Filippo* (1783) – that is, in the direction of Romanticism, conceived in French terms.

Hölderlin's translations *Oedipus der Tyrann* and *Antigone* appeared in 1804 with his "Notes" on these Sophoclean plays.[8] His own earlier drama *Empedokles* (in its several versions), set in ancient Greek Sicily, was influenced partly by Sophocles' *Oedipus at Colonus*. A highly foreshortened explanation of the ancient philosopher's decision to resist election to kingship and instead to depart in sacrificial death in Hölderlin's tragedy is that Empedocles dares to mark awareness of the separation between the human and the divine. He institutes the memory of the lost divine in a cultic act, thereby reconciling nature and spirit, his own heroic role and the people he leads, his own times and what will be lasting in history. The third version, *Empedokles auf dem Ätna*, relates the historical event even more expressly to an overarching mythic paradigm that transcends the human conflict of the age. The departing victim, like Christ (who in Hölderlin's poetry is an avatar of Dionysus closing Antiquity), points the way into a new order. While Hölderlin comprehended tragedy as a sacred union occurring in an act of consciousness, he veered away from the pathway of Enlightenment humanistic tragedy of the "soul" in order to restore a primary mythic relationship with the divine. Behind his rediscovery of ancient tragedy we can detect the Romantic ground-pattern of a process in which historical singular existence and mythic universality first correspond, then fall apart, but are reunited on a higher level. Schiller codified the problem of modern separation from nature or loss of the divine in his treatise *Über naive und sentimentalische Dichtung* (On Naive and Sentimental Poetry, 1795), just as German high Romanticism was arriving on the scene. Kleist reconsidered the inherently circular or spiral motion of overcoming the gap between the pure beauty of a mindless puppet (absolute nature) and God (absolute spirit) in his essay "Über das Marionettentheater" (On the Marionette Theater, 1810). But Hölderlin reendowed the experiencing structure of the human mind with a mythic significance that was eternal and inhered in nature.

Hölderlin's "Anmerkungen" (Notes) on the Sophoclean tragedies set forth his view that these plays embodied actual stages in the emergence of the "tragic" epoch and that the Greek idea inevitably was transformed for us by its passage into the Christian era. Hence there were two kinds of tragedy in the present world, the ancient Greek and the modern Hesperian. We could never simply return to or even imitate that earlier happening. It literally reshaped consciousness; we became different by virtue of it in historical-developmental terms. In Oedipus' "närrisch wilde Nachsuchen nach einem Bewußtsein" (foolishly wild search for a consciousness), we glimpse the raging of the power of nature in the union of God and man. The "grenzenlose Eineswerden durch grenzenloses Scheiden sich reiniget" (infinite becoming-as-one purifies itself through infinite separation). At an axial zero point, or "caesura," the rupture occurs in *Oedipus* which is occasioned by the protagonist's knowing; this is the categorical reversal in the Greek world after which Man "hiermit im Folgenden schlechterdings nicht dem Anfänglichen gleichen kann" (simply cannot, in what follows, be like what he was at the beginning). Hölderlin's thought anticipates such later attempts to formulate a view of tragedy and history as that which Camus advanced in his lecture of 1955 "On the Future of Tragedy." To Camus's mind, both the Greek century from Aeschylus to Euripides and the European from Shakespeare to Calderón "mark a transition from forms of cosmic thought impregnated

---

[8] For a detailed analysis, consult Jeremy Adler, "On Tragedy: 'Notes on the *Oedipus*' and 'Notes on the *Antigone*' [of] Friedrich Hölderlin, Translated with an Introduction," *Comparative Criticism*, 5 (1983), 205-30 (Introduction) and 231-44 ("Notes").

with the notion of divinity and holiness to forms inspired by individualistic and rationalist concepts. [...] literarily, the works move from ritual tragedy and from almost religious celebration to psychological tragedy. [...] Both revolt and an order are necessary" to constitute genuine tragedy. However, once playwrights destroy the balance in tragedy that springs from recognition of a divine order that imposes absolute limits on man, tragic art falters and subsides.[9]

Hölderlin's heroine Antigone is acting in the existential wilderness we enter after the "caesura," but paradoxically her story is thus also the threshold of a humane age of suffering, a quest to understand the rupture. Hölderlin brought this second phase of tragedy into line with the longer-term "Hesperian" (i.e., Western European) tendency by interpreting the dramatic conflict in the *Antigone* as a "revolt" against the societal hardening which, dialectically, countered the rupture, the terrifyingly chaotic moment of revelation. His view of Antigone as the heroine who asserts a religious principle of reconciliation and love in opposition to Creon's ethos of the state and power was echoed independently in Wagner's interpretation of the Oedipus trilogy, notably in the *Ring*.[10] Hölderlin's idea that the Greek experience exhibits the tension between archaic (Oriental) and Hellenic (Occidental) factors in our development recurred in Nietzsche's analysis of culture in *Die Geburt der Tragödie aus dem Geiste der Musik* (The Birth of Tragedy out of the Spirit of Music, 1st ed., 1872).

The case of Niccolini illustrates a general direction in which certain classicistic writers would steer appreciation of Greek tragedy. He began translating Aeschylus in 1816 and, like A.W. Schlegel, but contrary to La Harpe, esteemed the sublimity of Aeschylean tragedy. In *Edipo nel bosco delle Eumenidi* (Oedipus in the Grove of the Eumenides), Niccolini preserved the cult aspects and mysticism of his model Sophocles, yet – in the spirit of Chénier – adopted the modern idea of reconciliation between Oedipus and Polynices and converted Oedipus' revelations into a revolutionary condemnation of princely absolutism. Eventually, against his remaining neoclassical scruples, Niccolini gave recognition to the greatness of Shelley's *Cenci* in an Italian adaptation, named specifically after the heroine *Beatrice Cenci* (1844). Shelley's play attributed the monstrosity of crime directly to the father as a cruel authority figure and to the corrupt system of papal Rome which he reflects. The children, in seeking to end the Oedipal curse that taints the family, take a step that indeed constitutes a rupture in human affairs; they enact the drama of revolution against a false order that must be ritually cleansed. Niccolini, like Shelley, recognized that the Oedipal aggression against the parent could be "modernized" in parallel to the French Revolutionary model of the execution of the King.

Social and National Consciousness

The attitudes about the folk and prerational creativity that Andreeva and Hanak treat in their essay as a complex widely shared across Europe, and the artistic phenomena of *costumbrismo* that

---

[9] I cite from the English edition of Albert Camus, *Lyrical and Critical Essays*, ed. Philip Thody, trans. Ellen Conroy Kennedy (New York: Vintage, 1970), pp. 295-310. Camus uses the term "Romantic drama," without any illustrations, to designate what is a lesser mode of representation concerned with the "struggle between good and evil."

[10] For a thorough contextual account of Wagner's ideas as a late Romantic, see L.J. Rather, *The Dream of Self-Destruction: Wagner's "Ring" and the Modern World* and *Reading Wagner: A Study in the History of Ideas* (Baton Rouge and London: Louisiana State Univ. Press, 1979 and 1990).

Dowling treats as characteristic of Spanish writing, belong to a larger realm of Romantic historical imagination. Through their fascination for folklore, so Andreeva and Hanak find, the Romantics continued the Enlightenment belief in natural law and idealization of the "noble savage," and combined this with the newer organicist view of history and culture which especially Herder had advanced, but without surrendering the consciousness of their own modernity and their sense of separation from the "naive." Folklore provided models of what had been possible in the lost child-like state of humanity. Inevitably, the Romantic search in folkways for authentic expressions of "the indwelling law" (Coleridge) and their emphasis on the deep-rooted character of a people helped foster nationalism. Andreeva and Hanak illustrate how widely the new interest in folklore permeated the Slavic lands, and how diverse were the levels and modes of literary engagement with folklore. First, they establish the extent to which nineteenth-century authors in East and Southeast Europe either took up and reworked significant materials out of the national past – a past reconceived or to some degree invented in terms of ethnic identity – or began to employ folkloristic motifs in works of high literature as a means of subserving mood, character delineation, and emplotment, and for other ends in a broad range of genres (lyrical poetry, ballad, romance, legend, etc.). It was against this background that playwrights could anticipate audience receptivity to folkloristic elements in drama.

Andreeva and Hanak demonstrate the international flow of the new artistic sensibility in drama through the fortunes of the story of Genevieve of Brabant. Müller used the popular chapbook and puppet play sources to create his Storm-and-Stress tragedy *Golo und Genovefa* (1781). Although the play was set in the Middle Ages, Müller focussed on the portrayal of how a lover of weak character – transparently a modern "fatal man" – turns into a villain. Tieck then figured as the seminal writer linking Storm and Stress and Romanticism. His more lyrical medievalizing martyr play *Leben und Tod der heiligen Genoveva: Eine Tragödie* (Life and Death of Saint Genevieve: A Tragedy, 1798) focussed on the intensity of life and faith in the past. Adapted via a lesser, intermediary version, the same subject-matter served, in the Bulgarian play, *Long-suffering Genevieve*, as a vehicle to express the desire for national rebirth and liberation from the Turks. Tieck's use of "arbitrariness" (*Willkür*) in another sophisticatedly "childlike" play, *Der gestiefelte Kater* (Puss-in-Boots, 1797), was partly motivated by the desire to exhibit the nonrational logic of the imagination, but he also saw the potential to smuggle social and political, as well as poetological, commentary onboard under the guise of childlike nonsense. In general, folkloristic elements could serve to clothe messages far removed from the simplicity of ordinary life. Thus "folklore" as a complex came to bind literary realms from actual children's rhymes and stories to elegant fictions and allusive plays.

Romantic philologists such as the Grimm brothers contributed enormously to the advancement of a more rigorous analysis of folk art, but we do not obtain an accurate picture of the interests of many sophisticated writers before 1850, if we apply the results of such efforts retrospectively as if later scholarly attitudes determined binding categories for the discrimination of "genuine" folklore during the heyday of Romanticism. The confusion over the authenticity of Macpherson's Ossianic poems, which impressed Goethe but were challenged by Johnson, illustrates a rather common relationship to folk materials still evident in the Romantic decades. Although the mythological subject-matter indeed derived from ancient Irish lore shared in the West of Scotland, Macpherson freely edited traditional Gaelic poems and inserted passages of his own invention. In essence he was coloring with modern sentiments and coopting for high art materials which, over time, had slipped from that status in an earlier culture and survived as archaic, exotic remnants of folk culture – from the viewpoint of the dominant society. When Brentano and Arnim published the song collection *Des Knaben Wunderhorn: Alte deutsche Lieder* (1806-08), they were not yet able or willing to distinguish between actual products of folk inspiration and works that sprang from the conscious artistry of past centuries, and when the spirit moved them, the editors did not hesitate to shape up poems they deemed too lapidary. In fact, in European literary history there have been many periods of borrowing of materials which have floated up and down in a variety of once recognized hierarchical systems of art. Some materials of venerable age return after sea changes and appear to belong to the folk, although in real history they have already passed through prior incarnations in high culture.

A case in point is the story in the popular play *Los amantes de Teruel* (The Lovers of Teruel), which lives on in Hartzenbusch's Romantic version. In Iberia this work enjoys the reputation of being "archetypically" Spanish in its sentiments, but in large measure that may be because Hartzenbusch retains the basic motifs of the universally understandable tragedy of a woman forced to marry during the absence or incapacitation of her lover, ingredients found throughout Europe over the centuries in both folk art and high art. Earlier Spanish plays on the subject include Rey de Artieda's *Los amantes* (1581) and Tirso's and Montalbán's identically titled *Los amantes de Teruel* (both 1635). Insofar as Scott's *The Bride of Lammermoor* (1819) and Donizetti's opera *Lucia di Lammermoor* share the basic story form with fellow Romantic Hartzenbusch's play, we see that "Spanishness" and "Scottishness" (even when transposed in Italian!) belong to a generic complex that is capable of adaptation to fit any nationalist requirements.

The new imaginative relationship to an original natural context that is thought to have lent its indelible stamp to national character could be pushed far, yielding distinct attributes upon which poets could draw to construct a nativist or nationalist myth. Dowling explains the fortunes of the visual mode of the picturesque in Spain where, starting from its association with wild nature and the sublime in Italian and Spanish painting at the beginning of the eighteenth century, it gradually was adapted to theatrical art as a means to express the organic feeling of place and the Romantic spirit. By the 1830s the drama was widely conceptualized as a sequence of painterly scenes, so that many Spanish plays were ready-made for conversion into the "mixed" art of the opera. This is striking in a play such as the Duke of Rivas's *Don Alvaro, o La fuerza del sino* (1834), the source for Verdi's *La forza del destino*. Rivas breaks the neoclassical structure into a flowing pictorial series, the analogy to which one finds in comedies of the day and in the popular *zarzuela* (operetta).

Voisine-Jechova's essay indicates the equal importance of chivalric plays and plays depicting scenes of daily life in Bohemian drama around 1800 – plays often based on secondary foreign authors like Zschokke and Kotzebue and performed mainly in amateur theaters, in a cultural world where Baroque taste still lingered. Eventually Štěpánek used the Romantic historical elements to create a schematic moral drama with its own artificial diction and opened the way toward "modern" Czech Romanticism. In Bohemia, too, the transposition of drama into opera was an opportune way to reach the town audiences and cultivate a sense of national identity. Romanticism was a principal force in the creation of a national identity in Brazil. As Rela has shown in the introduction to his collection of *costumbrismo* theatrical works, plays of this sort helped shape the cultural physiognomy and profile the particularities of language during the decades in which Brazil was separating definitively from the Portuguese world.[11]

---

[11] Walter Rela, *Teatro costumbrista brasileño: Martins Pena, Macedo, Alencar, França Júnior, Artur Azevedo* (Rio de Janeiro: Instituto Nacional do Livro, 1961).

In thinking of the picturesque as a means of projecting a national self-awareness, it is useful to recall that the Spanish Romantic drama evolved in an atmosphere charged with the politics of the Revolutionary and Napoleonic era. Like the Italians, the Spanish reacted in a double register, both *against* French dominance and, in a reflexive manner, *in response to* French reception of new currents in Europe as the lead example. Thus the initial Spanish debate over A.W. Schlegel's ideas about their own Baroque theater (spurred by translation of his *Lectures* in 1818) was not settled in favor of Romanticism until the 1830s when the French themselves demonstrated greater receptivity to the new tendencies. Both the Duke of Rivas and Martínez de la Rosa began their careers as dramatists during the French siege of Cadiz in 1812. Rivas's early opposition to the neoclassical unities was doubtlessly reinforced through his experience of the example of Shakespeare during exile in England. His *Don Alvaro* (1834) was remarkable for using dialect as well as high Castilian, intermingling verse and prose, and linking Storm-and-Stress intensity with a Spanish sense of fatefulness. A politician of humble family, Martínez de la Rosa started from an orientation to Alfieri. After witnessing the inroads of German Romanticism on the scene in France, he converted to the newer fashion. His greatest success, *La conjuración de Venecia*, with its lavish painterly settings, produced in Madrid in the same year as Rivas's *Don Alvaro*, solidified the hold of their new kind of drama that fused narrative and pictorial elements.

Typical of the active lines of communication between the Old and New Worlds and the common denominator of politics was the career of the Mexican-born Gorostiza, a politically adroit playwright whose witty comedies supported liberal sentiment during his time in Madrid. Upon the fall of the liberalizing forces in Spain and Mexico's successful bid to gain independence from the mother country, Gorostiza adapted by serving as a diplomatic intermediary for Mexico in Europe. The Revolution of 1820 in Portugal helped precipitate the career of the dramatist Almeida-Garrett, who gained valuable impressions during his years of exile in England and France when reactionary forces twice regained power in his homeland. His eventual appointment as inspector general of theaters (1836), his founding of a conservatory for theater art, and his assiduous efforts to train a new generation of playwrights and performers lent lasting momentum to his Romantic reforms. Portuguese "Arcadianism," which in the drama meant pieces based on French neoclassical norms and Voltairean tragedy, served even liberal playwrights as a vehicle during the first two decades of the nineteenth century. With Shakespeare and Scott and other contemporaries of the North in mind, Garrett reached back into the romance of the Portuguese past for patriotic (anti-Spanish) themes – in plays such as *Dom Filipo de Vilhena* (1840) and *Luiz de Sousa* (1844) – to create a drama freed from neoclassical constraints and capable of conveying the new sense of Romantic individualism. Because of the relatively late breakthrough in Portugal, the mother country exercized only negligible influence on the shaping of Romanticism in Brazil.

While Furst takes as her point of departure the leading signs of aesthetic renovation in Germany with its early reception of Shakespeare, Carlson's essay on nationalism looks at the same context from the perspective of the shaping of cultural self-images. He reminds us that Rousseau, like Herder, was suspicious of arbitrary state structures or artificial cosmopolitanism in the eighteenth century and anticipated Romantic ideas of a naturally rooted commonwealth which required its own communal forms. Klopstock's "bardic" history play, *Die Hermannsschlacht* (Hermann's Battle, 1769), reflected the widespread craving to create a national identity in the fragmented German territories during Storm and Stress. In contrast, certain of Schiller's "German Classical" plays such as

Die Jungfrau von Orleans (1801) and *Wilhelm Tell* (1804) once again centered on the struggle of a Rousseauesque hero against despotism. The fluctuation between these polarities continued in German Romantic literature, but the Napoleonic invasions did much to galvanize Romantic opinion in Germany and Scandinavia for promotion of their distinct cultural identity in drama, and such great writers as Kleist were swept up in the new enthusiasm. A remarkable period of history plays ensued, stretching from Brentano to Grillparzer.

After an uneasy relationship since the Congress of Vienna, the Revolution of 1830 enabled Belgium to separate from the Netherlands, with final recognition ratified in 1839. Already in firm possession of a national identity, the liberal Dutch felt no immediate attraction to Romantic drama as a vehicle for developing it anew and remained rather conservative in theatrical terms, drawing eclectically on all their neighbors, mixing pre-Romantic German and French plays, bourgeois sentimentalism and melodrama, and historical pageantry. The plays of Bilderdijk, often linked to specific political moments in the nation's life, such as the tragedy *Willem van Holland* (1808), formed an important early strand in the Dutch repertory around which a national orientation could form. In the Netherlands, as so often was the case elsewhere in Europe, the reception of Shakespeare was crucial for a swing toward national subjects and Romantic structural features by the 1830s. Post-Napoleonic patriotism in Bohemia and Hungary meant promoting Czech and Magyar cultural identity against German dominance. In Spain, Italy, and Russia – as in Germany – this meant overcoming French tradition, even while imbibing largely French-inspired lessons of liberal modernity. Thus the German example of championing the Golden Age writers was welcomed in a Spain which, like Germany, had fought to be liberated from French occupiers in the first two decades of the nineteenth century. The task of defining national consciousness set forth by the Russian historian Karamzin influenced Pushkin's foundational work, the tragedy *Boris Godunov*, which was too liberal in sentiment for the censors in the repressive atmosphere of the 1820s. As Szegedy-Maszák indicates in his essay, one of the first powerful plays of nineteenth century in Hungarian, Katona's *Bánk Bán* (Governor Bánk), took up the well-known story of the noble who had to cope with the perplexities of maintaining order and justice in the absence of the king. In dealing with the national past Katona succeeded in creating a remarkable range of highly individualized characters. This play established a sense of a Hungarian identity rooted in its own antiquity, as well as of the complexity of the history underlying actual Europe.

At the end of the eighteenth century, Italy consisted of a patchwork of states as did Germany, and its North was caught between the rival Austrian and French intruders. Italian sentiment – for example, in the works of Alfieri – swung from regarding the French as liberators to denouncing them as betrayers of republican ideals. Similarly, when the Austrians replaced the French, the Italians interpreted the lessons from German Romanticism, aided by such mediators as Madame de Staël, as justifying their own right to cultivate Italian national identity. Manzoni's play *Il conte di Carmagnola* (1820) embodied the spirit of twinned liberalism and patriotism in Milan which influenced Stendhal and was congenial to Byron, both major figures on the scene. The liberal republican message in Byron's historical dramas *Marino Faliero, Sardanapalus*, and *The Two Foscari*, despite their neoclassical form, reciprocally appealed to the Italian Romantics, inspiring among others the opera composers Rossini, Donizetti, and Verdi, and influencing the tragedian Niccollini's turn toward Romanticism. Hugo's advocacy of a new theater imbued by liberalism gave a specifically political twist to Stendhal's suggestion in *Racine and Shakespeare II* (1825) that great events in

French history could be an important source for Romantic tragedy. The playwrights of the Young Germany movement, moving away from national pride to contemporary political concerns such as repression and censorship after the Congress of Vienna, reflected the Hugolian concept of drama as a weapon for liberal thought, rather than either Schillerian idealism or German Romanticism of the Napoleonic period.

The New European Protagonists

Beyond doubt among the most important effects of Romanticism were deep alterations in the way that the nineteenth century henceforth would elaborate any typology of human life. To begin with, certain contemporary social and psychological roles were stamped or redefined by Romanticism. And in depicting fictive or real figures of the past, Romantic writers by and large permanently changed the very optics of nineteenth-century vision. Such formative earlier revolutions as Renaissance humanism and the Enlightenment were filtered to some extent through interposed Romantic lenses. Even opponents of the Romantic mentality in any aspect of its multifarious influence had to recognize it as a potent new factor in European civilization. A significant part of nineteenth-century cultural energies thus went into digesting and coping with Romantic phenomena, until eventually enough time passed so that artists on the threshold of Modernism could pay renewed serious attention to many tenets and qualities of art that Realism and Naturalism failed to banish.

Any census of the protagonists appearing in Romantic plays eventually runs up against the difficulty of separating figures who pertain primarily to the realms of romance and history and have a preponderantly social or political significance from those through whom the dramatists express a cosmological or metaphysical vision or strive to reconstitute myth. (Because this second general category of protagonists remains important for Modernist "neo-idealist" directions in the drama, I shall consider it below separately in regard to Symbolist theater and theater of the Absurd.) For similar reasons, a comparatist will often find it difficult to distinguish "historically" grounded from "mythologically" grounded characters or to determine any necessary accord of either with distinctive generic modes (tragedy, comedy, opera, history plays). It is not illegitimate to regard popular Romantic drama as a vehicle primarily for presenting the Romantic character as a factor in culture. But as I shall argue below, that approach fails to take adequate account of the advances in genre concept and formal experimentation which constitute a large part of Romantic creativity and are relevant for the twentieth century, and perhaps well beyond.

It is in the realm of "character" that Romanticism connects so obviously with predilections of the Enlightenment and Revolutionary age. The person of extraordinary sensibility who faced the trials of existence in eighteenth-century plays and novels is the immediate ancestor. The Romantics thematized the special role of the artist as hero in the inevitable contention of love and creativity against hardness and philistinism. Often the struggle was between the forces of progress and reaction, and frequently the artist would by temperament be a revolutionary sympathizer. (Some important exceptions will be discussed below in connection with "cosmic" drama.) The border-line between the idealist, the artist, and the outlaw fluctuated beguilingly. Hugo's Ruy Blas, for example, combined glamorous attributes of the free-booting individualist with the lover and patriot, ready to sacrifice himself out of selfless devotion.

Many of these central roles were transmitted to a wider international public as staple subject-matter through opera in the post-Romantic era. Opera subserved the longer-term process of amalgamating eighteenth-century and nineteenth-century materials into a popular Romanticism broadly conceived. For example, Schiller's (in German terms) "Classical" tragedy *Don Carlos* (1787) bridged aspects of Enlightenment, Storm and Stress, and Romanticism with its juxtaposition of the passionate king's son and his intellectual friend, the Marquis de Posa, and its celebration of their aborted plan to liberate the Netherlands as a step in a greater campaign to restore man's lost freedom and dignity. Verdi's *Don Carlo* (première 1867) then simplified and reimbedded the themes and types in European consciousness. Büchner's *Dantons Tod* (1835) was the first major play examining the process by which the Revolution began to devour its own makers during the Terror.

This general proposition was conveyed across the threshold of the twentieth century by the far less complicated story-line in Giordano's opera, *Andrea Chénier* (première 1896), based on the life of the actual Romantic poet who first supported the Revolution but then denounced the bloodthirsty Jacobins and was executed in 1794. Through its emerging malice, exhibited in the vileness of the mob and its manipulators, the Revolution takes on the attributes of fate in the opera, while death as a sacrificial act ennobling the lovers Chénier and Maddalena lends a Christian aura to their martyrdom. Although Giordano's work lacked Büchner's deeper existential probing into the perverse strangeness of history, it helped perpetuate the typology that was essential to the survival of *Dantons Tod* in its own right and its rediscovery by the Expressionists. A similar longer-term relationship can be detected between a popular opera like Puccini's *Tosca* (première 1900), based on Sardou's maudlin story set in Rome in 1800, and the depictions of a corrupt, repressive Italy in the "Gothic" manner so widespread among Romantics such as Shelley. In their warmth and resolution, the singer Floria Tosca and the painter Mario Cavaradossi exemplify the liberal heritage in general, and not just the evanescent golden age of youthful fervor represented by the artist crowd in Puccini's *La Bohème* (1896). The lasting example of Werther as a tragic victim of sensibility was reinforced by a century of operatic versions from Kreutzer's now forgotten adaptation (1792) to Massenet's still popular one (1892).

Dramatic Modes and Paradigms

Surely one of the most fascinating moments of creative convergence in the history of Romantic theater was Tieck's brilliant production (Berlin, 1843) of Shakespeare's *A Midsummer Night's Dream*, set on a specially designed, multilevel stage, and its action carefully integrated with Mendelssohn's still beloved, accompanying music that the composer had completed for the occasion. The interpretive-expressive symbiosis of language, music, and drama that the two artists Tieck and Mendelssohn strove to bring about represents a collaboration close to opera proper. The structural shift toward an absolute fusion of poetry and music in opera of the Romantic age will be considered below. The importance of opera as a vehicle of Romantic contents and story-forms is obvious if we think only of the many libretti based on Romantic dramas and novels that have survived into the modern repertory.

As a popular medium opera also illustrates the general readiness of the Romantic age to bring romance and history into closer alliance. Romantic reconstitution of a "lost" Middle Ages meant permitting the realities of medieval faith, passion, and society (so far as the artist could construe them) to shine forth in their own right uncensored. One full generation after Goethe's Storm-and-Stress history play *Götz*, we see the greater openness to medieval values and beliefs in a brace of plays by Protestant authors from Tieck's *Genoveva* (1798) to Kleist's *Käthchen von Heilbronn* (1810). Before Werner's conversion to Catholicism, he treated the world-historical juncture of the Reformation, too, as part of the cultural romance in the spectacle play *Luther oder die Weihe der Kraft* (Luther or the Consecration of Power, 1806) and accommodated it to the Calderonian vogue. Schiller's *Wallenstein* trilogy (1799) was by any measure the most ambitious attempt at the turn of the century to analyze an axial moment in the history of the German peoples. Schiller moves progressively from the realm of the masses in the camp, into the sphere of the officers, and finally into the inner sanctum of the star-crossed man of destiny, the great general of the Thirty Years' War. Although the playwright thought of his work as pertaining to a German Classicism, Europe at large came to view the tragic history play as an exemplary Romantic model. For example, as its translator and champion, Constant had to bide decades and introduce *Wallenstein* gradually to the French audience.[12] In German late Romanticism, beyond the portrayal of a superdimensional hero, Grabbe's *Napoleon oder die hundert Tage* (Napoleon and the Hundred Days, 1830) showed the possibility of attaining epic proportions in the representation of history, matching the capacity of the novel, through the sheer energy of its mass scenes. The bridge from the Romantic tradition of searching, complex historical drama to Realism was crossed by Grillparzer in such works as *König Ottokars Glück und Ende* (King Ottokar's Fortune and End, 1825) and *Ein Bruderzwist im Hause Habsburg* (Fraternal Strife in the House of Hapsburg, published 1872).

It goes without saying that the artist as spiritual guide and benefactor, as tormented genius, or as the perplexed or tainted revolutionary or ruler entered into the nineteenth-century novel as a stock figure, as easily as into opera. As Cox notes in his essay, Romantic tragedy in the drama interfaced with the genre of the tragic novel. The Romantics protested against the old neoclassical "rules" as constitutive of a genre because they were grasping for a tragic "vision" instead; hence tragedy could be and was attempted in a multiplicity of forms. For Cox the Romantic high tragedy originated from views on history, nature, and the mind which we think of as primary characteristics of the paradigm shift at the end of the eighteenth century. It sprang from two fountainheads: one was the sense of being caught between the loss of a meaningful order of the past and a breakthrough to the creation of a new order, and the other was the experience of the inherent problems of subjectivity. Whereas Shelley's *Prometheus Unbound* projected "imagination's dream of what ought to be," *The Cenci* was the nightmare haunting the imagination. In Byron's *Cain* the Romantic protagonist faced not a divine order but the chaos that followed its collapse, the uncertainty that forced the hero to create his own order.

As early as the 1770s, Goethe's *Götz* demonstrated the isolation of the hero in resistance to the crushing power of a deep historical shift. In the following decade, Schiller's *Die Räuber* (The Bandits) portrayed the contest between awareness of a heroic past and a debased present. Several decades later, Musset's *Lorenzaccio* explored the conflict between inner identity and external reality, the gap between the traditional hero and the would-be Romantic hero. With Beddoes's *Death's Jest-Book*, Cox illustrates the general crisis when the act of creating the self as hero in the present

---

[12] For a detailed account, consult Lilian R. Furst, *The Contours of European Romanticism* (Lincoln: Univ. of Nebraska Press, 1979), chs. 5, "Benjamin Constant's *Wallenstein*," and 6, "Two Versions of Schiller's *Wallenstein*."

shut off access to a visionary future or the divine. With Wordsworth's *The Borderers* and Coleridge's *Remorse*, Cox demonstrates the case of the destructive mode of analytic consciousness; and with *Lorenzaccio*, the trap inherent in the structure of historical time. Büchner's *Danton's Death* could be added to Cox's illustrative plays as an example of history providing the opportunity for tragic failure and being the showplace of the reduction of society to the lower drives, when humankind is misled by the lure of revolutionary transfiguration.

By the 1720s, dramatists as different as Voltaire and Bodmer had attempted to tame the subject-matter of Sophocles' *Oidipus Tyrannos* and resituate its ancient protagonist in the camp of sensitive rebels against any authority that was divorced from human reality and needs. The "fate tragedy" became intertwined with the Gothic vogue in Walpole's play *The Mysterious Mother* (1758). In his essay on the special topic of "fate drama," Hoffmeister points to the underlying pattern of Oedipal conflict that made certain Shakespearean and Calderonian plays (e.g., *Hamlet, Macbeth, La vida es sueño, La devoción de la cruz*) apt successors to the Oedipus story in the Romantic canon. In many instances, fate drama enabled a Romantic author to rescue important values still held in common with the Enlightenment, such as individual freedom and responsibility, or to return, as a Christian, to writing plays supposedly in the spirit of the Greeks. A curse, a dire secret, dangerous misunderstandings, or other conditioning factors on which the plot hinged permitted a shift away from any conviction regarding social empowerment or the applicability of reason. Sometimes this collapse of confidence expressed anxiety or outrage over oppressive situations, and not a genuine sense of numinous powers. But fate drama was sometimes a channel for the attraction to a numinous realm. The Christianizing countercurrent of German Romanticism – the thematic complex of sin, need for grace, and divine justice appearing in Werner's fate tragedies – attained an important climax in Grillparzer's first play *Die Ahnfrau* (The Ancestress, 1817).

Secularized, the "curse" resurfaced in Naturalist drama later in the century, sometimes as a hereditary factor, sometimes as a deforming pressure exerted by the social system, sometimes as the protagonist's psychology or philosophy (e.g., the hero's misconception of his public role in Ibsen's *An Enemy of the People*, 1882). Because metaphysical concerns often lurked beneath the surface of rational or scientific convictions, Naturalism became in some respects a conduit for late-Romantic anxieties. Thus Büchner's unfinished *Woyzeck* gripped the Expressionist imagination of the early twentieth century through its critique of heartlessly pursued science, as well as through its piercing insight into the existential misery of disadvantaged members of the underclass.

Through the example of the powerful antiheroes of Elizabethan and Jacobean tragedy – to whom, as Garber reminds us, Milton's Satan must be added – English literature contributed a distinctly more intense tradition of the person who is his own fate or acts as fate for others.[13] The penetration of British and German Gothicism into popular theater in France occurred mainly through the sensational melodrama, the typical plot involving intrigue and counter-intrigue, a fatal agent and his intended victim. But Romantic authors such as Hugo were attracted to the genre more because of its possibilities for psychological study. As the fate genre appeared south of the border in the 1830s, Spanish authors largely interpreted fate as "a disastrous combination of character and insurmountable circumstances"; thus, in Hoffmeister's view, Rivas's *Don Alvaro* stands out as a play in which only the fatal man knows everything about his own background. As Voisine-Jechova notes in her

---

[13] See ch. 2, "Places for the Mind," in Frederick Garber, *The Autonomy of the Self from Richardson to Huysmans* (Princeton: Princeton Univ. Press, 1982).

essay, the fate genre is found even earlier in the Slavic territories, for instance, in Vocel's *Harfa* (The Harp, 1825). Štěpánek's *Bratrovrah* (The Fratricide, 1821) introduced the problem of taboo violation reminiscent of the Byronic searching into criminality as a source of metaphysical insight. In Klicpera's *Soběslav, selský kníže* (Sobeslav, the Peasant Prince, 1826), the wavering Hamletic hero pulled the drama toward a "modern" kind of Romanticism.

Flaherty's essay connects the theory of acting to fundamental debates in Romantic aesthetics that hammered at issues posed in the late eighteenth century. In line with Herder's hypothesis that the ancient Greek poets such as Orpheus were shamans who gained sway over the imagination, German writers wondered whether the modern play and its performance could conjure some similar entrancement. This theme was internalized self-reflexively in Tieck's plays among others, which asked whether drama like children's games had its own order distinct from real social existence, and whether playing was a kind of possession. However, the notion of autonomous "playing" was just one of the rival views widespread in the later eighteenth century. The idea of gaining emotional distance was a variant corollary that was drawn from the awareness of living in the "sentimental" age (in Schiller's sense of the term). Wilhelm von Humboldt, A.W. Schlegel, and Solger were among those who valued the French example of controlled artistry above the German example of affective surrender to nature. Schlegel argued that, in fact, the ancients' stage artistry was controlled in all respects. However, that might mean that the mimetic doctrine and naturalism contradicted the very essence of theatrical art. Solger went further by viewing the cathartic power in drama as a religious phenomenon, but stressing the balance to be struck between enthusiasm and irony. Flaherty takes us on a fascinating excursus into attempts to use drama as a healing art in the belief it might enable people to tap into dream states beneficially.

Romantic theories of acting and Romantic psychology thus overlapped in many instances. Hoffmann's *Seltsame Leiden eines Theater-Direktors* (A Theater Director's Unusual Sufferings, 1819) represents a major juncture where the theory of acting merges with interest in manifestations of the unconscious overriding normalcy, in the puppet as emblematic of a secretly controlled player, and in therapeutic possibilities of play. Besides being a prime example of the Tieckian genre of fantastic comedy in its use of *commedia dell'arte* motifs, Hoffmann's *Prinzessin Brambilla: Ein Capriccio nach Jakob Callot* (1821) is also, in Flaherty's words, a psychodrama about "the performing artist who desperately needs to learn self-awareness, discipline, and irony." That sense of half-observing one's own impulses, I would add, frequently applies to the situation of the "subject" in Romantic literature at large. In this respect, Flaherty's essay confirms the findings of Burwick and Schmeling.[14] Diderot in France and Lamb in England are among the notable Romantic theoreticians who recognize that the great actor must be completely disciplined and self-possessed, even distanced from the part, in order to perform it as an act of art.

In his essay on opera as a special form of drama, Weisstein looks at the concept of opera in the nineteenth century not in terms of its major themes but of its obvious connection with the Romantic aspiration to fashion a multimedia vehicle. Clearly, as he points out, the crosscultural and intergeneric borrowing of resources for a host of specific operatic works made opera in the aggregate as drama into perhaps the densest kind of European "intertextuality." One result is a virtually inevi-

---

[14] French theories of acting and illusion have been treated in great detail in Maurice Descotes, *Le Drame romantique et ses grands créateurs* (Paris: Presses Universitaires de France, 1955). A valuable reexamination of the importance of Diderot in a broader context is found in Burwick, *Illusion and the Drama*, ch. 2., "Illusion and the Players: Diderot, Tieck, and Lamb."

table imprecision in defining what constitutes the Romantic core, since scholars can include works for their subject-matter at one end of a spectrum and for certain musical qualities at another. Weisstein assumes a deliberately "purist" stance in order to sort out the canon according to strict criteria of a genuine fusion of the creative forces (composer/playwright) and of the chief arts (text/music). As a result of giving such preponderant weight to the Romantic drive for totalization, he segregates virtually all of Italian and French operas as deviating in some respect from the goal of the wholly unified, through-composed *Gesamtkunstwerk*. Usefully, in the process of sorting, he also notes other generic categories that are applicable to specific works – even if they otherwise fall from the strict formalistic standard – e.g., the dramatic fairytale. In this structuralist exercise, Weisstein illustrates how certain works ordinarily cited as primary Romantic operas, e.g., Weber's *Der Freischütz*, were pulled in some measure toward other generic poles (melodrama, *Nummernoper*, etc.), whereas in clear contrast Wagner's *Der fliegende Holländer* broke through to the new unity. Weisstein advances the yet more daring suggestion that Berlioz's original version of the *Symphonie fantastique* would qualify as a quintessential *Gesamtkunstwerk*, because the composer was author of a matching literary program and conceived of the total work as a musical autobiography. What links the two ventures is the implicit dream structure of each – a factor that recurs in neo-Romantic works such as Strindberg's *Ett Drömspel* (A Dream Play, 1901).

Regional Varieties

The present volume attempts to build bridges across some of the barriers to a broader history of Romantic drama. Critical attention hitherto has concentrated on the traditions of separate nations within the enormous European area or has tended to be limited to smaller blocks of closely related cultures. The Romantic "golden triangle" of Britain, France, and Germany still attracts the most scrutiny in comparative studies, while other parts of Europe are less frequently examined in a larger context. The essays by Bisztray on Swedish, Danish, and Norwegian literature, Carlson on Italian, Dowling on Spanish, Voisine-Jechova on Czech, Szegedy-Maszák on Hungarian, and Gershkovich on Russian all contribute importantly to building the more adequate context that future comparative studies require. These scholars profile not only features characteristic of Romanticism in the particular culture, but also crucial features shared by spiritual affinity with or in response to creativity elsewhere in Europe. Esslin then demonstrates how comparative studies can draw together evidence from Western and Eastern, as well as Northern and Southern, Europe in a larger framework and thereby illuminate important relationships.

It is against this European backdrop that Plant, Pladott, and Carilla place the fascinating details of the expansion of Romanticism into the New World, as it was carried in English and Spanish. There are certain common patterns in the development of North, Central, and South America: First of all, in contrast to the relatively concentrated French and Portuguese language blocks in the New World, the English and even more so the Spanish language were spread over formidably vast and variegated territories. These different regions had their own distinct population mixes and were already acquiring their own sense of local identity before the Romantic age. Second, in the aggregate, New World writers and theater people had ample opportunity to travel to and from, and to work in, Britain or Spain; and newcomers or visitors from the old countries, too, kept the lines of contact vibrant. Third, despite such ready contact, the inroads of any intellectual and aesthetic movement was slowed and diluted, both because of the wide dispersal of New World cultural centers, and their absorption in their immediate political concerns. The entire expanse of the New World was deeply marked by the several Independence movements leading to separate nationhood, and often reinforcing links with Revolutionary themes in Europe, notably with the French tradition. Fourth, while the traditional or acculturated English and Spanish speakers in the Americas succeeded in naturalizing important European themes and forms, they discovered compelling new matter that sprang directly from their experience of creating new homelands. Among the special factors was the immediacy of dealing with and/or merging with aboriginal peoples who in Europe were still, in the main, understood only as cultural clichés or literary figments – e.g., as examples of exotic paganism or the "noble savage." From Ottawa to Buenos Aires, Romanticism became connected with the accruing knowledge that countries in the New World represented a complex development in cultural relations consequent upon the Renaissance age of exploration and modern empire-building. On the one hand, they existed as a kind of reflection of Europe and European dreams and concerns; on the other hand, they were on a pathway of separation and elaboration of new internal patterns.

In his treatment of the constellation of Spanish-speaking nations from Mexico to Argentina, Carilla demonstrates something of the inner logic of the evolution of the New World through his own cultural sentiments. He feels drawn to the subject of the interaction between the dominant Spanish and the pre-Colombian indigenous languages, but must lament the loss of most translations into or out of New World native idioms and of some few original dramas composed in them. As inheritor, he is proud of the forging of a distinct civilization of mixed European and native peoples in the Western hemisphere, but is bothered by the scant survivability of Latin American drama of the Romantic age. Spanish became an international, instead of national, language; however, it thereby preempted the establishment of any completely original native drama in the colonies, since local forms of Spanish did not grow into viable, distinct literary languages.

Carilla's strong "nativist" sympathies incline him to focus mainly on the negative aspects of cultural power that inhered in the institutional and geocultural realities of the Hispanic world and helped determine such an outcome, and to slight the productive aspects of the symbiosis between Latin America and Europe. In his account we are reminded that, although translations into local tongues occurred, the religious theater of the *autos* and the secular *comedias* were transportable only in Spanish. The rudimentary facilities for theater in Latin America, the wide distances between metropolitan centers, the scattered public who had only Spanish in common, the concomitant lack of any dense network of newspapers and magazines in which to discuss and promote drama, and the long stretches of political instability impeded any grand flourishing. Nonetheless, Carilla presents us with an impressive inventory of playwrights, actors, impressarios, and critics who made such big cities as Mexico, Lima, and Buenos Aires into notable citadels of dramatic art despite all the obstacles. He points out the success of major Latin American authors such as Gorostiza (Mexico), Pardo (Peru), and Samper (Columbia) in Spain, demonstrating the international character of the age. The story of the lively presence of Spanish, French, and Italian visitors in the theaters of Hispanic America, notably in Argentina, runs through the footnotes. There we can also glimpse the international network which allowed works in Spanish to be published and circulated in exile from major non-Spanish capitals such as London, Paris, and Brussels, as well as the continuing significance of Madrid for many writers born in the New World.

Nowadays numerous critics – long after the intervening nationalistic evolution of various segments of the New World – decry as "oppressive" and "(neo)imperialistic" any former commonality or remnant reciprocity which their nations may have enjoyed with whichever old country. The more doctrinaire nativist persuasion, holding that New World authors were destined to throw off the suffocating hold of Europe and release the deeper unique essence determined by the original indigenous peoples in the particular landscapes, is currently found throughout North and South America. Neo-Marxian and postmodernist critics have widely borrowed nativist tenets and adapted them to fit a cultural crusade against "wicked" European elements in contemporary societies and to privilege the claims of underclass and "Third World" peoples in general. From the comparatist's perspective, however, this sort of mystique is just one of the natural results of an earlier imbibing of European Romantic teachings – e.g., organicity, the authenticity of the folk, etc.

Carilla notes that Romantic historical drama in Latin America was initially concerned more with favorite European subject-matters such as (in rough order of prominence) the Middle Ages, modern society, and Antiquity, but later turned increasingly to colonial topics, the saga of the Conquest, and the several movements of Independence. Readers will recognize that, recycled and transposed into recent Latin American fiction, these interests have been reborn through the "foundational romances" of the 1960s onward. In generic terms of the Romantic period, the retardation effect of importation of literary changes into the colonies brought about a situation for drama somewhat resembling that in Bohemia or Russia at the start of the nineteenth century. There was a closeness and mixing of Classic and Romantic materials. Melodrama and *costumbrismo* were the principal binding modes. Besides the imperishable Baroque playwrights Lope and Calderón, the major contemporary Iberians such as Larra, García Gutiérrez, Zorilla, and Hartzenbusch were staple fare in Latin America, as were popular French authors such as Hugo and Dumas in translation. The great Shakespeare and influential Schiller were known in Spanish versions via second-rate French mediators.

Plant acknowledges an analogous set of problems in defining what constitutes Canadian Romantic drama in English. Although a remarkable number of plays were composed by Canadians, the drama in Canada (whose formal incorporation as a nation dates from 1867) exhibited a delayed momentum. From one perspective, the Revolutionary period amounted to a civil war subdividing the dominant British people into two large blocks on the North American continent, but the migration between these territories and traffic back and forth over the Atlantic meant a great degree of sharing of trends and themes before the new nations had sorted out their distinct attributes. An illustration of the early common roots is Roger's play *Ponteach, or the Savages of America* (London, 1766), subsequently claimed as part of the literature of both Canada and the United States. It exhibited the loosely applied Shakespearean fashion accepted everywhere in the English-speaking world and already sweeping Germany. Its Rousseauesque theme of the resistance of innately good people to a corrupt white civilization was to remain an embedded commonplace on both sides of the forty-second parallel and pass into cinematic lore. Some dramatists like Mair, writing in the later nineteenth century, transposed this conflict to portray the sinister republican Americans as the corrupt forces that threatened the decent Indians and Canadians. The predominant genres in the Canadian repertory were the nationalistic idyll, the melodrama of endangered virtue, and fate drama. A gradual fusion of Gothic and exotic tastes occurred in accord with the rising Victorian fascination for psychological forces.

Pladott finds a very significant confirmation of the strong libertarian and republican sentiments in the United States in the early passion for plays such as Payne's *Brutus* (1818) that depict ancient political heroism and revolt. To the extent the American nation liked to style itself as Roman in virtues, the neoclassical streak at the highest political level (e.g., in the images and pronouncements of figures like Washington and Jefferson) rubbed off on literature. No less a reviewer than Walt Whitman later read Bird's *Gladiator* (1831) as a tract applicable to the Abolitionist cause. In contrast to opinion in the many Spanish-speaking nations further south, in the United States the call for an American dramatic literature freed from foreign rules started virtually with the young republic. Pladott explicates Stone's *Metamora* (1830) in some detail not just as an example of the favorite subject-matter of the conflict between a corrupt encroaching civilization and a threatened native way of life, but as a deeper Romantic probing of the irreconcilable gap that had opened between two orders of "writing" or signification – the natural and the rational. Just as the drama served for projecting ethnic identity in Eastern Europe, so a special genre of "Yankee" plays, grounded in folklore, grew out of the later eighteenth century and helped promote the self-congratulatory American myth into the twentieth century: the picture of "unfettered thinking" and "vigorous feeling" as against European "aridity" and "effeteness"; the contrast between beneficent rural life and urban blight, between native genius and shallow sophistication. Another special dramatic genre of "frontier" plays firmly established itself, matching countless novels and tales. The conflict or antinomy was shifted from that between England and America or city and country to that between the socially restrictive, cultured East and the free-spirited West within the continental United States. Pladott stresses that it was greater interest in such phenomena as the natural endowments of resourceful adventurers and pioneers that blocked any widespread reception of the reflective Byronic hero or European victim figures like Woyzeck in North America. In general, American dramaturgy in the nineteenth century was not drawn to polarities such as the sublime and grotesque, nor into the realms of dream and elaborate irony (which, I should add, certainly cannot be said for the course of narrative fiction in the United States).

Carilla does not treat the case of Brazil which stood apart from its Spanish-speaking neighbors, both before and after it gained formal independence in 1822. In Brazil, the creation of a national literature through innovation and experiment meant turning away from older Portuguese to newer British, French, and German models, and more specifically from Portuguese "arcadianism" and neoclassicism to Romanticism in the drama. The Real Teatro de São João, inaugurated in 1813, produced Iberian, French, and Italian works appealing to eighteenth-century taste. The formative moment of change arrived in the mid-1830s when Gonçalves de Magalhães (1811-1882) lectured on Brazilian literature in Paris and Dos Santos founded the National Theater in Rio. The former's instantly successful *Antônio José ou o poeta e a Inquisição* (Antônio José or the Poet and the Inquisition, 1838) was the first Romantic tragedy with a nationalistic theme in Brazil. It was soon followed by Martins Pena's (1815-48) comedy *O juiz de paz na roça* (The Justice of the Peace on the Plantation, 1838), establishing a strong *costumbrista* tradition. Romantic melodrama with Brazilian themes thrived at mid-century. Melodrama became a significant vehicle for critical social and political statements in superior artistic achievements such as *Mãe* (Mother, 1862), Alencar's (1829-77) plea against slavery. Brazilian Romanticism was stronger in lyric poetry and in narrative than in drama, so that the inroads of Decadence and Symbolism were felt most powerfully in poetry and fiction, whereas the payout for dramatic literature was delayed into the twentieth century.

By contrast, as Szegedy-Maszák's essay shows, Hungarian Romantic drama both was prolific, and boasted masterpieces worthy to vie with the best of Europe at large. While the quantitative change could be attributed, as in Brazil, to the greater suitability of Romanticism for developing the vogue of the national past, there was still considerable early resistance to historical drama of great merit. A case in point would be Katona's *Bánk Bán* (Governor Bánk, 1820), at first neglected, but eventually recognized for its purity of language, fine characterization, and variety of social and philosophical types. Kisfaludy's historical plays were more successful by being more melodramatic and colorful, while Vörösmarty excelled in the lyrical drama and fairytale. In the last category, his *Csongor és Tünde* (Csongor and Tünde, 1829-31) was the most innovative, anticipating the quest paradigm and imaginative structures of Symbolist drama and increasing in influence into the twentieth century. Madách's *Az ember tragédiája* (The Tragedy of Man, 1859-60) is the subject of several essays in our volume because of its special rank and one of the major "cosmic" dramas (Esslin) that attempted "encyclopedic" totalization (Szegedy-Maszák). The play fuses a master-repertory of literature, as digested by a learned poetic mind, and a philosophic inquiry into the nature of mankind, documented through excerpts from the archive of history. But perhaps more important: it is suffused with an ambiguity that has continued to prompt interest and debate. On the one hand, it echoes the act of faith closing Goethe's *Faust*; on the other hand, it seems to foreshadow the Nietzschean and Existentialist attitudes toward history – especially the need for art as a representation of lasting value in the face of a universe possibly empty of any tangible values except inexorable natural laws. Szegedy-Maszák's searching analysis of this great work forthrightly confronts the task of making qualitative judgments about the stature of major plays across the enormous range of the entire civilization.

Segel, too, is concerned to bring some balance into the discussion of canonicity which hitherto has been dominated by criticism focussing on West European literatures. He sets forth with considerable verve the reasons why Polish dramatic literature was so profoundly steeped in Romanticism that in Poland the distance between the great playwrights of the nineteenth century and those of the twentieth is perhaps the least for any nation. Many Polish artists shared the experience of exile in Western nations, above all in France. These long sojourns not only tied them intimately to Romantic trends at important cultural centers like Paris; their circumstances promoted writing dramas in Polish as poetic testaments and experiments, rather than as works geared primarily for stage production. They were predisposed to accept the Romantic idea of liberating the established genres and creating a drama for the mind. Segel's corollary thesis that Russia, in contrast to Poland, boasted very little by way of Romantic drama comes as no surprise. The case of Russia is indeed interesting because of a curious parallel with France and Italy. In all these nations a powerful neoclassical tradition was entrenched well into the nineteenth century, and the demonstrable Romantic swing in the theater dated first from the 1820s. In a recent book, Karlinsky has ably presented the extreme thesis that the truer, deep-seated Russian tradition was neoclassical and that, in effect, it was the enormous influence of the Romantic critic Belinsky which succeeded in shifting attention away from this core, thus conjuring a mistaken sense of a stellar period that might be achieved through Romantic drama.[15]

Gershkovich's essay in our volume takes issue with attempts such as Karlinsky's to deny the power of the salient masterworks, Griboedov's comedy *Gore ot Uma* (Woe from Wit, 1823-24) and Pushkin's tragedy *Boris Godunov* (1825), which at a stroke qualitatively asserted Romanticism in a

---

[15] Simon Karlinsky, *Russian Drama from Its Beginnings to the Age of Pushkin* (Berkeley, Los Angeles, London: Univ. of California Press, 1985).

cultural atmosphere of spiritual ascent. The fact that many stylistic phases of drama were telescoped together in a cultural surge was, Gershkovich reminds us, not unusual for Eastern Europe. Symptomatic was that both authors were fascinated by Goethe's *Faust I* with its "Prologue in the Theater" which thematized the poet. In the figure Chatsky, Griboedov created the first great Romantic individualist in Russian literature, a man full of "Byronic" contradictions (too many for the programmatic cultural critic Belinsky!). Chatsky's character expressed something more radical than was admitted in the accommodative views of Romantics like Küchelbecker who could not digest the Western cult of "egotistic" life and developed a "service mentality" later axiomatic in left-wing circles. Griboedov instead expressed the freedom of the creative artist and the liberation of the human personality from the authoritarian ethos of the state. In fact, Chatsky's inner agonies and utter isolation at the end make him into a *pharmakon* and bring the bittersweet comedy to the verge of tragedy.

Carlson's separate essay on Italy complements Furst's by tracing the far more gradual reception of Shakespeare south of the Alps against the sway of French ideas, but also by showing how rivalries such as that between the Venetians Goldoni (who praised the English and Spanish but was supported by Voltaire) and Gozzi (a partisan of the *commedia dell'arte* as a national tradition, whom Baretti, the pro-English, anti-French critic favored), obscured the pre-Romantic seeds in both. The success of neoclassical tragedy replete with Shakespearean echoes – once this was established by the works of Alfieri and his followers Monti and Foscolo in the waning eighteenth and dawning nineteenth century – brought about a situation that bore some resemblance to the special juncture of German *Klassik*. German "Classicism" of the 1780s and 1790s was led by Goethe and Schiller, both of whom had emerged from Storm and Stress, and was continued by Hölderlin; it overlapped with the rise of Idealism in philosophy, marked by the appearance of Kant's major treatises, and with the rapid unfolding of full-fledged Romanticism from around 1795 onward. In the plays associated with *Klassik* we see a reconstitution of the humane heritage of the Enlightenment. *Klassik* was concerned with the harmony of the self, its place in an intelligible world, and the search for truth; it stressed emotional profundity, the need for a balance between thought and action, and the moral and aesthetic education of the human race. The triumph of human nobility over the threat of the barbaric is exemplified in Goethe's *Iphigenie auf Tauris* (final version 1786-87), while the tragic consequences of the split between heart and mind is examined in Schiller's *Don Karlos, Infant von Spanien*, in 1787; and a decade later, Hölderlin begins his several *Empedokles* fragments (1797ff.), in which he probes the nature of a breaking-point in human consciousness and the anguish of the visionary (or poet) through whom the human heritage is deepened. In Italy, there was no figure comparable either to Goethe or Hölderlin, but Alfieri bore clear resemblances to Schiller. Alfieri thus furnished at home the model of the liberal, and soon ardently patriotic, precursor whom the Italian Romantics could install as a pillar in their literary temple.

Two significant reinforcements of opinion occurred in the Napoleonic period. The German Romantics took over the earlier Storm-and-Stress approval of Gozzi and interpreted him in the light of their own development of Romantic irony. And German ideas were mediated directly to Italy through Mme de Staël and A.W. Schlegel, taking root most notably in the liberal stronghold Milan and the circle gathered around the journal *Il Conciliatore*. Influenced by the German view of literary works as organic forms, and drawing from Italian history, Manzoni's play *Il Conte di Carmagnola* (1820) appeared at just the right moment – after the Austrian suppression of *Il Conciliatore*. It was hailed as a model at home and abroad, gaining a crucial positive review from Goethe. Upon his return from Milan to Paris, Stendhal's interest in the Italian Romantics predisposed him to champion the cause of Shakespeare vigorously in the battle royal that was opening between the partisans of French neoclassicism and advocates of a Romantic revolution in the theater. What Carlson describes in the case of Italy is a prime illustration of the continuous process in Europe whereby reception of newer generic impulses did not necessarily occur in a direct or single set of artistic decisions in any one recipient nation, but as a result of often intermittent sharing and feedback as ideas flowed over a network of multiple channels. His study demonstrates why a comparative approach is better suited to the assessment of the complex patterns of responses to primary, secondary, tertiary, and even longer delayed phases of change.

Neomythological Creation

The importance of historical plays has been discussed above, but here I turn to another expression of the Romantic drive for universality that went beyond fascination for the pageantry of history. This was the conversion of ancient and early modern figures into archetypes, the creation of new mythological imaginative space, and the recognition of a suprapersonal intertextuality by which we are connected to older mythic insights.[16]

The Goethean model of a symbolic drama with an epic sweep of several millenia is at the heart of what Esslin terms "cosmic drama" and Szegedy-Maszák calls lyrical drama in "encyclopedic form." My own essay devoted to *Faust II* concentrates on showing how Goethe draws together the multiple strands in the evolution of European drama. These include the dazzling liberation of the poetic mind from any constraints of the neoclassical unities or even conventional notions of time and space, the constant heightening of our imaginative involvement by reminding viewers of the kind of illusion at work, the recourse to mythological, magical, and fairytale moments, the encounter with turning-points in the evolution of civilization, and overt and covert conflation of mythological and symbolic references. The lyrical modulation of larger rhythms and the shifting amongst modes and devices of the theater, including elements from the opera and masque, contribute to the aggregate "symphonic" effect. In its entirety (Preludes, and Parts I and II), *Faust, a Tragedy* impressed the later nineteenth century as having a special stature like that of Dante's *Divine Comedy*: it was unique in its monumentality and it constituted an epic summation for its age. In the critical vocabulary of the 1980s, *Faust* could be considered to be a grand junction of European intertextuality.

As Esslin indicates, the response to the challenge of *Faust* was intense at a surprisingly early date on the part of several major writers whose work was epoch-making for their respective nations: Krasiński for Poland, Madách for Hungary, and Ibsen for Norway. Krasiński's *Nieboska komedia* (Undivine Comedy, 1835) used the resuscitated Baroque framework of a world theater and an epic

---

[16] On major protagonist figures associated with ancient or early modern mythologemes – e.g., Oedipus, Prometheus, Faust, Don Juan – consult: Gerald Gillespie, "Romantic Oedipus," in *Goethezeit: Studien zur Erkenntnis und Rezeption Goethes und seiner Zeitgenossen; Festschrift für Stuart Atkins*, ed. Gerhart Hoffmeister (Bern, München: Francke, 1981), pp. 331-45; Jane K. Brown, "Faust," in *European Romanticism: Literary Cross-Currents, Modes, and Models*, ed. Gerhart Hoffmeister (Detroit: Wayne State Univ. Press, 1990); and Gerald Gillespie, "The Devil's Art" and "Prometheus in the Romantic Age," in *European Romanticism*, pp. 77-95 and 197-210.

progression through the ages in order to follow the evolution of "Man" in various personae who exhibit stages of experience and discovery, as well as the struggles of the Romantic spirit against inimical principles and forces. Scenes from Goethe's *Faust* often shine through the episodes of the *Undivine Comedy* which are set sequentially in Antiquity, the Middle Ages, Renaissance, and modern times. But all moments have an underlying immediate historical subtext that obsesses the conservative Polish nationalist. Krasiński is concerned over the onmoving political and social crisis which the Revolutionary and Napoleonic period has bodied forth. In his related essay, Segel reminds us that the monumental works of the great Polish Romantic playwrights – above all, Mickiewicz's *Dziady, Część trzcecia* (Forefathers' Eve, Part III), Słowacki's *Kordian*, and Krasiński's *Nieboska komedia* – became the foundation of twentieth-century Polish dramatic literature and are still a vital force. Whether reinvoked or parodied, the visionary forms and religious and mystical strains of Romanticism have not passed from the Polish stage.

Esslin has cogently shown that Madách's *The Tragedy of Man* (1862) resembles Krasiński's *The Undivine Comedy* in adapting the world-theater framing and other specific features from *Faust* in the service of the Hungarian artist's own vision of human development. His Adam and Eve recur in many roles in constant interaction with avatars of Lucifer, humanity's shadow, down to the artist's present world. *The Tragedy of Man* is an impressive outline of the great epochs, achievements, and failures on the Faustian scale of several millennia. Eventually the plotline of history moves by way of a dreary world of socialism, as the threatening future, into a vision of the crisis of confidence in the purpose of life, set in a bleak ice age. But the play closes completing its own hermeneutic circle when Adam, awakening in despair from his encyclopedic "dream" of the meaninglessness of history, has to go out through the gates of Eden into the saga of human destiny. Esslin underscores the fact that, despite the involvement of supernatural agencies, both Krasiński and Madách fix their gaze on history as a secular contest of forces that has emerged naturally from Christian civilization. Esslin notes that the Modernist novel, especially Joyce's *Ulysses* and *Finnegans Wake*, took over the attempt to synthesize the waking and dreaming of an entire culture and to suggest an eternal cyclic process rather than a Hegelian linear dialectic. Szegedy-Maszák emphasizes that persistent basic roles and philosophic points of view recur as variations on paradigms in the otherwise historically distinct individuals of the successive ages in *The Tragedy of Man*; thus as early as in the dialogue between Lucifer and Adam we detect, for example, aspects of the contemporary nineteenth-century clash between values of Romantic Liberalism and Positivism. Another kind of semantic layering is the effective palimpsest constituted by the fusion of literary sources as varied as Shakespeare, Milton, Tocqueville, Byron, John Stuart Mill, et al.

In the essay on Scandinavian drama, Bistray emphasizes that, although Ibsen rejected certain clichés of a Norwegian "national" Romanticism (complacent blending of historicism and folklore) and travestied the Romantic hero cult in *Peer Gynt* (1867), he never abandoned the underlying concept of the quest itself – the Faustian pattern of striving. Using Nemoianu's terms, we can say that *Peer Gynt* pertains to the bittersweet variety of late or post-Romantic works which are severely undercut by Romantic irony and prominently thematize a self-debilitating inner critique. The episodes on Peer's pathway of degredation finally take the inadequate dreamer beyond symbolic native realms such as that of the trolls into foreign parts where he engages in further exotic acts of exploitation (e.g., dealing in Negro slaves, posing as a prophet in Africa, etc.), before his return to Norway as a disillusioned old man. Only the abiding pure love of Solveig balances out the criminal tendency of the egotistical worldling. The play's themes of the authentic core of humanity which Solveig incarnates, of the polarity between natural strength and sickly presumption, and of the "buttonmoulder" who recasts spoiled matter express an essentially cyclic idea of the drive for human realization.

Dissolving the Generic Boundaries of Drama

The essays by Schmeling, Nemoianu, and Esslin carry us from the first moments of Romantic experimentation with form to the Modernist threshold when widespread changes in tone, substance, and structure evidence some of the longer-range consequences for European drama. In broadest terms, despite important resistance to Romantic concepts throughout the nineteenth century, Romanticism slowly overcame the Realist code and broke the grip of rational illusion and historical teleology in the theater. Especially by establishing dream processes as an organizing principle, Romantic drama prepared a way of envisioning the world that was congenial to the age of psychology that dawned in its Modern form in the psycho-anthropological and psycho-historical approaches of Nietzsche, Bergson, Freud, and Jung. The movement between the licit day-world and other realms (nightmare, fairytale, mythological tenebrae, etc.) were daring around 1800; dream and mythic reverie became staple means of imagination in the theater by 1900. Romanticism also had an immense impact through a variety of attempts to make, not just the novel, but the drama too, into an all-embracing super-genre, an instrument of Romantic totalization. Howarth and others in this volume have dealt with Hugo's theory that drama, by encompassing both the grotesque and the sublime, could unify all phenomena and polarities of existence. Esslin and others have shown that Goethe's *Faust* actually achieved its own quasi-mythic status as an act of totalization and realized the wildest hopes for a *Gesamtkunstwerk* – a score of years before Wagner completed the other commanding *Gesammtkunstwerk* of the nineteenth century, his mammoth opera tetralogy, *Der Ring des Nibelungen* (The Nibelung's Ring). The latter did not have the thematic richness and density of *Faust*, but it was revolutionary nonetheless in its own right because, in addition to new Romantic myth-making in reflection upon older myth, Wagner demonstrated the Romantic associational technique of the leitmotif in an epic tour de force.

Both *Faust* and the *Ring* are self-mirroring symbolic stories. My separate essay (as mentioned *supra* in the section "Neomythological Creation") examines how Goethe outbid the Romantics by having his work intermittently engage in destruction of its own illusions and illusions within illusions. In the *Ring*, Wagner did not explicitly break the dramatic illusion, which maintained the ostensible plot continuity of his reworked Nordic-Germanic medieval materials. Rather he counted on the literary knowledge which the more competent members of the audience would bring to bear. Half a century separated the *Ring* from Novalis's famous syncretic and synthetic myth, "Klingsohr's Fairytale," the neomythological work-within-the-work at the core of the medievalizing novel *Heinrich von Ofterdingen* (1800). With good reason Wagner expected us to appreciate his conflations of mythological identities – for example, Brünnhilde with Antigone – and to interpret the action as a philosophical and metaphysical allegory of the collapse of Western civilization bearing on the spiritual welfare of his own times; and this is exactly what superior readers did, such as Shaw in *The Perfect Wagnerite* (1898).[17]

---

[17] See especially ch. 7, "The Insurrection of Woman," in L.J. Rather, *Reading Wagner*.

Our "re-reading" the ancient stories bundled in the *Ring* for a modern lesson about the tragic madness of capitalism and statism creates an ironic tension that approaches, but is not as radical as, that in Goethe's *Faust*. *Faust* is inherently closer to the non-preaching, self-resolving irony that appeared in the fantastic comedies of the young Tieck. Goethe exhibits theater transformed simultaneously into anti-theater and meta-theater: a self-beholding act of theatrical imagination. Later Romantics whose writing was in progress between the completed *Faust I* and *Faust II* often responded primarily to the earlier Tieckian breakthrough. The final complexity of Goethean cosmic drama was not yet evident to them. For example, Büchner's indebtedness is clear from the lyrically melancholy comedy *Leonce und Lena* (written 1836), which commingles motifs from Tieck, Shakespeare, and Byron with influences from Brentano's *Ponce de Leon* (1804) and Musset's *Fantasio* (1833), and probes existence as captivity in the play. In *Don Juan und Faust* (publ. 1829), Grabbe takes the further important step of *merging* the mythological spheres of these Northern and Southern archetypes who were the brain-children of early modern Europe. Thereby he ties onto meta-theater of the Goethean direction, presenting the cultural protagonists of different pasts together in the same imaginative space, the space of a theater of the mind.[18]

The possibility of a theater of the mind appeared in the comedies which Tieck wrote in the last years of the 1790s. These independently anticipated in poetic practice the idea of Romantic irony which the theoretician Friedrich Schlegel started formulating in the *Athenäum-Fragments* (1778-1800). Tieck's *Puss-in-Boots* erased any boundaries between the contemporary day-world and realms of fantasy (fairytale, magical opera, etc.), and self-critically demonstrated its own operations as an enacted illusion, even while one of its prominent themes carried to exuberant extremes was the paradoxical collapse of the play in progress, the very play we are witnessing. In Tieck's *The Land of Upsidedown*, the *commedia dell'arte* clowns seize control of the play, a theatromaniac member of the audience exchanges places with a disgruntled player, and at one point the vulgar public, by rushing onto the stage to defend the revolutionaries against the director's plan to restore poetic values, gets trapped forever behind the untimely lowered curtain in a metaphysical limbo. Earlier Scaramouche, the tyrant clown, grows dizzy witnessing a play-within-the-play, within which in turn a play-within-the-play is staged. Tieck's *Prinz Zerbino* raised the stakes by depicting the paradox of a drama wherein the noblest protagonist, the melancholic son of the lucky Gottfried from *Puss-in-Boots*, seeks in vain to wind the play back to a better passage or annul it. The improbable, virtually random plot and theater machinery cannot be stopped, nor can the characters opt out of the play. Yet curiously, as the Prince wanders in search of some extra-dramatic redemption, he encounters figures from different spheres of literature and history, ancient to modern, who are not much help in counseling him about his existentialist dilemma.

Connections with Symbolist Drama

Whether actions and feelings are subject to irony exercized on the authorial plane or internally by participants in the play, recognizable in the situation of many Romantic protagonists such as Prince

---

[18] On Grabbe's anticipation of a variety of modern dramatists such as Jarry and Valéry, see Gerald Gillespie, "Faust en pataphysicien," *Journal of European Studies*, 13 (1983), 98-110.

Zerbino, is a pervasive existential anxiety. Often their condition is explicitly Hamletic. Whereas the title figure of Goethe's novel *Wilhelm Meisters Lehrjahre* (Wilhelm Meister's Apprenticeship, 1796) ultimately works his way through the Hamlet problem, innumerable heirs to Romanticism remain like Hamlet "sicklied o'er with the pale cast of thought" right into the twentieth century. Bonaventura's narrator Kreuzgang is indelibly stamped by the Hamlet role and identifies it with the Oedipus and Don Juan stories as well in *Die Nachtwachen* (The Night Watches, 1804). Feeling one-self to be fictional, like a character in a play, is a key attribute of the Hamletized Romantic mind. We encounter the Symbolist version of this condition in Laforgue's story "Hamlet, ou les suites de la piété filiale" (1885), included in the *Moralités légendaires* (1887). The story, which is governed by Romantic irony, takes us straight into the nightmarishly decadent world of the "actual" Hamlet who is absorbed in and lives virtually only through the play he has written based on the recent hideous crimes in his family. The angry "actual" Laertes murders this otherwise insignificant and ineffectual haunted prince in a grisly fashion, and the real world goes lustily about its business. It is the modern artist, likewise alienated from life's strange cruelty, who in turn is Hamlet's haunted descendant. Joyce's Stephen recognizes himself as an avatar of Hamlet in *Ulysses* (1922), and his own personal Shakespeare obsession, which recapitulates that of the nineteenth century from Goethe over Mallarmé to Freud, reimbeds the tradition in a new Modernist framework.[19]

The Hamletic mind is symptomatic of the general movement away from older values of "nature" and "reality" to the mind itself and spirituality. To the extent that Romantic drama, too, like Romantic narrative, drifted from the older organicist to the newer psychological polarity, it pulled away from sentimental-verisimilar conventions of character portrayal and toward dream structures, lyrical composition, and symbolic fairytales. These trends were essential precursors en-abling the eventual formation of a distinct Symbolist theater.

A central conflict in much of Symbolist theater is the struggle against death and the void or against life as an absurd illusion.[20] The stage becomes the locus of synaesthesia; form, color, music, gestures, and (by allusion or implication) scents suggest "correspondences" and mystery. An inner landscape is projected, but the play's motifs and discourse are veiled in ambiguity. The use of silences to modulate the flow increases the importance of the lyrical element. Actors are treated pri-marily as poetic mediums; there is no impetus to engage in ordinary "characterization" or to impart a standard ideological message. Mallarmé's fragment *Hérodiade* (written 1864ff.) exemplifies the closeness of the poem or prose-poem and lyrical drama in Symbolism. As the artist wrote to an ac-quaintance, the aim of his new poetics was to *"Peindre non la chose, mais l'effet qu'elle produit. Le vers ne doit donc pas, là, se composer de mots, mais d'intentions, et toutes les paroles s'effacer devant les sensations [...]"* (*paint not the thing but the effect it produces*. In that case, though, the verse is not to be composed of words but of intentions, and the words all to give way to the sensa-tions [...]). The epical and rhetorical expansion of such drama is reached in Villiers de l'Isle-Adam's *Axël* (1894) that upholds the "Decadent" ethos in elaborate detail set forth in long monologues. The middle ground in formal terms is occupied by works like Hofmannsthal's *Der Tor und der Tod*

---

[19] See Gerald Gillespie, "Afterthoughts of Hamlet: Goethe's Wilhelm, Joyce's Stephen," in *Comparative Literary History as Discourse*, ed. Mario Valdés, Daniel Javitch, and A. Owen Aldridge (Bern: Lang, 1992), pp. 286-304.

[20] For a broader treatment of Western Europe, cf. Hartmut Köhler, "Symbolist Theater," in *The Symbolist Movement in the Literature of European Languages*, ed. Anna Balakian (Budapest: Akadémiai Kiadó, 1982), pp. 413-24; its categorized bibliographies and index of authors and artists make this vol. in the *Comparative History* series an especially valuable resource.

(Death and the Fool, 1893). It opens with the esthete Claudio wondering about the meaning of existence and ends with his realization, too late, of the need to live and feel to the utmost; Death, a sophisticate, arrives, produces the lost images of his mother, sweetheart, and best friend, and leads all away. Rilke's *Die weiße Prinzessin* (The White Princess, 1898) and the early Claudel's *Tête d'Or* (Golden Head, 1890) continue this type of poetic dialogue on existential questions, while Blok derives his play *Balaganchik* (The Puppet Show, 1905) directly out of his own poem.

The dream-like or visionary play was suited for elaborating allegorical fantasies or exploring psychological states. Both ancient myth and fairytale were apt vehicles. Hofmannsthal's interest in abnormal, neurotic, and libertine characteristics was registered in such plays (libretti) as *Elektra* (1903) and *Oedipus und die Sphinx* (1906). A non-rational logic and esoteric quality were hallmarks in Maeterlinck, one of the most influential Symbolist playwrights. In his *Les Aveugles* (The Blind, 1891), an allegory on the skepticism of modern civilization, a dozen men and women wander morosely through the world guided only by obsolete symbols and are abandoned in a dark forest by their chief mentor, a dead Catholic priest. His *Pelléas et Mélisande* (1892), set in a medieval forest, resonates with the lyrical pathos which Tieck's play *Genoveva* introduced a century earlier. Golaud, grandson of old king Arkel, finds Melisande weeping by a fountain and marries her although her identity remains a secret. When his brother Pelléas is seized by love which she chastely reciprocates, Golaud kills him in a rage, and Melisande dies of a broken heart. In *L'Oiseau bleu* (The Blue Bird, 1908), Maeterlinck invokes a Symbolist theme color that was established in Romanticism, going back to Novalis's *Heinrich von Ofterdingen*.[21] The fairy Berylune sends the unhappy woodcutter's children, Tyltyl and Mytyl, accompanied by the (loyal) Dog and (treacherous) Cat, in search of the Blue Bird. After exploring the Land of Memory, Place of Night, and Kingdom of the Future, the disconsolate questers return home to find the Blue Bird in a cage and release it. Yeats went back to the "sacred books," including Celtic myth, as in the lyrical tragedies *The Countess Cathleen* (1892) and *Deirdre* (1907), to create a modern religious drama that did not depend on doctrinaire allegiances but on a deeper universal symbolic power.

The longer-term absorption of Romantic "anti-realist" tendencies can be detected in certain crossovers between and amongst Symbolist, Naturalist, and Expressionist theater.[22] The dark streak of Romantic negation was no less persistent than the hope for transcendance or salvation; and Romantic probing into the psyche for matter and structure brought forth disturbing as well as entrancing discoveries. Strindberg's *Fadren* (The Father, 1887) and *Fröken Julie* (Miss Julie, 1888) are classics of Naturalist theater because of their unswerving examination of primary psychological conflicts as a kind of pathology. Yet in his late period the playwright's obsession with emotion, instinct, and passion carried him into the domain of Symbolist fantasies, in his case, fantasies with strong Expressionist traits. The archetypal pattern of the journey and such tendencies as titanism and satanism are as important as any specific biographical allusions in the trilogy *Till Damascus* (To Damascus, 1898-99), a pilgrimage play. *Brott och brott* (Crime and Crime, 1899), dealing with the destructive power of evil thought, still shows the influence of contemporary French theater in the depiction of social context. Besides conveying Strindberg's sense of the malevolence at the

---

[21] The emergence of a poetic tonality dominated by blue around 1800, and the persistence of blue as a master reference in literature and painting into Modernism, is traced by Angelika Overath, *Das andere Blau: Zur Poetik einer Farbe im modernen Gedicht* (Stuttgart: Metzler, 1987).

[22] For a thorough treatment of Expressionist theater, consult the *Comparative History* volume, *Expressionism as an International Literary Phenomenon*, ed. Ulrich Weisstein (Budapest: Akadémiai Kiadó, 1973).

heart of life, *Dödsdansen* (The Dance of Death, 1901) has horrific, nightmarish qualities fore-shadowing the grotesque, farcical brand of "comedy" which we now associate with Ionesco, Dür-renmatt, Ruibal, and other practitioners of the Absurd. *Svanevit* (Swannwhite, 1901), orienting toward the example of Maeterlinck, uses the resources of magic and romance to enable expression of the precious miracle, love.

It is worth citing the playwright's own preface to *Ett drömspel* (A Dream Play, 1901) because of its constellation of terms bridging Romanticism and Modernism and its hovering between a Sym-bolist and Expressionist treatment of the generic "roles" through which the human story is played out as a play-within-a-play:

> Författaren har i detta drömspel med anslutning till sitt förra drömspel *Till Damaskus* sökt härma drömmens osammanhängande men skenbart logiska form. Allt kan ske, allt är möjligt och sannolikt. Tid och rum existera icke; på en obetydlig verklighetsgrund spinner inbillningen ut och väver nya mönster: en blandning av minnen, upplevelser, fria påhitt, orimligheter och improvisationer.
>
> Personerna klyvas, fördubblas, dubbleras, dunsta av, förtätas, flyta ut, samlas. Men ett medve-tande står över alla, det är drömmarens; för det finns inga hemligheter, ingen inkonsekvens, inga skrupler, ingen lag. Han dömer icke, frisäger icke, endast relaterar; och såsom drömmen mest är smärtsam, mindre ofta glättig, går en ton av vemod, och medlidande med allt levande genom den vinglande berättelsen. Sömnen, befriaren, uppträder ofta pinsam, men när plågan är som stramast, infinner sig uppvaknandet och försonar den lidande med verkligheten, som huru kvalfull den än kan vara, dock i detta ögonblick är en njutning, jämförd med den plågsamma drömmen.[23]

> (Following the example of my previous dream play *To Damascus*, I have in this present dream play sought to imitate the incoherent but ostensibly logical form of our dreams. Anything can happen; everything is possible and probable. Time and space do not exist. Working with some insignificant real events as a background, the imagination spins out its threads of thoughts and weaves them into new patterns – a mixture of memories, experiences, spontaneous ideas, impossibilities, and improvisa-tions.
>
> The characters split, double, multiply, dissolve, condense, float apart, coalesce. But one mind stands over and above them all, the mind of the dreamer; and for him there are no secrets, no inconsis-tencies, no scruples, no laws. He does not condemn, does not acquit; he only narrates the story. And since the dream is more often painful than cheerful, a tone of melancholy and of sympathy with all living creatures runs through the pitching and swaying narrative. Sleep, which should free the dreamer, often plagues and tortures him instead. But when the pain is most excruciating, the moment of waking comes and reconciles the dreamer to reality, which, however agonizing it may be, is a joy and a pleasure at that moment compared with the painful dream.)[24]

The idea of the superiority of the creative dreaming mind and its "sympathy with all living crea-tures" strikes both a Tieckian and a Schopenhauerian note. Further Romantic echoes reverberate in the paragraphs that Strindberg added in the director's copy of the play for its first staging in 1907. Calderón and Shakespeare are reverently invoked for their insights into life as a dream. The play is explicitly compared to a symphonic composition in which voices carry the thematic development. From one perspective, in its intensity, anguish, and structure, this work is a prime example of Expressionism. But readers familiar with the Romantic cosmic drama which Esslin discusses will

---

[23] August Strindberg, *Samlade Skrifter* (Stockholm: Albert Bonnier, 1916), XXXVI, 215.
[24] August Strindberg, *Selected Plays*, trans. and ed. Evert Sprinchorn (Minneapolis: Univ. of Minnesota Press, 1986), p. 646.

recognize the affinity of Strindberg's universal dream vision to the totalizations striven after by Krasiński, Madách, Ibsen, et al. in the wake of Goethe. The play consists of a privileged beholding of, and experiential involvement in, the world on the part of the daughter of the god Indra within an overtly neomythic frame; the Poet, whose role is internalized in the dream, has the task of translating what she tells him. The quest and pilgrimage paradigm recur in *Stora landsvägen* (The Great Highway, 1910). Its symbolic roles are not numerous, but include biblical, classical, and Oriental characters. Strindberg may compress the cosmic drama in order to make a fervent personal statement in old age, but the freedom with which he assigns basic human traits and ideas to his symbolic figures resembles the technique which we see later in Wilder's absurdist *By the Skin of Our Teeth* (1942), influenced directly by Goethe (and Joyce) and concerned about a general crisis in human development. As Bisztray remarks, although from one perspective Ibsen and Strindberg qualify as Naturalists, they had an enormous impact on turn-of-the-century neo-Romantic and Symbolist playwrights throughout Europe.

This effect began to be felt in Russia in the 1880s as the first translations of the great Scandinavians were being read. Naturalism and Symbolism came simultaneously; for example, translations of Maeterlinck and Hauptmann in the 1890s, and Hofmannsthal, Wedekind, Schnitzler, D'Annunzio, Wilde, and Shaw in the 1900s. In certain respects the short-lived Russian Symbolist drama can be regarded as a delayed experiencing of the more radical kind of Romantic experimentation not at all prominent in the earlier moment of Russian Romanticism proper. Significantly, the master of psychology Chekhov was attracted toward Maeterlinck as a dramatist of states of mind but repelled by the moralist Ibsen. There is evidence that at the end of his life Chekhov (d. 1904) was moving toward an "anti-realist" art such as the Symbolists then developed before World War I. The lines were drawn by Briusov's attack on the Moscow Art Theater in 1902, and Meyerhold's resignation from it, eventually to head for a while Komissarzhevskaya's new establishment, a Symbolist citadel. Meyerhold's staging of Sologub's *The Triumph of Death* in 1907, a brooding tragedy set in the time of King Pepin, was a decisive turning-point for Russian drama. In an essay, "Literary Intimations of a New Theater" (1906), Meyerhold asserted that "literature" was the innovative force that again and again broke up rigid old forms of drama. He saw the importance of Blok's creation of a "grotesque theater" out of the puppet concept, using *commedia dell'arte* figures, and he later experimented with the *commedia* as a means of renewal through stylization. Meyerhold viewed Gozzi and Tieck as the pioneers of a self-sufficient theater, liberated from mimetic servitude to life. The Symbolist theoretician Ivanov sought, as a believing Christian, to harness Nietzsche's Dionysian principle to a rebirth of a drama with mythic and religious power, and speculated on ways to rechannel Wagner's music-drama more effectively. Fulfilling the call for a Bacchic drama was Annensky's *Thamytris Kitharodos* (1906), in which the Muses finally blind their rival, the music-beset poet who fails to respond to a Nymph's love and so by his misstep enters a strange vatic realm. Although Blok eventually turned away from lyrical drama on the grounds it was leading to a weakening of dramatic power, his *The Rose and the Cross* (1912), set in medieval Languedoc and Brittany, remained a captivating example of the poetic evocation of a lost world, such as Tieck had introduced in *Genoveva*. Besides the possibility of a *Gesamtkunstwerk*, Bely was interested in creating the modern equivalent of the mystery play. In its anti-naturalist bias, Russian Symbolism emphasized the integration of painterly, operatic, and balletic features and turned, like Romanticism, to a recovery of the qualities of high cultural moments of the past – the drama of ancient Greece, the Middle Ages, the Elizabethan era, the comedy of Molière and Italy. Russian Symbolism also anticipated features of a drama of the Absurd in ways that bore a curious resemblance to the transition in Spain between the Generation of 1898 and Valle-Inclán.

Connections with Absurdist Drama

The chapters "Romantic Irony and the Grotesque" and "Romantic Irony and Modern Anti-Theater" in the Garber volume deal with the relevance of two major older streams of dramatic "absurdism" that prepared the ground for the Modernist and Existentialist waves which today enjoy the status not of an aesthetic revolution but of a canonical tradition.[25] Eighteenth-century writers who were fascinated by religious and folk imagination, and by the Gothic, horrific, and grotesque, and writers who were ready to disregard neoclassical norms of order, harmony, propriety, and rational illusion in favor of fictionality, artifice, fantasy, and irregularity, commingled to form one broader stream. In the longer term more was involved than admiring Shakespeare's "irregularities" as an instance of the power of nature manifested through a genius, as Storm and Stress had, although that bias was of lasting effect. A different momentum began to gather in works such as Möser's treatise *Harlekin, oder Vertheidigung des Groteske-Komischen* (Harlequin, or a Defense of the Grotesque-Comic, 1761), praising *commedia* clowns, "Baroque taste," and opera *because* they are "unnatural."

A significant twist was given to the high Romantic view of drama as an imaginative act of illusioning and disillusioning in the strange German novel *The Night Watches of Bonaventura* (1804). At midpoint, in an interpolated work, a botched tragedy entitled *Man*, the liberated clown engages in a theoretical diatribe on the now accelerating, downward slide of drama over the ages from mendacious tragedy into meaningless farce.[26] This plunge out of belief and dignity into horror and nightmare manifests the mysterious triumph of truth as inexorable negation. The savage clown proclaims himself the successor to Oedipus and Hamlet in our human play going nowhere. The odd first-person narrator, the watchman Kreuzgang, peers in a perpetual nocturne at the city of man as at a hellish vision by Breughel, Michelangelo, or Callot. An ex-puppeteer, he regards the French Revolution – just as Jean Paul suggests in the same year – as a colossal farce, a macabre *Grand Guignol* extravaganza. Although less bizarre than Kreuzgang, the title figure of Büchner's *Danton's Death* (1835) bears a clear resemblance insofar as he progressively deconstructs the absurd drama of the Revolution as an insider. This kind of agonizing had a special appeal for the Expressionists who rediscovered both the (then still) anonymous author "Bonaventura" and Büchner. *Danton's Death* was not staged until 1902, when its late Romantic disillusionism could resonate with such Modernist works as Strindberg's *A Dream Play*.

The second stream of Romantic "absurdism" bubbled to the surface by 1800 in Tieck's exposure of the artificial reality of the play sphere. Following *Puss-in-Boots* and *The Land of Upsidedown*, Romantic "disillusioning" in the Tieckian vein consisted of more than a humorous examina-

---

[25] Gerald Gillespie, in *Romantic Irony*, ed. Frederick Garber (Budapest: Akadémiai Kiadó, 1988), pp. 322-42 and 343-57. On aspects of modernist "anti-art" at large and in the theater, consult the indispensable two-part *Les Avant-gardes littéraires au XXe siècle*, ed. Jean Weisgerber (Budapest: Akadémiai Kiadó, 1984).

[26] Anon. [=August Klingemann], *Die Nachtwachen des Bonaventura*, trans. and ed. Gerald Gillespie (Austin: Univ. of Texas Press; Edinburgh: Edinburgh Univ. Press, 1972), ch. 8. After decades of controversy over the authorship of *The Night Watches*, Bonaventura was finally identified in the 1980s as the Brunswick theater director August Klingemann (1777-1831). Klingemann first produced Goethe's *Faust* (1827) and was a major factor in reshaping the canon of dramatic literature.

tion of the relationships among authors, audiences, works, genres, and conventions. A dominant authorial consciousness juxtaposed or interwove such scrutiny with other subject-matters within an encompassing frame-play, it dissolved the boundaries between the real and the imagined within the fiction, and it suggested analogies to the interactions of inner and outer life beyond the theater walls. Among the favorite models for the artist's ironic self-awareness were Shakespeare's *A Midsummer Night's Dream* in dramatic literature and Cervantes's *Don Quixote* in narrative fiction. As has been discussed above, a crucial moment in the evolution of Romantic fantastic comedy occurred when Tieck internalized the theme of the failure or collapse of the theatrical production in the play itself. This theme of nullification ultimately reached out to include the authorial mind. The audience, too, eventually was induced to consider whether its members could really share anything substantial on an intersubjective basis, if, like the projected self-destructing illusion before them, their own mentation was a tenuous arbitrary figment.

Prior comparative scholarship has not called attention in any consistent and thorough manner to the fact that several of the eminent modernist innovators credited with introducing the Theater of the Absurd in their respective languages had a strong interest in German drama of the Romantic period. The cases of the playwrights Jarry, Pirandello, and Wilder exemplify not only three directions of dramatic absurdism and its reception in three nations; these writers, whose careers as an aggregate stretch from the end of the nineteenth century to World War II, represent three successive generations who enjoyed such a connection. The vogue of Beckett, Dürrenmatt, and Ionesco belongs to the postwar period, when the concept of the Theater of the Absurd was popularized by Esslin's seminal book (1961).[27]

It is instructive to consider the many-stranded ancestry of Wilder's play *By the Skin of Our Teeth*. His work is a response to the specter of a human catastrophe which many feared totalitarianism and World War II might portend. It is a fascinating example of the embracing of absurdity to conjure an affirmative mood. Wilder was an admirer of Goethe's *Faust* rather than of the absurdists Jarry and Pirandello, and the lessons of that masterwork helped him in restoring the connection between the cosmic purview of drama and drama as an arbitrary, visionary construct. He had also studied Joyce's use of dream logic in *Ulysses* to create a universal encyclopedic work. Wilder turned the absurd around into an affirmation ("credo quia impossibile"), in a hidden rebirth of the resolving beneficent irony of high Romanticism. He did so a decade before Beckett's existentialist masterpiece, *Waiting for Godot*, threw the switches again in a direction that had been anticipated in the late Romantic mode of "nihilistic" irony.

[27] Martin Esslin's book, *The Theatre of the Absurd*, 3rd ed. (Harmondsworth: Peregrine, 1987), remains the foundational and indispensable guide.

GENERAL BIBLIOGRAPHY

Note: The following list is not intended to be exhaustive but to provide a starting point. The individual essays in this volume should be consulted for further items. Among the titles cited below, many are helpful in furnishing more comprehensive, categorized, or specialized bibliographies on Romantic drama and its cultural variations – for example: Heinz Kindermann, *Theatergeschichte Europas*, Vol. VI; Joseph W. Donahue, Jr., *Dramatic Character*; W.D. Howarth, *Sublime and Grotesque*; Barry V. Daniels, *Revolution in the Theatre*; Laurence Senelick, *National Theatre in Northern and Eastern Europe*; Jeffrey N. Cox, *In the Shadows of Romance*; Frederick Burwick, *Illusion and the Drama*.

Romantic Poetics and Cross-Currents

Theory of Drama

Albrecht, W.P. *The Sublime Pleasures of Tragedy: A Study of Critical Theory from Dennis to Keats*. Lawrence: University Press of Kansas, 1975.

Baader, Horst. "Diderots Theorie der Schauspielkunst und ihre Parallelen in Deutschland." *Revue de Littérature Comparée*, 33 (1959), 200-23.

Bach, Max. "Sainte-Beuve critique du théâtre de son temps." *PMLA*, 81 (1966), 563-74.

Billaz, André. "Le *Cours de Littérature dramatique* de A.W. Schlegel: Note sur la traduction française de 1814." *Revue d'Histoire Littéraire de la France*, 70 (1970), 610-18.

Burwick, Frederick. *Illusion and the Drama: Critical Theory of the Enlightenment and Romantic Era*. University Park: Pennsylvania State University Press, 1991.

Carlson, Marvin. *Theories of the Theatre: A Historical and Critical Survey, from the Greeks to the Present*. Ithaca and London: Cornell University Press, 1984. (See especially chs. 11-17.)

Chambers, Ross. *La Poétique du théâtre dans la littérature européenne (XIXe et XXe siècles)*. Sydney: University of Sydney, 1971.

Clark, Barrett H. *European Theories of the Drama*. Rev. ed. New York: Crown Publishers, 1965.

Daniels, Barry V. *Revolution in the Theatre: French Romantic Theories of Drama*. Westport, Conn.: Greenwood, 1983.

Descotes, Maurice. *Histoire de la critique dramatique en France*. Tübingen: Place, 1980.

Dukore, Bernard. *Dramatic Theory and Criticism: Greeks to Grotowski*. New York: Holt, Rinehart, & Winston, 1974.

Durán, Agustín, 1789-1862. *Discurso sobre el influjo que ha tenido la crítica moderna en la decadencia del teatro antiguo español* [...]. Introd. and notes by Donald L. Shaw. Exeter: University of Exeter, 1973.

Hobson, Marian. "Du Theatrum Mundi au Theatrum Mentis." *Revue des Sciences Humaines*, no. 167 (July-Sept. 1977), 379-94.

Magnanini, Emilia. "La teoria del dramma romantico fra Russia ed Europa." *Rivista di Letterature Moderne e Comparate*, 39 (1986), 213-33.

Petrocchi, Giorgio. *Le poetiche del romanticismo: Corso de lezioni per l'anno academico 1972-73*. Roma: Elia, [1973].

Petrocchi, Giorgio. *Lezioni di critica romantica*. Milano: Il saggiatore, 1975.

Scelfo, Maria Luisa. *Le teorie drammatiche nel Romanticismo: Tra Manzoni e Hugo*. Catania: Marino, 1984.
Schmidt, P. "Romantisches Drama: Zur Theorie eines Paradoxons." In: *Deutsche Dramentheorien*. Ed. Reinhold
    Grimm. 2 vols. Frankfurt a.M.: Athenäum, 1971. I: 245-69.
Schyberg, Fredrik. *Dansk teaterkritik indtil 1914*. Copenhagen: Gyldendal, 1937.
Senelick, Laurence. *Russian Dramatic Theory from Pushkin to the Symbolists*. Austin: University of Texas Press,
    1981.
Valette, Rebecca M. "Benjamin Constant, Dramatic Theorist." *French Review*, 37 (1964), 426-31.
Westling, Christer. *Idealismens estetik: Nordisk litteraturkritik vid 1800-talets mitt mot bakgrund av den tyska
    filosofin från Kant till Hegel*. Uppsala: n.p., 1985.
Zamfirescu, Ion, *Teatrul romantic european*. Bucureşti: Editura Eminescu, 1984.

Cross-Cultural Studies

Bauer, Roger. "Du drame 'bourgeois' au drame 'romantique.'" In: *Change in Language and Literature: Proceed-
    ings of the Triennial Congress of FILLM*. Eds. M. Szabolcsi and J. Kovács. Budapest: Akadémiai Kiadó,
    1966. pp. 153-78.
Bauer, Roger. "Von Schillers *Wallenstein* zu Benjamin Constants *Wallstein*, oder: Die Zwänger der klassizisti-
    schen Konvention." In: *Der theatralische Neoklassizismus um 1800: Ein europäisches Phänomen?* Ed.
    Roger Bauer, with Michael de Graat and Jürgen Wertheimer. Bern, Frankfurt a.M., New York, Paris: Lang,
    1986. pp. 184-95.
Bauer, Roger. "Das Schicksal im Schauerdrama: Von Lillos *Fatal Curiosity* zu Zacharias Werners *Der vierund-
    zwanzigste Februar* und Pixérécourts *Le Monastère abandonné*." In: *Inevitabilis Vis Fatorum: Der Triumph
    des Schicksalsdramas auf der europäischen Bühne um 1800*. Ed. Roger Bauer. Bern, Frankfurt a.M., New
    York, Paris: Lang, 1990. pp. 249-58. (See also Bauer's Foreword, pp. 5-13.)
Bauer, Roger, and Wertheimer, Jürgen, eds. *Das Ende des Stegreifspiels/Die Geburt des Nationaltheaters: Ein
    Wendepunkt in der Geschichte des europäischen Theaters*. München: Fink, 1983.
Burwick, Frederick. "Romantic Drama: From Optics to Illusion." In: *Literature and Science: Theory and Prac-
    tice*. Ed. Stuart Peterfreund. Boston: Northeastern University Press, 1989.
Carlsson, Anni. *Ibsen, Strindberg, Hamsun*. Kronberg/Ts.: Athenäum-Verlag, 1978.
Castle, Terry. "Phantasmagoria: Spectral Technology and the Metaphorics of Modern Reverie." *Critical Inquiry*,
    15 (1988), 26-61.
Čiževskij, D. *Comparative History of Slavic Literatures*. Trans. by R.N. Porter and M.P. Rice; ed., with a fore-
    word, by Serge A. Zenkovsky. Nashville: Vanderbilt University Press, 1971. (Chapter 10, pp. 118-50, de-
    voted to Slavic Romanticism.)
Clayton, J. Douglas. "From Gozzi to Hoffmann: German Sources for *commedia dell'arte* in Russian Avant-Garde
    Theatre." In: *The Science of Buffoonery: Theory and History of the* commedia dell'arte. Ottawa: Dovehouse,
    1989. pp. 117-33.
Cope, Jackson I. "Harlequin's Reinvasion: Garrick, Goldoni, and the Germans." In: *Dramaturgy of the Dae-
    monic: Studies in Antigeneric Theater from Ruzante to Grimaldi*. Baltimore: Johns Hopkins University
    Press, 1984.
Cox, Jeffrey N. *In the Shadows of Romance: Romantic Tragic Drama in Germany, England, and France*. Athens:
    Ohio University Press, 1987.
Dédéyan, Charles. *Le Drame romantique en Europe: France, Angletere, Allemagne, Italie, Espagne, Russie*.
    Paris: Société d'Edition d'Enseignement Supérieur, 1982.
Dietrich, Margret. *Europäische Dramaturgie im 19. Jahrhundert*. Graz, Köln: Böhlau, 1961.
Du Bruck, Alfred. *Gérard de Nerval and the German Heritage*. London, The Hague, Paris: Mouton, 1965.
Fraper, F.W.M. *The Rise and Fall of French Romantic Drama with Special Reference to the Influence of Shake-
    speare, Scott, and Byron*. London: Constable, 1923.
Frenzel, Elisabeth. "Mussets *Lorenzaccio* – ein mögliches Vorbild für *Dantons Tod*." *Euphorion*, 58 (1964), 59-
    68.

Frye, Prosser Hall. *Romance and Tragedy: A Study of Classic and Romantic Elements in the Great Tragedies of European Literature*. Lincoln: University of Nebraska Press, 1961.

Galster, Bohdan. *Paralele romantyczne; Polsko-rosyjskie powinowactwa literackie*. Wyd. 1. Warsaw: Państwowe Wydawnictwo Naukowe, 1987.

Gershkovich, A.A. "Teatr i natsional'naya Kul'tura (k postanovke problemi)." In: *Teatr v National'noy Kul'ture Stran Isentralnoy i Ugovostochnoy Europi XVIII-XIX vv*. Moscow: Nauka, 1976.

Gershkovich, A.A. "Le Théâtre est-européen à la Charnière des Lumières et du Romantisme." *Neohelicon*, 3, nos. 3-4 (1975), 51-67.

Getto, Giovanni. "Il teatro di Schiller e il romanzo di Manzoni." *Lettere italiane*, 15 (1963), 399-426.

Gillespie, Gerald. "Romantic Irony and the Grotesque." In: *Romantic Irony*. Ed. Frederick Garber. Budapest: Akadémiai Kiadó, 1988. pp. 322-42.

Gillespie, Gerald. "Romantic Irony and Modern Anti-Theater." In: *Romantic Irony*. Ed. Frederick Garber. Budapest: Akadémiai Kiadó, 1988. pp. 343-57.

Gilman, Sander L. "Very Little Faust...: Parodies of the German Drama on the Mid-Nineteenth Century British Stage." *Arcadia*, 8 (1973), 18-44.

Gravier, Maurice. "Georg Büchner et Alfred de Musset." *Orbis Litterarum*, 9 (1954), 29-44.

Grieder, Theodore. "The German Drama in England, 1790-1800." *Restoration and Eighteenth-Century Theatre Research*, 3 (1964), 39-50.

Hays, Michael. "Comedy as Being/Comedy as Idea." *Studies in Romanticism*, 26 (1987), 221-30.

Jechová, H. *L'Image poétique dans le movement romantique slave*. Paris: Didier, 1982.

Johnston, Brian. "Revolution and the Romantic Theater." *Theater Three*, 4 (Spring 1988), 5-20.

Jost, François. "German and French Themes in Early American Drama." *Journal of General Education*, 28 (1976), 190-222.

Kindermann, Heinz. *Theatergeschichte Europas*. VI: *Romantik*. Salzburg: Mueller, 1964.

Klapper, Roxanne. *The German Literary Influence on Byron*. Salzburg: Institut für Englische Sprache und Literatur, 1974.

Klapper, Roxanne. *The German Literary Influence on Shelley*. Salzburg: Institut für Englische Sprache und Literatur, 1975.

Kuleshov, V.I. *Romantizm v slavianskikh literaturakh*. Moskva: Izd. Moskovskogo Universiteta, 1973.

Kuzemińska, W. *Bohaber mityczny w powieśiach polskich i francuskich*. Warsaw: Państwowe Wydawnictwo Naukowe, 1985.

Llorens Castillo, Vicente. *Liberales y románticos: Una emigración española en Inglaterra (1823-1834)*. 2nd ed. Madrid: Castalia, 1968.

Locker, Malka. *Les Romantiques: Allemagne, Angleterre, France*. Paris: Presses du temps présent, 1964. (First published 1958 in Yiddish.)

Lombard, C.M. "French Romanticism on the American Stage." *Revue de Littérature Comparée*, 43 (1969), 161-72.

Magnuszewski, J. "Polski romantyzm a literatury zachodnioslowianskie." In: *Z polskich studiow slawistycznych*. Warszawa: Państwowe Wydawnictwo Naukowe, 1963. pp. 105-29.

Martonyi, Eva. "Des Lumières au romantisme: Mise au point des recherches hongroises sur le XIXe siècle." *Romantisme*, 36 (Spring 1982), 79-92.

Mortier, Roland. *Diderot en Allemagne 1750-1850*. Paris: Presses Universitaires de France, 1954.

Nagavajara, Chetana. *August Wilhelm Schlegel in Frankreich*. Tübingen: Niemeyer, 1966.

Nineteenth Century Theatre Research, I (1973) ff. (Bibliography.)

Orsini, G.N.G. "Coleridge and Schlegel Reconsidered." *Comparative Literature*, 15 (1964), 27-41.

Panne, M.C. van de. *Recherches sur les rapports entre le romantisme français et le théâtre hollandais*. Amsterdam: H.J. Paris, 1927.

Partridge, Eric. *The French Romantics' Knowledge of English Literature (1820-1848), According to Contemporary French Memoirs, Letters and Periodicals*. Paris: Bibliothèque de Littérature Comparée, 1924. Reprinted: New York: Franklin, 1968.

Paulsell, P.R. "Ludwig Tieck's *Der gestiefelte Kater* and the English Burlesque Drama Tradition." *Michigan Germanic Studies* 2, (1986), 144-58.

Pipkin, James, ed. *English and German Romanticism: Cross-Currents and Controversies*. Heidelberg: Winter, 1985.

Plard, Henri. "A propos de *Leonce und Lena:* Musset et Büchner." *Études Germaniques*, 9 (1954), 26-36.

Quigley, Martin. *Magic Shadows: The Story of the Origin of Motion Pictures*. Washington, D.C.: Georgetown University Press, 1948.

Richardson, Alan. *A Mental Theater: Poetic Drama and Consciousness in the Romantic Age*. University Park, PA: Pennsylvania State University Press, 1988.

Rokem, Freddi. *Theatrical Space in Ibsen, Chekhov and Strindberg: Public Forms of Privacy*. Ann Arbor: University of Michigan Research Press, 1986.

Rusack, Hedwig Hoffmann. *Gozzi in Germany: A Survey of the Rise and Decline of the Gozzi Vogue in Germany and Austria, with Special Reference to the German Romanticists*. New York: Columbia University Press, 1930.

Senelick, Laurence, ed. *National Theatre in Northern and Eastern Europe, 1746-1900*. Cambridge: Cambridge University Press, 1991.

Shilstone, Frederick W. "Byron's 'Mental Theatre' and the German Classical Precedent." *Comparative Drama*, 10 (1976), 187-99.

Sőtér, István and Irene Neupokoeva. eds. *European Romanticism*. Budapest: Akadémiai Kiadó, 1977. (Transl. from the Russian first edition of 1974; contribution on drama.)

Steiner, George. *The Death of Tragedy*. London: Faber, 1961.

Stokoe, F.W. *German Influence in the English Romantic Period 1788-1818, with Special Reference to Scott, Coleridge, Shelley, and Byron*. New York: Russell & Russell, 1963.

Thompson, John. *Alexandre Dumas père and the Spanish Romantic Drama*. Baton Rouge and London: Louisiana State University Press, 1938.

Valentin, Jean-Marie. *De Lessing à Heine: Un siècle de relations littéraires entre la France et l'Allemagne*. Metz: Metz University Press, 1986.

Wertheimer, Jürgen. *"Der Güter gefährlichstes": Zur Krise des Dialogs zwischen Aufklärung und Romantik*. München: Fink, 1990.

Wikander, Matthew M. *The Play of Truth and State: Historical Drama from Shakespeare to Brecht*. Baltimore: Johns Hopkins University Press, 1986.

Wittmann, Anna M. "Closure in European Romantic Drama." Diss. University of Alberta, Edmonton, 1984.

Wootton, Carol. "The Deaths of Goethe's Werther and De Vigny's Chatterton." *Revue de Littérature Comparée*, 50 (1976), 295-303.

Shakespeare/Elizabethan Drama

Ades, John I. "Charles Lamb, Shakespeare, and Early Nineteenth-Century Theater." *PMLA*, 85 (1970), 514-26.

Badawi, M.M. *Coleridge: Critic of Shakespeare*. New York: Cambridge University Press, 1972.

Bate, Jonathan. "The Politics of Romantic Shakespearean Criticism: Germany, England, France." *European Romantic Review*, (Summer 1990).

Bate, Jonathan. *Shakespeare and the English Romantic Imagination*. Oxford: Clarendon Press, 1986.

Bauer, Roger, ed., with Michael de Graat and Jürgen Wertheimer. *Das Shakespeare-Bild in Europa zwischen Aufklärung und Romantik*. Berne, Frankfurt a.M., New York, Paris: Lang, 1982.

Bochner, Jay. "Shakespeare in France: A Survey of Dominant Opinion, 1733-1830." *Revue de Littérature Comparée*, 39 (1965), 44-65.

Coiscault-Cavalca, Monique. "Les Romantiques français et les Elisabéthains." *Les Lettres Romanes*, 19 (1965), 121-35, and 20 (1966), 38-56, 125-41, 230-46.

Getto, Giovanni. "Manzoni e Shakespeare." *Lettere italiane*, 19 (1967), 187-236.

Hoheisel, Peter. "Coleridge on Shakespeare: Method Amid the Rhetoric." *Studies in Romanticism*, 13 (1974), 15-23.

Jacobus, Mary: "'That Great Stage Where Senators Perform': Macbeth and the Politics of Romantic Theatre." *Studies in Romanticism*, 22 (1983), 353-87.

Jolles, F. "Shakespeares *Sommernachtstraum* in Deutschland: Einige Betrachtungen über den Vorgang der Assimilation." *German Life and Letters*, 16 (1962-63), 229-37.

Knight, G. Wilson. *Byron and Shakespeare*. London: Routledge & Kegan Paul, 1966.

Lamb, Margaret. "That Strain Again: Shakespearean Comedies by Musset and Büchner." *Educational Theatre Journal*, 27 (1975), 70-76.

Lott, Nelda Jackson. "The Tragedies of Scott, Lamb and Coleridge: Their Elizabethan Heritage." Diss. University of South Mississippi, 1971.

Oliver, A. Richard. "Charles Nodier's Cult of Shakespeare." *Orbis Litterarum*, 17 (1962), 154-65.

Patterson, Charles I., Jr. "Charles Lamb, Shakespeare, and the Stage Reconsidered." *Emory University Quarterly*, 20 (1964), 101-7.

Pennink, Renetta. *Nederland en Shakespeare, achttiende eeuw en vroege romantiek*. 's-Gravenhage: Nijhoff, 1936.

Pichois, Claude. "Préromantiques, Rousseauistes et Shakespeariens (1770-1778)." *Revue de Littérature Comparée*, 33 (1959), 348-55.

Sauer, Thomas G. *A.W. Schlegel's Shakespearean Criticism in England, 1811-1846*. Bonn: Bouvier, 1981.

Schanze, Helmut. "Shakespeare-Kritik bei Friedrich Schlegel." *Germanisch-romanische Monatsschrift*, Neue Folge, 15 (1965), 40-50.

Shaw, Marjorie. "Shakespearian Performance in Paris in 1827-8." In: *Studies in French Literature Presented to H.W. Lawton by Colleagues, Pupils and Friends*. Eds. J.C. Ireson, et al. Manchester University Press; New York: Barnes & Noble, 1968. pp. 301-13.

Shokoff, James. "Charles Lamb and the Elizabethan Dramatists: A Reassessment." *The Wordsworth Circle*, 4 (1973), 3-11.

Stopp, Elisabeth. "Eichendorff und Shakespeare: Festvortrag zur Jahresversammlung der Eichendorff-Gesellschaft, 7. April 1972." *Aurora*, 32 (1972), 7-23.

Tomkins, A.P. "The Elizabethan Revival: A Study of the Contribution of Elizabethan Drama to the Romantic Movement." Diss. Kings College, Cambridge, 1956-57.

Wasserman, Earl R. "Shakespeare and the English Romantic Movement." In: *The Persistence of Shakespeare Idolatry*. Ed. Herbert M. Schneller. Detroit: Wayne State University Press, 1964. pp. 77-103.

Williams, Simon. *Shakespeare on the German Stage*. Cambridge: Cambridge University Press, 1990.

Calderón and Golden Age

Brüggemann Werner. *Spanisches Theater und deutsche Romantik*. Münster: Aschendorff, 1964.

Brüggemann, Werner. "Zur deutschen Calderón-Forschung des 19. Jahrhunderts." *Spanische Forschungen der Görres-Gesellschaft*, 25 (1970), 176-272.

Behler, Ernst. "The Reception of Calderón Among the German Romantics." *Studies in Romanticism*, 20 (1981), 437-60.

Franzbach, Martin. *Untersuchungen zum Theater Calderóns in der europäischen Literatur vor der Romantik*. München: Fink, 1974.

Getto, Giovanni. "*I promessi sposi*, i drammaturghi spagnoli e Cervantes." *Lettere italiane*, 22 (1970), 425-99.

Hardy, Swana L. *Goethe, Calderón und die romantische Theorie des Dramas*. Heidelberg: Winter, 1965.

Meregalli, Franco. "Consideraciones sobre tres siglos de recepción del teatro calderoniano." *La literatura desde el punto de vista del receptor*. Amsterdam: Rodopi, 1989. pp. 65-84.

Nougué, André. "Le Théâtre de Tirso de Molina dans la première moitié du XIXe siècle espagnol." *Bulletin Hispanique*, 71 (1969), 585-90.

Cultural Streams

Czech, Slovak

Hrbata, Zdeněk. "Motiv hradu v českém romantismu." *Slavia*, 55 (1986), 39-47.

Ivanov, Miroslav. *Záhada rukopsiu královédvorského.* Prague: Novinář, 1970.

Kimball, Stanley Buchholz. *Czech Nationalism: A Study of the National Theatre Movement, 1845-83.* Urbana: University of Illinois Press, 1964.

Kopecký, M. "Deutschsprachige Darstellungen der tschechischen Literatur im ersten Drittel des 19. Jahrhunderts." *Zeitschrift für Slawistik*, 31 (1986), 518-25.

Máchal, Jan. *Slovankské Literatury,* Vol. II. Praha: Matice Česká, 1925.

Měšťan, Antonín. *Geschichte der tschechischen Literatur im 19. und 20. Jahrhundert.* Köln: Böhlau, 1984.

Novák, Arne. *Czech Literature.* Trans. Peter Kussi; ed. William E. Harkins. Ann Arbor: Michigan Slavic Publications, 1976.

Otruba, Mojmír, ed. *Rukopisy královédvorský a zelenohorský: Dnešní stav poznání.* Sborník Národního muzea v Praze. Řada C (Literární historie), svazek XIII-XIV. Prague: Academia, 1969.

Panovavá, E. "Charakter prechodu od klasicizmu k romantizmu v slovenskej poézii v konfrontácii s ruskou literatúrou." *Slavica slovaca*, 17 (1982), 133-140.

Dutch, Flemish

Albach, Ben. "De Romantiek en het Toneel in de tijd van François-Joseph Pfeiffer." *Negentiende eeuw,* 8 (1984), 131-53.

Haak, A.C. "Enige 19e-eeuwse beschouwingen over toneelvernieuwing." *Scenarium*, 7 (1983), 16-22.

Hunningher, Benjamin. *Een eeuw Nederlands toneel, 1840-1940.* Amsterdam: Querido, 1949.

Leeuwe, Hans H.J. de. "De geschiedenis van het Amsterdamsche toneel in de negentiende eeuw (1795-1925)." In: *Zeven eeuwen Amsterdam.* Ed. A.E. d'Ailly. Vol. V. Amsterdam, no date. pp. 113-55.

Leeuwe, Hans de. "International Bibliography of the Dutch and Flemish Theatre: Publications in English, French and German." *Theatre Research*, 12 (1972), 175-90. (About 40 items on the nineteenth-century theater.)

Tindemans, Carlos. *Mens, gemeenschap en maatschappij in de toneelletterkunde van Zuid-Nederland, 1815-1914.* Gent: Koninklijke Academie voor Nederlandse Taal- en Letterkunde, 1973.

English, American, Canadian

Booth, Michael. "A Defence of Nineteenth-Century English Drama." *Educational Theatre Journal*, 26 (1974), 5-13.

Brier, Peter. "Dramatic Characterization in the Essays of Charles Lamb." *Coranto*, 8 (1973), 3-23; 9 (1973), 17-31.

Brinckmann, Christine. *Drama und Öffentlichkeit in der englischen Romantik: Eine Untersuchung zum Verhältnis von Theater- und Lesedrama.* Frankfurt a.M.: Lang, 1977.

Brophy, Robert J. "*Tamar, The Cenci,* and Incest." *American Literature*, 42 (1970), 241-44.

Brown, Laura. *English Dramatic Form 1660-1760: An Essay in Generic History.* New Haven: Yale University Press, 1981.

Cave, Richard Allen, ed. *The Romantic Theatre: An International Symposium.* Gerrards Cross, Bucks.: Colin Smythe; Towata, N.J.: Barnes & Noble, 1986.

Chiang, Oscar Ching-Kuan. "Idealism in Plays Written by Early Nineteenth-Century Poets." Diss. St. John's University, 1972.

Clancy, Charles J. *A Selected Bibliography of English Romantic Drama.* Folcroft, PA.: Folcroft Library Editions, 1978.

Conolly, L.W. *The Censorship of the English Drama 1737-1824.* San Marino: The Huntington Library, 1976.

Conolly, Leonard W., and Wearing, J.P. *English Drama and Theatre 1800-1900: A Guide to Information Sources.* Detroit: Gale, 1978.

Donohue, Joseph W. *Dramatic Character in the English Romantic Age.* Princeton: Princeton University Press, 1970.

Donohue, Joseph W., Jr. "Character, Genre and Ethos in Nineteenth-Century British Drama." *Yearbook of English Studies,* 9 (1979), 78-101.

Evans, Bertrand. *Gothic Drama from Walpole to Shelley.* Berkeley: University of California Press, 1947.

Fletcher, Richard M. *English Romantic Drama 1795-1843: A Critical History.* New York: Exposition Press, 1966.

Fréchet, René. "Lamb's 'Artificial Comedy'." *Review of English Literature,* 5, no. 3 (July 1964), 27-41.

Gottlieb, Erika. *Lost Angels of a Ruined Paradise: Themes of Cosmic Strife in Romantic Tragedy.* Victoria, British Columbia: SonoNis Press, 1981.

Harris, A.L. "English Tragedy in the Early Romantic Period, 1790-1830." M.A. thesis. University of London, 1955.

Irvin, Eric. "Nineteenth Century English Dramatists in Australia." *Theatre Notebook,* 30 (1976), 24-34.

Kosok, Heinz, ed. *Das englische Drama im 18. und 19. Jahrhundert: Interpretationen.* Berlin: Schmidt, 1976.

Orel, Harold. "The Relationships between Three Poet-Dramatists and Their Public: Lord Byron, Thomas Talfourd, and Robert Browning." In: *The Nineteenth-Century Writer and His Audience.* Eds. Harold Orel and George J. Worths. Lawrence: University of Kansas Publications, 1969. pp. 31-49.

Otten, Terry. *The Deserted Stage: The Search for Dramatic Form in Nineteenth-Century England.* Athens: Ohio University Press, 1972.

Parkayastha, Pratyush Ranjan. *The Romantics' Third Voice: A Study of the Dramatic Works of The English Romantic Poets.* Salzburg: Institut für englische Sprache und Literatur, 1978.

Rafroidi, Patrick. *L'Irlande et le romantisme: La littérature irlandaise-anglaise de 1789 à 1850 et sa place dans le mouvement occidental.* Paris: Editions Universitaires, 1972.

Reiman, Donald H., ed. *The Romantics Reviewed: Contemporary Reviews of British Romantic Writers.* 9 vols. New York and London: Garland, 1972.

Rees, Leslie. *The Making of Australian Drama: A Historical and Critical Survey from the 1830s to the 1970s.* Sydney: Angus & Robertson, 1973.

Rowell, George. *The Victorian Theatre: A Survey.* 1956. Reprint, Oxford: Clarendon Press, 1967.

Steiner, F.G. "Problems in the Relationship between the Rise of Romanticism and the State of Tragedy, 1790-1820." Diss. Balliol College, Oxford, 1954-55.

Trewin, J.C. "The Romantic Poets in the Theatre." *Keats-Shelley Memorial Bulletin,* 20 (1969), 21-30.

Zaic, Franz. *Die Verstragödie in der englischen Vorromantik.* Wien, Stuttgart: Braumüller, 1968.

French

Affron, Charles. *A Stage for Poets: Studies in the Theatre of Hugo and Musset.* Princeton: Princeton University Press, 1971.

Bassan, Fernande. "Le Drame romantique." *Nineteenth Century French Studies,* 7 (1979), 165-80.

Bowman, Frank Paul. "Notes towards the Definition of the Romantic Theater." *L'Esprit créateur,* 5 (1965), 121-30.

Bourgeois, René. *L'Ironie romantique: Spectacle et jeu de Mme de Staël à Gérard de Nerval.* Grenoble: Presses Universitaires, 1974.

Brown, Frederick. *Theater and Revolution: The Culture of the French Stage.* New York: Viking, 1980.

Brun, A. *Deux proses de théâtre: drame romantique, comédies et proverbes.* Gap: Ophrys, 1954.

Carlson, Marvin A. *The French Stage in the Nineteenth Century.* Metuchen, N.J.: Scarecrow Press, 1972.

Carlson, Marvin A. *The Theatre of the French Revolution.* Ithaca, N.Y.: Cornell University Press, 1966.

Christout, Marie-Françoise. *Le Merveilleux et le théâtre du silence en France à partir du XVIIe siècle.* The Hague: Mouton, 1965.

Cooper, Barbara T. "Master Plots: An Alternative Typology for French Historical Dramas of the Early Nineteenth Century." *Theatre Journal*, 35 (1983), 23-31.

Descotes, Maurice. *Le Drame romantiques et ses grands créateurs*. Paris: Presses Universitaires de France, 1955.

El Nouty, Hassan. "Théâtre et anti-théâtre au dix-neuvième siècle (trois héritiers de Vitet: Musset, Gobineau, Henry Monnier)." *PMLA*, 79 (1964), 604-12.

Evans, David Owen. *Le Drame moderne à l'époque romantique (1827-1850): Les problèmes d'actualité au théâtre à l'époque romantique; le théâtre pendant la période romantique*. Paris, 1923 and 1925. Reprint Genève: Slatkine, 1974.

Fouchard, J. *Le Théâtre à Saint Domingue*. Port-au-Prince: Imprimerie de l'État, 1955.

Frappier-Mazur, Lucienne. "La Métaphore théâtrale dans *La Comédie humaine*." *Revue d'histoire littéraire de la France*, 70 (1970), 64-89.

Gould, Evlyn. *Virtual Theater from Diderot to Mallarmé*. Baltimore: Johns Hopkins University Press, 1989.

Howarth, William Driver. *Sublime and Grotesque: A Study of French Romantic Drama*. London: Harrap, 1975.

John, S.B. "Violence and Identity in Romantic Drama." In: *French Literature and Its Background*. Ed. John Cruikshank. (= *The Early Nineteenth Century*, IV.) London, New York, Oxford: Oxford University Press, 1969.

Jones, Michèle H. *Le Théâtre national en France de 1800 à 1830*. Paris: Klincksieck, 1975.

Kelly, L. *The Young Romantics: Paris 1827-37*. London: The Bodley Head, 1976.

Kodler, Eric H. *Literary Figures in French Drama (1784-1834)*. The Hague: Nijhoff, 1969.

Le Breton, André. *Le Théâtre romantique*. Paris: Bibliothèques de la Revue des cours et conferences, 1924.

Lelièvre, Renée. "La commedia dell'arte vue par George et Maurice Sand." *Cahiers de l'Association Internationale des Études Françaises*, 15 (1963), 247-59.

Lelièvre, Renée. "Fantastique et surnaturel au théâtre à l'époque romantique." *Cahiers de l'Association Internationale des Études Françaises*, 32 (1980), 193-204.

Leners, R. *Geschichtsschreibung der Romantik im Spannungsfeld vom historischen Roman und Drama: Studien zu Augustin Thierry und dem historischen Theater seiner Zeit*. Berne: Lang, 1987.

Matthews, Brander. *French Dramatists of the Nineteenth Century*. New York: Blom, 1968.

Starobinski, Jean. "Note sur le bouffon romantique." *Cahiers du Sud*, 61 (1966), 270-75.

Steiner, Gerhard. *Jakobinerschauspiel und Jakobinertheater*. Stuttgart: Metzler, 1973.

Yarrow, P.J. "Three Plays of 1829, or Doubts about 1830." *Symposium*, 23 (1969), 373-83.

German, Austrian

Arntzen, Helmut. *Die ernste Komödie: Das deutsche Lustspiel von Lessing bis Kant*. München: Nymphenburger Verlagshandlung, 1968.

Bauer, Roger. "'Das gemißhandelte Schicksal: Zur Theorie des Tragischen im deutschen Idealismus." *Euphorion*, 58 (1964), 243-59.

Bauer, Roger. *La Réalité, Royaume de Dieu: Études sur l'originalité du théâtre viennois dans la première moitié du XIXe siècle*. München: Hueber, 1965.

Bennett, Benjamin. *Modern Drama and German Classicism: Renaissance from Lessing to Brecht*. Ithaca and London: Cornell University Press, 1979.

Burckhardt, Sigurd. *The Drama of Language: Essays on Goethe and Kleist*. Baltimore: Johns Hopkins University Press, 1970.

Carlson, Marvin A. *The German Stage in the Nineteenth Century*. Metuchen, N.J.: Scarecrow Press, 1972.

Catholy, Eckehard. *Das deutsche Lustspiel: Von der Aufklärung bis zur Romantik*. Darmstadt: Wissenschaftliche Buchgesellschaft, 1982.

Guthke, Karl. *Geschichte und Poetik der deutschen Tragikomödie*. Göttingen: Vandenhoeck & Rupprecht, 1961.

Harding, Laurence. *The Dramatic Art of Ferdinand Raimund und Johann Nestroy*. The Hague: Mouton, 1974.

Homann, Renate. *Selbstreflexionen der Literaturstudien zu Dramen von G.E. Lessing und H. von Kleist*. München: Fink, 1986.

Houston, G.C. *The Evolution of the Historical Drama in Germany during the First Half of the Nineteenth Century*. New York: Haskell, 1972.

Kafitz, Dieter. *Grundzüge einer Geschichte des deutschen Dramas von Lessing bis zum Naturalismus*. 2 vols. Frankfurt a.M.: Athenäum, 1982.

Kaufmann, F.W. *German Dramatists of the Nineteenth Century*. New York: Books for Libraries Press, 1970.

Kindermann, Heinz. *Theatergeschichte der Goethezeit*. Wien: Bauer, 1948.

Kistler, Mark. *Drama of Storm and Stress*. New York: Twayne, 1969.

Klingenberg, Karl Heinz. *Iffland und Kotzebue als Dramatiker*. Weimar: Arion, 1962.

Kluge, Gerhard. "Das Lustspiel der deutschen Romantik." In: *Das deutsche Lustspiel*. Ed. Hans Steffen. Göttingen, Zürich: Vandenhoeck & Ruprecht, 1968. I: 181-23.

Kluge, Gerhard. "Das romantische Drama." In: *Handbuch des deutschen Dramas*. Ed. Walter Hinck. Düsseldorf: Bagel, 1980. pp. 186-99.

Körner, Josef. *Romantiker und Klassiker: Die Brüder Schlegel in ihren Beziehungen zu Schiller und Goethe*. Darmstadt: Wissenschaftliche Buchgesellschaft, 1971.

Kraft, Herbert. *Das Schicksalsdrama: Interpretation und Kritik einer literarischen Reihe*. Tübingen: Niemeyer, 1974.

Lea, Charlene A. *Emancipation, Assimilation and Stereotype: The Image of the Jew in German and Austrian Drama (1800-1850)*. Bonn: Bouvier, 1978.

Leber, Elsbeth. *Das Bild des Menschen in Schillers und Kleists Dramen*. Bern: Francke, 1969.

Leopoldseder, Hannes. *Groteske Welt: Ein Beitrag zur Entwicklungsgeschichte des Nachtstücks in der Romantik*. Bonn: Bouvier, 1973.

Neubuhr, Elfriede, ed. *Geschichtsdrama*. Darmstadt: Wissenschaftliche Buchgesellschaft, 1980. (Contains choice essays on Schiller, Grillparzer, Grabbe, Büchner, Hebbel, Goethe, and the Young Germany authors.)

Prudoe, John. *The Theatre of Goethe and Schiller*. Towata, N.J.: Rowan & Littlefield, 1973.

Rapp, Eleonore. *Die Marionette im romantischen Weltgefühl: Ein Beitrag zur deutschen Geistesgeschichte*. Bochum: Deutsches Institut fürs Puppenspiel, 1964.

Škreb, Zdenko. "Die deutsche sogenannte Schicksalstragödie." *Grillparzer-Gesellschaft*, 9 (1972), 193-237.

Steinmetz, Horst. *Die Trilogie: Entstehung und Struktur einer Großform des deutschen Dramas nach 1800*. Heidelberg: Winter, 1968.

Storz, Gerhard. *Klassik und Romantik: Eine stilgeschichtliche Darstellung*. Mannheim, Wien, Zürich: Bibliographisches Institut, 1972.

Thalmann, Marianne. *Provokation und Demonstration in der Komödie der Romantik: Mit Grafiken zu den Literar-Komödien von Tieck, Brentano, Schlegel, Grabbe und zum Amphitrion-Stoff*. Berlin: Schmidt, 1974.

Wiese von, Benno. *Deutsche Dramaturgie des 19. Jahrhunderts*. 4th ed. Tübingen: Niemeyer, 1969.

Wiese, Benno von. *Die deutsche Tragödie von Lessing bis Hebbel*. Hamburg: Hoffmann und Campe, 1961.

Ziegler, K. "Stiltypen des deutschen Dramas im 19. Jahrhundert." In: *Formkräfte der deutschen Dichtung vom Barock bis zur Gegenwart*. Ed. Hans Steffen. Göttingen: Vandenhoeck & Rupricht, 1967.

Zobel, Konrad. "Popular Romantic Repertoire: The Josefstadt Theatre in Vienna, 1846-1848." *Theatre Studies*, 22 (1975-76), 17-25.

Hungarian

Arany, János. *Összes művei*. Vol. X. Budapest: Akadémiai Kiadó, 1962.

Babits, Mihály. *Az európai irodalom története*. Budapest: Nyugat, 1936.

Babits, Mihály. *Esszék, tanulmányok I-II*. Budapest: Szépirodalmi Könyvkiadó, 1978.

Horváth, János. *Tanulmányok*. Budapest: Akadémiai Kiadó, 1956.

Kemény, Zsigmond. *Élet és irodalom: Tanulmányok*. Budapest: Szépirodalmi Könyvkiadó, 1971.

Lukács, György. *A modern dráma fejlődésének története I-II*. Budapest: Franklin-társulat, 1911.

Németh, Béla G. *Türelmetlen és késlekedő félszázad: A romantika után*. Budapest: Szépirodalmi Könyvkiadó, 1971.

Sőtér, István. *Nemzet és haladás: Irodalmunk Világos után.* Budapest: Akadémiai Kiadó, 1963.
Staud, Géza. *A magyar színháztörténet forrásai I-III.* Budapest: Színháztörténeti Intézet, 1962-63.
Szegedy-Maszák, Mihály. *Világkép és stílus: Történeti-poétikai tanulmányok.* Budapest: Magvető Könyvkiadó, 1980.
Szegedy-Maszák, Mihály. "Romanticism in Hungary." In: *Romanticism in National Context.* Eds. Roy Porter and Mikuláš Teich. Cambridge: Cambridge University Press, 1988.

Italian

Bottoni, Luciano. *Drammaturgia romantica: Il paradigmi culturali.* Pisa: Pacini, 1980.
Bottoni, Luciano. *Drammaturgia romantica: Il sistema letterario manzoniano.* Pisa: Pacini, 1984.
Carlson, Marvin. *The Italian Stage from Goldoni to D'Annunzio.* Jefferson, N.C., and London: McFarland, 1981.
Pullini, G. *Teatro italiano dell' ottocento.* Milan: Società Editrice Libraria, 1981.
Santangelo, Giorgio. *Il dramma romantico in Italia.* 2 vols. Palermo: Manfredi, 1971-72.

Polish

Janion, Maria. *Romantyzm. Rewolucja, Marksizm.* Gdańsk: Wydawnictwo Morskie, 1972.
Janion, Maria and Maria Żmigrodzka. *Romantyzm i historia.* Wyd. 1. Warszawa: Państwowy Instytut Wydawniczy, 1978.
Kleiner, Juliusz. *Sentymentalizm i preromantyzm: studia inedita z literatury porozbiorowej, 1795-1822.* Wydanictwo Kraków: Literackie, 1975.
Komozowski, Jaroslaw. *Polskie Zycie teatralne na Poddu i Wolyniu do 1863 roku.* Wrodaw: Zaklad Narodowy im. ossolińskich, 1985.
Kridl, Manfred, ed. *A Survey of Polish Literature and Culture.* New York: Columbia University Press, 1956.
Krzyżanowski, Julian. *Polish Romantic Literature.* Freeport, N.Y.: Books for Libraries Press, 1968.
Segel, Harold. trans. and ed. *Polish Romantic Drama.* Ithaca: Cornell University Press, 1977. Introduction, pp. 7-71.
Straszewska, Maria. *Romantyzm.* Warszawa: Państwowe Zakłady Wydawnictw Szkolnych, 1969.
Urbankowski, B. *Mysl romantyczna.* Warszawa: Krajowa Agencja Wydawnicza, 1979.
Weiss, Tomasz. *Romantyczna genealogia polskiego modernizmu; rekonesans.* Wyd. 1. Warszawa: Państwowy Instytut Wydawniczy, 1974.

Portuguese and Lusobrazilian

Coutinho, Afrânio. *An Introduction to Literature in Brazil.* New York: Columbia University Press, 1969.
Franca, José Augusto: *Le Romantisme au Portugal: Étude de faits socio-culturels.* Paris: Klincksieck, 1975.
Hulet, Claude Lyle. *Brazilian Literature.* 3 vols. Washington, D.C.: Georgetown University Press, 1974. III: 183-378.
Rela, Walter. *Teatro costumbrista brasileño.* Rio de Janeiro: Instituto Nacional do Livro, 1961.
Sousa, J. Galante de. *O teatro no Brasil.* Rio de Janeiro: Tecnoprint Gráfica, 1968.
Vieira-Sanentel. *Tendências da literatura dramática do século 19; João da Câmara, um caso exemplar.* Ponta Delgada: Azores University Press, 1981.

Russian and Ukranian

Anikst, A. A. *Istoria Uchenii o Drame: Teoria Drami v Rossii ot Pushkina do Chekhova.* Moscow: Nauka, 1972.
Brown, William Edward. *A History of Russian Literature of the Romantic Period.* 4 vols. Ann Arbor: Ardis Publishers, 1986. I, chs. 1-3; III, ch. 3; IV, ch. 6.

Čiževskij, Dmitrij. *Comparative History of Slavic Literatures.* Trans. R.N. Porter and M.P. Rice; ed. S.A. Zenkovsky. Nashville: Vanderbilt University Press, 1971.

Clayton, J. Douglas. *Issues in Russian Literature before 1917.* Columbus, OH: Slavica, 1989.

Ivashkiv, Vasilii. *Ukrainskaya romanticheskaya drama 30-80 ch. godov XIX v.* Akad. Nauk Ukrain. SSR, Inst. Literatury Im. T.G. Shevchenko, 1987.

Karlinsky, Simon. *Russian Drama from Its Beginnings to the Age of Pushkin.* Berkeley, Los Angeles, London: University of California Press, 1985.

Leighton, Lauren G. *Russian Romanticism: Two Essays.* The Hague: Mouton, 1975.

Lotman, Yuri M. "The Theatre and Theatricality as Components of Early Nineteenth-Century Culture." In: Lotman, Iurii Mikhailovich. *The Semiotics of Russian Culture.* Ed. A. Shukman. Ann Arbor: Dept. of Slavic Languages and Literatures, 1984.

Pomar, Mark G. "Russian Historical Drama of the Early Nineteenth Century." Diss. Columbia University, 1978.

Roberti, Y.C. *Histoire du théâtre russe jusqu'en 1917.* Paris: Presses Universitaires de France, 1981.

Schultze, B. *Studien zum russischen literarischen Einakter: Von den Anfängen bis A.P. Čechov.* Wiesbaden: Harrassowitz, 1984.

Warner, Elizabeth A. *The Russian Folk Theatre.* The Hague, Paris: Mouton, 1977.

Scandinavian

Dahl, Willy. *Norges litteratur. I: Tid og tekst 1814-1884.* Oslo: Aschehoug, 1981.

Engdahl, Horace. *Den romantiska texten: En essä i nio avsitt.* Stockholm: Bonnier, 1986.

Marker, Frederick J. and Lise-Lone. *The Scandinavian Theatre.* Oxford: Blackwell, 1975.

Senelick, Laurence, ed. *National Theatre in Northern and Eastern Europe, 1746-1900.* Cambridge: Cambridge University Press, 1991.

Skitser til romantikkens teater. København: Gads, 1967.

S.E. Europe

Alterescu, S., ed. *Abridged History of Romanian Theatre.* Bucharest: The Institute for the History of Art and Editura Academiei, 1983.

Călin, Vera. *Romantismul.* Rev. and aug. ed. Bucharest: University of Bucharest, 1975.

Duda, Gabriela (et al.). *Structuri tematice şi retorico-stilistice în romantismul românesc (1830-1870); sub îngrijirea şi cu un studiu introductiv de Paul Cornea.* Bucureşti: Editura Academiei, 1976.

Genov, Krust'o Todorov. *Romantizmut v bulgarskata literatura.* Sofia: Bulgarska akademiia na naukite, 1968.

Ionescu, Medea. *A Concise History of Theatre in Romania.* Trans. D.S. Lecca. Bucharest: Editura Ştiinţifică şi Enciclopedică, 1981.

Lord, Albert B. "The Nineteenth-Century Revival of National Literatures: Karadžič, Njegoš, Radičević, the Illyrians and Prešeren." In: *The Multinational Literature of Yugoslavia.* Ed. Albert B. Lord. New York: St. John's University Press, 1974. (= *Review of National Literatures,* 5, no. 1 [Spring 1974], 501-11.)

Mîndra, Vicu. *Clasicism şi romantism în dramaturgia românească, 1818-1918: Privire istorică asupra unui secol de literatură teatrală.* Bucureşti: Editura Minerva, 1973.

Senelick, Laurence, ed. *National Theatre in Northern and Eastern Europe, 1746-1900.* Cambridge: Cambridge University Press, 1991.

Vičev, Dobry. "Methodologische Fragen der Rezeption der deutschen Literatur in Bulgarien bis 1878." *Bulgaronemecki literaturni i kulturni vzaimootnošenia pres XVIII i XIX vek.* Sofia: Bulgarskata Akademia na naukite, 1985.

Spanish, Catalan, and Hispanic American

Abreu Gómez, E. "Un aspecto del teatro romántico." In: *Contemporáneos* (México), nos. 30-31 (1930).

Arrom, José Juan. *Historia de la literatura dramática cubana*. New Haven: Yale University Press, 1944.

Arrom, José Juan. *Historia del teatro hispanoamericano: Época Colonial*. México: Ediciones de Andrea, 1967.

Berenguer Carisomo, Arturo. *Las ideas estéticas en el teatro argentino*. Buenos Aires: Instituto Nacional de Estudios de Teatro, 1947.

Borges Pérez, Fernándo. *Historia del teatro en Costa Rica*. San José de Costa Rica: Imprenta Española, 1942.

Caldera, Ermanno. *Il dramma romantico in Spagna*. Pisa: Università di Pisa, 1974.

Caldera, Ermanno. *La commedia romantica in Spagna*. Pisa: Giardini Editori, 1978.

Carilla, Emilio. *El romanticismo en la América hispánica*. 2 vols. 3rd ed. Madrid: Gredos, 1975.

Castagnino, Raúl H. *Crónicas del pasado teatral argentino, siglo XIX*. Buenos Aires: Editorial Huemul, 1977.

Castagnino, Raúl H. *El teatro en Buenos Aires durante la época de Rosas*. Buenos Aires: Academia Argentina de Letras, 1989.

Castagnino, Raúl H. *Sociología del teatro argentino*. Buenos Aires: Editorial Nova, 1963.

Castagnino, Raúl H. *Literatura dramática argentina, 1717-1967*. Buenos Aires: Editorial Pleamar, 1968.

Croce, Elena. *Il romanticismo spagnolo: La splendida eredità di un romanticismo povero*. Roma: Bulzoni, 1986.

Dauster, Frank N. *Historia del teatro hispanoamericano, siglos XIX y XX*. 2nd ed. muy ampliada. México: Ediciones de Andrea, 1973.

Díaz Plaja, Guillermo. "Perfil del teatro romántico español." *Estudios Escénicos*, 8 (1963), 29-56.

Gies, David Thatcher. *Theatre and Politics in Nineteenth-Century Spain*. Cambridge: Cambridge University Press, 1988.

Henríquez Ureña, Pedro. *La cultura y las letras coloniales en Santo Domingo*. Buenos Aires: Universidad de Buenos Aires, 1936.

Jones, Willis Knapp. *Breve historia del teatro Latinoamericano*. México: Ediciones de Andrea, 1956.

Kosove, Joan Lynne Pataky. *The "Comedia Lacrimosa" and Spanish Romantic Drama (1773-1865)*. London: Tamesis, 1977.

María y Campos, Armando de. *Entre cómicos de ayer*. México: Editorial "Arriba el Telón," 1949.

Mangaña Esquivel, Antonio. *Teatro mexicano del siglo XIX*. México: Fondo de Cultura Económica, 1972.

Mansour, George. "Toward an Understanding of Spanish Romantic Drama." *La Chispa '83: Selected Proceedings*. Ed. Gilbert Paolini. New Orleans: Tulane University, 1983. pp. 171-78.

Marrast, Robert. "Le Drame en Espagne à l'époque romantique de 1834 à 1844: Contribution à son approche sociologique." In: *Romantisme, Réalisme*. Lille: Centre d'Études Ibériques et Ibéro-Américaines du XIXᵉ Siècle, 1978. pp. 35-45.

McClelland, Ivy L. *The Origins of the Romantic Movement in Spain*. 2nd ed. New York: Barnes & Noble, 1975.

Merarini, P. et al. *El teatro romántico (1830-1850): Autores, obras, bibliografía*. Bologna: Atesa, 1981.

Mérimée, Paul. *L'Art dramatique en Espagne dans la première moitié du XVIIIe siècle*. Toulouse: France-Ibérie Recherche, 1983.

Miguel i Vergès, G.M. *Els primers romàntics de poisos de llengua catalana*. Barcelona: Leteradura, 1979.

Moncloa y Covarrubias, Manuel. *Diccionario teatral del Perú*. Lima: Badiola y Berrio, 1905.

Montaner, Joaquín. *El teatro romántico española*. Barcelona: Instituto de Teatro Nacional, 1928.

Olavarría y Ferrari, Enrique. *Reseña histórica del teatro en México (1538-1911)*. 2nd ed. 5 vols. México: Editorial Porrúa, 1961.

Ordaz, Luis. *El teatro en el Río de la Plata desde sus orígenes hasta nuestros días*. rev. ed. Buenos Aires: Ediciones Leviatan, 1957.

Ordaz, Luis. *Historia de teatro argentino*. Buenos Aires: Centro Editor de América Latina, 1982.

Pasarell, E.J. *Orígines y desarrollo de la afición teatral en Puerto Rico*. San Juan de Puerto Rico: Editorial Universitaria, 1951.

Peers, Edgar Allison. *A History of the Romantic Movement in Spain*. 2 vols. New York and London: Hafner, 1964.

Pla, Josefina. *El teatro en el Paraguay. Primera parte: de su fundación a 1870*. Assunción: Diálogo, 1967.

Posada, Miguel García. *Teatro y poesía en el romanticismo*. Madrid: Cincel, 1981.

Rela, Walter. *Breve historia del teatro uruguayo*. Montevideo: Proyección, 1988.

Rela, Walter. *Contribución a la bibliografía del teatro chileno (1804-1960)*. Montevideo: Universidad de la República, 1960.

Rela, Walter. *Teatro uruguayo, 1807-1979*. Montevideo: Alianza Cultural Uruguay – EE.VV., 1980.

Real Ramos, César. "De los 'desarreglados monstruos' a la estética del fracaso: Prehistoria del drama romántico." *Anales de Literatura Española*, 2 (1983), 419-45.

Reyes de la Maza, Luis. *Cien años de teatro en México, 1810-1910*. México: Secretaria de Educación Pública, 1972.

Reyes de la Maza, Luis. *El teatro en México entre la Reforma y el Imperio (1858-1861)*. México: UNAM, 1958.

Reyes de la Maza, Luis. *El teatro en México durante la Independencia (1810-1839)*. México: UNAM, 1969.

Reyes de la Maza, Luis. *El teatro en México durante el Segundo Imperio (1862-1867)*. México: UNAM, 1959.

Rivero Muñiz, J. *Bibliografía del teatro cubano*. La Habana: Biblioteca Nacional, 1957.

Rosa-Nieves, Cesário. *El romanticismo en la literatura puertorriqueña*. San Juan, P.R.: Instituto de Cultura Puertorriqueña, 1960.

Rosenblat, R. and A. Blanco Amores. "Diez años de actividad teatral en Buenos Aires 1852-1862." In: *Cursos y Conferencias* (Buenos Aires), 32 (1947).

Rubio Jiménez, Jesús. *El teatro en el siglo XIX*. Madrid: Playor, 1983.

Sáez, Antonia. *El teatro en Puerto Rico: Notas para su historia*. San Juan de Puerto Rico: Editorial Universitaria, 1950.

Saz, Agustín del. *Teatro hispanoamericano*. 2 vols. Barcelona: Editorial Vergara, 1963-64.

Sebold, Russell P. "Contra los mitos anticlásicos españoles." *Papeles de Son Armadans*, 35 (1964), 83-114.

Tapia, John. *The Spanish Romantic Theatre*. Lanham, M.D.: University Press of America, 1980.

Zavala, Iris M. *Romanticismo y realismo*. Barcelona: Crítica, 1982.

Themes, Styles, Genres

Avant-Garde, Absurdism

Esslin, Martin. *The Theatre of the Absurd*. 3rd ed. Harmondsworth: Penguin, 1987.

Jean Weisgerber, ed. *Les Avant-gardes littéraires au XXe siècle*. 2 vols. Budapest: Akadémiai Kiadó, 1984.

Melodrama/Spectacle

Accorsi, M.G. "Il melodramma melodrammatico." *Sigma*, 30, no. 1, (1980).

Booth, Michael. *English Melodrama*. London: Jenkins, 1965.

Booth, Michael. *Victorian Spectacular Theatre 1850-1910*. Boston: Routledge & Kegan Paul, 1981.

Brooks, Peter. *The Melodramatic Imagination*. New Haven: Yale University Press, 1976.

Dapino, G., ed. *Il teatro italiano: Il libretto del melodramma dell' ottocento*. Turin: Einaudi, 1983.

El Nouty, Hassan: *Théâtre et pré-cinéma: Essais sur la problématique du spectacle au XIX siècle*. Paris: Nizet, 1978.

Heilman, R.B. *Tragedy and Melodrama: Versions of Experience*. Seattle: University of Washington Press, 1968.

Howarth, W.D. "Word and Image in Pixérécourt's Melodramas: The Dramaturgy of the Strip Cartoon." In: *Performance and Politics in Popular Drama*. Ed. D.J. Bradby et al. Cambridge: Cambridge University Press, 1980.

Mondeville, G.E. "The Origins and Early Development of Melodrama on the London Stage 1790-1840." M.A. thesis, Columbia University 1946.

Rahill, Frank. *The World of Melodrama*. University Park, PA: Pennsylvania State University Press, 1967.

Ritter, Naomi. *Art as Spectacle: Images of the Entertainer since Romanticism*. Columbia, Mo.: University of Missouri Press, 1989.

Saxon, A.H. "The Circus as Theatre: Astley's and Its Actors in the Age of Romanticism." *Educational Theatre Journal*, 27 (1975), 299-312.

"Le Spectacle romantique." *Romantisme,* 38 (Autumn 1982). (Special number.)

Thomasseau, Jean-Marie. *Le Mélodrame.* Paris: Presses Universitaires de France, 1984.

Opera/Ballet

Aschengren, Erik. "The Beautiful Danger: Facets of the Romantic Ballet." Transl. by N. McAndrew. *Dance Perspectives*, 58 (Summer 1974), 1-52.

Black, Michael. *Poetic Drama as Mirror of the Will.* London: Vision Press, 1977.

Borchmeyer, Dieter. *Das Theater Richard Wagners.* Stuttgart: Reclam, 1982.

Casaell, Austin B. "Maeterlink's and Dukas' *Ariane et Barbe-Bleue*: A Feminist Opera." *Studies in Romanticism,* 27 (1988).

Conrad, Peter. *Romantic Opera and Literary Form.* Berkeley: University of California Press, 1977.

Dent, E.J. *The Rise of Romantic Opera.* Ed. Winton Dean. New York: Cambridge University Press, 1976.

Donakowski, Conrad L. *A Muse for the Masses: Ritual and Music in an Age of Democratic Revolution, 1770-1870.* Chicago: University of Chicago Press, 1977.

Fries, Othmar. *Richard Wagner und die deutsche Romantik: Versuch einer Einordnung.* Zürich: Atlantis Verlag, 1952.

Goldin, D. "Aspetti della librettistica italiana fra 1770 e 1830." In: *Die stilistische Entwicklung der italienischen Musik zwischen 1770 und 1830 und ihre Beziehungen zum Norden.* Analecta Musicologica, 21. Rome, 1972.

Kerman, Joseph. "Opera, Novel, Drama: The Case of *La Traviata.*" *Yearbook of Comparative and General Literature*, 27 (1978), 44-53.

Kimbell, D.R.B. *Verdi in the Age of Italian Romanticism.* Cambridge: Cambridge University Press, 1981.

Lang, Paul Henry. *Music in Western Civilization.* New York: Farrar & Rinehart, 1941. Chs. 15-18.

Mittenzwei, Johannes. "A.W. Schlegels 'Vocal-Farbenleiter' und ihre Auswirkungen auf Fr. Schlegels Drama *Alarcos.*" In: Mittenzwei. *Das Musikalische in der Literatur.* Halle (Saale): VEB Verlag Sprache und Literatur, 1962.

Rather, L.J. *Reading Wagner: A Study in the History of Ideas.* Baton Rouge and London: Louisiana State University Press, 1990.

Rinaldi, M. *Le opere più note di Giuseppe Verdi.* Florence: Ilschki, 1986.

Robinson, Paul A. *Opera and Ideas.* New York: Harper & Row, 1985.

Siora, N. "Szenische Bauweise des Erzählers Eichendorff nach dem Opernvorbild Glucks und Mozarts." Diss. Frankfurt a.M., 1973.

Troy, C.E. *The Comic Intermezzo: A Study in the History of Eighteenth-Century Italian Opera.* Ann Arbor: University of Michigan Press, 1978.

Wendler, Ursula. "Eichendorff und das musikalische Theater: Untersuchungen zum Erzählwerk." Diss. Bonn, 1969.

Myth and Neomythology

Bequero, Arturo. *Don Juan y su evolución dramática.* Madrid: Editora Nacional, 1966.

Casto, Robert C. "Shelley as Translator of *Faust*: The 'Prologue'." *Review of English Studies*, 26 (1975), 407-24.

Cowen, Roy C. "Grabbe's Faust – Another German Hamlet?" *Studies in Romanticism*, 12 (1973), 443-60.

Dédéyan, Charles. *Le Thème de Faust dans la littérature européenne. IV.: Du romantisme à nos jours.* Paris: Minard, 1961.

Eggenschwiler, David. "Byron's *Cain* and the Antimythological Myth." *Modern Language Quarterly*, 37, no. 4 (1976), 324-38.

Fraisse, Simone. "Le Thème d'Antigone dans la pensée française au XIXe et au XXe siècles." *Bulletin de l'Association Guillaume Budé*, 4 (1966), 250-88.

Gillespie, Gerald. "Afterthoughts of Hamlet: Goethe's Wilhelm, Joyce's Stephen." In: *Comparative Literary History as Discourse: In Honor of Anna Balakian.* Ed. Mario Valdés. Berne: Lang, 1992. pp. 286-304.

Gillespie, Gerald. "The Devil's Art." In: *European Romanticism: Literary Cross-Currents, Modes, and Models.* Ed. Gerhart Hoffmeister. Detroit: Wayne State University Press, 1990. pp. 77-95.

Gillespie, Gerald. "Faust en Pataphysicien." *Journal of European Studies,* 13 (1983), 98-110.

Gillespie, Gerald. "Prometheus in the Romantic Age." In: *European Romanticism.* Ed. Gerhart Hoffmeister. Detroit: Wayne State University Press, 1990. pp. 197-210.

Gillespie, Gerald. "Romantic Oedipus." In: *Goethezeit: Studien zur Erkenntnis Goethes und seiner Zeitgenossen; Festschrift für Stuart Atkins.* Ed. Gerhart Hoffmeister. Bern, München: Francke, 1981. pp. 331-45.

Harvie, James A. "The Promethean Syndrome." *Comparative Literature Studies,* 13 (1976), 31-39.

Hoffmeister, Gerhart. "Goethe's *Faust* and the Theatrum Mundi Tradition in European Romanticism." *Journal of European Studies,* 13 (1983), 42-55.

Jeanne, René "Napoléon et le théâtre." *Europe,* 48 (April-May 1969), 275-301.

Kohlschmidt, Werner. "Das Hamlet-Motiv in den *Nachtwachen des Bonaventura.*" In: *Dichter, Tradition und Zeitgeist.* Bern, München: Francke, 1965. pp. 93-102.

Mandel, Oscar. *The Theatre of Don Juan.* Lincoln: University of Nebraska Press, 1963.

Moisan, J. "Hamlet à la lumière du romantisme allemand." *Carleton Germanic Papers,* 15 (1987), 31-39.

Schondorff, Joachim, ed. *"Antigone": Sophokles, Euripides, Racine, Hölderlin, Hasenclever, Cocteau, Anouilh.* Introd. Karl Kerényi. München: Langen-Müller, 1966.

Schondorff, Joachim, ed. *"Ödipus": Vollständige Dramentexte, mit einem Vorwort von Karl Kerényi.* Bd. II: *Hölderlin-Hofmannsthal-Gide-Cocteau-Eliot.* München: Langen-Müller, 1968.

Stamm, Rudolf. "Lord Byron's *Cain:* Mysterium der Versuchung." In: *Zwischen Vision und Wirklichkeit: Zehn Essays über Shakespeare, Lord Byron, Bernard Shaw, William Butler Yeats, Thomas Stearns Eliot, Eugene O'Neill und Christopher Fry.* Bern, München: Francke, 1964. pp. 85-98.

Voisin, Marcel. "Gautier, Nerval et le Second Faust." *Revue des Langues Vivantes,* 36 (1970), 406-11.

Watson, Harold. O.S.B. "Saint-Beuve's Molière: A Romantic Hamlet." *French Review,* 38 (1965), 606-18.

Wesche, Ulrich. "Goethe's Faust and Byron's Manfred: The Curious Transformation of a Motif." *Revue de Littérature Comparée,* 50 (1976), 286-90.

Symbolism

Block, Haskell M. *Mallarmé and the Symbolist Drama.* Detroit: Wayne State University Press, 1963.

Carpenter, William. *Vers le théâtre intérieur.* Stanford: Humanities Honors Program, 1981.

Cassiana Lacerda, Carollo, ed. *Decadismo e simbolismo no Brasil: Crítica e poética.* 2 vols. Rio de Janeiro: Livros Técnicos e Científicos, Editora, 1981.

Green, Michael, ed. and trans. *The Russian Symbolist Theatre: An Anthology of Plays and Critical Texts.* Ann Arbor: Ardis, 1986.

Hoffmann, Paul. "Zum Begriff des literarischen Symbolismus." In: *Literaturwissenschaft und Geistesgeschichte: Festschrift für Richard Brinkmann.* Tübingen: Niemeyer, 1981. pp. 489-509.

Ireson, J.C. "Towards a Theory of the Symbolist Theatre." In: *Studies in French Literature Presented to H.W. Lawton by Colleagues, Pupils and Friends.* Eds. J.C. Ireson, et al. Manchester University Press, New York: Barnes & Noble, 1968. pp. 135-56.

Kalbouss, George. *The Plays of the Russian Symbolists.* East Lansing, Michigan: Russian Language Journal, 1982.

Köhler, Hartmut. "Symbolist Theater." In: *The Symbolist Movement in the Literature of European Languages.* Ed. Anna Balakian. Budapest: Akadémiai Kiadó, 1982. pp. 413-24.

Lemaître, H. *Du Romantisme au symbolisme: L'Age des découvertes et des innovations, 1790-1914.* Paris: Bordas, 1982.

Riffaterre, Michael. "Un exemple de comédie symboliste chez Victor Hugo." *L'Esprit créateur,* 5 (1965), 162-73.

Playwrights

Alencar

Aguiar, Flávio. *A Comédia Nacional no Teatro de José de Alencar*. São Paolo: Atica, 1984.

Almqvist

Romberg, Bertil. *Carl Jonas Love Almquist*. New York: Twayne, 1977.

Andersen

Marker, Frederick J. *Hans Christian Andersen and the Romantic Theatre: A Study of Stage Practices in the Pre-naturalist Scandinavian Theatre*. Toronto: University of Toronto Press, 1971.
Grønbeck, Bo. *Hans Christian Andersen*. New York: Twayne, 1980.

Arnim

Falkner, G. *Die Dramen Achim von Arnims: Ein Beitrag zur Dramaturgie der Romantik*. Zürich: Atlantis Verlag, 1962.
Streller, Dorothea. "Achim von Arnim und *Auch ein Faust*." *Jahrbuch der Sammlung Kippenberg*, n.s. 1 (1963), 150-62.

Bilderdijk

Jong, Martien J.G. de. *Bilderdijks verborgen werkzaamheid als dramatisch dichter*. Diss. University of Gent, 1958.
Jong, Martien, J.G. de. *Tussen Klassicisme en Romantiek*. Onuitgegeven prijsvraagverhandeling voor de Koninklijke Vlaamse Academie, 1964.
Jong, Martien J.G. de. "Nationale Treurspelen uit de nalatenschap van W. Bilderdijk." In: *Verslagen en Mededelingen van de Koninklijke Vlaamse Academie voor Taal- en Letterkunde*. Nieuwe Reeks. Gent: Secretariaat der Academie, 1960. pp. 551-617.
Jong, Martien J.G. de. *Taal van lust en weelde: Willem Bilderdijk et la littérature italienne*. Brussell: Presses Universitaires de Namur, 1973.
Leeuwe, Hans H.J. de. *Bilderdijk: Het drama en het tooneel*. Utrecht: A. Oosthoek, 1990.

Boker

Gallagher, Kent G. "The Tragedies of George Henry Boker: The Measure of American Romantic Drama." *Emerson Society Quarterly*, 20, no. 3 (1974), 187-215.
Smith, Peter Mann. "A Study of The Sociological and Cultural Milieu of George Henry Boker and the Critical Responses to the Nineteenth-Century Productions of His Plays." Diss. University of Denver, 1971.
Voelker, Paul D. "George Henry Boker's *Francesca da Rimini*: An Interpretation and an Evaluation." *Educational Theatre Journal*, 24 (1972), 383-95.
Zanger, Jules. "Boker's *Francesca da Rimini*: The Brothers' Tragedy." *Educational Theatre Journal*, 25, no. 4 (1973), 410-19.

Büchner

Benn, Maurice B. *The Drama of Revolt: A Critical Study of Georg Büchner*. Cambridge and New York: Cambridge University Press, 1976.

Hilton, Julian. *Georg Büchner.* London: Macmillan Press, 1982.
Richards, David G. *Georg Büchner and the Birth of the Modern Drama.* Albany: State University of New York Press, 1977.
Schmidt, Henry J. *Satire, Caricature, and Perspectivism in the Works of Georg Büchner.* The Hague: Mouton, 1970.
Zagari, Luciano. *Georg Büchner e la ricerca dello stile drammatico.* Torino: Edizioni dell'Albero, 1956.

Byron

Ashton, Thomas L. "Marino Faliero: Byron's Poetry of Politics." *Studies in Romanticism,* 13 (1974), 1-13.
Blackstone, Bernard. *Byron: A Survey.* London: Longmans, 1975.
Brisman, Leslie. "Byron: Troubled Stream from a Pure Source." *English Literary History,* 42 (1975), 623-50.
Brogan, Howard O. "Byron and Dr. Johnson, that Profoundest of Critics'." *Bulletin of New York Public Library,* 79, no. 4 (1976), 472-87.
Carr, Thomas Y. "Byron's Werner: The Burden of Knowledge." *Studies in Romanticism,* 24 (1985), 375-98.
Cooke, M.G. "The Restoration Ethos of Byron's Classical Plays." *PMLA,* 79 (1964), 569-78.
Corr, Thomas Joseph. "Views of the Mind (of Reason and Imagination) as Structural and Thematic Principles in the Works of Byron." Diss. Duquesne University, 1974.
Eggenschwiler, David. "The Tragic and Comic Rhythms of *Manfred.*" *Studies in Romanticism,* 13 (1974), 63-77.
Ehrstine, John W. *The Metaphysics of Byron: A Reading of the Plays.* The Hague: Mouton, 1976.
Kahn, Arthur D. "Seneca and Sardanapalus: Byron, the Don Quixote of Neo-Classicism." *Studies in Philology,* 66 (1969), 654-71.
Lim, Paulino M. *The Style of Lord Byron's Plays.* Salzburg: Universität Salzburg, 1973.
Robinson, Charles E. "The Devil as Doppelgänger." In: *The Deformed Transformed: The Sources and Meaning of Byron's Unfinished Drama. Bulletin of the New York Public Library,* 74 (1970), 177-202.
Sperry, Stuart M. "Byron and the Meaning of *Manfred.*" *Criticism,* 16 (1974), 189-202.
Steffan, Truman Guy. *Lord Byron's "Cain": Twelve Essays and a Text with Variants and Annotations.* Austin and London: University of Texas Press, 1968.
Steffan, Truman Guy. "Seven Accounts of the Cenci and Shelley's Drama." *Studies in English Literature,* 9 (1969), 601-18.
Taborski, Boleslaw. *Byron and the Theatre.* Salzburg: Universität Salzburg, 1973.
Tandon, B.G. *The Imagery of Lord Byron's Plays.* Salzburg: University of Salzburg, 1976.
Tannenbaum, Leslie. "Lord Byron in the Wilderness: Biblical Tradition in Byron's *Cain* and Blake's *The Ghost of Abel.*" *Modern Philology,* 72 (1975), 350-64.
Twitchell, James. "The Supernatural Structure of Byron's *Manfred.*" *Studies in English Literature,* 15 (1975), 601-14.
Zelenak, Michael X. "Cursed with Consciousness: The Romantic Ego and Promethean Despair in Byron's Drama." *Theater Three,* no. 4 (Spring 1988), 21-30.

Dumas (père et fils)

Bassan, Fernande. *Alexandre Dumas, père, et la Comédie-Française.* Paris: Lettres Modernes, Minard, 1972.
Bassan, Fernande. "Dumas Père et le drame romantique." *L'Esprit créateur,* 5 (1965), 174-78.
Maurois, André. *The Titans: A Three-Generation Biography of the Dumas.* Trans. G. Hopkins. New York: Harper, 1957.

Eichendorff

Demuth, Otto. *Das romantische Lustspiel in seinen Beziehungen zur dichterischen Entwicklung Eichendorffs.* Prag: Bellmann, 1912; reprint, Hildesheim: Dr. Gerstenberg, 1973.

Goethe

Carlson, Marvin A. *Goethe and the Weimar Theatre*. Ithaca, N.Y.: Cornell University Press, 1978.
Hinderer, Walter, ed. *Goethes Dramen: Neue Interpretationenen*. Stuttgart: Reclam, 1980.
Höfler, Otto. "Goethes Urteil über die Romantik (Vortrag)." *Anzeiger*, 108 (1971), 249-80.
Hoffmeister, Gerhart. *Goethe und die europäische Romantik*. München: Francke, 1984.
Keller, Werner, ed. *Aufsätze zu Goethes "Faust I."* Darmstadt: Wissenschaftliche Buchgesellschaft, 1974.
Keller, Werner, ed. *Aufsätze zu Goethes "Faust II."* Darmstadt: Wissenschaftliche Buchgesellschaft, 1992.
Van Abbé, Derek. *Goethe: New Perspectives on a Writer and His Time*. London: Allen & Unwin, 1972.

Grillparzer

Geissler, Rolf. *Ein Dichter der letzten Dinge: Grillparzer heute*. Wien: Braumüller, 1987.
Grillparzer: A Critical Introduction. Cambridge: Cambridge University Press, 1972.
Naumann, Walter. *Grillparzer: Das dichterische Werk*. Stuttgart: Urban-Bücher, 1956.
Wagner, Eva. *An Analysis of Franz Grillparzer's Dramas*. Lewiston: Mellen Press, 1992.

Heiberg

Fenger, Henning and Frederick J. Marker. *The Heibergs*. New York: Twayne, 1971.
Ingerslev-Jensen, Povl. *P.A. Heiberg*. Herning: Kristensen, 1974.

Hölderlin

Benn, M.B. "The Dramatic Structure of Hölderlin's *Empedokles*." *Modern Language Review*, 62 (1967), 92-97.
Binder, Wolfgang. "Hölderlin und Sophokles." *Hölderlin-Jahrbuch*, 16 (1969-70), 19-37.
Böschenstein-Schäfer, Renate. "Hölderlins Gespräch mit Böhlendorff." *Hölderlin-Jahrbuch,* 14 (1965-66), 110-24.
Hempelmann, Gernot. *Dichtung und Denkverzicht: Hölderlin als Tragiker*. Hamburg: Lüdke, 1972.
Hochmuth, Ingeborg. "Menschenbild und Menschheitsperspektive in Hölderlins Trauerspielfragmenten *Der Tod des Empedokles*." *Wissenschaftliche Zeitschrift der Friedrich-Schiller Universität Jena*, 21 (1972), 437-46.
Hölscher, Uvo. *Empedokles und Hölderlin*. Frankfurt a.M.: Insel, 1965.
Pezold, Klaus. "Zur Interpretation von Hölderlins *Empedokles*-Fragmenten." *WZUL*, 12 (1963), 519-24.
Simon, Jürgen. *Der Wechsel der Töne im Drama: Beobachtungen zu Hölderlins Trauerspiel "Der Tod des Empedokles."* Tübingen: Huth, 1967.
Staiger, Emil. "Der Opfertod von Hölderlins Empedokles." *Hölderlin-Jahrbuch*, 13 (1963-64), 1-20.

Hoffmann

Eilert, Heide. *Theater in der Erzählkunst. Eine Studie zum Werk E.T.A. Hoffmanns*. Tübingen: Niemeyer, 1977.
Funk, E. "E.T.A. Hoffmann und das Theater." Diss. Wien, 1957.
Schnapp, Friedrich. "Aus E.T.A. Hoffmanns Bamberger Zeit: Fünf Theater-Kritiken von Adalbert Friedrich Marcus (September-Dezember 1809), entdeckt und mitgeteilt von Friedrich Schnapp." *Literaturwissenschaftliches Jahrbuch der Görres-Gesellschaft*, 7 (1966), 119-43.

Holberg

Engelstad, Carl Fr. *Ludvig Holberg: Gjøgleren, granskeren, gåten*. Oslo: Aschehoug, 1984.
Engster, H. *Der Januskopf des Bürgers: Eine gesellschafts-geschichtliche Analyse von L. Holbergs Komödie "Yeppe poa Berget."* Bern-Frankfurt a.M.: Lang, 1978.

Grandjean, Mariannne. *Ludvig Holbergs kunstsyn og dramaturgi.* København: Teatervidenskabelige Institut, 1980.

Hugo

Butor, Michel. "Le Théâtre de Victor Hugo." *Nouvelle Revue Française*, 12 (1964), 862-78, 1073-81.
Chahine, Samia. *La Dramaturgie de Victor Hugo (1816-1843)*. Paris: Nizet, 1971.
Doyle, Ruth Lestha. *Victor Hugo's Drama*. Westport, Conn.: Greenwood Press, 1981.
Howarth, W.D. "Victor Hugo and the 'Failure of French Romantic Drama'." *L'Esprit créateur*, 16 (1976), 247-56.
Lyons, Constance L. "Tragedy and the Grotesque: Act IV of *Ruy Blas*." *French Review*, 45, Special Issue no. 4 (Spring 1972), 75-84.
Wentzlaff-Eggebert, Harald. *Zwischen kosmischer Offenbarung und Wortoper: Das romantische Drama Victor Hugos*. Nuremberg: Erlangen-Nuremberg University Press, 1984.

Ibsen

Durbach, Errol. *"Ibsen the Romantic": Analogues of Paradise in the Later Plays*. Athens, GA: University of Georgia Press, 1982.
Johnston, Brian. *Text and Supertext in Ibsen's Drama*. University Park: Pennsylvania State University Press, 1989.
Marker, Frederick J. *Ibsen's Lively Art*. Cambridge: Cambridge University Press, 1989.

Katona

Arany, János. *Bánk bán-tanulmányok* (1859). In: *Arany János Összes Művei*. X. Budapest: Akadémiai Kiadó, 1962. 275-329.
Gyulai, Pál. *Katona József és "Bánk banja."* Budapest: Franklin-társulat, 1883.

Kleist

Clausen, Mary Anne Holmgren. "Theater in the Poetic World of Heinrich von Kleist." Diss. Bryn Mawr, 1976.
Crosby, Donald. "Kleist's Prinz von Homburg – An Intensified Egmont?" *German Life and Letters*, 23 (1969-70), 315-20.
Frank, Luanne T. "Kleist's Achilles: Hilfskonstruktion or Hero?" In: *Husbanding the Golden Grain: Studies in Honor of Henry W. Nordmeyer*. Eds. Luanne T. Frank, and Emery E. George. Ann Arbor: The University of Michigan, 1973. pp. 82-96.
Garland, Mary. *Kleist's Prinz Friedrich von Homburg: An Interpretation through Word Pattern*. The Hague: Mouton, 1968.
Geary, John. *Heinrich von Kleist: A Study in Tragedy and Anxiety*. Philadelphia: University of Pennsylvania Press, 1968.
Henkel, Arthur. "Traum und Gesetz in Kleists *Prinz von Homburg*: Ein Vortrag." *Neue Rundschau*, 73 (1962), 438-64.
Henschel, Arnold J. "The Primacy of Free-Will in the Mind of Kleist and in the *Prinz von Homburg*." *German Life and Letters*, 17 (1963-64), 97-115.
Jancke, Gerhard. "Zum Problem des identischen Selbst in Kleists Lustspiel *Amphitryon*." *Colloquia Germanica*, (1969), 87-110.
Lupi, Sergio. "*Il Prinz von Homburg* di Heinrich von Kleist ovvero La Coscienza ritrovata." *Studi Germanici*, 6 (1968), 25-73.

Parker, John J. "A Motif and Certain Peculiarities of Style in Heinrich von Kleist's *Prinz Friedrich von Homburg.*" *Journal of the Australasian Universities Language and Literature Association*, 23 (1965), 103-10.

Politzer, Heinz. "Kleists Trauerspiel vom Traum: *Prinz Friedrich von Homburg.*" *Euphorion*, 64 (1970), 200-20.

Rheinfelder, Hans. "Tragödie ohne Sühnetod: Kleists *Prinz von Homburg* und Rotrous *Venceslas.*" In: *Miscellanea di studi in onore di Bonaventura Tecchi, a cura dell'Instituto Italiano di Studi Germanici Roma.* 2 vols. Rome: Edizioni dell' Ateneo, 1969. pp. 349-66.

Schaub, Martin. *Heinrich von Kleist und die Bühne.* Zürich: Juris, 1966.

Schneider, Karl Ludwig. "Heinrich von Kleists Lustspiel *Der zerbrochene Krug.*" In: *Das deutsche Lustspiel.* Ed. Hans Steffen. Göttingen: Vandenhoeck & Ruprecht, 1968. pp. 166-80.

Schrimpf, Hans Joachim. "Tragedy and Comedy in the Works of Heinrich von Kleist." *Monatshefte*, 58 (1966), 193-208.

Schunicht, Manfred. "Heinrich von Kleist: *Der zerbrochene Krug.*" *Zeitschrift für deutsche Philologie*, 84 (1965), 550-62.

Seeba, Hinrich C. "Der Sündenfall des Verdachts: Identitätskrise und Sprachskepsis in Kleists *Familie Schroffenstein.*" *Deutsche Vierteljahrsschrift für Literaturwissenschaft und Geistesgeschichte*, 44 (1970), 64-100.

Sembdner, Helmut, ed. *Kleists Aufsatz über das Marionettentheater: Studien und Interpretationen.* Berlin: Schmidt, 1967.

Steller, Siegfried. *Das dramatische Werk Heinrich von Kleists.* Berlin: Rütten & Loening, 1967.

Szondi, Peter. "*L'Amphitryon* de Kleist, une 'comédie d'après Molière'." *Revues des Sciences Humaines*, no. 113 (1964), pp. 37-49.

Tatar, Maria M. "Psychology and Poetics: J.C. Reil and Kleist's *Prinz von Homburg.*" *Germanic Review*, 28 (1973), pp. 21-34.

Thalheim, Hans-Günther. "Kleists *Prinz von Homburg.*" *Weimarer Beiträge*, 11 (1965), 483-550.

Thalmann, Marianne. "Das Jupiterspiel in Kleists *Amphitryon.*" *Maske und Kothurn*, 9 (1963), pp. 56-67.

Turk, Horst. *Dramensprache als geordnete Sprache: Untersuchungen zu Kleists "Penthesilea."* Bonn: Bouvier, 1965.

Wittkowski, W. "Weltdialekt und Weltüberwindung: Zur Dramaturgie Kleists." In: *Deutsche Dramentheorien.* Ed. Reinhold Grimm. 2 vols. Frankfurt a.M.: Athenäum, 1971.

Kotzebue

Mandel, Oscar. *August von Kotzebue.* University Park: Pennsylvania State University Press, 1990.

Schumacher, Hans, ed. *"Die deutschen Kleinstädter": Ein Lustspiel in vier Akten (1803).* Berlin: de Gruyter, 1964. (Background information, bibliographical and interpretative materials, pp. 84-110).

Lamartine

Le Hir, Yves. "Aspects du langage dramatique dans *Saül* de Lamartine." *Revue des Sciences Humaines*, 34 (1969), pp. 577-83.

Madách

Barta, János. *Madách Imre.* Budapest: Franklin-társulat, 1942.

Horváth, Károly, ed. *Madách-tanulmányok.* Budapest: Akadémiai Kiadó, 1978.

Lotze, Dieter P. *Imre Madách.* Boston: Twayne, 1981.

Lukács, György. *Madách tragédiája* (1955). In: *Magyar irodalom – magyar kultúra: Válogatott tanulmányok.* Budapest: Gondolat Könyvkiadó, 1970. pp. 560-73.

Sőtér, István. *Alom a történelemröl: Madách Imre és "Az ember tragédiája."* Budapest: Akadémiai Kiadó, 1965.

Manzoni

Caretti, Lanfranco. *Manzoni e la critica*. Bari: Laterza, 1969.
Caretti, Lanfranco. *Manzoni: Ideologia e stile*. Torino: Einaudi, 1972.
Salvadori, Giulio. *Il dramma reale d'Alessandro Manzoni*. Brescia: Morcelliana, 1962.

Martins Pena

Damasceno, Darcy. "Martins Pena e o drama romântico." *O Estado de São Paulo,* Supplemento Literário, Mar. 1, 1969. p. 4.
Lyday, Leon F. "Satire in the Comedies of Martins Pena." *Luso-Brazilian Review*, 5, no. 2 (1968), 63-70.

Mickiewicz

Robinson, Marc. "Who Cares about Mickiewicz?" *Theater Three*, no. 4 (Spring 1988), 51-64.

De la Motte Fouqué

Chambers, Walker W. "Die Dramen von Friedrich de la Motte Fouqué." *Maske und Kothurn*, 10 (1964), 521-31.

Musset

Calen, A. "The Place of *Lorenzaccio* in Musset's Theatre." *Forum for Modern Language Studies*, 5 (1969), 225-31.
Gans, Eric Lawrence: *Musset et le "drame tragique": Essai d'analyse paradoxale*. Paris: Corti, 1974.
Gochberg, Herbert. *Stage of Dreams: The Dramatic Art of Alfred de Musset (1828-1834)*. Geneva: Droz, 1967.
Jansen, Steen. "Alfred de Musset, Dramaturge: *A quoi rêvent les jeunes filles* et la technique dramatique d'*Un spectacle dans un fauteuil*." *Orbis Litterarum*, 21 (1966), 222-54.
Jeúne, Simon. "Musset caché." *Revue d'Histoire Littéraire de la France*, 66 (1966), 419-38.
Lebois, André. *Vues sur le théâtre de Musset*. Avignon: Aubanel, 1966.
Rütten, Raimund. "Individuum und Gesellschaft in Alfred de Mussets *Lorenzaccio*." *Germanisch-romanische Monatsschrift*, N.F. 23 (1973), 67-93.
Sices, David. *Theater of Solitudes: The Drama of Alfred de Musset*. Hanover, N.H.: New England University Press, 1974.
Stackelberg, Jürgen von. "El *Lorenzaccio* de Alfred de Musset: Interpretación de un drama romántico." *Finis Terrae*, Año X, no. 38, (1963), 57-71.

Nerval

Bonnet, Henri: "Nerval et le théâtre d'ombres." *Romantisme*, 4 (1972), 54-64.
Cox, Jeffrey. "Killing Kotzebue: Nerval's *Leo Burckhart* and the Ideology of Literary Deaths." *European Romantic Review* (Summer 1990).
DuBruck, Alfred. "Nerval and Ranpack." *Romance Notes*, 11 (1969), 286-90.
Sullivan, Dennis G. "The Function of the Theater in the Work of Nerval." *Modern Language Notes*, 80 (1965), 610-17.

Pushkin

Brown, William Edward. *A History of Russian Literature of the Romantic Period*. 4 vols. Ann Arbor: Ardis, 1986. III, ch. 3.

Rassadin, Stanislav Borisovich. *Dramaturg Pushkin*. Moskva: Iskusstvo, 1977.
Tinyanov, U. *Pushkin i ego sovremenniki*. Moscow: Nauka, 1969.

Schiller

Liebfried, Erwin. *Schiller*. Frankfurt a.M.: Lang, 1985.
Borcherdt, Hans Heinrich, ed. *Schiller und die Romantiker: Briefe und Dokumente*. Stuttgart: Cotta'sche Buch-
handlung Nachf., 1948.
Ugrinsky, Alexej, ed. *Friedrich von Schiller and the Drama of Human Existence*. Westport, Conn.: Greenwood
Press, 1988.

Schlegel, A.W. and F.

Ehrlich, L. "Die frühromantische Dramaturgie August Wilhelm Schlegels." In: *Wissenschaftliche Zeitschrift der
Universität Halle*, 18 (1969), 157-69.
Hoffmeister, Gerhart. "A.W. Schlegels Rezeption des europäischen Barockdramas: Zum Problem der Fremdaus-
legung und Selbstprojektion – mit einem Anblick auf Friedrich Schlegel." In: *Europäische Barockrezeption*.
Ed. Klaus Garber et al. Wiesbaden: Harrassowitz, 1991. pp. 437-454.

Shelley

Barcus, James E., ed. *Shelley: The Critical Heritage*. London and Boston: Routledge & Kegan Paul, 1975.
Bennett, James R. "*Prometheus Unbound*, Act I, 'The Play's the Thing'." *Keats-Shelley Journal*, 23 (1974), 32-
51.
Cameron, Kenneth Neill. *Shelley: The Golden Years*. Cambridge, Mass.: Harvard University Press, 1974.
Coats, Sandra Whitaker. "Gothic Elements in Shelley's *Prometheus Unbound*." Diss. Texas A&M University,
1971.
Curran, Stuart. *Shelley's Cenci; Scoripons Ringed with Fire*. Princeton: Princeton University Press.
Duerkson, Roland A. "Shelley's 'Deep Truth' Reconsidered." *English Language Notes*, 13, no. 1 (1975), 25-27.
Dyck, Sarah. "The Presence of that Shape: Shelley's *Prometheus Unbound*." *Costerus*, 1 (1972), 13-80.
Elliott, Barbara. "Shelley and the Romantic Reviewers: The Relevance of Poetry and Criticism in the Early Nine-
teenth Century." Diss. Rice University, 1974.
Flagg, John Sewell. *"Prometheus Unbound" and "Hellas": An Approach to Shelley's Lyrical Dramas*. Salzburg:
Universität Salzburg, 1972.
Hughes, Daniel. "Shelley, Leonardo, and the Monsters of Thought." *Criticism*, 12 (1970), 195-212.
Hurt, James R. "*Prometheus Unbound* and Aeschylean Dramaturgy." *Keats-Shelley Journal*, 15 (1966), 43-48.
Rickert, Alfred E. "Two Views of *The Cenci*: Shelley and Artaud." *Ball State University Forum*, 14, no. 1
(1973), 31-35.
Singh, Sheila Uttam. *Shelley and the Dramatic Form*. Salzburg: Universität Salzburg, 1972.
Thorn, Arline R. "Shelley's *The Cenci* as Tragedy." *Costerus*, 9 (1973), 219-28.
Webb, Timothy. "Shelley and Cyclops." *Keats-Shelley Memorial Bulletin*, 23 (1972), 31-37.
Zimansky, Curt Richard. "This Proper Paradise: A Study of Shelley's Symbolism and Mythology." Diss. Indiana
University, 1972.

Strindberg

Johnson, Walter. *August Strindberg*. New York: Twayne, 1976.
Morgan Margery. *August Strindberg*. New York: Grove Press, 1985.
Sprinchorn, Evert. *Strindberg as Dramatist*. New Haven: Yale University Press, 1982.

Turco, Jr., Alfred. "An Enemy Like Him – Nietzsche, Strindberg, and *The Dance of Death.*" *Theater Three*, 4 (1988), 65-94.

Tieck

Beyer, H.G. "Ludwig Tiecks Theatersatire *Der gestiefelte Kater* und ihre Stellung in der Literatur- und Theatergeschichte." Diss. München, 1960.
Gillespie, Gerald. "Young Tieck and the Romantic Breakthrough." *Theater Three,* 4 (Spring 1988), 31-44.
Kemme, H.-M. "Ludwig Tiecks Bühnenreformpläne und -versuche und ihre Wirkung auf die Entwicklung des deutschen Theaters im 19. und 20. Jahrhundert." Diss. Berlin, Freie Universität, 1971.
Lüdeke, H. *Ludwig Tieck und das alte englische Theater.* Frankfurt a.M.: Mortiz Diesterweg, 1922. Reprint Hildesheim: Dr. Gerstenberg, 1975.
Nef, Ernst. "Das-Aus-der-Rolle-Fallen als Mittel der Illusionszerstörung bei Tieck und Brecht." *Zeitschrift für deutsche Philologie*, 83 (1964), 191-215.

Vigny

Barbera, Giuseppi, ed. *Théâtre.* Milan: Gastaldi, 1967.
Dale, R.C. "*Chatterton* is the Essential Romantic Drama." *L'Esprit créateur*, 5 (1965), 131-37.
Daniels, Barry Vincent. "Alfred de Vigny and the French Romantic Theatre." Diss. Cornell University, 1973.
Daniels, Barry V. "An Exemplary French Romantic Production: Alfred de Vigny's *Chatterton.*" *Theatre Survey*, 26 (1975), 65-88.
Kushner, Eva. "Histoire et théâtre chez Vigny." *L'Esprit créateur,* 5 (1965), 147-61.

Vörösmarty

Babits, Mihály. *Az ifjú Vörösmarty; A férfi Vörösmarty* (1911). In: *Esszék, tanulmányok.* Budapest: Szépirodalmi Könyvkiadó, 1978. I: 208-55.

Wordsworth

Owen, W.J.B. "*The Borderers* and the Aesthetics of Drama." *Wordsworth Circle,* 6 (1975), 227-39.
Pipkin, James. "*The Borderers* and Wordsworth's Emblems of Solitude." *Southern Review* (Adelaide), 9, no. 2 (1976), 79-92.
Pollin, Burton L. "Permutations of Names in *The Borderers,* or Hints of Godwin, Charles Lloyd, and a Real Renegade." *Wordsworth Circle*, 4 (Winter 1973), 31-35.
Priestman, Donald G. "*The Borderers*: Wordsworth's Addenda to Godwin." *University of Toronto Quarterly,* 44 (1974), 56-65.
Sharrock, Roger. "*The Borderers:* Wordsworth on the Moral Frontier." *Durham University Journal,* 25 (1964), 170-83.
Storch, R.F. "Wordsworth's *The Borderers*: The Poet as Anthropologist." *Journal of English Literary History*, 36 (1969), 340-60.
Thorslev, Peter L., Jr. "Wordsworth's *Borderers* and the Romantic Villain-Hero." *Studies in Romanticism*, 5 (1966), 84-103.

INDEX

This index is selective. It concentrates on artists and authors of the late eighteenth to early twentieth century relevant to the volume's prime topics. Some earlier figures of interest to the Romantics are noted, but, with rare exceptions, the index omits persons active beyond Modernism and their works. Generally, names and works appearing in the annotations are not listed.

Entries in part one observe the naming customs of the cultures in question; however, figures from antiquity and figures better known in English by their penname or title will be listed under the common Anglicized form. Readers should look for names from Russian and other languages written in Cyrillic characters under more than one system of transcription both in the main text and in the index (e.g., Meyerhold as well as Meierkhol'd, Ševčenko as well as Shevchenko, and so forth). Only German umlauts will be interpreted as equivalent to the marked vowel plus e. Otherwise, except in the initial position, if a letter is modified by a diacritic mark, that will not affect the alphabetical order. The prefix Mc will be considered equivalent to Mac; the abbreviation St., to Saint or Sainte; German eszet (ß), to a double s.

In part two, titles beginning with the definite or indefinite article in any language will ordinarily be listed under the first word after the article. (For example, Madách's play, *Az ember tragédiája* under the noun *ember*, not the direct article *az*; Strindberg's *Ett drömspell* under the noun *drömspell*, not the indirect article *ett*; Verdi's opera *La forza del destino* under *forza*; and so forth.) In the infrequent case of a reference to a name or title in an annotation, only the relevant page number is indicated.

INDEX OF NAMES

INDEX OF TITLES